About the Editors

TONY MEENAGHAN is a Lecturer in Marketing at the Graduate School of Business, University College Dublin. His main research interest is marketing communications and in particular commercial sponsorship. He has published on these and related topics in such journals as the *European Journal of Marketing*, the *International Journal of Advertising*, the *Journal of Advertising Research*, the *Journal of Product and Brand Management* and the *Irish Marketing Review*. He is the author of *Commercial Sponsorship*, published in 1983 by MCB University Press, the joint editor of *Perspectives in Marketing Management in Ireland*, published in 1994 by Oak Tree Press and the sole editor of *Researching Commercial Sponsorship*, published in 1995 by ESOMAR.

PAUL O'SULLIVAN is Director of the College of Marketing and Design at the Dublin Institute of Technology, having previously lectured in media communications and advertising there for a number of years. His main research interests are in integrated marketing communications and in communication strategies for small entrepreneurial companies. He has published on these topics in a number of journals and is a co-author of *Marketing Practice in the Republic of Ireland and Northern Ireland* (Co-operation North, 1992) and of *Marketing Planning for Small Business* (Irish Goods Council, 1983). He is a member of the Board of the Project Development Centre, Dublin, a Director of the Bolton Trust and a Director of the Small Enterprise Seed Fund and is currently a member of the Higher Education Authority.

Irish Studies in Management

Editors:

W.K. Roche
Graduate School of Business
University College Dublin

David Givens
Oak Tree Press

Irish Studies in Management is a new series of texts and research-based monographs covering management and business studies. Published by Oak Tree Press in association with the Graduate School of Business at University College Dublin, the series aims to publish significant contributions to the study of management and business in Ireland, especially where they address issues of major relevance to Irish management in the context of international developments, particularly within the European Union. Mindful that most texts and studies in current use in Irish business education take little direct account of Irish or European conditions, the series seeks to make available to the specialist and general reader works of high quality which comprehend issues and concerns arising from the practice of management and business in Ireland. The series aims to cover subjects ranging from accountancy to marketing, industrial relations/human resource management, international business, business ethics and economics. Studies of public policy and public affairs of relevance to business and economic life will also be published in the series.

Marketing Communications in Ireland

Edited by
Tony Meenaghan
and
Paul O'Sullivan

Oak Tree Press

Dublin
in association with
Graduate School of Business
University College Dublin

Oak Tree Press
Merrion Building
Lower Merrion Street
Dublin 2, Ireland

© 1995 Individual Contributors and
the Graduate School of Business, University College Dublin
and:
"Couponing and Coupon Redemption: Problems and Perspectives" by Marie Louise O'Dwyer and Mary Lambkin; and
"Branding: Regaining the Initiative" by John Fanning: © 1994 and 1995 *Irish Marketing Review*
"Fear Appeals: Segmentation is the Way to Go" by Valerie Quinn, Tony Meenaghan and Teresa Brannick: © 1992 *International Journal of Advertisers*.

A catalogue record of this book is
available from the British Library.

ISBN 1-86076-006-6

All rights reserved. No part of this publication may be reproduced or transmitted in any form or by any means, including photocopying and recording, without written permission of the publisher and the individual contributors. Such written permission must also be obtained before any part of this publication is stored in a retrieval system of any nature. Requests for permission should be directed to Oak Tree Press, Merrion Building, Lower Merrion Street, Dublin 2, Ireland.

Printed in Ireland by Colour Books Ltd.

Contents

LIST OF CONTRIBUTORS xxi
FOREWORD, John Fanning xxiii
INTRODUCTION, Tony Meenaghan and Paul O'Sullivan xxvii
ACKNOWLEDGEMENTS xxxv

PART 1:
MARKETING COMMUNICATIONS
— CONCEPTS AND CONTEXT

1: Marketing Communications in Transition,
   Tony Meenaghan 1

   Introduction 1
   Changes in the Media 2
      Above-the-Line Activity 2
      Above-/Below-the-Line Expenditure Reallocation 5
      A Media Explosion 6
      Increased Clutter 10
      Media Inflation 11
   Changes in Client Perspectives 13
      The Growing Power of the Retailer 13
      Corporate "Shortermism" 15
      Increasing Number of Similar Brands 15
   Changes in the Supply/Production Industry 16
      The Growth of Specialist Agencies 17
      The Growth of Media Specialists 17
      The Traditional Advertising Agency 19
      Production Costs 20
      Globalisation 21
   Changes in the Audience 21
      Audience Control of Media 21
      Increased Audience Sophistication 22
      Audience Fragmentation 23
   Conclusions 23
   References 24

2: Advertising as Communication, *Katriona Lawlor* — 29

Communication Models 29
Theory of Meaning 31
Signs 32
Model of Meaning...33
    Intention..34
    Text 40
    Interpretation 41
Conclusions..44
References 45

3: Managing Marketing Communication — The Client Perspective, *Michael Carey* — 49

Introduction...49
Strategic Planning and the Role of Marketing Communications 50
Resource Allocation — Loaves and Fishes...52
Support Agencies — Building Partnerships 53
    Account Management..55
    Creative Services..55
    Media Services 56
    Planning and Research Services 56
    Financial and Administrative Services 56
Alternative Client Structures — Responding to Change 56
Types of Communication...59
    Advertising...59
    Promotions 60
    Sponsorship..61
    Public Relations...61
    Other Types of Marketing Communication 62
Importance and Role of Evaluation...62
Conclusion 63

4: Communications in a Business-to-Business Framework, *Seán de Búrca* — 64

Introduction...64
The Business-to-Business Market..65
The Business-to-Business Communications Mix 67

Contents

The Role of Advertising in a Business-to-Business Framework 69
   Advertising in General Business and Trade Publications 71
   Developing Effective Business-to-Business Advertisements 73
   Advertising in Directory Listings and Buyers' Guides 76
Sales Promotions in a Business-to-Business Framework 77
   Trade Fairs and Exhibitions 77
   Product Literature 80
   Seminars and Demonstrations 81
   Sales Promotion and Incentives 81
   Speciality Advertising 82
Direct Marketing in a Business-to-Business Framework 82
   Direct Mail 83
   Direct-Response Advertising 83
   Telemarketing 84
Public Relations in a Business-to-Business Framework 84
   Publicity 86
   Sponsorship 87
Personal Selling 88
   The Impact of Personal Communications 88
Conclusions 92
References 92

PART 2:
ADVERTISING: THE PLAYERS

5: **The Advertising Agency — Function and Direction,**
   Ian Fox and Iskandar Abdullah   **99**

The Evolution of Advertising 100
   Origins of the Advertising Agency 102
Types of Advertising Agency 102
   The Creative Department 103
   The Media Department 103
   The Client-Service Department 103
   Other Kinds of Agency 104
How Agencies Charge their Clients 105
The Agency at Work 107
   The Brief 108
   Traffic 108
   Creating the Idea 110

   Production 110
   Finance 111
  Issues for the Future 111
   The Multinational Advertising Agency 111
   Media 113
   Legal 113
  References 114

6: Media Strategy — Selecting and Scheduling Media in Ireland, *Peter McPartlin*   115

  Introduction 115
  The Irish Media Market 116
  Television 118
  Radio 119
  Press 119
  Outdoor 121
  Cinema 121
  Advertising-Revenue Shares 122
  The Media Process 123
  Strategic Media Planning 124
  Reach and Frequency 129
  Implementation Media Planning 130
   Choice of Individual Media Vehicles 130
   Size and Length 132
   Position 132
  Sample Media Schedule 132
  Media Buying/Execution 134
  Evaluation 136
  Media — No Turning Back 136
  Fragmentation 137
  What Next for Media? 139
  Computers in Media 141
  A Media Glossary 143
  References 145

7: Creative Strategy in Advertising, *Iskandar Abdullah and J.P. Donnelly* — 146

Introduction 146
The Planning Process 147
   What is Advertising Creativity? 147
   Creative Strategy Planning 147
The Creative Briefing Process 152
   The Creative Brief 152
   Developing the Single-Minded Proposition 158
Evaluating the Advertising 162
   The Big Idea 162
   Creative Evaluation 165
Conclusion 166
References 167

8: Examining Client/Agency Relationships in an Irish Context, *Tony Meenaghan and Barbara Patton* — 168

Introduction 168
From "Purchase" to "Relationship" in Marketing 168
Client/Agency Relationships in Marketing 169
The Stages of the Client/Agency Relationship 170
   Selection Stage 170
   Maintenance Stage 171
   Dissolution Stage 174
The Client/Agency Relationships in an Irish Context 176
   Agency Selection 176
   Maintaining the Client/Agency Relationship 177
Perceived Weaknesses of Agencies 179
Improving the Client/Agency Relationship 180
Critical Elements of the Client/Agency Relationship 181
   Creativity 181
   Sourcing of Services through Agency 181
   Agency Remuneration 183
   Understanding of Client's Business 184
   Dissolving the Relationship 184
Summary 185
References 186

9: **Media Research in Ireland,**
Áine O'Donoghue and Tom Harper 190

Introduction 190
TAM (Television Audience Measurement) 191
   The Establishment Survey 192
   Panel Design 192
   People-meter 193
   Processing 194
   Reporting 194
   JNLR (Joint National Listener Research) 196
   JNRR (Joint National Readership Research) 200
   Use of Media Research Data (Radio and Print) 204
   Cinema Research 205
   JNPR (Joint National Poster Research) 205
Media Research — All Ireland 206
References 208

10: **The Role of Marketing Research in Advertising,**
Phelim O'Leary and Des Byrne 209

Pre-Advertising 211
Advertising Development 213
Advertising Expression 214
Effectiveness Tracking 214
Concluding Comments 215
References 217

11: **Co-operative Advertising — Client, Channel and**
Agency, *Paul O'Sullivan and Peter Doran* 218

Introduction 218
Forms of Co-operative Advertising 219
   Horizontal Co-operative Advertising 219
   Ingredient Producer Co-operative Advertising 220
   Vertical Co-operative Advertising 220
When Should Co-operative Advertising Be Used 221
Channel Co-operation and Conflict 223
Channel Behaviour 224
Channel Conflict 225
   The Dual-Signature Problem 227
Promotion Strategy and Channel Management 227

Contents

        Field Study 228
        Findings 229
    Conclusion 235
    References 236

12: The Regulatory Environment for Advertising in Ireland, ***Duncan Grehan***   **238**

    The Regulatory Framework 238
        Sources of Regulation 239
        The Regulators of Advertising 241
        The Objectives of Regulation 243
    Regulation of Advertising Practices 245
        Misleading Advertising 245
        Comparative Advertising 247
    Sanctions for Breaches of Advertising Regulations 250
    Regulation and the Evolving Environment for Advertising 254
    References 256

13: Issues Facing Advertisers in Ireland, ***Elizabeth Reynolds and Fred Hayden***   **257**

    The Irish Advertising Market 257
    Critical Issues Facing Irish Advertisers 259
        Production Costs 260
        Media Research 262
        Expanding Range of Media Opportunities 263
        Media Costs 265
        The Emergence of Media Monopolies in Ireland 267
        Regulatory Issues 268
        Agency / Client Issues 268
    Summary 270
    References 271

14: From Exporting to Globalisation — Issues in International Communications, ***Frank Bradley, Eamonn Clarkin and Dympna M. Hughes***   **274**

    Introduction 274
    Nature of Global Advertising 275
        Definition of International Advertising 276
        The Growth in Global Advertising 276
        Communications Options for the International Company 277

Internationalisation Options 278
Conditions for Successful Communications Strategies 279
   Impact of Position in the Business System 279
   Standardised and Differentiated Marketing Communications .. 279
International Communications among Selected Irish Companies .. 283
   From Sub-Supply to Branded Trade Marketing 284
   From Single Market Brand to Multi-Market Branding 285
Barriers to Irish Global Brands 286
   Market Size and Cost of Marketing Communications 286
   Channels of Distribution 286
   Short-Term Promotions 288
   Impact of Market Focus 288
   Impediments to Cultural Convergence and Market
   Homogenisation 289
   Country of Origin Effect 290
Conclusions 291
References 293

PART 3:
COMMUNICATION STRATEGY

15: Branding: Regaining the Initiative, *John Fanning*   297

Changing Brand Fortunes 298
The Brand in Perspective 298
   A Brief History of Branding 298
   What is a Brand? 299
   The New Threat to Brands 300
The New Threat from Retailers 302
   First Crisis in Early 1970s 302
   Second Crisis in Early 1990s 303
   The Threat from Consumers 305
   The Threat from Marketing: Brand Management 307
Regaining the Initiative 309
   Overcoming the Threat from Retailer Brands 309
   Increasing Marketing Literacy among Consumers 312
   Overcoming the Weaknesses of the Brand-Management
   Function 314
Conclusions 315
References 316

16: Advertising and the Development of Marketing Imagery, *Tony Meenaghan*   318

Introduction 318
Types of Marketing Images 319
From Identity to Image 320
The Concept of Branding 321
Adding Brand Values 322
Advertising — Its Role in Marketing Imagery 323
Creating Imagery in Advertising 326
    Message Content 327
Methods of Creating Brand Imagery in Advertising 328
    Metaphors and Symbols 328
    The Brand Name 329
    Slogans/Copy 330
Media/Media Vehicle Effect 330
    Media Effect 331
    Media-Vehicle Effects 331
Conclusion 333
References 334

17: Strategic Corporate Identity and Corporate-Image Research in Ireland, *John D. Byrne*   338

Introduction 338
Image and Identity 338
Marketing Implications of Corporate Image 339
    The Strategic Nature of Corporate Identity 341
Globalisation and the Changing Environment for Irish
Corporations 342
Corporate Publics 343
Communications in Corporate-Identity Creation 344
Planning for Corporate-Image Development 345
Researching Corporate Image 346
Evaluating Effectiveness 349
Electricity Supply Board (ESB) — A Case Study 350
    Introduction 350
    Supply-Industry Restructuring 350
    ESB's Corporate-Reorganisation Programme 351
    Corporate-Image-Tracking Research Carried Out by ESB 352

    Dimensions of ESB's Corporate Image...352
    Analysis of Results...353
    ESB — Tracking Awareness and Image-Dimensions
    Awareness..353
    Reliability...355
    "Moving with the Times"..356
    "Responsible Attitude Towards the Community".........................357
    "Well-Managed Company"..358
Conclusions..359
References 360

18: Corporate Change: The Convergence of Internal and External Communications Strategies, *Kevin Bourke* 361

Introduction...361
Planning and Design..362
    Historical Background..362
    The Change Process..364
    Long-Term Perspective...366
    Marketing Action Programme (MAP)..366
Internal Marketing Programmes 369
    Involvement and Assimilation 369
    "Superthought"...370
    Making Marketing Effective...371
Externalising the Message 371
    Corporate Identity...372
    Design 374
    Launch 375
    Roll-out 376
Internal Research and Conclusion 376
    Research..376
    The Learning Organisation..380
Conclusion 380

19: Fear Appeals: Segmentation is the Way to Go, *Valerie Quinn, Tony Meenaghan and Teresa Brannick* 382

Introduction...382
Fear Appeals in Advertising 383
Inconsistencies in the Research 384

Contents

> Using Fear Appeals — Important Considerations 386
> Fear Appeals and Market Segmentation 387
> Research Methodology 388
> Emerging Results 388
> Commentary 394
>> The Impact of Fear Appeals on Students at Different Educational Levels...394
>> The Impact of Fear Appeals on Male Students Compared to Female Students 395
> Conclusion 395
> References 396

20: Advertising and the Senior Market, *Darach Turley* 398

> Introduction 398
> Seniors and the Media 399
> Programme Preferences 402
> Viewing Motivation 405
> Advertising and the Senior Market 407
>> The Portrayal of Older People in Advertisements 408
>> Appeals in Senior Advertising 409
>> Attitudes of Seniors towards Advertising..................411
>> Impact of Advertising on Seniors 412
>> Models in Senior Advertising 412
> Conclusions 414
> References 415

21: Disturbing the Stability of Purchasing Patterns: The Key to Successful Launching of FMCG Brands, *Cathal Brugha and Kevin Donnelly* 420

> The Nature of FMCG Purchasing 420
> Repertoire Buying 421
> Consumer Flows 423
> The Stability Index 424
> The Effect of New Brand Launch on Market Stability......424
> Achieving Product Trial 426
> Communication Strategy: Creating Uncertainty 428
> Types of Uncertainty 429

Incumbent Reaction to New Brand Challenges 431
Summary 432
References 433

PART 4:
MARKETING COMMUNICATIONS — BEYOND THE LINE

22: Sales Promotion — An Irish Perspective,
Laura Cuddihy, Kate Uí Ghallachóir and
Fred Hayden **437**

Introduction 437
Role of Sales Promotion in Marketing Strategy 440
Structure of Sales-Promotion Industry in Ireland 443
Companies' Allocation to Non-Media Advertising 446
Consumer Promotions 447
Order Fulfilment and Promotions-Handling Process 450
Trade Promotions 451
Planning a Campaign 452
Budgeting for Sales Promotion 454
Evaluation of Sales Promotions 455
Legal Issues in Sales Promotions in Ireland 456
References 457

23: Couponing and Coupon Redemption: Problems
and Perspectives, *Marie Louise O'Dwyer and*
Mary Lambkin **459**

Types of Sales Promotion 460
Coupon Use and Growth 461
Coupon Redemption 463
The Coupon Redemption Process 464
Research on Couponing 465
    Deal-Proneness 466
    Factors Influencing the Coupon-Redemption Rate 467
Method of Coupon Distribution 468
    Nestlé 470
Coupon Value 471
Couponing Effort and Timing 472

Contents   xvii

	The Impact of Coupon Use on Sales	474
	Cow & Gate	476
	Future Research	477
	Conclusions and Implications	478
	References	479

24: Public Relations and Publicity, *Francis X. Carty*   481

Defining Public Relations	482
Problems and Perspectives	485
Grunig's Four Models of Public Relations	486
Publicity	488
The Press Release	490
Handling the Bad News	491
Evaluating Media Coverage	492
Conclusions	498
References	493

25: Managing Sponsorship Effectively, *Tony Meenaghan*   495

Introduction	495
Background	495
Sponsorship — An Industry in Transition	496
Developing Range of Sponsorship Media	497
Changing Perceptions of Sponsorship	498
Increased Sophistication of Management Practice	500
Developing Sponsorship-Support Industry	500
The Sponsorship Management Process	501
Marketing and Marketing Communications Strategy	501
Objective-Setting in Sponsorship	502
Sponsorship Selection	503
Sponsorship Budget	507
Sponsorship Exploitation, Implementation and Integration	507
Measuring Sponsorship Results	509
Measuring the Level of Media Coverage Gained	509
Measuring Communications Effects in Sponsorship	509
Measuring the Sales Effects of Sponsorship	511
Conclusions	513
References	513

26: Exhibiting Planning and Practice, *David Shipley* — 516

- Introduction 516
- An Exhibiting Planning Framework 518
- Recent Research Findings 523
- Summary and Conclusions 528
- References 529

27: Direct Marketing — Irish Perspectives, *Michael McGowan* — 532

- The Challenge of Definition 532
- The Defining Characteristics of Direct Marketing 534
- The Media of Direct Marketing 536
- Trends in Direct Marketing Media 537
- Factors that have Influenced the Growth of Direct Marketing in Ireland 538
- Technology Developments 539
- The Benefits Associated with Using Direct Marketing 541
- The Future for Direct Marketing 541
  - *Interactive (Electronic) Marketing Media* 542
  - *Customer Loyalty* 543
  - *Telephony-Based Direct Marketing* 543
- Factors that Will Influence the Growth of Direct Marketing in Ireland, 1995–2000 543
- References 545

28: Store Atmospherics and the Rituals of Consumption, *Paul O'Sullivan and Donald C. McFetridge* — 546

- Retail Change 547
- Atmospherics 548
  - *Atmospheric Elements* 551
  - *Consumer Profiles and Consumer Values* 557
- Development of the Concept 559
- Concluding Remarks 561
- References 562

PART 5: ADVERTISING — EFFECTS AND OUTCOMES

29: Advertising Effectiveness — The Holy Grail?, Peter Nash — 567

Introduction 567
How Advertising Works 568
    Linear-Sequential Models 569
    Human-Needs Models of Advertising 569
    Advertising Objectives 572
A New Model of Effective Advertising 573
    Effective Advertising is as Easy as ABC 573
    A. Creating Awareness 574
    B. Branding Advertising Effectively 576
    C. Achieving On-Strategy Communication 578
Marketing Research Can Help Create Effective Advertising 578
    Research is Integral to the Creative Process 578
    Qualitative Research 579
    Quantitative Research 579
    Advertising Tracking 580
Advertising Effectiveness — A Local Example 581
Conclusions 583
References 583

30: Playtime TV: Advertising-Literate Audiences and the Commercial Game, Stephanie O'Donohoe — 585

Introduction 585
The Concept of Advertising Literacy 585
    Advertising-Literacy Skills: Previous Research 586
    Advertising-Literacy Skills: Practitioners' Impressions 588
The Implications of Consumers' Advertising Literacy 592
    Advertising Uses and Gratifications among Young Adults 595
Conclusions 599
References 601

31: The Social and Economic Effects of Advertising in Ireland, Caolan Mannion and Damien McLoughlin — 604

The Economic Effects of Advertising in Ireland 605
    Advertising and the National Economy 605
    The Role of Advertising in Market Entry and NPD 607

Advertising and the Irish Media 609
  The Advertising–Sales Controversy 610
  Advertising and the Consumer's Decision Process 611
  Advertising and Higher Prices 613
The Social Effects of Advertising in Ireland 615
  Public-Service Advertising 615
  Sports, Education and the Arts 616
  Subverting Society's Agenda 617
  Advertising and Social Values 618
  Can Advertising Manipulate Consumer Purchase? 621
Advertising and Another Society 623
  The New Challenges to Public Policy 625
Conclusions 626
References 627

List of Contributors

Iskandar Abdullah is a Lecturer in Marketing at University College Dublin and Pertanian University, Kuala Lumpar, Malaysia and was formerly Account Director with J. Walter Thompson in Tokyo, Sydney and Singapore.

Kevin Bourke is a consultant with Genesis Corporation and was formerly, General Manager, Group Marketing, AIB Group.

Frank Bradley is R&A Bailey Professor of International Marketing, University College Dublin.

Teresa Brannick is a Newman Scholar in the Department of Marketing at University College Dublin.

Cathal Brugha is a Lecturer in Management Information Systems at University College Dublin.

Des Byrne is a Director of Behaviour and Attitudes Ltd., Dublin.

John Byrne is Manager, Customer Research, Electricity Supply Board, Ireland.

Michael Carey is Marketing Director, Irish Biscuits Ltd.

Francis X. Carty is Lecturer in Public Relations, DIT, Aungier Street, Dublin.

Eamonn Clarkin is Planning Director, Irish International Advertising.

Laura Cuddihy is a Lecturer in Sales Management, DIT, Mountjoy Square, Dublin.

Sean de Búrca is a Lecturer in Marketing at University College Dublin.

Peter Dolan is a Marketing Executive with Grafton Group plc.

J.P. Donnelly is Managing Director, Dimension Marketing Services.

Kevin Donnelly is Executive Director, Taylor Nelson AGB plc.

John Fanning is Managing Director, McConnell's Advertising Services Ltd., Dublin.

Ian Fox is Director of the Institute of Advertising Practitioners in Ireland (IAPI).

Duncan Grehan is the Principal of Duncan Grehan and Partners, Solicitors, Dublin.

Tom Harper is Managing Director, Media Audits, Ireland.

Fred Hayden is Chief Executive, Association of Advertisers in Ireland, Ltd.

Dympna Hughes is Marketing Services Manager Europe with Boartlongyear, AG, Germany.

Mary Lambkin is a Lecturer in Marketing at University College Dublin.

Katriona Lawlor is a Lecturer in Marketing Communications at DIT, Mountjoy Square, Dublin.

Caolan Mannion is Marketing Research Executive, Dataquest, Westborough, MA, USA.

Donald McFettridge is a Lecturer in Retail Management at University of Ulster.

Michael McGowan is Marketing Manager, Kompass Ireland.

Damien McLoughlin is an Assistant Lecturer in Marketing at Dublin City University Business School.

Peter McPartlin is Media Director, Irish International Advertising.

Tony Meenaghan is a Lecturer in Marketing at University College Dublin.

Peter Nash is Marketing Research Manager, Guinness Ireland Ltd.

Áine O'Donoghue is Managing Director, MRBI Ltd.

Stephanie O'Donohoe is a Lecturer in Marketing at the University of Edinburgh.

Marie Louise O'Dwyer is a Lecturer in Marketing at Waterford Regional Technical College.

Phelim O'Leary is a Director of Behaviour and Attitudes Ltd., Dublin.

Paul O'Sullivan is Director of the College of Marketing and Design, DIT, Mountjoy Square, Dublin.

Barbara Patton is Head of Marketing, Irish Permanent plc.

Valerie Quinn is Marketing Projects Manager at R & A Bailey, Ireland.

Elizabeth Reynolds is a Lecturer in Marketing at University College Dublin.

David Shipley is Professor of Marketing at Trinity College Dublin.

Darach Turley is a Lecturer in Consumer Behaviour, Dublin City University.

Kate Uí Ghallachóir is a Lecturer in Marketing Strategy, DIT, Mountjoy Square, Dublin.

Foreword

Almost 25 years ago, after working in London for a few years mainly in the area of advertising planning research I decided to try my luck back in Dublin. The general consensus in London was that I was making a huge mistake. It was pointed out to me that the Republic of Ireland had the same population and per capita income levels as the Tyne Tees region in the UK and that there wasn't exactly a huge amount of advertising agency activity in Newcastle. It was generally assumed that it would only be a matter of time before Dublin went the same way as Newcastle.

Twenty-five years later the pessimistic predictions have been proved false. Although the marketing services sector in Ireland has had it share of casualties and redundancies during that period, compared with other centres like London and New York, it has proved surprisingly resilient. The fact remains that unlike the Tyne Tees region there is still a vibrant marketing services industry Ireland:

- There have been notable international Irish brand successes, e.g. Bailey's Irish Cream, Kerrygold and Jameson and there's now a new group of emerging brands like Ballygowan, Goodfellas and Kilkenny Irish Beer.

- Irish advertisements regularly feature in international creative awards festivals.

- Irish promotional campaigns and direct marketing programmes have achieved an extraordinary level of success in the more recently established award festivals in these areas.

- Irish executives working in the marketing services area are in constant demand for promotion to head office or to take charge of larger markets. Even more significant during the past year, at least two major multinational companies have located key elements of their pan-European marketing programmes in Dublin.

Clearly, therefore, the level of expertise in the Irish marketing services sector is on a par with that anywhere else in Europe and I believe that this book with its well-documented case histories, covering almost every aspect of marketing communication, offers conclusive evidence of the professionalism and sophistication of marketing practice in Ireland.

It may be interesting to speculate on why this professionalism and sophistication has come to characterise marketing practices in Ireland.

The first and most important reason is that we had no choice. The significant minority of companies that market their products and services in the Irish market have always located both their strategic marketing thinking and their marketing service agencies in Britain. Improvements in electronic communications make that option much easier — the minority in 1970 could easily have become the majority in the 1990s. The only reason why this has not occurred is that Irish companies in the marketing services sector have been forced to match standards set in London. This is no mean achievement. Whatever doubts there may be about the strategic marketing capacity of British businesses, there can be no doubt that their marketing services sector has achieved worldwide acclaim for its high standards of excellence. We were therefore forced into being able to match the performance of our nearest neighbour.

The revolution in marketing education was another significant factor. Here the pioneering role of the Marketing Institute was critical. Thousands of students have enrolled with the Institute over the past 20 years, and over 2,500 have qualified from their demanding Graduate Course. Marketing education has also mushroomed in the universities, the Dublin Institute of Technology and the RTCs. Almost every major marketing academic from around the world has been brought over to Ireland by the Marketing Institute for day-long courses or seminars during this period. The Marketing Society has also played its part by regularly organising meetings addressed by the most prominent practitioners from the UK and further afield. In the relatively small, homogeneous Irish marketing environment the most advanced thinking, the latest theories and the best practise are disseminated in a very short time.

Understanding the consumer is the cornerstone of marketing thinking, and without market research this would be impossible. Another reason for the success of the marketing services sector in Ireland is a highly sophisticated, diverse and well-developed market-research industry. The Marketing Society, which acts as a controlling body for market research, has maintained standards at a very high level, and visiting marketing experts are often surprised by the degree of sophistication of both qualitative and quantitative data in Ireland. Perhaps the most visible manifestation of marketing-research excellence is the measurement of media, and here Irish statistics on readership, listenership and viewership compare very favourably with any other market in the world.

Unfortunately a consistent record of success during the past twenty-five years is no guarantee that we will even survive the relatively short period to the new Millennium. The increasing centralisation of power in global companies, and the tendency to locate power in the centre of large concentrations of population and away from smaller countries, like Ireland, means that our industry will continue to face enormous challenges in the future. Our survival is not, and perhaps never will be, of major concern to the political and public service establishment, but perhaps we should make our case more often:

1) *Strategic Requirement for the Irish Industry.* Without a strong indigenous marketing services sector it will be much more difficult for Irish companies to create brands in Ireland capable of being marketed abroad. Green Isle is a good example of an Irish company set up in the recent past, which created a number of very strong brands in Ireland — e.g. Donegal Catch — and was ultimately able to launch the highly successful Goodfellas Pizza on the Irish market and then into the UK. The Irish marketing services sector played a vital role in the development of these brands.

2) *Employment.* It is notoriously difficult to obtain accurate figures on the number of people employed in the marketing services industry. However, it is probably between 4,000 and 5,000, depending on how one defines people who are employed in companies using the services of the marketing communications sector. This is a significant number of jobs, but the industry is also responsible for a much wider range of sub-contracting work and it is possible that up to 20,000 people, from typesetters and printers to actors and songwriters, are dependent on the marketing services sectors for a significant source of their income.

3) *Quality of Life.* A distinctive Irish marketing communication voice relieves us to some extent from the drab uniformity of the homogenised, standardised, pasteurised, Los Angelised world which threatens to engulf us all. People who live on this island, and a great many who choose to visit us, rightly value what has been referred to as the Irish "design for a living". The way we

communicate with ourselves is part of that design. We should try to protect it.

Ultimately our best defence will continue to be our own professionalism. This book is both a celebration of that professionalism and an enduring record, which will be of lasting use to successive generations of marketing practitioners and students.

John Fanning
September 1995

Introduction

Tony Meenaghan
Paul O'Sullivan

An appraisal of the state of the art and the practice of marketing communications in Ireland is both appropriate and timely. Appropriate because the marketing communications industry is a significant sector in the Irish economy, involving the vital interests of clients, media, agencies and an extensive services-support industry, all interacting in an intensely competitive and dynamic environment. This book represents the first comprehensive inventory of marketing communications activity in Ireland, addressing as it does process and practice in the marketplace within the framework of ideas provided by contemporary communication discourse. Thus the book aims to provide both a map of the industry and a series of benchmarks of good practice to guide entrants to the profession and students of communication issues.

The current appraisal may be regarded as timely because the very nature of marketing communication activity in Ireland and in the larger global economy is itself changing in response to radical developments in the marketplace, in technology and in the corporate needs that form a frame of reference for the industry. It is now accepted wisdom that the fractured marketplace of today requires the communication "practitioners of the future to be equipped with new theories, strategies and skills" (Duncan, Caywood and Newson, 1993: Appendix, 1).

A number of important marketplace changes have been the subject of wide debate amongst practitioners and theorists and are addressed directly within this book. These include growing audience fragmentation, increased media proliferation, escalating cost of new and traditional media, restructuring of agencies and agency functions, globalisation of markets, and the diffusion of new technologies which recreate and redefine marketing relationships. Furthermore, the decreasing impact and credibility of messages in a cluttered environment, the sophistication of consumers as message receivers, and the increasing power of the retailer, all demand a response in terms of overall communication strategy, and advertising strategy in particular.

Part of the response to these influences involves a redefinition of what constitutes marketing communication options and media, and of the very target market itself. As one commentator has put it:

> The lines between news and advertising are blurring: newspapers are going electronic; catalogues appear as videos; telephone lines are becoming media channels; the mass media are engaging niche markets; a profitable audience of only one person now is not unimaginable. Public relations professionals are using advertising and marketing tactics; advertising agencies own public relations firms; direct marketing and promotion are no longer below-the-line after-thoughts; and some marketing managers are as much concerned with stakeholders as they are with customers (Duncan, Caywood and Newson, 1993: 1).

The challenge for marketing managers is not alone to master the new communication options, but also to co-ordinate their application to ensure coherent and effective outcomes. Different communication and promotion tools reach different segments, and must be co-ordinated to assure optimal market coverage. New realities require new responses, and Integrated Marketing Communications (IMC) has emerged "as a potential solution to these needs for co-ordination of multiple and diverse marketing tools targeted to multiple and diverse audiences" (Stewart, 1995: 1).

The concept of integrated marketing communications (IMC) brings together all the various promotional activities, traditionally planned and implemented as separate or loosely affiliated campaigns, in an integrated, planned and targeted programme of communication activity. What is implied here is not merely the creation of a loose liaison between specialists on the client's side or indeed on the agency/services side. Nothing short of a paradigm shift will accommodate the reconsideration of the fundamental relationship of marketer to customer and of both with the mediators who stand between them.

With the customer as the raison d'être of corporate existence, the defining focus will be on relationship building and the traditional notion of communication activity as grounded on the stimulation of transactions becomes obsolete.

> To build relationships with customers rather than merely to be involved in transactions, the marketer must integrate communi-

cation forms to build a consistent approach that in turn will build a relationship (Schultz, Tannenbaum, and Lauterborn, 1993: 40).

It is clear then that if the integrated marketing communication approach is to be realised old assumptions must exit, assumptions about the role of advertising and sales promotion, about the organisation of advertising and public relations departments, about agencies and what they do, about the media and most of all, about accountability (Schultz, Tannenbaum, and Lauterborn, 1993: 13).

The marketing educator must similarly rise to the challenge of providing a conceptually unified and integrated programme of communication study. This volume draws together the perspectives of practitioners and academics, seeking to provide both inventory and prospect for Irish marketing communications. The contributors in many instances anticipate the issues that will arise in the practice of the individual communication disciplines, and also the problems associated with the effective integration of communication approaches by clients, in the decades ahead.

This book is structured into four major sections each incorporating a number of papers by academic specialists, senior marketing practitioners and authoritative figures from the agency world and the advertising services industry.

The first section examines key concepts and the overall context within which marketing communications operates. It evaluates the impact of economic, technological and social change on our understanding of how communications works and what the predicted outcomes of the current movement towards reconfiguration of the industry and of the relationships within it are likely to be. Tony Meenaghan examines changes in a number of interrelated areas including the media, the client community, the audience in the marketplace and the marketing services sector, in order to provide a research-based snap-shot of the current state of the industry. Katriona Lawlor explores recent approaches to the study of advertising as communication, drawing on post-modernist discourse to present a meaning-based model, which places the reader of the advertisement at the centre of the discussion. Michael Carey offers a practitioner's view of the strategic needs that clients seek to fulfil in their communication activity directed towards enhancement of their brand franchise and brand equity in an FMCG environment. The business-to-business framework of communications is reviewed by Sean de Búrca in a paper which presents a typology of business-to-business communication techniques and argues for the integrated application of marketing communication tools in a highly targeted way in order to establish and defend vital relationships.

Against this background, section two considers from a managerial perspective the changing role of each of the respective players in the contemporary Irish advertising industry. Ian Fox and Iskandar Abdullah examine the function, role and direction of the agency, articulating the nature of external and internal relationships, and the processes involved in the creation of effective advertising. The central relationship, that of client and agency, is examined by Tony Meenaghan and Barbara Patton, utilising current Irish research findings which provide insight into the factors influencing relationship establishment, maintenance and dissolution. Iskandar Abdullah and J.P. Donnelly analyse the tensions that may arise between the parties in developing and delivering effective advertising, and they identify the creative briefing process as crucial to the achievement of campaign goals.

Phelim O'Leary and Des Byrne argue that the role of marketing research in the overall advertising process must never be allowed to become technique fixated or to become an end in itself. However, in its proper place it can make a significant and highly relevant contribution at a number of junctures in the advertising chain, and they particularly emphasise the role of research, especially qualitative research, in the development of strategy.

Current practice in the selecting and scheduling of media is outlined by Peter McPartlin who considers the various claims of qualitative judgment and quantitative-based decision-making in realising both the targeting and creative objectives of advertising. The media-research industry generates the media-research data which is the currency by which advertising space is bought and sold and Áine O'Donoghue and Tom Harper provide a definitive reading of the joint industry structures and the individual research surveys which meet the needs of clients, agencies and media owners alike. Paul O'Sullivan and Peter Dolan examine the complex relationship of partners in the distribution value chain where the Irish research evidence shows that the objectives of the individual players are seldom fully complementary when the creation and implementation of co-operative communication campaigns are at issue. Frank Bradley, Eamonn Clarkin and Dympna Hughes consider the problems involved in developing an international communication strategy in an increasingly global marketplace, arguing that global campaigns demand flexibility in addressing the conditions of each individual market. For Irish companies the choice will lie on a continuum between exporting to a number of markets with relatively limited ambitions, and creating a lasting brand franchise in a selected number of key target markets.

This section concludes with two papers which review the overall context in which advertising operates in Ireland. In an examination of the regulatory framework of advertising, Duncan Grehan identifies the key statutory and voluntary regulatory arrangements, and outlines the implications of technological change for the industry and the regulators. Elizabeth Reynolds and Fred Hayden evaluate critical issues facing advertisers in Ireland today, ranging from cost factors to legislative constraints to relationships with the agency.

In the third section, issues of communication strategy are considered. John Fanning re-asserts the primacy of the brand as the focus of marketing effort, and argues that building the long-term brand franchise remains the core objective of marketing activity. Tony Meenaghan suggests that image creation is a critically important area of modern marketing, and he examines the various forms of marketing imagery and the role that advertising strategy has in developing such images. In two, strongly case-based, papers John Byrne and Kevin Bourke explore the role of communication in the management of strategic corporate identity in ESB, and in the implementation of radical corporate change in the AIB Group respectively.

Segmentation forms a common theme in papers which use current Irish research to consider issues of appeal strategy and campaign targeting. Valerie Quinn, Tony Meenaghan and Teresa Brannick conclude that fear appeals remain a potent creative option, particularly when message strategy and content are targeted according to the identified market segments. Darach Turley argues that the marketers of mainstream consumer brands may have ignored the very substantial senior market segment up until now, but cannot continue to do so given that the 55+ age cohort is the generation that has determined the status of today's successful brands over its life span through the exercise of a form of consumer veto. There are major implications in terms of targeting, appeal strategy and role portrayal for the marketer of mainstream consumer brands. Kevin Donnelly and Cathal Brugha suggest that consumers purchase from a repertoire of brands within which any new brand must seek to take its place. They argue that it is only through the disturbance of purchase patterns that a new brand can succeed, and that communication strategy must focus on creating uncertainty in the minds of consumers, using a front-loaded launch-support package.

The fourth section represents a broadening of focus to encompass the totality of marketing communications methods available to the marketing manager. The blurring of the traditional "line" between advertising and other elements of the conventional marketing communication mix has been a feature of practice over recent years. Managers have taken a more integrated approach to achieving communication objectives, and the industry has responded with a reconfiguration of agency form and function. The weight of budget spend has oscillated between advertising and non-media appropriations, but the long-term trend would suggest that emerging options such as sponsorship and direct marketing will take their place alongside advertising, sales promotion and public relations in the future.

Laura Cuddihy, Kate Uí Ghallachóir and Fred Hayden examine the Irish sales-promotion sector, detailing a managerial approach to the creation of campaigns, and outlining the options available for achieving both tactical and strategic ends. Marie O'Dwyer and Mary Lambkin consider the potential of couponing within a sales promotion campaign, utilising recent Irish research to place problems in an overall perspective. Francis X. Carty addresses issues of definition in the field of public relations and publicity and evaluates a number of models for the management of relationships, corporate communication and reputation. He argues that public relations can be an agent of change, a path to the resolution of problems and a core competence for the management of conflict. Tony Meenaghan sees commercial sponsorship as a particularly potent marketing communications medium, provided that those managing it have a clear vision of its role and potential, and adopt a rigorous approach to all aspects of campaign design and implementation. David Shipley suggests a similar planning framework to guide exhibiting practice based on recent in-depth research with Irish and British exhibitors. The dramatic rise of direct marketing is mapped by Michael McGowan in a detailed examination of the characteristics of the activity, the trends now emerging, and the factors that will drive likely future developments in an Irish context. Paul O'Sullivan and Donald McFettridge re-appraise the evidence regarding the impact of store atmospherics on store choice and in-store behaviour, and conclude that while retailers are sophisticated in the use of atmospherics, researchers have failed to address many of the key issues despite the obvious potential for cross-disciplinary work with other academic specialists.

The fifth section considers the effects and outcomes of advertising in terms of the achievement of objectives, the actual response of consumers to advertisements and the wider social and economic impact of activity by the industry. Peter Nash reviews the literature on how advertising works and how appropriate objectives are set and realised, and he provides insight into a highly effective advertising campaign for the Guinness brand. Stephanie O'Donohoe argues that consumers not only understand the rules of the advertising game, but also use their understanding to play with ads in ways that practitioners may not intend and academics are only beginning to appreciate. Caolan Mannion and Damien McLoughlin examine the social and economic effects of advertising, detailing the costs and benefits involved, and exploring the nature of consumer ambivalence towards advertising, with particular reference to the emergence of a new information-driven society.

It is anticipated that students, practitioners and commentators will find much that will be of value in the individual papers contained in this volume. The contributors are senior practitioners in the field and academics actively engaged in researching marketing communications processes and outcomes. The editors hope that this first comprehensive attempt to examine a dynamic and important sector of the economy will aid current understanding, as well as stimulating a debate which may influence in some small way industry practice, public policy and the direction of future research.

REFERENCES

Duncan, T., Caywood C. and Newsom, D. (1993): *Preparing Advertising and Public Relations Students for the Communications Industry in the 21st Century*, A Report of the Task Force on Integrated Communications, Chicago, IL: Northwestern University.

Schultz, D.E., Tannenbaum, I. and Lauterborn, R.F. (1993): *Integrated Marketing Communications*, Lincolnwood, Chicago: NTC Business Books.

Stewart, D. (1995): *The Market-Back Approach to the Design of Integrated Communications Programs: A Change in Paradigm and a Focus on Determinants of Success*, Working Paper, Department of Marketing, University of Southern California, Los Angeles, CA.

Acknowledgements

A volume such as this is ambitious both in scope and scale, and the realisation, even in part, of those ambitions is largely due to the generosity of the academics and practitioners who have contributed their expertise, experience and insight so willingly and generously. The fusion of theory and practice involved in bringing together the work of the many specialists from the industry with the research insights provided by academic commentators required an exceptional spirit of co-operation, patience and even tolerance on the part of the contributors. We wish to thank them all sincerely for making their time, their knowledge and their understanding available to the larger public.

A particular word of appreciation is due to Fred Hayden, Chief Executive of the Association of Advertisers in Ireland (AAI) Ltd., for the provision of wise counsel and continued support throughout the enterprise, and for making available the results of researches conducted under the aegis of the AAI. We would like to thank John Fanning of McConnell's Advertising Services both for contributing a paper to the book and for agreeing to write the foreword to the overall collection. Thanks are also due to Ian Fox of the Institute of Advertising Practitioners in Ireland (IAPI), and to the members of other industry bodies for the generous provision of pertinent information and advice.

There are many individuals within the agency sector and the marketing-support industry who have been unstinting in providing information, in answering and clarifying queries and in guiding our steps in bringing this project to fruition. Their active interest in the venture, no less than their co-operation, is greatly appreciated.

We would also like to thank the editors of the journals who kindly allowed us to reproduce material. In particular, we would like to thank Aidan O'Driscoll, editor of the *Irish Marketing Review*, for his unstinting generosity in this regard. Thanks are also due to the editor of the *International Journal of Advertising*.

We owe a particular debt of gratitude to Professor Bill Roche, Research Director of the Graduate School of Business at UCD for his support and enthusiasm for this project and for the larger project of creating a rigorous and relevant management literature, which will be of value to students and members of the business community.

This volume could not have reached the publication stage in the available time without the dedication and commitment of Mary Mulcahy who worked as research assistant on the project. Her infinite patience and meticulous attention to detail in helping to prepare the text for publication are greatly appreciated.

Finally we wish to thank David Givens and his colleagues at Oak Tree Press for their professionalism, forbearance and support at all stages of this venture.

The book represents a collaboration between acknowledged experts in communication practice, and academic researchers who are actively engaged with the issues addressed. This collaboration has provided a particularly satisfying dimension to the task of editing this book. We trust that the papers, individually and collectively, will provide equally satisfying, stimulating, and in some instances even provocative, reading.

Tony Meenaghan
Paul O'Sullivan
September 1995

Part 1

Marketing Communications — Concepts and Context

1
Marketing Communications in Transition

Tony Meenaghan

INTRODUCTION

The term "marketing communications" is currently used in marketing to describe the totality of methods of communication and persuasion available to the marketing manager. As such, it is broader than just advertising, incorporating the other elements of the marketing communications mix, namely sales promotion, personal selling and public relations. This umbrella term supplants other rapidly ageing classifications of communications activity in marketing, such as "above-" and "below-the-line" advertising and "media" and "non-media" advertising. It further provides a flexible and inclusive framework for an examination of this fast-changing area of marketing management.

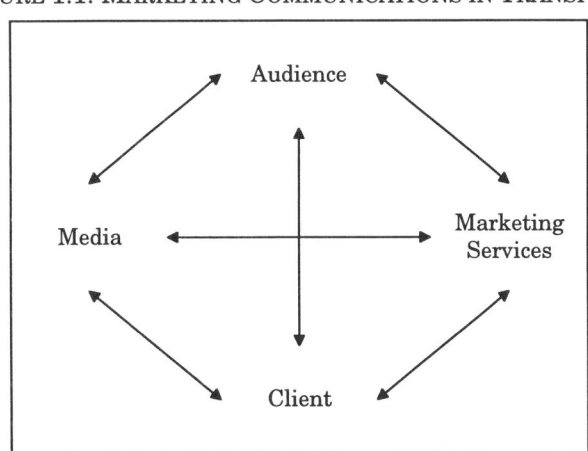

FIGURE 1.1: MARKETING COMMUNICATIONS IN TRANSITION

Few areas of human experience have been subject to change of the same scale and pace as that wrought in recent times in the field of human communications. Consequently, marketing, together with its attendant field of marketing communications, is in a state of considerable transition (Duncan, Caywood and Newson, 1993). The purpose of this paper is to examine the changes currently underway in a number of sectors of the marketing communications industry. These interrelated sectors as indicated in Figure 1.1 above, include the media, clients, audience and the marketing services sector which services/ supports this industry. As the effects of change pervade all economies and impact on companies of greatly varying scale, this paper will present evidence from both the Irish and larger international market.

Given that the focus of the paper is marketing communications in transition, Figure 1.2 is instructive in that it provides a research-based snap-shot of the various elements that currently constitute the marketing communications industry (excluding personal selling). It further illustrates the relative emphasis accorded to the individual components of marketing communications, in that the figures indicated under each heading represent the value of that activity in the UK market for the year 1992.

CHANGES IN THE MEDIA
Above-the-Line Activity

There has been little evidence of major change taking place in the traditional above-the-line media in Ireland. Table 1.1 below, which portrays the allocation of expenditure in Ireland to the various above-the-line media between 1988 and 1994, shows an increasing market-share in this sector for television, radio and the regional press. A declining percentage of above-the-line expenditure is currently allocated to both the magazine and outdoor sectors, while a temporary levelling off of television spend in 1990 and 1991 was largely attributable to the effects of the Broadcasting Act, 1990, which is discussed more fully below. The level of cinema advertising, though minuscule in percentage terms, continues to grow as it does in most developed economies.

Traditional above-the-line advertising has endured considerable recessionary effects. In the major economies in the US market, advertising as a percentage of Gross Domestic Product (GDP) fell from 2.42 per cent in 1987 to 2.16 per cent in 1993 (*The Economist,* August 1994). Similarly in the UK market in 1991, media advertising as a percentage of GDP was at its lowest point since 1985 (Briggs, 1993). While the recent past may have been particularly difficult for media advertising, projections suggest a more encouraging future in the US market. Industry experts Veronis, Suhler and Associates (1994)

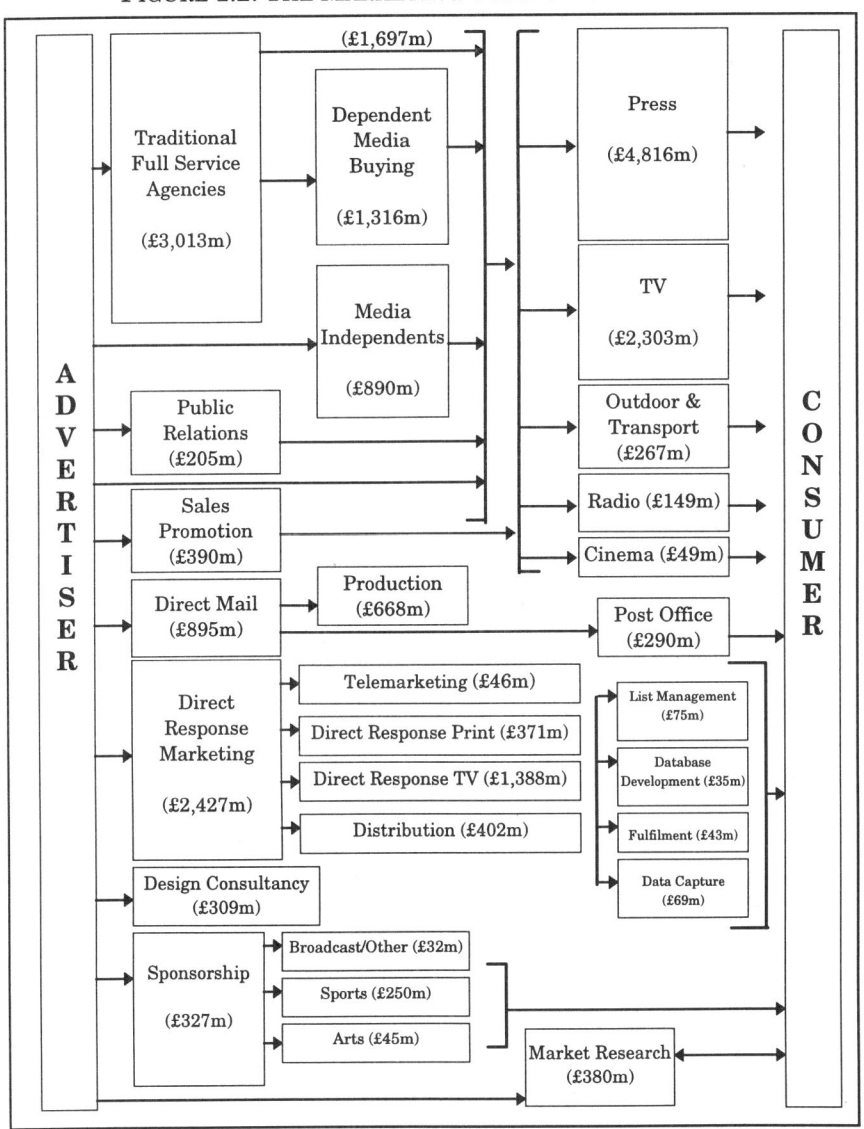

FIGURE 1.2: THE MARKETING COMMUNICATIONS MAP

Advertiser			Consumer
Traditional Full Service Agencies (£3,013m)	Dependent Media Buying (£1,316m) [£1,697m]	Press (£4,816m)	
	Media Independents (£890m)	TV (£2,303m)	
Public Relations (£205m)		Outdoor & Transport (£267m)	
Sales Promotion (£390m)		Radio (£149m)	
		Cinema (£49m)	
Direct Mail (£895m)	Production (£668m)	Post Office (£290m)	
Direct Response Marketing (£2,427m)	Telemarketing (£46m)	List Management (£75m)	
	Direct Response Print (£371m)	Database Development (£35m)	
	Direct Response TV (£1,388m)	Fulfilment (£43m)	
	Distribution (£402m)	Data Capture (£69m)	
Design Consultancy (£309m)			
Sponsorship (£327m)	Broadcast/Other (£32m)		
	Sports (£250m)		
	Arts (£45m)	Market Research (£380m)	

Source: Adapted from Snowden, S. (1992): "The 1992 Marketing and Communications Map", *Admap*, 27(10): 51.

suggest a compound annual growth of 6.3 per cent for the period 1993–98 in the US market as against 2.3 per cent over the period 1988–93, while worldwide advertising expenditure is forecast to grow by 6.7 per cent in 1995 (Zenith Media Worldwide, 1994; *The Economist,* August 1994).

TABLE 1.1: ESTIMATES OF IRISH ADVERTISING EXPENDITURE IN IRELAND, 1990–94

Year:	1990		1991		1992		1993		1994	
Medium	£m	%	£m	%	£m	%	£m	%	£m	%
National Newspapers	63.0	38.0	64.0	37.0	70.5	37.0	74.5	36.0	79.5	35.5
Regional Newspapers	6.0	4.0	6.5	4.0	7.5	4.0	8.0	4.0	8.5	4.0
Magazines	10.0	6.0	9.0	5.0	9.0	5.0	10.0	5.0	11.5	5.0
Television	51.0	31.0	56.5	32.0	64.5	35.0	71.5	34.5	78.5	35.0
Radio	20.0	12.0	24.0	14.0	24.5	13.0	27.0	13.0	28.0	12.5
Outdoor	13.0	8.0	13.0	7.5	14.0	7.5	15.0	7.0	15.5	7.0
Cinema	0.8	0.5	1.0	0.5	1.0	0.5	1.2	0.5	2.3	1.0
Total (rounded)	163.8		174.0		191.0		207.2		223.8	

Source: Association of Advertisers in Ireland Ltd. (1995): based on Central Statistics Office, National Newspapers of Ireland, and Advertising Statistics of Ireland data.

In Ireland, above-the-line media advertising has not suffered to the same degree as happened in other major economies. This can perhaps be attributed to the fact that Ireland is an under-advertised economy with a per-capita expenditure of $150.8 in 1994, compared to $251 in Spain and $325.5 in Switzerland in the same year. (*UK Marketing Pocket Book*, 1994). This observation is further evidenced by the fact that for 1995 advertising expenditure in Ireland as a percentage of Gross Domestic Product (GDP) is forecast at 0.76 per cent compared to 1.40 per cent in the UK (Zenith, 1995). In recent years media advertising has seen an annual increase in value terms of 8 per cent (Hayden, 1995). However when this figure is reduced to take into account very high levels of media inflation and national price inflation (based on the consumer price index), the volume increase in terms of expanded time and space bought has been more modest.

Above-/Below-the-Line Expenditure Reallocation

One of the most significant changes in the world of marketing communications in recent times has been the extent of the reallocation of marketing communications expenditure from above- to below-the-line media options. In the US market, traditional media advertising in 1992 accounted for 25 per cent of all advertising expenditure compared to 42 per cent in the mid-1970s (Shergill, 1993). In the US packaged goods industry, consumer and trade promotions now account for 70 per cent of communications expenditure (Donnelley Marketing Inc., 1992). Less dramatic, though no less significant, evidence of this reallocation of expenditure is available from the Irish market. Research carried out by the Marketing Development Programme (MDP) at University College Dublin on behalf of the Association of Advertisers in Ireland in 1993 showed that non-media advertising (NMA) accounted for 38 per cent of total advertising expenditure, with the total estimated value of non-media advertising for 1992 being given as £117 million. Arising from this study, the break-down of expenditure to various forms of non-media advertising is shown below in Table 1.2.

TABLE 1.2: BREAKDOWN OF NMA EXPENDITURE, 1992

Non-Media Activity	1992 Expenditure (£ m)
Point of Sale	34
Direct Mail	19
Exhibitions	18
Competitions	15
Added Extra	10
Extra Product/Money-Off	8
Demonstrations	7
Sampling	6

Source: A Report on the Extent and Trends of Non-Media Advertising in Ireland (1993), UCD Marketing Development Programme for the Association of Advertisers in Ireland Ltd.

As is the case with above-the-line expenditure, the NMA budget is variously allocated to a combination of trade and consumer promotions, with a reported 62 per cent of NMA expenditure allocated to final consumers and 38 per cent to the trade sector (MDP, 1993). However this general pattern varies quite widely by industrial sector. For instance, the food sector directs 77 per cent of its non-media advertising to the end consumer. In the US market, it is reported that packaged goods manufacturers in 1993 directed their budgets as follows: 25.2 per cent to media advertising, 46.9 per cent to trade promotion and 27.9 per cent to consumer promotion, indicating the importance of NMA expenditure to that sector (Donnelley, 1994).

Indications from the US market suggest that the rate of growth in promotions expenditure will lessen in the coming years. Industry forecasters, Veronis, Suhler and Associates (1994) suggest that projected annual compound growth will be 3.2 per cent over the period 1993–98, compared to 4.3 per cent over the 1988–93 period. This is somewhat lower than the projected growth rates for media advertising previously cited.

A Media Explosion

From the development of the printing press to the creation of radio and television, technological advance has always been a key catalyst in the development of new media. This is evident in the recent utilisation of satellite for broadcast purposes and will again prove true with the advent of the much heralded super-highway as technological advance continues to provide alternative access routes to consumers (McPartlin, 1995; Merkle, 1995). For the purposes of analysing this media explosion, attention will be focused under two separate headings, namely:

- The fragmentation of traditional media
- New media developments.

Fragmentation of Traditional Media

Media fragmentation, brought about by technological advance, increased leisure-time availability and related life-style changes, is significantly altering access routes to target markets. Two major factors have been instrumental in the fragmentation of traditional media. The first is an expansion of new media vehicles in each medium — increasing number of press titles, for example. The second factor is media overspill from other markets, which, while long a problem for advertisers, is greatly exacerbated by technological developments.

Fragmentation resulting from an expansion of media vehicles is evident in the following examples. In the UK market, BRAD (British Rate and Data) indicates that there was a 53 per cent increase in the number of magazines available in 1993 as compared to 1984, with 694 more consumer and 1,746 more business and professional titles (*Magazine News*, 1994a). In the category "women's magazines", the Audit Bureau of Circulation (ABC) in the UK now audit 45 different magazine titles (ABC, 1993). The extent of fragmentation that has developed in the German market is indicated by the fact that there are 8,000 magazines available in that marketplace (*Magazine News*, 1994b).

In Ireland the radio sector has greatly expanded with Radio Éireann giving way to Radio One, 2FM and FM3 under the aegis of RTE. Further expansion of the sector has resulted from the establishment of the Independent Radio and Television Commission (IRTC), which today licenses 21 independent commercial stations and a number of community radio stations.

While technological development has facilitated the expansion of media vehicles, it has been the primary factor facilitating media overspill, particularly in the broadcast media. In recent times, Europe has seen a massive expansion in the television sector. In 1980 there were 67 television stations broadcasting in Europe, but this had increased to 157 by the early 1990s (Perry, 1994). By the year 2000, it is predicted that there will be some 500 television stations servicing the European market (Barrett, 1995). This expansion has had several related effects. One result was that the number of broadcast hours on European television increased threefold in the period 1985–92 (Antenna, 1993). Another inevitable consequence of this scale of development is media overspill. For example, 60 per cent of Swiss households now have a choice of 40 television stations, many from outside the state (Morand, 1995).

The television market in most economies is now serviced by both terrestrial and satellite stations. In the case of the Irish market, increased station choice is derived from the considerable expansion of foreign television stations available on cable and satellite-dish services. There are more than 400,000 cable-receiving subscribers (Irish Multi-Channel Operators Associations, 1995; O'Brien and Roper, 1995) and 60,000 satellite-receiving dishes (Sky Television, 1995) currently in service in Ireland. While subscribers in many areas of the Republic of Ireland have received more than the RTE channels for some years now, the extent of media fragmentation is evident in the fact that subscribers to Cablelink in the Dublin area can now receive 13 channels on the basic service and a further five on a pay-to-view basis. Current levels of television-station penetration in Ireland are indicated in Table 1.3

TABLE 1.3: TELEVISION-STATION PENETRATION, 1988–93

Year	RTE 1/ Network 2	BBC1	BBC2	UTV	HTV	CH4	S4C	Sky One	Sky News
1988	100	58	58	50	9	49	8	31	—
1989	100	61	61	53	10	52	7	30	4
1990	100	64	64	54	11	57	8	32	23
1991	100	63	63	53	12	53	10	34	31
1992	100	65	65	53	12	53	9	37	33
1993	100	66	66	57	10	57	7	16*	15*
1994	100	68	67	62	8	63	5	36	38

* Cable services curtailed in this period
Base: All TV Homes = 100%
Source: AGB TAM (1994).

The press sector in Ireland has similarly been affected by an expanding range of domestically produced titles and overspill from the UK market (Walsh, 1995). Traditional titles such as *The Irish Independent, The Irish Press* and *The Irish Times* have had to compete with new Irish titles such as the *Star, Sunday World, Sunday Tribune* and *Sunday Business Post* (McConnell's Media Facts 1995, Palmer 1995). The extent of overspill from the UK is evident from the fact that the *Daily Mirror* now sells approximately 50,000 copies in the Irish market while "Sundays" such as the *Sunday Times* and the *News of the World* sell some 58,205 and 166,583 units respectively, with sales of the latter almost twice the sales of the *Sunday Tribune* (National Newspapers of Ireland, 1995*)*. The effect of this competitive pressure has been to render many Irish titles unprofitable and in the case of the Irish Press Group, to render the future of its titles precarious (*Business and Finance*, 1995).

New Media Developments

As marketers continue to seek alternative access routes to target markets, new media opportunities have developed. Certain of these, such as cable and satellite broadcasting, have resulted from technological advance, while other media developments have stemmed from corporate desire for more cost-efficient access to markets. Notable amongst these is commercial sponsorship which is valued at $10.8 billion worldwide (SRI, 1994). The explosive growth in this medium is graphically illustrated by the fact that the UK sponsorship market was valued at £4 million in 1970 (Buckley, 1980) but by 1994 it was valued at £450 million (Mintel, 1994). Pro-rata expenditure on sponsorship for the Republic of Ireland would be in the order of £20–£25 million per annum. These estimates of direct spending do not include the support spend necessary to promote the sponsor's association with an event. Industry suggestions are that for effective sponsorship a figure at least equivalent to the direct costs must be invested in support promotions, which greatly increases the marketing investment in this medium. The percentage of total advertising expenditure going to sponsorship varies considerably by country. In the UK, the relevant percentage is 4.3 per cent, in the US 3.3 per cent, and in Italy 7.0 per cent (ISL Marketing, 1992).

Product placement is another example of advertisers seeking alternative routes to markets. Product placement is the inclusion/presentation within programmes, normally television shows or films, of goods and services as part of realistic scene creation. In effect, programme or film producers offer, for monetary return, to show/use particular products or services in their productions, which ultimately are seen by consumers. Its recency, growth and main market are indicated by the fact that 35 placement agencies were established in the US between 1982 and 1990 (Swain, 1990). Its potency can be seen by the fact that a brand such as Ray Ban sunglasses increased its sales from 18,000 units to over 4 million units as a result of being placed in over 160 movies per year, such as *Risky Business*, and *Top Gun*. Its impact on conventional advertising is indicated by the report that only £370,000 was spent advertising sunglasses in the main British media in 1989, less than half the figure for 1985, even though sales were worth £43 million (Lees and Rayment, 1990).

Interactive games of the Sega and Nintendo variety provide a particularly potent access medium to the youth market (Brown, 1994). These interactive games represent a new form of channel to particular audiences, and to date some 100 interactive advertising campaigns have been carried on computer games, such as Predator football boots on "FIFA International Soccer", Pepsi/7-Up on "Formula 1 Grand Prix", Coca-Cola on the Olympics game and Snickers on the Nintendo game "Biker Mice from Mars".

These games differ from traditional advertising media in several respects. Advertising on this medium could be described as non-linear, being threaded through and appearing within the context of the game, with the message often changing as the game is progressed by the player. Furthermore, the medium delivers not just a captive, but an involved receiver. Unlike traditional media advertising, players are their own media schedulers, determining their own frequency and intensity of exposure. A final distinction is that this medium delivers an almost exclusively young, male-biased audience. It is reported that some 82 per cent of 5–19-year-olds play interactive games on a weekly basis, with the UK Leisure Software market being valued at £850 million in 1994, and its power as a medium is evident in that the PGA European Tour Game reached 57 per cent of 16–18-year-old boys (Bobroff, 1995).

Advertising on the Internet provides an access medium to a different segment of society, with the longer-term probability of total market coverage, perhaps under another technological iteration. Currently, advertising on this medium is something of an unknown quantity for advertisers, agencies and regulators, but this communication channel has the potential to be the ultimate overspill medium and this looks likely to represent the future direction of advertising media.

Increased Clutter

One of the inevitable consequences of the explosion in media and media vehicles is increasingly cluttered channels of communication to selected audiences. A recent Marketing Society (Ireland) newsletter (*Perspectives*, 1994) suggests that by the age of 20, the typical North American has seen 800,000 ads on television. Were one also to include ads carried in media other than television, the net result is an incredibly cluttered, noisy environment with obvious consequences for those attempting to gain the attention of selected audiences and ultimately to persuade them to behave as suggested. Recent commentary on this cluttered advertising environment would also indicate that viewer recall of advertising has fallen (Micklethwait, 1990). A further development among all consumers of advertising, inevitably linked to clutter, is the change in consumer attitudes to advertising. Recent research indicates that consumers are becoming more hostile towards advertising in general, and increasingly fail to see the resultant benefits of it (Pollay and Mittal, 1993; Mittal, 1994).

Media Inflation

Media costs, measured on the cost of reaching 1,000 members of the targeted population (CPT), show Ireland to be a reasonable cost environment in which to mount an advertising campaign but reveal some sharp differences between media. This is evident from Table 1.4 which compares the relative costs of European media. As indicated, television costs in Ireland are approximately half the European average, but colour-press advertising costs are some two-and-a-half times the European average. A comparison of costs across all media with our nearest market, the UK, is instructive, showing media costs in Ireland generally to be greater than those pertaining in the UK.

TABLE 1.4: ADULT CPTS INDEXED ON THE EUROPEAN AVERAGE

Country	TV All-Time	Newspaper Mono	Newspaper Colour	Radio All-Time	Cinema
Belgium	153	84	101	60	92
Denmark	155	135	101	204	117
Finland	124	111	130	225	95
France	68	206	86	89	104
Germany	124	106	117	50	62
Greece	29	117	152	21	237
Ireland	52	114	262	61	137
Italy	109	76	67	—	—
Netherlands	69	64	96	44	129
Norway	233	114	136	210	62
Portugal	52	66	92	—	—
Spain	121	65	63	52	125
Sweden	172	87	173	—	100
Switzerland	173	143	394	589	144
UK	76	34	77	65	93
Europe	100	100	100	100	100

Source: Marsh, F. (1991), "Irish TV half European Average", *Irish Marketing Journal*, December: 10–11.

Whilst the figures presented in Table 1.4 may appear attractive from a relativist perspective, they are unlikely to provide much solace to domestic focused Irish marketers who have incurred significant production costs and who have witnessed substantial media inflation in recent years. The level of media inflation which has affected the Irish media market is indicated in Table 1.5.

TABLE 1.5: FIVE-YEAR INDEX OF IRISH MEDIA COSTS

Year	Consumer Price Index*	RTE			
		RTE TV	Radio 1	2FM	Cinema
1990	100.0	100	100	100	100
1991	103.6	132	108	109	95
1992	106.0	153	135	123	98
1993	107.6	153	129	129	96
1994	110.1	145	128	146	86
	Sunday	Mornings	Evenings	Regionals	Magazines
1990	100	100	100	100	100
1991	106	103	119	102	122
1992	109	111	132	126	118
1993	112	118	130	123	119
1994	118	122	142	128	122

* *Source*: CSO annual averages. McConnell's, Media Facts, 1995.

Media inflation associated with RTE television can be attributed to the Broadcasting Act introduced in 1990. This Act, which had the objective (through the capping of RTE revenue) of diverting advertising spend from RTE toward other media, particularly the developing local-radio sector, had the effect of boosting the advertising revenue to spill-over media such as UTV and Channel Four and, more importantly for Irish advertisers, driving up local media rates (AAI, 1992; DKM, 1991; DKM, 1992). While the rate of inflation in television has fallen following the withdrawal of the Broadcasting Act in 1993, in the early 1990s Irish advertisers were faced with media cost inflation which annually ran at several multiples of the national inflation level as indicated by the consumer price index.

Media cost inflation was rampant in Ireland in the early 1990s, and there can be little doubt but that media inflation has been a major factor affecting advertising worldwide over recent decades. In the US market in 1970, a 60-second slot around the *Bewitched* television programme cost $5,200 and a 30-second slot around *Peyton Place* cost $2,750. By 1994 a 30-second slot around the programme *Seinfield* cost $390,000 (Mandese, 1995).

CHANGES IN CLIENT PERSPECTIVES

Changed client perspectives have contributed to the state of turbulence in marketing communications. A number of these developments can be identified as follows.

The Growing Power of the Retailer

It has long been recognised that in many industries the balance of power once so lovingly guarded by the manufacturer has swung irreversibly in favour of the retailer. The loose collection of disorganised and independent retailers, no match for corporate monoliths of a previous era, has now been replaced by highly focused, highly demanding retail power blocks. Mayer (1991) reports that by the end of the 1980s five chains sold half of all non-food, non-durable consumer goods in the US market. In the Irish market, 5 per cent of shops control 61.3 per cent of food turnover, while 30 per cent of shops control 52 per cent and 62.8 per cent of turnover in the chemist and liquor sectors respectively (A.C. Nielsen, 1994). In the UK in 1992, 5 per cent of shops controlled 70 per cent of turnover in the grocery sector (A.C. Nielsen, 1995). This concentration of consumer demand with a small number of retail buyers has impacted on the marketing communications industry. Several manifestations of this impact can be illustrated.

The Repositioning of Retailer Brands.

Having used their power to force many manufacturers to produce generic and own-label brands on their behalf, retailers are increasingly investing in their own brands. Improved product quality, redesign and repackaging has significantly narrowed the gap between manufacturer and retailer brands, with obvious consequences in terms of consumer choice (Murphy, 1994). With a vested interest in developing consumer franchise for their brands, the retailer often seeks to reduce the number of brands carried, delisting third and fourth ranked brands, thereby reducing the competition for the retailer brand, while simultaneously positioning it against the major brands in the category. Indeed, there is evidence that consumers increasingly perceive less difference between brand names and the alternatives. Studies by DDB Needham and Grey Advertising in the US market show a decline in those purchasing manufacturer brands and in those believing that such manufacturer brands assure quality (Landler, 1991). In fact, the upgrading of the retailer brand is a central feature of the marketing strategy of Irish supermarket chains.

Pressure to Re-channel Communications Expenditure

Retailers, concerned to impact on their own bottom-line, are pressing major national brand owners to invest in below-the-line expenditures which boost sales through their outlets. Retailer concerns for sales performance are often at variance with those of national brand owners who wish to invest in media advertising to boost the equity in their brands, thereby differentiating these manufacturer brands from retailer brands. Not only are powerful retailers forcing manufacturers to redirect their communications budgets to sales promotions, but they are also charging national brand owners for access to shelf-space. This practice, once prevalent in the Irish supermarket trade, often referred to as "hello money" or a slotting allowance, is proof positive of retailer power and consequent influence over marketing-communications expenditure in Ireland.

The Retailer as Marketer

A third consequence of the increased power of the retail sector is the emergence of the retailer as marketer. Empowered by the concentration of purchasing expenditure, the retailer has also significantly gained from technological developments. Information provided by check-out scanners and bar-codes enables the retailer to monitor consumer choice in a manner rarely available to the manufacturer. This information, combined with that generated externally through tie-in promotions with cinemas, garages, etc. through schemes such as Superquinn's Superclub, dramatically improves available profiles on the modern consumer. This information provides the retailer with the ability to decide which manufacturer brands to stock and which manufacturer brands to copy as retailer brands, as well as enabling them to monitor the effectiveness of both their own and manufacturers' promotional efforts. In effect, technology is bringing the retailer closer to consumers and their preferences. In return, the retailer is changing from being the outlet for manufacturers' produce to taking on the catalytic role of informed, empowered marketer, with the manufacturer increasingly being relegated to the role of supplier. Inevitably, this role as marketer has caused retailers themselves to embrace wholeheartedly activity a range of marketing communications activity.

Corporate "Shortermism"

Responding to the pressures of stock-exchange values, corporations, particularly those in the Western World, have adopted a short-term orientation in corporate affairs. The corporate desire for ever-upward sales results translates into pressure on brand managers to deliver results that satisfy the financial markets. This factor, allied to the mobility of the brand management career, has led to a shift in expenditure to those methods of marketing communications which produce rapid sales responses. In effect, this shift in expenditure to consumer and trade promotions, while often delivering short-term sales gain (frequently unsustained when the promotion ends), results in reduced investment in media advertising, the key driver of brand equity (Jones, 1990). The irony is that financial markets, so recently obsessed with brands and their inherent equity, are now the pressure point which lead to a reallocation of communications expenditure to the detriment of longer-term brand equity. The corporate "shortermism" is articulated by Schultz (1991) as follows:

> Struggling to meet financial goals in markets that often grow no faster than the population as a whole, packaged-goods companies have been riding hard on their brand managers to produce quarterly sales results — people are saying: "I can't wait for the advertising to work. I've got to turn these dollars around more quickly". Driven by these demands the brand manager in turn is demanding "value" from the advertising agency, who is traditionally ill-equipped to service the sales-oriented short-term needs of clients (70).

In an Irish context this short-term orientation is often reflected in pressure from corporate headquarters abroad on local Irish operations to yield specific turnover requirements.

Increasing Number of Similar Brands

Despite the difficulties of securing demand, there is an ever-increasing supply of products available to consumers with these products being largely homogeneous in terms of customer benefits.

The increasing supply of products can be related to several factors including increased competition in market sectors brought about by globalisation and the product-development activities of retailers. In 1975, the average US supermarket carried approximately 9,000 items, but currently some 3,000 new products are introduced each year, with some US supermarkets now carrying up to 30,000 items (*The Economist*, 1992). While some of this expansion can be attributed to an increased number of categories carried, it none the less indicates the extent to which companies are seeking continual product innovation as the route to success. Increasingly, those products being offered to the marketplace are similar. This is because technological advance no longer offers the certainty of sustained competitive advantage, with the result that many product alternatives are largely indistinguishable. A recent example of this phenomenon is the emergence of new yellow fats technology in Ireland and its rapid imitation by Irish processors. One US commentator, Rothenberg (1989), suggested that there were 150 cereal brands each with sales of $1 million or more in that marketplace.

In an environment where product innovation no longer provides sustained competitive advantage, continued customer loyalty must be generated by factors above and beyond functional innovation. Convinced believers in advertising argue that the key to a longer term customer franchise is through continued investment in brand equity through sustained media advertising (Lannon, 1994).

Given the multiplicity of factors affecting their decision, national brand owners now appear like rabbits caught in the headlights of an oncoming car, knowing that they should move but unsure as to which direction. The sales-promotions route, while delivering short-term sales results which impress the stock exchange, denigrate the brand equity and move it perilously close to the upgraded retailer brand. Investment in brand equity through media advertising will only deliver in the longer term, with less tangible returns in the interim causing stock-exchange anxieties. A further complication of this strategy is that it is likely to incur the wrath of the retailers who prefer the promotions route which will impact on their bottom line.

CHANGES IN THE SUPPLY/PRODUCTION INDUSTRY

As a result of the fusion of various pressures, such as technological advance, increased consumer sophistication, and the changing regulatory environment, as well as increasing client pressure for value, the supply/production industry which services marketing communications is the subject of fundamental adjustment. A number of specific changes can be identified.

The Growth of Specialist Agencies

An inevitable consequence of the shift in expenditure to below-the-line options is the increased reliance by advertisers on the services of specialist agencies. As such, the communications industry is now serviced by specialist agencies in the fields of direct marketing, promotions and sponsorship, amongst others.

Indeed, in many of the world's major advertising markets, even the specialists are specialising, with agencies dedicated to the internet, interactive media, and to sub-sectors of new media such as popular music sponsorship. While traditional agencies have attempted to minimise the income loss by either establishing or taking over specialist service agencies, the net outcome is increased servicing of client needs by specialist agencies, whether they are independents or advertising-agency subsidiaries.

The Growth of Media Specialists

The expansion and contraction of services have long been a feature of the history of advertising agencies worldwide, oscillating from the full-service one-stop-shop to the "hot shop" concentrating solely on creative output. One of the more notable trends in recent times has been the emergence of the media specialist, who increasingly has taken on one of the key services offered by traditional advertising agencies.

Advertisers, driven by a demand for efficiency in expenditure, are increasingly utilising the services of media specialists to place advertising created by the traditional agency. This emerging trend is more evident in the case of the multinational brands where the advertising is often produced in one market — the US, for example — and then circulated for media placement in each national market, either through an international media buying specialist or a local equivalent. In Western Europe in 1990, it was estimated that 34 per cent of media buying was handled by media specialist companies — that is, those not integrated into a full-service agency. In markets such as France, Italy and Spain, the share of advertising buying undertaken by media specialists was in the region of 80 per cent (Summers, 1994). Media specialists can be one of three types:

1) Genuinely independent specialist companies such as Carat International

2) Agency-owned media "dependants", such as Zenith and Initiative, owned by Saatchi and Lintas respectively

3) Media buying clubs such as the Media Partnership in the UK which buys on behalf of several traditional agencies such as JWT, Ogilvy and Mather, BBDO and DDB. Table 1.6 shows the relative shares of media buying by media specialists and clubs, on the one hand, and traditional agencies, on the other.

TABLE 1.6: MARKET SHARE OF MEDIA SPECIALISTS, 1990

Country	Specialists* %	Clubs %	Agencies/Others %
Austria	8	19	73
Belgium	13	36	51
Denmark	17	—	83
Finland	37	—	63
France	40	32	28
Germany	20	4	76
Greece	2	40	58
Italy	27	12	61
Netherlands	25	17	58
Norway	42	—	58
Portugal	24	39	37
Spain	72	19	9
Sweden	60	—	40
Switzerland	4	6	90
UK	30	—	70
Total	34	13	53

*   Including agency-owned and independents.
Source: Green, A. (1992): "Death of the Full-Service Ad Agency", *Admap*, 21(1): 22

The penetration of media specialists in the Irish market is apparent from a recent IAPI study which indicates that 16 per cent of major

Irish advertisers place their media buying with a media independent, compared to 3 per cent five years earlier (IAPI, 1994). In the Irish market, media-buying agencies can be subdivided into "independents" such as All-Ireland Media, The Media Bureau and GT Media and "dependants" such as Zenith and Initiative. Some media buying in the Irish market is also undertaken directly from the UK, particularly in the press sector.

The Traditional Advertising Agency

While advertising agencies have long been faced with changing environmental conditions, the variety of factors and the speed of change currently impacting on the industry has serious consequences for the traditional advertising agency. Squeezed between value-seeking, marketing-oriented clients, better-educated and more sophisticated consumers, and a variety of niche competitors offering specialist services, the traditional advertising agency is reassessing its position in the marketing communications industry.

The challenge for the traditional advertising agency is to redefine its role in an increasingly changing industry. The extent of its dilemma is obvious. Media advertising, the preserve of the traditional agency, is falling as a percentage of all marketing communications expenditure. In 1991, expenditure on media advertising in the UK accounted for 1.47 per cent of gross domestic product (GDP), its lowest level since 1985 (Briggs, 1993). Between 1987 and 1992 media advertising had a five-year historical growth rate of 6.5 per cent, while the specialist activities of public relations and direct marketing rose by 12 per cent and 11.2 per cent respectively (Briggs, 1993). With media independents often undertaking the placement of advertising on a commission level of 2–3 per cent, traditional full-service agencies are being undercut in this aspect of service. The result is declining agency profitability with the Institute of Practitioners in Advertising (IPA) in the UK indicating that industry net profit (before interest) fell from 2.2 per cent in 1988, to 1.9 per cent in 1989, and to 1.55 per cent in 1990 (Briggs, 1993).

Furthermore, there is evidence that agency/client relationships are increasingly of shorter duration. *Media International* estimates that in 1985, 50 per cent of major accounts stayed with the agency for 10 years or more, but today that percentage is less than 25 per cent (Briggs, 1993). Further research results indicating that the traditional agency/client relationship is under pressure are presented in a 1994 survey of major Irish advertisers, which reported that while 59 per cent of advertisers were likely to stay with a full-service agency over the 5-year period to 1999, 28 per cent of respondents were unlikely to do so, and a further 13 per cent were not sure (IAPI, 1994).

Faced with an increasingly turbulent marketplace, the traditional full-service agency must undergo fundamental adjustment in order to survive (Byles, 1992; Feldwick, 1992). The onus is now on the traditional agency to move from a product orientation to being more customer-responsive — in effect to introduce the values sought by clients such as flexibility, speed, and accountability allied to the ability and willingness to suggest solutions outside the agency's traditional area of service (*Marketing*, 1994). Given the importance of delivering on these objectives in order to survive, the organisational focus is on "re-engineering" the agency by introducing project managers in a less hierarchical structure with an emphasis on outsourcing the requisite talents. A recent perspective on the dilemma facing the traditional agency suggests that:

> To survive in the next decade, a new breed of agency will have to emerge.... The new agency will be half the size of the old agency, more flexible and with the ability and desire to work across twice as many areas and be more cost-efficient.... Agencies will need to change their attitude, become more client focused and learn to empathise with client needs (Cawley Nea Ltd., 1993).

Production Costs

While technological advance has benefited many aspects of advertising creation, such as computer-aided design, film and television production, as well as all aspects of press advertising, the reality is that the production costs of advertising are escalating. In fact, in many economies they are outstripping increases in media rates. In the UK market, media rates for press display advertising increased by 24 per cent between 1981 and 1991, while production costs increased by 59 per cent. This escalation is even more marked in the case of television where advertising production costs increased by 97 per cent over the decade to 1991, as against increased media costs of 55 per cent over that period (Henry, 1993). Increased production costs are a major concern for indigenous Irish advertisers whose costs must be allocated over smaller audience numbers relative to their counterparts in other European and international markets, who allocate production costs over much larger audiences. This represents an added motivation for clients to shift their communication spend towards promotion where initial production costs are lower.

Globalisation

As client companies have altered their focus from individual markets to contemplate the global consumer, the communications industry servicing the client has similarly felt the need to readjust. This is evident in the development of global advertising agencies which now are selected to service clients on an all-market basis (Turnbull and Doherty-Wilson, 1990), with many major Irish agencies now having an association with multinational groups. It follows from this development that campaigns are planned with a global consumer in mind, in terms of creative advertising work and media planning as well as the range of subsidiary services.

In this regard, Irish advertisers increasingly tend to focus beyond the Republic of Ireland market with 34 per cent of all major advertisers having an all-Ireland — that is, Republic of Ireland plus Northern Ireland — focus to their advertising in 1994 as compared with five years previously (IAPI, 1994). By 1999, 44 per cent of major Irish advertisers expect that their campaign focus will be on an all-Ireland basis, while 41 per cent expect their campaign to have a joint British and Irish focus (IAPI, 1994).

CHANGES IN THE AUDIENCE

The audience, which is the focus of all marketing communications activity, is changing in several key ways.

Audience Control of Media

Technological innovation is delivering to the audience greater control of the media. While increased media opportunities afford the consumer greater choice, other developments also empower the audience. In the case of television, video recording machines (VCRs) enable the consumer to decide what programmes will be seen and the time of viewing, with in-built facilities to "zip" advertising. In 1988, VCR penetration in Ireland was 26 per cent of households, while multi-set penetration was 16 per cent. By 1994, VCR penetration had increased to 59 per cent with multi-set penetration increasing to 29 per cent (Harper, 1994; Irish Tam Establishment Survey, 1994). In a similar manner, the advent of remote control units has led to greater audience control of the broadcast media, with penetration of units in

Irish homes increasing from 5 per cent in 1981 to 73 per cent in 1994 (Irish Tam Establishment Survey, 1994).

The advent of the super-highway, which uses the home or office personal computer as a central information management point, will further empower consumers who will eventually be able to determine their preferred viewing, bypassing the offerings of the local broadcast station, cinema, and video outlet. The net result of these changes is the surrender of control of media to the audience, who will then decide to download the output of these media on their own terms, and not those of the media owner.

Increased Audience Sophistication

While early theories of advertising effects tended to view the audience as "passive palsies" (Bauer, 1971) who would succumb to persuasion through repetition of communication, modern advertising theory tends to regard the consumer in a more positive light, as educated, confident, and mature (King, 1991; Friestad and Wright, 1994; O'Donohoe, 1994). In effect, it is now fashionable to refer to the "sophisticated consumer" as an integral part of the communications process (Lannon and Cooper, 1983). Much of modern advertising tends to presume an intelligent, sophisticated audience as a party to the communication process: a consumer complete with intellectual, as well as financial, predispositions, who is advertising-literate and plays an active, rather than a passive or submissive, role in modern communications. This recognition has had a dramatic effect on the creation of modern advertising. A particularly important section of the audience is the youth market. The young are the recipients of volumes of commercial messages unparalleled in previous generations. One marketing consultant specialising in this market sector suggests that:

> People under 25 feel disenfranchised by politics, but empowered by consumer choice. They are more sussed, more ad literate, marketing literate, and they know more about brands, they have more information. Today's teens are well versed in participating in the commercial world. Probably their only area of power is as a consumer (Benson and Armstrong, 1994: 55).

In a similar vein, research conducted in the UK by J. Walter Thomson, the Henley Research Centre, and Millward Brown has led to the description of the 1990s consumer as the "thoughtful butterfly" (McMurdo, 1993). This consumer is more sceptical and thoughtful about the choice of brand, willing to consider the merits of own-label alternatives, and concerned with quality and benefits other than mere badge status. From a communications point of view "the thoughtful butterfly" represents a more difficult target. This person is literate, sceptical and even dissatisfied about advertising techniques and can no longer be relied upon to consume the mass media used to deliver the brand message. Such consumers manifest less stability in absorbing marketing output, being apt to switch between many modes of purchasing and consumption behaviour inside short periods, thereby bringing greater uncertainty to planned attempts to reach markets defined on the basis of traditional segmentation.

Audience Fragmentation

Audience fragmentation represents one of the inevitable consequences of media proliferation, as audience sizes diminish with increased media opportunities. Research conducted into the effects of television-station proliferation (Buck, 1989) shows that there is a threshold point beyond which greater channel choice does not lead to more viewing. In effect, the total pool of audience viewing tends to remain stable, with newer channels cannibalising audience from existing stations. Between 1970 and 1989, the share of audience held by the three major US networks had fallen from 90 per cent to almost 60 per cent, with the share of audience held by cable networks increasing from 3 per cent to 22 per cent over the period. In 1995, the Head of Sponsorship at Sky Television (Ward, 1995) reported that in recent years there had been a 500 per cent increase in the number of channels available in the UK, resulting in 3,000 per cent more advertisements, but only an 8 per cent increase in overall viewing. The inevitable outcome is considerable audience fragmentation and a highly cluttered environment.

As the situation pertaining in the US market unfolds in European broadcasting, there is likely to be a move from conventional broadcasting to *narrowcasting*, with both methods of access to audiences competing side by side over time for audiences which will increasingly exhibit loyalty to programmes and lifestyle reflections, rather than to stations per se.

CONCLUSIONS

All aspects of the marketing communications industry are currently undergoing fundamental change. Changes in the media have led to a diversity of access routes to targeted consumers, with advertisers turning to non-media advertising, because of the escalating cost of both producing and placing traditional media advertising. Consumers of advertising are now perceived as better educated and more mature than previous generations. This sophisticated consumer has brought about an increased reliance on research as the basis for strategy development in both marketing and advertising. Audiences are increasingly fragmented, capable of being reached more cost-effectively through specialist media in an environment that has become more cluttered.

Today's marketers are better informed, and increasingly managing their marketing communications actively, rather than relying on their agency to handle it on their behalf. Driven by corporate desire for increased profitability, modern advertisers are becoming more demanding of the agencies operating on their behalf. This has had major ramifications for the traditional agency, which, faced with competition from highly efficient specialist agencies and media independents, is experiencing a breakdown in traditional methods of remuneration, allied to demands for greater accountability and quality in the service provided. The trends evident in the larger global context are reflected in the microcosm of the global economy which is modern Ireland.

REFERENCES

A.C. Nielsen (1994): *Nielsen Retail Census*, Dublin: A.C. Nielsen.

A.C. Nielsen (1995): *The Retail Pocketbook*, Henley-on-Thames: A.C. Nielsen in association with NTC Publications.

Association of Advertisers in Ireland (1992): *Report and Review*, Dublin: AAI.

Antenna Report on Broadcasting (1993): London: Nomad Productions.

Audit Bureau of Circulation (1993): *Consumer Press Circulation Review*, Serial 124, December, Hertfordshire.

Barrett, M. (1995): "Broadcast Sponsorship-Chairman's Introduction", Sponsorship Europe '95 Conference, Conrad Hilton Hotel, Brussels, 6–7 April.

Bauer, R.A. (1971): "Games Profile and Audience Play", *Innovative Behaviour and Communication*, New York: Holt, Rinehart, and Winston.

Benson, R. and Armstrong, S. (1994): "These People Know What You Want", *The Face*, July: 52–7.

Bobroff, D. (1995): "Playing the Game? Sponsoring Interactive Media", Sponsorship Europe '95 Conference, Conrad Hilton Hotel, Brussels, 6–7 April.

Briggs, M. (1993): "Why Agencies must Change", *Admap*, 28(1): 21–2.

Brown, M. (1994): "Watch out Sonic, the Admen are coming", *The Independent*, 18 October: 29.

Buck, S. (1989): *The Future for Old and New Television Channels in the UK, Some Clues from Around the World*, London: AGB Research.

Buckley, D. (1980): "Who Pays the Piper?", *Practice Review*, Spring: 10–14.

Byles, D. (1992): "Full-Service Agencies Effectiveness and Evaluation", *Admap*, 27(8): 35–7.

Cawley Nea Ltd. (1993): *The New Order in Irish Advertising*, Dublin: Cawley Nea Ltd.

DKM Ltd. (1991): *Economic Impact of the Broadcast Act*, 1990, June, Dublin: DKM.

DKM Ltd. (1992): *Issues in Irish Broadcast Policy*, August, Dublin: DKM.

Duncan, T., Caywood C. and Newsom, D. (1993): *Preparing Advertising and Public Relations Students for the Communications Industry in the 21st Century. A report of the Task Force on Integrated Communications*, Chicago, IL: Northwestern University.

Donnelley Marketing Inc. (1992): *Fourteenth Annual Survey of Promotional Practices*, New York: Donnelley Marketing.

Donnelley Marketing Inc. (1994): *Sixteenth Annual Survey of Promotional Practices*, New York: Donnelley Marketing.

Economist, The (1992): "The Party's Over", 1 February: 69.

Economist, The (1994): "Hubris and Humble Pie", 27 August: 51–2.

Feldwick, P. (1992): "Full-Service Agencies-Coherence and Fragmentation", *Admap*, 27(5): 37–8.

Friestad, M. and Wright, P. (1994): "The Persuasion Knowledge

Model: How People Cope with Persuasion Attempts", *Journal of Consumer Research*, 21, June: 1–27.

Green, A. (1992): "Death of the Full-Service Ad Agency", *Admap*, 27(1): 21–4.

Harper, T. (1994): "The Changeable Irish TV Audience", *Admap*, 29(4): 40–42.

Hayden, F. (1995): Personal discussion, July, Dublin, The Association of Advertisers in Ireland (AAI).

Henry, H. (1993): "How Production Costs have Outstripped Media Rates", *Admap*, 28(1): 15–18.

IAPI (Institute of Advertising Practitioners in Ireland) (1994): *A View from the Top*, IAPI Conference, April, Dublin: Behaviour and Attitudes.

Irish Multi-Channel Operators Association (1995): Personal contact, Dublin.

Irish Tam Establishment Surveys (1994): Dublin: AGB/TAM.

ISL Marketing (1992): Annual Estimates of Sponsorship Markets, London.

Jones, J.P. (1990): "The Double Jeopardy of Sales Promotions", *Harvard Business Review*, September/October: 145–52.

King, S. (1991): "Brand Building in the 1990's", *Journal of Consumer Marketing*, 8(4): 43–52.

Landler, M. (1991): "What Happened to Advertising", *Business Week*, 23 September: 68–9.

Lannon, J. (1994): "What Brands Need Now", *Admap*, 29(9): 38–42.

Lannon, J. and Cooper, P. (1983): "Humanistic Advertising — a Holistic Cultural Perspective", *International Journal of Advertising*, 2(2): 195–213.

Lees, C. and Rayment, T. (1990): "Shade Wars: How Big Money Goes Riding on a Film Star's Nose", *The Sunday Times*, 22 July: 5.

Magazine News (1994a): "Datafile", London: Periodical Publishers Association, 25, February: 26–7.

Magazine News (1994b): "Datafile", London: Periodical Publishers Association: 26, April: 10–11.

Mandese, J. (1995): "The Buying and Selling", *Advertising Age*, Special Collector's Edition, 50 years of Advertising, Spring: 20.

Marketing (1994): "Trouble in Adland, Part I", 5(4), May: 18–21.

Marketing Development Programme (1993): *A Report on the Extent and Trends of Non Media Advertising in Ireland*, University College Dublin.

Marsh F. (1991): "Irish TV half European Average", *Irish Marketing Journal*, December, 10–11.

Mayer, M. (1991): *Whatever Happened to Madison Avenue?*, Boston: Little, Brown and Company.

Merkle, H (1995): "The Place of Advertising in Tomorrow's Technology", EALA Conference, organised by Association of Advertisers in Ireland, March, 31.

McConnell's Media Facts (1995): Dublin: McConnell's Advertising Service Ltd.

McMurdo, L. (1993): "Chasing Butterflies", *Marketing Week*, 21 May: 28–31.

McPartlin, P. (1993): "Virtual Hitchhiking on a Superhighway", *Marketing*, 6(3), March: 20–21.

Micklethwait, J. (1990): "Assault on the Heartland — The Fight for Marketing Budgets in America", in "Survey of the Advertising Industry", *The Economist*, 9 June: 3.

Mintel (1994): *Special Report on Sponsorship*, London: Mintel Publications.

Mittal, B. (1994): "Public Assessment of TV Advertising: Faint Praise and Harsh Criticism", *Journal of Advertising Research*, 24(1), January/February: 35–53.

Morand, G. (1995): "Broadcast Sponsorship-Session Introduction", Sponsorship Europe '95 Conference, Conrad Hilton Hotel, Brussels, 6–7 April.

Murphy, J. (1994): "Own Label Making Life Hot for Branding", *Irish Marketing Journal*, November: 8–9.

National Newspapers of Ireland (1995): *Estimated Circulation of British Newspapers in Ireland*, Dublin.

O'Donohoe, S. (1994): "Advertising Uses and Gratifications", *European Journal of Marketing*, 28(8/9): 52–75.

O'Brien, D. and Roper J. (1995): "Capital-hungry Cable Offers Rich Pickings", *Sunday Tribune*, (Business Section) 9 July: 3.

Palmer, D. (1995): "Space Invaders: The International Challenge to Media in Ireland — A Threat or an Opportunity", IAPI Media Conference, Jury's Hotel, Dublin, 24 March.

Perry, J. (1994): "European Lessons About TV's Future", *Admap*, 29(6): 18–23.

Perspectives (1994): Marketing Society of Ireland, 1(2), June.

Pollay, R.W. and B. Mittal (1993): "Here's the Beef: Factors, Determinants, and Segments in Consumer Criticism of Advertising", *Journal of Marketing*, 57(3), July: 99–114.

Rothenberg, R. (1989): "The Turmoil on Madison Ave, A Special Report", *The New York Times*, 3 October: 1A.

Schultz, D.E. (1991): quoted in Landler, M. (1991): "What Happened to Advertising?", *Business Week*, 23 September: 68–70.

Shergill, S. (1993): "The Changing US Media and Marketing Environment Implications for Media Advertising Expenditures in the 1990s", *International Journal of Advertising*, 12(2): pp. 95–115.

Sky Television (1995): Dublin office, Personal contact.

Snowden, S. (1992): "The 1992 Marketing and Communications Map", *Admap*, 27(10): 50–51.

SRI (Sponsorship Research International) (1994): *Annual Estimates of Sponsorship Expenditure*, London: SRI.

Summers, D. (1994): "Clout of a Specialist", *Financial Times*, 15 December.

Swain, G. (1990): "Cue the Coke", *Daily Mirror*, June: pp. 16–17.

Turnbull, P. and Doherty-Wilson, L. (1990): "The Internationalisation of the Advertising Industry", *European Journal of Marketing*, 24(1): 7–15.

UK Marketing (1994): *Pocket Book '94*, London: Advertising Association UK.

Veronis, S. and Associates (1994): *Communications Industry Forecast*, New York: Veronis, S. and Associates: 46.

Walsh, G. (1995): "What the Competition Authority Cut Out", *Business and Finance*, 22 June: 32–4.

Ward, M. (1995): "Selling Change — Broadcast Sponsorship in a Multi-media World", Sponsorship Europe '95 Conference, Conrad Hilton Hotel, Brussels, 6–7 April.

Zenith Media Worldwide, (1994): *Advertising Expenditure Forecasts*, London: Zenith.

2
Advertising as Communication

Katriona Lawlor

Traditional communication models are linear and transactional. They assume that the message sent is more or less received as was intended by the sender. The postmodern approach to communication is concerned with how a receiver interacts with, and interprets meaning from a text. Therefore, sometimes understandably, students of advertising become confused and believe that they are studying two separate concepts: communication and meaning. Instead they are utilising two approaches to the study of advertising as communication/meaning.

The communication transaction or transmission approach focuses on the intention of the advertiser and how this can be most effectively achieved. In order to be persuaded, a consumer must be "hit" a number of times by a message before eventually recalling the advertiser's message. This approach attempts to offer guidelines to the advertiser as to how communication works and how it could be improved and made more effective.

The postmodern approach to communication is concerned with meaning and consumer reading of ads. Meaning is concerned with the connection of objects, events, symbols and myths in ads with the rest of the individual's life. Centre of attention shifts from what is important to the advertiser to what is meaningful to the reader, or as Lannon (1985) put it, it is not so much what advertising does to the consumer, but what consumers do with advertising.

This paper briefly outlines the early communication models and then presents a meaning-based model, which is adapted to incorporate various issues that arise in the discussion of advertising as communication.

COMMUNICATION MODELS

Early communication models assumed that the message sent by the sender to the receiver, was perceived exactly as the source intended.

"Bullet" theory is an appropriate name for this approach wherein it was assumed that the receiver was passive and waiting to be "hit" by the message. The Laswell communication model (1948) shown in Figure 2.1 was the first to establish the essential components of communication. This model consisted of four components. The first three elements are common to all approaches to the study of communication.

FIGURE 2.1: HOW COMMUNICATION WORKS

WHO?	SAYS WHAT?	HOW?	TO WHOM?	WITH WHAT EFFECT?
Source	Message	Channel	Audience	Reaction

Source: Laswell, H.D. (1948): *Power and Personality*, New York: W.W. Norton.

Models such as the Shannon and Weaver (1949) communication model shown in Figure 2.2 — generally considered in most marketing textbooks — include the following elements:

FIGURE 2.2: ELEMENTS IN THE COMMUNICATION PROCESS

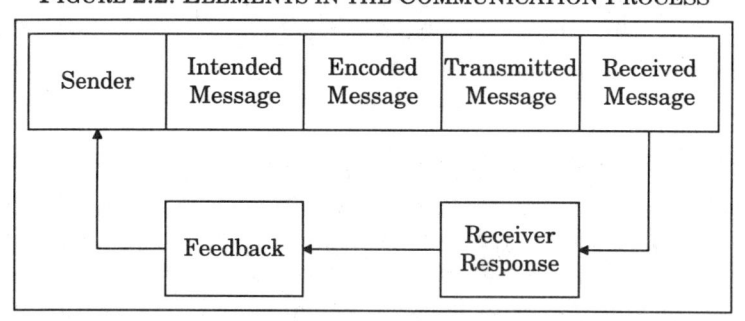

Sender	Intended Message	Encoded Message	Transmitted Message	Received Message
	Feedback		Receiver Response	

Source: Shannon, C. and Weaver, W. (1949): *The Mathematical Theory of Communications*, Champaign: University of Illinois Press.

The model suggests that at the start of the communication, in this case the advertising process, the advertiser will decide what the intended message is going to be — that is, the message that the advertiser wants to get across to a target audience. This message is put into a transmitted format or encoded into various signs to suit the characteristics of the media where the ad is to appear. The message is also pitched at a level that the target audience will understand. The final stage is where the target audience decodes the ad, and the advertiser hopes that, at the end of this process, the intended message is the same as the decoded message. However, as Boulton points out

> ... the limitations of language and human intelligence are such that we all have some difficulty in saying what we mean and all have some difficulty in being certain that we understand what the other person means (Boulton, 1971: 83).

The decoding process and the meaning people take from ads depends on many different factors, such as the experiences that a person brings to the interpretation of an advertisement.

THEORY OF MEANING

Product and advertising meaning is based not only on an individual's evaluations of the product or ad itself but also on the cultural perspective of the individual (McCracken, 1987). Sanders also supports this view:

> Behaviour can best be achieved by tapping into cultural meanings as they are used in the immediate interaction situation (Sanders, 1987: 72).

Cultural determinants of meaning include social interaction (Levy, 1959) and codes used to create product symbolism, such as aesthetic, social and logical codes (Durgee, 1986). Thus, the contemporary view of the brand sees it no longer as a bundle of utilities, but rather as a bundle of meanings. Consumers receive impressions of brands from a range of sources varying from interpersonal to television, music, peers, film. Lannon (1994: 161) describes this process of communication from varying sources as "mosaics of meaning".

It is clear from the above commentators that methods of determining communication effectiveness, such as recall and rating scales, are inadequate in determining the real relationship between, and significance of, the brands communication and the consumer. An alternative method can be found in meaning-based models of communication that focus on what was decoded from the ad and the interpretative framework used in the analysis of meaning.

Theories of meaning are derived from philosophy and linguistics. Both disciplines attempt to say what meaning is, and form the roots of the field of enquiry known as semiotics. The subject matter of semiotics is concerned with the meaning of a sign. Semiology is the study of any system of signs; the sign can be verbal or non-verbal:

> Semiotics studies all cultural processes as processes of communication (Eco, 1979: 8).

Cleaveland (1986: 228) describes a semiotic analysis as "an unfolding of the meaning of a set of words". The words derive their meaning from three separate sources:

1) The semantic analysis: this is the translation by the audience of words into ideas

2) The syntactic analysis: interpretation of words by their structure sequence in a sentence

3) The pragmatic analysis: this is the audience's interpretation of the context of the words.

Semiology and its application to advertising is based upon the theories put forward by the two pioneers in the field, De Saussure (1916) and Pierce (1931).

SIGNS

Pierce's (1931) and De Saussure's (1916) theories are built around the concept of sign. Each proposes how a sign represents and refers to the thing it stands for. Saussure's definition of sign is composed of two elements, — the signifier, which is the material object, and the signified, which is a mental concept or reference. The relation between signifier and signified is signification. It is the process of signification between both sign and signified that enables the interpreter to assign meaning.

> Signification is more or less codified, and ultimately we are left with open systems which scarcely merit the designation "code" but are merely systems of hermeneutic interpretation (Guiraud, 1975: 25).

In advertising, the role of signification is the transference of meaning, usually from the denotative level of language to the connotative. For example, in the ad for Milk Tray chocolates, the explicit and denotative meaning is that ladies "love Milk Tray". But the implicit meaning is that the man is prepared to risk life and limb to show the woman how much he loves her. The signifier is chocolates, the signified is love, and signification between the two is that women value gifts that express love.

The sign is not simply the separate components of signifier and signified, but the relation (or signification) of both. Signs only have meaning if what they signify is of value to a target audience. Therefore, the full meaning of a word includes the value of the word in a given cultural system.

MODEL OF MEANING

Croghan's Real Model of Meaning (1986: 11) focuses on the social process of meaning rather than the structural relationship between items of text (1986: 11). The model is explained in terms of three levels and is given as:

Level 1: (Author) Intention (Purpose)

Level 2 Text

Level 3: (Reader) Interpretation (Effects)

The first level identifies the initiator and intention of the communication. The second level is the text, which is not simply written material, but also an expression of meaning that may be verbal or non-verbal. Text could be a human body, a conversation or written material. The third level is interpretation or how the reader reads either level 1 or 2, or both 1 and 2. In deriving meaning from a communication, the reader may or may not refer to levels 1 and 2. Croghan illustrates the model using the example of a rape judgment where the judge reduced the convicted man's sentence because he claimed that the woman contributed to the crime because of the clothes she wore. The judge in this case was concerned with levels 2 and 3 of the model. Various interest groups protested about the judgment claiming that what the woman wore was her own business — these groups were concerned with levels 1 and 2 of the model.

The model can be applied to advertising. The advertiser is inclined to assume that ads are created according to their intention as specified in an advertising brief — the agency or creative people then develop text and this is interpreted. It is hoped that the effects of the creative interpretation correlate positively with the intention of the advertiser: ads may be interpreted in the same way as the judge interpreted the rape crime. The reading of the ad is confined to levels 2 and 3 when people process or interpret some social aspect of the ad or text, such as music. Other consumers may immediately recognise the intention of the advertiser (level 1) and produce an automatic defence which blocks further processing of the ad. The three levels in this model need to be described in more detail to show how meaning is ascribed and derived in advertising.

Intention

The first level of meaning in the model is concerned with the intention of the author. The author in advertising may be one or more of several people — for example, advertiser, art director, visualiser, photographer, copywriter. If meaning is to be assigned on the basis of intention, one must ask whether or not the intention makes meaning explicit in terms of the text used. The advertiser considers two sets of factors in deciding how to express the intended meaning. The first of these relates to how people derive meaning — the advertiser must consider how people process meaning from ads. Secondly, the advertiser must consider how best to convey the meaning in the ad — this will include analysis of creative research and will be based in part on the advertiser's own past experience of what is most effective.

Processing Meaning

Advertisers need to know how consumers react to ads and what they do with ads if they are to fulfil their intention successfully. The advertiser's intention is usually stated within an advertising brief in the form of a statement of objectives. The literature on the setting of objectives in advertising is based on theoretical models which claim to show how advertising works in achieving certain effects with consumers — these are usually referred to as *hierarchy-of-effects* models (see Figure 2.3).

Hierarchy-of-effects models integrate psychological concepts from the fields of learning, motivation and attitude theory. In a review of the evolution of these models, Barry (1987) delineates three phases of development. The first period was from 1870–1929. The main model that emerged during this period was the AIDA (awareness, interest, desire, and action) model proposed by Strong (1925). The basic principle of this phase was that the ad should be exactly like a salesperson and should be a substitute for a sales presentation, by creating awareness of a product, leading to generation of interest, and desire for the product, which then, it is hoped, will lead to purchase. On first sight, there would appear to be four separate objectives and distinct intentions. However, they do, in fact, constitute a continuum focused on achieving sales — all models at this time were premised on the notion that sales was the intended outcome of marketing communication activity. Later theorists such as Colley (1962) and Kotler (1991) describe the AIDA model as a communication-school model, but this description incorrectly takes the emphasis away from "sales". Communication-school models, are based on the idea that a given campaign has the objective of creating awareness or interest or desire or action, but AIDA sees the action/sale as the intended outcome of all campaigns.

FIGURE 2.3: RESPONSE-HIERARCHY MODELS

Stages	AIDA Model[a]	Hierarchy-of-Effects Model[b]	DAGMAR Model[c]	Communications Model[d]
Cognitive Stage	Attention ↓ ↓ ↓	Awareness ↓ Knowledge ↓	Unawareness ↓ Awareness ↓ Comprehension ↓	Exposure ↓ Reception ↓ Cognitive Response ↓
Affective Stage	Interest ↓ ↓ Desire ↓	Liking ↓ Preference ↓ Conviction ↓	Conviction ↓	Attitude ↓ Intention ↓
Behaviour Stage	Action	Purchase	Action	Behaviour

Source: (a) Strong (1925), (b) Lavidge and Steiner (1961), (c) Colley (1962), (d) Kotler (1991).

These first-phase hierarchy models reflect the kind of psychological theory that Pavlov (1927) expounded as his stimulus-response theory. Stimulus-response theory in advertising suggests that the consumer does not think about the ad and that it is possible to condition an audience to a stimulus via repetition, to cause a conditioned response. The audience's ability to read an ad is wholly discounted and the campaign is based on the notion that the advertiser can sell, manipulate or create the desired response by simply repeating the ad and maintaining high-frequency levels.

The true communication-school models belong to the second phase (1929–68). Typical models are the Dagmar model (Defining Advertising Goals for Measured Advertising Results) produced by Colley (1962), and the Effects Model, created by Lavidge and Steiner (1962). The principle underlying the second phase is that consumers pass through a series of stages in processing an advertisement — from awareness to comprehension, conviction, liking and action. The advertiser determines which of these stages the consumer is currently at in relation to the product and designs a campaign to move the consumer nearer to purchase. The main contribution to this phase came from Lavidge and Steiner when they utilised attitude theory to explain how people move from unawareness of a product to ultimate purchase. If, for instance, the advertiser's intention is to improve awareness and comprehension, then the cognitive component of an attitude must be changed, so an informational campaign is used. If, on the other hand, the intention/objective is to improve liking or conviction, then the affective component of attitude must be changed and a persuasive campaign is used. If the objective is to influence purchase (the action or connotative stage), sales-promotion devices may be used (Palda, 1966).

Barry (1987) refers to the third phase (1969 to the present) as providing challenges to traditional models. The second-phase hierarchy models had relied heavily on attitudinal theory, which suggests that consumers consciously and deliberately evaluate attributes and information before making a decision. People learn from information, form their attitudes, and behave accordingly — a traditional view of fairly rational humans. Unfortunately, there is little evidence that advertising works in this way (Driver and Foxall, 1986). Much of attitude theory is based on Fishbein's work, yet even Fishbein himself questions the premise that attitude causes behaviour. He suggests that after 70–75 years of attitude research we might reasonably conclude that people align their attitude to behaviour, rather than behave as a direct result of attitude (Fishbein, 1980).

The main principle of this third phase was first put forward by Krugman (1965) who describes the consumer as a passive processor of information. The most typical, and perhaps the most important, model developed in this phase is Ray's (1973) Three Orders Hierarchy. Ray argued that the "low-involvement hierarchy" offers a case where people learn, behave, and then form an attitude. Ehrenberg's (1974) model similarly addresses the very common low-involvement situations: it describes a three-stage process of awareness, trial and reinforcement or repeat buying. In this situation, advertising is said to work via Skinner's (1938) theory of operant conditioning. Operant conditioning is different from classical conditioning in that it considers the effect of the environment on the individual. A consumer who is not reinforced or does not like the product after trial, will not purchase again.

In overview, it is possible to see how in the three distinct phases during the past 100 years, an advertiser might have approached the problem of conveying intended meaning very differently, according to the underlying understanding of human psychology then current.

Creative Appeals

When the advertising objectives have been set, advertisers must determine how to transfer their intention to the consumer. Everything in an ad may have meaning, but not all meaning is the product of intention. Colour may have meaning, but from the advertiser's point of view there may not be a specific intention behind choice of colour. Intention will be represented by choice of creative mix "which is composed of those advertising elements the company controls to achieve its advertising objective" (Bovee and Arens, 1989: 233). The creative mix arises from consideration of target audience, product concept, communications media and the advertising message. While each of these four areas must be considered in deciding on how to achieve the stated objectives creatively, the advertising message is the main concern of this discussion.

Creative strategy is fundamentally concerned with message strategy, which in turn focuses on *content* and *layout*. Many commentators, such as Frazer (1983), Aaker and Norris (1982), Vaughn (1980), Rossiter and Percy (1987) have been concerned with developing message-content typologies. However, these typologies consider how an individual processes message content, rather then considering the effects of a particular layout on information processing.

Layout of ads has been studied from a stylistic viewpoint to illustrate artistic change over time, rather than in terms of the effects of various layouts on consumers. Research studies of layout and design by commentators such as Leiss, Kline and Jhally (1986), Feasely and Stuart (1987) are generally based on content analysis. More empirical research is required to examine the combined effects of style/

presentation with message content, to show how both affect the way in which people process information.

The choice of a creative appeal to carry an advertiser's intention is ultimately concerned with how the ad triggers the referent system of the receiver. Advertising is based on the principle that receivers have the ability and knowledge to connote from denotative meanings in ads. Take, for example, a typical shampoo ad featuring a girl washing her hair in a stream in a pastoral setting. The denotative meaning would be that the shampoo washes hair effectively, and the connotative that it is a natural product because of its association with nature. Other connotative meanings may be that the product is not artificial and is sophisticated, and that the individual has an opportunity to get back to nature by using this product.

Williamson (1978: 24) sees this connotative capacity as extremely important because "it is the first function of an ad to create differentiation between one particular product and others in the same category". Choice of symbols and people in an ad show not only what the product is, but also what it is not: the use of nature, for instance, implies a natural product and not an artificial product. The referent system allows for the transference of meaning from the signifieds to the signifiers. A product is given meaning because of the person or thing with which it is associated.

Mythology, Black and White Magic

Barthes (1973) explains meaning and the transference of meaning from signified to signifier through the concept of mythology:

> In myth, we find again the tri-dimensional pattern which we have just described: the signifier, the signified and the sign. But myth is a peculiar system, in that it is constructed from a semiological chain which existed before it: it is a second-order semiological system (Barthes, 1973: 114).

The concept of mythology describes the process of transformation of meaning in advertising. The sign in one system becomes the signified in another. Advertisements of the 1950s were thus relatively straightforward and could be evaluated within a first-order linguistic system, where the product was shown and demonstrated with explicit statements of attributes. Advertisements of the 1990s, however, rely on a second-order semiological system (i.e. of mythology) where the sign value or signification of a celebrity, film, music or sport is implicitly the signifier of meaning for a product.

The question for advertisers and practitioners is whether people can and do "read" mythology in ads. Barthes (1973) addresses this issue and outlines three ways in which myths are read in ads. The first is where the user of the myth (the advertiser) utilises the empty signifier, in order to create the signification that will be applied to the second-order meaning. The second way of reading a myth takes it from the perspective of the receiver of the message, where the receiver sees the full intention behind the choice of myth. In effect, this mode of interpretation means that the message is demythologised. The third way of receiving the myth is where the receiver/reader reads the myth as intended by the author. Further research is needed to determine effects of the second and third modes of reading ads. The concern for the advertiser is whether demythification will produce a negative intention to purchase a product. Wells (1986) introduced a parallel concept, which he labelled the "schemer's schema", a concept similar to demythification, where the audience is aware of the advertiser's/ marketer's intention and puts up a guard against persuasion.

Mythology can take many forms in advertising. One of the forms most frequently encountered is the working of magic (Williamson, 1978) and black and white magic (Leiss, Kline and Jhally, 1986; Myers, 1987). Magic is used as a process — spotty skin changes into beautiful clear skin; people become younger and better.

> Advertisements draw upon the entire magical repertoire, including contagious magic, charms to avoid dire consequences, taboos, command over the supernatural, incantation (jingles) and even the devil's blandishments (Leiss, Kline and Jhally, 1986: 23).

Williamson (1978) describes several kinds of magic in ads: "alchemy", where a lot of magic comes from a little product use; "spells", where the magic potency of the product produces the desired transformational effect; the "Genie in the Lamp" and the "World in the Bottle" where people, time and feelings can all be contained in the product; and the "Crystal Ball/Magic Circle", where the crystal ball is used to access the future.

Magic that is concerned with showing changing relations between people and objects is referred to as "black and white magic". White magic is a term used to indicate the ability of the product to take on some aspect of nature — the product will therefore bring nature to the user. Black magic gives the product the ability to improve interpersonal relations (Leiss, Kline and Jhally, 1986). Myers (1987) takes a broader view of black magic when she claims that critics of the advertising profession proclaim it as the new demonology, "the false god that despite ourselves we worship" (1987: 84). Black magic is therefore anything that perverts the truth, the presentation of a falsified reality that transforms people's lives. An extension of the black-magic critique of advertising lies in a comparison between advertising and the Marxist theory of fetishism.

According to Marx, every object has a use value and an exchange value: use is the functional performance of the product, and exchange the value of the good in comparison to the value of other goods:

> Life and meaning are attached to objects that might seem worthless in themselves. In all societies but our own we call this fetishism (Williamson, 1978: 150).

Fetishism is the creation of magical, material values regarded as inherent in the product — it is a bringing of the product to life. In effect, it is the value-added concept that many marketers strive for. Value-added is the adding of intangible attributes to a product through promotion, to differentiate the product and give it more value to the consumer.

The advertising literature and, in particular, the research literature, with the notable exception of Williamson's work, has failed to highlight the importance of the referent system (or even implications of one referent system being used rather than another), which is capable of subverting the desired intention of the advertiser. The referent is the knowledge and values that receivers attach to people and objects in our society or culture. It is what allows us to connote meaning from one event to the next. Many advertisements depend on a person's ability to transfer meanings from symbols to products: by using a personality such as Madonna, the advertiser attempts to tap the values that a particular sector of the market associate with Madonna, in the hope of successfully transferring these values or images to the product. Advertisers need to know what referent systems are triggered and whether there is a transference of meaning from these referent systems to the product. It is only by considering the referent system that advertisers will know what is likely to happen to their intention.

Text

Second-level meaning focuses on text — not just hard-copy text, but the whole social communication within text. The "text" in advertising can be visual or verbal, or both visual and verbal. Meaning at this level may, in fact, be derived more from non-verbal material than verbal text.

The text in advertising is essentially intertextual. It will contain and use signs and symbols from other aspects of culture (films, books, etc.) to create brand values and product meanings. This intertextuality involves the re-reading of signs, and proposes the notion that any one text is read in relation to others — "Intertextuality exists in the space between texts" (Fiske, 1987). There is no need to have explicit knowledge of the previous text, because people build up cultural images that allow for the reading of an image created in a particular space into another and different text at a different time. Marilyn Monroe and Madonna convey a similar image: sexy blonde females; James-Bond-type men another. The reader does not need to have explicit knowledge of each individual text that conveyed these images, because previous knowledge of these types of people is read across texts. An advertising receiver encountering these images can "read" them even without having seen the classic Monroe films or read the Ian Fleming novels.

If intertextual signs falsify original signs, the question might be asked as to whether we ever have a final meaning available. The only path to final meaning is through looking at how an individual reads a text at a given moment in time. In the past, textual readings of ads have been given by Williamson (1978), Dyer (1982), and Langholz-Leymore (1987). These readings provide both method and reason for studying texts. However, of necessity, they lack the individual idiosyncratic interpretation of ads by members of the general audience, and instead rely on the author's own interpretation of the ads. Approaches to reading and experiencing ads which focus on the actual consumer, such as O'Donohoe (1994), and Lawlor (1992), need to be considered.

Interpretation

Interpretation is Croghan's (1986) third level of meaning and is concerned with how people read an ad or other text. Two different approaches emerge. The first is essentially the way in which rationalists explain meaning. Rationalists claim that surface meaning may differ, but that deep meaning is universal. Structuralists typify the rationalist approach. The second approach is exemplified by the major research contributions on the reading of television and the applicability of these studies to the reading of advertising. This involves a relativist approach, where it is believed that deep meaning differs and is not universal.

Structuralists study meaning from a universal perspective. Thus, Levi-Strauss constructs a system of universal thinking, and Barthes a system to show the significance or language of meaning. Such rationalists and structuralists believe that all languages are the same in deep structure, and only surface structure differs. The relativists, on the other hand, take an opposing view, stating that meaning differs across and between cultures.

Two of the main influences on structuralism have been Barthes (1973) and Levi-Strauss (1983). Both use the concept of myth to explain reading, and although both theories differ fundamentally, the focus of each is on the specific narrative at a given moment in time. Levi-Strauss's ultimate concern is with "the unconscious nature of collective phenomena" (22). He sought to discover thought processes that were universally valid for all humans. To seek out these thought processes he studied myth, because he believed that the thought processes in myth are primitive, and therefore uncontaminated by twentieth-century culture, which has forced modern man to adapt thought processes to technologies at the expense of the senses.

Barthes' (1973) system was also two-tiered, but focused on how meaning from one system or culture was transformed within a second system, thereby creating a new meaning, which he called "myth". His fundamental concern was with the ideologies that were used in both systems, and how the significance of the sign in the first system was lost when it was used in the second.

Structuralists believe that the structure of any form of communication reveals the message. For structuralists, communication can only be explained by examining the complex network of relations that link and unite parts of the communication. In applying the structuralist method to ads, it can be said that, as ads are the products of the human brain, there is a universal meaning somewhere beneath the surface features that is common to all.

> Structuralism claims that the symbolic function of the mind predetermines our ability to communicate (Konner, 1984: 157).

Langholz-Leymore (1987) specifically applies the structuralist method to advertising and believes that structural analysis of ads shows that, just as a new sentence conforms to existing rules of syntax, so too, ads must conform to the main signifier of the product category.

Langholz-Leymore (1987) argues that structural analysis must be undertaken for a system of ads. The system she uses is product categories:

> All the different claims of all the different brands operating in the market make up its advertising system. Individual advertisements are nothing but isolated pieces in a jigsaw puzzle (324).

For a fuller explanation and application of this method to advertising, see Leymore (1975) and Lawlor (1992).

In the 1970s and 1980s, there has been reaction in favour of relativists, mainly through contributions of ethnic studies from feminists and Blacks. These groups argue from a minority position that all linguistic worlds are different. The problem for the advertiser is one of creating ads that appeal to different conceptual worlds. Advertisers may appear to trivialise and ignore minorities who have beliefs different from the traditional American view (McCracken, 1987). Sapir (1949) and Whorf (1963) highlight the importance of relativity in culture, arguing that the real world centres around the language habits of the group:

> Human beings do not live in the objective world of social activity as ordinarily understood, but are very much at the mercy of the particular language which has become the medium of expression for their society (Whorf, 1963: 162).

Using the traditional reader strategy, a text is presented and analysed for deep/true meaning. It is assumed that the meaning is in the text, waiting to be uncovered. An alternative approach to reading is proposed by Iser (1978) who suggests that texts are made to mean through the process of reading. This suggests that reading is not a property of the text, but the result of interaction between reader and text. Allan (1987) refers to this as a reader-oriented approach to text. Reader-oriented approaches to meaning derived from text stem from phenomenology, a branch of philosophy that is concerned with the perceiving individual and the world of people and texts that are perceived.

Ingarden (1984) was one of the first researchers to take a reader-oriented approach to literary criticism, and takes an approach to reading similar to Croghan's (1986) three-level model. In this schema, the text starts as an intention of the author or addresser. Once the work is written, it becomes separate from the writer and awaits different possibilities of meanings from the reader. Iser concurs with

Ingarden's work and takes a semiotic approach to reading literature. The essential stance taken by these researchers is that the text is only one half of the perceptual equation: it is the object. The second half of the equation, the perceiving individual, has not yet received the same attention as has the text. Reader-oriented theorists differ over the focus of study. Ingarden and Iser focus on text and Fish (1980) and Holland (1975) on the individual reader. If reading is dependent on the interaction of the reader and the text, then perhaps it is time that researchers sought ways of focusing on the individual.

Other reader-oriented theorists such as Allan (1987) and Kaplan (1987) start out from the premise that reading of text involves viewer activation — how readers produce their own meaning. Nevertheless, the attention of much of the research is still focused on the text, and not the production of meaning from the individual. There is a need in advertising to examine the values and significance of what is in the ad from the viewer's perspective. The question remains unresolved as to whether viewers are reading values as shown, or projecting their own values, which may alter the meaning considerably.

CONCLUSIONS

This paper has presented the theoretical background to the study of advertising as communication. The model presented stresses the need to focus on three areas. The first is the intention. The intention in advertising may be the advertiser's, the creatives' or the apparent intention of the perceived main source in the ad. The study of intention will largely focus on its creative expression, raising issues such as: what did the source say? How did the source express its message? Why was a particular execution used to achieve an intention? The study of intention should examine the referent system of the viewer. Semiotics usefully describes the process of transformation of meaning. This process looks at how the sign in one system becomes the signified in another. Signs chosen must be capable of triggering the viewers referent system.

The second area is the text or ad. The text in advertising is concerned with both the hard copy and the social communication within the ad. Much is now being written on the intertextual nature of the text. The concern of the model presented in this paper is with the relationship between ads and the audiences that consume them. Historically, the question has been: what do ads do to people? An alternative view is to ask: what do people do with ads?

The third area is concerned with how the audience interacts with, and takes an idiosyncratic interpretation of, a text. The methods used to study interpretation may fall broadly into the approaches known as structuralism or relativism. Media studies research has advanced further in this type of inquiry than current advertising research, and can provide useful guidelines to the study of interpretation.

While this paper has concentrated on advertising as communication, the approach taken to the study of meaning could be applied to any aspect of marketing communication. The notion that consumers produce their own meanings while interacting with a text is of concern not just to advertisers and marketers, but also to society at large.

REFERENCES

Aaker, D. and Norris, D. (1982): "Characteristics of TV Commercials Perceived as Informative", *Journal of Advertising Research*, 22(2): 22–34.

Allan, R. (1987): "Reader-Oriented Criticism and Television", in Allan, R. (ed.), *Channels of Discourse*. London: Methuen: 74–112.

Barry, T. (1987): "The Development of the Hierarchy of Effects: An Historical Perspective", in, Leigh, J. and Martin, C. (eds.), *Current Issues and Research in Advertising*, Ann Arbor MI: Association of Consumer Research: 251–96.

Barthes, R. (1973): *Mythologies*, London: Paladin.

Boulton, M. (1971): *The Anatomy of Language*, London: Routledge and Kegan Paul.

Bovee, L., and Arens, W. (1989): *Contemporary Advertising*, Homewood IL: Irwin.

Cleaveland, C. (1986): "Semiotics: Determining What the Advertising Message Means to the Audience." in Sentis, K. and Olson, J. (eds.), *Advertising and Consumer Psychology*, New York: Praeger: 227–41.

Colley, G. (1962): *Defining Advertising Goals for Measured Advertising Results*, New York: Association of National Advertisers.

Croghan, M. (1986): "Where Did Limbo Go? The Analysis of Real Theory of Meaning", *Essays in Language, Literature and Area Studies*, University of Bradford, 7, Autumn: 1–15.

De Saussure, F (1916): *Cours de Linguistique Générale: Course in General Linguistics* (translated by) Harris, R., London: Duckworth (1983).

Driver, J., and Foxall, G. (1984): *Advertising Policy and Practice*, London: Holt Rinehart and Winston.

Dyer, G. (1982): *Advertising as Communication*, London and New York: Methuen.

Durgee, J. (1986): "How Consumer Sub-Cultures Code Reality: A Look at Some Code Types." in Lutz, J. (ed.), *Advances in Consumer Research*, Ann Arbor MI, Association for Consumer Research, 13: 332–7.

Eco, U. (1979): *A Theory of Semiotics*, Bloomington, IN: Indiana University Press.

Ehrenberg, A. (1974): "Repetitive Advertising and the Consumer", *Journal of Advertising Research*, 14(2), April: 25–34.

Feasely, F. and Stuart, J. (1987): "Magazine Advertising Layout and Design: 1932–1982", *Journal of Advertising*, 16(2): 20–25.

Fish, S. (1980): *Is There a Text in This Class*, Cambridge, MA: Harvard University Press.

Fishbein, M. (1980): "An Overview of the Attitude Construct", in Hafer, G. (ed.), *A Look Back, A Look Ahead*, Chicago, IL: American Marketing Association: 1–19.

Fiske, J. (1987): *Television Culture*, London: Methuen.

Frazer, R. (1983): "Creative Strategy: A Management Perspective", *Journal of Advertising*, 12(4): 36–41.

Guirand, P. (1975): *Semiology*, London: Routledge and Kegan Paul

Holland, N. (1975): *5 Readers Reading*, New Haven, CT: Yale University Press.

Ingarden, R. (1984): *The Literary Work of Art*, (translated by) Grabowicz, G., Evanston, IL: North Western University Press.

Iser, W. (1978): *The Act of Reading: A Theory of Aesthetic Response*, Baltimore, MD: Hopkins University Press.

Kaplan, A. (1987): "Feminist Criticism and Television", in Allen, R. (ed.), *Channels of Discourse*, London: Methuen: 211–53.

Konner, M. (1984): *The Tangled Wing: Biological Constraints on the Human Spirit*, London: Penguin Books.

Kotler, P. (1991): *Marketing Management: Analysis, Planning and Control*, Englewood Cliffs, NJ: Prentice Hall.

Krugman, H. (1965): "The Impact of Television Advertising: Learning Without Involvement", *Public Opinion Quarterly*, 25: 349–56.

Langholz-Leymore, V. (1987): "The Structure is the Message", in Umker-Sebeok, J. (ed.), *Marketing and Semiotics*, Berlin: Mouton de Gruyter: 319–31.

Lannon, J. (1985): "Advertising Research: New Ways of Seeing." *Admap*, October: 520–24.

Lannon, J. (1994): "Mosaics of Meaning: Anthropology and Marketing", *Journal of Brand Management*, 2(3): 155–67.

Laswell, H.D. (1948): *Power and Personality*, New York: W.W. Norton: 37–51

Lawlor, K. (1992): "A Semiotic Reading of Ads" (unpublished), PhD Thesis, Dublin City University.

Lavidge, R. and Steiner, G. (1961): "A Model for Productive Measurements of Advertising Effectiveness", *Journal of Marketing*, 25: 59–62.

Levi-Strauss, C. (1983): *Structured Anthropology*, Chicago IL: University of Chicago Press.

Leiss, W., Kline, S. and Jhally, S. (1986): *Social Communication in Advertising*, New York: Methuen.

Levy, S. (1959): "Symbols for Sale", *Harvard Business Review*, 37, July/August: 117–24.

Leymore, V. (1975): *The Hidden Myth Structure and Symbolism in Advertising*, London: Heinemann.

McCracken, G. (1987): "Advertising: Meaning or Information." in Wallendorf, M. and Anderson, P. (eds.), *Advances in Consumer Research*, Ann Arbor, MI: Association of Consumer Research, 14: 121–4.

Myers, K. (1987): *Understains, The Sense of Seduction of Advertising*, London: Comedia.

O'Donohoe, S. (1994): "Leaky Boundaries: Intertextuality and Young Adult Experiences of Advertising", Conference Paper for Changes in Advertising and Consumption since the 1950s, Centre for Consumer and Advertising Studies, University of East London.

Palda, K. (1966): "The Hypothesis of a Hierarchy of Effects: A Partial Evaluation", *Journal of Marketing Research*, 3(1): 13–24.

Pavlov, I. (1927): *Conditioned Reflexes. An Investigation of the Psychological Activity of the Cerebral Cortex*, (translated by) Anwerp, G.V., London: Oxford University Press

Pierce, C.S. (1931): in Hartsonne, C., Weiss, P and Bucks, A. (eds.), *Collected Papers*, Cambridge, MA: Harvard University Press.

Ray, M. (1973): "Marketing Communication and The Hierarchy of Effects", in Clarke, P. (ed.), *New Models for Mass Communication Research*, Beverley Hills, CA: Sage Publications, 2: 147–176.

Rossiter, J., and Percy, L (1987): *Advertising and Promotion Management*, Singapore: McGraw-Hill.

Sanders, C. (1987): "Consuming as Social Action: Ethnographic Methods In Consumer Research", in Wallendorf, M. and Anderson, P. (eds.), *Advances in Consumer Research*, Ann Arbor, MI: Association of Consumer Research, 14: 71–5.

Sapir, E. (1949): "Language." in Mandelbaum, D. (ed.), *Language, Culture and Personality, Selected Essays*, Berkeley, CA: University of California Press: 1–44.

Shannon, C. and Weaver, W. (1949): *The Mathematical Theory of Communications*, Champaign, IL: University of Illinois Press.

Skinner, B.F. (1938): *The Behaviour of Organisms: An Experimental Analysis*, New York: Appelton-Century Crofts.

Strong, E.K. (1925): *The Psychology of Selling*, New York: McGraw Hill.

Vaughn, R. (1980): "How Advertising Works: A Planning Model", *Journal of Advertising Research*, 20(5), October: 27–33.

Wells, W. (1986): "Three Useful Ideas", in Lutz, R. (ed.), *Advances in Consumer Research*, Ann Arbor MI: Association for Consumer Research, 13(9): 11.

Williamson, J. (1978): *Decoding Advertisements Ideology and Meaning in Advertising*, London: Marion Boyars.

Whorf, G. (1963): *Language Thought and Reality*, Cambridge, MA: MIT Press.

3

Managing Marketing Communication — The Client Perspective

Michael Carey

INTRODUCTION

The client perspective on the planning and implementation of marketing communications will inform the work of the various agency professionals engaged to create and implement campaigns. However, there is often a lack of appreciation of the extent to which the marketing-communication activity impacts upon every aspect of the workings of a professionally-run marketing function in a fast-moving consumer good (FMCG) company.

Everything done by a manager responsible for a brand can ultimately be categorised under the heading "marketing communication". Each marketing decision and every communication initiated by that brand manager will have either a developmental or a damaging impact on the overall image of that brand in the eyes of at least one of the publics with which the brand is involved.

Three very important messages emerge from that realisation. The first and the most important is that there must be consistency in everything done to a brand. This is a basic principle of professional brand management. Lack of consistency will lead to conflicting brand images and to a weak brand personality. Brands are fragile animals that must be protected from other brands, they must be built in the minds of the consumers. Inconsistency in that development may, at best, be a waste of resources and, at worst, lead to that valuable asset, the brand equity, being damaged beyond repair. The second message relates to the nature of the audience for marketing communication. The primary audience is, in many cases, the consumer. However, other publics must be considered, such as the trade (buyers, store management, etc.) the media, industry (corporate Ireland) and government. In addition, a further target for marketing communication is the internal customer (salesforce, production management, finance, etc.). Finally, the third message is that the level of responsibility given to the manager who is making decisions on issues affecting the brand is immense. Good brand management will lead to a healthy profitable company. Poor brand management may damage the company's most valuable assets and so lead to commercial disaster. The challenge presented to the manager responsible for the brand's marketing communication is thus significant, making that role one of the more rewarding in many Irish FMCG companies.

It is important to note that there is little of substance written on this topic in the Irish context. The views within this paper are based upon direct experience gained in Ireland and the UK in a number of FMCG and service companies. The points made here are therefore more relevant in the consumer-products context, though many of the issues are common to other industries and sectors.

STRATEGIC PLANNING PROCESS AND THE ROLE OF MARKETING COMMUNICATIONS

Marketing-communication plans take their place in a hierarchy of total company objectives and strategy. This hierarchy is built upon two dimensions — time and scope. The example below illustrates the structure of the strategic planning process in Irish Biscuits, part of the large French food company, Groupe Danone.

FIGURE 3.1: TIME DIMENSION OF PLANS

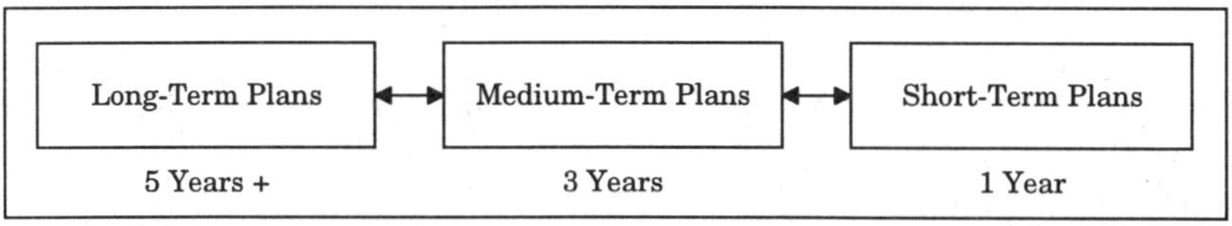

Long-Term Plans	Medium-Term Plans	Short-Term Plans
5 Years +	3 Years	1 Year

The first variable is that of *time*. The planning cycle, which takes place annually, begins with each operating company (Irish Biscuits, in this case), outlining its long-term objectives in unquantified directional terms. These are discussed with Groupe Danone and agreed. Based on these agreed long-term objectives a three-year plan (called the Strategic Action Plan) is completed, again by the operating company, and agreed. The first year of that plan is then specified in great detail with budgets set for volume sales, costs, prices, advertising spends and promotional activity. Marketing-communication objectives will appear in each of these time perspectives. In the long-term plan, the issues will resist specific definition and will relate to such broader problems as the target corporate image that the operating company wants to achieve. As the periods reduce, the objectives become more specific and quantifiable, such as raising the score achieved in research for the perception of Irish Biscuits as an "innovative food company" from 70 per cent to 90 per cent. In the short-term plan, the communication objectives are very detailed. Typical objectives might be the implementation of an advertising plan in April of the year in question, in which the company aims to reach 70 per cent of biscuit purchasers on average three times each with a new advertisement for cream crackers.

FIGURE 3.2: BUSINESS SCOPE DIMENSION OF PLANS

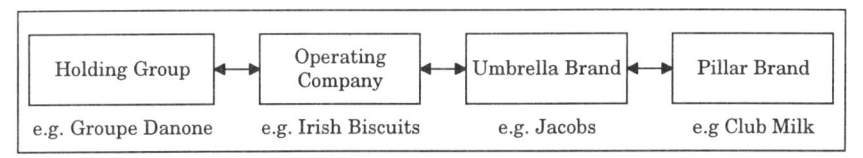

Holding Group	Operating Company	Umbrella Brand	Pillar Brand
e.g. Groupe Danone	e.g. Irish Biscuits	e.g. Jacobs	e.g Club Milk

The second variable is *scope*. The plans (at all time horizons), are produced at a number of levels of product or business scope. These range from plans for Groupe Danone, plans for Irish Biscuits Limited, plans for the Jacob's brand and plans for "pillar brands" (i.e. key brands on which the umbrella brand Jacob's is supported), such as Club Milk. Again, the marketing-communication objectives will differ for each level with different target audiences for each (e.g. Irish Biscuits' primary target is the trade customers, while Club Milk's primary target is the grocery shopper), different media used (Groupe Danone may use the main financial press while Jacob's brand may use a mainstream consumer medium such as television) and different types or modes of communication (e.g. Irish Biscuits may focus resources on PR activity, while Club Milk will mix advertising and promotional activity).

In addition to time and scope, a key influence on the communications activity of an individual brand, e.g. Kimberly, is the overall strategic objective for that product group — in this example, Mallows. That overall strategic objective is set through careful analysis of the present position of that brand in terms of how attractive the market sector is, and how Irish Biscuits has performed in that sector.

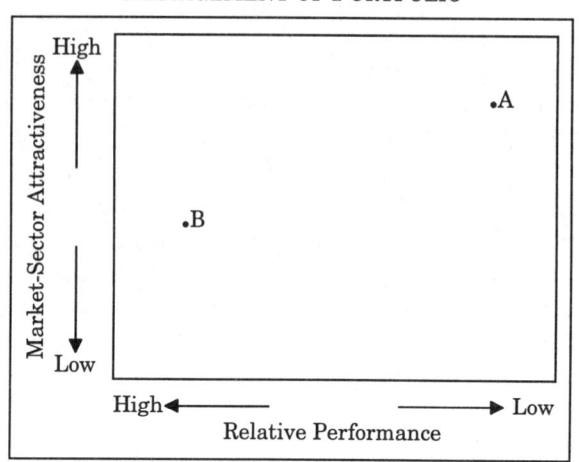

FIGURE 3.3: SETTING PRODUCT GROUP STRATEGIES THROUGH MANAGEMENT OF PORTFOLIO

[Figure: A 2x2 matrix with vertical axis "Market-Sector Attractiveness" ranging from Low to High, and horizontal axis "Relative Performance" ranging from High (left) to Low (right). Point A is in the upper-right (high attractiveness, low performance). Point B is in the middle-left area (moderate attractiveness, moderate-to-high performance).]

At Irish Biscuits, management has developed a detailed model which measures these two aspects of the product-sector portfolio. The map which is created shows clearly the present position of each product group, and so helps to diagnose the correct overall strategic objectives. For example, a product sector positioned at A is one that is highly attractive, yet the performance is relatively poor. The objective for that sector may be "to build share/performance". Alternatively, a product sector in position B is quite attractive and has seen extremely good performance, so the objective for that sector may be "to defend its share and grow the sector".

Based on this analysis, the overall objective is set. In the context of that objective, the marketing-communications strategy is developed. Thus, if the underlying strategic objective for Club Milk is to grow its share of the biscuit count-line market significantly, the marketing-communication strategy will include heavy investment in main media support, promotional activity that aggressively achieves high level of trial of the brand, and an active PR programme that keeps the brand high in the minds of the target consumer.

RESOURCE ALLOCATION — LOAVES AND FISHES

The allocation of resource between the competing needs of the brands in a company's portfolio is a complex and inexact activity. Inevitably, more funds are required than are available and choices must be made.

The starting point in a company such as Irish Biscuits is the setting of product-sector strategies as described above. Based upon the task which must be achieved, a level of funding can be estimated. For example, if the overall objective is to double the brand's market share, then the resources required will be very significant. If the strategy is to "milk" the sector, the resources required will be small.

Another major consideration for allocation of funds across the portfolio of products is the nature of the sector in which the product competes. If the competitive set is one that is driven by brand image built by heavy advertising support, then it may be necessary to have a very large budget. For example, in soft drinks, a canned brand aimed at teenagers (Pepsi, for example) requires very heavy advertising spends if it is to remain in the consumer's mind, while squash brands (Miwadi, for example) do not operate in such a competitive set, and so require less investment.

A distinction can be made between "top-down" and "bottom-up" budgeting. With a top-down approach, the senior management will look at the available total budget and make an overall allocation. In bottom-up budgeting, each brand manager will present plans which will require a minimum budget allocation. These are then totalled to give an overall budget requirement. In practice, a combination of these two is normally used. Proposals are developed by brand managers who compete for a portion of a fixed total budget.

In many Irish companies, the resources for marketing communication are divided between two functions in the company — sales and marketing. It is vital in such instances for these two functions to work closely together to achieve an acceptable level of consistency.

SUPPORT AGENCIES — BUILDING PARTNERSHIPS

A number of external agencies play a crucial role in successful development and implementation of marketing-communication strategies. The relationship between these agencies and the client company must be a very close and positive one if the quality of the work produced is to be optimised. The most important agencies are those responsible for advertising, public relations, and promotions. In some instances, these areas are handled by independent specialists, while a number of agencies offer full-service — in other words, they employ a range of individuals who together service the company's total communication needs. On the other extreme, within some of these three areas the level of specialisation has gone further. For example, a number of specialised advertising companies have set up in recent years in Ireland, and these offer only creative development or media planning/buying or strategic planning. In such instances, the client selects a number of advertising specialists who together develop and implement the advertising strategy.

There is no perfect type of agency. The full-service agency will meet the needs of some clients best, while specialists suit others. Whatever structure of agency is selected by the client, it is very important to work closely with the selected agency as "partners". Building such relationships is best achieved by involving the agencies in the development of the overall communication strategy, and so generating a level of commitment to the projects. In addition, involving the agencies at an early stage will also help to achieve a level of consistency between the different types of communication, keeping all communication in line with the overall strategy.

The selection of an agency to handle one or all elements of the client's communication needs must be done with great care, as such arrangements will most likely stay in place for a number of years and will, if successful, have a major impact on the future direction of the company's marketing-communication strategy. The "normal" approach to the selection of an agency is to invite a shortlist of agencies to "pitch" for the business. In this process, the client will brief the agencies to carry out a project (which may be a single piece of creative work or a media strategy). The work of each of the competing agencies is then presented to the client who selects one of the agencies to work with from then until the next review. This approach is often criticised as being very unrealistic and false (i.e. there is little interaction between client and agency as the initial work is being done) and excessively expensive for the agencies (as only the selected agency tends to get paid for the initial work).

The pitch approach has the advantage of providing a platform to discuss some relevant issues so that the client can form an opinion on the abilities of the agency's personnel. The selection criteria used by the client will include:

- The personal chemistry between the client and the account handling team
- The ability of the account handlers/planners to understand the client's business
- The perceived ability of the agency's creative team
- The perceived ability of the media planners/buyers
- The fee structure/level.

Having commenced the relationship with the agency, it is important to establish procedures that will allow both a level of control on the activities of the account and a level of freedom for creativity. Most agencies will have suitable procedures in place which will include contact reports of all client/agency meetings, regular work-in-progress reports and reviews of past activities.

On an annual basis, most clients will formally review the performance of the agency. Some clients also request the agency to review its own performance in terms of clarity of briefing, response to creative work and the level of understanding of the communication issues. The formal review will seek to measure every aspect of the service provided by the agency. An example of an instrument to structure such an evaluation is that used by McConnell's Advertising Services, which has held the Irish Biscuits account for many years. The client provides a score of how the agency performs on each of the following dimensions:

Account Management

1) Knowledge and understanding of the business

2) Commitment to and involvement with the account (interest, enthusiasm, time spent on account)

3) Contribution to helping achieve business goals (strategic thinking, marketing counsel, problem-solving, quality of advertising briefs)

4) Organises and delivers total agency resources

5) Contributes innovatively and with initiative

6) Responsiveness to day-to-day needs and requests of the client

7) Cost-consciousness (keeps within prescribed budgets, cares about client's money).

Creative Services

1) Effectiveness of creative services (freshness, originality, impact in the marketplace)

2) Effective translation of concept into execution

3) Quality of execution (production values, writing, finished art)

4) Knowledge and understanding of business by creative staff.

Media Services

1) Knowledge and understanding of business

2) Translation of marketing and creative ideas into an effective media plan.

3) Contributes innovatively and with initiative

4) Media-buying efficiency

5) Working procedures (thoroughness, timeliness, responsiveness).

Planning and Research Services

1) Contribution to development of advertising strategy (in relation to business, marketing, creative and media objectives)

2) Quality of research advice (efficiency and practical value of research recommended and provided)

3) Contribution to the evaluation of advertising effectiveness

4) Contributes innovatively and with initiative

5) Overall quality (thoroughness, timeliness, responsiveness).

Financial and Administrative Services

1) Effective billing and accounting procedures

2) Effective estimating and control of production and other variable costs

3) Effective secretarial services

These issues are discussed openly and honestly between the agency management and the client so that all perceived problems can be addressed before they damage the relationship or the quality of work produced by the agency.

ALTERNATIVE CLIENT STRUCTURES — RESPONDING TO CHANGE

Clients' marketing departments differ in structure depending upon the size of the company, the type of business it is in and the role of the marketing function in that company. For small businesses, the marketing function may be carried out by the managing directors. As companies become bigger, it is necessary to create a separate commercial function which may include both sales and marketing. Many large companies continue with such a combined sales/marketing structure while others split these roles and create two departments.

The client structures have evolved over time, with some aspects of the older structures returning to popularity in recent years. In the early 1960s, marketing as a business function was virtually unknown in Ireland. As commercial media developed, many consumer-brand companies rapidly developed their marketing resources. Some of Ireland's most successful marketers started their career in sales and added the additional marketing roles. This led in some cases to the two functions being managed together. As these companies evolved and the marketing activities became more complex, the functions split into two. Today, a number of companies have responded to the changing retail structure and have again combined sales and marketing. Trade or channel marketing (the communication with the trade customers rather than the consumer) has taken on some of the key account sales functions. In at least one company in Ireland, highly-trained individuals combine the roles of brand managers and key account managers. The marketing-communication responsibility of these managers will include both consumer and trade-customer communication activity, thus in a sense returning to the structures of the 1960s.

In Irish Biscuits, the roles are divided, with a sales director heading up the selling functions and a marketing director controlling the marketing functions. The marketing department is structured on the hierarchical model illustrated in Figure 3.4 below.

The role of the marketing director is to direct the function and, together with the other directors of the company, to plan, agree and co-ordinate the overall company strategy. Reporting to the marketing director are two senior managers, each of whom manages a defined range of products where they have responsibility for the full marketing mix. They are supported by brand managers who focus their attention on a more limited range of products and act as the general managers of their brands, with responsibility for planning and implementing all activities relating to those brands. A marketing services manager is responsible for services to the departments (general market research, data analysis, etc.). The marketing assistant's role is to work on specific projects on any one of the brands depending upon the short-term resource needs of the brand managers. While the ultimate responsibility for all marketing activity is with the marketing director, much of the advertising, PR and promotional planning is handled by the marketing managers and the brand management team, with implementation becoming the focus of the brand manager's job.

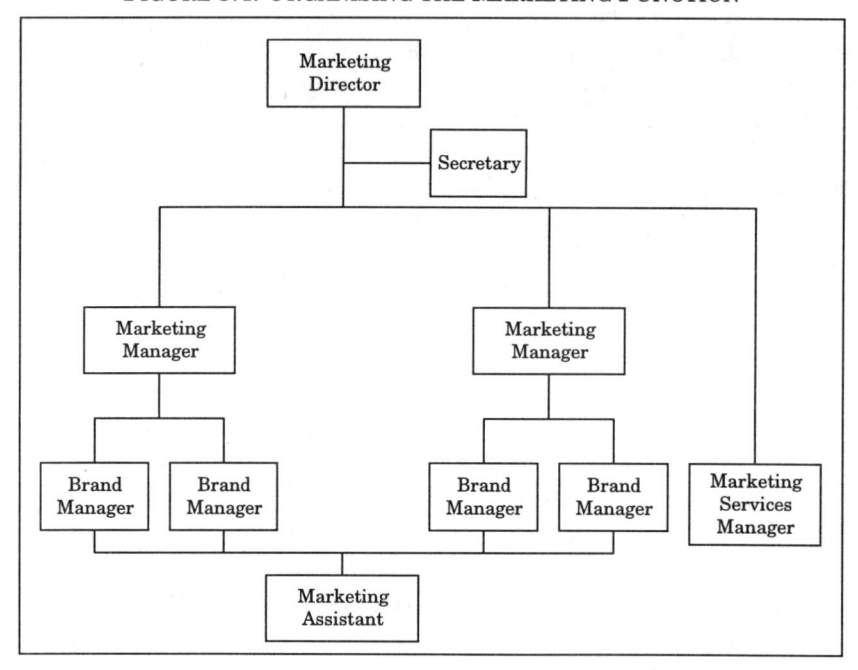

FIGURE 3.4: ORGANISING THE MARKETING FUNCTION

```
                    Marketing
                    Director
                        |
                        |——— Secretary
                        |
            ┌───────────┴───────────┐
        Marketing                Marketing
        Manager                  Manager
            |                        |
      ┌─────┴─────┐         ┌────────┼────────┐
    Brand       Brand     Brand    Brand    Marketing
   Manager     Manager   Manager  Manager   Services
                                            Manager
                        |
                    Marketing
                    Assistant
```

An alternative structure to this is that of the marketing department in Cantrell and Cochrane. A number of years ago, that department was restructured to take account of the complexities of a company in the drinks industry with a combination of grocery products and licensed trade products, and a combination of brands owned by the company (e.g. Club Orange, TK) and brands owned by international companies produced/sold under a franchise agreement (e.g. Pepsi, Schweppes). The matrix structure was developed to create a suitable focus on each aspect of that business. Reporting to the marketing director were five senior managers who worked together as a team, requiring a high degree of co-operation. The matrix structure is outlined in Figure 3.5 below.

The marketing-communication responsibility was split, with consumer advertising and PR being the responsibility of the product group managers, while consumer promotions and trade marketing were carried out by the trade marketing managers.

Whatever structure is used, it is crucial to maintain a consistency between the activities of a number of managers. This is achieved by agreeing clear overall direction for brand development, so that the managers are fully committed to the strategy they are planning and implementing. This in turn will help to develop clear briefs for the agencies, which will result in a high quality of work.

FIGURE 3.5: A MATRIX APPROACH TO MARKETING ORGANISATIONS

	1) Product Group Manager Owned Brand (both trade sectors)	2) Product Group Manager Franchised Brand (both trade sectors)	3) NPD Manager (both trade sectors)
4) Grocery Trade Marketing Manager (all brands)			
5) Licensed Trade Marketing Manager (all brands)			

Once again, there is no correct structure for all companies. Different needs will be served by different structures with different allocation of responsibility for marketing communication.

TYPES OF COMMUNICATION

As outlined above, marketing communication covers a wide range of activities. These activities include consumer advertising, promotions, sponsorship, PR and a host of other elements such as direct mail, packaging designs and corporate image. Some very brief comments on each of these from a client's perspective are offered below.

Advertising

The management of the advertising activity of the client company involves two main elements: Copy and Media. The copy is the material used, the message of the advertising. The media is the route by which that copy reaches its target audience. Working closely with an advertising agency (either a full service agency or a collection of independent specialists) will provide the client with solutions for both of these main elements of advertising.

A particular issue facing brands that are managed from an Irish base (with little or no access to advertising copy from outside the country) is the relative cost of the production of the commercials and the cost of media. Brands such as Jacob's Fig Rolls, Club Orange and Bachelors Beans must creatively develop and produce commercials specifically for the Irish market. It would not be unusual for brands such as these to pay up to £200,000 for one 30-second television commercial. The annual media budget for brands such as these may also be about £200,000. The allocation of up to 50 per cent of the total advertising budget to the production costs of the advertisement leads to very difficult budgeting decisions. The advertisement must be of similar production values to the imported alternative if it is to compete in a very competitive marketplace, so cheaper advertisements are simply not an option. The disadvantage to the Irish brand is enormous. For a UK-based brand, production cost will most likely not exceed 10 per cent of the total budget available. A brand marketed in Ireland by a UK company will, in effect, be capable of almost twice the level of media investment as an Irish brand of the same size and profitability, if the ad used in the UK can be used here or inexpensively localised. To minimise the effect, the Irish brand must extract a two- or three-year life from its ad. Imported international brands may have many advertisements available from which they can select the most appropriate for the Irish market. Careful creative use of funds is therefore a very necessary aspect of the Irish brand manager's role.

Promotions

To be effective, promotions must be consistent with the overall communication strategy. Too many companies fail to optimise their promotion budgets, through engaging in inappropriate activity which does little to reinforce the brand's values. In other cases, brands have become *overdependent* on short-term extra "free" promotional offers which may, in the long term, undermine the inherent values of the brand. Offering, say, 20 per cent extra free is a very effective short-term volume-generating activity in sectors such as biscuits and soft drinks. However, continuous use of such a promotion leads to the consumer expecting the extra quantity at the standard price, and when the promotion is withdrawn, the consumer may perceive the reintroduction of the standard-sized product as a massive price increase. Thus, promotional activity that was intended to build the brand values will damage them instead.

Good sales promotions, which build upon at least one aspect of the brand's personality, will assist in achieving the longer-term communication objectives. Thus, a promotion for Pepsi which uses a connection with teenagers' interests — such as a major rock music concert — (assuming that it is correctly implemented) will be a more efficient use of the budget than a promotion based on the theme of "natural ingredients", for example.

Sponsorship

Many Irish companies use sponsorship to support other forms of marketing communication. Sponsorship often allows the client to present a very credible message to its target audience. Careful selection, achieving close association between the brand and the sponsored event through image-fit and audience-fit, can greatly assist in the creation of the intended brand image. The Budweiser sponsorship of the Irish National Basketball League successfully links the brand with the Americana imagery of top-class basketball. Similarly, the Calor Kosangas sponsorship of the Housewife of the Year Awards brings together the brand with a key target audience, gaining excellent coverage for a limited budget.

The criteria used to select an effective sponsorship include:

- Credibility/stature of the event
- Link between the brand's target audience and the event's target audience
- Ability to include the brand name as the official name of the event
- Exclusivity and extent of branding to be allowed
- Extent of guaranteed media coverage
- Potential for customer/client entertainment
- Professionalism of the organisation running the event
- Costs (both direct costs and additional support costs)
- Options to renew the sponsorship.

While selection and management of sponsorship events is now becoming highly professional in Ireland, it is not unusual to see inappropriate brand sponsorships which appear to be determined by the personal interest of the company's senior management. Such events should not be confused with real brand-building sponsorship.

Public Relations

Professional public relations can help to achieve the overall marketing-communication objectives by changing or reinforcing the corporate or brand image. Careful management of relations with the consumer and trade media will lead to the target audience's impression of the company/brand moving in the intended direction. All media are capable of being carefully managed, but it must be done with care so that the long-term relationship with the media is maintained and the credibility of the brand is not undermined. Best results are achieved by fully understanding the needs of the media and supplying them with the type of information they require in the form that is most useful to them.

The relationship between a PR consultancy and a client should be as close as that of an advertising agency and client. If the consultancy really understands the client's business, they can develop a full programme of activity which maximises all major PR opportunities and keeps the company or brand to the forefront of its target audience's mind.

Other Types of Marketing Communication

Everything done by a manager responsible for a brand can be categorised under the heading Marketing Communication. Fulfilling the overall marketing-communication objective will include elements such as the graphic design of packaging, and general corporate-image management. The role played by design in brand creation is often understated, given that consumers encounter design aspects of a product at the very outset. For fast-moving consumer goods, the packaging will have more contact with the consumer than most of the other elements of marketing communication. Good, well-considered packaging design can successfully position the product at the intended level, while badly-developed design can undermine the brand's positioning, making achievement of overall communication objectives considerably more difficult. The area of general corporate image is also very important in advancing those objectives. Company logo, letterheads and business cards will all affect the perception of the company and must be managed consistently with the overall objective in mind.

IMPORTANCE AND ROLE OF EVALUATION

Much can be learned from structured post-evaluation of the use of marketing-communication tools. This can only be completed if, as part of the pre-planning, measurable objectives were set. An organisation and its management can therefore build upon the experience of each marketing-communication project, to make the next one more successful. However, such evaluations should not take up too much of management time. If overevaluation takes place, little time will be left to do things that will build the brand. Evaluation is important but will be damaging if it becomes too much of an activity in its own right. The exercise of common sense in selecting the type and form of evaluation will help to avoid such pitfalls.

Evaluations in the area of marketing communication may include reviews of effectiveness of media buying; on-going monitoring of brand awareness; image monitoring to measure the achievement of a campaign against pre-set targets; and measurement/analysis of redemption levels of various types of sales promotions. The information gained from all such evaluations must be actionable if it is to be used to improve future activities. Gathering vast quantities of data for its own sake will just distract from the job of building the brands.

CONCLUSION

It is clear that "marketing-communication" activity is central to the responsibilities of those involved in the marketing management function in an FMCG manufacturer or distributor. The most crucial issue is that a diverse set of activities must be co-ordinated to achieve an overall consistent message for the target audience. Consistent activity will have a synergistic influence on the achievement of brand objectives. An effective marketing department will work as partners with key outside agencies to achieve those synergies.

4
Communications in a Business-to-Business Framework

Seán de Búrca

INTRODUCTION

Business-to-business communication refers to all promotional activities in which a firm may engage to communicate with existing and potential customers. Traditionally, personal selling was considered the dominant tool in the business-to-business communication mix. However, this paper concentrates its attention on the other communication techniques used in the business-to-business communication mix. The role of personal selling is considered, but from the perspective of the impact of interpersonal communication and interaction in business-to-business markets.

While some businesses use traditional consumer media such as television, radio and newspapers, most business-to-business communication tends to concentrate on print media such as general business publications, trade publications, professional journals, directory listings and buyers' guides. Of course, other forms of business-to-business communication include direct marketing, sales promotion and public relations. Direct marketing activities such as direct mail, telemarketing, catalogues and data sheets are becoming an increasingly popular form of the business-to-business communication mix. In addition, business-to-business sales-promotion activities — such as trade fairs, exhibitions, seminars and demonstrations — play a vital communication role. Finally, public relations is considered a significant, credible, low-cost and highly effective business-to-business promotional tool. When these techniques are properly planned and controlled, they can enhance a company's image, build recognition for its products and services, reach unknown or inaccessible buying influences, and generate new sales prospects.

The focus of this paper is to review the techniques that business-to-business marketers use to communicate with present and prospective customers. It places considerable emphasis on the applied aspects of communications in a business-to-business framework. A typology of business-to-business communication techniques is presented and discussed from an applied industry perspective, paying particular attention to their application in the Irish market. The paper concludes with a discussion of the managerial implications of the impact of interpersonal contacts for the business-to-business communication mix.

THE BUSINESS-TO-BUSINESS MARKET

Understanding the organisational buying process is fundamental to the development of an effective business-to-business communications strategy. Organisational buyers apply a wide range of rational and emotional buying motives to the purchasing process. Traditionally, the literature has focused on the buying process, the buying situation, buying motives and the buying centre concept. Robinson, Faris and Wind (1967) identify an eight-stage decision-making process, as shown in Table 4.1.

TABLE 4.1: AN EIGHT-STAGE BUSINESS-BUYING PROCESS

Stage 1	Need Recognition
Stage 2	Product Type and Quantity
Stage 3	Writing Detailed Specification
Stage 4	Vendor Search and Evaluation
Stage 5	Proposal Analysis
Stage 6	Proposal Evaluation and Supplier Selection
Stage 7	Order Routine
Stage 8	Vendor Feedback and Evaluation

Source: Robinson, P.J., Faris, C.C. and Wind, Y. (1967): *Industrial Buying and Creative Marketing*, Boston: Allyn and Bacon.

The buying process identified above requires various types of skills and buying participants. The implications for an effective communications strategy are that sellers need to isolate by stage who these influencers are and what degree of influence they exercise over the decision-making process.

Furthermore, organisational buyers engage in three different types of buying situations: straight rebuy; modified rebuy; and new task. Each buying situation is characterised by different buying motives, the buyer-centre composition, and the complexity of the buying process. As a result, the implications for marketing communications need to be recognised. In addition, organisational buying motives differ by product and by buying-centre participant. Buying motives are diverse and complex and each member of the buying centre has different expectations, and consequently evaluates a seller's business proposition differently.

To be successful, marketing communications strategy must address the significant variation in information needs of those individuals involved in the purchasing decision as it progresses through the various stages of the buying process. A major task confronting the business-to-business marketer is to identify those individuals who are involved in the purchasing decision process. These decision-makers make up the decision-making unit (DMU) and are referred to as the buying centre. Effective marketing communications is influenced by the number and background of influencers in the buyer centre who may cut across functional lines and assume several different roles during the purchasing-decision process. Various buying roles are played by individuals in the buying centre and have a major affect on selling strategies. Webster and Wind (1972) identified a number of buying-centre roles, such as deciders and influencers, which they labelled primary roles, and users, buyers and gatekeepers, which they labelled secondary roles.

The influence of the above traditional literature on organisational buying is further compounded by purchasing's influence on buyer behaviour. The position of purchasing and its status within the organisation has a significant influence on industrial-buying behaviour. International material shortages, skyrocketing costs of materials and energy, fluctuating nationalistic moods, conflicting social goals, profit squeezes, and greater government regulation of business during the 1970s brought about a recognition of the importance of the purchasing function. Contributing to this recognition and the growing status of purchasing is the realisation that efficient and effective purchasing, through the use of material-requirements planning and just-in-time inventory control systems, is a key factor in maintaining profiles and alleviating cash-flow problems (Reeder, Brierty and Reeder, 1987).

However, a recent Irish survey of corporate purchasing,

commissioned jointly by the Irish Institute of Purchasing and Materials Management and the Marketing Institute, found that the role of purchasing in Irish firms was far from a strategic one. Evidence from this study suggests that the most significant obstacle to achieving best value for money appears to be that the purchasing department is involved in the purchasing decision at too late a stage to affect the outcome significantly (de Búrca and McLoughlin, 1995).

The discussion so far has focused on the traditional literature found in most business-to-business marketing textbooks. This traditional approach to marketing, which developed in a consumer context, was transferred to the analysis of business-to-business markets. This view of marketing, which focuses on an active marketer assembling a mix of variables, which are then launched towards a relatively homogeneous passive group of many potential consumers, restricts the understanding of the reality of much of what occurs in business markets. A number of researchers interested in industrial markets were struck by the fact that the prevailing view in the literature was of a world that just did not tally with their own experience (Ford, 1990). This group of researchers became known as the IMP group (Industrial Marketing and Purchasing). Research conducted by the IMP research group in their five-country study of business relationships points to a number of important influences in business markets. Evidence from this study indicates that most firms operate in markets where a limited number of customers account for a considerable proportion of the firm's sales. The interaction between companies is seen as occurring within the context of a relationship between the companies. These relationships are often close, complex and long-term, and are built out of the history of the companies' dealings with each other. Thus, they can be described in terms of adaptations, commitments, trust and conflict. The nature of interaction between companies over time means that a lot of different problems must be dealt with. Every relationship is a chain of episodes in which the past and the future matter. This connectedness and interdependency in business relationships provides an alternative context in which to assess the allocation of resources to establish, maintain and develop such interorganisational relationships.

THE BUSINESS-TO-BUSINESS COMMUNICATIONS MIX

Business firms communicate with a varied set of publics, including customers, prospects, employees, shareholders and the general public. Consequently, a wide variety of communication techniques is used to address these target markets (Figure 4.1). These techniques are rarely used alone. Instead, they must be integrated with other components in order to achieve strategic goals. However, some techniques account for a greater share of the average firm's communications budget.

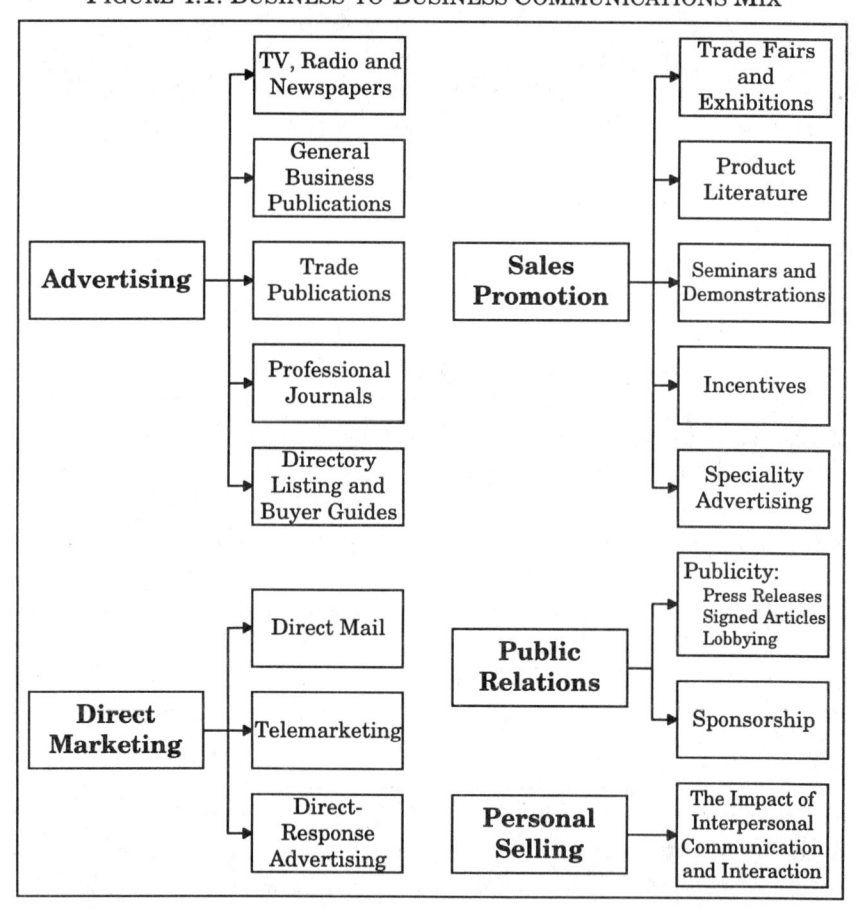

FIGURE 4.1: BUSINESS-TO-BUSINESS COMMUNICATIONS MIX

Advertising
- TV, Radio and Newspapers
- General Business Publications
- Trade Publications
- Professional Journals
- Directory Listing and Buyer Guides

Sales Promotion
- Trade Fairs and Exhibitions
- Product Literature
- Seminars and Demonstrations
- Incentives
- Speciality Advertising

Direct Marketing
- Direct Mail
- Telemarketing
- Direct-Response Advertising

Public Relations
- Publicity: Press Releases, Signed Articles, Lobbying
- Sponsorship

Personal Selling
- The Impact of Interpersonal Communication and Interaction

Kotler (1994) identified five competing concepts under which organisations conduct their marketing activity:

1) The production concept
2) The product concept
3) The selling concept

4) The marketing concept

5) The societal marketing concept.

These concepts reflect a company's orientation towards the marketplace. Traditionally, personal selling was considered the dominant tool in most business-to-business communications mixes. Several arguments are proffered to justify this dominant position. The traditional belief is that given the technical complexity of business products, the relatively small number of potential buyers, and the extensive negotiation process, the primary communications vehicle in business-to-business marketing is the salesperson. This view predominantly reflects what Kotler identified as a selling concept or orientation towards the marketplace. In doing so, the concept assumes that customers typically show buying inertia or resistance and need to be coaxed into buying.

However, experience has taught marketing managers that even the best salespeople cannot sell what customers do not want. As a result, it is better to concentrate on what the market wants rather than attempting to sell what the company makes. This is not, however, to deny the importance of personal selling as a communications vehicle in business-to-business marketing. Instead, the challenge for the business marketer is to create a communications mix that can help direct the sales force to prospective customers and enhance the effectiveness of the salesperson's interactions with personnel in the buying firm, in order to achieve sales and profit objectives. Therefore, a comprehensive programme of personal and non-personal forms of communications must be co-ordinated to achieve the desired results. The next section presents a review of the business-to-business communications mix from an applied industry perspective, paying particular attention to its application in the Irish market.

THE ROLE OF ADVERTISING IN A BUSINESS-TO-BUSINESS FRAMEWORK

To understand the role of advertising, it is vital to recognise the forces that shape and influence organisational buying decisions. Organisational buying is typically a joint decision. Research to date has traditionally focused on the influence of the buying centre, which suggests that a business marketer has to focus on a variety of individuals for any particular purchase. As a result, it is often not feasible for salespeople to make contact with everyone in the buying centre.

Therefore, advertising can play an effective role in reaching inaccessible or unknown buying influencers. Business-to-business advertising can enhance sales effectiveness, increase sales efficiency, create awareness and assist potential prospects to self-select and, therefore, increase the overall efficiency of the selling effort.

Effective advertising enhances the sales call by arousing interest in the supplier's offering and by helping to create supplier preference. Siebert (1970: 209) states that:

> ... when buyers are aware of a company, its reputation, its products, and its record in the industry, sales people are more effective.

Furthermore, research by Morrill (1970) indicated that when buyers were exposed to a firm's advertising, their opinion of the firm improved, sales per call were higher, and the firm's sales personnel were rated considerably higher on product knowledge, service and enthusiasm.

The impact of advertising on sales efficiency can be felt in two ways (Hutt and Speh, 1995). Firstly, suppliers need to remind actual and potential buyers of their product and make them aware of new products or services. Additionally, because there is often little or no product differentiation between many suppliers, buyers need to be reminded of suppliers' unique capabilities, such as dependability and reliability of service. Secondly, the cost of reaching large numbers of buyers by engaging in personal selling can be prohibitive and often unjustifiable. Research undertaken by de Búrca and Lambkin (1993) on sales-force management in Ireland, found that, taking an average rate of incentive pay of 20 per cent, together with an average salary for sales people of £17,750 and estimates of other costs, the total annual cost of a field sales representative, was approximately £43,500. Extrapolating further, it can be seen that the cost of an average-sized sales force of 10 representatives would be approximately £435,000 per year. Add to that the cost of sales management and sales administration at a ratio of, say, 0.5:1.0 and the total annual cost of selling accumulates to a very significant level of overhead for many Irish companies, and one whose productivity requires careful scrutiny.

Business-to-business advertising is an effective means of creating awareness of suppliers as well as their product offerings. Indeed, Hutt and Speh (1995) view the buying process, from a communications standpoint, as taking potential buyers sequentially from unawareness of a product or supplier to awareness, to brand preference, to conviction that a particular purchase will fulfil their requirements, and, ultimately to actual purchase. Effective advertising can alert potential purchasers to their needs and identify suppliers with product offerings as possible solutions to those needs. Trade-magazines are rated as the most important source of information for these buyers.

In addition, business-to-business advertising assists potential prospects to self-select, that is, respond to the advertisement by requesting additional information. As a result, the business marketer can assist these prospects and possibly convert them to customers.

In conclusion, advertising does not substitute for effective personal selling, rather it should supplement, support, and complement that effort. However, personal selling is constrained by its costs and should not generally be used to create awareness or to disseminate information. These tasks can be capably performed by advertising. On its own, advertising cannot generally create product preferences — this requires demonstration, explanation and operating testing. Similarly, conviction and actual purchase can be ensured only by personal selling. The business-to-business advertising task is to play a supporting role in creating awareness, providing information, and uncovering important leads for salespeople (Hutt and Speh, 1995).

Advertising in General Business and Trade Publications

Business publications are classified as either horizontal or vertical. Horizontal publications are directed at a specified task, technology, or function, whatever the industry — for example, *Marketing News*, *Advertising Age*, and *Purchasing*. Vertical publications deal with a specific industry and may be read by almost everyone in the company (Bovee and Arens, 1982). In addition to the above, a number of general business publications such as *Business and Finance*, *The Sunday Business Post*, *The Economist*, *Fortune*, *Business Week* and the *Wall Street Journal* tend to be read by business professionals across all industries, because of their general business content. The choice of one or other, or all, is dictated by the desire to penetrate a particular industry, reach common influencers across industries, or optimise the goals of reach and frequency (Reeder et al., 1987).

In Ireland, a comprehensive computerised index to business magazines can be searched by company, subject or specific product, and is available in all Dublin Public Libraries (DPLNET). The service is also available on Minitel. In addition, there is a range of national and international statistics (CSO, OECD, UN, EU), as well as a range of Irish Government publications, legislation and Dáil Reports. Indeed, all areas of local and national government are covered on DPLNET. Many professions organise their members through professional bodies such as the Institute of Accountants, Marketing Institute, Association of Advertisers in Ireland and the Institute of Purchasing and Materials Management. The majority of businesses are members of trade associations such as RGDATA. These associations produce publications containing listings, statistics and contact addresses which can be used by suppliers of goods and services likely to be purchased by the interest group in question. Indeed, one issue per annum tends to be the definitive directory of trade buyers. Furthermore, many of these trade magazines publish special editions often at the end or beginning of the year, which provide good articles on the current state of, and expected developments in, their respective industries.

The Institute of Public Administration (IPA) *Yearbook and Diary* is widely regarded as the most comprehensive source of information in Irish life. For example, a typical use of the IPA directory informs us that *Checkout Magazine* provides information on the food trade in Ireland and is issued to food and associated manufacturers, suppliers and distributors, multiple outlets, wholesalers, cash and carries, group and independent grocery stores. Indeed, the publishers of these magazines produce an annual *Checkout — Yearbook and Buyers' Guide*. Typical material from this is a comprehensive analysis of Ireland's major food and drink categories, critical forces shaping the future of European retailing and detailed data on individual companies, listing such things as main products, brand names and relevant management contacts. Another example of a yearbook is the *MAPS Directory*, produced by the Association of Advertisers in Ireland. Primarily aimed at users of advertising services, this volume also details a wide variety of business and consumer publications which, in turn, can point to further sources of data for the marketer wishing to target customers in that segment.

There are several other publications that draw together data and statistics from a variety of government, semi-state, private research, commercial and academic bodies. Sources include the Central Statistics Office, Eurostat, the Economic and Social Research Institute, Forbairt, the Irish Trade Board, Joint National Listenership Research, Joint National Readership Research and Irish TAM. While much of the information is taken from readily available sources, some

Communications in a Business-to-Business Framework

would not be so easily accessed by the individual researcher. In summary, trade publications, especially yearbooks, are an invaluable source of marketing information for those sectors that they serve.

Developing Effective Business-to-Business Advertisements

The effectiveness of business-to-business advertising has been the subject of much study, but firm conclusions remain elusive. However, a systematic approach to the development of business-to-business advertisements enables a company to manage effectively the various decisions confronting such an approach.

FIGURE 4.2: MODEL FOR DEVELOPING EFFECTIVE BUSINESS ADVERTISEMENTS

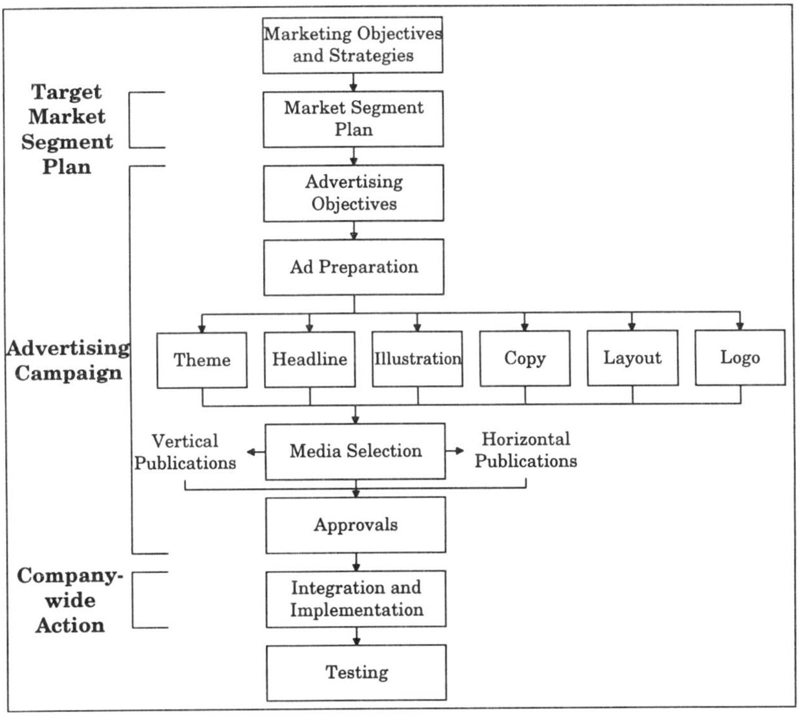

Source: Mahin, P.W. (1991): *Business-to-Business Marketing*, London: Allyn and Bacon: 339.

The advertising decisions model in Figure 4.2 identifies three critical elements that must be considered (Mahin, 1991):

- A market segment plan
- A professionally prepared advertisement campaign
- A co-ordinated company response.

However, it must be borne in mind that advertising is only one aspect of the entire marketing strategy and must be integrated with other components in order to achieve a firm's strategic goals.

Market Segment Plan

Knowing the target audience is a vital prerequisite to advertisement preparation. Indeed, business suppliers and influencers, such as top management, technical personnel and purchasing agents, have different information needs. Consequently, only when the audience is identified is it possible to select an advertising theme, write copy and choose the proper medium.

Advertising Objectives

An advertising objective is defined by Bellizi and Lehrer (1983: 19) as

> ... a time-related, concise statement of the intended outcome of a particular advertising action, phrased in terms of what should happen in the mind of the prospect as a result of reading the advertisement.

The advertising objective must, therefore, fulfil a marketing-strategy objective and respond to the roles to which business-to-business advertising is best suited, that is, creating awareness, providing information, influencing attitudes, and reminding buyers of company and product existence.

The objective must speak in unambiguous terms of a specific outcome. Every effort should be made to state objectives that are specific, measurable and obtainable. Two important business advertising objectives are to open the prospect's doors for the salesperson and make it easier to close the sale. Other objectives tend to focus on building product or company image, to increase brand awareness, to differentiate products from competitors, to launch a new product, and to generate sales leads.

Advertisement Preparation

Having decided on the advertising objectives, a number of elements concerning the preparation of the advertisement have to be considered, such as, the theme, the headline, the illustration, the copy and the layout. The theme should highlight the major benefits and should possess the following traits (Bellizzi and Lehrer, 1983):

- Should attract attention
- Should stop the reader
- Should be readily understood
- Should be brief, that is, emphasising a few benefits only.

In addition, these authors contend that the headline should communicate something of value to the prospect. It is important to remember that the headline is the words that are read first, and therefore they should attract the reader's primary attention. As a result, headlines often emphasise product innovations or improvements, or state competitive comparison and/or product-application information.

Illustrations are designed to work in unison with the headline. The collective purpose is to arouse interest, capture attention, and define the ad's primary focus. A study by Bovee and Arens (1982) indicated that a single dominant illustration occupying 60–70 per cent of the total ad space had the highest stopping power.

An advertisement copy must effectively communicate the unique selling proposition and substantiate product claims. Given the technical nature of many business products the specific wording of the "copy" poses a major problem, as the technical expertise of the target audience can vary substantially. Bellizzi and Lehrer (1983) identified three approaches:

- Direct narration of a product's application (straight exposition)
- A case history that identifies the actual experience of a user
- Testimonials that are similar to case histories except that the user customer is always a recognised industry leader.

The advertisement's layout contains the following elements: illustration, headline, copy, charts and signature, and through its visual attractiveness, can arouse interest and motivate readership (Bellizzi and Hite, 1986).

Finally, the logo or signature identifies the advertisement's sponsor and acts as a trademark. However, the logo is often remembered and can, therefore, assist in distinguishing individual brand identities.

Media Selection

Three main types of periodical print media are used by businesses: trade magazines, professional publications and the press. These publications can be classified as horizontal or vertical. Business-to-business advertisers are faced with a difficult choice, given the huge number of publications on offer. The criteria used usually include the following:

- The publication's served market
- Its total circulation
- Proportion of paid circulation to total circulation
- Proportion of editorial pages to total pages published
- Number of inquiries generated from advertisements placed in the past.

Approvals, Integration, and Implementation

It is essentially top management's responsibility to ensure that stock, trained intermediaries and salespeople are in place, with up-to-date product literature and price lists, before the advertising campaign is launched.

Testing

An advertisement's headline, illustration, and message are usually pretested with a sample audience to ensure message clarity and comprehension.

Advertising in Directory Listings and Buyers' Guides

One of the most important ingredients of modern business is information. Information is vital for business strategy, international competitiveness and the identification of technological opportunities. A comprehensive range of international trade directories and buyers' guides covering most countries is readily available in most business libraries. The Irish *IPA Yearbook*, discussed earlier, lists many trade and professional journals and organisations and is a most useful starting point for detective work. Some of the more common trade directories in use are Kompass, Thoms and Dun and Bradstreet. In addition, the Forbairt information services have compiled a database containing information on over 7,000 Irish manufacturing companies, and acts as a most useful source of information on manufacturers and suppliers of particular products. Technological advances, in the form of CD ROMs and on-line services, have greatly improved the accessibility of these resources. Companies ordinarily, but not always, pay for a listing of their products and services in such directories. The main advantage of directory advertising is that it is a highly credible medium and, for many buyers, their basic purchasing tool. One disadvantage is that unless buyers purchase directories to use, advertising in this medium is not seen (Reeder et al., 1987).

SALES PROMOTIONS IN A BUSINESS-TO-BUSINESS FRAMEWORK

Business-to-business advertising budgets are designated primarily for trade publications and direct-marketing activities. However, these programmes are reinforced by sales-promotion activities, such as, trade fairs and exhibitions, seminars and demonstrations, premium and incentives and speciality advertising.

Trade Fairs and Exhibitions

Trade fairs have a long history, dating at least from biblical times (Hanlon, 1977). The contemporary significance of trade fairs is evident from the absolute scale of trade-fair activity. Of the 2,000 major trade fairs held worldwide each year, 60 per cent take place in Europe, 10 per cent in North America, 20 per cent in South East Asia, and the remaining 10 per cent in Latin America, Africa and Australia (Palka, 1992). The industry is expected to grow by half again over the next decade (Trade Show Bureau, 1991).

In general, companies that participate in trade fairs come to display, describe, and sometimes demonstrate, their products and services to customers, distributors, suppliers, and the press. Bello and Barksdale (1986) highlight a number of advantages and disadvantages. On the advantage side, trade fairs deliver high-quality target audiences to exhibitors in an efficient manner. Consequently, exhibitors can generate hundreds of contacts in a few days. These contacts tend to be qualified buyers, since attendance is often restricted to a specific industry. Trade fairs allow buyers to compare competitive offerings, ask questions and engage in negotiation, and thus facilitate and often accelerate the buy–sell process. On the other hand, these authors point to a number of disadvantages. In particular, buyers can be confused by competing and often conflicting "market noise" at trade fairs. In addition, as salespeople are away from their territories, customer service can deteriorate temporarily with existing accounts. Finally, trade fairs can be a costly means of communicating with the market.

The effectiveness of trade fairs, however, depends on the role they are to play in the overall promotional mix and how well trade-fair objectives are established. Companies use trade fairs to achieve a variety of objectives, to support selling and non-selling objectives. To support selling objectives, trade fairs are useful for:

- Identifying prospects
- Gaining access to key decision-makers
- Disseminating information on products, services, and company personnel
- Actually selling products.

To support non-selling objectives, trade fairs are a viable vehicle for:

- Obtaining information on and encouraging interests of suppliers
- Gathering information regarding competitors' proposed products and prices
- Influencing distributors
- Testing and evaluating customer reactions to products
- Training new sales and marketing personnel through exposing them to customers and competitors
- Maintaining and enhancing corporate morale (Reeder et al., 1987).

Because trade fairs differ with respect to the opportunities they provide to achieve each of these objectives, managers need a clear understanding of their goals in order to select the trade fairs in which to participate.

Trade fairs are a unique element of the promotional mix because they are the only technique that encourages large numbers of unknown prospects to visit a seller's place of business (booth). This represents a reverse buy–sell situation, since the buyer comes to the seller rather than vice versa. The benefit to the seller is significant new-order-getting opportunities at very low-per-contact-reached costs. Average cost per contact is estimated at half that of a traditional sales call. In addition to trade fairs, some companies promote their products at exhibitions.

Exhibitions include displays of a company's products at a meeting, convention or conference to individuals not necessarily in the same trade as the exhibitor, and in public areas where exposure to appropriate individuals is likely, such as, airport terminals.

Recent research conducted by the UCD Marketing Development Programme (1995), and commissioned by the Association of Advertisers in Ireland Ltd. (AAI), assessed the satisfaction levels of members and non-members of the AAI with trade fairs. The survey findings revealed that overall the majority of respondents (66 per cent) were satisfied with trade fairs as a promotional medium. The main reasons why these companies exhibited were:

- To meet new customers
- To enhance company image
- To promote existing products.

Alternatively, the main reasons why companies chose not to exhibit were cost, and that exhibitions were irrelevant to their respective industry. The research indicated that the main perceived advantage of exhibitions as a form of promotion was the large captive audience and the opportunity to meet new customers.

Similarly, the main perceived disadvantage was the overall cost involved in such an activity. As a result, this influenced the decision whether a company exhibited or not. The success of trade fairs was primarily evaluated by the number of contacts made and the sales leads generated. However, Ames and Hlavacek (1987) illustrate the relative cost-effectiveness and reach of the various tools used for business-to-business communications (see Figure 4.3).

The breadth of coverage increases as costs per contact decrease. However, total cost goes up proportionately. Research conducted on trade fairs as a means of marketing communications offering unique possibilities to the business-to-business marketer was investigated by Coogan (1994). This study examined the effectiveness and use of the three largest Irish trade-only fairs, *vis-à-vis* other industrial promotional tools. The evidence from this research indicates that the majority of companies rate trade fairs as an effective promotional tool. The results confirm that the vast majority of firms use exhibitions as a strategic, three-dimensional medium within their total marketing communications mix. They set clear quantifiable objectives, apply strategic vision on show selection, use an appropriate budgetary technique and conduct all-important evaluative research on their participation.

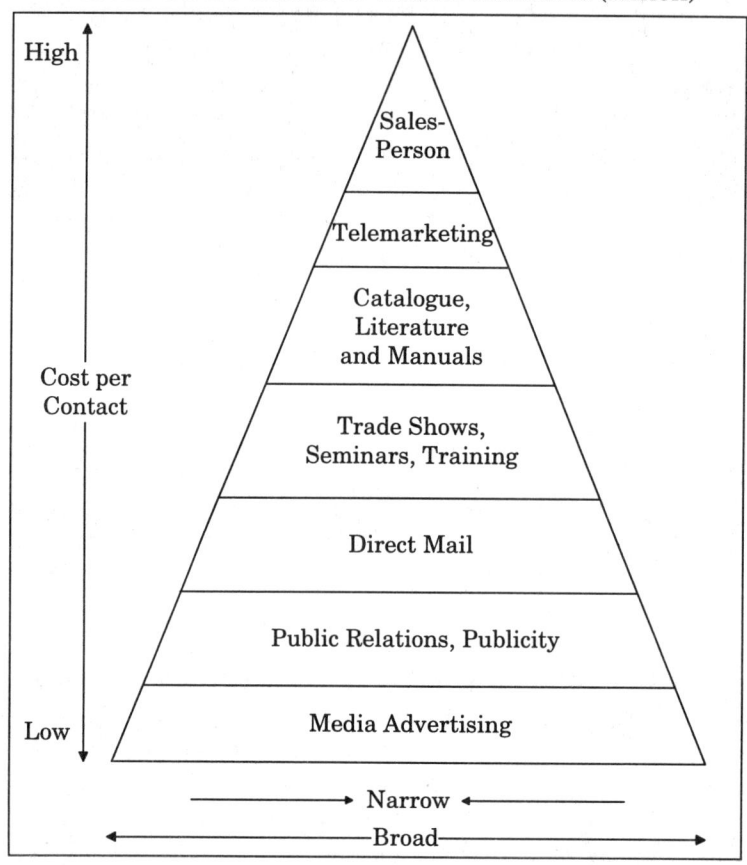

FIGURE 4.3: COVERAGE OF TARGET AUDIENCE (REACH)

```
                    Sales-
                    Person
                  Telemarketing
                 Catalogue,
                 Literature
                 and Manuals
              Trade Shows,
              Seminars, Training
            Direct Mail
        Public Relations, Publicity
        Media Advertising
```

Cost per Contact: High → Low
Narrow → Broad

Source: Ames, B. and Hlavacek, J.D. (1987): "Managing Marketing for Industrial Firms", in Rothschild, M.L. (ed.), *Marketing Communications*, Toronto: DC Heath and Co.: 68.

Product Literature

Product literature includes materials describing a company's products and services, including catalogues, brochures, specification sheets, price lists, parts lists, instruction, service manuals and pre-recorded audio or video tapes. Product literature gives the buyer detailed purchasing information about a product's specification, performance capabilities, and features. This information is particularly important during three critical stages of the buy cycle: specification writing, vendor search and evaluation, and proposal analysis (Mahin, 1991).

Buyers use catalogues and brochures to compare products, product applications and prices of potential suppliers. In addition, catalogues provide support for distributors because it is not always possible for them to carry in stock all the items a manufacturer supplies. Furthermore, data-specification sheets provide detailed technical information on such things as product dimensions, efficiencies, performance data, and cost savings, and are an important complement to the personal selling effort.

The effectiveness of product literature can be difficult to measure. However, customers are very quick to point out shortcomings in a company's product literature.

Seminars and Demonstrations

This form of communication includes presentations made by technical personnel at professional meetings, travelling seminars sponsored by the company and presented in several cities, fixed-location demonstrations centres, and visits by customer personnel to plant sites. The primary purposes of these activities are to communicate information about new products and technologies, and to demonstrate vendors' capabilities (Cardozo, 1982).

Sales Promotion and Incentives

While promotional contests and "giveaways" are quite common in consumer marketing, they are also used, though less frequently, in business-to-business markets. The effectiveness of these materials is difficult to measure, in large part because clear objectives for their use are not stated, and measurements are not specified (Cardozo, 1982). However, most marketers report favourable customer response to particular sales-promotion campaigns, particularly those involving reseller support. In addition, most customers willingly accept "free lunches" and other forms of hospitality and entertainment. Indeed, with regard to the promotion instrument used by sponsors, the ability to provide corporate hospitality was the most important promotional aspect of sponsorship for Irish industrial goods companies (Crowley, 1991). However, extensive entertainment and expensive gifts may not be appropriate in most industries. Premiums and incentives are generally used to build goodwill during reorder or post-order stage.

Speciality Advertising

In contrast to premiums, which are items of value and normally related to the products they are intended to sell, speciality advertising consists of useful, low-cost giveaways such as calendars, ballpoint pens, cigarette lighters or other gifts given to prospects by salespeople. Since the item will have the firm's name and address on it somewhere, and possibly contain an advertising message, it is also classified as an advertisement (Reeder et al., 1987).

DIRECT MARKETING IN A BUSINESS-TO-BUSINESS FRAMEWORK

Direct marketing is defined by Jenkins (1984: 12) as:

> ... an interactive system of marketing in which the marketer establishes direct relations with the customer via interactive communications.

Within the business-to-business promotional mix, direct marketing includes the following activities: direct mail, direct response advertising and telemarketing. Of course, personal selling is considered to be another form of direct marketing. However, personal selling will be discussed separately later. In contrast to most media advertising, which is non-personal, direct marketing is a personalised form of communications.

Direct marketing offers the business marketer numerous benefits, including:

- Better maintenance of customer files because these are a prerequisite for all direct marketing programmes

- Faster response time as direct marketing programmes link the buyer directly with the seller

- Enhanced sales productivity ratios as telemarketers are able to initiate four to six times the number of sales contacts possible for an outside sales force (Jenkins, 1984).

Effective direct marketing requires application of a concept known as database marketing. In essence, database marketing involves getting accurate and precise information about customers and prospects so that the business marketer can direct the appropriate marketing efforts with the correct appeal to the selected target market. Maintaining and upgrading the database is an ongoing task requiring considerable effort. However, mailing lists may be compiled in-house from trade publications and industrial directories or purchased from mailing-list houses such as Dun and Bradstreet.

Direct Mail

Direct mail is a separate advertising medium that is used to communicate a message to selected target markets. It can accomplish all of the major advertising functions, but its real contribution is in delivering the message to a precisely defined prospect. Direct mail is commonly used for:

- Corporate-image promotion
- Product and service promotion
- Sales-force support such as lead generation and re-inforcing the sales call
- Distribution-channel communication (Hutt and Speh, 1995).

The primary benefits of direct mail are its selectivity, personalisation, flexibility and high readership. A major disadvantage of direct mail is that it can be screened out from its intended audience or treated as "junk mail". Furthermore, direct mail does not reach the hidden influencers as advertising in trade publications might do. Hence, direct mail should complement print advertisements, not be a substitute for them (Mahin, 1991).

Direct-Response Advertising

Business marketers also use direct-response advertising as another element of the direct-marketing mix. Bennett (1978: 58) defines direct-response advertising as: "... any advertisement that seeks an immediate action or response and allows the customers to respond directly to the advertiser".

Typical responses include an immediate purchase, a salesperson's visit, or, perhaps, product literature. Direct-response advertising is differentiated from general advertising by its shorter time-frame, its goal of eliciting an immediate customer response, and its ability to identify each customer by name, address, and place of business (Mahin, 1991).

Telemarketing

Telemarketing is becoming an increasingly popular form of business-to-business direct marketing. With the rising costs of sales call, discussed earlier, many business-to-business marketers are turning to telemarketing as a way of reaching buyers cost-effectively. Telemarketing is a combination of three key elements — telecommunication devices, information systems, and trained personnel — in a dynamic customer-oriented process that seeks new orders and enhanced customer service (Mahin, 1991).

The Irish Direct Marketing Association contends that there are over 2,000 people employed directly in call-centre orientation environments in Ireland. Companies such as FEXCO in Killorglin, Co. Kerry handle European-wide VAT refunds and Irish Prize Bonds. In addition, Dell and Coca-Cola manage specific service desks from Dublin.

When used effectively, telemarketing can generate sales' leads, qualify customers, and substitute for some personal sales calls. It can be used to enhance the effectiveness of publication and direct-mail advertising. When a toll-free number is included in print and direct-mail advertising, prospects can easily respond and get immediate information while the advertised message is still fresh in their minds.

PUBLIC RELATIONS IN A BUSINESS-TO-BUSINESS FRAMEWORK

Public Relations is considered a significantly credible, low-cost, and highly effective business-to-business promotional tool. Publicity is an output of public relations and includes company press releases, editorial and signed articles and lobbying activities. In some firms, public relations also involves sponsorship of special events. The effectiveness of public relations and publicity is attributed to its third-party credibility, as a non-paid-for communication of information about the company or its products and services. However, there are some direct costs involved in some public-relations activities. For example, someone has to write the article or prepare the news release and arrange for it to be placed in the right publication. In addition, public-relations consultants and lobbying costs are forms of direct costs. Williams (1983: 209) concludes that the effectiveness of public relations varies across the hierarchy of communications, and he contends that:

Its highest effectiveness occurs during the cognitive stages of building awareness and imparting knowledge. It is least effective during the preference, conviction, and purchase stage (209).

There are many different approaches to public relations. On the one hand, there are companies run by individuals who shun public relations, even at the expense of their business. The 1995 dispute at Dunnes Stores is a case in point, where the company did not employ any public relations on its behalf. The company's only public defence of its industrial-relations strategy was to take out advertisements in the newspapers to put its case. In contrast, MANDATE, the trade union in conflict with Dunnes Stores, had a very effective campaign. It presented its case in a calm, rational manner and avoided the extreme rhetoric that is sometimes the hallmark of such industrial disputes. Eventually, Dunnes Stores hired public relations expert Pat Henaghan who coaxed the company into issuing its first press statement in the firm's 51-year history, announcing it would attend the Labour Court hearing into the dispute.

Public relations can play a proactive and reactive role. A number of companies in Ireland use the proactive approach to public relations, creating a strong positive image for themselves. For example, in the education field, Michael Smurfit's support of University College Dublin's Graduate School of Business and the Tony O'Reilly funding of the O'Reilly Hall in UCD and the O'Reilly Institute in Trinity College stand out as positive examples of proactive public relations. A number of companies — such as Tara Mines and Intel — position themselves as being environmentally friendly through the sponsorship of educational materials and of river improvement.

Similarly, it may be better to have a considered, detailed piece about your company in one business publication, rather than a series of snippets in several titles. Furthermore, even though listenership and readership figures decline in the summer months because of holiday time, such times can be ideal for making announcements because there is a greater certainty that they will be picked up, and will command more space in newsprint and time on radio or television than at another time of year.

Finally, the reason why a company considers an opening or an award of an ISO certificate to be newsworthy, including the presence of a government minister at the event, could be the very reason why a business editor decides to put the photograph in the bin. It is often not appreciated how many similar events the same minister attends.

A business editor may decide that in the previous fortnight the publication has carried too many pictures of the minister "cutting the tape", surrounded by men in suits.

Publicity

Publicity is an output of public relations and includes company press releases, editorials, signed articles and lobbying activities. Business firms issue press releases, such as background information for the press and public on the company, its products, technology and the industries in which it participates. These press releases serve as a supporting promotional tool to personal selling and have a synergistic effect with advertising by preceding it and thereby enhancing the advertisement's effectiveness.

At a recent conference held by the Association of Advertisers in Ireland, and in conjunction with the Dublin Chamber of Commerce, the Deputy Editor of the *Sunday Business Post*, Aileen O'Toole, suggested that a press release about a company should begin with whatever is news, such as an official opening, an expansion, an award, or an acquisition, by explaining what has happened clearly and succinctly (O'Toole, 1995).

O'Toole suggests that a press release should give an amount of background detail on the company.

> Never assume that your business is so well known that you can afford to leave out the basics, such as the company's full name, location, an explanation of what it does, the number of employees, where its main markets are, when it was established, how it has developed and so on. This allows a journalist to put the news development in some sort of context.

Editorial material and signed articles about a company or its products and services are considered vital sources to generate sales leads and bring about better relationships with customers. Evidence indicates that industrial customers rate technical editorial material in trade journals as an important source of information in the buying process (Williams, 1983).

Lobbying involves dealing with legislators and government officials to promote or defeat legislation and regulations. Some companies maintain an extensive lobby presence at various levels of government, primarily to provide information to administrators and legislators whose actions affect the company or its industry. Indeed, companies often pool their efforts through an industry association. In the US, where lobbyists are legally registered companies, this form of influence is readily acceptable. Obvious examples of such proactive lobbying activity are the National Rifle Association and the tobacco industry.

In Ireland, the phenomenon of public-affairs consultants is not so transparent. However, extensive lobbying happens and cases are made at all political levels on behalf of companies. For example, the Association of Advertisers in Ireland Ltd. (AAI) made its views known concerning the broadcasting legislation, and is credited with having a significant impact on the Green Paper. Furthermore, there is a substantial lobbying industry at European Union (EU) level, based in Brussels, making inputs at policy level and in debates prior to the framing of legislation.

Sponsorship

Sponsorship has emerged as a significant form of marketing communications over the past number of years. The growth has stemmed from increasing supply of sponsorship opportunities and the demand from the corporate sector for effective communications media.

Recent research among major Irish companies (Crowley, 1991) examined the priority that sponsors attached to the various corporate audiences and how this related to the promotional instruments used to exploit sponsorship opportunities. In a business-to-business context, a number of interesting findings emerged. Industrial-type companies used sponsorship as a form of communication to the business community. These companies tended to be small in scale and would seem to indicate the extent to which smaller companies are more likely to use sponsorship as a medium to facilitate business-to-business marketing and a particularly appropriate medium for their very specific audiences.

Schuman (1986) in a study of American sponsors found that sponsors sought to communicate with a whole variety of corporate audiences. The evidence from the Irish study confirmed this and found that the audiences targeted and the objectives to be satisfied varied with the sponsor's industrial background. Predominantly, business-to-business sponsorship concentrated its communications objectives on community relations (29 per cent), corporate responsibility (21 per cent), awareness/recognition (17 per cent) and image/reputation (11 per cent) (Crowley, 1991).

In addition, the Crowley (1991) study attempted to analyse audience importance by industrial sector. While the study recognises the small number of companies in these categories, nevertheless the notable features were:

- The relatively high priority attached to suppliers by sponsors in the agricultural and food sector
- The importance of the workforce public as a very important target for sponsors in the retailing sector
- The low priority attached to the local community by the chemical and pharmaceutical sector, given the potential for criticism as a sponsorship target audience
- The absence of any interest by the transport or construction sectors in the general public as an audience.

Finally, the study found that, with regard to the promotion instrument used by sponsors, the ability to provide corporate hospitality was the most important promotional aspect of sponsorship for industrial goods companies. Sponsorship is big business in Ireland. Several companies are actively engaged in major sport and arts sponsorships. Smurfit is involved in a number of sponsorships which go to the core of Irish life from an educational, cultural and sporting perspective. Its sponsorship of the Irish St Ledger is a major form of corporate hospitality, where the company invites every buyer across its whole range of businesses to a day's racing and entertainment. In addition, Guinness Peat Aviation's (GPA) sponsorship of the Dublin International Piano competition is an internationally and highly acclaimed sponsorship. Other examples such as Opel's sponsorship of soccer, Wessel and Cable's sponsorship of the Irish Championship Hurdle and Guinness's sponsorship of the GAA hurling championships are a few of the more obvious sponsorship activities in which Irish companies are engaging.

In conclusion, the emergence and now virtually universal acceptance of sponsorship as a component in the business-to-business marketing mix results from the capacity of sponsorship to perform certain key marketing tasks particularly well, especially its ability to achieve corporate hospitality.

PERSONAL SELLING
The Impact of Personal Communications

Personal contacts are at the heart of interaction between organisations and serve as the primary medium of communication in both buying and selling. Apart from their function for two-way information exchange, personal contacts facilitate other elements of interactions, such as product adaptations and changes in production, distribution and commercial systems. Price, delivery and other factors are often subject to negotiation and this occurs through interorganisational contacts (Turnbull, 1979).

A number of research studies have highlighted the importance and significance of interpersonal communication and interaction in business-to-business markets (Levitt, 1967; Ford, 1980; and Häkansson, 1982). These studies point to one reason for the greater importance of interpersonal communication in business-to-business markets: namely, that both buyers and sellers need a greater volume and quality of information and this information need exists at all stages of the decision process. In addition, these studies provide evidence of the value accredited to personal contacts and interpersonal communication in lowering buyers' perceived risk, improving suppliers' credibility, and in providing a valuable source of information about supply markets. Indeed, personal contacts between buyers and the technical and general management staff of suppliers were considered as important as sales representation both before and after a supplier was chosen. However, these studies did not indicate why interpersonal communications was so important. Thus, while there had been a recognition of the importance of interpersonal communications, very little research attempted to address the "why" question. As a consequence, a qualitative empirical research investigation into the nature and roles of interpersonal contact was carried out in three UK supply companies by Turnbull (1979). The main objective of the research was to determine the opinions of supplier personnel as to why personal contacts were important to the supplier and in what way they were thought to be important to the customer companies. It emerged very clearly that not only are personal contacts seen as very important for suppliers, but also that they serve a variety of purposes for both buyers and sellers. Turnbull (1979) classified these roles and related the roles to different aspects of the marketing situation, as illustrated in Table 4.2 below.

The information-exchange role plays a vital part in reducing the uncertainty found by buyers in placing an order for a product or service. Häkansson, Johanson and Wootz (1976) refer to the phenomenon as "need uncertainty". Turnbull (1979) argues that

> ... the perceived risk may be reduced by the exchange of information on technical, commercial and organisational matters. The information exchange flow is enhanced in the face-to-face situation

and the parties to the exchange are able to seek out and evaluate information about the competence and credibility of each other (328).

TABLE 4.2: BASIC RELATIONS BETWEEN PERSONAL CONTACT ROLES AND ASPECTS OF THE MARKETING SITUATION

	Task-related		Non-task-related
	Product-related	Supplier-related	
Short-Term	Information Exchange	Assessment	Ego-enhancement
Long-Term	Adaptation	Crisis insurance	Social

Source: Turnbull, P.W. (1979): "Roles of Personal Contacts in Industrial Export Marketing", *Scandinavian Journal of Management*, 16.

The assessment role for both buyers and sellers is equally surrounded by risk. This process can be improved through interacting with the other party in both formal and informal situations.

Negotiation and adaptation are normal roles, often involving daily personal contacts, both at the time of the original order and subsequently.

The crisis insurance role of personal contacts is deliberately established by companies to handle major problems, which cannot be resolved through existing channels. These contacts can be at a higher management level, or at a different level, to facilitate change or gain preferential treatment.

It is important to distinguish the task-related roles from the more personal or non-task-related. The roles discussed above can be classified as the formal. However, the reasons why personal contacts are important to buyers and sellers have as much to do with non-task-related roles, such as the social role and ego-enhancement role.

Social relationships often develop as a consequence of instrumental interaction, however, the development and regular contact maintained, is justified on the grounds that it makes work more congenial.

The ego-enhancement role occurs where somebody deliberately establishes contact with senior people in supplier or buyer organisations because of the belief that such contact will enhance their status in their own organisation.

Relating these roles to different aspects of the marketing situation, Turnbull (1979) distinguishes task- and non-task-related roles, both in the short term and the long term, and further classifies the task-related roles from focusing on the product to focusing on the supplier (Table 4.2). These inter-organisational personal contacts serve to allow what Turnbull (1979) describes as "Marketing Service Communication" to take place.

In conclusion, further evidence from this research indicated that the multiple roles that personal contacts performed, in the form of "Marketing Service Communication" varied according to the complexity of the product technology, the stages of development of relationship, the relative importance of the supplier or customer to the other party, and unexpected discontinuities and crises.

Research conducted by the IMP (Industrial Marketing and Purchasing) research group in its five-country study of supplier–customer relationships in European industrial markets (Häkansson, 1982) drew attention to the roles that personal contacts play in developing and maintaining supplier–customer relationships. Interpersonal contacts between supplier and customer companies are identified in the IMP interaction model as performing vital roles in problem-solving, in exchanging social values and information, and in demonstrating commitment to, and establishing credibility with, the other party. Research based on a subset of the IMP database, concerning 49 British suppliers of industrial goods and their customer contacts in France, Germany, Italy, Sweden and the UK, analysed the nature of personal contacts, focusing upon their frequency, breadth and the managerial levels involved (Cunningham and Homse, 1986). The author contends that an analysis of interpersonal contacts along these dimensions enables management to recognise the resource implications for the communications mix of interpersonal contacts. The complexity and resource implications of supplier–customer relationships is evident from the research results, which showed that, for each customer, an average of eight supplier staff and nine customer staff were involved in the network of interpersonal contacts across functions such as sales, design, quality control, manufacturing and finance. On average, face-to-face meetings between suppliers and customer staff occurred almost weekly in the domestic market and once every two months with foreign customers. At least three levels of management in supplier and customer companies were involved. The complexity, resource implications and organisational problems of managing interpersonal contacts between companies is clear from the above research.

CONCLUSIONS

The focus of this paper was to review the techniques that business-to-business marketers used in communicating with current and prospective customers. A typology of business-to-business communication techniques was presented and discussed from an applied industry perspective. Particular attention was given to the impact of interpersonal contacts for the business-to-business communications mix.

As business firms have to communicate with a varied set of publics — from customers, to prospects, to shareholders, to employees and the general public — no one communication tool is considered appropriate. Instead, the challenge for the business marketer is to create a communications mix that enhances a company's image, builds recognition for its products and services, reaches unknown or inaccessible buying influences, and generates new sales prospects. Given the traditional and dominant role of personal selling, the business-to-business communications mix should seek to help direct the sales force to prospective customers and enhance the effectiveness of the salesperson's interactions with personnel in the buying firm in order to achieve sales and profit objectives. In short, each technique should supplement, support and complement the company's offer by utilising an integrative communications platform.

Finally, this paper concludes that there is a clear requirement for management to identify the impact of interpersonal contacts, especially for the communications-mix budget, to ensure that resources are being directed at appropriate markets and customers in order to establish and defend vital relationships.

REFERENCES

Ames, B.C. and Hlavacek, J.D. (1987): "Managing Marketing for Industrial Firms", in Rothschild, M.L. (ed.), *Marketing Communications*, Toronto: D C Heath and Co.: 678.

Bellizzi, J.A. and Hite, R.E. (1986): "Improving Industrial Advertising Copy", *Industrial Marketing Management*, May: 117.

Bellizzi, J.A. and Lehrer, J. (1983), "Developing Better Industrial Advertising", *Industrial Marketing Management*, February: 19.

Bello, D.C. and Barksdale, H.C., Jr. (1986): "Exporting at Industrial Trade Shows", *Industrial Marketing Management*, August: 197–8.

Bennett, P.D. (1988): *Dictionary of Marketing Terms*, Chicago; American Marketing Association.

Bovee, C.L. and Arens, W.F. (1982): *Contemporary Advertising*. Homewood, IL: Irwin: 688–9.

Cardozo, R.N. (1982): "Industrial Marketing Communications", *Harvard Business Review*, Note 9-583-086.

Coogan, James (1994): "Trade Exhibitions in the Marketing Communications Mix: The Irish Dimension", in *Student Marketing Digest: Current Research in Marketing*, Dublin Institute of Technology, College of Marketing and Design, 3: 13–34.

Crowley, M.G. (1991): "Prioritising the Sponsorship Audience", *European Journal of Marketing*, 25(11): 11–21.

Cunningham, M.T. and Homse, E. (1986): "Controlling the Marketing-Purchasing Interface: Resource Development and Organisational Implications", *Industrial Marketing and Purchasing*, 1(2): 3–27.

de Búrca, S. and McLoughlin, D. (1995): "The Major Constraints and Barriers in Developing a Strategic Role for Purchasing: A Survey of Corporate Purchasing in Ireland", IMP Conference, Manchester, September.

de Búrca, S. and Lambkin, M. (1993): "Sales Force Management in Ireland", *Irish Marketing Review*, 6: 53–63.

Ford, David, (ed.) (1990): *Understanding Business Markets: Interaction, Relationships and Networks*, London: Academic Press.

Ford, David (1980): "The Development of Buyer–Seller Relationships in Industrial Markets", *European Journal of Marketing*, 15(5/6): 339–54.

Häkansson, H. (ed.) (1982): *International Marketing and Purchasing of Industrial Goods: An Interaction Approach*, New York: Wiley: 10–27.

Häkansson, H., Johanson, J. and Wootz, B. (1976): "Influence Tactics in Buyer–Seller Processes", *Industrial Marketing Management*, December: 319–32.

Hanlon, A. (1977): *Trade Shows in the Marketing Mix: Where They Fit and How to Make Them Pay Off*, Shrewsbury, MA: Hawthorn Books.

Hutt, M.D. and Speh, T.W. (1995): *Business Marketing Management*, Forth Worth: Dryden Press: Paper 16.

Jenkins, V. (1984): *The Concept of Direct Marketing*, Garden City, NY: Hoke Communications, Inc.; Published by *Australia Post*: 12.

Kotler, P. (1994): *Marketing Management*, Englewood Cliffs, NJ: Prentice Hall: 15–29.

Levitt, T. (1967): "Communications and Industrial Marketing", *Journal of Marketing*, 31(5): 15–21.

Mahin, P.W. (1991): *Business-to-Business Marketing*, London: Allyn and Bacon.

Morrill, J.E. (1970): "Industrial Advertising Pays Off", *Harvard Business Review*, March/April: 4–14.

O'Toole, A. (1995): "Using the Media", Business-to-Business Conference, Dublin Chamber of Commerce and The Association of Advertisers in Ireland Ltd. June.

Palka, K. (1992): "Trade Secrets", *Business Traveller*, October: 34.

Reeder, R.R., Brierty, E.G. and Reeder, B.H. (1987): *Industrial Marketing*, London: Prentice Hall: Paper 15.

Robinson, Patrick J., Faris, Charles C. and Wind, Yoram (1967): *Industrial Buying and Creative Marketing*. Boston, MA: Allyn and Bacon: 12–18.

Schuman, P. (1986): "The Power of 'Perceptual Marketing', An Analysis of Sponsorship as Components of Marketing and Corporate Relations Programs", New York University, unpublished thesis.

Siebert, J.C. (1970): "Advertising and Selling Objectives for Industrial Markets", in Coram, T.C. and Hill, R.W. (eds.), *New Ideas in Industrial Marketing*, London: Staples Press: 209.

Trade Show Bureau (1991), "The Projected Growth of the Exposition Industry: A 10-Year Forecast," Research Report IT12.

Turnbull, P.W. (1979), "Roles of Personal Contacts in Industrial Export Marketing", *Scandinavian Journal of Management* 16: 325–37.

UCD Marketing Development Programme (1995): *Report on Exhibitors' Satisfaction with Irish Trade Shows and Exhibitions and Guidelines for Successful Exhibition Participation*, Graduate

School of Business, University College Dublin, Blackrock, Co. Dublin.

Webster, Frederick E. Jr., and Wind, Yoram (1972): *Organizational Buyer Behavior*, Englewood Cliffs, NJ: Prentice Hall.

Williams, J. (1983): "Industrial Publicity: One of the Best Promotional Tools", *Industrial Marketing Management*, July: 209.

Part 2

Advertising: The Players

5

The Advertising Agency — Function and Direction

Ian Fox
Iskandar Abdullah

If I were starting my life all over again I am inclined to think I would go into the advertising business in preference to any other (Franklin D. Roosevelt).

"Advertising consists of messages, paid for by those who send them, intended to inform or influence people who receive them" (Pollard, 1988: 1). Over the past century, and particularly since the expansion of television in the 1960s, the role of the advertising agency has become central to the successful creation of these messages. Even within the small Irish market, there is a lively and professional advertising industry.

There are over 50 companies calling themselves advertising agencies, though the number operating at a "proper" service level would be below this. The CSO Annual Survey (latest year 1992) received data from 41 companies employing 883 people, with a total turnover of £174 million. A 1994 estimate (Advertising Statistics of Ireland, 1995) suggests that the total media spend in the Republic of Ireland was £246 million, though this includes advertising not placed through agencies, and does not allow for the considerable discounts on rate cards available from the national press. The employment level of 883 is also misleading: many of the services once performed within the advertising agency are now purchased from outside, third-party companies. Photography, typography, print and television production, artwork and illustration would be the prime examples of this phenomenon. This means that the real figure for employment could be twice or even three times as high, if the main outsourced services were to be included. As with most industries, a small number of large agencies handle a disproportionate share of the business, though there is no one company near a monopolistic situation. The advertising agency business in Ireland is largely based in Dublin, though some agencies exist in smaller cities to satisfy the needs of local clients.

A listing of the top 20 Irish advertising agencies, ranked based on television buying with RTE, is shown in Table 5.1. This table not only indicates the volume of television advertising placed by the top 20 agencies, it also seeks to indicate which agencies were affiliated with multinational agency groups, either through being owned by, or having an association with, a multinational agency, and secondly, which agencies were full-service agencies and which were specialist providers.

In this paper we will try to capture some of the colour and vitality of advertising as it grew. We will also examine the organisation of an advertising agency, and trace how work is progressed through an agency. The final part will discuss the future directions of organisational structures for advertising agencies.

THE EVOLUTION OF ADVERTISING

In ancient times, all advertising was vocal. Dunn (1965) wrote that in ancient Greece, street criers selling cattle chanted advertising rhymes which must have sounded like today's jingles. According to Wood (1958), early New York was filled with cries such as:

> Clams! My clams I want to sell today,
> The best clams from Rockaway!

After the criers, came signs. Signs carved in clay, wood or stone were hung in front of shops, so that passers-by could see what products the merchant offered. Some signs were symbolic. In medieval England, a coat of arms designated an inn, a sign of three nuns embroidering meant a draper's shop, a gilt arm wielding a hammer signified a goldsmith, and three pigeons and a sceptre meant a thread-maker. In Rome, a boy being whipped was a sign for a school (Wood, 1958).

One advertising historian, Henry Sampson, mentioned that the first newspaper ad appeared in 1650 in London, offering a reward for the return of 12 stolen horses (Dunn, 1965). Later, ads appeared for coffee, chocolate, tea, real estate and medicine. Such advertising was targeted at a specific audience, who were customers of coffee-houses where the newspapers were read. In the US, the first newspaper ad appeared in the *Boston Newsletter* in 1704.

TABLE 5.1: TOP 20 AGENCIES' ADVERTISING SPEND ON TELEVISION IN IRELAND, JANUARY–DECEMBER 1994

Placing	Agencies	Type	Affiliations	Type
1	McConnell's	FS		
2	Zenith Media Ireland	MD	Saatchi & Saatchi/Bates	O
3	Initiative Media	MD	IPG Group	O
4	Peter Owens	FS		
5	DDFH&B	FS	J. Walter Thompson	A
6	McCann Erickson	FS	McCann-Erickson	O
7	Wilson Hartnell	FS	Ogilvy & Mather	O
8	AIM	MI		
9	Arks Ltd	FS	Lopex	O
10	QMP	FS	DMB&B	A
11	Des O'Meara	FS		
12	MGC	MI		
13	Irish International	FS		
14	Young International	FS	Lopex	O
15	CDP	FS		
16	The Media Bureau	MI		
17	Dimension	FS	McConnell's	O
18	BMPDDB Needham	FS		
19	The Media Centre	MI		
20	TMD London	MI		

Key: FS = Full-service agencies
      MD = Media Dependent
      MI = Media Independent
      O = Owned by
      A = Association

Source: RTE Sales and Marketing, 1995.

Advertising agencies sprang up in Ireland not long after their appearance in New York and London. Henry Crawford Hartnell set up his company — Wilson Hartnell — in 1879, and a number of other businesses soon followed, including O'Keefes, Parkers and Kennys; all but the last named are still trading. Advertisers in the nineteenth century included Arnotts of Henry Street, Rowntrees' recently launched Fruitgums and Jacobs' Cream Crackers. The most famous figure in early Irish advertising is fictional: Leopold Bloom, in Joyce's *Ulysses*. He is depicted as a space broker in 1904 — a time when an interest in the text and appearance of the advertisements was becoming as important as the sale of newspaper space. On Bloomsday, he is busily concocting an advertisement for the "House of Keyes" and runs foul of the editor of *The Freeman's Journal* in his efforts to obtain a free editorial "puff" for his client.

Origins of the Advertising Agency

The original advertising "agents" were agents for newspapers and magazines, and not for the advertisers. They were media brokers, involved in selling advertising space to anyone they could persuade to advertise, in return for commissions (MacCabe, 1984). Historian Ralph Hower (1949) in summarising the role of the agency in the 1800s, wrote:

> The advertising agency came into existence because of the ignorance of both publisher and advertiser, [which] together with their genuine economic need for assistance, presented an opportunity for profit. The agency facilitated the purchase and sale of space.... In a larger sense, however, the agency's chief service in this early period was to promote the general use of advertising, and thus to aid in discovering cheaper and more effective ways of marketing tools (Hower, 1949: 19).

The advertising agency no longer acts as a media broker for publishers, but is a principal in law itself. It has the task of creating the advertisements on behalf of the client companies, and placing them in the appropriate media so as to reach the maximum target audience at the lowest possible price.

TYPES OF ADVERTISING AGENCY

The model for an advertising agency is fairly consistent throughout the developed world. As with so many aspects of Irish business, the country's proximity to the huge UK market means that Irish agencies tend to be modelled on the London style, which is itself much influenced by organisation structures prevalent in New York. As many international client companies have been operating in the Irish market for a long time, the Irish agency has had to provide a standard of service of an acceptable international level, even though Ireland is a small market with tiny budgets by UK or US standards. A single, large London advertising agency would have a turnover greater than the entire Irish advertising industry. A critical difference in the Irish agency world is that there are far fewer specialist agencies than in larger economies — in London, for example, there are agencies specialising solely in industrial or financial accounts.

The classic full-service advertising agency has three main functional units, which will be dealt with below.

The Creative Department

This is where the advertising is created by writers (copywriters) and artists (art directors), often working in teams. In larger agencies, there may be many such teams, and an overall Creative Director will be responsible for general standards. In the large agencies in London or New York, with 1,000 or more employees, a complex infrastructure is needed to maintain standards and meet deadlines.

The Media Department

This is where the recommendations as to how to spend the advertising budget are devised, and, once the media plan is approved, media schedulers/buyers carry out the work of placing the advertisement and monitoring the effectiveness of the campaign. The expertise involves the use of extensive statistical research data and personal bargaining skills to optimise the benefits of the available budget. For its size, Ireland has a sophisticated range of media research data available.

The Client-Service Department

This provides the interface between client and agency. The account executive acts as the salesperson for the agency, and also as the client's representative within the agency. The most important task is to write the advertising brief. A well-targeted brief is essential in developing a good campaign, but the account executive also has to present the agency's ideas to the client, ensuring that the work remains faithful to the brief and is ready on time and within budget. Most agencies will assign a client-service team to an account comprising at least an Account Director and Account Executive but even within the small Irish market, the team can increase in number, depending on the complexity of the client account involved.

Depending on the size of the agency, each of these three main functional units will contain various skilled personnel at senior and assistant level. The function of the Finance Department is to manage the agency's finances, while the administration department is responsible for the provision of in-house services and despatch. An example of an organisation chart of a full-service Irish agency is shown in Figure 5.1.

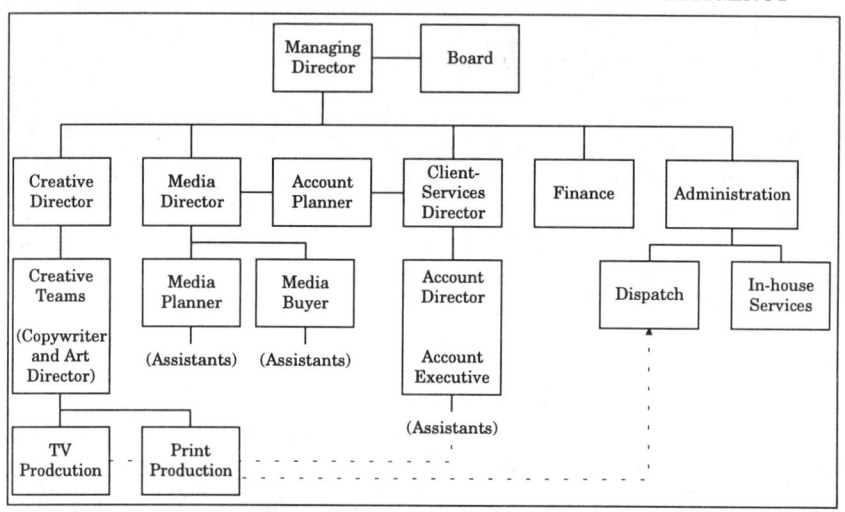

FIGURE 5.1: ORGANISATION CHART FOR FULL-SERVICE AGENCY

```
                          Managing Director ── Board
    ┌──────────┬──────────┬──────────┬──────────┬──────────┐
 Creative    Media      Account   Client-     Finance   Administration
 Director    Director   Planner   Services
                                  Director
    │           │         │          │                      │
 Creative    Media      Media     Account              Dispatch  In-house
 Teams       Planner    Buyer     Director                       Services
 (Copywriter
 and Art    (Assistants)(Assistants) │
 Director)                         Account
    │                              Executive
 TV        Print                      │
 Prodcution Production            (Assistants)
```

Other Kinds of Agency

It is possible for an agency to specialise in one, or in a limited number, of the principal services provided by advertising agencies. The most common form of this specialist agency which has emerged over the past decade is the Media Independent. These companies grew out of the needs of international advertisers who simply wanted to place advertising which had been generated for international campaigns in the Irish market, and who felt that they would get a more competitive price from a company specialising in media buying only. Following the global success of the media-buying specialist, large international communication groups which contain a number of agencies have set up their own media-buying operations, handling the function for their own group member and in some cases for other advertisers and agencies. These agencies, because of their links with established full-service agencies became known as Media Dependants, of which the Saatchi-associate Zenith Media is the largest and best known in Ireland. This agency undertakes media buying for its two associated Dublin agencies: Saatchi and Saatchi and the Bates agency.

There are arguments for and against the placement of advertising through a media buying specialist. Full-service agencies feel that they can provide the value for money and breadth of service, while the media specialists believe that with their lower overhead and buying power they have the edge in terms of offering superior client value. As indicated in Table 5.1 above, of the Top 20 television buying agencies in Ireland in 1994, 13 were full-service agencies, 2 were media dependants and 5 were media independents.

Another form of agency is the company acting as full-service in name, which in fact sub-contracts one or more key services to outside specialist providers. It is quite possible for a skilful individual or group of individuals to set up a small company, buying creative services from a third party, and using media specialists for media buying. Some of today's successful full-service agencies started out in much this manner. There is a small number of such agencies operating successfully in the Irish market at the moment.

Obviously, in the larger international market, agency types and affiliations all become far more complicated, with companies buying over other agencies or service units, until it is difficult to determine who owns exactly what agency name today. Whilst the international agencies have become increasingly important in Dublin — some through a complete ownership, others through a minority shareholding in an Irish agency — it is remarkable that out of the 13 full-service agencies in the television buying Top 20 for 1994, six are still wholly Irish-owned, two have a partial overseas shareholder, and only five are fully-owned by international agency groups, as can be seen by reference to Table 5.1. Of course, this does not include Saatchi and Bates, whose media buying goes through Zenith as a media dependant.

HOW AGENCIES CHARGE THEIR CLIENTS

The traditional way in which advertising agencies earn their money is through the "Commission System". This evolved from the origins of the advertising agent: in the nineteenth century, these agents would buy a whole page or a half-page of space from a newspaper for a particular day, and then divide it up and sell it to individual clients. Because agents were acting as space brokers, they got a special commission for undertaking this risk, and in most cases it was calculated as 15 per cent of the official rate-card value of the same space. Thus, on a £100 worth of space, the agent would get a commission of

£15, the media owner would earn £85, while the price to the advertiser was £100.

In essence, the agency to this day earns the majority of its income from the commissions it obtains from the media, which by and large remain at 15 per cent. For many years, there has been talk of the demise of the commission system — even conferences in the 1960s were predicting its immediate end. Its detractors argue that the size of the media budget may have little relationship to the work actually undertaken by the agency. Many believe that clients should be charged proper fees, just as is the case with architects, solicitors or accountants. Despite the logic of this argument, clients have been slow to change, mainly because of the difficulty in assessing what is a reasonable fee.

What has happened, however, is that clients have been bargaining with agencies to reduce their charges, and this has led to an erosion of the 15 per cent rate of commission. A large client may suggest that a full 15 per cent on an account requiring little work is too high a fee, and because of the intensely competitive nature of the business, agencies increasingly have been negotiating their charges and reducing the amount of commission that they keep, rebating the remainder to the client or adding it to the client's media budget.

The result has been a complex series of price wars. Many advertising commentators abhor this descent into bargaining, arguing that advertising is about creating the right advertisement to maximise the client's sales, not about price-cutting. Defenders of the system believe that such reductions inevitably lead to a deterioration in the service levels provided and the quality of staff employed, and can lead to a downward spiral into mediocrity in terms of creativity. The Institute of Advertising Practitioners in Ireland, which is the industry body for the main full-service agencies and would represent some 80 per cent of the total business, has been concerned that companies, in their enthusiasm for business, might price their contracts below a profitable level, and has conducted a number of surveys to establish industry norms for its members.

Traditionally, some 80 per cent of the client's advertising budget goes into the media-buying campaign, and 20 per cent into the cost of producing the advertisements. This is a generalisation, of course, and the ratio will vary greatly according to the size of the account and whether international material can be used, or whether original Irish advertisements have to be produced. In addition, the production of television commercials is far more costly than press, outdoor and radio advertisements, and this can also shape the media/production ratio. However, as well as income from media commission, the agency is in a position to add to its earnings through its mark-up on the production costs.

Production costs in advertising can be complex, with many parties involved. There are the clear, third-party matters like the production of a block or plate for printing, the production of posters, or the recording of a radio commercial. Here the agency can nominate a mark-up, usually around 20 per cent. As well as material produced outside the agency, many agencies will also charge for the time spent by the agency's creative team in creating an advertisement — this is usually agreed in advance and it is up to the agency to keep within that total budget or forfeit any extra time. Finally, the client may agree that there is an unusually large amount of work to be undertaken, and supplementary fees may be added to the original budget estimates — some clients, for example, prefer to commission market research through an agency, and specific fee arrangements would have to be agreed for this.

As a generalisation, it could be claimed that agencies, in addition to the commission on media which they retain, probably earn a further 20 per cent of 20 per cent — or 4 per cent of the total — in gross margin on production costs. Income from media commission and mark-ups on advertising production is the sales income which the agency receives to run its company. Net margins are considerably lower, and an advertising agency, with its high payroll cost, will often record a final net profit below that which many industries would find acceptable. For example, the Central Statistics Office 1992 figure puts total agency remuneration in 1992 at £174 million, but notes that payroll costs came to £17.4 million — exactly 10 per cent of total agency gross income (Central Statistics Office, 1994). When this cost is deducted from the 15 per cent commission and the production gross margin, net profit is quite small, particularly when price wars force reductions in commissions and other agency charges. While figures for the net profitability of Irish advertising agencies are not currently available, Briggs (1993) reports that the net profitability (before interest) of UK advertising agencies was 2.2 per cent in 1988, 1.9 per cent in 1989, and 1.55 per cent 1990.

THE AGENCY AT WORK

The three main departments within an agency have been briefly described earlier. However, in order to understand the operations of an advertising agency, the basic steps in progressing a campaign through an agency will be traced. This is illustrated in an activity-flow diagram in Figure 5.2.

The Brief

The first task is to agree a brief with the client. There are various briefing systems in use, but in essence all are attempts to answer the classic *"who, why, where, when, how much?"* questions. Preparing the brief is a primary function of the Client-service personnel, with the Account Director spending time on bringing this to fruition. If consumer information is required, this will be commissioned from a market-research company directly by the client or through the agency. Once the brief has been completed, the work of creating the advertisements gets underway.

In the large, international agencies, there may be so many people involved on an account that there is a need to appoint one individual who concentrates on the research data and the brief — for this the role of Account Planner was created. This is a hybrid job and is the only really new agency position to be created in the world of advertising since television production started. The account planner must possess media skills, marketing skills and a lot of clear strategic thinking. Irish agencies in general tend to be too small in scale to afford such a specialist, and the task is often undertaken by the Account Director in liaison with the Media Director.

Traffic

Once the brief is agreed, the work commences. The Traffic Manager (often doubling as the Production Manager), who is responsible for overseeing the campaign through the agency, will open a "Job Bag" or similar cost centre, so that all costs can be allocated to the job. Timetables will then be agreed with the various departments for the project and the Traffic Manager will administer them throughout the whole campaign. The Traffic Manager must work closely with the Creative Director to agree allocation of time among the creative staff, in order to ensure that the work is ready on schedule. Planning may seem tedious, but it is the surest way of reducing problems and cost over-runs later.

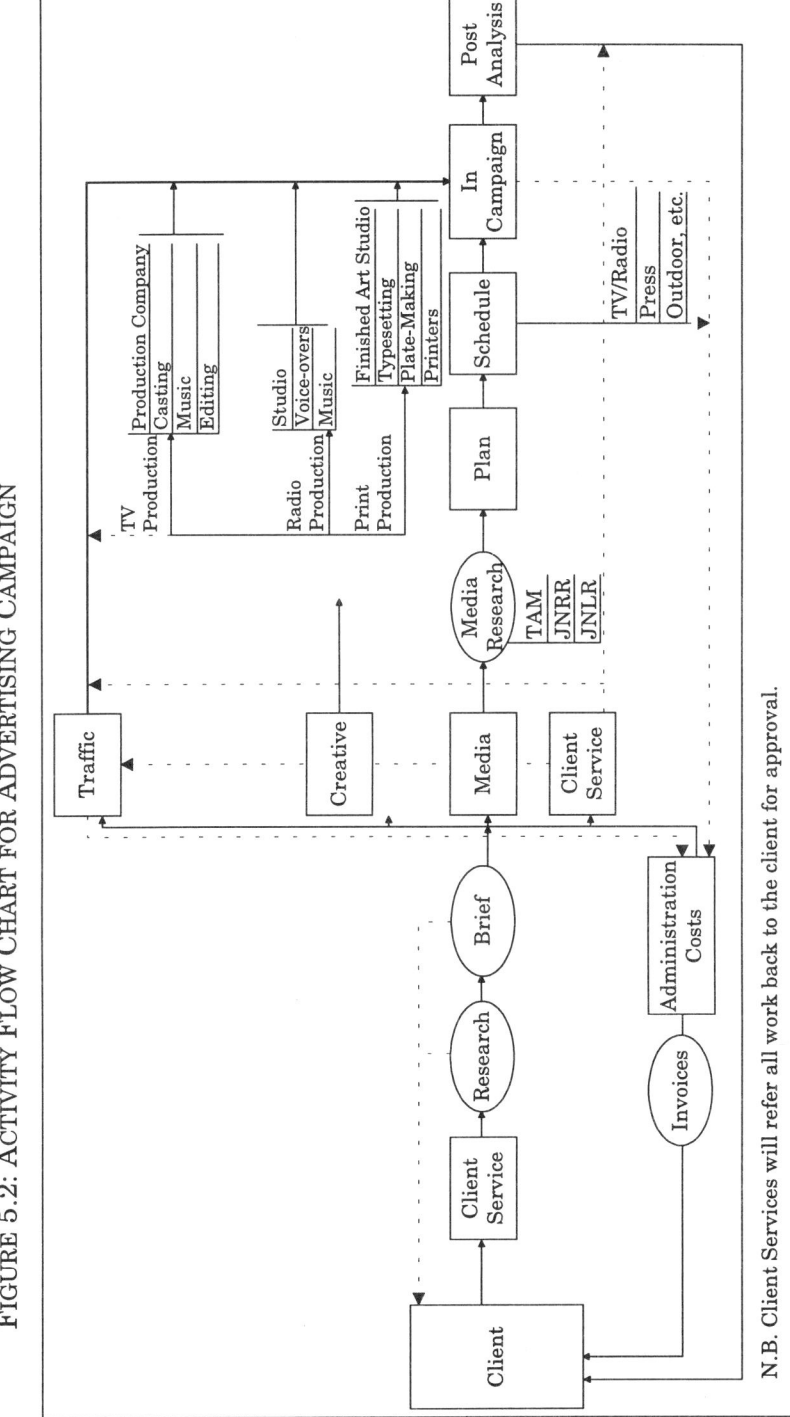

FIGURE 5.2: ACTIVITY FLOW CHART FOR ADVERTISING CAMPAIGN

N.B. Client Services will refer all work back to the client for approval.

Creating the Idea

Now a creative team begins work, based on the brief as given. It usually involves two people — a copywriter and an art director. Writers tend to operate on their own, but art directors often have assistants to help with sketches and "storyboards" (a strip-cartoon describing a television commercial). In a large agency, a number of teams may work on a project simultaneously to produce a range of possible answers, though this is an expensive process. Eventually, some concepts are prepared for the client's reactions; such concepts may be tested among consumers by a research company before the final concept is agreed.

Production

When an idea is approved, the work moves on to its production stage. There are three main streams here: television, radio and print.

Television Production

In the main, an agency will employ a third-party television production company to organise and undertake the production of a commercial; some larger agencies have their own subsidiaries which will undertake this work as well as radio production. It is usual that the agency will obtain competitive quotes, as the sums involved can run into six figures quite easily. In the small Irish market, the client-service team usually looks after the organisational side of the production, and the creative team supervises the actual casting, shooting, editing and agreeing of the final version of the commercial. The client will generally seek a close involvement at all stages of this production process. Again, the main criterion is careful planning in advance to minimise last-minute changes and extra costs.

Radio Production

While obviously less expensive than television, the careful production of a radio commercial is also particularly rewarding. Usually the copywriter acts as the radio producer, hiring a sound recording studio and supervising the actors. In some instances, the full creative team will participate and the client-service people will ensure that the client is happy with the choice of voices and other production inputs.

Print Production

The traditional Production Department handles the print matters in the agency. Some production departments also become involved in television or radio production, but usually only in their function of traffic control and chasing the progress of the work against the usually tight deadlines. The main work of the production department is ensuring that all print advertisements appear to the highest possible standard, and that the printers maintain the best reproduction levels during the run. As many clients place the production of point-of-sale and other print items through their agencies, the print buyer can have a busy schedule in costing work, obtaining quotes and supervising the actual printing. The department usually looks after dispatch and many of the small but important ancillary activities of the agency.

Finance

In a business with such a complexity of charges, a good accounting system is essential. Larger agencies will utilise the services of a computer manager as the use of electronic systems increases. The principles of administration are the same as in any other company producing goods or services. The main problem is ensuring that the people involved keep a good record of their time spent on a particular job and of the many items and services sourced from third-party suppliers.

ISSUES FOR THE FUTURE

The Multinational Advertising Agency

Inevitably, as a small economy, Ireland is unlikely to set the trends for the future of the advertising world at large. However, advertising agencies in Ireland have been quick and effective in keeping pace with international trends. To an extent, this is forced on them, as any moderately-sized Irish agency will have one or more international clients who will tend to impose their creative and production standards on the Irish agency. The proximity of London, as already noted, helps to maintain high advertising standards, even within the very limited budgets available.

The increasing internationalisation of the business is the biggest global change that advertising has been experiencing, and will continue to face in the next decade. Many international clients demand that their service companies, such as accountants, lawyers and advertising agencies, have matching facilities in each country in which they operate. This has led to increased international agency involvement even in a small country like Ireland. It can be seen from Table 5.2 that a major international agency grouping such as WPP, through its subsidiary agencies J. Walter Thompson and Ogilvy and Mather, has offices in 65 and 61 countries respectively. While these two agencies are represented in the Irish market through DDFH&B and Wilson Hartnell (see Table 5.2), there are many international agency "names" which are still not represented in the Irish market, though it can be expected that the trend towards internationalisation of the advertising-agency business will continue, with inevitable consequences for independent Irish agencies.

TABLE 5.2: MULTINATIONAL AGENCIES WITH OFFICES IN MORE THAN 40 COUNTRIES

Group	Agency	No. of Countries	No. of Clients in more than 10 Countries
WPP	Ogilvy & Mather	61	27
	J. Walter Thompson	65	23
Omnicom	BBDO	63	25
	DDB Needham	74	16
Interpublic	Lintas	49	14
	Lowe Group	54	6
	McCann-Erickson	90	34
Cordiant	Saatchi & Saatchi	69	22
		57	19
Others	Bozell	56	18
	DMB&B	57	8
	Leo Burnett	50	13
	Euro RSCG	47	13
	FCB Publicus	51	14
	Gray	67	36
	Young & Rubicam	61	19

Source: WPP Group plc (1994): *Annual Report and Accounts*, London: 49.

Following discussions with leading multinational agencies, the consultant Rein Rijkens (1992) has made the following observations about the future of advertising:

- The increased use of international creativity will reduce the need for creative work at a local level.
- The standard 15 per cent commission is already diminishing and may become the exception rather than the rule.
- Agencies' profits from international accounts will therefore drop and they will seek more profitable work involving original creativity from local accounts.
- This will encourage the seeking out of niche markets not occupied by the international brands.
- Media decisions will tend to be left to the local agencies but they will have to be sensitive to the growing use of external satellite channels outside their control.

Media

On the media side, further fragmentation can be expected. Ireland is a tiny market, no larger than many European cities. While extra television channels may deliver greater audience choice, from an advertising point of view this will only serve to divide up a small population still further, making it increasingly expensive to reach audiences. Whatever else happens, the real cost of reaching a target audience is likely to rise far faster than normal price inflation.

Legal

In the area of regulation, there will be an increasing range of controls exercised by Brussels. While these may be introduced for altruistic or political reasons, they are likely to place restrictions on aspects of advertising. As the Director of the World Federation of Advertisers, Paul de Win, put it in 1991:

> Everywhere today, Governments are seeking to improve the well-being of their people by encouraging individual development. But these Governments are also passing regulations, restrictions and even bans that are detrimental to the development of local, national and international industries and commerce. They forget that this industrial development is fundamental to the improved well-being of both the individual and the nation.

With new pressures coming from the enlarged European market, particularly the often regulation-oriented views of the Scandinavian bloc, advertising will remain a difficult, volatile and endlessly fascinating business. Whether Jerry della Femina's famous 1970 adage "the most fun you can have while keeping your clothes on" will continue to be true remains to be seen.

REFERENCES

Briggs, M. (1993): "Why Agencies Must Change", *Admap*, 28(1): 20–22.

Central Statistics Office (CSO) (1995): *Business of Advertising Agencies 1992*, Dublin: CSO; see also IAPI, 1994 Annual Report.

de Win, P. (1990/91): "Winning Formula", *Media & Marketing Europe*, December/January.

Dunn, W. (1965): *Advertising, Its Role in Modern Marketing*, New York: Holt, Rinehart and Winston.

Hower, R.M. (1949): *The History of an Advertising Agency*, Cambridge, MA.: Harvard University Press.

MacCabe, B.F. (1984): "The Advertising Agency", in Hart, N.A. and Connor, J.O. (eds.), *The Practice of Advertising*, London: Heinemann: 36–56.

Pollard, M. (1988): *Advertising*, London: Penguin.

Rijkens, R. (1992): *European Advertising Strategies*, London: Cassell.

Wood, J.P. (1958): *The Story of Advertising*, New York: The Ronald Press Company.

6

Media Strategy — Selecting and Scheduling Media in Ireland*

Peter McPartlin

INTRODUCTION

It is, perhaps, not unfair to say that in the recent past many marketing people considered the media element of the advertising process to be a bore — jargon-led, unaccountable and littered with Xs on grids. But an underlying shift is taking place in Irish marketers' advertising priorities. Many more are paying greater attention to the planning and buying of their media campaigns and, as a result, are placing their media advisors under greater scrutiny. Increased interest in what was once only of major concern to big spenders, such as Guinness, Unilever and Mars, has grown amongst almost every medium-sized to large-scale advertiser in the country.

This has resulted from a number of key developments. Firstly, the continued pressure on marketing and advertising budgets and an increasing recognition by companies that expenditure on media is often the biggest single financial investment they make — eclipsing even expenditure on the lifeblood of many businesses, research and development. Secondly, media-rate inflation has become more pronounced in recent times, particularly in the television sector. Advertisers have thus found it extremely difficult to maintain traditional exposure levels and/or "share of voice" versus competitors. It is estimated that the average rate of media-cost inflation in Ireland since 1990 has outstripped that of general consumer prices by a factor of almost three to one. In the television arena, for example, an

---

* Note: This paper includes terminology used in the planning, buying and analysis of media. A glossary of the most frequently-used terms is included at the end of this paper, while further explanations may be found in Chapter 9 of this book: "Media Research in Ireland".

advertiser spending £130,000 supporting its brand in 1990 would have had to spend close to £200,000 in 1994, just to maintain the same exposure levels — a period when the consumer price index rose by 11 per cent.

The final factor relates to a measurable decline in audience levels across almost all of the major Irish media. In the print sector, newspaper sales and readership remain under severe strain from the combined effects of UK competition, rising covering prices and the ubiquity of news on the audiovisual media.

Audience levels on television have also been under pressure as the viewing public becomes less passive and tolerant of the traditional programming fare. With the aid of remote-control handsets and VCRs, viewers are taking active editorial decisions, which very often impact on the commercials shown. This is borne out by an increasing number of media studies which suggest that the television set is playing a less intrusive part in people's lives, and that possibly up to 40 per cent of those counted as "watching TV" are not!

The media market is a complex one (See Figure 6.1 below). The breadth and depth of Irish media have expanded considerably in the past decade, as has the number of ways in which individual media can be bought and sold. In television, for example, in addition to the basic prime-time and afternoon segments there is now breakfast time, morning time and night time, which have developed in line with the extension of broadcasting hours. Prices vary for the same television spot or press space, and audiences' viewing, reading and listening habits fluctuate from one day to the next. And because such large sums of money are involved in the media planning and buying process, even minor errors of judgment can result in considerable wastage of valuable advertising budgets.

The aim of this paper is to explore the increasing complexity of Irish media from an advertising viewpoint, to outline the contribution of media planning to the development of advertising solutions and to identify the role and tasks of the media planner and buyer within the advertising process.

THE IRISH MEDIA MARKET — DYNAMIC, COMPLEX AND COSTLY

The Republic of Ireland, like every other country in Europe, has its own unique marketing and media conditions which shape the manner in which Irish advertising campaigns are planned and executed. For a country of its size and relatively small population density, Ireland

Media Strategy — Selecting and Scheduling Media in Ireland   117

FIGURE 6.1: THE MEDIA MAZE

Broadcast

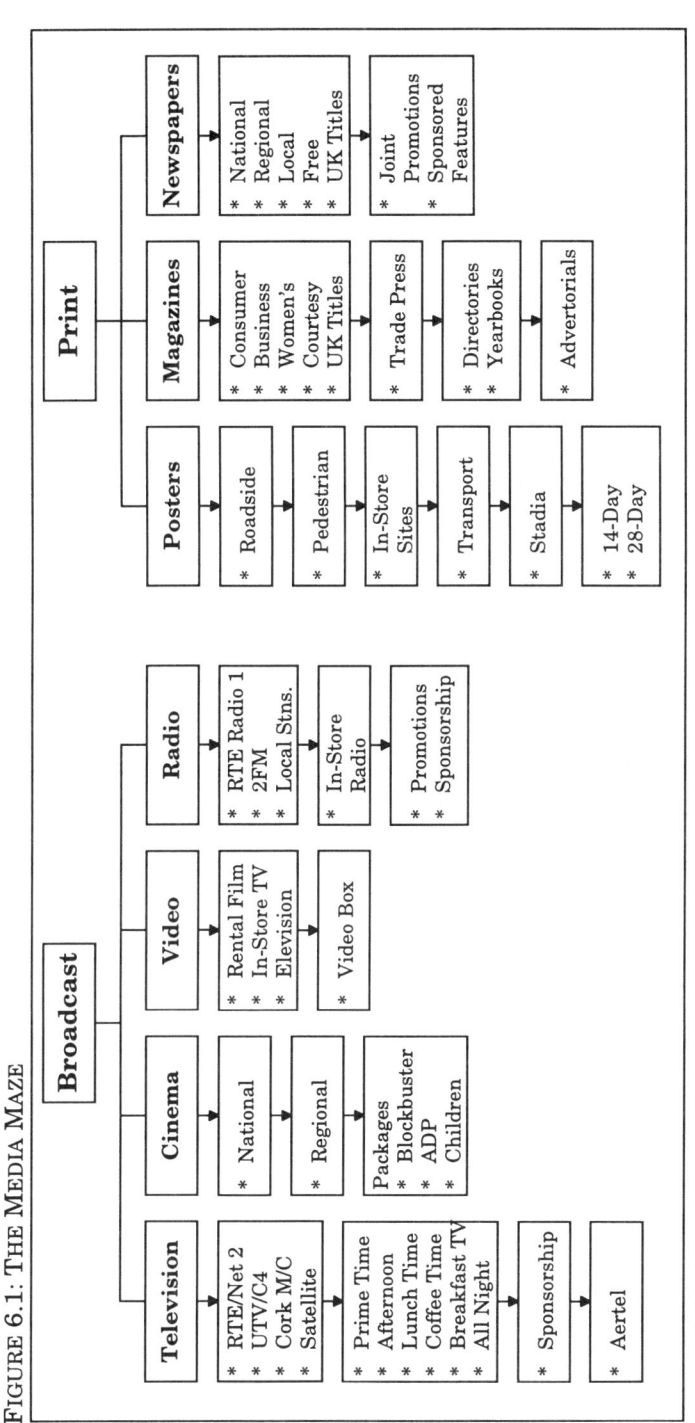

- **Television**
  - RTE/Net 2
  - UTV/C4
  - Cork M/C
  - Satellite
  - Prime Time
  - Afternoon
  - Lunch Time
  - Coffee Time
  - Breakfast TV
  - All Night
  - Sponsorship
  - Aertel

- **Cinema**
  - National
  - Regional
  - Packages
    - Blockbuster
    - ADP
    - Children

- **Video**
  - Rental Film
  - In-Store TV
  - Elevision
  - Video Box

- **Radio**
  - RTE Radio 1
  - 2FM
  - Local Stns.
  - In-Store Radio
  - Promotions
  - Sponsorship

Print

- **Posters**
  - Roadside
  - Pedestrian
  - In-Store Sites
  - Transport
  - Stadia
  - 14-Day
  - 28-Day

- **Magazines**
  - Consumer
  - Business
  - Women's
  - Courtesy
  - UK Titles
  - Trade Press
  - Directories
  - Yearbooks
  - Advertorials

- **Newspapers**
  - National
  - Regional
  - Local
  - Free
  - UK Titles
  - Joint Promotions
  - Sponsored Features

Source: Irish International Advertising.

arguably ranks alongside Italy as the most complex media market in Europe. Recent years have seen some major developments which have heightened this complexity for advertisers.

TELEVISION

Perhaps the greatest degree of complexity exists in the television sector. In the early 1970s, the vast majority of homes in the Republic could receive only one national television station — RTE 1. Today, as well as the two RTE channels, over seven in ten television homes can now receive the four main UK stations (BBC 1 and 2, ITV and Channel 4) (Irish TAM, 1994a). In addition, a range of satellite channels (Sky One, Sky News, Super, Children's Channel, Eurosport and MTV) are available through cable in around one-third of homes, most of which are on the heavily-populated eastern and southern coasts (Irish TAM, 1994b). All of these combine to bring over 220 hours of daily programming to television viewers in urban areas like Dublin and Cork, not including the additional fare from the two subscription-based Sky movie and sports channels, which have been vigorously promoted by local cable operators and satellite-dish retailers.

Viewing is measured by the Television Audience Measurement (TAM) system in the Republic, which is funded by RTE, the advertising agencies and media independents. It provides detailed programme and commercial break data for the two RTE channels and limited information on viewing of the imported television services. The Irish are amongst the most avid television viewers in Europe, devoting an average of 3.2 hours per day to the range of channels on offer (Irish TAM, 1994b). Historically, RTE's two channels have accounted for the largest share of viewing in the multichannel homes, regarded by many advertisers as the most important for marketing success. Several factors, however, have combined to place this position under threat in recent times.

As well as the increased popularity of programming on the imported channels, RTE's ability to fund competitive and attractive home productions and to compete for alternative imported programmes is arguably being eroded by the subsidy that it is obliged to make to the new Irish language television service (to be launched in 1996). Also in doubt is its future share of the broadcasting licence fee which the 1995 Green Paper on Broadcasting has intimated may be shared with other public-service broadcasting providers. A weakened RTE is of major concern to indigenous advertisers and their agents, as it is likely to raise the entry costs to mass-market television to unacceptably high levels. Also worrying is the continued growth of video-recorder ownership (59 per cent of homes) and remote-control handsets for channel changing (73 per cent of homes) (Irish TAM, 1994a), with many studies indicating their negative effect on the impact of television commercials.

With the launch of the independent commercial television channel, TV3, still in doubt, many advertisers, particularly those marketing products and services on a 32-county basis, continue to rely on a mix of RTE and in-spill commercial services like Ulster Television (UTV) and Channel 4 to reach large audiences in the Republic.

RADIO

Commercial radio in one form or another has existed in the Republic since the 1920s. This longevity and the extent of daily listenership by the population to national stations like RTE Radio 1 and 2FM, has meant that commercial radio enjoys a position of primacy amongst the range of options available to advertisers in Ireland. The launch of the country's network of 21 local independent stations in 1990 has further spurred the growth in advertising spending with commercial radio, while eroding RTE's audience share in the process.

With over a one-third share of adult prime-time listenership, according to the Joint National Listenership Research (JNLR, 1994), the local independents have stimulated the advertising market through a variety of options, including programme sponsorship and on-air promotions, as well as traditional spot package advertising. The demise of the national independent radio operator, Century, in 1991, has not dulled advertisers' enthusiasm for the medium, nor the ambitions of the many business consortia which await the Independent Radio and Television Commission's (IRTC's) decision to re-award the national franchise.

Pirate radio stations have begun to re-emerge to fill the audience gap left by the legitimate mainstream operators. These, along with the long-wave pop station, Atlantic 252, have succeeded in building an impressive audience base amongst urban teenagers and young adults. (According to TGI (Target Group Index) in 1994, Atlantic 252 has an average "listened yesterday" reach of 37 per cent amongst 15–24-year-olds.)

PRESS

If the major broadcast media have prospered in Ireland over the past decade, it has largely been at the expense of newspapers. On the one hand, national newspaper sales and readership levels have been generally pressurised by rising cover prices, cheaper UK imports and an increasing loss of the "newspaper habit" by sections of the population. At the same time, sluggish investment in new print technology and more expensive audience-delivery rates, combined with a greater belief in television's effectiveness by many FMCG advertisers, have stunted the medium's ad-revenue growth. The much-publicised problems of Irish Press Newspapers are perhaps an extreme example of the difficult climate that all newspapers have faced in varying degrees.

In spite of these mitigating circumstances, the press sector remains remarkably resilient, with particular titles performing against the odds. In overall sales and readership terms, *The Sunday Independent* (circulation: 278,212) (ABC, 1995) has enjoyed a decade of continued growth thanks to an editorial mix of high-profile and highly-opinionated columnists. At the other end of the Sunday market, *The Sunday Business Post* (32,436) (ABC, 1995) has successfully established a niche for fresh and provocative business coverage. *The Irish Times* (95,310) (ABC, 1995) continues to dominate daily newspaper readership amongst the AB social class, while *The Star* (76,392) (ABC, 1995), the joint publishing venture between Independent Newspapers and the UK Express Newspaper Group, has successfully carved out a strong populist following against UK imports like *The Daily Mirror* and *The Sun*.

Recent improvements in the economic climate have resulted in a healthy rise in newspapers' traditional ad revenue mainstays, such as property, recruitment and classifieds. Elsewhere in the press sector, the market also supports some 40 plus regional weekly newspapers and a variable number of city-based free titles. Most rely on direct advertising support from local businesses and regional "upweights" of national press campaigns. Consumer magazines, with few exceptions, have generally found it difficult to grow their sales base beyond 25,000 in the Irish market. Relatively high cover prices and competition from attractive UK alternatives have been natural obstacles for many Irish publishers. However, the resurgence of the two mass-market weeklies, the *RTE Guide* (180,899) (ABC, 1994) and *Woman's Way* (66,000) (ABC, 1994), has consolidated advertiser confidence in the medium, particularly in the food, cosmetics and beverages areas.

Newspaper and magazine audiences are measured by the industry-funded Joint National Readership Research (JNRR) which reports on the average issue readership of a selection of the indigenous titles only, across a range of demographics and special interest groups.

OUTDOOR

The Irish outdoor sector is largely dominated by two European poster giants, the French-owned David Allen Holdings and More O'Ferrall. However, the public-transport poster company, CAN, and smaller companies like Metro and Salepoint occupy key positions in a medium where, for many advertisers, location is everything. The medium has shown itself to be very resilient and responsive to the many attacks on its revenue base over the years. In the early 1980s, government legislation banned tobacco from poster advertising and, in turn, freed up hundreds of key sites that the cigarette companies had held on a long-term basis. New advertisers, penalised by the high entry levels to television and the erosion of audiences in multichannel homes, took to the medium with vigour.

The advent of more affordable colour facilities in the national press and the launch of local radio caused a fall in demand in the late 1980s/early 1990s. Since then, however, the poster contractors have responded with the introduction of superlites (illuminated bus-shelter sites), point-of-sale units, large 96-sheet panels and ad frames on the country's bus fleet. These, together with site classification and audience-measurement data (through the JNPR), and 28-day or 14-day campaign options, have placed the medium on a sounder footing for growth.

CINEMA

Despite an increase in the array of television channels available to the average Irish household and the sharp rise in VCR penetration, cinema attendances have been amongst the most buoyant in Western Europe. Ireland has one of the highest per capita admission levels in the EU at 2.9 (Screen International, 1994) visits per annum. The introduction of the multiplex to Ireland by UCI in 1989 and increased investment in the quality of screens and cinemas by other cinema owners have been partially responsible for attracting new and lapsed customers to the medium. These have largely coincided with the re-emergence of the highly popular Hollywood blockbuster like *Batman* and *Jurassic Park*, as well as features with a distinctly Irish flavour, like *The Commitments* and *In the Name of the Father*.

Although its audience levels are relatively small compared to television, cinema is particularly favoured by advertisers because of its attractive, young age profile and its trend-setting reputation. For that reason, the medium attracts a large proportion of its advertising revenue from large brand companies in the beer, soft drinks and clothing categories.

ADVERTISING REVENUE SHARES

Irish media expenditure has grown modestly since 1990 as can be seen by reference to Figure 6.2. The market has never really experienced the highs or the lows that have been evident in the UK advertising sector in the same period. Media spending here is naturally linked to economic confidence, but also, in recent times, the country's involvement in major sporting events like the soccer World Cup tournaments of 1990 and 1994. (In the first half of 1994, for example, total display advertising expenditure rose by 10 per cent on 1993 (ASI, 1994)).

FIGURE 6.2 MEDIA EXPENDITURE IN THE REPUBLIC OF IRELAND

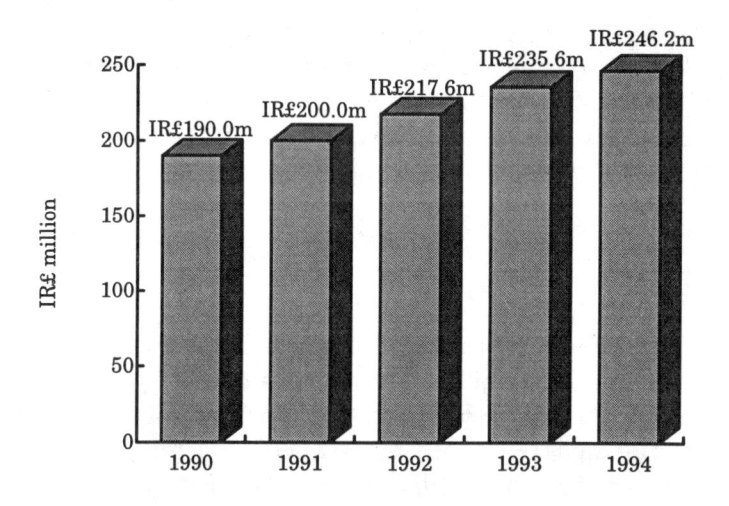

Year	IR£ million
1990	IR£190.0m
1991	IR£200.0m
1992	IR£217.6m
1993	IR£235.6m
1994	IR£246.2m

Based on rate card estimates of expenditure.
Source: Advertising Statistics Ireland Ltd.

The majority share of advertising spend is still taken by the national press (Figure 6.3), followed by RTE television. However, television has enjoyed a greater level of growth in the past five years. Relative to other European markets, radio accounts for a disproportionately higher share of media expenditure in Ireland. In contrast, consumer magazines, with a 6 per cent share, are below the European average because of the relatively few large circulation titles in the market. Cinema, with only a 1 per cent share of spend, has experienced the sharpest growth in real terms, albeit from a small base.

FIGURE 6.3: MEDIA EXPENDITURE SHARES 1994 — REPUBLIC OF IRELAND

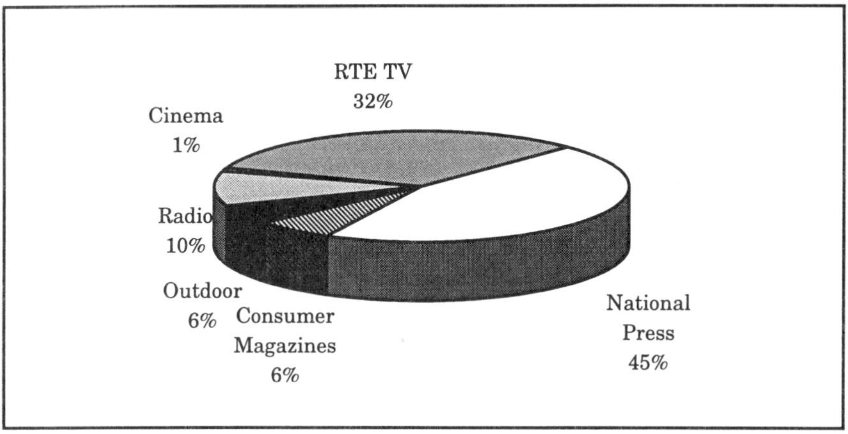

- RTE TV 32%
- Cinema 1%
- Radio 10%
- Outdoor 6%
- Consumer Magazines 6%
- National Press 45%

Source: Based on rate card estimates of expenditure. Total IR£246.2 m. Advertising Statistics Ireland Ltd.

THE MEDIA PROCESS

In the simplest interpretation of the media function, an advertiser attempts to reach as many of a defined target audience as possible (coverage or reach), as often as possible (frequency) and at the lowest possible cost (efficiency). As Sissors and Surmanek (1982: 1–3) note:

> Media planning consists of a series of decisions made to answer the question for advertisers: What are the best means of delivering advertisements to prospective purchasers of my brand or service?

The role of media planning has changed in advertising agencies. Today, media planning ranks in importance with marketing and creative planning, but in the early days of advertising agency operations media planning consisted of simple, clerical-type tasks. There were fewer media available in those days, and little research on media audiences had been done to guide planners in decision making. Planning today is an executive function because it has become so much more complex and important than it was years ago. Today's planners must have a greater knowledge base from which to draw to formulate media plans. The planners must not only know more about media, which have increased tremendously in number, but also know more about marketing, research and advertising than did their predecessors. Most important, planners are called upon not only to make decisions, but to defend them as the best ones that could be made from among many alternatives.

The various stages through which a media plan evolves vary from agency to agency, and within agencies, from account to account. These variations will largely depend on the nature and complexity of the brief to be addressed and the level of involvement of the media team with the development of the overall advertising and creative solution.

STRATEGIC MEDIA PLANNING

Media choices and decisions should ideally reflect the advertiser's marketing strategy and tactics as well as the advertising objectives and creative approach. Usually, therefore, the best solutions are found if the media planning and buying are an integral part of the overall process. An understanding of how advertising works is also a fundamental part of good media planning. At the outset, an accurate and comprehensive advertising brief is vital to the success of every other stage of the media process (see Abdullah and Donnelly, Chapter 7 of this book). Typically this should include information on:

- The brand, its consumer proposition and the market in which it competes
- The role of advertising within its marketing mix
- Target market data, including distribution and consumption patterns and, ideally, consumers' attitudes towards the brand
- Seasonal factors that might influence timing
- Promotional plans, if any
- The available budget.

From an analysis and discussion of the brief, advertising objectives are usually defined. They can involve any of the following:

- Increasing sales
- Launching a new product
- Shifting attitudes or changing behaviour
- Building awareness
- Boosting share of voice/visibility
- Forcing distribution
- Encouraging direct response

The size of the available budget, to a significant extent, serves to limit the opportunities open to the media planner. The other limiting factor is usually a creative one. Decisions about which basic medium or group of media to use are usually joint decisions between the creative and media teams, but obviously with a strong influence from the client service and planning personnel, as well as the advertiser. The media-selection process is usually, therefore, a trade-off between what the creative team, client and client service executive believe is instinctively right for the brand and its message, and what the media team knows is appropriate in targeting terms and is affordable in practice.

The size and nature of the target audience is a primary consideration in the selection process. Ideally it needs to be defined in terms of lifestyle, life-stage and relevant behavioural characteristics (or psychographics) as well as by basic demographics. The media target audience is often different from that defined by the advertising strategy. This is because most media deliver quite a broad mix of people who do not often correspond directly to the prospective or lapsed users of the advertised brand. Comprehensive multimedia research such as Target Group Index (TGI) is, therefore, helpful in identifying key sub-groups within the total audience of a particular medium.

Unless the planner actually knows the media consumption habits of the strategic target audience, the media target tends to be defined as a broader group, the media habits of which the planner does know — for example, beer drinkers rather than Budweiser drinkers.

Ring (1993: 110) identified an essential judgment skill of media planners/buyers as the ability to use their understanding, experience and expertise to minimise wastage — that is, people seeing advertising that is not primarily targeted at them.

As Ring notes, this involves three stages:

1) Deriving a media target from the strategic advertising target
2) Seeing what media these people consume, using quantified media research
3) Making more subjective judgments about whether these media/titles/programmes suit the brand, its marketing and advertising objectives, and the particular ads.

As well as the target audience and the size of the available budget, the following are some of the other main factors that influence the inter-media decision:

- *Creative Preference* — Has creative work been developed with a particular medium in mind? Is there a requirement for colour, sound, movement and detailed information? (For instance, it is doubtful that the Guinness Stout "Anticipation" commercial, featuring actor Joe McKinney and the Guaglione soundtrack, would have been as successful without the initial benefit of television exposure.) Are there new media opportunities appropriate to the target audience? It is the media person's responsibility both to discourage the "creatives" from producing extravagant and spectacular solutions when the budget is minimal, and to keep them aware of new media ideas or new ways of using established media.

- *Client Preference* — Very often, the advertiser will have preconceived ideas of what media are right for the campaign (for example, electrical-appliance chain stores such as Power City and D.I.D. devote the largest proportion of their media expenditure to newspapers, while Kellogg concentrates primarily on television, presumably influenced by the effectiveness of previous campaigns in those media). If the media planner knows these to be demonstrably wrong, either for budgeting or targeting reasons, then the onus is on the planner to argue the case rationally for an alternative selection.

- *Type of Product* — The way in which different media are consumed and the atmosphere or environment they create for the message can dramatically affect responses to advertising. It is important, therefore, to try and match the characteristics of the medium (and not just its audience levels) to those of the advertised product (for example, BMW spend most of their limited Irish advertising budget only in *The Irish Times*).

- *Competitive Activity* — The agency team, guided by the media planner, must decide whether it is best to pursue an offensive or defensive competitive strategy. This involves examining the media selection and weights of expenditure of competitors and deciding whether their media approach should be followed, or whether they should be avoided by advertising in media where visibility or "share of voice" can be heightened (for example, Rehab Lotteries have tended to concentrate media support for their "instant win" games on selected local radio stations because of the national dominance and greater spending power of the National Lottery).

- *Timing* — Predetermined launch dates or long creative development time often militate against the use of particular media. For example, lead times or copy dates for full colour in national press or limited availability of posters sites during the summer period may result in alternative media having to be selected.

- *Retail Influence* — The support of the retail trade, particularly the grocery multiples, is usually essential to the success of a new brand. Very often, the promise of television support for a new product launch can be a potent influence and a signal to the retailer of advertiser confidence. For example, when Mona Yogurt was launched in 1984, a heavy television and outdoor campaign was conducted to drive distribution with a sceptical retail trade.

Tables 6.1 and 6.2 provide a basic quantitative and qualitative ranking of the various strengths of the major media groups: television, radio, national press and outdoor.

TABLE 6.1: QUANTITATIVE RANKING OF THE MAJOR MEDIA

	TV	Radio	National Press	Outdoor
Coverage	1	2	3	4
Frequency/Repetition	3	2	4	1
Cost Efficiency	2	1	4	3
Audience/Wastage	2	2	2	3
Low Entry/Production Costs	4	1	2	3

Source: Irish International Advertising.

TABLE 6.2: QUALITATIVE RANKING OF THE MAJOR MEDIA

	TV	Radio	National Press	Outdoor
Intrusiveness	Very Good	Good	Fair	Fair
Emotive Power	Very Good	Good	Good	Fair
Branding Ability	Very Good	Fair	Good	Good
Image Builder	Very Good	Fair	Good	Good
Providing Detailed Information	Fair	Fair	Very Good	Poor
Consumer Reaction	Good	Good	Good	Fair

Source: Irish International Advertising.

In a study of media practice within Dublin advertising agencies, Kennedy (1992) established a ranking of the factors influencing the inter-media selection process in order of decreasing influence (Table 6.3). The overall ranking differed between the various sized agencies, with the larger agencies more cost- and budget-oriented than middle-sized and smaller agencies, which placed greater emphasis on qualitative factors such as creative input, editorial climate and product fit.

TABLE 6.3: FACTORS INFLUENCING INTER-MEDIA SELECTION

Factor	Relative Score
Reach	2.00
Budget Size	2.21
Creative Scope	3.35
Cost-Efficiency	3.42
Cumulative Frequency	4.28
Product Fit	4.71
Competitor's Media Use	5.28
Editorial Climate	6.21
Marketing Flexibility	6.28
Trade Reaction	6.92
Sales History	7.28
Technical Capabilities	7.64

Based on a sample of 25 agencies with total annual billings of £98 million.

Source: Kennedy, I. (1992): "The Processes of Planning and Buying Media in Dublin Advertising Agencies", *Student Marketing Digest*, 1: 118–27.

REACH AND FREQUENCY

One of the most difficult tasks with which media planners are faced is setting the optimum levels of reach (how many people can be exposed to the campaign) and frequency (how often they should be reached). In the case of the former, it is difficult to be precise, as there is little hard evidence from research or experimentation that can provide definitive guidance. In general though, it is held that high reach is necessary for new product launches in order to generate awareness of the new brand. In such situations, it is often necessary to opt for a reach level that is higher than the brand-awareness level desired, on the basis that not everyone exposed to the medium will be exposed to the advertisement and the brand name. Advertising in support of sales promotion campaigns also tend to need high degrees of reach as consumers need to be made aware of when or where certain deals or offers are available.

The main consideration in planning reach levels tends to be the available budget. No matter which media are selected, a fixed level of expenditure limits the amount of reach possible. Here the planner calculates the amount of target reach that each medium can deliver, plus the amount of follow-on support or continuity required, to set a reach level. The establishment of an effective level of frequency is an even more pressing concern for the planner. However, in this instance a great deal of thinking and research exists on the subject. Common sense suggests that it is unlikely that one exposure to an advertisement will have a substantial effect. Consequently, this has led to a belief in the advertising business that high frequency or repetition is a necessary part of the persuasion process in selling a product. The more frequently a persuasive message is seen or heard, the more likely the consumer is to see the merits of the advertised brand and be convinced to buy it. Therefore, one goal of frequency is to surpass the threshold, or first few exposures, to the point where the audience member will absorb the message. Research has shown that there are threshold levels, although it is not known precisely whether the threshold is one, two, three or more exposures.

As Sissors and Surmanek (1982: 156–7) note:

> The frequency level must vary because certain situations may require higher or lower levels. This uniqueness of the advertising message, for example, can affect frequency. The more innovative and unusual it is, the more likely that consumers will notice it and pay attention to it. The converse is also true. A rather ordinary ad message might need many more than four exposures to be seen

and remembered. In all discussions on frequency levels, the planner must be aware that creative executions vary from brand to brand and the creative element can argue for more or less frequency than the competition uses.

Another consideration affecting the frequency level is the perceived value of a brand compared with the values of competitors' brands. When a brand has an important and easily perceivable benefit not shared by competitors, then less frequency may be necessary. In other words, the brand has an easily exploited advantage over competitors. But when a brand is very much like all other brands in a product category, more frequency may be necessary for the message to be noticed or remembered.

The noise level in a product category also plays a role in deciding how much frequency is needed. If many similar brands are being advertised simultaneously, consumers may find it difficult to recall the message for any one brand amid the confusion caused by the noise level of competitors. On the other hand, when few competitors advertise, less frequency may be required.

Some planners feel that a frequency level should be based on the level of that used by a brand's most serious competitive threat. Or, the competitor who is the most vulnerable to a brand's promotional attack efforts should be singled out. The frequency level of that competitor should be equalled or surpassed, with the objective of gaining an advantage.

In summary then, the amount of reach and frequency needed for a given media campaign is based as much on judgment and experience as on hard fact.

IMPLEMENTATION MEDIA PLANNING

When the basic media-selection process has been completed and a media strategy has been devised, the planner must make a number of intra-media decisions (such as where to place the advertising within a chosen medium or group of media) in order to arrive at the brief for the media buying team. The tactical issues that must be addressed at this stage basically involve the selection of individual titles, television and radio stations, deciding on commercial lengths and print sizes and setting parameters on the most appropriate positions within the media.

Choice of Individual Media Vehicles

Industry research such as the national readership survey (JNRR) and television audience measurement (TAM) can help to identify which are the best publications or programmes to use for the task in hand. Generally, the choice of individual media is determined by their reach and relative cost-efficiency in delivering the target audience, but also by their perceived effectiveness for accomplishing particular tasks. As a basic step, a cost-per-thousand analysis or cost-ranking exercise is usually done against the available audience data and the likely advertising rate costs (Table 6.4).

TABLE 6.4: NATIONAL PRESS — COST RANKING/ADULTS ABC1

		Readership		11" x Col. B/W Cost	C/000
		000	%	£	£
1.	Sunday Independent	440	55	4,158	9.45
2.	Sunday Tribune	174	22	2,288	13.15
3.	Irish Independent	274	34	3,806	13.89
4.	Sunday Press	211	26	3,432	16.27
5.	Irish Times	213	26	3,900	18.31
6.	Sunday Business Post	85	11	1,606	18.89
7.	Sunday World	159	20	3,476	21.86
8.	Evening Herald	105	13	2,530	24.10
9.	Cork Examiner	63	8	1,760	27.94
10.	Evening Press	78	10	2,200	28.21
11.	The Star	50	6	1,804	36.08
12.	Irish Press	53	7	1,980	37.36
13.	Cork Evening Echo	24	3	1,100	45.84

Source: JNRR, 1994. Rate Cards at July 1995

As Ring (1993: 116) notes, however:

> Media schedules aren't established solely on the basis of cost ranking; qualitative judgements also apply. Specifically these involve the planner/buyer's judgement on:
> - Whether a given title is particularly likely to be read by buyers of the advertised brand.
> - Whether it's a particularly suitable context for the brand. Brands and their advertisements take colour from the company they keep. This is normally called the environment. (An example in an Irish context here would be an international perfume brand using the smaller circulation *Image* magazine versus the larger selling *Woman's Way*.)

- Whether it is particularly suitable for the advertising or campaign objectives (e.g. Levi jeans are unlikely candidates for advertising on RTE Radio 1).
- Market conditions; circulation and readership forecasts; soft and hard markets and so on.

Size and Length

Creative and communication considerations are obviously important in decisions on ad size or commercial length. Within the available budget, the media planner has to weigh up the probable penalties of the medium's rate structure against the likely effectiveness of a larger size or longer spot length. The planner knows that as space size increases, likely coverage and frequency levels tend to decrease. The creative view on this tends to be simply "bigger is better". Size, however, is not everything and there have been some examples of successful campaigns that have had impact through the clever use of small spaces creatively rendered and positioned appropriately. There is also some evidence to suggest that many broadcast commercials do not need to be as long in order to convey at least the more fundamental elements of their message.

Position

Setting parameters on the desired positions within each of the selected media is an important part of the process, with the media planner basically aiming to put the advertising "in danger of being seen". Decisions on the most appropriate positions are usually made on the basis of the likelihood of greater audience availability in a mood receptive to the advertising. A basic example here would be advertising for a long-haul airline being placed in or near an editorial feature on the Far East or a television spot for a home-insurance company in a programme on crime prevention.

To help with decisions on media positioning, research is available such as detailed minute-by-minute television programme ratings and, occasionally, page-traffic studies for press, which indicate the relative importance of different parts of a publication's editorial, while outdoor has site classification and traffic data.

SAMPLE MEDIA SCHEDULE

Figure 6.4 is the typical shape of a media plan that might be used to promote the opening of an adult cinema (i.e. 18 cert) "thriller". In most cases like this, the support activity tends to be concentrated into the week preceding the opening and the opening weekend itself, in order to maximise audience interest and word of mouth. Press, outdoor and television are usually the main media used for major film launches — with print media being used to brand the film, its stars and the screens at which it will play, and television to convey the nature and excitement of the production.

FIGURE 6.4: SAMPLE MEDIA SCHEDULE

Client: Blockbuster Movies Inc.
Product: Adult Thriller
Period: March 1995

IRISH INTERNATIONAL ADVERTISING SCHEDULE

Medium	Size/Length	Unit Cost £	No.	Total Cost £	March 3–22
Republic of Ireland					Campaign Achievement — 1+ Cov / Av. Freq.
					Cinemagoers 81% / 1.9
					Adults 18–24 80% / 1.7
Press					
Sunday Independent	10" x 4	930	1	930	5
Sunday World	8" x 3	912	1	912	5
Evening Herald	Page	1,030	1	1,030	7
"	10" x 4	510	1	510	
The Star	Page	900	1	900	10
Moviegoer	"	700	1	700	10
Big Ticket	Page Colour	800	1	800	
				5,782	
Outdoor					
Adshel/Dart	4-Sheet		26/25	1,930	
Adshel — Dublin	"		72	1,900	
6-Sheet — Dublin/Cork	6-Sheet		40	5,600	
				9,430	
Television					
RTE 1/Network 2	30/10 secs	(60 : 40 Ratio)		8,000	120 TVRs — Adults
				8,000	Total Launch TVRs Including Overspill = 142; Estimated 1 + Coverage = 58%; Av. Frequency = 2.1
Total Republic of Ireland				IR£ 23,212	

In this hypothetical instance, the film has a young adult bias (i.e. the audience which accounts for usually two-thirds of regular cinemagoers) and the press selection reflects this with the three tabloid newspapers (Sunday World, Evening Herald and Star) and the movie magazines (The Big Ticket and Moviegoer) being used to reach them. The Sunday Independent is selected to reach a slightly broader audience through its larger circulation and readership. The press combination, through a special JNRR computer analysis, is expected to provide an opportunity for 81 per cent of regular cinema-goers and 80 per cent of 18–24 year olds to see an advertisement at least once. The average frequency, amongst those who will be exposed to the advertising, is just under 2 — a level which is usually sufficient for a major film that has received pre-launch publicity.

Posters are used to build street presence and awareness, particularly in the main cities like Dublin and Cork, which usually account for half of box-office receipts. On this plan, 4 sheets (101m x 152m) and 6 sheets (120m x 180m) are used at Dublin Dart stations and city-centre bus shelters, reflecting the travel patterns of young adults. A mix of 30 seconds and 10 seconds are used on RTE Television with a weighting of exposure in favour of the longer commercial. The television activity is concentrated into 9 days with an estimated ratings weight of 120 adult TVRs. Together with anticipated overspill of ratings from UTV/Channel 4, the burst is expected to provide 58 per cent of adults with at least 1 opportunity-to-see. A planner will estimate the likely cost of this from previous experience, air-time demand and likely viewing levels at the time of activity.

MEDIA BUYING/EXECUTION

With agreement reached on these various factors, the media buyer must then work to a buying strategy and implement tactics that will deliver the media schedule targets. The primary aim of the buyer is to deliver the media objectives in the most effective and efficient way. This involves competitive negotiation with the relevant media with the flexibility and keen awareness to avail of opportunities for the campaign as they arise. The buyer/seller interface is very often a crucial but underestimated part of the whole media process. The regularity of contact, the mutual trust, understanding and respect between both parties, are all factors that can influence the delivery of the final media plan.

The media owner's rate is usually the start point of discussion between the agency media buyer and the sales representative, with the former endeavouring to gain the most advantageous price and position within the available budget, and the latter aiming to increase the medium's budgetary share or revenue yield. Price/value for money and positioning within the medium are, therefore, important aspects of any media negotiation and, generally, across most media they are influenced by:

- Volume of business from the particular client

- Exclusivity of the business to the medium

- A new revenue source for the medium

- The relative demand for space or air-time in the period dictated by the advertiser.

Because of the relative levels of demand and space availability, negotiation generally takes place at an early stage for national radio and outdoor campaigns, and much closer to the date of insertion for newspaper activity. However, a requirement for prime solus positions or full-colour facilities in particular titles can influence the timing of press commitment.

Television buying tends to demand greater and more continuous input from media buyers, largely because of the manner in which the medium is sold and also because of the greater availability of data with which to measure buying performance. Negotiation of television campaigns is usually done within the confines of the "pre-empt" rate structure on RTE or a pre-agreed audience/price deal with UTV and Channel 4. The pre-empt rate card is a structured bidding system whereby spots are only secured at a level nominated by the buyer if no one else bids for that break at a higher rate. Pre-emption usually takes place up to two working days before transmission. RTE currently operates a tier of 17 different rates, although in reality individual spot prices will usually range across three or four levels.

Television buyers tend to book a large proportion of their spot requirements in advance in order to avail of early booking incentives. However, even booking early does not guarantee spots that are not bought at the top of the pre-empt rate structure. The pre-empt system has heightened the emphasis on buying skill and experience within the television medium, as buyers must be capable of assessing a variety of ever-changing factors that can influence the price and quality of television campaigns and know the most appropriate time and price level at which to commit.

EVALUATION

The media process is generally completed with a post-campaign analysis. This evaluation at its basic level usually includes:

- An examination of the media market conditions pertaining to the campaign
- Actual campaign achievements in audience and cost terms versus projections
- Discounts negotiated or savings achieved
- Competitive activity.

If advertising tracking data (e.g. Financial Services Monitors, Millward Brown, etc.) are available, then the effects of the campaign on awareness, image or even sales may be included for presentation to the client.

The foregoing description of the media planning and buying process would appear to indicate a fairly methodical series of logical steps guided by hard fact. However, as Ring (1993: 119) notes:

> ... most media strategies and schedules are built on an impressive edifice of experience, prejudice, received wisdom and, in some instances, common sense.

MEDIA — NO TURNING BACK

> We are now moving into the era of the media planner. And the omnipotence of the media planner may be the phenomenon of the 1990s (O'Reilly, 1990).

So said Heinz Chief Executive, Dr Tony O'Reilly, in a business address on advertising in early 1990. This was perhaps the most public acknowledgement that the balance of power or, more correctly, the balance of priorities in advertising, had begun to shift in favour of media, around the end of the 1980s. The media contribution began at last to move out of the dark ages when it was something to be seen and not heard.

Today, many Irish clients and their agencies have embraced this global trend and become more sophisticated in both their definition of their target customers and the development of communication strategies and approaches to reach them. Until fairly recently, labelling audiences by the standard range of demographics would have been ns of computers and computerised planning models (see "Computers in Media" section below).

FRAGMENTATION

It is generally felt that media fragmentation, cost inflation and the increasing disinterest and cynicism of audiences towards traditional options are all conspiring to forge the next significant change in media planning (Figure 6.5

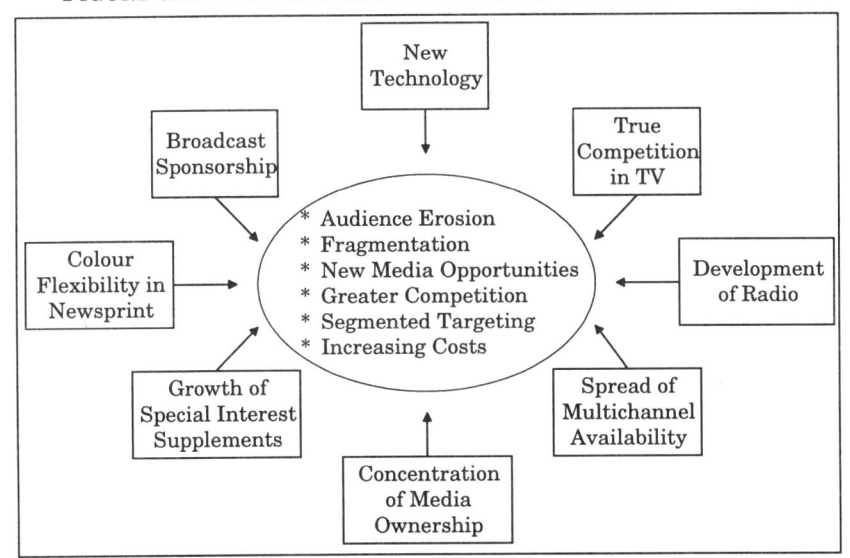

FIGURE 6.5: THE CHANGING DYNAMICS OF THE MEDIA MARKET

Surrounding boxes pointing to central oval:
- New Technology
- Broadcast Sponsorship
- True Competition in TV
- Colour Flexibility in Newsprint
- Development of Radio
- Growth of Special Interest Supplements
- Spread of Multichannel Availability
- Concentration of Media Ownership

Central oval:
* Audience Erosion
* Fragmentation
* New Media Opportunities
* Greater Competition
* Segmented Targeting
* Increasing Costs

Source: Irish International Advertising.

In the past, when advertisers had limited media choice, the primary focus for many was on message content and, therefore, creativity. Today, in an age of expanded media choice, there is an increasing focus on media context and, therefore, planning. Here the media plan becomes an influence on, and not just a consequence of, the creative brief and execution. The key lesson being learnt on the fragmentation issue, from Ireland, the UK, and elsewhere, is that giving audiences greater media choice does not result in greater levels of media consumption. Rather, what has generally happened is that people re-sort or manage their range of media options within an allotted time frame. An increase in "light media consumers", who are often young and affluent, has meant that it has become more difficult to reach desired groups of consumers with, for example, television advertising.

In these circumstances, an advertiser and media planner have basically three options in attempting to recreate the effect of the coverage-led campaign of old (Cox, 1994):

1) Spend more money in alternative media, to upweight exposure amongst "lighter" consumers, (e.g. using specific radio stations, magazines or poster sites)

2) Target and buy more efficiently in the original media selection

3) Modify the media selection and strategy (6).

The relatively slow growth in Irish advertising expenditure, however, indicates that few advertisers are likely to consider spending in line with rate inflation. At the same time, the increasing number of media specialist companies has focused attention on cheap media buying over media effectiveness, with clients now generally expecting enhanced results on comparably smaller budgets. Consequently, media planners are realistically faced with a choice from the latter two options — i.e., to target and buy more efficiently or to adapt the media selection strategy.

The common media strategy of trying to dominate a medium or range of media through a heavy advertising spend is now no longer practical or affordable. The large growth in commercial messages competing for attention, and the seemingly inexorable rise in media-rate inflation, have effectively seen to that. "Relevance", it would appear, is now much more important than "Dominance". Communities of consumers are now fragmenting from the old style "16–34s" or "ABC1" descriptors into communities of common interests such as football fanatics, "Internetters", squash players, rave-goers, etc. This makes it more appropriate, if more challenging, to determine the relevance of the media to a product, the image of those media and the consumer perception of both. The questions that will increasingly be asked include:

- How can the communication involve and stimulate a potentially disinterested consumer, already exposed to hundreds of advertisements each day?

- Is exposure alone enough?
- Will the advertising perhaps only be effective if exposed to a consumer in the right frame of mind and at the right time?

WHAT NEXT FOR MEDIA?

Developments in the Irish advertising business have tended to reflect, either consciously or unconsciously, and at a slower pace, those in the UK. The growth of media-specialist buying companies and the centralisation by major advertisers — e.g. Guinness, Gilbeys, Unilever, Coca-Cola — of their media buying are two such examples.

Since the late 1980s, however, the emphasis in the UK has moved from one of media-buying scale and muscle to media planning and strategy.

In 1989, a fledgling agency, Howell Henry Chaldecott Lury (HHCL) was the first to appoint a media strategist to head up its media service. Despite initial industry scepticism and even hostility, HHCL soon began to achieve a reputation for radical creative solutions complemented by radical media planning. Its campaign for the launch of the banking service, First Direct, was a case in point. The agency developed a distinctive and fresh approach that did not rely on the traditional mix of full pages, large poster sites and lavish 30/60 second television spots. Small size press ads and short-length television spots were created and placed strategically (with the help of qualitative rather than quantitative research) and with high frequency. The result enabled a new bank to be launched at a fraction of the normal cost and a sizeable customer-base to be built.

There was much criticism of HHCL's apparent overdependence on the use of focus groups and qualitative research, rather than industry data, for developing media strategies. Today, however, most UK media planners have moved away from using quantitative data alone in the search to communicate more effectively with their target markets and to shape their strategies accordingly. For example, two years ago, Nissan UK launched the Micra with a highly-targeted mix of quirky creative, small-space press ads and outdoor, while also in 1992, Boddingtons beer opted for short television spots and colour pages only on back-cover positions of quality review sections. In both cases, the brands underspent the competition but still achieved the required awareness and response levels. Media strategy had clearly emerged as a competitive point of difference when placed at the heart of the advertising process.

In Ireland, the sharp growth in the number of television channels, radio stations, magazines, newspaper sections and supplements, combined with a "convergence in content", has greatly expanded the media repertoire of audiences and encouraged them to move towards greater selectivity. The availability of video recorders, remote-control devices, portable televisions, programmable radios and teletext has enabled the once captive consumer to escape and has given consumers the freedom to choose the media they want, when they want it. For them and for advertisers there is no turning back.

If fragmentation continues at this pace, mass-coverage media opportunities will become highly-prized and premium commodities. (In the UK, for example, there are currently efforts being made by the ITV sales houses to place fixed price premiums on peak-time shows like *Coronation Street* because of the sheer size of the audiences they deliver.) And this is all before the so-called new media such as interactive television, video on demand and advertising on the Internet, gain a grip on the mainstream market.

There is clearly an opportunity in these circumstances, for smaller and more targeted media to gain if they can deliver a desired audience. There is also an opportunity here for media planners to be positioned as genuine communication advisors and not just pedestrian "number crunchers" and "cost-per-thousand merchants". Clients need to be encouraged to think beyond coverage, frequency and discount to consider communication effectiveness. They also need to be persuaded that unless there is a clear and relevant media strategy underpinning a campaign, then wasting money is almost assured.

In the near future, the traditional media skills of planning, buying and analysis across basically five types of media (television, radio, cinema, press and outdoor) will no longer be enough. Understanding and evaluating the wider range of media options available to clients; planning campaigns in consultation with direct marketing or database specialists; and having to negotiate everything from sponsorship to product placement deals will be almost prerequisites for media experts.

As Sissors and Surmanek (1982: 3) noted over a decade ago:

> Media planning is not so much a matter of being able to answer such relatively simple questions as where to place advertisements or how many advertisements to run each week, as it is a matter of proving that optimal decisions were made under a given set of marketing circumstances. Advertisers demand such explanations and media planners must be able to provide them. Today's media planners have changed as requirements for planning have

changed. The new planner must have breadth of knowledge, marketing understanding, research familiarity, creative planning awareness and media acumen to do the job competently.

These will increasingly be the real points of difference between the good, the bad and the average media advisors of the future, and not how far they can go in winning media discounts and commissions.

COMPUTERS IN MEDIA

The proliferation of media options (and related media research) and the demands by advertisers for greater efficiencies and certainty in their media activity, have resulted in greater investment and reliance by agencies and media-buying companies on computerised planning and analysis systems. Today, computer programmes help to create improved media schedules, handle complex data analyses and, within particular media, indicate the best options or strategies for achieving targets.

In the Irish market, most, if not all, of the computer-based information systems are concerned with historical analysis of audience data or competitor advertising activity, rather than with being predictive. The following are some of the most commonly-used support programmes or databases, in the Irish context:

- *TAM On Line* — provides overnight RTE TV audience ratings across a range of audiences. Campaign analysis of client or competitor activity is also possible, with reach, frequency and campaign weight in ratings terms being provided

- *Remit* — a computerised model for evaluating radio campaigns, either actual or hypothetical, based on the JNLR survey data

- *Telmar/JNRR* — a computer bureau service, which provides coverage and frequency evaluations of press schedules using the JNRR survey data

- *TGI/Choices* — a software package, which enables cross-referencing, reach, frequency and media ranking exercises to be conducted on the Target Group Index brands, demographics, lifestyles and attitudinal data

- *DaRTE* — a direct access facility to RTE, which enables television buyers to verify daily air-time availability and campaign status as well as logging historical television viewing trends on audience shares, programme profiles, etc.

- *ASI On Line* — provides computerised analyses of competitive expenditure by advertiser, product category and individual medium.

In the UK and other large media markets such as France and Germany, more advanced computerised planning and optimisation systems have been developed. Many of these systems are centred on the television medium because of the wealth and continuity of audience data available. The planning systems generally provide estimates of coverage and frequency needed to meet a planner's initial requirements (e.g. demographics, TVRs, channels, dayparts, etc.). The optimisation systems, on the other hand, allow the user to determine what the likely campaign coverage will be, given the schedule parameters, or the best way to achieve a given objective (e.g. what is the best channel and day-part distribution of spend to maximise the desired frequency range?)

The latest generation of computerised systems in Europe is even more sophisticated and designed to provide guidance on more complex planning problems. Large media-buying companies such as Carat and Optimedia have been in the vanguard of the development of proprietary planning systems in an effort to gain a competitive business advantage. Optimedia, for example, has begun developing a programme that helps advertisers determine the necessary weight of advertising by market across Europe. Known as Optitac, this media optimisation system first analyses in detail the media tactics used by competing brands in a particular market sector, then relates these tactics to the particular life-stage of a product and its advertising campaign.

The smaller scale of the Irish market has limited the development of such systems here. However, some Irish agencies have made tentative steps to construct their own proprietary planning models. For example, Irish International's "ARMADA" (Advertising Recall and Media Activity Data Analysis) system is designed to relate advertising awareness data to the coverage and frequency performance of television campaigns and thus guide future advertising-support weights.

A MEDIA GLOSSARY

Audit Bureau of Circulations (ABC) — This organisation audits and publishes newspaper and magazine circulation data on a regular basis. Audits are carried out and certified by chartered accountants, and provide advertisers with a basic guarantee of circulation or sales figures for ABC member publications.

Average Issue Readership — The number of people who claim to have read or looked at one or more copies of a specific publication during the issue period in question (i.e. last month, last week, or yesterday, depending on whether the publication is a monthly, weekly or daily).

Controlled Circulation — The distribution, usually free of charge, of a publication to a specifically-defined audience selected for its members' position, job function, profession or some other attribute that allows the publishers to provide a viable free magazine.

Cost-per-Thousand — A measure of efficiency used for intra-media decision-making, where the costs of delivering 1,000 of the target market through various candidate media or air-time breaks are compared.

Cost Ranking — A listing of a selection of publications based on the price that is to be paid divided by a defined reader-audience, ranked from cheapest to most expensive. The media planner will make a media selection from the cost-rank, taking into account any planning constraints. Additionally, planners may well weight the raw ranking list to reflect their client's or their own subjective view (e.g. on editorial capability or reproduction quality).

Coverage — The number of people in a target audience who are likely to have the opportunity to be exposed to a particular medium (or a schedule of media vehicles). Usually expressed as a percentage of the target audience.

Duplication — An audience level that is common or overlaps between two or more different media.

Frequency — The estimated number of times a target audience has the "opportunity-to-see or hear" a campaign or advertisement expressed over a period of time. Frequency is usually expressed as a single average "opportunities-to-see" (OTS) figure, or more fully as a frequency distribution range for a given media schedule.

Frequency Distribution — The range of "opportunities-to-see or hear" a particular advertisement that a target audience has of the scheduled media. Usually stated in terms of the percentage via the target audience who have 1 OTS, 2 OTS, 3 OTS, etc.

Impact — The actual exposure to the advertisement of a member of the target audience, i.e. when an "opportunity-to-see" is deemed to have been taken.

Opportunities-To-See (OTS) — The chance of seeing a particular medium and, therefore, an advertisement within the medium. Two types of opportunities-to-see figures may be found on a given schedule. Firstly, an average OTS figure, which is the gross OTS divided by the coverage. On a television schedule this might appear as 450 TVRs yielding 90 per cent coverage and, thus, an average OTS of 5. It is a somewhat misleading and misused figure as it is often construed to mean that 90 per cent of the target audience will see the advertisement 5 times, whereas in fact, 90 per cent will see it once, a smaller percentage seeing it twice and so on (see frequency distribution).

The second type of OTS figure relates to this frequency distribution where coverage is indicated at a certain level of frequency such as 65 per cent at 3+ OTS, which simply means that 65 per cent of the target market will have the opportunity-to-see the advertisement three or more times.

Pre-emption — Most television contractors operate a pre-empt structure whereby a commercial spot can be bought at one of a number of predetermined price levels. Any advertiser paying less than the top rate may, therefore, lose its spot to a higher bidder. The pre-empted spot will either be moved to an available break at the station's discretion or cancelled completely, thus enabling the buyer to choose another spot or increase the bid for the original spot.

Profile — The composition of a medium's total audience, usually expressed in demographic terms (e.g. class, age, sex, location, etc.).

Psychographic — A description of consumers or audience members on the basis of some psychological trait, characteristic of behaviour or lifestyle. Psychographics are used to differentiate among prospects with the same demographic characteristics.

Reach — The estimated number of a target audience likely to be exposed to a media vehicle or schedule.

Television Rating (TVR) — The estimated audience at a given time to a programme or commercial break, expressed as a percentage of the population or audience universe.

REFERENCES

ABC (1995): Audit Bureau of Circulations, Dublin, July–December.

ASI (1994): Advertising Statistics of Ireland, Dublin.

Cox, S. (1994): "Commercial Radio and the Future Media Marketplace", *Admap*, 29(10): 34–7.

Irish TAM (1994a): Irish TAM Establishment Survey, May, Dublin: AGB/TAM.

Irish TAM (1994b): *Report on Viewing Trends*, Dublin: AGB/TAM.

Kennedy, I. (1992): "The Processes of Planning & Buying Media in Dublin Advertising Agencies", *Student Marketing Digest*, 1: Dublin Institute of Technology (DIT): 118–27.

Ring, J. (1993): *Advertising on Trial*, London: Pitman Publishing.

Screen International (1995): *The Irish Cinema Audience*, Dublin: Screen International.

Sissors, J and Surmanek, J (1982): *Advertising Media Planning*, Chicago, IL: Crain Books.

White, R. (1993): *Advertising: What It Is and How To Do It*, London: McGraw Hill International.

7
Creative Strategy in Advertising

Iskandar Abdullah
J.P. Donnelly

INTRODUCTION

The purpose of this paper is to examine how creative strategies are planned and, consequently, how a creative piece of advertising is developed. It is intended that this paper will be useful both to clients who should understand how the agency works in order to produce more effective briefs, and thus improve their advertising, and to agency personnel who are charged with developing and producing great advertising for their clients.

The promotion of such mutual understanding may hardly seem necessary to the superficial observer who is conscious of clients and agencies ostensibly working in intimate co-operation. However, the history of advertising is characterised by client/agency conflict regarding the nature and effectiveness of the advertising created by the one on behalf of the other. There are many instances of advertisements winning awards for creativity but failing to impress the client in terms of their effects on sales or on other objectively quantifiable outcomes. Advertisements are often judged on their creativity, and clients themselves are often initially attracted to agencies that have a reputation for delivery of creativity. The client, however, lives in a world of contingency where the demands of the marketplace necessitate a shorter-term horizon and a tendency to see objectives in terms of bottom-line impacts, even where it might be acknowledged that creativity is an important contributor to the campaign. There can often be a very real tension between perceived "effectiveness" (the domain of the company) and "creativity" (the domain of the advertising creator).

The first section will examine creative-strategy development and determine the necessary background information. The second section deals more specifically with the creative brief, specifically its objectives, structure and content. Finally, the third section is concerned with the creative process itself, the big advertising idea and the steps necessary to evaluate creativity in advertising.

THE PLANNING PROCESS
What is Advertising Creativity?

Belch and Belch (1995: 268) describe advertising creativity as "the ability to generate fresh, unique, and appropriate ideas that can be used as solutions to communication problems". In other words, to be "appropriate", a creative idea must be relevant to the target audience, the product, and the competitive frame in which the product lives.

People who work in the creative side of advertising are often faced with many tough challenges. Not only are they required to communicate the benefits of a product or service, but they must come up with the advertising message that will interest the audience and make the resultant ads memorable. This involves having a *creative strategy* to determine *what* the advertising message will communicate and to set guidelines as to *how* the *creative execution* should say what it is supposed to say. While there should be no necessary conflict between *what* and *how*, it is often the case that a balance must be found between "creative" advertising, which captures the consumer's imagination, and "effective" advertising, which persuades the consumer to have a purchase preference.

Creative-Strategy Planning

The attempt to mediate between these potentially opposing forces where a campaign is seeking to create both creative advertising and effective advertising might be described as *Creative-Strategy Planning*. There are several components to the development of the creative brief — these include understanding of the brand or service; understanding the consumer; understanding the competition; and finally, understanding the role and capability of advertising in the marketing and communications mix.

Understanding the Brand

In any competitive market, people's choice between brands normally depends on the *total impression* that they have of each brand. They do not usually run through a catalogue of relative virtues and vices as they stop before the shelves or shop windows. In most markets, people establish buying habits or have a mental short-list involving a repertoire of brands from which they would normally choose. The strength and nature of the total impression of a brand governs whether or not it is on the short-list and whether it tends to be first, second or third on that list.

At the heart of every successful brand is a strong product benefit — in other words, the reason why consumers should buy one brand over another. Traditionally, this was based on a very real and rational reason for buying a product — for example, a more effective detergent for stains, a more economical car, a creamier tasting beer. However, in today's commercial environment there is a plethora of products offering similar benefits, and it has therefore become harder to differentiate a product from its competitors. As a result, the addition of emotional benefits to the rational claims has become a more important part of the differentiating process. Today, the successful brands are likely to be those which can create a brand personality that will persuade consumers to prefer one brand over another, through advertising, which creatively combines the emotional and rational in a coherent and effective communication.

If advertising is, to an extent, shaped by a brand's established personality, then to develop outstanding advertising it is necessary to understand thoroughly how that personality has been built over time. This totality of a brand's appeal will most likely have developed by combining three different types of appeals:

1) *Appeal to the Senses (Reactions)*: How the brand looks, tastes, feels, sounds (either in the pack or as a product in use)

2) *Appeal to the Reasons (Beliefs)*: These are the rational reasons that a person has to justify choice of a brand — that is, what the brand does, what it is for, what it contains, how it performs

3) *Appeal to the Emotions (Feelings)*: These are the psychological rewards of using the brand, what mood it evokes or satisfies, what its associations are.

In many instances, all three appeals interact with one another and are linked together to form the *personality of the brand*. Just as each person is unique, so must the brand be. It is not so much that each specific appeal is different from that of competitors, but more that it must be unique in its particular blend of appeals to the senses, the reasons and the emotions. Thus, the way in which people respond to a brand's advertising may depend on their attitude to that brand, which has been developed over time. A useful checklist of questions to ensure a comprehensive understanding of the brand is as follows:

- How did the brand come about?
- What is the history of the brand?
- What media and media levels has it had to support it over its past?
- Who knows about the brand?
- Who did use and who now uses the brand?
- What is their current attitude towards the brand and why?
- How do they behave when purchasing the brand?
- How do they use it?

Understanding the Consumer

The second component that must be understood in creative-strategic planning is a thorough understanding of the relevant consumer. No brand can appeal to all people all the time. But it is not normally possible to divide the consumers of a product type into well-defined and neat segments of Brand-A users, Brand-B users, etc. As was observed above, most consumers in most markets have a short-list or repertoire of brands from which they normally choose and these short-lists can themselves change over time.

The reason why exclusive brand loyalty does not always exist is that the *non-discriminating* appeals of the brand usually apply more or less equally to all brands in a market, while the *discriminating* appeals are not usually quite important enough to divide consumers permanently into exclusive groups, or perhaps, to offset a tempting price cut or special offer. A discriminating appeal is one that creatively bestows on the brand a personality that makes it stand out from competing brands in the same category. A non-discriminating appeal is one that merely replicates standard or dated appeals for brands in the category.

The long-term objective of advertising, therefore, is to get a brand on to the consumer's short-list, or if it is already there, to move it up in terms of preference from third or fourth place to first or second. This means that one needs to understand consumers and their attitudes to the brand, as well as the relationships between consumers and competitive brands. This means going beyond the simple demographic categorisations of consumers into ABC1, Families with two children, etc. To articulate the composition of a target group fully, they must be classified in terms of the way in which live, what their values are (especially in relation to the product category in question), what their usage patterns are. Then it is possible to develop a mental image of an individual, *a target person instead of a target group*, and to write advertising specifically directed to *that person*. Most of the information gathered from the earlier checklist relating to the "Understanding of the brand", will be useful for this purpose.

Understanding the Competitive Frame

Just as it is necessary to analyse the company's own brand in order to develop a creative strategy, it is equally important that a similar process be carried out for competitive brands. It is important to understand the relationship that competitor brands have with their consumers and with the target market, the specific values inherent in these brands, and their strengths and weaknesses. Finally, it is important to make an assessment of competitors' communication strategy, encompassing all aspects of communication from message content to preferred media.

It might also be useful to examine competitive brands from an overall business point of view. By carrying out a SWOT Analysis (strengths, weaknesses, opportunities and threats) it is possible to determine a competitor's rationale behind advertising and communication strategies and also the competitor's likely future reaction to the strategy, which might be pursued in relation to one's own brand.

The Role of Advertising in the Marketing Mix

Clearly, the role of advertising must be complementary to the achievement of the brand's objectives. A given ad can of course perform more than one role, but the fewer the tasks the advertisement is asked to perform, the more effective the resultant communication will be. In general, the creative brief for advertising is likely to have a specific short-term objective that must be met while the campaign simultaneously contributes to a longer-term strengthening or modification of the brand's personality. It is important that advertising roles should not be defined simply in terms of increasing sales, but rather to achieve a specific task that will ultimately persuade consumers to prefer and purchase the brand.

The J. Walter Thompson advertising agency identified five advertising objectives and consequent roles as follows (Clements, 1986):

1) *Direct Action. "I should do it now"*: Where the objective is to gain immediate purchase. For example, the required response to a coupon ad should be to clip out the coupon and take it to the shop, or call the freephone number. The desired response would be: "Brilliant, I'll do that right now!"

2) *Interest. "I should find out more"*: Where the objective of the advertising is to encourage the target person to find out more about the brand. For example, an objective for car advertising is often to get consumers into the showroom where they can personally experience the car and where the dealer can clinch the sale. The desired response would be: "Sounds interesting, I must find out more".

3) *Trial. "What a good idea"*: Where the objective is to get the target group to try the brand for the first time. This could be for a new brand, for a reformulated or repositioned brand, or for the extended usage of an old brand. It could also be for brands where the target group is changing and where, therefore, new potential users are continually moving into the category. Promoting trial will involve the communication of new features, either functional or symbolic, and the desired responses would be: "That would be just the thing for me!"

4) *Remind and Intensify. "Yes, that is why I buy that brand"*: Where the objective is to strengthen brand loyalty and to get repurchase, based on reminding the target group why they first bought the brand. Most repeat-purchase markets have a short-list of brands that are bought in complex patterns and cycles. So one of the major tasks of advertising is to jog people's minds about how much they were satisfied by the brand in the past. The desired response would be: "Ah, that reminds me, I must buy it again".

5) *Modify. "I wonder"*: Where the objective is to change attitudes to a brand. This is the most difficult task for advertising as it must first overcome scepticism and previous assumptions, then build a new response. The desired response would be: "I've never thought of it like that before".

Having defined specifically what the objective being pursued is, the next important question is to determine whether advertising alone is capable of achieving this task. Often, many marketing and advertising practitioners try to resolve problems with their product/brand by merely changing the advertising or just increasing their investment in advertising, without taking into account fundamental product problems, which may be the root of the dilemma.

THE CREATIVE-BRIEFING PROCESS
The Creative Brief

So far, the emphasis has been on the need to understand the brand, the target audience, the competitors and the role of advertising in planning and developing creative strategy. The provision of this information is usually the responsibility of the client as part of the brief to the agency but it is often necessary to involve the advertising agency in that process. The subsequent development of the creative strategy will be the responsibility almost exclusively of the advertising agency, and should complement the client's marketing plan. The focus of the creative strategy is, firstly, on the consumer, and secondly, on the personality of the brand.

Every piece of advertising produced should be created to meet the objectives and guidelines contained in the creative strategy. Therefore, the creative strategy should explain how the creative material should work and *how* it should be judged. The creative strategy sets objectives in terms of *what* should be in the minds of targeted consumers in order to influence them to regard a brand favourably. As a result, the advertising agency often has a greater in-depth understanding of the consumer than the client because advertising, to be effective, must talk one-to-one with the consumer on the consumer's terms. Therefore, the primary expertise of the agency should lie in its understanding of the consumer, of the advertising process and of how it fits in the marketing mix. The resultant thinking and understanding is then summarised in a creative briefing document, or Creative Brief.

How is the Creative Brief Written?

Consider a situation where an account executive in an agency has just returned from a meeting with the Client. In that meeting, the agency was requested to propose an advertising campaign for the coming year and was given the necessary information relating to the brand. Back at the agency, the account executive sets down some ideas and prepares to initiate an internal process by conducting a "creative briefing" with the creative team, which includes the creative director, copywriter, art director and other "creatives" deemed appropriate. To facilitate this process a *creative brief* is needed. The "brief" is a one- or two-page document, which contains all the essential information that the creative team will need, and which targets information for the media team.

For the creative department to develop the desired advertising effectively, it needs background knowledge of the brand and a high-quality strategic overview of the market situation, in order to get the creative "juices" flowing. As well as receiving this strategic input, the creative team must be made aware of the outline proposals regarding the media to be used in the campaign.

The creative brief should bring life to the creative strategy, and it should, therefore, be written in a language that the consumers can understand. The language must also be succinct and precise, with every word carefully chosen. This is not easily achieved as there are pitfalls that must be avoided. The first of these is that the use of a "consumer" language register can lead to unfocused thinking in the form of a long list of multiple responses which the campaign might possibly wish to elicit from consumers. The second pitfall is that too often the creators of advertising will tend to focus exclusively on an emotional response, because they either forget the basics of the brand or because they believe that consumers will think that functional differences are tired and of limited appeal.

What is in the Creative Brief?

The actual contents of the creative brief vary from agency to agency, but the basic ingredients tend to be the same because all briefs must address the same issues (Clements, 1986). In general, the advertising brief should succinctly answer the following questions:

- What are the key facts (The market background)
- Who are we talking to? (The target person)
- Where are we in their minds? (Current attitudes)
- What is the problem advertising must solve? (Role of advertising)
- What is the Single-Minded Proposition (Key consumer benefit)
- What is the support? (Evidence)
- What is the key response? (Consumer takeaway)
- What is the personality of the advertising? (Desired brand image).

What are the Key Facts?

The brief will present the market-background data, which essentially involves a summary of the market environment, the brand's performance to date, key information on competitors, and relevant background information on the brand itself. It is important that this information is precisely written, and possibly bullet-pointed. Some briefs just select one key fact that is important for the overall direction of the campaign, and this can be useful in stressing the key problem that needs to be solved.

Who is being Addressed?

The problem with usual target-group descriptions is that they do not tell creative people enough about the type of person to whom the appeal is to be directed. They may describe who the target customers are, but usually do not say much about how such customers think or feel. Statistical descriptions of the target market may be useful for understanding the market trends, or for defining the role of advertising, and in such descriptions are certainly essential to the making of media decisions. But when it comes to creating the advertisement itself, there is a need to get behind the statistics to see the consumer as a person in a fuller human form.

There is a need to develop a mental image of an individual, a *target person,* instead of a *target group*. Describe the target person in human terms by painting a word picture that brings that person to life. A good brief should give insights into the target consumer's beliefs and motivations that will allow the creative advertising to "hook on to" some motivating quirk in the consumer's mind. However, experience has shown that many account executives love to write extensive and detailed target-person descriptions, focusing on occupation, home furnishings, leisure activities, etc. This approach misses the point, which is the relationship between the brand and the person. We should be interested in other aspects of the consumer's life only in so far as they provide relevant clues to the brand relationship.

Where is the Brand in the Consumer Mind?

The answer to this question will involve a summary of the key attitudes that the target consumer has towards the company's brand and those of the competition. It is a short-list of the key strengths and weaknesses, written in consumer language. If the aim is to get responses from the target consumers, then it is necessary to know what consumers think about the brand and to clearly identify "what makes them tick" in relation to the product category and its constituent brands. Successful marketing must trade in the realm of consumer perception. It is important, therefore, to recognise that perception is something that usually cannot be changed overnight, and any form of attitudinal change can only occur as a result of a long-term, consistent communication campaign.

What is the Problem the Advertising Must Solve?

This focuses on what the advertising must accomplish. In a sense it answers another question, "Why is the advertisement being run?". Sometimes it is phrased in terms of a problem in order to ensure that the team thinks in terms of strengthening rather than just maintaining the position of the brand. It examines the role of the advertising and provides a realistic assessment of the objectives for the advertising. If the problem definition is wrong, then whatever advertising is developed will also be wrong — the key to writing it is to be totally honest and as specific as possible.

Focusing on the problem forces personnel to identify the key issues or opportunities facing the brand which the advertising is being required to address. However, this requires considerable judgment on the agency's part because advertising should not react to every marketing problem. *Advertising is not a solution to every marketing problem.*

The Single-Minded Proposition

This is the most important element of the brief, as it captures the strategic thrust of the advertisement. Essentially, this is the benefit that will differentiate one brand from another. As such, it will probably be the result of detailed strategic thinking, which ultimately must be crystallised into a single-minded proposition — in other words, the more simple the thought, the more effective the communication. Later into this paper, several techniques used by advertising agencies around the world to develop the correct proposition are examined in detail. As a matter of course, the proposition should be expressed in a way that best stimulates the creative team. Figure 7.1 is illustrative in terms of providing a thought process for developing a good proposition.

FIGURE 7.1: POSSIBLE BRIEFS TO MICHELANGELO

You are no doubt familiar with the frescoes on the ceiling of the Sistine Chapel. They are one of the greatest works of art of all time, painted by the Renaissance genius, Michelangelo. We can imagine the *briefs* he might have been given for this work by his client, Pope Julius II, or the Pope's account man, Cardinal Alidosi.

a) "Please paint the ceiling."

There is no doubt that this is what Michelangelo was being asked to do but this brief gives him no hint as to what the solution to the request might be. It leaves all the decisions and thinking to the artist before he can put paint to plaster.

b) "Please paint the ceiling using red, green and yellow paint."

This brief is worse. Not only does it still not tell him what to paint, it gives him a number of restrictions without justification — restrictions which will inevitably prove irksome and which will distract him from his main task.

c) "We have got terrible problems with damp and cracks in the ceiling and would be ever so grateful if you could just cover it up for us."

This is much worse. It still does not tell him what to do, and it gives him irrelevant and depressing information which implies that no one is interested in what he paints because it will not be long before the ceiling falls in anyway. How much effort is he likely to put into it?

d) "Please paint biblical scenes on the ceiling incorporating some or all of the following: God, Adam, Angels, cupids, devils and saints."

Better. Now they are beginning to give Michelangelo a steer. They have not given him the full picture yet (if you will pardon the pun) but at least he knows the important elements. This is the sort of brief that most of us would have given. It contains everything the creatives need to know but it does not go that step beyond, towards an idea, towards a solution.

Here is the brief which Michelangelo was actually given, more or less...

"Please paint our ceiling, for the greater glory of God and as an inspiration and lesson to his people. Frescoes which depict the creation of the world, the Fall, mankind's degradation by sin, the Divine wrath of the deluge and the preservation of Noah and his family."

Now he knows what to do and is inspired by the importance of the project, he can devote his attention to executing the detail of the brief in the best way he knows.

Source: O'Malley, D. (1989): *Creative Briefing, How to Plan Advertising*, London: Cassell in association with the Account Planning Group: 77–95.

What is the Supporting Evidence?

This section should state the reason why the brand will deliver the benefit promised by the advertising. It is an essential part of the advertising and should always be used. The support should be *rational*. For instance, it can come from the ingredients in a product, the way it is made, the way it performs, its position in the market, and so on. Sometimes the support can be *emotional* — for example, reassuring, exciting, caring. In some instances, the nature of the advertising executions themselves may be all the support that the brand needs. In general, the support combines both the rational and the emotional evidence.

What is the Key Response?

This is the consumer promise stated in consumer-response terms. It is written in one or two sentences. It is the summary thought which consumers need to take away from the advertising to enhance their perceived value of the brand.

Response is not a simple concept. It covers what the target person notices about a brand — its colour, shape, taste, strength, price and so on. Sometimes these responses are categorised as target *reactions* (appeals to the sense), target *beliefs* (appeals to the reason) and target *feelings* (appeals to the emotion).

What is the Personality of the Advertising?

A brand's personality is a long-term statement about its emotional and rational positioning in the consumer's mind. Advertising must reflect and build on the personality of the brand. The advertising personality is a statement of those traits to be included in the advertising. This is often best described in terms of a person. Such a "person" should not necessarily be confused with a description of a typical person in the target group, but should best describe the brand and the images we wish to define for the brand which will appeal to the target.

Ultimately the creative brief is probably the most important document that the account executive and creative team will develop. It is the strategy for the advertising, and therefore reflects our understanding of where the brand is, where it is going and how it is intended that advertising should change the attitude of consumers.

The written briefing document is merely a summary or a checklist through which the client service person takes the creative team. As part of the briefing process, there should be considerable debate between these two parties in order to ensure that the creative team fully understands the background to the brief. It is useful to have competitive product samples and historic advertising to explain the direction further. The creative process develops from the information contained in this one- or two-page document. Highly creative advertisements do not result from pure inspiration.

An organised approach to creative thinking was developed by James Webb Young, a former creative vice-president at the J. Walter Thompson advertising agency. He compared the process of producing ideas to that of manufacturing a motor car, when he said that "the production of ideas runs on an assembly line"; that "in this production the mind follows an operative technique which can be learned and controlled"; and that "its effective use is just as much a matter of practice in the technique as is the effective use of any tool".

According to Young's (1974) Model, the creative process involves five stages:

1) *Immersion*: The collection and analysis of information pertinent to the communication problem

2) *Digestion*: Taking the information and "turning it over in the mind"

3) *Incubation*: Placing the problem on "conscious hold" to let the subconscious work

4) *Illumination*: The point where the creative ideas begin surfacing as a result of steps 1–3 above

5) *Verification*: Analysing the idea to see whether it could be modified to fit our purpose.

Young's approach is still regularly used and certainly has influenced thousands of people who have worked for the J. Walter Thompson agency worldwide, as well as many others in the industry.

Developing the Single-Minded Proposition

As discussed throughout this paper, the quality of thought generated during the process is the most important factor in writing a creative brief. Over the past 50 years, several approaches have been developed to help guide the thought process in order to stimulate better the creative team's search for a major selling idea: that is, the "big creative idea" which demonstrates the strategic thinking behind the brand. These approaches include Leo Burnett's *inherent drama*; Rosser Reeve's *unique selling proposition*; David Ogilvy's *brand image*; Jack Trout and Al Ries' *positioning*; and Saatchi and Saatchi's *sources of propositions*. A brief description of each of these approaches is now given.

Burnett's Inherent Drama

Leo Burnett, founder of the Leo Burnett agency in Chicago, believed that the secret of effective advertising was finding the inherent drama in a product. According to him, one must understand the "reason" why a manufacturer made the product and why the consumer should purchase it. Once this is understood, the job of advertising is to take the Inherent Drama of the product–consumer interaction and produce arresting, warm and believable ads, without relying on gimmicks, tricks, or borrowed interest.

One of the best-known examples of such an approach is Leo Burnett's work for Green Giant peas. In order to communicate the special care taken in the company's harvesting and packaging process given the consumer's desire for freshness, Green Giant peas were advertised as "harvested in the moonlight" (Dunn and Barban, 1990).

Reeves's Unique Selling Proposition

The concept of a *unique selling proposition* (USP) was developed by Rosser Reeves, former chairman of Ted Bates advertising agency in New York. According to him, a successful advertising campaign has to be built on the product's USP, which he described as having three parts (Reeves, 1961):

1) Each advertisement must make a proposition to the consumer. Not just words, not just product puffery, not just show-window advertising. Each advertisement must say to each reader, "Buy this product and you will get this benefit."

2) The proposition must be one that the competition either cannot, or does not offer. It must be unique either in the brand or the claim.

3) The proposition must be strong enough to move the mass millions, that is, pull over new customers to the brand.

Once it was identified, Reeves believed that the USP should be stressed repeatedly in the ads and retained indefinitely in a campaign. One of his most famous USPs was the M&M candies claim, "melts in your mouth, not in your hands".

For such an approach to work, the brand must have a truly unique attribute or special benefit that can be used in the claim. This may require research to seek out that USP, but it should be noted that unsubstantiated uniqueness claims may lead to unnecessary legal battles.

Ogilvy's Brand Image

Brand personality is the total impression that people have of a product, and this is commonly referred to as *an image*. David Ogilvy, one of the most respected creatives in the history of advertising and one of the founders of the Ogilvy and Mather agency, argued that a brand image could be developed for every product through advertising. He based his approach on the belief that images are not inherent in products, but are instead qualities that the consumer associates with them. According to him, people buy physical and psychological benefits, not products. Advertising should, therefore, be focused on a long-term investment in the development and retention of brand image, even if it means short-term sacrifices (Ogilvy, 1964). In *Confessions of an Advertising Man*, he wrote:

> Every advertisement should be thought of as a contribution to the complex symbol which is the brand image. The manufacturer who dedicates his advertising to building the most sharply defined personality for his brand will get the largest share of the market at the highest profit. By the same token, the manufacturers who will find themselves up the creek are those short-sighted opportunists who siphon off their advertising funds for promotions (Ogilvy, 1964: 100).

Various products and services have used image advertising very successfully, including cigarettes, airlines, financial services and clothing.

Ries and Trout's Positioning

Another approach to developing the big idea is a concept introduced by Jack Trout and Al Ries (1981) called *positioning*. They believe that advertising should be created to gain a perceptual foothold in the consumer's mind by establishing something memorable and distinctive about the brand against competitor brands. Brands can be positioned on the basis of attributes, price, quality, usage, product users, and product class. Any of these can be the source of the "big idea", which will be the basis for creative strategy, and which will gain a place for the brand in the mind of the consumer. The important thing for Ries and Trout is that positioning could be best described in one word.

It is advisable to be aware that positioning is sometimes confused with the brand-image approach, but in reality it is a broader concept. In effect, positioning is the logical outgrowth of image analysis, in that it involves utilising what is known about the brand's image, the competition, and the target group. Therefore, it is helpful to analyse brand image before utilising it as the basis of a positioning strategy, which will determine what is to be communicated.

Saatchi and Saatchi's Sources of Proposition

Saatchi and Saatchi outline several areas from which the proposition might be developed. These are indicated below:

- *Product Characteristics* — Ingredients, texture, performance in use, packaging, availability (or rarity), disposable/refillable, country of origin

- *User Characteristics* — Celebrities use it, experts use it, most people use it, exclusive use

- *Ways of Using the Product* — to share, to give, to treat yourself

- *How the Product is Made*

- *Surprising Facts about the Product, Users or Usage* — for example, the nib is polished with walnut shells

- *Price Characteristics* — better value because it lasts longer, money-off offers, it's cheaper, it's more expensive

- *Image Characteristics* — High quality, good value, friendly, exotic, contemporary

- *Satisfying Psychological/Physiological Needs* — thirst, hunger, sex, social status, self-confidence, being a good mum, being a good wife/husband

- *Product Heritage* — Established in 1796, old-fashioned quality, founders of the firm

- *Disadvantages of Non-use* — how you could lose out, the risk of damage, missed opportunity

- *Direct Comparison with Competitors* — product comparisons
- *Newsworthiness* — new, improved, anniversaries, topical events
- *Generic* — claiming a characteristic of all brands for yourself, e.g. refreshment.

EVALUATING THE ADVERTISING
The Big Idea

"Trends in advertising come and go, but one rule remains intact and unchallenged: The Big Idea makes a big difference", according to Fred Danzig (1988), editor of *Advertising Age*. He goes on to say that:

> Advertisers pay agencies big money and hope that at some point, a Big Idea, that awesome bolt of creative lightning that can cut through the clutter and power sales to higher levels will strike (Danzig, 1988: 9).

Danzig and many other practitioners believe that for an ad campaign to be effective, it must contain that *big idea* which attracts the consumer's attention, gets the desired response, and makes the brand different from the competitors'. That is a real challenge for the creative team because for many products it is difficult to find anything interesting to say about them. Despite this problem, the "big idea" has become the basis of some very successful advertising campaigns. Some of these classic examples include:

Avis	"We try harder"
Coca-Cola	"It's the real thing"
Pepsi	"The choice of a new generation"
British Airways	"The world's favourite airline".

In most cases, these are international campaigns where the "big idea" has proven sufficiently universal and flexible to serve as the core proposition in global communications campaigns. The following are some good examples in the Irish context:

- Telecom Éireann's "Telephone Lines" is a more recent campaign which uses line drawings of famous personalities, such as Jack Charlton and Dave Fanning, to demonstrate its latest domestic telephone products and services.
- Green Isle's Goodfellas Pizza was not necessarily a big advertising idea, but a "big positioning". It carefully chose its Italian-American

positioning as a means of differentiating itself from other frozen pizzas and making it more accessible and mainstream. The advertising idea then simply demonstrated this positioning through the American family characters at Sal's pizza restaurant who are enjoying the product so much that they can hardly stop to talk — as a result the pizza is simply "too good for words".

FIGURE 7.2: GOODFELLAS AD

Goodfellas
"Wedding Cake"
Television: 30 seconds

SFX: (Special Effects)	*(entering with a big band swoosh) Italian/American-style music Sound of street party, people laughing, shouting and talking. There's a real buzz.*
Bride:	No, no. I love *you* more.
Groom:	Nah. I love you more.
Bride:	How much more?
Sal:	Love? Who needs it? We got Goodfella's ...
Ma:	... American-style pizza. But when you gonna get yourself a nice girl, huh? All your brothers, they marry. And you? You breaka my heart.
SFX:	*This fades under as the sound of the guys at the next table fades in. The guys are all laughing and grinning at Sal because he's being henpecked.*
Mikey:	Sure, Sal. Get married.
Joey:	You got the tomatoes. The cheese.
Mikey:	Pizza like this, I'd marry you myself.
Sal:	*(with a grin)* You Mammalook.
Denise:	Hey. Who stole my pepperoni?
Sal:	Ba da bing!

Kids:	(*nodding and laughing*) Mmmmffff!
SFX:	*Cook places pizza wedding cake on top table.*
Bride:	(*stunned into silence*)
Groom:	(*stunned into silence*)
Sal:	It's too good for words.
Sal (*over*):	Goodfellas American-Style Pizza. From stores with ice compartments.

- Lyons Tea — The Black and White Minstrels campaign was very famous for many years as an image representation for all Lyons promotions. While the campaign was enjoyed for its fun and novelty and had strength in its ability to transfer across other forms of communication, it had no real connection with the brand proposition. Nevertheless, at the time, Lyons was really the first brand to utilise mainstream television and could establish and own this positioning.

- ESB — "Electricity Brings Living to Life" was the theme used to demonstrate ESB's role in Irish society. It cleverly plays on homely situations — such as the father getting up in the middle of the night to feed the baby, the girl getting ready for her debs night, the emigrant son coming home — but actually translates into practical examples of how electricity contributes to everyday life.

These ideas have helped these companies and brands to develop a long-term sustainable advantage over their competitors. While not all advertising requires a big idea, it does give a distinct advantage to the brand by strengthening the differentiation factor through communication.

Creative Evaluation

It is often extremely difficult for clients to evaluate advertising without being subjective, or perhaps intimidated by a powerful creative team. So, when judging advertising it is important to remember that the "big idea" is an expression of the benefit or proposition which has been agreed for the brand. To ensure compliance with this, it will be necessary to refer to the brief agreed at the outset. While it is easy to be awed by the emerging advertising proposals, it is necessary to bring objectivity to the decision process, and to recognise the "big idea". Unilever developed the following training guidelines as a means of insuring proper client briefing and ultimately achieving effective advertising:

- Is there a big idea? Is it memorable? Is it relevant?
- Does it discriminate the brand from its competitors?
- Will it involve the target audience?
- Does it develop a relationship?
- Does it feel genuine?
- Is it simple and clear? Single-minded?
- Is the brand name integrated or inseparable from the idea?
- Does it make full use of the medium's capabilities?
- Is the idea campaignable?
- Are the style, manner and tone consistent with the brand's personality?

A client who can answer *Yes* to all of these questions should agree to run with the proposals because it is likely that this relatively simple idea will result in a very effective advertising campaign.

CONCLUSION

This paper has tried to provide a full understanding of how the creative process should work and how client and agency might go about putting in place a long-term advertising campaign. The emphasis in this paper has been on the considerable work that should go into the background strategy formation and the client brief to the agency. A format for a creative brief has been identified based on industry practice, and detailed guidelines provided on it should be developed and written. Finally, the paper has reviewed a number of approaches to the "big creative idea" and proposed a checklist against which good advertising can be evaluated.

The authors would stress the importance of sourcing and interpreting good-quality research data which can offer important insights about the target market. There is also a general need for more discussion on what advertising can and cannot do, and what represents a good advertisement. The present observations are offered in the hope that any clarification of the complex process involved in developing the creative strategy and creative brief can only serve to encourage the development of good, effective, creatively exciting advertising.

REFERENCES

Belch, G.E. and Belch, M.E. (1995): *Introduction to Advertising and Promotion: An Integrated Marketing Communications Perspective*, Homewood, IL: Irwin.

Bullmore, J. (1991): *Behind the Scenes in Advertising*, Henley-on-Thames: NTC Publications.

Clements, G. (1986): *Seminar Proceedings*, J Walter Thompson Seminar on T-Plan and Planning Cycle, Kuala Lumpur, Malaysia: 13–24.

Danzig, F. (1988): "The Big Idea", *Advertising Age*, 9 November: 16.

Dunn, S.W. and Barban, A.M. (1990): *Advertising: Its Role in Modern Marketing*, Orlando, FL: The Dryden Press: 274.

McDonald, C. (1992): *How Advertising Works: A Review of Current Thinking*, Henley-on-Thames: NTC Publications.

O'Malley, D. (1989): *How to Plan Advertising*, London: Cassell in association with the Account Planning Group: 77–95.

Ogilvy, D. (1964): *Confessions of an Advertising Man*, New York: Atheneum: 100–102.

Reeves, R. (1961): *Reality in Advertising*, New York: Alfred A. Knopf: 47–8.

Ries, A. and Trout, J. (1981): *Positioning, The Battle for Your Mind*, New York: McGraw-Hill.

White, R. (1993): *Advertising: What it is and How to Do it*, London: McGraw-Hill.

Young, J.W. (1975): *James Webb Young's Technique for Producing Ideas*, Lincoln, IL: NTC Publications.

8
Examining Client/Agency Relationships in an Irish Context

Tony Meenaghan
Barbara Patton

INTRODUCTION

Since the emergence of advertising as a mode of business communication, three key relationships have come to exist between the major parties to the advertising equation — client, agency and media. The client/agency interface represents a critically important relationship, as does that forged between the agency and the media, with the direct relationship between client and media being considerably less prevalent. From the establishment of the first advertising agency in Philadelphia in 1841, the client/agency relationship has evolved as economic, technological and social factors have impacted. Throughout that time, the agency referred to in discussions on the client/agency relationship has been the traditional full-service agency, and it is this relationship which is the primary focus of this paper, which examines the client/agency relationship over the various stages of its life from selection through to maintenance and eventual dissolution. The paper will further seek to examine those variables which determine the quality and duration of the client/agency relationship and will utilise evidence available from Irish sources.

FROM "PURCHASE" TO "RELATIONSHIP" IN MARKETING

Traditionally, the focus of attention in marketing was directed towards "the single analysis of a single discrete purchase, and not the relationship between the buying firm and the selling firm" (Wilson and Mummalaneni, 1986: 9). However, in more recent times, the relationship between the buyer and seller has come to prominence in the marketing literature. This can be recognised in the Network approach to marketing analysis in Scandinavia, (Anderson and Soderlund, 1988) and the work of the Industrial Marketing and Purchasing (IMP) Group in Europe (Häkansson and Johanson, 1984; Turnbull and Wilson, 1989; Häkansson, 1982; Cunningham and Turnbull, 1982). The acceptance of the need to focus on *the relationship* as the primary basis for marketing exchange arose rather belatedly amongst US academics (Dwyer, Sehuer and Fego, 1987; Webster, 1992; Ganesan, 1994; Morgan and Hunt, 1994) and derived largely from discussions within the services marketing literature, rather than as a due recognition of research themes instituted in European marketing many years earlier. Indeed, it is probably true to suggest that relationship marketing is the dominant paradigm in the marketing literature today (Barnes, 1995; Gummesson, 1995; McKenna, 1991).

It is reassuring that a more holistic view of marketing exchange is now being pursued as it is absolutely vital to incorporate this approach as central in the explanation of exchange in services marketing. Exchange in many service contexts involves a long-term commitment and a continued stream of interactions between buyer and seller (Lovelock, 1983; Glynn and Lehtinen, 1995). Indeed, in a services context, the intrinsic quality of the buyer/seller relationship is of vital importance because of essential characteristics of a service product itself. These features include intangibility (Shostack, 1982; Crosby et al., 1990), heterogeneity (Berry, 1980), perishability (Boone and Kurtz, 1995), as well as the necessary inseparability of production and consumption, with the buyer, in effect, entering into the production process of the service provider (Grönroos, 1982). In effect, these are instances where the quality of the relationship is often used as a surrogate indicator of the quality of the service provided.

CLIENT/AGENCY RELATIONSHIPS IN MARKETING

Given the nature of the service product exchanged between client and agent in an advertising context, the focus of attention inevitably falls on the nature of the relationship between these parties. Indeed, the client/agency relationship is perhaps distinctive among buyer/seller relationships because of the ephemeral nature of the "service product" and the related high dependence on interpersonal dynamics. An effective client/agency relationship is reliant on an effective personal relationship, with the existence of trust and respect between the parties being central. Weilbacher (1983) suggests that:

> ... it is because of the difficulty of predicting and measuring the productivity of advertisements and advertising campaigns that industry attention often focuses on the relationship between the advertiser and his agency (8).

This relationship is often complex, formed at different levels and developing at different paces. It can occur on both structural and personal bases. Structural variables are concerned with the relative size of organisation, the number of contact points, the nature of the client's product or service and the management structure and systems of each organisation, as well as the type and intensity of agency services required (Michell, 1988a). The personal bases are concerned with the quality of the relationships between contact personnel, the quality of understanding of one another's position and the desire for the on-going maintenance of the relationship.

> The client/agency relationship is a system in which the climate of the relationship is central, both influencing and being influenced by the ways agency and advertiser personnel work together and the quality of the work they produce (Wackman et al., 1986/7: 24).

THE STAGES OF THE CLIENT/AGENCY RELATIONSHIP

Three different stages of the client/agency relationship can be identified viz. the selection stage, the maintenance stage and the dissolution stages.

Selection Stage

The selection of an agency is a critical decision for a client, and various approaches to selection are proposed. These are largely based on the client company's understanding of its own needs and a matching process to find the agency of "best fit" (Dunn, Barban, Krugman and Reid, 1990; Bolen, 1984). These guidelines generally involve:

- An examination of the structural elements of an agency i.e. numbers employed, size of billings, etc.
- Range and depth of services provided and their compatibility with client needs
- The relative size of the prospective account within the agency portfolio

- The possible existence of conflicting accounts
- The distinctive skills of the agency
- The performance rating of the agency as reflected in terms of industry status, and reputation reflected in industry awards, trade press commentary and recommendations.

The primary selection criterion is often "creativity". This fact is illustrated in the results of a recent UK survey (Taylor, 1994) which showed that being "fundamentally committed to creative excellence" was what most client companies sought in a new agency. This is mirrored in the actual comments of two UK advertisers who recently appointed new agencies. A spokesperson for Microsoft (UK) suggested that "EuroRSCG impressed us with its invention and creative culture", while the cable channel TLC suggested that its new agency "has a good handle on the sort of creative solutions we need" (Taylor, 1994). Creativity however, is often difficult to measure, particularly in the pre-relationship phase, and other criteria contribute to the final decision. Agency selection is arrived at by a combination of qualitative (people-based) and quantitative (structural) judgments. Qualitative judgments will take the form of perceived agency understanding of the business, agency reputation, agency style and culture as reflective of one's own, and empathy with account personnel. Quantitative judgments will deal with structural factors: size of billings, handling of competing accounts, etc.

Available research on the topic of agency selection (Cagley and Roberts, 1984; Wackerman, Salmon and Salmon, 1986/87; Taylor, 1992; Mitchell, 1988a; O'Beirne, 1987) suggests that clients look first at the structural factors of agencies under consideration, and second at their "people quality". However, if the "people quality" is deficient, it is unlikely to be compensated for by structural factors, while certain structural deficiencies could be ignored when the "people quality" is high. As agency selection is, in effect, a relationship selection rather than a service selection per se, these qualitative judgments may outweigh quantitative measures.

Maintenance Stage

It is generally agreed that, as Hallett (1979) defined it: "the real business of an advertising agency is keeping clients happy". While this at first may appear to be a glib statement, it is in fact an accurate summary of the role of the agency. In an area where objective measurement of advertising in general, and creativity in particular, is almost impossible to achieve, the client perception of satisfaction is what maintains a relationship.

Central to this satisfaction is a good personal relationship with agency personnel. This is cemented by commitment demonstrated on both sides. Three issues, which sometimes threaten this commitment, but which can be turned in to opportunities, are costs, creativity and agency-performance measures. Where cost becomes an element of uncertainty between client and agency, the result can be a weakening of trust. Indeed, client satisfaction with cost, as a measurable element, is central to the client/agency relationship. This conclusion receives widespread support in available research (Wackerman, Salmon and Salmon, 1986/87; Taylor, 1992; Syedain, 1992). Moreover, a recent campaign magazine survey of client companies in the UK (Taylor, 1994) showed that "cutting costs" was the second most important way in which agencies could improve their service.

In the same survey (Taylor, 1994), bringing forward "unprompted original ideas" was believed to be the most important way in which the agency could improve its service to the client. Creativity is ultimately what the client is seeking in a relationship, but the creativity of the agency is itself influenced by the quality of the client/agency relationship. This influence is captured in a statement, used by Michell (1984b) in his research, with which clients agreed: "Good advertising depends on clients displaying high trust and low fear toward the agency".

The maintenance of the client/agency relationship is dependent on both the quality of service provided and the interpersonal relationships between contact personnel. Figure 8.1 provides an overview of the variables deemed central to the maintenance of "good" client/agency interpersonal relationships, as well as the list of the respective researchers who have sought to investigate these variables in the client/agency context. This listing is useful in understanding the interpersonal aspects of the relationship. To manage the relationship effectively, the following recommendations are made:

- Agree and define the role and responsibilities of both client and agency. This lessens the chance of misunderstandings and disappointments arising after the first bloom of enthusiasm fades in a new client/agency relationship.
- Ensure that there is open and regular communication.
- Facilitate grievance procedures on both sides. Sometimes a

personal relationship between two people operating the account on a day-to-day basis may not allow for dissatisfaction to be expressed — until it grows into a problem. Institute a system of redress.

- Achieve strong account executive compatibility with the client, and high perceived quality, i.e. similarity and expertise.

FIGURE 8.1: VARIABLES USED TO DEFINE "GOOD" CLIENT/AGENCY INTERPERSONAL RELATIONSHIPS

Independent Variable	Author(s)	Year
Attention	Wackman et al.	1987
Communications	Schein	1970
Involvement	Michell	1984
Intensive Interaction	Souder	1981
Compatibility	Evans	1973
	Michell	1984
	Michell	1987
	Cagley	1986
Interpersonal Compatibility	Cagley & Roberts	1984
Synergism	Cagley & Roberts	1984
Personal Chemistry	Michell	1984
	Wackman et al.	1987
Lack of Personal Conflict	Michell	1987
Mutual Understanding	Cagley & Roberts	1984
Integrity	Cagley & Roberts	1984
Integration Skills	Lawrence & Lorsch	1967
Leadership Skills	Wackman et al.	1987
Flexibility	Cawson	1980
Reputation	Cagley & Roberts	1984
Personnel Quality & Standards	Michell	1987

Source: Halstead, D. (1990): "A Conceptual Model of Successful Agency–Advertiser Relationship", *AMA Winter Educators' Conference — Marketing Theory and Applications*, Proceedings Series D., Lichtenhal et al. (eds.), Chicago: American Marketing Association: 90.

- Pay close attention to costs, billing and accurate, regular reporting to clients. This also assists the building of trust.

- Manage the creative process effectively and institute client training if possible. Client training can help improve the expertise of the client, thus helping the relationship.

- Agree agency performance measures and initiate reviews against these measures. Again, this clarifies the understanding of each participant and also introduces an element of objectivity into the account performance.

Dissolution Stage

The ending of a client/agency relationship is a relatively commonplace occurrence, despite the considerable personal and financial costs incurred by both sides. The underlying cause for these terminations seems to derive from the fact that an agency fails to meet or to continue to meet the expectations of its client. These expectations may or may not have been stated explicitly at the outset. In research carried out by Doyle et al. (1980), the most common reasons provided by UK clients, in descending order, as justification for changing agency were:

1) Dissatisfaction with agency performance

2) Changes in client policy

3) Changes in client management

4) Changes in agency management

5) Changes in agency policy.

The most important reason for moving account — "dissatisfaction with agency performance" — was an aggregate of several variables, including amongst others, standard of creative work, standard of account-agency management, weakness of campaigns, poor agency marketing advice, and the agency not getting close enough to the client. Agencies, on the other hand, take an opposite view and believe that the primary factors for loss of an account are changes which have occurred within client organisations (change of management, change of strategy etc.) and are not related to agency performance (Doyle et al., 1980).

Other factors which influence the relationship are structural factors. Direct positive correlation has been found between the account size, the client size and the agency size. The implication of this is that if a client organisation grows in size or increases its account size (or vice versa), then its agency relationship will be threatened. The reverse also holds where an agency may change, perhaps by merger or takeover. An overview of relationships suggests that the stronger the social and structural bonds between client and agency, the healthier and more stable the relationship. If these bonds are allowed to weaken, the relationship may dissolve.

The reality of client/agency relationships is that they are entered upon in a warm glow of enthusiasm and high expectation, and require constant attention and nurture to ensure their continuance. This is implicit in Levitt's (1983) observation regarding marketing relationships in general:

> A healthy relationship maintains and preferably expands, the equity and the possibilities that were created during courtship. A healthy relationship requires a conscious and constant fight against the forces of decline. It becomes important for the seller regularly and seriously to consider whether the relationship is improving or deteriorating, whether the promises are being completely fulfilled, whether he is neglecting anything, and how he stands *vis-à-vis* his competitors (90).

Recent research conducted amongst UK advertisers (Taylor, 1994) would seem to suggest that clients regard the lack of constant and conscious attention as the major reason for changing agency (see Table 8.1).

TABLE 8.1: REASONS FOR CHANGING AGENCY

	Percentage
It is not devoting enough time/resources to your account	87
It has lost its enthusiasm for your product/service	85
It is working on a conflicting account	61
There is a personality clash	44
It lacks integrated communication skills	32
It lacks the technology to service your account	15
You change agency regularly as a matter of course	2

Source: Taylor (1994).

THE CLIENT/AGENCY RELATIONSHIP IN AN IRISH CONTEXT

To date, little recent research focusing on the client/agency relationship has been undertaken in an Irish context. In order to facilitate understanding of this relationship, a research study was undertaken, which focused on aspects of the relationship seen from the client perspective. In effect, the primary objective of the research was to examine client perceptions of, and satisfaction levels with, Irish advertising agencies — variables at the core of the client/agency relationship. The research, which was undertaken between May and August 1992, had both qualitative and quantitative dimensions. The qualitative research consisted of a series of 11 depth interviews with informed and experienced respondents from either side of the client/agency relationship. The quantitative research consisted of a mailed questionnaire to 160 advertisers. The sample was chosen to reflect varying client types in terms of turnover, marketing budget and industry sector, with a final response rate of 52 per cent of mailed respondents being achieved.

While a considerable body of valuable information regarding client perceptions of agencies was unearthed in the research study, this paper concentrates on those results which elucidate each of the various stages of the client/agency relationship.

Agency Selection

The questionnaire encouraged client respondents to suggest their own criteria for agency selection, rather than seek aided responses from a predetermined criterion list presented in the questionnaire. It sought responses on this issue only from those clients who had changed advertising agency in the previous three years. The results of this survey concur with earlier Irish research on this particular topic (O'Beirne, 1987) and those available in the larger world arena (Michell, 1988a; Cagley and Roberts, 1984) in emphasising the role of creativity, the "people factor" and empathy with the client's business as key factors in the agency selection decision. See Table 8.2 below.

The results also confirm the existence of certain structural variables affecting the decision, such as ability to offer strategic advice, reputation, fee structure and range of services. These structural factors have been identified in studies by both Michell (1988b) and Wackman, Salmon and Salmon (1986/87) in the US market.

TABLE 8.2: REASONS FOR AGENCY SELECTION

	Percentage
Creativity	23
Relationship/People Factor	21
Corporate Decision	12
Know our Business	12
Offer Strategic Advice	8
Reputation	8
Reduced Fees	5
Fresh Approach	5
Media Buying	3
Full-Service	3
Total Number	100

Maintaining the Client/Agency Relationship

As stated, client satisfaction with the service delivered by the agency is central to maintaining the client/agency relationship. Overall, Irish advertisers were satisfied with their current relationship with their agency, with 75 per cent of respondents expressing themselves "very satisfied" or "satisfied", 15 per cent neutral and only 10 per cent dissatisfied with the client/agency relationship. When asked to select the statement that best described their relationship with their agency, the responses suggested that, while the relationships were generally co-operative and trusting, a degree of wariness underlying the relationship was detectable. See Table 8.3 below.

TABLE 8.3: DESCRIPTION OF CLIENT/AGENCY RELATIONSHIPS

Description	Percentage Using Descriptions
Co-operative	58
Trusting	42
Arm's Length	17
Wary	17
Changeable	11
Other	2

The results of the qualitative research also indicated high levels of satisfaction with current agency relationships. Most respondents seemed to derive personal satisfaction from the relationship with their agency, almost as one might from working with a close business partner or "like-minded" person. All clients were intensely committed to their companies and their products, and insofar as their agency demonstrated the same commitment, they shared a common sense of purpose.

Qualitative Comments

> I love it when the agency are knocking on the door, saying hey, we thought of something, we know you didn't ask for it — but we want to show it to you.

> An agency that shows that maybe on a Saturday morning walking up Grafton Street, that someone had an idea for your brand — that they' re thinking and that they care.

Trust between client and agency appeared to be of particular importance and was a central feature of strong client/agency relationships. Trust seemed to coincide with the expression of satisfaction with other elements of agency services, such as creativity and general costs and the openness and maturity of the relationship. An agency working well for a client makes the advertiser look well and, in turn, a satisfied client ensures that the agency contact-handling personnel are successful within the agency. This mutually supportive dimension of the relationship was important, with the converse situation also being true.

Qualitative Comments

> Trust is an essential part of our relationship — you can't work without it.

> Any agency that makes the brand manager look good will be favoured.

Overall, Irish advertisers appeared to be generally satisfied with the services provided by Irish agencies. There was, however, some degree of contradiction regarding the cost of services provided, with 87 per cent agreeing with the description "expensive" and 49 per cent in agreement that Irish agencies were often "guilty of overcharging", yet 62 per cent agreeing that "the agencies provided good value for money". This confusion was also found in the qualitative results and may have arisen from the fact that the service provided is often not susceptible to objective measurement and generally not capable of comparison. This in turn may reflect clients' unease about value in an area of service that is difficult to quantify. Overall, however, the image of Irish agencies as seen by clients was positive, as indicated in Figure 8.2.

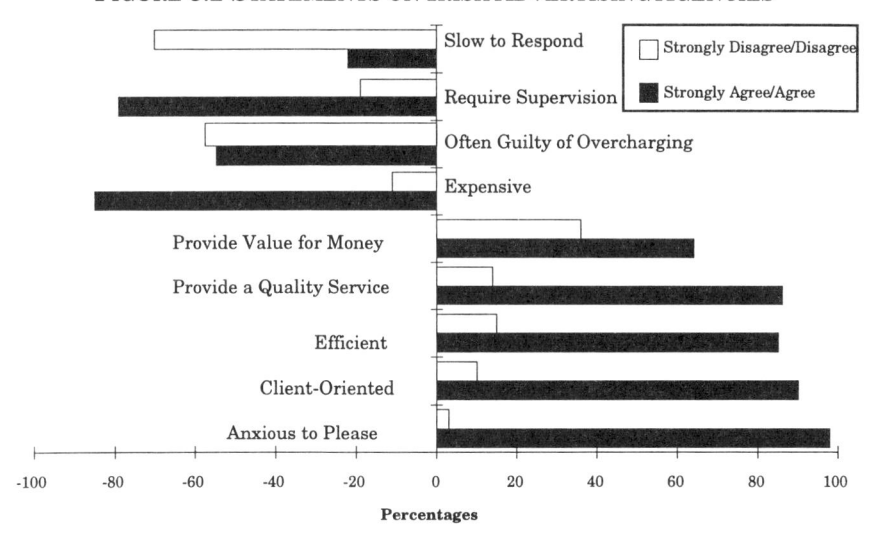

FIGURE 8.2 STATEMENTS ON IRISH ADVERTISING AGENCIES

[Bar chart showing percentages of Strongly Disagree/Disagree and Strongly Agree/Agree for the following statements: Slow to Respond, Require Supervision, Often Guilty of Overcharging, Expensive, Provide Value for Money, Provide a Quality Service, Efficient, Client-Oriented, Anxious to Please. X-axis ranges from -100 to 100 Percentages.]

The high levels of satisfaction with their advertising agencies shown in the research was also found in a 1994 IAPI (Institute of Advertising Practitioners in Ireland) study of top Irish advertisers. The expression of satisfaction ratings with Irish advertising agencies were: excellent (22 per cent), very good (50 per cent), good (19 per cent), fair (6 per cent) and don't know (3 per cent). Indeed, these clients in this 1994 survey expressed themselves more satisfied with agency performance than they were five years previously.

PERCEIVED WEAKNESSES OF AGENCIES

Identifying where agencies fail to meet client expectations is a necessary first step in improving the relationship. In this research study, respondents were asked to identify the weaknesses of their agency. The responses are indicated in Table 8.4.

Clients, rating their agencies on dimensions deemed important to them, see their agencies as being weak on key service variables such as service, cost, listening ability, creativity and knowledge of the client's business.

TABLE 8.4: PERCEIVED WEAKNESSES OF ADVERTISING AGENCIES

	Percentage
Service	23
Expensive	19
Not Listening/Arrogant	13
Creativity	11
Don't Know Our Business	11
Not Proactive	9
Limited Services/No Below Line	6
Pushing Advertising Solutions	5
Don't Offer Strategic Advice	3
Total Number	100

IMPROVING THE CLIENT/AGENCY RELATIONSHIP

Maintaining the present state of the relationship is not an adequate objective for other than a handful of client/agency interfaces, in that resting on one's laurels and failing to pay due attention to client expectations, will inevitably lead to the demise of the relationship. Asked to indicate ways in which relationships could be improved, clients responded as indicated in Table 8.5.

TABLE 8.5: WAYS OF IMPROVING THE RELATIONSHIP

	Percentage Agreeing
Agency to be More Proactive	48
Agency to Understand Our Business Better	40
Agency to Offer Strategic Advice	36
Agency to Improve Creativity	35
Agency to Reduce Charges	30
Client to Get Close to Creatives	26
Agency to Meet Deadlines	20
Increase Amount of Contact	19
Change the Account Executive	5

The results are largely self-explanatory, except to point out that overall it appears that clients have expectations on key dimensions of the service which need to be constantly met to ensure the maintenance of the relationship.

CRITICAL ELEMENTS OF THE CLIENT/AGENCY RELATIONSHIP

As well as examining overall satisfaction levels with the relationship, the research also focused on specific elements deemed critical to the maintenance of the client/agency relationship. The elements examined here are creativity, range of services, agency remuneration and understanding of client's business.

Creativity

The majority of respondents considered creativity to be excellent or good, both in agencies in general (62 per cent) and in their own agency in particular (67 per cent), with only 10 per cent of respondents suggesting "room for improvement" or "poor creativity". It was notable that satisfaction with agencies on this criterion in general was such that clients may need to look to other elements of service in order to discriminate between agencies.

Qualitative Comments

> You buy creativity because it's the only thing you can't do yourself.
>
> It should normally come from a synergy or an empathy between the agency and the client.
>
> It's so much a given that I would start to look at other things — like how will they understand my business.

Sourcing of Services through Agency

The range of services, as well as their actual quality is a vital factor in the client/agency relationship. Fifty-seven per cent of survey respondents bought non-advertising services through their agency, while 43 per cent bought only advertising services through their agency. Those who bought non-advertising services as well as advertising, indicated that the most important services were those listed in Table 8.6 below.

Clients buying non-advertising services through their agency sought two broad categories of services. The first were the traditional below-the-line-type services, such as sales promotions, print, literature, design and direct mail, while a second category of service might usefully be described as marketing services, which included market research, new-product development assistance, as well as strategic advice.

TABLE 8.6: NON-ADVERTISING SERVICES BOUGHT THROUGH AGENCY

Service	Percentage Purchasing through Agency
Design	66
Sales Promotion	55
Print Buying	53
Direct Mail	34
Market Research	23
New Product Development	17
Marketing Consultancy	13
Public Relations	2
Sponsorship	2
Strategic Advice	2
Point of Sale	2

However, while many clients employed their agency as a one-stop shop for marketing services, the research also indicated the extent of client purchasing from specialist providers. Table 8.7 below shows the range and rank order of services bought independently of the advertising agency.

These results, based on all respondents, show the extent to which specialists are employed to provide non-advertising services such as market research, public relations, sales promotion and design. The results also highlight two areas of concern for the advertising agency as specialists are employed to provide traditional advertising-agency services. The first is media buying where, because of the near commodity nature of the product, competition from specialists must be a realistic expectation. More alarming, from an agency point of view is the usage of creative specialists by clients.

The qualitative research gave some clues both as to the motivation for sourcing services and the attitudes to their delivery amongst advertisers. Sourcing non-advertising services through a full-service agency, while convenient, posed problems for the client. These problems centred around cost, competence, motivation and management, as can be seen from the accompanying comments.

TABLE 8.7: SERVICES PURCHASED THROUGH SPECIALISTS

Service	Percentage Purchasing from Specialists
Market Research	82
Public Relations	62
Sales Promotions	57
Design	55
Print Buying	24
Marketing Consultancy	17
Creativity	15
Media Consultancy	12
Media Buying	11

Qualitative Comments

You might get consistency from an advertising agency, but you lose value for money.

I think advertising agencies are good at what they do — advertising, and that's it.

I would prefer to keep them separate — play one off against the other to a certain extent. Otherwise, they could become a little safe.

It's not glamorous enough for them, they're only interested in making ads.

I have a long-term commitment to my advertising agency. Advertising is a long-term process. I have a short-term commitment to my promotions agency. I wouldn't want to get bogged down in a relationship with one promotions agency.

I think they (sales promotions agencies) are at an early stage of development and they have a long way to go.

Agency Remuneration

While all client respondents did use the commission system as the main method of payment, they generally were not in favour of the commission system as a method of agency remuneration, with only 12 per cent in favour, 53 per cent not in favour and 35 per cent neutral.

Indeed, those not in favour and those neutral on the topic of agency remuneration gave specific reasons for their dissatisfaction as indicated in Table 8.8.

TABLE 8.8: REASONS FOR DISSATISFACTION WITH THE COMMISSION SYSTEM

Reason Given	Percentage
Commission is Not Earned	38
Too Expensive/Costly	29
Should Be Negotiable	20
Agencies Push Advertising	13

There was considerable dissatisfaction with the commission system as it currently operates, but its future appears to be secured by the lack of a workable alternative approach. Some survey respondents did suggest negotiated commission rates as an acceptable alternative.

Qualitative Comments

> There is a balance in this — but at the moment I feel that the balance is too much in favour of the agencies and too little in favour of the clients.
>
> Seems funny that the reason you talk to an agency is because you want them to generate ideas for you, and that's the very thing you don't pay them for.

Understanding of Client's Business

The majority of respondents (65 per cent) believed that generally Irish agencies understood their clients' business well or very well, but a worrying 34 per cent thought that Irish agencies, in general understood their clients' business "poorly". When asked about their own advertising agency 85 per cent of client respondents thought that their own agency understood their business well or very well. The other 15 per cent, who were less satisfied, represented potential defectors from their agencies on this key dimension of service.

Dissolving the Relationship

Failure to deliver on client expectations in terms of service, and the consequent deterioration of interpersonal relations between client/

agency personnel, will inevitably lead to the client moving agency. The results of research on the motivation for dissolving the client/agency relationship as given by Irish advertisers who had changed agency in the previous three years is shown in Table 8.9 below. While poor creativity and personal-relationship factors are to be expected, the high incidence of "international realignment" and conflict of interest are somewhat peculiar to the time period, in that many independent Irish agencies were becoming affiliated with larger global agency groups at the time of the research.

TABLE 8.9: DISSOLVING CLIENT/AGENCY RELATIONSHIPS

	Percentage
Poor Creativity	33
International Realignment	16
Relationship/People Factor	13
Conflict of Interests at Agency	9
Want All Business with One Agency	7
Agency Inflexible/Can't Change	7
Client Staff Change	4
Agency Staff Change	2
Other	9
Total Number	100

SUMMARY

The relationship between the client and the advertising agency represents a particularly interesting example of a services marketing interaction. This is because of the creative nature of the advertising product, the interpersonal relationships involved and the frequency of contact and duration of the arrangement. Three distinct phases of the relationship can be identified: selection, maintenance and dissolution. Both personal and structural variables form the bases of the relationship and, as in all purchasing situations, it is the extent to which the advertising agency fulfils the expectations of the client that is the key determinant in maintaining the relationship.

In general, Irish advertisers appear to be well satisfied with the quality of service provided by Irish advertising agencies. The motivations for entering upon, maintaining and exiting from, relationships with agencies are broadly similar to those found in other developed markets where the factors of creativity, costs and the quality of account servicing are central to good client/agency relationships.

REFERENCES

Anderson, P. and Soderlund, M. (1988): "The Network Approach to Marketing", *Irish Marketing Review*. 3: 63–8.

Barnes, J. (1995): "Establishing Relationships — Getting Closer to the Customer May Be More Difficult Then You Think", *Irish Marketing Review*, 8: 107–16.

Berry, L. (1980): "Services Marketing is Different", *Business*, 30, May/June: 58–69.

Bolen, W. (1984): *Advertising*, New York: John Wiley.

Boone, L.E. and Kurtz, D. (1995): *Contemporary Marketing*, 8th ed., Chicago, IL: Dryden Press.

Cagley, J. (1986): "A Comparison of Advertising Agency Selection Factors: Advertiser and Agency Perceptions", *Journal of Advertising Research*, June/July: 39–44.

Cagley, J.W. and Roberts, R. (1984): "Criteria for Advertising Agency Selection: An Objective Appraisal", *Journal of Advertising Research*, 24(2), April/May: 27–31.

Cawson, D.R. (1980): "Pitching and Spinning: or How to Choose and Use Your Agency", *Advertising and Marketing*, 17: 2–6.

Crosby, L., Evans, K. and Cowles, D. (1990): "Relationship Quality in Services Selling: An Interpersonal Influence Perspective", *Journal of Marketing*, 54(3): 68–80.

Cunningham, M. and Turnbull, P. (1982): "Inter-Organisational Personal Contact Patterns", *International Marketing and Purchasing of Industrial Goods*, by IMP Project Group, Häkansson, H. (ed.): New York: John Wiley and Sons: 304–16.

Doyle, P., Corstjens, M. and Michell, P. (1980): "Signals of Vulnerability in Agency–Client Relations", *Journal of Marketing*, 44, Fall: 18–23.

Dunn, W., Barban, A., Krugman, D. and Reid, L. (1990): *Advertising*

— *Its Role in Modern Marketing*, 8th Edition, Chicago: Dryden Press.

Dwyer, R.F., Schuer, P.H. and Fego, O. (1987): "Developing Buyer/Seller Relationships", *Journal of Marketing*, 51, April: 11–27.

Evans, G.S. (1973): "Comparative Organisational Analysis of Advertising Agencies: The Effect of Size on Management Style", *Journal of Advertising*, 2: 26–31.

Ganesan, S. (1994): "Determinants of Long-Term Orientation in Buyer–Seller Relationships", *Journal of Marketing*, 58, April: 1–19.

Glynn, W. and Lehtinen, U. (1995): "The Concept of Exchange: Interactive Approaches in Services Marketing", in Glynn, W.J. and Barnes, J.G. (eds.), *Understanding Services Management*, Dublin: Oak Tree Press: 89–118.

Grönroos, C. (1982): "An Applied Service Marketing Theory", *European Journal of Marketing*, 16(7): 30–41.

Gummesson, E (1995): "Relationship Marketing: Its Role in the Service Economy", in Glynn, W.J. and Barnes, J.G. (eds.), *Understanding Services Management*, Dublin: Oak Tree Press: 244–68.

Hallett, T. (1979): "An Agency is Only as Good as the Advertiser who Employs It", *Marketing Week*, 5 December.

Halstead, D. (1990): "A Conceptual Model of Successful Agency–Advertiser Relationship", in Lichtenthal, D., Wilson, D. and Spekman, R. et al., *1990 AMA Winter Educators' Conference — Marketing Theory and Applications*, Proceedings Series, Chicago: American Marketing Association: 89–93.

Häkansson, H. (1982): "An International Approach", in Häkanssson, H. (ed.), *International Marketing and Purchasing of Industrial Goods*, Chichester, UK: John Wiley.

Häkansson, H. and Johanson, J (1984): "A Model of Industrial Networks", Working Paper, Department of Business Administration, University of Uppsala, Sweden.

Häkansson, H. (ed.), IMP Project Group (1982): "The Interaction Model", *International Marketing and Purchasing of Industrial Goods*, New York: John Wiley: 14–23.

Institute of Advertising Practitioners in Ireland (IAPI) (1994): "A View From The Top", IAPI Conference, April.

Lawrence, P.R. and Lorsch, J.W. (1967): "Differentiation and Integration in Complex Organisations", *Administrative Science Quarterly*, 11: 1–47.

Levitt, T. (1983): "After the Sale is Over", *Harvard Business Review*, September/October: 87–93.

McKenna, R. (1991): "Marketing is Everything", *Harvard Business Review*, January: 65–79.

Michell, P (1984b): "Accord and Discord in Agency–Client Perceptions of Creativity", *Journal of Advertising Research*, 24(5): 9–21.

Michell, P. (1987): "Creativity Training: Developing the Agency–Client Creative Interface", *European Journal of Marketing*, 21(7): 44–56.

Michell, P. (1988a): *Advertising Agency–Client Relations: A Strategic Perspective*, London: Croom Helm.

Michell, P. (1988b): "Influence of Organisational Compatibility on Account Switching", *Journal of Advertising Research*, June/July: 33–38.

Morgan, R. and Hunt, S. (1994): "The Commitment–Trust Theory of Relationship Marketing", *Journal of Marketing*, 58(3): 20–38.

O'Beirne, L. (1987): "Evaluative Criteria Used by Major National Advertisers in Agency Selection", (unpublished) MBS dissertation, University College Dublin.

Schein, E.H. (1970): *Organisation Psychology*, Englewood Cliffs, NJ: Prentice-Hall.

Shostack, L.G. (1982): "How to Design a Service", *European Journal of Marketing*, 16(1): 55.

Souder, W.E. (1981): "Disharmony between R and D and Marketing", *Industrial Marketing Management*, 10, 67–73.

Syedain, H. (1992): "Clients Fear Agency Sting", *Marketing (UK)*, 2 April: 25.

Taylor, T. (1992): "The Campaign Report: Choosing an Agency", *Campaign*, 31 January: 9–22.

Taylor, T. (1994): "Survey Results — The Campaign Report", *Campaign*, 25 September: 3–6.

Turnbull, P.W. and Wilson, D.T. (1989): "Developing and Protecting Profitable Customer Relationships", *Industrial Marketing Management*, 18: 233–8.

Wackman, D., Salmon, C. and Salmon, C. (1986/87): "Developing an Advertising Agency–Client Relationship", *Journal of Advertising Research,* 11: 14–67.

Webster, F.E. (1992): "The Changing Role of Marketing in The Organisation", *Journal of Marketing,* 56, October: 1–17.

Weilbacher, W. (1983): *Auditing Productivity — Advertiser/Agency Relationships Can Be Improved,* New York: Association of National Advertisers Inc.

Wilson, D.T. and Mummalaneni, V. (1986): "Bonding and Commitment in Buyer–Seller Relationships: A Preliminary Conceptualisation", *Industrial Marketing and Purchasing,* 1(3): 44–58.

9
Media Research in Ireland

Áine O'Donoghue
Tom Harper

INTRODUCTION

A good advertisement will only achieve results if it is carried in media which effectively maximise the number of prospective buyers who will see or hear the commercial. Media Research, therefore, is concerned with profiling media audiences, not only in terms of total numbers, but also in terms of the types of people that form those audiences. In Ireland, media research is controlled by a number of joint industry committees. These committees commission independent research companies to provide audience data. The research is funded by the media owners, and they, in turn, use the data to sell space to advertisers via advertising agencies. So, in effect, media research data become the currency by which advertising space is bought by advertisers and their agencies and sold by media owners. The surveys are designed to show the estimated thousands of the population (or of sub-groups of the population) who will have an opportunity to see or hear an advertisement.

The major joint industry media research contracts in Ireland are:

- TAM — Television Audience Measurement (funded by RTE and Institute of Advertising Practitioners in Ireland — IAPI). The research contract is currently held by AGB TAM.

- JNLR — The Joint National Listenership Research (funded by RTE, and the independent radio stations franchised by the IRTC). The research contract is currently held by the Market Research Bureau of Ireland (MRBI) Ltd.

- JNRR — The Joint National Readership Research (funded by the major newspapers and magazines). The research contract is currently held by Lansdowne Market Research Ltd.

- JNPR — The Joint National Poster Research (funded by the main poster-site companies). The research contract is currently held by Irish Marketing Surveys Ltd.

TAM (TELEVISION AUDIENCE MEASUREMENT)

About 96 per cent of private households in the Republic of Ireland own a television set. This represents just over one million television homes with a potential television audience over three years of age of 3.2 million. Estimates, based on the annual television establishment survey, show that multi-set ownership has jumped from 16 per cent in 1988 to 29 per cent in 1994 and VCR penetration has almost doubled, reaching 60 per cent of television homes in 1994, as can be seen from Figure 9.1. All television homes in Ireland receive the two national stations, RTE 1 and Network 2, but about 70 per cent of homes are multichannel, receiving UK stations and/or satellite stations. Forty per cent of these multichannel homes receive their signal from cable systems and 30 per cent from off-air aerials.

FIGURE 9.1: VCR AND REMOTE CONTROL OWNERSHIP, 1983–94

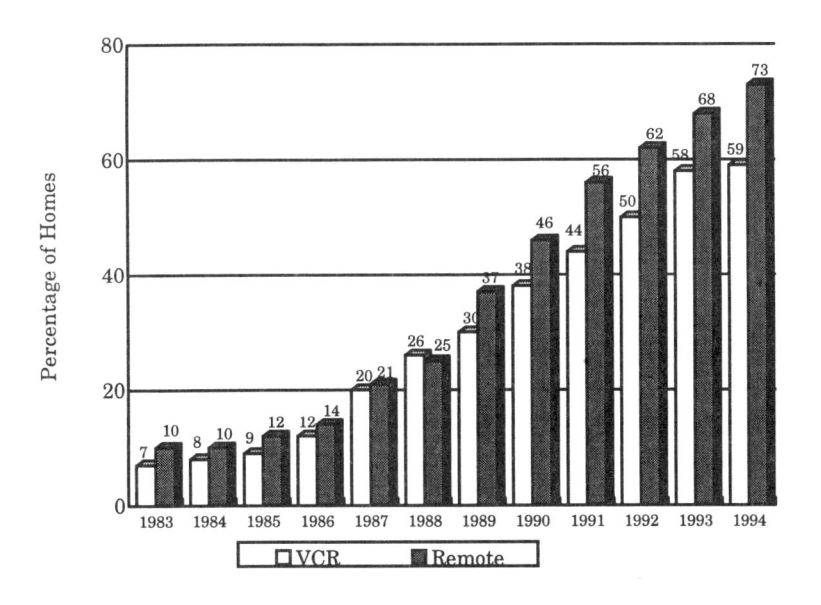

Base: Total Television Homes.
Source: The Establishment Survey (1995): Dublin: AGB TAM.

The method used to measure television audiences in the Republic of Ireland is one of the most sophisticated techniques available in media research today. This method is similar to that used in most other European countries. The TAM contract is normally awarded for a period of five years. From 1962 to 1996, this contract was held by AGB, a UK-affiliated research group. After a tendering process in 1995, the TAM contract was awarded to AC Nielsen for the 1996–2001 period. In spite of the change in contractors, the general methodology remains the same. The method is also the same in Northern Ireland where viewing is measured by BARB (Broadcast Audience Research Board Ltd.), the British contractor.

The Establishment Survey

Once a year, a survey is conducted to establish the nature of the television market. The survey is a large, multi-stage probability sample with about 2,500 interviews conducted throughout the Republic of Ireland. The purpose of the survey is to estimate the important television viewing statistics and to provide a list of names and addresses. This list is used as a pool of potential recruits for the television measurement panel.

For the design of the Establishment Survey the country is divided into regions (Dublin, Rest of Leinster, etc.) and further clustered into urban and rural areas. Primary sample points are selected for these areas (DEDs — District Electoral Divisions), and then a systematic random sample of homes is selected from the electoral register. The head of the home or the housekeeper is interviewed regarding television-related ownership and reception method, as well as relevant demographic information. This data can then be used to determine which homes to recruit for the daily measurement panel.

Panel Design

Television-viewing data is monitored from a continuous panel of homes over time. Once the sample size has been determined, a panel is designed to represent the universe that is measured from the establishment survey. For example, if the establishment survey finds that 30 per cent of homes have two or more television sets, then the panel will have 30 per cent of respondents with two or more sets. These panel controls are grouped into primary controls — those with a direct influence on viewing, such as number of sets and household size — and into secondary controls — those that have an indirect influence on viewing, such as social class and age of housekeeper. In the Nielsen contract for 1996, 600 homes have been selected and in each home the specially designed data collection meter has been installed.

People-meter

Figure 9.2 portrays the typical television-collection people-meter. It is called a people-meter because it is designed to measure people's viewing, and not just the number of homes viewing. The meter has a remote unit which has a button for each person in the sample home. The central computer will store the demographic master file used to link each person's age, sex, social class and any other personal data to their viewing data. One part of the meter sits on top of the television set and flashes a display to the panel members, i.e. "Who is Viewing". The meter constantly sends the viewing data down the mains in the home to the storage unit. This storage unit is linked to the telephone line, and each night the central computer dials all panel homes and collects the viewing data. A special telephone connection is installed in the panel home so that the phone does not ring during the night. Some meter systems can also collect audience appreciation data from

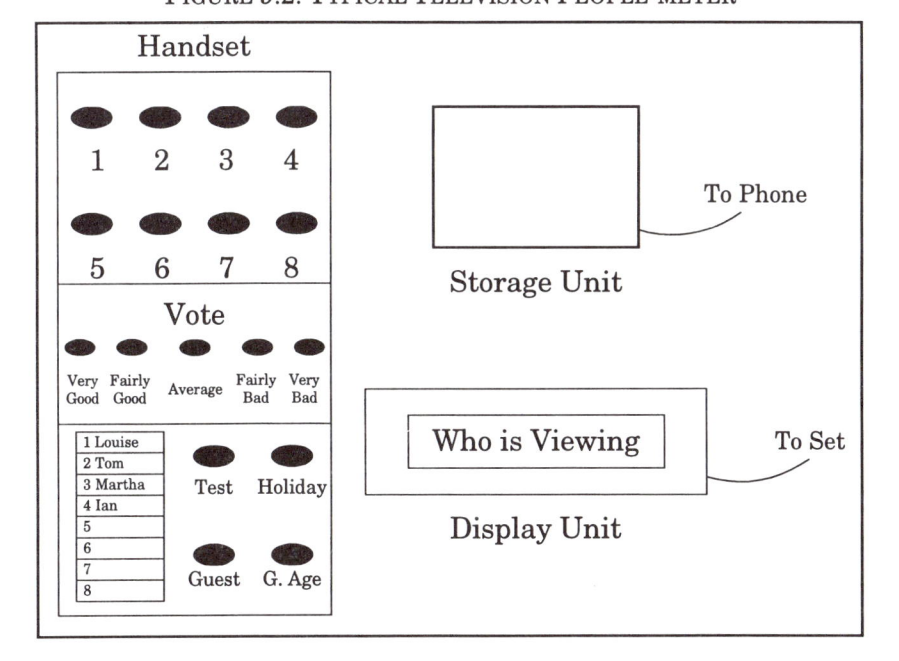

FIGURE 9.2: TYPICAL TELEVISION PEOPLE-METER

each of the viewers — for example, on a five-point scale of very good to very bad. Once all the data has been downloaded to the central computer, the processing routines are started.

Processing

Processing is largely a data-reduction exercise. Viewing data are collected person by person, second by second for all stations viewed. The viewing data are taken from this "raw" stage and cleaned and processed to "reporting level". For example, in some cases the television set can be turned on and there may be seconds or even minutes before the panel members push their assigned buttons. Rules and methods for processing this kind of "uncovered viewing" must be employed. Panel members are then counted and "weighted", based on the actual return for that day versus the expected return (as set out in the panel controls). Cleaned weighted data are then stored in a minute-by-minute format, ready for reporting.

Reporting

The minute-by-minute data are matched to the broadcaster's transmission log for reporting purposes. For example, the transmission log has the start and end times for all programmes broadcast on RTE 1 and Network 2. If the *Nine O'Clock News* starts at 21.01 and ends at 21.25, the programme rating for all desired demographics will be the average minute rating for these 25 minutes. The start and end times of a commercial break are also used to provide the commercial spot ratings.

The basic data provided from the television panel are ratings. If there are 600 housekeepers on the panel, and 200 watch the *Nine O'Clock News*, the TAM rating will be 33.3. Reporting of the information can be grouped into two levels — programme use and commercial use. In the case of programme reporting, broadcasters use the data in many different ways. Schedulers must decide where to broadcast programmes (which station and what time of day). Analysis of how people watch television through such methods as "ebb and flow" and "programme profiles" helps programme placement and the commissioning of programmes. An example of the programme data is indicated in Table 9.1.

Commercial reporting arises from the fact that the advertising industry uses the television data in many different ways. For example, advertising agencies will have the ability to run *Reach* and *Frequency* reports on all campaigns. Competitive activity reports are also available and top-ranking programmes can be listed for many different demographic groupings.

TABLE 9.1: PROGRAMMES PROFILES REPORT: ULSTER SOAPS

Area: Ulster
Profile: Adults by Age
Currency: Consolidated

Period: 27/03/95–09/04/95
(2 consecutive weeks)
Channel Factor: Excluded

		All Adults	Adults 16–24	Adults 25–34	Adults 35–44	Adults 45–54	Adults 55+
Eastenders	Av TVR	23.7	25.6	27.8	22.9	22.8	20.7
	Index	100	108	118	97	96	88
	Profile	100.0	19.0	23.1	17.2	14.1	26.5
	000	268	51	62	46	38	71
	Share	52	68	61	59	47	39
Coronation Street	Av TVR	36.6	25.9	36.5	30.3	35	47.4
	Index	100	71	100	83	95	130
	Profile	100	12.4	19.6	14.8	14.0	39.2
	000	415	52	81	61	58	163
	Share	78	78	86	74	72	78
Brookside	Av TVR	11.9	9.9	18.3	9.2	7.9	12.5
	Index	100	83	153	77	66	105
	Profile	100.0	14.5	30.2	13.8	9.7	31.8
	000	135	20	41	19	13	43
	Share	27	34	43	24	20	21

Read: Average TVR: (Television Rating Point) 36.6 per cent of adults watched *Coronation Street* on average over the 2-week period.

Index: The index or bias indicator shows that *Coronation Street* has an older audience profile (130) for 55+ as opposed to 71 from adults 16 to 24.

Profile: The profile row indicates that of the 415,000 adults watching *Coronation Street*, 12.4 per cent of those were between in the 16–24 age group.

000: 415,000 adults (36.6 per cent of all adults) watched *Coronation Street* on average over the 2-week period.

Share: *Coronation Street* obtained 78 per cent of all adults viewing at the time of transaction.

Source: BARB/Nielsen.

With the evolution of personal computers and window-based applications, the manipulation and analysis of the extensive television database is rendered quite achievable. The television audience data can be easily downloaded onto users' PCs and examined in the client's own office.

JNLR (Joint National Listener Research)

The JNMR (Joint National Media Research) programme, established in 1972, examined the audience for both radio and print media. However, in 1989 this programme was subdivided, giving way to two separate programmes, the JNRR (Joint National Readership Research) and the JNLR (Joint National Listenership Readership), which focused on the print and radio media respectively. Consequently, the joint industry body which controls the radio listening media research in the Republic of Ireland today is the JNLR. Its management committee comprises representatives of RTE, the National Broadcasting Authority; representatives of the IRTC, the Independent Radio and Television Commission responsible for issuing franchises to local stations, to community stations, and still holding an unallocated franchise for a national radio station; IAPI, the Institute for Advertising Practitioners in Ireland (advertising agencies); and AAI, the Association of Advertisers in Ireland (client companies). The research programme was established in 1990 after the IRTC had issued licences to some 25 local stations throughout the country.

The two major methodologies for collecting audience data on radio — "day-after recall" and the "diary method" — were assessed and pilot-tested prior to the decision being made to conduct the JNLR research on the basis of the day-after recall method. This method is widely used throughout Europe — in Germany, France, Spain, Italy and Switzerland — while the diary method is used in the UK, Belgium, Denmark and the Netherlands. In using the day-after recall methodology the survey aims to measure the audience to every legal radio station broadcasting in Ireland, quarter hour by quarter hour throughout the day, with wider time blocks (half hours and hours) being used in the late evening and through the night.

Informational Coverage

The persons interviewed in the research, which is conducted on the basis of in-home, face-to-face interviews, are asked whether or not they listened to all the legal stations operating in their area on the day prior to interview. The RTE stations listed are RTE Radio 1, 2FM, Raidio na Gaeltachta, FM3, Atlantic 252 and, in the Cork region, RTE Radio Cork. The IRTC station(s) measured in each area is (or are) the named station(s) franchised for the area in which the respondent lives.

Any radio-listening outside these named stations is further recorded in two major groups — listening to other franchised local stations (the spillover from one franchise area to another) and listening to any other station (this would include overseas stations and any pirate stations operating in the franchise area).

Having identified the stations listened to on the day prior to interview, the respondent is shown a list of the programmes transmitted by each of these stations on the previous day and asked to look through the schedule and indicate all the times during the day when they listened to the particular station. This listenership is recorded on a detailed grid as indicated in Figure 9.3. The actual time at which a block of listening commenced and the specific time at which it finished are recorded on the grid. At editing stage, these commencement and finishing times are inspected, and the full quarter hour of listening is recorded for a station where a respondent had listened to eight or more minutes in the block (in half-hour blocks the minimum listening period for inclusion is 16 minutes).

FIGURE 9.3: SAMPLE RADIO LISTENERSHIP SCHEDULE

STATION LISTENED TO									
MONDAY–FRIDAY Listened YESTERDAY		RTE Radio 1	Radio 2FM	Home Local Station	Other Local Station	RTE FM3	Raidio na Gaeltachta	Atlantic 252	Any Other Station
01	7am–7.15	01	03	08	09	10	11	12	13
02	7.15–7.30	01	03	08	09	10	11	12	13
03	7.30–7.45	01	03	08	09	10	11	12	13
04	7.45–8am	01	03	08	09	10	11	12	13
05	8am–8.15	01	03	08	09	10	11	12	13
06	8.15–8.30	01	03	08	09	10	11	12	13
07	8.30–8.45	01	03	08	09	10	11	12	13
08	8.45–9am	01	03	08	09	10	11	12	13

The JNLR Sample

The statistical sample of persons aged 15+ used by the JNLR is approximately 6,500 per annum. The initial sample size is 5,000, distributed proportionally over the entire country. The number of respondents emerging in each local franchise area is then inspected, and additional interviews are allocated to smaller areas to ensure that a minimum of 200 interviews are conducted in every franchise area. The Dublin sample is built up to a minimum size of 2,000. This building up of the sample is to ensure that all data emerging from the research are based on sub-samples of not less than 200. The sampling procedure is a stratified random process designed to select wards or District Electoral Divisions (DEDs) throughout the country. Within each of these chosen wards/DEDs, a single address is randomly selected and each address forms the starting point for a cluster of 10 interviews. The interviews at each of these sampling points is quota controlled for age, sex/marital status and socioeconomic class.

There is considerable discussion within the radio-research industry about the appropriateness of having a further control variable, i.e. working/non-working. However, as the social class and employment-status data available in Ireland are not provided by the Central Statistics Office cross-analysed by age groups, the JNLR survey operates on the basis that half of all urban interviews are conducted after 5 p.m. to ensure that the sample is representative of those in work. All interviews are conducted face-to-face in respondents' homes, with interviewers calling at every *nth* house from the initial randomly-selected sampling point, to fill the quota of interviews.

The JNLR Report (Source: JNLR/MRBI, 1994)

The JNLR report provides a series of measures on the impact of radio. The data is provided nationally; for Co. Dublin; for Co. Cork; and for the national area excluding counties Dublin and Cork. Data are provided in the report for every station relevant in each of those areas. The specific measures reported are:

- Reach
- Share
- Programme Reach and Average Audience
- Listenership by quarter-hour blocks.

Reach

The Reach of a station is defined as the number of people in the population who listened to the station on the day prior to interview. This listening can be for any period — long or short — and totals can of course add to more than 100 per cent. See Figure A.

FIGURE A: REACH

		Total	Male	Female
	Universe Est (000)	2647	1300	1346
		100%	100%	100%
	Sample	6639	3236	3403
	Av. Weekday "Yesterday" L'ship			
	Any Radio	2345	1171	1174
		89%	90%	87%
	RTE Radio 1	1024	504	520
		39%	39%	39%
	2FM	743	396	347
		28%	30%	26%
	RTE Radio Cork*	36	19	16
		12%	13%	11%
	Home Local Station	1169	599	570
		44%	46%	42%
	Other Local Station	241	133	107
		9%	10%	8%

- Estimated 000 of population aged 15+
- Sample of persons interviewed
- 1,024,000 (or 39% of all aged 15+) listened to RTE Radio 1 on an average weekday
- 44% of adults listened to their own local radio station (i.e., the one franchised for their home area)

* Universe is Co. Cork.

Share

The Share data show the proportion of all listening on an average day to each individual station measured, and will always add to 100 per cent. See Figure B.

FIGURE B: SHARE

		Total	Male	Female
	National — 7am–7pm — All Adults			
	Any Radio	100%	100%	100%
	RTE Radio 1	37%	34%	39%
	2FM	21%	23%	20%
	RTE Radio Cork	1%	1%	1%
	Home Local Station	36%	36%	37%
	Other Local Station	5%	6%	4%

- 21% of all listening on an average weekday is to 2FM

* Universe is Co. Cork.

The JNLR Report also provides a series of other key audience statistics.

Programme Reach and Average Audience

Programme Reach shows the proportion of people listening to each individual programme or time block, and will normally be higher than the audience to any one quarter hour in the block. The second measure related to programmes is Average Audience — that is, the average of the audiences in each specific quarter hour of the programme.

Quarter-Hour Audience Figures

The most detailed set of data in the report is the audience levels in percentage terms and in estimated thousands to every station by every quarter hour of the day (and by half hour or hour period in the late evening and throughout the night).

SIG (Special Interest Group) Data

Finally, in addition to the radio data, the JNLR also collects a considerable volume of data on product purchase and lifestyle issues, and audiences to various stations are published for all of these lifestyle groups.

JNRR (Joint National Readership Research)

Media research on the print industry in Ireland is also controlled by a joint industry body — the JNRR. Its management committee comprises representatives of the main Irish newspapers, the main Irish magazines, IAPI and AAI. The print survey — JNRR — is in existence since 1989. The research is designed to generate two main classes of information about readership — *reading frequency* and *average issue readership*.

The key issues in readership research are the determination of the frequency of reading or looking at a publication, and the recency of exposure to each publication. The principle of measuring readership is to attempt to establish, at each interview, whether or not the person interviewed has looked at any copy of the publication in question during a period back from the day of interview equal to the interval at which the publication appears. Thus, for each daily paper, the survey establishes whether or not the person interviewed looked at a copy of it "yesterday", (in the case of daily newspapers, interviews conducted on Mondays treat reading on the previous Saturday as "yesterday" in line with standard international practice). For each Sunday paper or weekly magazine, the research identifies whether or not the respondent had looked at a copy in the "past seven days", and for each monthly magazine whether or not the respondent had looked at a copy during the previous "four weeks". Each of these reading occurrences is described as "average issue readership" which is commonly referred to simply as "readership".

Informational Coverage

The JNRR research is based on in-home, face-to-face interviews, where interviewees are asked to look through a series of masthead cards showing each of the 22 publications covered in the research, and are asked to indicate on a frequency scale, the point which best corresponds to the frequency with which they read or look at each publication. The mastheads are then presented for a second time and respondents asked to indicate when they last read or looked at each publication.

The JNRR Sample

The sample design for the JNRR survey is a multi-stage probability sample. The first stage of the sample design involves the selection of primary sampling units (district electoral divisions, wards or groups of these). The second stage involves the selection of approximately 6,500 names and addresses of electors from within these primary sampling units. The third stage involves the selection of an individual for interview at the address selected in the second stage.

In some households where the number of individuals aged 15+ is greater than the number of electors (i.e. 18+) in the Register of Electors for that address, a second individual aged 15–24 also becomes eligible for interview. With some selected addresses not being possible to locate (or being demolished/vacant etc.) and the presence of two respondents for interview in some homes, the total sample of possible respondents emerges at approximately 6,600 individuals. Interviews are conducted with over 75 per cent of these — those not interviewed being unavailable during the time of the research, away temporarily or refusing to co-operate in the survey.

The JNRR Report (Source: JNRR/Lansdowne, 1994)

The JNRR report provides information on the publications measured under the following headings:

- Coverage
- Profile
- Cumulative Coverage
- Duplication/Sole Readership

Coverage

The coverage of a publication is defined as the number of people in the population who read or looked at any copy of it, anywhere during a period equal to the publication interval — yesterday for daily papers; past week for weekly papers, etc.

FIGURE C: PUBLICATION COVERAGE

The total number of people interviewed during the course of the survey → Sample

The estimated adult population in the Republic of Ireland aged 15+ expressed in thousands → Universe Est

This figure is a "grossed up" estimate of the population aged 15+ who read or looked at an Irish morning newspaper anywhere during a period equal to the publication interval (i.e. yesterday) → Morning Newspapers / Any Morning

21% of the adult population aged 15+ read or looked at the Irish Independent "yesterday" → Irish Independent

	Total	Male	Female
Sample	5044	2460	2584
Universe Est	2646	1300	1346
	100%	100%	100%
Morning Newspapers / Any Morning	1289	657	632
	49%	51%	47%
Irish Independent	566	295	271
	21%	23%	20%
Irish Press	167	81	86
	6%	6%	6%
Irish Times	265	135	130
	10%	10%	10%
The Star	319	158	161
	12%	12%	12%
Cork Examiner	203	103	100
	8%	8%	7%

Profile

The profile of readers of each publication shows the proportion of all readers of that publication who fall into the particular demographic groups — for example, the proportion of readers who are male and the proportion who are female (adding to 100 per cent). See Figure D.

FIGURE D: READER PROFILE

		Total	Any Morning	Morning Newspapers Irish Ind.	Morning Newspapers Irish Times
This figure shows all adult readership of any Irish morning newspaper	Sample	5044	2519	1138	558
The estimated adult population in the Republic of Ireland aged 15+ expressed in thousands	Universe Est	2646 100%	1289 100%	566 100%	264 100%
	Sex Male	1300 49%	657 51%	295 52%	135 51%
Of the 1,289,000 readers of any Irish morning newspaper, 454,000 or 35% are housewives	Female	1346 51%	632 49%	271 48%	130 49%
	Housewife	968 37%	454 35%	196 35%	92 35%

Cumulative Coverage

Cumulative readership takes into account regular and occasional readers, as well as the average issue readers. In other words, it takes into account the following:

- That not everyone who reads a certain issue of a publication, reads the next issue of that publication
- That the second issue will be read by some people who did not see the first issue; that the third issue will be seen by some people who did not see either the first or the second, and so on.

Duplication/Sole Readership

Duplicated readership is the estimated number of people who read two or more titles within a publication category — that is, those who read two or more morning newspapers, evening newspapers etc. Sole readership means the number of people who read one title only within a publication group — that is, one morning newspaper, one evening newspaper etc.

SIG (Special Interest Group) Data

Just as in the case of the JNLR survey, the JNRR also collects a considerable volume of data on product purchase and life-style issues, and readership data for all of these lifestyle groups are provided in the report.

Use of Media Research Data (Radio and Print)

The primary use of Media Research Data is to provide independent data, acceptable both to media owners and to advertisers, as a basis for buying and selling advertising space. It highlights the appropriateness of specific media to reach particular target groups. In the case of listenership, for instance, it will indicate the relevance of sports programmes as a slot for advertising geared towards males. It will show the estimated thousands of males listening to specific sports programmes on all, or any, of the stations covered in the research. Similarly, from the readership research data, one can see the estimated thousands of ABC1s who read each daily newspaper, and this allows the media space buyer in an advertising agency to buy space cost-effectively to maximise the number of ABC1s who will have an *opportunity to see* (OTS) their client's advertisement.

While the fundamental statistics presented in the reports show gross opportunities to see/hear an advertisement, the data collected also form the basic measurements required for schedule evaluation models. These models help the media buyer to calculate the overall reach and frequency likely to be achieved by a proposed schedule — for example, from the JNLR, what reach and average frequency will be achieved within Co. Dublin, with:

- 4 slots in the *Gay Byrne Show* (Radio)
- 2 slots during *Liveline*
- 3 slots on 98FM between 10.00 and 13.00
- 3 slots on FM104 between 10.00 and 14.00.

The *Reach* figure for such a schedule will indicate the total number of persons who will have any opportunity to hear the 12 broadcasts of the advertisement. *Frequency* will show, for the people reached, the average number of opportunities that each one will have to hear the broadcasts.

With these schedule-evaluation programmes developed by a US company, TELMAR, media buyers can evaluate a range of alternative schedules to find the one that provides maximum reach, or maximum frequency, or which is the least expensive in achieving a desired level of reach or frequency.

Cinema Research

Over the decade 1985–95, the cinema audience has been one of the fastest growing media audiences in Ireland. Research into the market is based on admission tracking and is done by linking to one of the other media surveys such as the JNRR. RSA Advertising commissions an independent research company to conduct continuous weekly admission audits. Actual weekly admission figures are collected for a representative sample of cinemas and grossed-up to estimate the total cinema-going audience on a monthly reporting basis. Cinema admissions for the period 1987–94 are indicated in Figure 9.4. The JNRR includes a question intended to estimate reach and frequency and the cinema-going profile. The cinema audience is largely young with the under 35s making up over 80 per cent of the admissions.

FIGURE 9.4: CINEMA ADMISSIONS IN THE REPUBLIC OF IRELAND, 1987–94

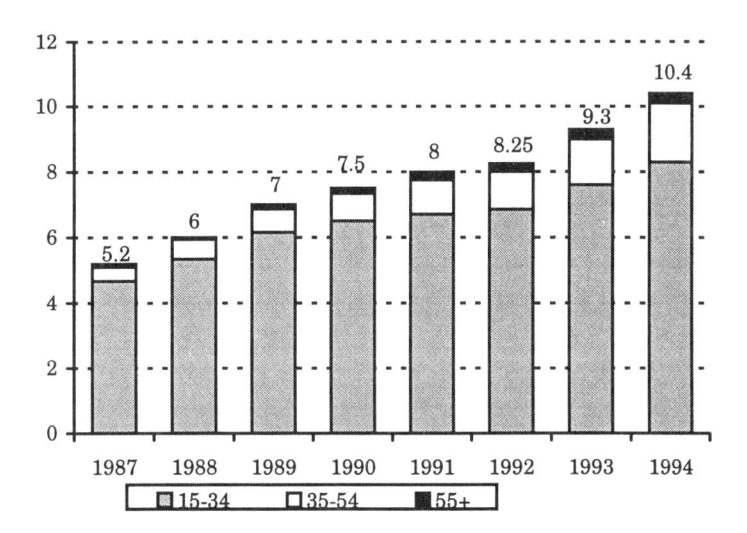

Source: RSA Advertising.

JNPR (Joint National Poster Research)

The JNPR Committee controls the research on posters in Ireland. It is the only research project which covers the Republic of Ireland and Northern Ireland using a broadly identical research technique. The research, which has been developed over the past number of years, is divided into two phases.

Phase I involves an evaluation of each poster site on a set of assessment criteria, for example:

- Solus or multiple site
- Head on, or angle of deflection
- Height from ground
- Illuminated or not, etc.

From this data a visibility score is calculated for each site — a score of 100 being the maximum score for a non-illuminated site, while illumination adds a further 30 points, giving a score of 130 as the maximum for an illuminated site. The scores are calculated for all of the major poster sizes — 4 sheets, 6 sheets, 12s, 48s, 96s and Europanels. Phase II of the research is designed to measure "passages past sites". It is based on in-home interviews with representative samples of the population, to determine their travel behaviour and journey patterns.

These journey patterns are analysed *vis-à-vis* poster sites and the data derived from these special analyses of travel behaviour, and more specifically of passages past eligible poster sites, are modelled in order to develop a formula for the subsequent estimation of the outdoor advertising audience. This formula can be used to estimate cover and frequency for outdoor campaigns of any weight over periods of 2, 4, 6, 8 or 12 weeks. A report is available in the form of a ready reckoner from which estimates for varying-size campaigns can be derived. The report contains estimates of the cover (reach) and average frequency (opportunities to see — OTS) for National, Dublin, and Main Urban campaigns. Table 9.2 below shows estimates of cover and frequency among *men* on a National campaign. Taking the first line of the table as an example, it can be seen that a national 4-week campaign of 20 million OTS (column 1) would give 12 million OTS for men (column 3). This campaign weight is estimated to cover (reach) 33 per cent of men at least once, with an average frequency of 27.5 times (columns 4 and 5). It would cover 24 per cent of men at least 10 times and 16 per cent at least 20 times (columns 6 and 7).

MEDIA RESEARCH — ALL IRELAND

The first thing that strikes anyone looking at media research in Ireland is that for a portfolio of surveys, all pursuing the same issue, the various research approaches are all strikingly different. Matters

TABLE 9.2: OUTDOOR ADVERTISING AUDIENCE RESEARCH COVERAGE AND FREQUENCY ESTIMATES, ALL MEN

National Campaign 4 Weeks		All Men	1+ OTS		10+ OTS	20+ OTS
(1)	(2)	(3)	(4)	(5)	(6)	(7)
OTS (millions)	*Av. No. Of Sites	OTS	Cov. %	Freq. (No.)	Cover %	Cover %
20	33	12	33	27.5	24	16
30	50	17	38	35.5	30	22
40	67	23	42	42.8	34	27

* Derived from the average OTS per site over 4 weeks.
Source: Outdoor Advertising Audience Research/Irish Marketing Surveys Ltd.

need to be improved. Media research should be structured in such a way that it provides meaningful data on the relative impact of all media, and elaborates as fully as possible on media-consumption habits and patterns. None of the media-research surveys in Ireland provides any assistance to advertisers or agencies in their initial choice of media. These decisions continue to be based on the collective wisdom of advertising and marketing personnel. The early identification of shifts and trends in media-consumption behaviour is essential for good media-buying decisions, and this is not monitored in any comprehensive media-consumption survey.

One recently introduced survey — the Target Group Index (TGI) — makes an attempt to fill this requirement. This large-scale survey measures media consumption (all media) and product usage by each respondent. But even this survey is conducted in Northern Ireland and in the Republic of Ireland using separate sample designs and reporting.

Media "spillover" is recognised by most of the industry. About 65 per cent of homes in the Republic can receive the UTV/Channel 4 signal. About 30 per cent of homes in Northern Ireland can view RTE. UK press titles are available in the Republic. Current media surveys do not incorporate this cross-border media consumption phenomenon.

For the future, consideration must be given to an all-embracing, all-Ireland survey, which should address

- All media consumption from the viewpoint of the consumer
- Media consumption in the context of lifestyle/activities
- Cross-consumption of media.

This research would allow media buyers to choose the most appropriate media for an advertising campaign, and then to use the existing individual media surveys to buy the most effective time or space slots in order to maximise the impact of the campaign.

REFERENCES

The Joint National Listenership Research (1994): Dublin: Market Research Bureau of Ireland Ltd.

The Joint National Readership Research (1994): Dublin: Lansdowne Market Research Ltd.

The Establishment Survey (1994): *The Size and Nature of the Television Audience in Ireland*, Dublin: AGB Tam.

Outdoor Advertising Audience Research (1994): Dublin: Irish Marketing Surveys Ltd.

10

The Role of Marketing Research in Advertising

Phelim O'Leary

Des Byrne

Within the umbrella of activities that are embraced by the title of marketing, market research and advertising have become closely linked. Corporate organisational charts will often include departments described as "Advertising and Market Research", where individuals with responsibility for one discipline will have a corresponding responsibility for the other. (Perhaps unwittingly, this can lead to budgeting problems and anomalies: one total financial allocation to both activities may not be relevant to the real needs of either; it is inappropriate automatically to follow cuts or increases in advertising spend with proportionate changes in market-research activity.) Since the 1970s there has been considerable cross-traffic in personnel terms between market research and advertising. Many advertising agencies have in-house research departments and the advent of the Advertising Planner in advertising is a prime example of discipline interaction. Corresponding specialisation has occurred in the research world, with the arrival of companies, departments, individuals and techniques dedicated to advertising research.

At this juncture, it is as well to point out that the relationship between advertising and market research has not always been an easy or harmonious one, and the joint history has been marked by minor wars and intellectual squabbling. This is more properly the subject of a different paper, but suffice it to say that it is our opinion that the benefits of the interaction of market research and advertising far outweigh the disadvantages. However, it is also probable that friction will continue between the disciplines, a microcosm of the chaffing that occurs between the broader concepts of Art and Science, and particularly so when Art and Science definitions are indistinct in the areas of advertising and market research.

At a fundamental level, the role of market research in advertising is a subservient one. When it is engaged, its only purpose is to serve advertising, although obviously it may also provide information which will be employed in other arenas. By its very nature, the collection of market-research data results in abundance — it is here that analytical skill is required, in the isolation and illumination of significant data which will inform advertising.

As an aside, it is worth noting that the analysis of data that is conducted in an advertising context may differ qualitatively from that which is practised in more general market research. The search is essentially a quest for competitive advantage and, especially in FMCG markets where product quality and performance may have become constants, the creative dramatisation of brand values, even those which may seem superficially insignificant, or those which have remained "buried", may affect the required distinction.

In the practice of market research in advertising, the acknowledgement of the role of subservience is a critical one. It needs to be remembered that the aim is advertising, or, more specifically, better or optimum advertising. This holds true whether or not research is activated in the development of advertising, or in the evaluation of advertising which has become public. Thus, it is important for market research in advertising not to become overly self-focused or self-indulgent. For example, any tendency to become technique-fixated should be avoided and the selection of techniques should be relevant to the primary aim.

Market research has a role and relevance at different junctions in the advertising chain, which may be illustrated as in Figure 10.1. It should be noted that this figure represents a theoretical picture of an advertising and research chain. In our experience, it is unusual (although increasingly not rare) for the sequence to be followed in detail, in practice. For a variety of reasons, mainly related to budgets and timing, market research may only enter the chain at isolated points. In this case, it is our view that research will have a greater beneficial effect if introduced at an earlier, rather than later, stage. Indeed, our own experience would suggest that it is the earliest period that is most critical. The "Big Picture", the world in which a product, brand, service, company etc. exists, together with the dynamics of this world, contains within it the seeds of eventual advertising. It is insightful knowledge of this world which is the genesis of meaningful and effective advertising; conversely, misunderstanding at this fundamental level, or, worse, absence of knowledge, will insidiously work its way through the entire advertising-development process.

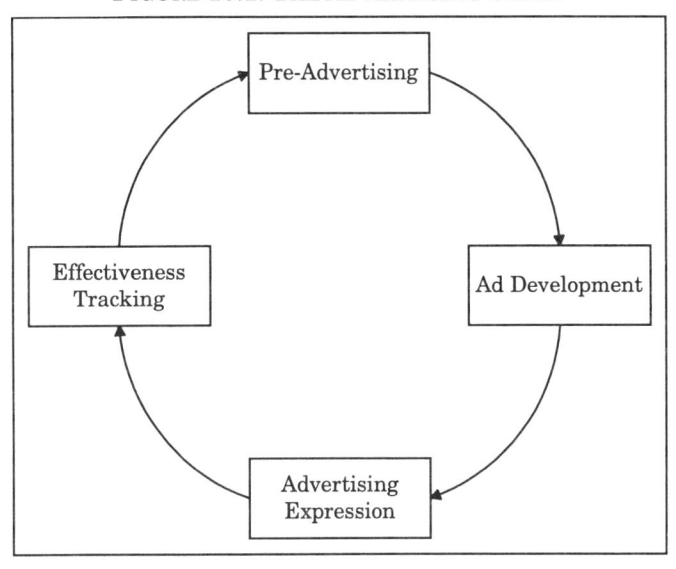

FIGURE 10.1: THE ADVERTISING CHAIN

[Figure: A circular diagram showing four boxes connected by arrows in a clockwise cycle: Pre-Advertising → Ad Development → Advertising Expression → Effectiveness Tracking → Pre-Advertising]

It may be helpful to describe in rather more detail the contribution of research at each of the phases in the chain.

PRE-ADVERTISING

This is sometimes referred to as pre-pre-testing. It is, as we have stressed, probably the most important link in the chain. Even the harshest critics of the contribution of research to advertising acknowledge the input of research in this area. The American copywriter John Lyon was no fan of research. He described it memorably as "the arteriosclerosis of the advertising process". Even from this decidedly uncomplimentary starting point, he acknowledged the vital importance of research in this area, in providing the sort of leads which are an essential prerequisite to designing highly-focused advertising.

Research in this area can, and ideally should, comprise a combination of qualitative and quantitative techniques. Here we need to explore the market in its broadest context to gain an understanding of the big picture and to see how consumers feel about the product field, the brands within it, and all of the functional and emotional aspects of the relationship between the consumer and those brands.

Qualitative research techniques can play a vital role in giving the necessary level of understanding and insight. In highly competitive markets, it will almost certainly be necessary to move beyond that, however, to a more formal quantitative segmentation of the market. One can get some idea of the sort of segmentation studies undertaken in this area from some of the examples illustrated in *Changing Attitudes in Ireland* (IAPI, 1991).

One of the segmentations described in that report divides people on the basis of their attitudes towards diet and health. Five key segments are identified:

- *Snackers*: people with a high interest in snack foods, take-aways and so on

- *Low-Fat Focus*: people with an interest in low-fat or diet options whenever they are available

- *Modernists*: people who are caught between these two tendencies

- *No Fat Concerns*: people who don't have to worry about what they eat

- *Conservatives*: people with very traditional tastes in this area generally.

This type of segmentation has significant implications for somebody marketing and advertising food or drink products.

Looking within these segments at consumption patterns of specific products and brands, one could readily show that diet yogurts (for example) are of most interest to people in the modernist and low-fat focus segments. However, a careful analysis of the information over time would have shown that low-fat yogurts developed more quickly in the low-fat-focus segment. In the initial phases, therefore, it was appropriate to gear advertising for diet yogurts to the specific mind-set of these early adopters. Over time, however, that segment became saturated and it became necessary to switch the point of attack. A decision of that sort must be a conscious and considered one, and the style of advertising may have to shift subtly to take into account the differences in outlook between the primary and secondary target groups. One may find that even elements as simple as the magazines that people read or the television programmes that they watch may differ, and the media plan would need to alter accordingly.

The essential elements in this phase of research are to define the primary target audience for the advertising, to gain an understanding of how the members think in general terms and with specific reference to the product category in question, and to develop an understanding of the triggers and barriers to increased consumption. These will form the essential planks in a marketing and advertising strategy.

ADVERTISING DEVELOPMENT

The advertising-development phase is likely to be primarily qualitative in nature. In many ways, it replicates the pre-advertising work but with a shift in emphasis to bring in an evaluation of the general advertising framework — i.e., advertising within the field. In much the same fashion as the pre-advertising work might have mapped individual brands within the sector, the work here would map competitive advertising.

The real breakthroughs, however, are likely to come from an exploration of new advertising ideas that are presented in very rough format, perhaps as rough storyboards or narrative tapes. This will lead towards a narrowing down of options.

This phase of research has to be very closely integrated with the earlier work in order to achieve maximum benefit. Researchers have to be very conscious that they are working with delicate stimulus material. Narrative tapes or rough storyboards can only give consumers some broad inclination of what is envisaged in the finished commercial. It will almost certainly be necessary to help consumers to bridge the gap between the stimulus and what the finished commercial is likely to look like. One helpful way of doing this is to have existing commercials rendered in rough storyboard format, and to use these in the early phases of a group discussion as a sort of dry run before presenting the new stimulus material.

Time and attention will need to be given to the development of the stimulus material. If, for example, a music soundtrack is deemed to be highly important to how the advertising is intended to work, then it is vital that this music be included in the process. More than that, it is essential that it should be as close as possible an approximation to what the final commercial will be like.

However good the stimulus material is, the researcher will have to be conscious of its limitations. This puts an enormous premium on proper briefing and consultation between the agency creatives who have developed the advertising material and the researchers. It is imperative that the researcher has a clear understanding of what the intended message is in the advertising. The job of the researcher, then, is to see to what extent the stimulus material gets that message across to consumers. (We use the term message in its broadest sense. It may be no more explicit than a feeling or mood that the commercial intends to induce.) One of the most important contributions a researcher can make is to identify the fact that certain intended messages are not getting through. The researcher's duty is then to make this clear and to ensure that the finished commercial will not run into the same problems.

There are many other tasks that researchers have to focus on. Does the advertising excite or not? Is the general tone of voice right for the consumer and, almost as importantly, for the brand itself? The final check question must be — "Does what is being conveyed in the advertising feed into the needs, wants or desires of consumers in relation to this product category and brand?" This is where the link between the pre-advertising research and the advertising development phase is most valuable.

ADVERTISING EXPRESSION

This is a phase that sometimes gets overlooked, particularly if budgets are tight. In very competitive markets, however, more and more attention is being given to research on later phases of the development of advertising executions. As the costs of television production in particular escalate, manufacturers are increasingly trying to maximise the effectiveness of their final commercials. In this final phase of the process, it is possible to use a rough cut of a finished commercial as the stimulus material to make absolutely sure that all of the elements are exactly as one would ideally wish them to be. There have been many instances recently where this late phase of research work has detected flaws in execution which could be corrected with significant benefit to the finished commercial.

EFFECTIVENESS TRACKING

We can all learn from our mistakes. We can learn from what we do right also. Procter and Gamble insist that when things are going right, you should find out why and put the lessons that you have learned to use in the future.

This is perhaps the most potent reason for tracking advertising effectiveness. Some people tend to see this in a very limited light:

what proportion of people recall our advertising, and can we link this with sales? These authors feel very strongly that it is necessary to go much deeper than this.

Anyone who has done the sort of pre-testing work that has been described earlier should have a clear understanding of how their advertising was intended to work. If it was intended to produce a change in people's understanding or in their feelings or in their relationship with the brand, then the tracking questions used should be designed to measure shifts on those particular points.

One useful checklist in this regard has been developed by Stephen King of JWT (McDonald, 1992). His *Scale of Responses Continuum* is set out in Table 10.1:

TABLE 10.1: SCALE OF RESPONSES CONTINUUM

	Desired	Typical Response
1.	Take action	Order now
2.	Seek information	"I must find out more about...."
3.	Relate to needs, wants, desires	Link brand to wants, etc.
4.	Bring to top of mind — recall previous satisfactions	"That reminds me"
5.	Modify attitudes	"I never thought of that before"
6.	Reinforce attitudes	"I always knew I was right to buy"

It can be seen clearly from Table 10.1 that variations in the planned objective of the advertising should produce variations in response. The point we are trying to stress is that the response measures should be specifically and directly geared to the way in which advertising was intended to work in the first place.

CONCLUDING COMMENTS

In this paper, we have attempted to summarise the contribution that research can make in the advertising-development chain. The phase of effectiveness tracking is not the end of the process. It is simply the entry point to the next phase of pre-advertising development work. Markets, brands and advertising do not stand still. It is a salutary exercise to look at reels of television commercials from 10 years ago. Most of these would not work today.

Practitioners talk of the role of advertising in "framing a brand". The idea is that the brand is a picture and the advertising is the frame that sets it off or, if it is out of synch, destroys the picture entirely. If the elements that are meant to work together fail to do so, then advertisers are almost sure to fall short of their goals. If they work together, there can be multiplier effect rather than a simple addition of the individual parts. In a 1994 *Admap* seminar on Advertising Effectiveness in London, Chris Baker, the convenor of the 1994 IPA Advertising Effectiveness Awards, used an interesting chart to demonstrate what he referred to as "joined-up thinking". His formula for greater advertising effectiveness is shown in Figure 10.2.

FIGURE 10.2: JOINED-UP THINKING

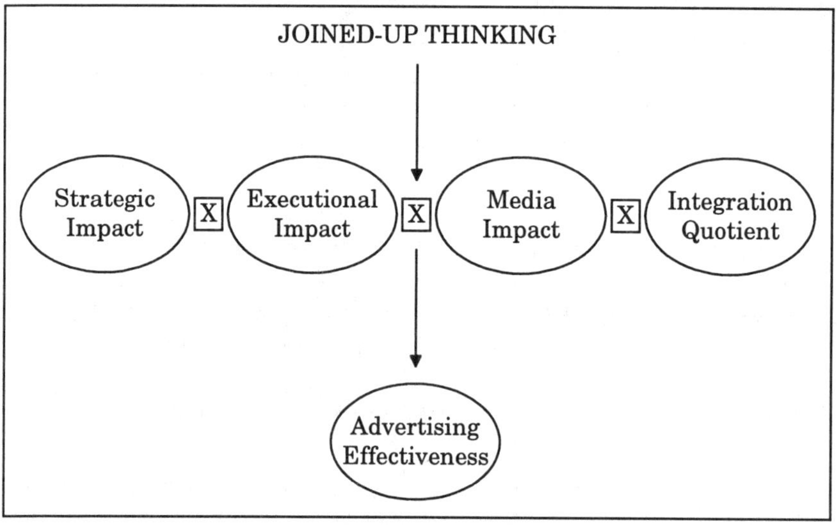

JOINED-UP THINKING

Strategic Impact [X] Executional Impact [X] Media Impact [X] Integration Quotient

↓

Advertising Effectiveness

What we hope we have demonstrated in this paper is that research can make an important contribution to all of these aspects of the advertising process (strategy, execution and media choice) which, when they are brought together successfully can create the sort of advertising impact that all advertisers and their agencies set out to achieve.

REFERENCES

Baker, C. (1994): "Factors Behind Success: The 1994 IPA Award Winner", *Admap*, 29(12): 9–13.

Byrne, D. (1991): *Changing Attitudes in Ireland, 1991*, Dublin: Institute of Advertising Practitioners in Ireland (IAPI): 17–9.

McDonald, C. (1992): *How Advertising Works*, Henley-on-Thames, Oxfordshire: NTC Publications Ltd.

11
Co-operative Advertising — Client, Channel and Agency

Paul O'Sullivan
Peter Dolan

INTRODUCTION

Co-operative advertising is an umbrella term which refers to various forms of jointly sponsored supplier/retailer advertising to the consumer. It represents an area of considerable potential in terms of improved marketing productivity for all parties involved, and its output, particularly in terms of press advertising, regularly intrudes upon consumers' attention.

Co-operative advertising is a feature of both industrial and consumer markets, and it is a communication tool of major significance for a range of goods involving both high- and low-involvement purchase situations, though primarily concerned with the former. It accounts for a significant part of the communications expenditure of both suppliers and retailers, and it may represent the single most important form of marketing communication in certain areas of the retail trade. Magrath (1992) points out that while there is little growth in US advertising budgets at national level, co-operative advertising is growing at 7 per cent per year, a rate far in excess of GNP growth.

Co-operative advertising is normally part of an overall programme of promotional support, which an individual manufacturer/distributor offers to a retailer and of itself it usually includes suggested advertising formats, materials for producing adverts, schedules of manufacturers' national advertising and promotion programmes and schedules of money allowances available.

Despite the scale and pervasiveness of the activity, very little research has been done on the planning, management and evaluation of communication campaigns grounded on co-operative approaches. This paucity of research activity is even more surprising when one considers that both the strategic and operational management of co-operative advertising campaigns represent a crucial interface of value chain partners and will often provide a flash point for tensions or an arena for the articulation and possible resolution of channel conflict.

The structure of Irish distribution for both durables and FMCGs represents a special case. Because of the limited scale of the consumer market and the relative openness of the economy to imports, Ireland has developed a large intermediate structure of distributors and wholesalers who act locally for foreign manufacturers. Channel relationships in Ireland tend to be complex and concerted channel action as required by a co-operative advertising campaign can be problematic.

FORMS OF CO-OPERATIVE ADVERTISING

Co-operative advertising may be formally defined as communication whose sponsorship and cost is shared by more than one party. Young and Greyser (1983) outline three principal categories of activity, as described below.

Horizontal Co-operative Advertising

This refers to advertising sponsored in common by a group of retailers or manufacturers. Varadarajan (1986) states that:

> It can be broadly viewed as a [campaign] characterised by the participation of and/or the pooling of promotional resources by two or more distinct entities designed to capitalise on joint opportunities for sales growth, profit, or realization of other objectives to the mutual benefit of the participants in the co-operative advertising sales promotion programme (61).

Current Irish examples of this type of activity include co-operative promotions in the coal distribution industry in order to create primary demand for a product category under pressure from environmentalists and regulators, and which is therefore losing favour with new-house builders. A further possible level of co-operation might involve an even more generic approach by all of the players in the overall Irish solid-fuel industry. It is notable that such activity is most likely to occur where the players have a well-defined common cause and where competitive tensions can be subsumed in the interests of the overall welfare of the sector. It is also facilitated where there is limited head-to-head competition and the individual players concentrate on servicing established stable distribution networks.

The presence of a co-ordinating body in an industry may also encourage horizontal co-operative activity. In some instances, the ongoing advertising activity in a sector may be funded through a levy on manufacturers and distributors; in other cases, the activity may involve ad hoc campaigns directed at particular communication or sales objectives.

A manufacturing company may both organise and fund a campaign which has a large horizontal component on behalf of its retailers, who, for their part, will contribute to the cost of the overall campaign. The joint radio campaigns in 1994 by a number of Opel dealers and the joint press campaigns by four well-known independent electrical dealers in the greater Dublin area, provide pertinent examples. The initiation of such campaigns usually falls to the manufacturer, and the activity is greatly facilitated by the relatively discrete nature of the territories served by the individual retailers. Manufacturers of up-market furniture and interior-design fittings, seeking to support fairly selective distribution networks, will regularly use this approach in the UK with most advertisements placings occurring in Sunday supplements and upmarket magazines.

Ingredient Producer Co-operative Advertising

This refers to advertising supported by raw-material manufacturers. The objective of such programmes is to help establish a branded end-product incorporating a branded major ingredient produced by the material manufacturer. Major campaigns of this sort do occur in both FMCG and durable consumer markets in the United States and are now becoming much more common in business-to-business markets.

Vertical Co-operative Advertising

This is advertising which in general is initiated and implemented by the retailer and partially/largely paid for by one or more of the suppliers. Haight (1983) defines it as follows:

> Vertical co-operative advertising reaches the consumer in the form of retail advertising, bearing the name of the retailer as signature, but including the name and often the distinctive emblem or logotype of the manufacturer or its brand (195).

Newhall (1992) argues that such co-operative advertising "brings national and multi-market advertisers right to where consumers live and shop" (40).

There are broadly two types of vertical co-operative advertising:

1) Customer- (i.e. retailer-) controlled programme: Any offer by a supplier to reimburse a retailer for all or part of the costs of advertising placed by the retailer which features the product or service of the supplier.

2) Supplier-controlled programme: Any offer by a supplier to create and place advertising featuring its own product or service over the names of one or more of its dealers, who are usually retailers.

The two approaches are not mutually exclusive in a supplier's overall strategy. Many companies offering support for a retailer-controlled programme will also make a supplier-controlled programme available to smaller retailers who do not themselves have sufficient resources to create and place their own advertisements. However, available trade and observation evidence suggests that the dominant form in the Irish market is the customer-controlled programme. This latter approach is so universal that until fairly recently it could probably have served as a definition of co-operative advertising itself, and because of its pervasiveness and relevance it is the main focus of this paper.

A combination of horizontal and vertical co-operative advertising can be relatively inexpensive for the retailer, but can have significant impact on the market. It may well be the only cost-effective way in which a small independent retailer can be represented in a national large-scale medium such as a national daily newspaper, a major magazine title or national commercial radio.

WHEN SHOULD CO-OPERATIVE ADVERTISING BE USED?

Generally, the objectives of co-operative advertising include the creation of demand for a company's product and the creation of sales at both trade and consumer levels. In this sense, it could be looked on as merely a short-term tool. However, there are instances where co-operative advertising is viewed as contributing to longer-term strategic goals.

Crimmins (1985) highlights the potential of co-operative advertising to service both short-term and long-term objectives — see Table 11.1.

TABLE 11.1: THE OBJECTIVES OF CO-OPERATIVE ADVERTISING FOR A SUPPLIER

Time Horizon	Intended Audience	
	Consumer	Trade
Short Term	• Immediate Purchase • Establish Price and Location	• Sell in • General Influence • Competitive Parity
Long Term	• Brand Message Reminder and Reinforcement • Image	• Trade Relationship • Position in Merchandise Mix

Source: Crimmins, E. (1985): *A Management Guide to Co-op Advertising*, New York: Association of National Advertisers.

Co-operative advertising is an essential element in a "push" promotional strategy, where manufacturers rely heavily on marketing intermediaries to perform the promotional activities. Large household appliances and many types of clothing purchase involving a considerable ego-investment are examples of situations where in-store merchandising and personal selling are critical to a supplier's overall promotional campaign. Co-operative advertising can play a significant role in such retailer-dependent marketing situations involving relatively expensive, infrequently purchased goods, particularly where there is selective distribution. These are usually classic high-involvement purchase situations with some degree of information search and probing by the customer to reveal the hidden attributes of the various product offerings.

Co-operative advertising will have less relevance in manufacturer-dependent marketing of frequently-purchased consumer goods where there is broad distribution through self-service retailers operating on classic FMCG principles. There will be a strong impulse component in consumer behaviour leading to such purchases, and the objectives of manufacturer communication will be to build the brand franchise and put a strong "pull" on the channel. Awareness of the brand and knowledge of its features/benefits are developed largely through national campaigns by the manufacturer. The main objective of advertising is to ensure that the consumer will consider the brand when a purchase occasion subsequently arises.

When that occasion does arise, local advertising, of which co-operative advertising is an important part, may have a role in communicating where the product is available and at what price. This information may be important for certain categories of product in moving the customer to action/purchase.

CHANNEL CO-OPERATION AND CONFLICT

Stern and El Ansary (1992) provide a working definition of marketing channels and the functions they serve as the means by which goods pass from the manufacturer to the ultimate consumer:

> Marketing channels can be viewed as sets of interdependent organisations involved in the process of making a product available for use or consumption. Not only do marketing channels satisfy demand, by supplying goods at the right place, quantity, quality and price, but they also stimulate demand through promotional activities of the units (retailers, wholesalers, manufacturers) composing them (3).

Channel members achieve performance targets primarily by ensuring that their activities are consistent with the needs and wants of their ultimate target market. Achieving such consistency at one level of the marketing channel implies performance requirements and expectations at other levels which must be met by proactive performance on the part of intermediaries.

Retailers, for example, often measure a key aspect of their performance productivity in terms of sales per square foot, sales per employee, or sales per transaction. To enable a retailer to achieve, for instance, a high yield of sales per square foot, manufacturers may have to incur heavy advertising expenditures and wholesalers may well be required to maintain high inventory levels.

Corey (1976) viewed a distribution system and its functioning from the opposite perspective — that of the manufacturer/supplier who built it:

> A distribution system is a key external resource. Normally it takes years to build, and it is not easily changed. It ranks in importance with key internal resources such as manufacturing, research, engineering, field sales personnel and facilities. It represents a key external commitment to a large number of independent companies whose business is distribution — and to the particular markets they serve. It represents, as well, a commitment to a set of policies and practices that constitutes the basic fabric on which is woven an extensive set of long-term relationships (528).

In addition to these differing perspectives, it should be recognised that a given channel may involve varying levels of intermediate activity, and systems may differ in terms of the number of vertical levels, the width of each and the specific functions performed by individual players at these levels.

CHANNEL BEHAVIOUR

Given that the supplier, the intermediaries and the retailers are separate, autonomous entities who interact for the achievement of common goals, it is clear that channel members are, to a greater or lesser extent, interdependent. Each channel member is dependent on the others in that the supplier usually has no direct link with the marketplace and the wholesaler/distributor or retailer does not usually produce goods. At the simplest level, an electrical retailer ultimately depends on Philips or Sony, for instance, to design appliances that will meet consumer needs. In turn, these international manufacturers depend, in the final analysis, on retailers in fairly localised markets to interact with consumers, persuade them to buy particular models, and provide after-sale service — delivery and installation, for example.

It is central to the understanding of marketing channel structure that there is a recognition that channels consist of such interdependent institutions or agents. This interdependency stems from the fact that channel members rely on each other to perform the marketing flows and functions. Functional interdependence requires a minimum level of co-operation in order to accomplish the channel task. Common sense indicates that firms, channels and industries cannot develop and be competitive or efficient without a reasonable relationship existing between their members to facilitate flows along this value chain.

Physical possession, ownership and *promotion* are typically forward flows from producer to consumer. Each of these moves down the distribution channel — a manufacturing company promotes its product to a wholesaler, which in turn promotes it to the retailer and so on. On the other hand, the *negotiation, financing,* and *risking* flows move in both directions whereas *ordering, payment,* and *market information* are backward flows from retailers to suppliers.

It is crucial for manufacturers to gain the co-operation of intermediaries and retailers in implementing promotion campaigns. Wholesalers and retailers alike must undertake promotional activities on behalf of the manufacturer. Co-operative advertising is one such activity, and it requires the working co-operation of a number of parties. The extent to which manufacturers, wholesalers and retailers successfully mesh these promotional activities depends on several factors. The margins offered, the extent of competition that the product faces, the amount of promotional material and assistance the supplier provides and the individual player's own promotional objectives determine how well the promotion will be co-ordinated by the value chain partners.

Where such co-operation does exist, Stern and El-Ansary (1992) point out that the partners can develop means to co-ordinate their planning, information systems and decision-making, and can negotiate appropriate levels of reward so that each individual member can justify the joint goals on independent criteria.

CHANNEL CONFLICT

Co-operating to achieve channel goals sometimes means giving up individual ones. Therefore, a tendency towards conflict in marketing channels is virtually inevitable. Although channel members are dependent on one another, they often act alone in their own short-run best interest. They often disagree on the roles that each should play, and the rewards that any one player should receive for fulfilling a particular role. Most commentators agree that this is a result of the functional and operational interdependence between the players. Co-operative advertising involves a reversal of certain flows along the chain (e.g. payment) and, not surprisingly, creates a heightened risk of tension and *channel conflict*. Conflict is generally characterised as a state of tension between two or more parties, resulting in stress, frustration, and potentially dysfunctional behaviours (Gaski, 1984).

However, the fact that the channel has been established and maintained is evidence that the individual members are capable of co-operation. In the process of co-operation, agreement is reached on many issues. Mallen (1973) observed that there exists a dynamic field of conflicting and co-operating objectives between member firms of a channel. He recognised that both conflict and co-operation can exist simultaneously and relations can at the same time be both co-operative and conflicting. For example, firms may wish to co-operate to achieve their respective goals, but may be in conflict over the best means of doing so. This requires at least a minimum level of trust to be established whenever an individual freely chooses to co-operate, thus placing that individual's fate in the hands of others.

The management of conflict in channels of distribution continues to be a major theme in the marketing literature and the debate has been nurtured in recent years by new insights regarding the benefits of networking and the potential of the relationship-marketing focus to shape total marketing activity. Such management requires an understanding by channel members of the underlying causes of tension. Etgar (1979) has shown that differences in perceptions and goals, differences in expectations, lack of channel-role clarity, and competition over resources are important causes of conflict among channel members. All may well be present as background to a given co-operative advertising campaign.

Such conflict may have serious consequences. The history of co-operative advertising in the United States is one of conflict and litigation between the "co-operating" parties, and much of the academic literature in the area is concerned with such litigation. Frazier and Summers (1986) found that retailers tend to respond to manufacturers' coercive powers by more frequently resorting to legalistic means. Similarly, Dant and Schul (1992) have found that internal and informal conflict resolution measures are preferred to third-party intervention because failure at the formal third party stage "usually means subsequent litigation" (50).

They list five problems that recur in the management of co-operative advertising campaigns:

1) The sharing of costs and messages between two organisations often results in conflict regarding message content, and occasionally in disputes regarding reimbursement arrangements from the manufacturer to the retailer.

2) In co-operative advertising programmes, the flow of money is from supplier (manufacturer) to customer (retailer) — the reverse of the norm, but the supplier must continue to maintain the goodwill of the customer for the larger purposes of overall retail marketing.

3) Money flows to the retailer to influence merchandising support decisions but it is also intended ultimately to influence consumers through the running of advertising messages.

4) Since both sponsoring businesses present a marketing message, a more complicated information-processing challenge is presented to the recipient. Very little is known about how consumers differentially respond to such a dual-signature advertisement.

5) There exists very little by way of formal evaluation methods for assessing co-operative advertising effectiveness.

The Dual-Signature Problem

The fourth of the problem areas identified above is of particular interest, in that it raises a number of issues regarding the consumer's response to co-operative advertisements. As Young and Greyser (1983) have observed.

> ... a key element in assessing the effectiveness of co-operative advertising in terms of consumer behaviour is knowing which cue or combination of cues is more relevant to the consumer when he or she considers a purchase decision (5).

The literature reveals that with a better understanding of this issue, a manufacturer may be in a position to make a more intelligent choice when confronted with a trade-off decision between sole-sponsored (national) advertising and jointly-sponsored retail (co-operative) advertising. Furthermore, as there is a lack of a shared view on the relative importance of each sponsor, there is often conflict between the two parties regarding the prominence of the manufacturer's or retailer's name in such advertisements.

This source of conflict in co-operative advertising programmes comes down to the issue of whether one of the cues has more impact on the consumer or is more beneficial during the time of the final purchase decision. There is not a single noteworthy European study published on consumer response to dual signatures. A recent Irish unpublished study involving the purchase of consumer durables (Matthews, 1993) has found that the manufacturer's brand name was dominant in terms of advertising response by consumers. The study further indicated that in a pre-purchase situation the manufacturer's-brand component of the ad had a greater influence on the sale of the goods but the store signature was more important to consumers in the post-purchase stage, as retailer after-sales service was deemed to be much more important than the manufacturer's guarantee.

PROMOTION STRATEGY AND CHANNEL MANAGEMENT

Strategic decisions regarding the appropriate communication mix to be used within a given marketing channel will be shaped by the objectives to be achieved with the defined target audience. The promotional activities undertaken within the distribution channel are briefly examined in terms of broad strategic options.

A *pull strategy* involves the manufacturer advertising directly to the ultimate consumer. The objective is that the consumer will request the product from their retailer, and eventually, the manufacturer will receive orders from the channel intermediaries. In other situations, manufacturers promote their products and services to their intermediaries who in turn promote them to the ultimate consumer. This alternative promotional approach is termed a *push strategy*.

The manufacturer provides the resources for a co-operative advertising campaign in order to "push" a product with the retailer. In theory the manufacturer should be in control of the relationship, acting as an effective channel leader. The reality is the retailer may struggle to use those resources to put a "pull" on their own retail brand and given that the retailer is the party most likely to be specifying and placing the advertisement, the retailer too has a considerable potential for control. A field study was undertaken to understand how actual channel behaviour in Ireland may provide an understanding of the issues that may help toward a resolution of some of these inherent conflicts.

Field Study

In September/October 1993, an exploratory primary research investigation by the present authors examined issues arising from the participation of suppliers and retailers in co-operative advertising programmes. The retail sector chosen was "brown goods" electrical retailing (i.e. television/video/home entertainment) partly because of the evident commitment by the sector to this form of advertising and partly because of tensions which were evident in the sector and which pointed to a degree of unease in the relationship between suppliers and retailers.

The emerging tensions within the sector at that time included a deep uncertainty as to the intentions of the ESB in electrical retailing; a feared entry of Dunnes Stores into the market at retail level; the recent breakdown of exclusive dealership arrangements between suppliers and retailers; the emergence of parallel imports as a threat to distributors; a number of recent spectacular business failures with major liabilities accruing to distributors and wholesalers; aggressive price competition; and a deep uncertainty as to the kind of strategic responses major suppliers and major retailers were likely to make in the immediate future. (Industry overview derived from Trade Sources, notably various issues of the monthly *Irish Electrical Industry Review* 1989–93). To an objective observer it would appear that the Irish electrical industry was over-subscribed at both supplier and retailer levels.

Advertising practice in the industry has tended to focus on price-cutting and special offers, and it could justifiably be suggested that both pricing and advertising strategy decisions appear to be often made simultaneously. As a consequence, much advertising output is low on creativity, blatant in its appeal strategy and largely devoted to putting across price reductions and one-off "spectacular" promotions. Industry figures have referred in public to the "imaginary and dubious RRPs" in many of these advertisements, and the lack of integrity implicit in an approach focused on getting traffic through the store door where high-pressure switch-selling might then be exercised. This price-led promotional activity has allegedly created a cut-price image for the entire consumer electronics industry, to the detriment of all.

The present study involved interviews with seven manufacturers/ importers (hereafter referred to as "suppliers") of brown goods and 25 retailers throughout Ireland. In total, there are 11 manufacturers with major brands in the Irish market. Eight of these were selected as representing the vast bulk of sales in Ireland. The supplier responses achieved represented all but one of these eight major players in the industry.

The retailers interviewed varied in type and included warehouse operators, specialists, department stores and a number of multiples. Individual firms operated in channels with quite different numbers of levels, but in all cases co-operative advertising allowances were available and the retailer had independent contact with the manufacturer's salesforce even where stock came through an intermediary. The study was thus only concerned with primary suppliers (manufacturers or their importers) on the one hand, and retailers on the other.

Findings

It emerged that substantial funds were allocated by suppliers (i.e. manufacturers/importers) for co-operative advertising activity, with one supplier providing well in excess of IR£500,000, four others IR£200,000–IR£499,000 and the remaining two providing over IR£100,000 for their retail partners in 1993. The proportion of the supplier's total advertising spend devoted to co-operative advertising varied, but in all cases this element represented a very significant part, and in a number of instances it represented over 80 per cent, of the total advertising budget of the supplier. In the case of one supplier (heavily dependent on a particular retail chain) the retailer's demands for a heavy co-operative advertising allowance — negotiated as part of the total terms of trade — absorbed almost all of the total advertising discretion of the supplier.

As might be anticipated, significant levels of allowance were directed to nine of the largest retailers — i.e., those with IR£1 million + turnover, and two of the retailers with a IR£400,000 turnover. One respondent was receiving over IR£100,000 a year, largely from a single supplier, with this being matched by a similar amount from his own resources. At the other end of the scale, what can only be regarded as gestural donations of IR£5,000 or less (four cases) and IR£1,000 or less (four cases) were made to the smaller retailers.

The reasons stated by retailers for participating in co-op programmes are detailed in Table 11.2 below. Nine possible reasons were offered to the retailer and they were asked to rank them in order of importance. All respondents had participated in co-operative activity in the previous 12 months.

TABLE 11.2: RETAILERS' REASONS FOR PARTICIPATING IN CO-OPERATIVE PROGRAMME

	Importance Ranking								
	Very Important							Not Important	
Reasons	1	2	3	4	5	6	7	8	9
Build Sales for Our Most Profitable Product	7	2	0	6	4	0	4	2	0
Meet Competitors' Efforts	0	0	1	5	4	6	7	1	1
Launch a New Product	1	4	4	6	2	5	1	2	0
Accede to Requests of Manufacturers	0	0	1	0	0	1	0	5	18
Build Sales in a Particular Region	2	1	6	2	3	4	3	4	0
Build Sales for Weaker Products or Lines	0	0	1	3	2	5	4	6	4
Even-out Peaks and Valleys of Demand	0	2	4	2	5	3	3	4	2
To Link Our Store with a Brand Image	6	9	5	1	1	0	2	1	0
To Boost Overall Sales	9	7	3	0	4	1	1	0	0
TOTAL	25	25	25	25	25	25	25	25	25

It is notable that the somewhat generalised reason of "Boosting Overall Sales" was ranked number 1 by nine retailers, with a further seven ranking it as number 2. In all, a total of 76 per cent of respondents gave this reason a first-, second- or third-place ranking. A greater degree of selectivity was evidenced by the strength of the preference expressed for "Build Sales for Our Most Profitable Product" with a total of nine first and second preferences. The only other significant rankings related to "Linking Our Store with a Brand Image" (probing suggested that this arose because of additional bonus allowances being made available from time to time to support a supplier's national brand campaigns) and "Launch a New Product" (probing again suggested a very similar rationale).

Particular attention in the analysis was paid to the category "Accede to Requests of Manufacturers", where definitively low scores were recorded. Whether these represent a stance of rugged independence by retailers or something closer to bloody-mindedness may be debatable. What is significant is that the 16 large retailers all placed this reason in either eighth or ninth place in the ranking. For them, such a request would clearly be treated with cool detachment, without any concession to possible loyalty or goodwill. The distribution of small retailer responses on this issue was somewhat wider, indicating perhaps a more tractable or more dependent population.

A parallel question was posed to the seven supplier respondents and the results are detailed in Table 11.3 below.

The suppliers responses counterpointed those of the retailers. Undifferentiated sales growth was cited in first place by four of the seven respondents and in second place by a further two. Thus, 86 per cent of respondents gave it a first or second preference in their ranking of reasons for participating in co-operative advertising activity. An instrument that might be regarded as providing the potential to focus on specific targets or outcomes is clearly being used without regard to these options.

There were reasonably strong indications that the supplier wished to strengthen the link with a given store but this may be no more than nostalgia for some of the benefits of the now abandoned tied-store system, rather than a real strategic priority. "Launching a New Product" was given some small degree of priority as a reason for co-operative advertising activity and there was some degree of concession to "Requests by Retailers", but overall there is little evidence of strategic thinking in the reasons offered.

TABLE 11.3: SUPPLIERS' REASONS FOR UNDERTAKING
CO-OPERATIVE ADVERTISING

	Importance Ranking									
	Very Important							Not Important		
Reasons	1	2	3	4	5	6	7	8	9	10
Build Sale for Our Most Profitable Product	—	—	3	2	—	—	2	—	—	—
Meet Competitors' Efforts	—	—	—	—	1	1	4	1	—	—
Launch a New Product	—	4	—	—	2	1	—	—	—	—
Accede to Requests of Retailers	—	—	—	—	2	4	1	—	—	—
Build Sales in Particular Region	—	—	—	1	1	—	—	2	2	1
Build Sales for Weaker Products or Lines	—	—	—	—	—	—	1	3	1	2
Even out Peaks & Valleys of Demand	—	—	—	—	—	—	—	1	3	3
To Persuade Store Execs. to Stock & Merchandise Particular Goods	1	—	3	1	—	—	—	—	1	1
To Boost Overall Sales	4	2	—	1	—	—	—	—	—	1
To Link Our Brand with an Individual Store	2	1	1	1	1	1	—	—	—	—
TOTAL	7	7	7	7	7	7	7	7	7	7

It emerged that only 48 per cent of the retailers interviewed used all of their co-operative advertising allowance, though another 28 per cent used at least 75 per cent and, in all, 92 per cent used more than 50 per cent of it. Under-use is a phenomenon identified in previous research in the USA and is very much a feature of the smaller retailers' activities in Ireland. It usually results in the larger retailers being allowed to exceed their stated allowances and absorb any unspent budget. Qualitative probing established a number of problems on the part of the small retailer relative to the uptake of budgets. The major ones involved:

- Getting the distributor actually to state concretely what the available allowances were
- Having to pay for the advertisement up-front but often waiting months for reimbursement
- Using manufacturers' scripts that paid scant regard to the branding needs of retailers themselves whose stores are mentioned only once in the script but who are expected to pay up to 50 per cent of the costs.

Suppliers say that they offer the co-operative advertising allowance to all retailers, but some admit to encouraging participation of the larger retail accounts only. De facto, the suppliers are merely giving concrete expression to the Pareto principle (i.e., an 80/20 sales strategy), but one outcome is that the smaller, perhaps more hard-pressed, retailer is rendered less competitive on yet one more dimension.

It is also clear from their responses that suppliers view the co-operative advertising campaign as essentially a *trade promotion* tool, with the vast majority of them expressing this view. By way of contrast, 60 per cent of retailers naturally viewed it as essentially a *consumer promotion* tool. This represents a classic case of conflicting perspectives, with two actors sharing a 50–50 activity and budget, though each has a different perspective on what is primarily being sought. While the two objectives are potentially quite compatible, it is particularly notable that 90 per cent of the large retailers viewed co-operative advertising in the context of consumer promotion only, and did not consider relationship-building through servicing the needs of a trade partner as even a worthwhile subsidiary objective. The reality is that many of these larger retailers will exploit the co-operative advertising budget to generate store traffic but deliver little by way of preferential support on the shop floor for the brands of their channel partner who shares the cost of the co-operative advertising campaign.

Table 11.4 indicates a strong bias towards particular media in the application of co-operative advertising funds by Irish electrical retailers. This mirrors the general finding in the literature which demonstrates that much of the aggregate co-operative spend in the US and Britain goes to newspaper advertising. Newhall (1992) states that the figures for that year for the US showed 64 per cent of the spend going to newspapers with the remainder going to radio, television, outdoor and "increasingly to direct mail" (40).

TABLE 11.4: WHERE DO RETAILERS SPEND THEIR CO-OP FUNDS?

Media Vehicle	Frequency	Percentage of Retailers
Newspaper	23	92
Catalogue	17	68
Radio	13	52
TV	2	8
Magazine	5	20
Outdoor	4	16
Other	5	20

Table 11.4 demonstrates that almost all retailers use newspapers — including city evening papers and provincial papers — as the primary medium. Catalogues and radio represent the only other really significant options. The pattern is even more striking when the *actual percentage* of funds allocated to each medium is considered. Respondent comment revealed that 65 per cent of their actual co-operative advertising funds are spent on newspaper ads, with 14 per cent on radio and 12 per cent on catalogues. Television attracted a minuscule 2 per cent of the total spend, but it should be remembered that this medium is likely to be used for the suppliers' national branding campaigns, and the co-operative advertising budget therefore helps to fill out the suppliers' media presence across a range of media as well as localising that presence. Television production and placement is expensive and is clearly beyond the resources of many retailers. The lead times on production are clearly not suited to the very short cycle implied by the tactical nature of retailers' advertising messages, and many of the products require a degree of active information search more suited to print media.

Both sets of respondents were asked to rate the importance of co-operative advertising in relation to achieving overall advertising objectives. The results are presented in Table 11.5.

Retail respondents clearly attached major importance to co-operative campaigns in the context of achieving their total objectives. Seventy-six per cent of respondents rated the activity as either "important" or "extremely important", a particularly significant figure given the problems that smaller retailers encounter in taking up such a budget. The suppliers, on the other hand, take a broadly contrasting view, with less than 30 per cent of respondents attributing "importance" of any sort to the activity in the context of achieving overall advertising objectives.

TABLE 11.5: IMPORTANCE OF CO-OPERATIVE ADVERTISING IN RELATION TO ACHIEVING OVERALL ADVERTISING OBJECTIVES

Response Category	Scale Value	Distribution of Responses	
		Supplier	Retailer
Extremely Important	1	0.0%	48%
Important	2	28.5%	28%
Neither	3	28.5%	20%
Unimportant	4	42.8%	4%
Extremely Unimportant	5	0.0%	0%
TOTAL		100%	100%

This is in many ways a remarkable state of affairs, given the significant budget lines committed to the activity. The indication in earlier tables that suppliers do not take a strategic view of the potential of the activity would seem to be borne out. They may well have arrived at the conclusion that co-operative advertising budgets are little more than rebates which retailers have come to expect and will demand as a matter of course, and which they, as suppliers, have no option other than to pay if they are to maintain some stability in the relationship. This, however, implies lack of strategic input in the decision-making for co-operative advertising campaigns, and a dangerous lack of overall control of messages in a retail sector (i.e. brown goods) that is in serious need of strong leadership and clearly-defined consensual objectives.

CONCLUSION

Co-operative advertising represents the most significant involvement in marketing-communication activity by large sections of the retail and distributive sectors. It is of major importance to the Irish newspaper industry as a revenue source and its output is encountered on a daily basis by Irish consumers in their routine usage of media. The Matthews (1993) study pointed to the fact that these advertisements carry a distinctive manufacturer's signature in the eyes of the consumer. Given the poor quality of creativity often encountered in these advertisements, and the lack of subtlety in the appeals they adopt, there must be a worry as to their longer-term impact on brand perception. There is a strong case for the ultimate supplier to view the activity on a more strategic level and to seek to integrate these heavy-cost campaigns more fully into the company's total marketing-communication programme.

REFERENCES

Bucklin, L.J. (1973): "A Theory of Channel Control", *Journal of Marketing*, 37(1): 39–47.

Corey, R.E. (1988): "Industrial Marketing: Cases and Concepts" in Kotler, P., *Marketing Management*, 6th ed., Englewood Cliffs, NJ: Prentice Hall: 528.

Glover, D.R. (1991): "Distributors' Attitudes Toward Manufacturer Sponsored Promotions", *International Marketing Management*, 2: 241.

Crimmins, E. (1985): "Who Should Control Co-op: Customer vs. Supplier", *Sales and Marketing Management*, 13 May.

Crimmins, E. (1970): *A Management Guide to Co-op Advertising*, New York: Association of National Advertisers.

Dant, R.P. and Schul, P.L. (1992): "Conflict Resolution Processes in Contractual Channels of Distribution", *Journal of Marketing*, 56(1): 38–54.

Etgar, M. (1979): "Sources and Types of Intrachannel Conflict", *Journal of Retailing*, 55(1): 53–8.

Etgar, M. (1978): "Selection of an Effective Channel Control Mix", *Journal of Marketing*, 42, July: 53–8.

Frazier, G.L. and Sheth, J.W. (1985): "An Attitude Behaviour Framework for Distribution Channel Management", *Journal of Marketing*, 49, Summer: 39–47.

Frazier, G.L. and Summers, J.O. (1986): "Perceptions of Interfirm Power and Its Use within a Franchise Channel of Distribution", *Journal of Marketing Research*, 23: 169–176.

Gaski, J.F. (1984): "The Theory of Power and Conflict in Channels of Distribution", *Journal of Marketing*, 48, Summer: 9–29.

Haight, W. (1983): *Retail Advertising Management and Techniques*, Jersey City, NJ: General Learning Press: 195–210.

Lusch, R. (1979): "Erase Distribution Channels From Your Vocabulary and Add Marketing Channels", *Marketing News*, 27 July: 12.

Magrath, A.J. (1992): "The Death of Advertising Has Been Greatly Exaggerated", *Sales and Marketing Management*, February: 23–4.

Mallen, B.E. (1973): "Functional Spin-off: A Key to Anticipating Change in the Distribution Structure", *Journal of Marketing*, 37, 18–25.

Mathews, S. (1993): "A Study Investigating Consumer Response to the Dual Signature in Co-operative Advertising", (unpublished) B.Sc. dissertation, College of Marketing and Design, DIT.

Milsap, C.R. (1985): "Conquering the Distribution Incentive Blues", *Business Marketing*, November: 122–5.

Newhall, J.S. (1992): "The Care and Feeding of a Cash Cow", *Sales and Marketing Management*, May: 40–47.

Nicholls, J.A.F., Rolsow, S. and Laskey, H.A. (1993): "Perceptual and Behavioural Channel Conflict: Are They Related?", *International Review of Retail Distribution and Consumer Research*, 3(1): 19–33.

Stern, L. and El-Ansary, A.I. (1992): *Marketing Channels*, Englewood Cliffs, NJ: Prentice Hall: 3.

Vaile, R.S. (1989): "Marketing Flows in Channels", in Stern, L., El-Ansary, A. and Brown, J. (eds.), *Management in Marketing Channels*, Englewood Cliffs, NJ: Prentice Hall: 14.

Varadarajan, P.R. (1986): "Horizontal Co-op Sales Promotion: A Framework for Classification and Additional Perspectives", *Journal of Marketing*, 50, April: 61–73.

Young, R. and Greyser, S. (1983): *Managing Co-operative Advertising: A Strategic Approach*, Lexington, MA: Lexington Books.

12

The Regulatory Environment for Advertising in Ireland

Duncan Grehan

Like most service industries, all aspects of advertising are subject to regulation. This paper will examine the regulatory environment for advertising in Ireland. Initially it will specify the regulatory framework including the sources of regulation, the nature of the regulators and the objectives of regulation. It will then proceed to examine the actual regulation of advertising practices, with particular reference to misleading advertising and comparative advertising. The sanctions available for breaches of advertising regulations will then be outlined and the paper will conclude with a consideration of issues arising from a changing environment and changing media technology.

THE REGULATORY FRAMEWORK

The regulation of the various aspects of advertising is either voluntary or compulsory. The process is regulated voluntarily so that private interests are defined and protected and so that the industry itself is not discredited. The terms of the relationships between the advertiser and the advertiser's agent, the agent and its consultants, sub-contractors and employees also require definition. Issues such as ownership of the rights to the advertisement or the advertising campaign and any goodwill attaching to it will be privately agreed. These are examples of aspects of voluntary regulation. Private contract interests in most cases will reflect and be governed by codes of practice developed and accepted voluntarily by the industry. It is widely acknowledged that the standard of the advertisement must be acceptable not only to the advertiser and agent, but also to the advertiser's market, the industry and the general public. The codes of standards balance the private and public interest. They are subject to, rather than above, the law. Compliance with the law is mandatory, not optional. The primary concern of the legislature in providing a statutory regulatory framework is to protect the interest of the public at large and the consumer in particular, and the national legislature has, to an increasing degree, been assisted by an expanding volume of European Union legislation.

Sources of Regulation

Advertising is therefore subject to both public regulation and private regulation.

Public Regulation

The sources of public regulation are extensive. European Union Regulations or Directives will generally override any conflicting provisions within Irish law and can create direct effects and rights even though not yet implemented by specific Irish law. An example of this is the strict liability imposed on tour operators for publishing any misleading information, under the Council Directive on package travel for which there has been no implementing Irish legislation although the deadline was 31 December 1992 (Directive 90/314). The principles found in the Treaty of Rome of free movement of goods and services, free competition and the right to establishment impact on the advertising industry, its participants and owners, and give rise to a need for a uniform or harmonised regulation. The idea is that there will be a uniform regulation within the Union as consumer tastes converge and as products ignore geographic borders.

The Irish Constitution of 1937 as amended (Article 29.4.5) concedes the supremacy of Community legislation in the event of any conflict between legislation "necessitated" by Community membership, the Constitution and the provisions of Irish domestic legislation. The Constitution, too, is a fundamental source of public regulation and it will cause any Irish legislation that conflicts with the principles, rights and duties that it guarantees to be struck down as void. These include the freedom of speech and of expression. They also include certain personal rights of the individual referred to in its Article 40.13, which are not expressly listed or enumerated but which have been confirmed by the Irish courts. A protection for the advertiser may yet prove to be the so-called unenumerated personal right to communicate, which was identified in a court case in the early 1980s in which a courier company challenged the monopoly of An Post to the right to deliver all stamped letters (Attorney General

v. Paperlink Limited, 1984, ILRM 343). Of equal significance to the industry is the unenumerated personal right of the individual to privacy (Kennedy v. Ireland, 1987, IR 587).

The sources of statutory provisions regulating advertising are numerous and incoherent and require codification. The most important source today, however, is perhaps the Consumer Information Act, 1978. Specific Acts may make provision for the implementation of laws or the regulation of particular practices in sectoral industries by way of Ministerial Order. In the absence of express statutory provision, regulation is sourced in the common law and the rights and restrictions will be defined by way of precedent court decisions which the courts will follow in the absence of statutory precision.

Private Regulation

Advertising is also regulated privately. In many instances, the parties involved will agree terms of their relationships and enter into contracts. Since the early 1980s the industry has turned to self-regulation to ensure and introduce certainty of standards, to protect itself, and to avoid costly, and often unsatisfactory, public regulation. The usefulness of such self-regulation has been recognised by the legislature, which created the Office of the Director of Consumer Affairs under the Consumer Information Act, 1978. One of the Director's statutory duties is to encourage and promote the establishment and adoption of codes of advertising standards (s. 9(5)(f)). The Code of Advertising Standards for Ireland was first published in 1981 by the Advertising Standards Authority for Ireland (ASAI), which published a fourth edition of it in July 1995. The practice of self-regulation is now firmly established, the objective being to review the current Code in five years' time, and thereby keep pace with technological and social changes. It applies to all media, unlike the equivalent Code in the UK which is restricted to non-broadcast media. It also incorporates a Code of Sales Promotion Practice.

The ASAI is an umbrella organisation and its founders include the leading newspaper and magazine publishers, the principal outdoor advertising companies, the national television broadcaster RTE, and the professional organisations for both the advertisers and the agencies. The professional bodies of many other industry sectors, such as direct marketing, catalogue mail-order trading, telemarketing, and financial services advertising, have since published codes of practice which generally also require compliance with the ASAI Code (the terms of which shall prevail in any conflict).

The broadcasting industry also promotes self-regulation. RTE has its own Code of Standards for Broadcast Advertising, although the Independent Radio and Television Commission has yet to bring its draft Code further, in compliance with its ageing statutory obligation to publish one, for the purposes of regulating advertising on licensed radio stations and the single independent television station permitted by statute (should one ever be established).

The Regulators of Advertising

The question of who regulates advertising may also be best explained by referring to public regulators and private regulators.

Public Regulators

The Appendix to the ASAI Code lists numerous statutes and ministerial Orders (and the competent Government Departments) regulating advertising. Many of those Acts set up structures for the regulation of specialist aspects of advertising with which they are concerned. The most important public institution to have been set up for the purposes of regulating advertising in the public interest was the Office of the Director of Consumer Affairs. Under the Consumer Information Act, 1978 (s. 9(6)), the Director has wide powers to monitor advertising practices and standards, to prosecute injunction or other court proceedings, to enter and search premises, to require the production of books and documents and to require the provision of information and of copy documents. The functions of the Director are to keep advertising practices under general review, to examine such practices, to require that practices which are likely to be misleading to members of the public in a material manner be discontinued, to institute High Court proceedings for the purposes of securing Orders in support of this work, to educate the public in relation to consumer protection legislation regulating advertising and to take and prosecute proceedings in respect of any breaches of, and offences under, the Merchandise Marks Acts, 1887–1970 and under the Consumer Information Act, 1978.

The Ministers of Departments with responsibility for the operation of legislation affecting advertising may also have statutory duties as regulators. Any of the functions of examining advertising practices and appointing officers to investigate practices are also shared with the Director of Consumer Affairs by the competent Minister who can remove the Director from office "at any time" (s. 9(4)(a)). Under the

1978 Act, for example, the Minister has responsibility to make so-called *Marking Orders* (s. 10) (requiring the provision of information or instructions in respect of goods and the prohibition of the supply of those goods in default), *Advertising Orders* (s. 11) (by which the Minister may require advertisements to include or exclude any particular information that seems to be necessary or expedient in the interest of the person to whom the advertisements are directed) and *Definition Orders* (s. 12) (by which words in advertisements may be deemed to have a certain meaning).

Proceedings in relation to any offence under any of the above Acts may also be brought by the corporation or county council in the area where the offence is committed. In other cases, the police will have an essential role in ensuring a respect for advertising law. Thus, breaches of the Gaming and Lotteries Act, 1956, by the promoters of illegal sales promotions or lotteries, will involve a complaint to and an investigation by the police. The complaint may be filed by the promoter's competitors, who may have a remedy for exemplary damages on the grounds that their livelihood and constitutional rights are prejudiced by these illegal activities.

Consumers too have a central role in the regulation and observance of the law and can refer complaints to the police or to the Director of Consumer Affairs or they can personally bring High Court proceedings and obtain injunctions and damages if an advertisement is misleading, under the European Communities (Misleading Advertising) Regulations, 1988.

Private Regulators

All parties involved in the production and publication of an advertisement will, for reasons of self interest rather than public interest, insist on regulation. They will be concerned to protect their own interest and, as in all contract matters, provision will be made for the definition of rights and duties and for the consequences of breaches of those duties. The ASAI and its Code provide an umbrella framework of self-regulation. Players can look to the Code for guidance on standards and restrictions on advertising conduct. The ASAI Secretariat provides a pre-publication vetting service. It also receives complaints and evaluates them, and drafts recommendations to the Complaints Committee which will then consider the complaint and will hear or receive submissions from affected parties. The Committee, which is composed of representatives from both the industry and the Office of the Director of Consumer Affairs, will impose sanctions where complaints are upheld.

The ASAI role as regulator can extend beyond the geographical borders of Ireland. One of its stated roles within the European Advertising Standards Alliance to which the self-regulatory bodies of the EU member states and other European countries belong is to demonstrate that self-regulation systems operate in the interests of the industry and consumers within the whole European single market. The ASAI invites complaints about advertisements on media based outside Ireland.

While compliance with the ASAI Code is voluntary, it is a condition of membership of the ASAI. The Code provides for an advertising standard which it states goes beyond that standard which is required by the law. The Secretariat and Complaints Committee will not investigate or take any steps, however, once legal action is in hand or the matter has been referred to the Director of Consumer Affairs. The Code provides for the processing of intra-industry complaints and it should be noted that under the Code, responsibility for compliance with it rests with the advertiser, even where the advertiser has delegated this duty to an advertising agent. The advertiser may seek a remedy in the courts against the agent should the advertiser, as a result of breach of contract or breach of duty by the agent, suffer any loss (whether as a consequence of the institution of an ASAI investigation or otherwise) arising from the advertisement being in breach of the Code. However, the placing by the Code of primary responsibility on the advertiser to ensure that the advertisement is up to the Code's standard, is also mirrored in the law, which requires the advertiser to establish the truthfulness of any statement advertised (s. 20 Consumer Information Act, 1978).

The Objectives of Regulation

It is assumed that the legislative objective is to ensure standards of advertising practice consistent with the interests of the common good, a flexible notion on which Western civilisation and the rule of law is founded. The actual objective is not apparent from any lengthy preamble or recitals in any particular Act for which, unlike "European" legislation, there is no convention, but may be found by reference to the Dáil Debates or Hansard. In protecting these interests, the legislature for over 100 years has introduced regulation to prevent misleading, untruthful, inaccurate or deceptive advertising. In recent years, since the foundation of the ASAI and the publication of its

Code, the industry standard to which all ASAI members subscribe, and which is set out as the fundamental tenet of the Code, is that all advertisements should be legal, decent, honest and truthful, be prepared with a sense of responsibility both to the consumer and to society, and respect fair competition.

The Code defines an "advertisement" as "a paid-for communication addressed to the public or a section of it, the purpose being to influence the behaviour of those to whom it is addressed. It is characteristic of an advertisement that an advertiser pays a third party to communicate the message" (1.2 (a) ASAI Code). There is no similar convenient definition of an advertisement within the law, given its diverse sources. The interpretation section of the Consumer Information Act, 1978 explains that an "advertisement includes a catalogue, a circular and a price list". Its definition of a "trade description" is much more extensive and helpful. It explains that "goods" include ships, vehicles, aircraft, lands, things attached to lands and growing crops. Instead of regulating misleading advertisements as to price, it refers to misleading "indications" of prices. There is a case to be made, therefore, that the policy objectives of the public regulation of advertising have become obscured by the age, structure and language of the legislation, making it inaccessible to the industry and the consumer, and offering restrictive access to lawyers because of the many sources to which reference must be made. If the consumer interest and the common good are these public-policy objectives, then regulation should be in compliance with the trend set by the European Community Directive on unfair terms in consumer contracts. Such legislation "should be drafted in plain, intelligible language", (Council Directive 90/13/EEC recitals and Article 4.2) and should be more easily sourced. The fourth edition of the ASAI Code, July 1995, has gone a long way towards meeting this objective. The essential difference, however, between the Code and the law is that the Code need not be as accurate in relation to definition and objectives as the law, because the Code is intended merely as a guide for good advertising conduct. Compliance with its standards could not be assured in the absence of public regulation and sanctions. The objectives of public regulation are threatened when inadequacies, inconsistencies, loopholes or absence of policing and enforcement activity are apparent. The Director of Consumer Affair's function to promote a respect for and knowledge of public regulation must be understood in this difficult context.

REGULATION OF ADVERTISING PRACTICES

Advertising practices, schemes and devices can only be carried on without personal and commercial risk if they are within the regulatory framework. The ASAI Code concerns itself with substantiation, legality, taste and decency, sexism, stereotyping, honesty, truthfulness, psychological pressure, the use of superlatives and testimonials, the use of fear and distress, the safety of individuals, the use of guarantees, and generally the exploitation of children and disabled persons. The Code has specific sections dealing with health and beauty, slimming products, children, alcoholic drinks, the provision of financial services and products, distance-selling including mail order and direct response, advertising of employment and business opportunities, occasional trading, and also the making of environmental claims. These are all areas in which the need for regulation is recognisable. Indeed, these self-regulating voluntary provisions in the Code could be ineffective and unenforceable in particular as against non-members of the ASAI were they not supported by legislation rendering illegal advertising practices that are contrary to the common good or against the interest of the consumer, or anti-competitive or in conflict with public-policy objectives like the observance of constitutional norms. Public regulation is not only important for public objectives, but also to secure and ensure and render certain private objectives, bargains and requirements and property interests. If an advertiser feels that a competitor has damaged the advertiser's reputation or infringed the advertiser's property rights or is in breach of contract or is carrying on an illegal activity to the advertiser's prejudice, then rather than looking to the Code and the ASAI complaints structure, the advertiser may look to the law for a remedy, both in terms of injunctions and in terms of compensation for injury and loss, neither of which are available from the ASAI structures. The advertiser will see whether the competitor is in breach of contract, in breach of the laws of tort by being deceptive, defamatory or misleading, or whether the competitor is in breach of the statutory law by engaging, for example, in misleading or illegal comparative advertising practices. The regulation of these two latter types of practices illustrates the degree and quality of public support.

Misleading Advertising

The objective of the Merchandise Marks Acts, 1887–1970, as amended by the Consumer Information Act, 1978, is to ensure truth, honesty and accuracy in the advertising or description of goods and services, and to ensure conformity of those goods and services to their published or advertised descriptions. Section 8 of the 1978 Act prohibits a person from publishing, or causing to be published, an advertisement for the supply in the course of a trade business or profession of goods, services or facilities, if the advertisement "is likely to mislead, and thereby cause loss, damage or injury to members of the public to a material degree". A person in breach of this prohibition is guilty of an offence as is any trader or professional who knowingly or recklessly makes a false "statement" concerning any business or service or profession (s. 6), or provides a false or misleading "indication" of the price of any goods or services (s. 7).

Under the European Communities (Misleading Advertising) Regulations, 1988 Article 4 (1), anyone, including the Director of Consumer Affairs, may, on notice to the party against whom the Order is sought, apply to the High Court for, and at the Court's discretion be granted, "an Order prohibiting the publication or the further publication of advertising, the publication of which is misleading advertising". In the case of *O'Connor (Nenagh) Ltd. & Ors.* v. *Quinnsworth* (15 March 1993, High Court, Mr Justice Keane), the Plaintiff was granted an injunction restraining the Defendant from publishing any advertisement misleading or likely to mislead by referring inaccurately to the prices or other terms upon which the Plaintiff's grocery goods were offered for sale. The court found it necessary to examine, analyse and explain what was misleading advertising in considering the Misleading Advertising Regulations where no definition is directly found. The court said that such definition was in fact to be found within the EC Council Directive 84/450/EEC which explains:

> Misleading advertising means any advertising which in any way, including its presentation, deceives or is likely to deceive the persons to whom it is addressed or whom it reaches and which, by reason of its deceptive nature, is likely to affect economic behaviour or which, for those reasons, injures or is likely to injure a competitor.

It should be noted that the 1988 Regulations provide that the applicant to the court is not required to prove any actual loss or damage or recklessness or negligence on the part of the advertiser. They also provide that, with a view to eliminating the continuing effects of misleading advertising, the court may require the publication of its decision in full and the publication of a corrective statement. They place the burden on the advertiser to substantiate the advertisement and the court may require the advertiser to furnish evidence as to the accuracy of any factual claims, and the court may deem such factual claim to be inaccurate if it is of the opinion that the evidence is insufficient. Exercising its discretion, the court is required to take into account the interests of all involved and, in particular, the public interest.

This burden of proof on advertisers to substantiate the truthfulness of their statements is found similarly in the Consumer Information Act (s. 20), which, while creating statutory offences, also provides statutory defences (s. 22) such as mistake, or reliance upon information supplied by third parties, accident, or some cause beyond the Defendant's control, or that all reasonable precautions and all due diligence had been exercised. Such liberal defence grounds seriously undermine the effectiveness of the prohibitions and offences as deterrents to sub-standard and misleading advertising practices.

Comparative Advertising

The manner in which the practice of comparing products in advertisements is regulated is unsatisfactory from the point of view of both the practitioner and the consumer. In general, comparative advertising is legal, and this is the position that has been taken by the ASAI Code and the courts and the Director of Consumer Affairs. However, it is up to the advertiser to ensure that it is legal. This can be difficult because of the many areas of law that must be taken into account and because the comparison must not offend against subjective concepts such as "fairness" and "the common good", the meaning of which in the circumstances of any particular case only a judge ultimately can determine. The comparison must not be deceptive or inaccurate, misleading or untruthful. These are all matters that tend to be subjective. The ASAI Code will assist in the definition of these concepts. It provides (2.54):

> Advertisers should not exploit or make unfair use of the goodwill attached to the name, trademark, brand, slogan or advertising campaign of any other person.

It states (2.55): "An advertisement should not so closely resemble another as to be likely to mislead or cause confusion". It states (2.47) that "comparisons are permitted in the interests of public information and vigorous competition". It provides (2.48) that "the elements of comparison should not be unfairly selected in a way that gives the advertiser an artificial advantage". Any claim that a product is superior or superlative relative to another must be capable of substantiation "with market share data or similar proof" (2.49). It provides: "Advertisers should not unfairly attack or discredit other businesses or their products" (2.50). In relation, therefore, to what comparative advertising is legal, the Code provides a coherent and useful guide. The sourcing of the laws that determine whether or not a comparison is legal, is far more complex.

The Consumer Information Act, 1978 sets out the circumstances in which it is a crime to engage in misleading advertising or in false and misleading price advertising, or the provision recklessly or knowingly of false or misleading statements as to services. The comparison should take care, therefore, not to mislead. It should not be libellous or contain inaccurate statements injurious to reputation. Its comparison should not constitute a passing off. The effect of the advertisement should not lead the public to believe that the advertised product in fact is another's product, and any such advertisement should not infringe any copyright, trademark or other intellectual property rights.

Active promotion and advertising by the proprietor of its product on a particular market can result in a proprietary interest in the goodwill that has been thereby created, and which is capable of protection. This protection may have to be sought by way of the expensive and time-consuming High Court passing-off action, combined with injunction relief. Unscrupulous advertisers may exploit the inevitable delays in the legal system to engage in illegal comparative advertising practices for so long as they are not prohibited. The sanctions of the law may be weighed up with the commercial advantages to the infringing advertiser, which can hide behind limited companies and extra-territorial jurisdictions, and the imprecision or incoherence of the legislation restrictive of comparative advertising. A perfect example is section 12 of the Trademarks Act, 1963, which has restrained any wider use of comparative advertising than its now traditional use by the motor industry or multinational household sanitary companies. It restricts the use of competitors' own trademarks for comparative advertising purposes and states that "an advertiser can not use a mark identical to or so nearly resembling another's mark if it is likely to deceive or cause confusion or if its use is likely to be taken as another's own mark". The trademark owner therefore has considerable protection and this in itself is restrictive of comparative advertising.

These issues are of concern to the European Parliament, Commission and Council who are drafting legislation on comparative advertising and who are amending the existing Directive, referred to above, concerning misleading advertising. In the recitals of the latest text to this draft (94/C 136/04), these concerns are expressed in summary in this manner:

(a) Given that consumers can and must make the best possible use of the internal market, the use of comparative advertising must be authorised under certain very stringent conditions in all Member States since this will help demonstrate the merits of the various products within the relevant range.

(b) Under such conditions comparative advertising can stimulate competition between suppliers of goods and services to the consumer's advantage.

(c) The freedom to provide services relating to comparative advertising must be assured.

(d) Comparative advertising, when it compares details which are relevant, always verifiable and neither misleading nor unfair, may be a legitimate means of informing consumers to their ultimate advantage.

(e) Criteria must be established to determine which practices in relation to comparative advertising are unfair and therefore may distort competition, cause damage to competitors and have an adverse effect on consumer choice.

(f) In particular, to prevent comparative advertising being used in an unfair and anti-competitive manner, only comparisons between competing goods and services of the same nature should be allowed.

(g) Trademarks (as per Article 5 of Directive 89/104/EEC) confer exclusive rights on the proprietor of a registered trademark, including the right to prevent all third parties from using in the course of such trade, any sign which is identical with, or similar to the trademark in relation to the identical goods or services or even, where appropriate, other goods. But it may be indispensable, in order to make comparative advertising effective, to identify the goods or services of a competitor making reference to a trademark or tradename of which the latter is a proprietor.

(h) Such use of another's trademark or tradename does not breach this exclusive right in cases where it complies with the conditions laid down by this particular (draft) Directive, and does not capitalise on the reputation of another's trademark but is intended solely to distinguish between them and thus objectively highlight differences.

It can be seen that the issues and conflicting interests with which the European legislators are grappling provide sufficient notice to the practitioner proposing to engage in legal comparative advertising, that the law restricting such practices is complex and uncertain.

It is in this context, therefore, that the High Court, in considering the 1988 Misleading Advertising Regulations, referred to above in the case of *O'Connor* v. *Quinnsworth* which related to comparative shopping-basket prices in competing supermarkets, stated that advertisers are perfectly entitled to mount price comparison campaigns, using named competitors, provided that the advertisers ensure that the comparisons "are accurate, both in fairness to the competitor and in the public interest".

This leading judgment is the current guide as to what comparative advertising practices may be permissible and as to the meaning of the provisions within the ASAI Code, the Irish statutes and the European Community Directives on misleading advertising and comparative advertising.

SANCTIONS FOR BREACHES OF ADVERTISING REGULATIONS

An indication of the consequences of non-observance of the regulations is important if one is to understand the regulatory system. It is not proposed to describe in any detail the consequences of breaches of contract, of duty, of statutory duties and of the criminal law, other than to point out that compensation is a remedy in civil law which will generally be measured by the evidence of the degree of loss and the consequences of the breach submitted by the party seeking the remedy from the court. The court will also exercise its equitable jurisdiction in relation to breach of contract or breaches of tort, both on the issues of whether or not, on the balance of convenience and the merits of the case and the issues to be tried, any interlocutory Orders of Injunction or otherwise are to be made to preserve the status quo pending the substantive later hearing of the action by the court, and in deciding issues such as costs, which generally the unsuccessful party will be ordered to pay to the successful party. The effectiveness of civil remedies will be influenced by the efficiency of the administration of the courts and the resources available, and the skill and diligence of the administrators and lawyers involved. The effectiveness of the civil remedy will often also be determined by the degree of precision or definition of the right which it is claimed has been infringed. If these rights are defined in "plain and intelligible language", whether in contracts or statute or in the opinion of witnesses to verbal contracts, the prospect of any effective remedy will improve.

The effective prosecution, enforcement and execution of the public law regulations, whether by the Director of Consumer Affairs, the Director of Public Prosecutions or otherwise, ought generally not to be an issue of financial resources. The public authorities should have available to them all of the resources, in terms of skills and finances of the State. In reality, however, the offices of public law enforcement suffer from staff shortages.

Self-regulation, therefore, is often the more effective and cost-efficient method of protecting a right and pursuing a complaint. The ASAI Secretariat and the Complaints Committee will deal with complaints from the public, even though they are not members. The ASAI emphasise that self-regulation and investigation of breaches of the Code do not amount to law enforcement. They are effective, however, insofar as the Complaints Committee publishes monthly case reports in which complaints are summarised, the position of the parties to the complaint is set out and the Committee's "decision" is published. These reports are distributed to all public media in which they are subsequently often published. Equally, the Board may exercise disciplinary measures over its members, and it may, as a matter of contract law with its members, impose a fine on the member in breach, or suspend the member from the privileges of membership, or expel the member. In the third edition of the Code, 1989 (Paragraph 26.5), it is stated that where the member does not agree to amend or withdraw an infringing advertisement, the Authority can arrange for the withholding, by all member media, of space or time from that advertiser, the notification of consumer protection agencies and the withdrawal of trading privileges.

The ASAI has no judicial function and has no statutory basis. It is a voluntary organisation which has been granted authority by its members to control and penalise delinquent members. It has no control over the activities of non-members, although it would certainly pursue a complaint against a non-member and invite that non-member to answer the complaint and publish its finding in its monthly case report, notwithstanding non-membership.

On the other hand, many of the statutory or public law controls on advertising create offences with consequences of fines and criminal convictions. In the case of misleading advertising or false or mis-

TABLE 12.1: ASAI CASE REPORT SUMMARIES

New PMPA Insurance	Häagen-Dazs Bailey's (Young Advertising)	Bord Gáis	R. Twining and Company
Telecover Motor Insurance	Ice Cream	Natural Gas	Fruit Tea Infusions
Golden Pages	Bus Shelter Superlites	Magazine	On-pack Promotion
AC/935/5	AC/935/24+	CB/955/1	AC/954/15
Complaint: The advert said "just pick up the phone ... we take all details, fill out the form for you and give you a quote". The complainant was told he could not be given a quote, but would be sent a proposal form, as he was seeking insurance for the first time. However, this restriction had not been mentioned in the advert (CAS B.5).	**Complaint:** The poster showed an apparently naked man and woman in an embrace, with the headline "Try something new". It was felt to belittle women, trivialise sex and lower standards (CAS B.3, Addendum 11).	**Complaint:** A Glasgow reader objected to a claim that natural gas "protects our world" — it was felt that while gas might be slightly less bad than other forms of energy, it was misleading to claim it protected the world. (CAS B.5).	**Complaint:** When the complainant peeled back the sticker for a "try me free" promotion, she discovered that it was valid in the UK only. This she considered misleading (CSPP 4.10 & 5.9).
Response: In some circumstances staff may ask for more details or written confirmation. An incorrect reason may have been given in this case, but this did not distract from the principle or policy in the advert.	**Response:** Consumer research among ABC1s from 19 to 35 in the UK and Ireland had shown that only 19 per cent found it more explicit than previous Häagen-Dazs adverts, and that only 6 per cent were offended by it.	**Response:** Natural Gas had helped to reduce harmful emissions by reducing dependence on more damaging fuels. Bord Gáis also listed a range of other contributions they had made to the environment.	**Response:** The packs in question had ended up in Ireland through a distribution error. The advertisers apologised, and indicated they would honour any applications from Irish consumers.
Conclusion: Upheld — the offer to "give you a quote" was expressed in an unqualified manner. A qualification should be included in future, which the advertisers agreed to do.	**Conclusion:** The research referred to one age group, mostly in the UK, but the medium used meant that the advert reached a much wider public, which may not necessarily have felt the same way. It was clear that some found it offensive — as the campaign was over, no further action was necessary, but care should be exercised in future.	**Conclusion:** Upheld — unqualified claims like this were justifiable only if the product caused no harm to the environment.	**Conclusion:** Upheld — a customer should be able to take account of any factor likely to affect a decision on participating in a promotion before they are committed to purchase.

Source: *Deadline* (1995): "Keeping the Standard", 3, Summer: 30.

leading trade descriptions, the offences may be prosecuted by the Director of Consumer Affairs. A person guilty of an offence under the Merchandise Marks Acts, 1887–1970, and under the Consumer Information Act, 1978 shall (per s. 17 of the 1978 Act) be liable on summary conviction to a fine not exceeding IR£500 or, at the court's discretion, to imprisonment for a term not exceeding six months or to both fine and imprisonment or, on conviction on indictment, to a fine not exceeding IR£10,000 or, at the court's discretion, to imprisonment for a term not exceeding two years, or to both the fine and imprisonment. The court may take into account any advertisement published by, or on behalf of, the person convicted, correcting any misleading advertisement or false or misleading description, statement or indication. In certain circumstances, the fine may be paid over to any party who has been injured by the offending conduct. Where the offender is a limited company or an association of persons, and the offence has been committed with the consent, or is a result of the neglect on the part of any director or manager or secretary or committee member of that company or association, then that person shall also be guilty of the offence of which the company or association has been found to be guilty and shall be liable to be proceeded with and punished either by fine or imprisonment (s. 19). A person guilty of an offence under the European Communities (Misleading Advertising) Regulations, 1988 may be liable on summary conviction to a fine not exceeding IR£1,000.

The Director of Consumer Affairs can issue seize and desist directions to offending advertisers or their publishers and distributors or other agents, and can require the withdrawal of infringing advertisement or descriptive materials (s. 9(b)). Examples of industry sectors whose advertising activities have been regulated by the Director of Consumer Affairs in this way include groceries, supermarkets, milk and food producers, financial services, banking and loan facilities, and tour operators and travel agents. Under the Consumer Credit Act the Director's powers and functions are broadened to control and license money-lending and to police the proposed restrictions on consumer-finance advertising. Where the requests of the Director are not observed or complied with, or are circumvented or are not dealt with on time, the Director may seek the assistance of Court Orders. The speedy granting of injunctions to the Director in response to the statutory entitlement of with the office, will be facilitated by the courts. The entitlement of any person to make an application for an injunction under Article 4 of the 1988 Misleading Advertising

Regulations is a considerable remedy, as often the interlocutory proceedings will resolve the issues between the parties, and a substantive hearing may not subsequently be necessary.

REGULATION AND THE EVOLVING ENVIRONMENT FOR ADVERTISING

The Director of Consumer Affairs, William Fagan, when addressing a recent conference of members of the ASAI, Irish advertising agents, advertisers and the European Advertising Lawyers Association stated:

> Advertising is the oil in the wheels of trade and competition. As ... somebody who is involved on a day to day basis in the enforcement of laws relating to advertising, I am very conscious of the dichotomy between the need to enforce the law and the need to ensure that there is not excessive regulatory intervention in the free operation of the markets (Fagan, 1995).

It is the concern of the legislators and their law-enforcers to balance the stimulation of competition in the market, which free advertising can provide, and the freedom to provide advertising services and the other personal rights guaranteed by the Irish Constitution and the Treaty of Rome, with concepts such as fairness, order, the public interest and the common good. This presents constant definitional problems, not exclusive to advertising law, which introduce uncertainties into the law and into the questions of what advertising is lawful and what is illegal. These uncertainties add to the cost of those required to comply with the law, a cost which is ultimately passed down to the consumer.

A marketing practice that is commonly used to increase the sale of products and services is the sales-promotion competition. The public enjoy these competitions and they are good for business. The problem is, however, that most of them are probably illegal lotteries and are breaches of the criminal law, as they are not and cannot be licensed under the Gaming and Lotteries Act, 1956. On the other hand, very few promoters of such lotteries, or their printers, publishers, exhibitors or broadcasters, are prosecuted for breaching the criminal law, although the penalty for each and every offence of which they are found guilty is a fine of a maximum IR£100 and/or three months imprisonment (s. 44 of the 1956 Act). It remains the case that the enormous expense involved in the design, administration, operation and advertising of these competitions, is at risk.

Uncertainties in the law, non-observance of the law and failure to prosecute breaches of the law, will result in disrespect for the law and will create an unhealthy business environment. Steps have been taken by the legislature to introduce legislation, such as the Consumer Information Act, 1978, to keep pace with changing market requirements. Public Regulation is greatly assisted by the common policy concerns that are being worked through with the enormous resources available to the European Union. The Community-wide regulation of advertising practices creates a market in which the industry can thrive.

Regulations that fall behind on altering market requirements and social changes are damaging to the industry and may no longer be in the common good, if only because they lead to disrespect for the law, the law-makers and enforcers. The industry must always lobby for legislation that will accommodate a healthy industry, utilising an advertising technology already available, which disregards the jurisdiction of national courts, the powers of national law-enforcement agencies, and which operates in a free, unrestricted and unregulated supranational terrain. The legislators must examine and seek means to control and regulate in the common good extraterritorial broadcasting to the Community and Irish market, the publishing and free movement of information via electronics, computers, data banks and satellite, and the increasing domination and trend to monopolisation of media and advertising space by transnational corporations.

When these problems are considered, the problems of regulating the traditional advertising media in Ireland such as the newspapers and magazines, outdoor advertising, and advertising on radio and on the single television station, pales into insignificance. It is true that the English television stations have broadcast advertisements received in Ireland without being subject to Irish public regulation for years. They have, however, at all times been subject to UK public regulation, to self-regulation and to private regulation, and injured parties have had access to UK legal systems and courts with which they are familiar to restrain any infringement of their rights by such forms of advertisement.

The developing media such as the Internet and satellite, which are now being harnessed by the industry, appear to be unregulated and have complete freedom. Their regulation is in the industry's own interest and it seems likely that self-regulation will again be introduced by the new media owners and participants to whom the rationale that the rule of order is preferable must be clear. The task of regulating the new media may require a reform of existing institutions which currently lack competence to legislate and administer at the speed desired by the market.

REFERENCES

Fagan, W. (1995): Sales Promotion and Comparative Advertising Law, Seminar sponsored by the Association of Advertisers in Ireland and the Institute of Advertising Practitioners in Ireland, Dublin, 31 March.

13
Issues Facing Advertisers in Ireland

Elizabeth Reynolds
Fred Hayden

Today's commercial environment is highly competitive. Whatever niceties may be employed in describing its role, the primary function of advertising is ultimately to sell goods and services. The purpose of this paper is to identify and examine the main issues facing Irish advertisers, describing in turn their nature and possible solutions available for their resolution. In order to provide the necessary context, this paper seeks initially to explore the current state of the Irish advertising market and to profile the major Irish advertisers for whom these issues are particularly pertinent.

THE IRISH ADVERTISING MARKET

Advertising expenditure for all advertisers in the Republic of Ireland reached IR£223.8 million in 1994 (AAI, 1995), an increase of 36.6 per cent over 1990. This was significantly ahead of the Consumer Price Index (CPI), which increased by 10.1 per cent over the same period. Growth in advertising expenditure probably reflects a number of factors, including the general economic well-being, an increased marketing emphasis in our commercial culture, and the plethora of new media opportunities created by media fragmentation and the development of new media. Turning to the current state of media advertising in Ireland, advertising in the national newspapers dominated expenditure with 46 per cent of total media spend in 1994. The second most important medium used by advertisers was television, with 35 per cent of total 1994 advertising expenditure. These two media overshadowed other key media outlets with 12.5 per cent and 7 per cent of expenditure being directed at radio and outdoor respectively in 1994.

Cinema, the fastest growing medium, still represents only 1 per cent of total expenditure.

In order to provide the necessary context to understanding the concerns of Irish advertisers, it is necessary to profile the major advertisers in Ireland in terms of sector and scale of expenditure. The total advertising expenditure figure of £233.8 million for 1994, includes all Irish companies, both public and private. This clearly implies that the advertising budgets of Irish advertisers are very small. Indeed, no more than 40 Irish advertisers have media budgets in excess of £1 million (ASI, 1994). Table 13.1 shows the top ten advertisers in volume expenditure terms in Ireland in 1993.

TABLE 13.1: TOP TEN ADVERTISERS IN IRELAND, 1993

Rank	Advertiser	IR£ m Spend	% Share of Total National Advertising Expenditure
1.	Government Departments	10.1	4.9
2.	Guinness Group Sales	4.9	2.4
3.	Procter and Gamble	4.6	2.2
4.	Power City	4.5	2.2
5.	Kellogg	4.2	2.0
6.	Electricity Supply Board	4.0	1.9
7.	Lever Brothers	3.3	1.6
8.	Gunne Auctioneers	2.7	1.3
9.	Cadbury	2.6	1.3
10.	Showerings	2.2	1.1
	Total	43.1	20.9

Source: Advertising Statistics of Ireland (1994).

Table 13.1 highlights the domination of Irish advertising by global consumer-product manufacturers and state-controlled companies (namely, Government Departments and Electricity Supply Board). Only two companies on this list can be considered as private indigenous Irish firms — Power City and Gunne Auctioneers. Expenditure by the major Irish advertisers is spread across the range of different media. Table 13.2 reveals the preferred media choices of the top 20 advertisers in Ireland who utilise a mix of media, such as television, radio, press and outdoor. Companies such as Kellogg, Procter and Gamble, Lever Brothers and Coca-Cola are heavy television advertisers, while companies such as Gunne Auctioneers, Dunnes Stores and Power City rely heavily on press advertising. Inevitably, the selection of media by major advertisers is particularly determined by cost structures, the extent of market coverage afforded, and the nature of the advertising message.

TABLE 13.2: MEDIA SHARE OF SPEND BY THE TOP 20 ADVERTISING COMPANIES IN IRELAND, 1993 (%)

Rank	Advertiser	TV	Press	Radio	Other	Total
1	Government Departments	28	53	13	6	100
2	Guinness Group Sales	41	23	5	31	100
3	Procter & Gamble	97	1	1	1	100
4	Power City	4	91	3	2	100
5	Kellogg	95	2	2	1	100
6	Electricity Supply Board	20	67	10	3	100
7	Lever Brothers	91	3	2	4	100
8	Gunne	—	99	1	—	100
9	Cadbury	77	—	12	11	100
10	Showerings	50	6	9	35	100
11	P.J. Carroll	—	100	—	—	100
12	Coca-Cola	60	1	15	24	100
13	Sherry Fitzgerald	—	100	—	—	100
14	Gallaher	—	100	—	—	100
15	Bank of Ireland	21	58	13	8	100
16	McKennas	7	87	4	2	100
17	Mars	91	2	1	6	100
18	Dunnes Stores	1	80	18	1	100
19	Rowntree Macintosh	82	—	4	14	100
20	Elida Gibbs	71	12	14	3	100

Source: Advertising Statistics of Ireland (1994).

CRITICAL ISSUES FACING IRISH ADVERTISERS

Given the scale of expenditure and the range of media chosen, Irish advertisers operating in an increasingly turbulent communications environment are currently faced with a range of issues which impact on the efficiency of their business operations.

Production Costs

One of the primary concerns facing Irish advertisers is that of production costs. This is particularly true given the small advertising budgets generally available to Irish advertisers. Production costs can be defined as the total costs, both fixed and variable, that must be invested in order to generate advertising material for use in the relevant medium. The essential ingredients of production costs are broadly similar from market to market. For example, it will generally cost a similar amount to produce an advertisement for a market of 65 million people, as represented by the UK market, as for a market of 3.5 million, as represented by the Republic of Ireland. The key elements of producing a television advertisement — such as studio costs, staff costs and editing costs — are broadly similar in most developed markets. Client concern with this issue is reflected in the results of a recent survey conducted by the Marketing Development Programme at UCD, on behalf of the Association of Advertisers in Ireland (AAI/MDP, 1992), which showed that 84 per cent of respondents singled out the area of production costs as one requiring urgent attention. Concern with this issue is not limited to a market disadvantaged in terms of scale, such as Ireland. Indeed, a recent worldwide study, conducted by the World Federation of Advertisers (WFA) across 35 countries, revealed that advertising production costs were the single biggest issue identified by all global advertisers (WFA, 1992). The disadvantage to Irish advertisers of disproportionate production costs is reflected in the fact that production costs as a percentage of media expenditure are 20 per cent for Irish advertisers, compared with an estimated percentage figure for the UK market of 9–10 per cent, and for the US market of 4–5 per cent (WFA, 1992).

Production costs, which represent an important source of revenue for Irish advertising agencies, were valued at £36 million in 1992 (CSO, 1994), a sum equal to 20.5 per cent of total media expenditure in that year, as can be seen from Table 13.3.

Since peaking in 1988, production costs have decreased over the years to 1992. This may reflect the high level of media inflation over the period, but may also suggest some cost efficiencies derived from advances in colour reproduction, video technology, graphics, animation, as well as the development of more interactive and user-friendly desk-top packages. Indeed, the volume of production work, particularly in the area of television, may have been curtailed by the climate introduced by the Broadcasting Act, 1990. The reduced availability of television minutage, and the related uncertainty regarding placement, inevitably led to a reduction in production in this medium.

TABLE 13.3: PRODUCTION COSTS AS A PERCENTAGE OF
TOTAL MEDIA EXPENDITURE

Year	1987	1988	1989	1990	1991	1992
Production/Total Media Cost Ratio	21.9	23.9	22.2	22.8	21.1	20.5

Source: Central Statistics Office (1994): *Business of Advertising Agencies*, Dublin: Association of Advertisers in Ireland.

It can be argued that the high level of production costs for media advertising has been a primary motivation for the redirection of marketing-communications budgets to below-the-line opportunities where production costs have less relevance. In the area of television, the production costs necessary to produce advertising of a quality comparable with that available to non-indigenous Irish companies, has perhaps meant that, in some instances, Irish advertisers may have chosen to forego their preferred media option of television, rather than hinder the image of their brand with inferior-quality production values. Indeed, multinational brand advertisers adopting a global communications strategy not only have the benefit of allocating the costs of producing advertising across a wide number of markets, but can also select the most cost-efficient market in which to commission production work. On the other hand, indigenous Irish advertisers, unable to benefit from a multi-country allocation of costs, are almost entirely in the hands of local Irish agencies and other suppliers for advertising production.

The cost to produce material for advertisers is based on a fixed percentage mark-up (17.65 per cent) by advertising agencies based on third-party invoices. The control of high production costs incurred by Irish advertisers is therefore a central element in the client/agency relationship. Trust, transparency and client satisfaction with agency costings are absolutely essential to the maintenance of a good relationship. A recent study of UK advertisers (Taylor, 1994) has indicated that the level of costs is the second most important concern for UK advertisers in their dealings with agencies. Considering that production costs in the UK are 9–10 per cent of media costs, the scale of concern for Irish advertisers must be obvious in this market where the production cost/media-cost ratio is twice as high as that appertaining in the UK.

Media Research

The availability of high-quality information on the audience for particular media is a fundamental prerequisite for developing an efficient advertising strategy. This truism which applies to all markets, is particularly true in an Irish context where certain aspects of media research are currently a concern for Irish advertisers. These concerns with media research are each examined in turn.

The Provision of Data on Irish Media Only

In a market which is the recipient of considerable media overspill from its nearest neighbour — the UK, and increasingly through technological advances from more distant markets — the Irish advertiser is hampered in the selection of efficient media by the lack of available information on media which do not originate from within the Republic of Ireland. In some instances, these valuable data are in fact collected through established Irish media research programmes — however, they are not generally made available to Irish advertisers. The lack of this information, while encouraging the consumption of domestic Irish media, means that Irish advertisers and their agencies are forced to work without access to data on key aspects of media planning.

Looking Beyond the Statistics

Whilst profiles of media consumption are inevitably of value in developing and delivering efficient advertising, there is a need for fuller descriptions of consuming publics. The availability of media-consumption statistics cross-related to consumer lifestyles, purchasing patterns and other marketing-related behaviours would simplify the task of the advertiser. Part of the argument given for the non-availability of this information has been the scale of the Irish market and consequent economic viability of funding such research. Recently, however, Target Group Index (TGI), so long a part of UK research services, has launched its research product in the Republic of Ireland market. TGI provides ongoing research information, linking patterns of media consumption with consumer purchase behaviour on a level previously unavailable to Irish advertisers and their agencies.

Media Research — The Island of Ireland

A third limiting factor with current media-research programmes in Ireland is that while Irish advertisers are increasingly planning their marketing programmes on an all-Ireland basis, media research is not available to support this developing practice. In order to facilitate this development, media research data needs to be comparable, consistent and standardised across the markets on both sides of the border. Such data need to be collected and presented for similar time-frames and in comparable formats. To date there has been little attempt to fuse media information, separately collected but similar in nature, into a coherent whole, which would enable the Irish advertiser to target the entire market of Ireland more efficiently.

Media Research — Who Pays?

Considerable sums of money are invested in media research in Ireland each year. Such research is undertaken in the Irish market by media owners, advertising agencies and Irish advertisers through their representative body, the Association of Advertisers in Ireland (AAI). The practice whereby media owners, agencies and advertisers together fund media research is not generally found in many other developed economies. The practice in many foreign markets is that media research is made available to advertisers as buyers of media time and space without their having to part-fund the collection of this information. The belief among advertisers in these markets is that research information on media audiences and media consumption patterns is the responsibility of media owners who ultimately benefit financially from the sale of their media product to advertisers as buyers. There can be no doubt but that advertisers need accurate media data to inform choice and, in particular, to determine the appropriateness of one medium over another, or one media vehicle over another. Whether advertisers should pay for such information is a separate issue, but it is an issue which Irish advertisers have chosen to see differently from their advertising counterparts in foreign markets at this time.

Expanding Range of Media Opportunities

As is the case with all developed economies, advertisers in an Irish context now face an expanding range of media opportunities. This can be linked to two separate, yet linked, developments — media fragmentation and the development of new media. Media fragmentation is inevitably influenced by technological advance which facilitates the supply of media. However, media fragmentation also reflects changing consumer demand for sophisticated and specialised lifestyle affiliations. In television, Irish consumers now have available an increased range of domestically produced programmes, together with an opportunity to enjoy considerable overspill in this medium, largely from the UK market. The fragmentation of traditional media also exists in the press sector, being particularly evident in the sub-sector that is magazines, while local radio as a medium has considerably expanded under the auspices of the IRTC. The second major source of expanded media opportunities derives from the range of new media again largely driven by technological advance. These include ATM machines, Teletext, interactive games and, increasingly, the Internet. Overall, Irish Advertisers are now faced with an expanded array of media choices, with the inevitability of further complex expansion in the future. The expanding range of media opportunities has several consequences for Irish advertisers.

- Modern consumers informed about available media choices will seek out a range of media vehicles — programmes, magazines, etc. — to reflect their lifestyles and interests. The difficulties of attempting to target the increasingly "media erratic" consumer are obvious.

- The recency of some of these new media has meant that advertisers — and, by extension, agencies — are often forced to make media choices without recourse to adequate independent information about the profiles of the audience which these media command. This is a further cause of concern with media research as currently available in Ireland. While such information is likely to be forthcoming at some future point, the advertiser of today is forced to operate to a large extent in an information vacuum for many of these new media.

- Irish advertisers, while enjoying greater media choice, now also face greater complexity in decision-making and the reduced effectiveness of fixed promotional budgets now directed over a greater range of media in search of specified target markets. The diminished effectiveness of promotional budgets derives from shrinking audiences for traditional media and media vehicles within these media. This means that, in order to achieve similar reach, coverage and frequency targets, the Irish advertiser must buy a larger array of media than was hitherto necessary.

- Though not an issue for major Irish advertisers operating through an agency, the range of media opportunities presents a bewildering and complex array of possibilities for advertisers who must seek to execute their own advertising strategy without the assistance of an agency. This phenomenon is manifest in the range of Irish companies now seeking to advertise on the Internet without any basic information as to its audience, its profile etc., other than the often-quoted and under-evidenced statistic that 30 million people worldwide are linked to this medium.

- A further negative consequence of an expanding range of media opportunities is the seemingly endless number of messages which assault the consumer's senses. This clutter has led to traditional style advertising delivering diminished impact, with increased pressure, not only for creativity in advertising, but also for creativity in media utilisation by advertisers.

- One of the often ignored features of an increasingly technology-friendly society is that newer media, when universally available, will enable Irish consumers to witness, evaluate, order and ultimately to consume their preferred products from sources beyond this island. This inevitable consequence of the global technological village will, in effect, provide stiffer levels of foreign competition for Irish advertisers in their own home market.

The phenomenon of expanded media opportunities is by no means entirely negative from the perspective of the Irish advertiser. Indeed, it can deliver a number of specific benefits. One of these is the more accurate, and perhaps more cost-efficient, targeting of specialised markets — witness the availability of regional advertising to direct messages via local radio, and the ability to enjoy greater selectivity and consequently less wastage in targeting specialist consumer groups through lifestyle magazines and programmes.

Media Costs

Inflation in the cost of media represents a significant area of concern for Irish advertisers. Indeed, media costs in Ireland have continued to rise, with increases significantly higher than the consumer price index over the period 1990–94 as indicated in Table 13.4.

Advertising costs in Ireland have significantly outstripped those incurred by other European advertisers in recent years. The scale of media inflation in Ireland can be seen by reference to the data presented in Table 13.4 which show that for RTE television and radio, the cost of media has increased by several times that manifested by the consumer price index. It is commonly agreed in the case of RTE television and radio that these costs resulted from government intervention through the Broadcasting Act, 1990, which limited the availability of advertising air time. The deletion of the offending legislation is unlikely to restore media costs levels to their original position. While these comments specifically apply to RTE, it is a fact that media cost inflation in all other media, with the exception of cinema, has also outstripped the CPI increases over the period.

TABLE 13.4: FIVE-YEAR INDEX OF IRISH MEDIA COSTS, 1990-94

Year	Consumer Price Index*	RTE TV	RTE Radio 1	2FM	Cinema
1990	100.0	100	100	100	100
1991	103.6	132	108	109	95
1992	106.0	153	135	123	98
1993	107.6	153	129	129	96
1994	110.1	145	128	146	86
Year	Sundays	Mornings	Evenings	Regionals	Magazines
1990	100	100	100	100	100
1991	106	103	119	102	122
1992	109	111	132	126	118
1993	112	118	130	123	119
1994	118	122	142	128	122

* Annual Averages.
Source: CSO Annual Averages, McConnell's Media Facts, 1995.

Indeed, the cost of media buying in Ireland, particularly on television, is affected by two aspects of RTE's policy. Firstly, RTE has available a lesser number of minutes of advertising time to programme time per hour than that available in many European countries. The problem of restricted minutage is further exacerbated by the fact that RTE television generally broadcasts 12/13 hours per day, compared to UK channels such as UTV and Channel 4, which broadcast 24 hours and 20 hours respectively.

While the Broadcasting Act of 1988 made provision for the establishment of a third television channel, TV3, the reality is that continued overspill from UK channels into Ireland since 1988 may have eroded the potential market for a third television channel in the Republic of Ireland.

The Emergence of Media Monopolies in Ireland

The Irish media market is currently composed of a series of dominant and near-monopoly suppliers in many of the key media. From an advertiser's point of view the danger is that such powerful monopoly positions will be reflected in increased prices charged for media space and time. A number of such media positions can be identified. The first is that of RTE and its continued dominant position in the Irish market. Despite increased competition, it continues to dominate the domestic sector in Ireland. However, technological advances in the form of cable and MMDS relays, as well as satellite receivers, have served to increase competitive pressures on RTE's dominant position.

The recent collapse of the Irish Press Group has also helped to create an increasingly monopolistic position for Irish Independent Newspapers, which now holds 26 per cent share of all newspaper circulation in Ireland — which equates to 36 per cent of all indigenous Irish newspaper circulation. Indeed, one of the probable consequences, should the Irish Press titles not be relaunched, is the copperfastening of the Independent Group's domination of the Irish newspaper sector. In the women's magazine market, Smurfit Publications holds a 55 per cent share of all Irish-produced women's magazines. Similarly in the outdoor media, More O'Ferrall currently hold a 61 per cent share of the small-sheet (4- and 6-sheet) poster market, whilst David Allen commands a 62 per cent share of the large-sheet (48-, 64-and 96-sheet) volume market. Table 13.5 highlights the concentration of outdoor media in Ireland.

As stated, the danger of monopolies is that because of their powerful position, costs charged for media space and time will increase, thereby making advertising in these media prohibitively expensive for many advertisers. Overspill media have helped to negate this monopoly power position, in that the Irish media monopolies, with the exception of outdoor media, are now forced to compete with international competitors. However, the very existence of such concentrated power in the hands of a few major media monopolies, and the attendant price consequence, are a major concern for Irish advertisers.

TABLE 13.5: SITE NUMBERS OF IRISH OUTDOOR COMPANIES

Company	96/64-Sheet	48-Sheet	32-Sheet	24/16-Sheet	12-Sheet	6-Sheet	4-Sheet	Total
More O'Ferrall	9	372	4	—	11	1,682	614	2,690
David Allen	89	1,387	81	14	53	—	24	1,571
C.A.N.	17	361	9	36	125	148	325	1,013
Salespoint	—	—	—	—	—	—	648	648
Metro	2	—	—	—	27	149	180	532

Source: *Deadline*, Summer 1995, 3: 27–8; and AAI estimates, 1995.

Regulatory Issues

In 1995, over 80 Government Acts impinge directly or indirectly on advertisers, along with a further 14 codes laid down by professional bodies or the advertising industry. The requirement for compliance with an increasing battery of regulatory controls is now a concern for advertisers, as greater information, knowledge and attention are needed to comply with increasingly rigid and complex regulations regarding advertising issues as diverse as claims in advertising, the portrayal of individuals and groups, the timing of particular categories of advertising — for example, alcohol — and advertising directed at specific groups, such as children. While already complex, the situation will be compounded further as new media become regulated while traditional media may well be forced to comply with an increased battery of regulatory controls. The consequences in terms of time and the cost of recourse to legal advice is an inevitable concern for advertisers.

An example of specific concern for Irish advertisers is the Gaming and Lotteries Act, 1956. Under current law, any consumer promotion which involves "chance" is in conflict with the law. This means that promotions originating in countries where the law is more liberal may have a competitive edge over indigenous-originated promotions. Intensive lobbying by Irish advertisers is currently underway in order to amend the Gaming and Lotteries Act, 1956 to bring it into line with other European countries, particularly the UK.

Agency/Client Issues

The relationship between advertisers and their advertising agencies has changed from a "company-to-agency orientation" to a "multiple-brand-to-multiple-agency" focus. Furthermore, clients seeking value are increasingly turning to specialists, such as creative houses and media specialists, to perform specific tasks, and an increased sales orientation among client companies has led to a greater usage of sales promotion and direct marketing houses. The net effect is an increased number of client/agency interfaces requiring to be managed. In order to maximise the efficient management of these interfaces, the advertiser requires a substantial depth and breadth of knowledge in each specialist area.

Agency Pitching Fees

Agency requests for pitching fees have recently emerged as a new and contentious issue for advertisers. Advertising agencies seeking to display their capabilities when "pitching" for a new account believe that the advertiser as prospective client should underwrite part of the costs incurred in preparing the agency pitch. This is particularly true for creative pitches involving television, where considerable expenditure is likely to be involved in preparing the necessary materials. Where the agency is seeking a new client account, or where a client account is being reviewed, agencies believe that a fixed fee for preparing a pitch involving substantial creative preparatory work should be recompensed. However, advertisers are generally reluctant to pay pitching fees to agencies because of the production costs involved and the belief that such expenditure represents promotional expenditure by a seller seeking to secure added business.

On the other hand, it might be conceded that there are some reasonable economic grounds for agreeing to a contribution to costs incurred, in particular for expensive creative pitches at a final agency-selection stage. This would encourage advertisers to be more efficient and circumspect in their selection procedure. However, it can also be argued that stricter selection procedures could mitigate against smaller agencies or agencies without a strong creative record. It could be further argued that in order to avoid this cost, global advertisers may source international material in preference to costly Irish production material. While debate on this topic continues, it remains a contentious client/agency issue with little prospect of a mutually acceptable solution emerging in the short term.

Agency Remuneration

Agency remuneration in the form of commission payments and fees has been, and will remain, an issue of concern to advertisers. Value-seeking advertisers are becoming increasingly cost-conscious with regard to all advertising costs. This consciousness is reflected in emerging remuneration methods based on fee payments whereby the agency is paid based on results achieved rather than according to the traditional commission system. Indeed, client payments to agencies, in return for services provided, increasingly involve negotiations and agreements concerning issues such as rebates on bulk media buying by the agency and other volume discounts achieved. With more frequent reviews of agency performance, and client obsession with costs, the topic of agency remuneration and the cost of agency services is currently a particularly difficult issue in client/agency relationships.

SUMMARY

Advertisers in all world markets are currently facing a highly complex advertising environment. The consuming public is sophisticated, informed and increasingly marketing literate, making the task of persuasion more difficult. Technology, changing lifestyles and demographic patterns have led to a myriad of new and developing media, rendering the task of targeting consumers more complex. Indeed, the proliferation of media and messages has ensured that it is harder to make an impact, and harder still to make an impact that lasts. Better and more accurate information on media consumption patterns, audience profiles, purchasing behaviour and advertising effectiveness is required to ensure cost-effective advertising strategies. Furthermore, advertising today must take place in an increasingly regulated environment.

While these are issues that concern all advertisers, there are also additional issues for advertisers operating in an Irish context. These include limited advertising budgets, inadequate broadcast media availability, an inflationary cost structure in terms of production and media, and various regulatory anomalies. The problems for indigenous Irish companies advertising in an Irish context are exacerbated by the fact that they must compete with multinational companies using advertising materials generated for a global stage.

REFERENCES

Advertising Statistics of Ireland (1993): "The Top Sixty Advertisers in Ireland", Dublin.

Association of Advertisers in Ireland (1990): *Report on Advertisers Concerns and Priorities for the 1990's*, Research conducted by The Marketing Development Programme UCD, Dublin: Association of Advertisers in Ireland.

Association of Advertisers in Ireland (1992): *Report and Review*, Dublin: Association of Advertisers in Ireland.

Association of Advertisers in Ireland (1992): *A Report on an Investigation of Production Costs Incurred by Advertisers in Ireland*, Research conducted by the Marketing Development Programme UCD, Dublin: Association of Advertisers in Ireland.

Association of Advertisers in Ireland (1993): *Report and Review*, Dublin: Association of Advertisers in Ireland.

Association of Advertisers in Ireland (1994): *A Report on the Extent and Trends of Non-Media Advertising in Ireland*, Research conducted by the Marketing Development Programme UCD, Dublin: Association of Advertisers in Ireland.

Association of Advertisers in Ireland (1994): "Managing Advertising Production Costs Seminar", Association of Advertisers in Ireland, July, Dublin.

Association of Advertisers in Ireland (1994): "The Domestic Advertiser — Our Needs — Seminar", Association of Advertisers in Ireland, November, Dublin.

Audit Bureau of Circulation (1994): *Circulation Review*, Berkhamsted, UK.: Audit Bureau of Circulation Limited.

Central Statistics Office (1985–93): *Report on Advertising Agencies Business for 1985 to 1993*, Dublin: Central Statistics Office.

DKM Ltd. (1991): *Economic Aspects of the Broadcasting Act, 1990*, Dublin: DKM.

DKM Ltd. (1992): *Issues in the Irish Broadcasting Act*, Dublin: DKM.

Green, A. (1992): "Death of the Full Service Agency", *Admap*, 27(1): 21–4.

Harper, T. (1994): "Quantitative Research" in Lambkin, M. and Meenaghan, T. (eds.), *Perspectives on Marketing Management in Ireland*, Dublin: Oak Tree Press: 369–79.

Harper, T. (1994): "The Changeable Irish TV Audience", *Admap*, 29(4): 40–42.

Hayden, F., Director, Association of Advertisers in Ireland (AAI), (1995): Personal Discussion, August.

Henry, H. (1993): "How Production Costs have Outstripped Media Rates", *Admap*, 28(1): 8–15.

IAPI (Institute of Advertising Practitioners in Ireland) 1995: "Space Invaders: The International Challenge to Media in Ireland, A Threat or an Opportunity", Address at IAPI Media Conference, April, Dublin.

Irish TAM Establishment Surveys (1993): Dublin: AGB/TAM.

Irish TAM Establishment Surveys (1994): Dublin: AGB/TAM.

Joint National Listenership Research (1994): "Summary of Results — 1993/1994", Dublin: Lansdowne Market Research.

Joint National Readership Research: (1994): "Summary of Results — 1993/1994", Dublin: Market Research Bureau of Ireland.

MAPS Directory (1995): *Media, Advertising, Promotions and Sponsorship 1994–1995*, Dublin: MAC Publishing Ltd. in association with AAI Ltd..

Marketing Society of Ireland (1994): *Perspective*, June, 1(2): 1.

Marketing Society (1993): *Marketing Society Register of Marketing Research Organisations*, Dublin: Marketing Society.

Mintel (1993): *Special Report on Sponsorship*, London: Mintel.

Meenaghan, T. and Mannion, C. (1994): "The Changing Face of Marketing Communications" in Lambkin, M. and Meenaghan, T. (eds.) *Perspectives on Marketing Management in Ireland*, Dublin: Oak Tree Press: 221–40.

McConnell's (1991): *Media Facts 1991*, Dublin: McConnell's Advertising Service Limited.

McConnell's (1992): *Media Facts 1992*, Dublin: McConnell's Advertising Service Limited.

McConnell's (1993): *Media Facts 1993*, Dublin: McConnell's Advertising Service Limited.

McConnell's (1994): *Media Facts 1994*, Dublin: McConnell's Advertising Service Limited.

McConnell's (1995): *Media Facts 1995*, Dublin: McConnell's Advertising Service Limited.

O'Connell, S. (1995) "Competition Body 'Powerless' in Poster Firm Deal" *Sunday Business Post*, 2 July: 29.

Taylor, T. (1994): "Survey Results — The Campaign Report", *Campaign*, 25 September: 3–6.

Walsh G. (1995): "What the Competition Authority Cut Out", *Business and Finance*, 22 June: 32–4.

World Federation of Advertisers (1992): *World Federation Members — A Survey of Their Concerns*, New Delhi: World Advertising Federation.

Zenith Media World-wide (1992): *Television in Europe to the Year 2000*, London: Zenith.

14
From Exporting to Globalisation — Issues in International Communications

Frank Bradley
Eamonn Clarkin
Dympna M. Hughes

INTRODUCTION

Companies launching new products and brands in international markets face a major competitive disadvantage in comparison with large, successful brands already established there. The problem is particularly acute for companies in small and peripheral markets, such as Ireland, where household population is smaller than that of medium-sized cities in France, Germany or the UK.

> Strong international brands represent the cumulative outcome of a large and sustained marketing investment, often stretching back over 50 years or more (Lambkin, Meenaghan and O'Dwyer, 1994: 167).

Indeed, debate on the question of whether Irish firms can, or should, invest in brand development and communication often concludes that it is virtually an impossible task. An alternative practice currently adopted by many large Irish food processors is proving to be a more attainable option. These companies have become sub-suppliers, passing the responsibility for branding to the custodian of the brand who has access to both financial and marketing power.

The question of whether to sub-supply or brand in the overall context of marketing communications, while generating considerable debate, has not yet been subjected to in-depth analysis or research.

The purpose of this paper is to initiate such an analysis by identifying the principal questions involved and by conducting a preliminary review of the evidence available internationally, while making particular reference to Ireland.

The paper is divided into three parts. In the first section, the options available to companies considering marketing their products abroad are outlined and the communication issues related to this process are discussed. In the second part, pertinent issues concerning international brands are reviewed in order to provide the context for a discussion of Irish products. The final section discusses the prerequisites for the successful transfer of products and the communication of their attributes abroad, and concludes by outlining some options for Irish firms which may help them to "leverage" their limited resources to communicate their product and services offerings effectively in international markets.

NATURE OF GLOBAL ADVERTSING

Terminology such as international, multinational, global and export, causes a certain amount of confusion when applied to advertising. Part of this ambiguity stems from the fact that many business firms operate wholly- or partly-owned subsidiaries in a variety of countries, through which they manufacture and market their products. Some concentrate primarily on exporting from either their home country or another manufacturing country; some conduct their marketing abroad through licensees or franchisees; while others engage in all these forms of marketing. Some people prefer the term "global" because many companies now employ global brand strategies. However, many of these companies have decentralised structures so that individual companies still retain considerable control over promotional activities in that country. In addition to the centralised control by advertisers, the increase in global brands has led to the centralisation of agencies. Multinational clients often favour the use of the same agency for the same brand in as many foreign markets as possible, leading to an increase in international media. However, not all markets are assigned equal levels of attention in terms of marketing communications (Hill and Shoa, 1994). All of these aspects, regardless of diversity, can be included under the rubric of "international" advertising because they involve the use of advertising in a foreign market. (Dunn et al., 1990).

Definition of International Advertising

International advertising can best be defined as the advertising activities of any profit or non-profit organisation in countries outside its home country (Dunn et al., 1990). It differs from domestic advertising in that it must communicate across additional communications barriers. International advertising also includes the growing international activities of advertising agencies, media, research firms, television production houses, and many other firms that serve the advertising industry in some way and also function internationally. What is now the International Advertising Association was until the 1950s the Export Advertising Association. This name-change places the debate surrounding the changes in advertising across countries in context. It recognises that advertising is becoming truly international — with much less advertising by exporters and much more advertising by advertisers, agencies and media operating in more than one country.

The Growth in Global Advertising

A review of the literature suggests a number of reasons for the growth in global advertising. Dunn et al. (1990) categorise them as follows:

1) The rise of the multinational corporation

2) Increase in global brands

3) Trade agreements between countries

4) Increased trade in goods and services

5) Worldwide improvement in living standards

6) Innovations in communications and transportation.

In regard to the first point, the rise of the multinational corporation has provided a stimulus for the growth of advertising, with this international advertising in turn crystallising the gains of these multinationals. Secondly, the increase in the number of global brands has also contributed to this development of international advertising. Thirdly, trade agreements between two or more nations tend to stimulate competition among the signatory nations, thus encouraging mass markets and an associated growth of advertising. The completion of the internal EU market illustrates this point. Fourthly, increased trade in goods and services has resulted in an increase in advertising to build demand. In this case, note the increased use of all forms of communications in developing countries in response to increased demand for goods and services resulting from rising incomes. Fifthly, worldwide improvements in living standards have increased the discretionary income of people around the world, which in turn feeds into advertising budgets. People throughout the world are beginning to insist on participation in the level of material well-being — once the exclusive prerogative of the West. Lastly, innovations in communication and transportation have facilitated the transmission of large amounts of data from overseas to head office. Such centrally controlled business firms represent major capital investments, and their success acts as a force to encourage other businesses to expand abroad.

Communications Options for the International Company

Innovative firms, having penetrated the domestic market, are often keen to exploit their business leads in foreign markets and translate these into sales and earning growth. Because the firm in international markets must deal with relatively high transaction costs, it is necessary to consider various ways of communicating aspects of the brand abroad. Initially, this may be achieved through exporting. As demand grows in foreign markets, the firm may increase its commitment progressively by moving through the spectrum of foreign sales subsidiaries, joint ventures or direct investments. In order to survive, however, it must continue to innovate. Hence the need to communicate effectively the winning attributes of its product or service offering. Firms internationalising through the use of a strong brand name must be aware, however, that continued investment is necessary to prevent the erosion of a brand over time.

In deciding on its options, the company engaging in international advertising usually considers three key factors: audience, budget and transferability of creativity. The first step involves an examination of the segments for the product or service in different markets. In this regard, it is noted that the profile of global products has increased because of similarities in viewing patterns across multiple markets (Martenson, 1987: 143). This means evaluating demographic profiles, interest groups, and business-to-business customers or trade buyers. As a consequence, regional factors may influence advertising decisions. Appeals which work in the north of England or in the north of Germany may not work in the southern parts of those countries.

These audience factors are more powerful discriminators than are national boundaries.

The second consideration facing Irish companies communicating brand attributes in foreign markets is the budget. In an ideal world, the budget is related to the task to be achieved, but rarely is the firm so free in its spending. Usually the company must determine what can be achieved at different expenditure levels for a given time period. The budget available suggests the type and mix of media and the penetration levels likely. The third consideration facing exporters refers to the difficulty of creating a successful international advertisement. Moving from one national market to another often means abandoning some accepted creative criteria in favour of new ones which are more comprehensible. There is also the need to emphasise visuals, which travel better than language — hence, the interest in standardising advertising. Visual appeals tend to be more successful as a standard ingredient of campaigns across multiple markets. At the same time, creative advertising must avoid the cultural traps associated with language, colour, humour, and the law likely to be encountered in national markets. It is difficult to discover universal appeals, but many successful companies have done so.

Internationalisation Options

The options facing indigenous Irish companies seeking to develop markets overseas for their products and services are restricted, therefore, and may be categorised under two broad headings — namely, sub-supply and brand development. The first such option is to sub-supply either primary or secondary processed products to an international marketing company which controls all responsibility for marketing and branding of the ultimate product abroad. This sub-supply option incurs limited marketing costs, and provides little or no control over the brand franchise in foreign markets. It is the route most commonly employed by Irish companies seeking markets overseas. Branding represents the other end of the spectrum when it comes to Irish businesses seeking to develop overseas markets. The ability to exploit this option tends to be a function of financial capability, investment and the ability to endure the vicissitudes of long-term competition.

Power over resources derives principally from size. Firms seek to grow to gain power and market dominance, while maintaining a balance between growth in resources and growth in demand. The four principal determinants of a firm's growth are market constraint, organisational objectives (Jain, 1989), managerial constraints and financial constraints. These manifest themselves both within — in the form of brand equity, type of product category, market size, market share and organisational skill — and externally, in the form of cultural differences, buyer-purchase motivations, national identity, and the competitive situation (Bradley, 1995: 30).

CONDITIONS FOR SUCCESSFUL COMMUNICATIONS STRATEGIES

Impact of Position in the Business System

An increasingly important topic in developing an approach to international markets is where and how to exploit the value-added in the business system (Carpano and Chrisman, 1995; Saimee and Roth, 1992). Successful firms continually make strategic decisions as to the appropriateness of allocating market resources to specific areas. Developing a successful international marketing strategy means optimising the product-market and the business-system resource allocation.

In seeking to achieve competitive advantage, management may try to identify those parts of the production process which contribute most to final product value for their selected customer segment, and concentrate on these. At the same time, they can explore the potential for providing more cheaply those elements of the product that cost the firm more to produce than their value to the customer. The potential for contracting out these activities to specialist sub-suppliers may be warranted. In these circumstances the international marketing strategy may involve careful resource allocation within the product-market and business systems. In turn, firms positioning themselves in different places on this trading spectrum require vastly different marketing-communication strategies.

Standardised and Differentiated Marketing Communications

Sociocultural distance as a barrier to internationalisation involves the notion of business distance which is multidimensional in nature. The various dimensions include not only the geographical distance and physical characteristics, but also economic and sociocultural differences. The greater the business distance and subsequent lesser information flow from the market, the fewer movements of products and people. This business distance has, to a certain extent, been diminished in recent years as a result of increased use of the media as a means of communication, and increased travel.

Consumer markets throughout the world are at different stages of development. It is recognised that a particular consumer market may be very advanced in one product area, but less advanced in others. The opposite may be the case in other markets. Two forces are, however, very influential in bringing about consolidation in some consumer markets: the pressure of convergence of consumer tastes and preferences, and the benefits to companies of brand building as a means of entering and competing in many international markets simultaneously (Levitt, 1983). The implications of product standardisation are best captured by one firm's definition of what it considers as an ideal Eurobrand:

> The same brand with the same packaging and the same price, the same copy strategy, the same creative and below the line promotion, with distribution in all European countries (Krum and Rau, 1993: 62).

This paper is concerned with the strategic role of marketing communications in assisting firms entering foreign markets successfully. In developing this aspect of their international marketing strategy, the firm must consider the value of a standardised approach or a differentiated approach. The extent to which a company standardises its approach will directly impact on its ability to open up opportunities for competitive advantage in primary and support activities of its value chain (Porter, 1986), "to rapidly enter foreign markets" and "to standardise its positioning strategies" (Carpano and Chrisman, 1995: 11–12). Although there is much evidence to support a standardised approach for some elements of the firm's marketing strategy, in many instances critical evaluation has focused on the principle rather than the execution of standardisation (Harris, 1994). Also the extent to which standardisation is practised will vary and it may be necessary to customise in a number of key areas to accord with specific market conditions.

> It is of little value for a firm to keep costs low by providing standardised products if they do not fit customers' needs or perceptions (Carpano and Chrisman, 1995: 12).

Standardised communications may also lack sufficient information to allow the buyer to make a choice. The larger the number of information cues (Resnik and Stern, 1977) — that is, messages that allow the buyer to discriminate among items to be purchased — contained in an advertisement, the more information is available (Mueller, 1991). Advertising which is not informative contains few such cues, but relies on slogans, pleasant scenery or humour as message content. While it may be easier to transfer slogans and the impact of attractive scenery across international markets, the difficulty arises in using information-laden advertising. Hence the interest among larger companies in standardising simple advertising messages. A standardised campaign based on a message of limited information content — for example, the association of Kerrygold butter with attractive green scenery or Harp Lager with Sally O'Brien's pretty face — may be successful. Messages containing a large number of information cues are likely to pose problems, however. It is usually very difficult in international markets to make product comparisons, because competitors are likely to be different from market to market. Similarly, a focus on a particular attribute may be meaningful in one market but not in another. The company faces a trade-off between standardisation and differentiation in advertising related to information content. High standardisation is associated with low information content, while low standardisation, or highly differentiated advertising across markets, permits high information content in the advertising. This trade-off is illustrated in Figure 14.1.

FIGURE 14.1: STANDARDISATION OF INFORMATION CONTENT TRADE-OFF IN INTERNATIONAL ADVERTISING

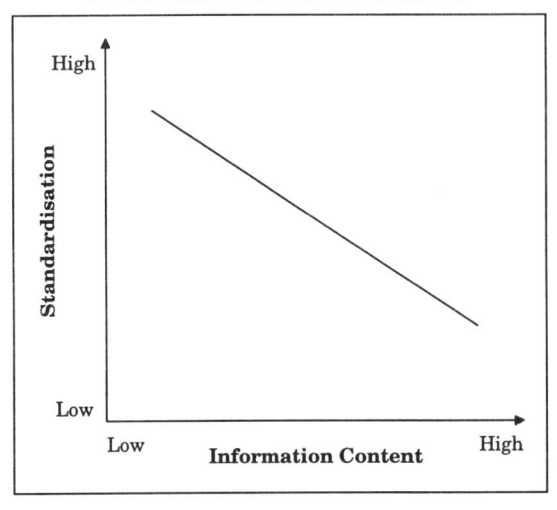

Although the trend is towards internationalisation, not all facets of the brand are equally open to standardisation across countries. Brand management refers to at least 18 specific areas of decision-making from brand-naming to advertising positioning. A 1992 Pan-European survey conducted by Eurocom/Kapferer of the 210 major brands reveals which facets are already global and which are purposely differentiated (Table 14.1). The underlying philosophy seems to be to "think global and act local" (Wind and Douglas, 1986), that is, "Think glocal". The car industry was found to represent a prototype of this behaviour, where the advertising global concept was the same but everything else — its creation and production — was different. The facets of brand management which were least globalised in the short term were variables such as direct-marketing and sales promotion. To what extent cross-cultural impediments have been the cause of this outcome has yet to be measured. At the other end of the spectrum,

TABLE 14.1 : GLOBALISING THE MARKETING MIX

Adaptations Most Frequently Made between Countries	Percentage
Sales Promotion	80
Relative Pricing	67
Direct Marketing	60
Media Mix	57
Advertising Execution	57
Below/Above-the-Line Ratio	50
Sponsoring	39
Packaging	36
Creative Idea	34
Distribution Channels	33
Brand Slogan	31
Brand Positioning/Promise	28
Product Features	28
Target Market	27
Brand Name	12
Brand Symbol and Emblem	10
Trademark/Logo	5

Base: 210 European Brands, 1992.
Note: Some numbers have been rounded.
Source: Adapted from Eurocom/Kapferer Pan-European Survey (1992).

globalisation is greatest for the logo, the symbolic character representing the brand (Kapferer, 1992). The strongest brands are those that experienced a maximum of tactical adaptations — they differentiate most of the direct-response facets of the marketing mix.

The successful outcome of these processes of convergence is dependent, to a large extent, on there being a high degree of cultural understanding and affinity between the partners. This affinity arises through communications between the parties involved. The international marketing aspect adds a new and complex dimension to the communications process. Successful buying and selling strategies are based on communicating the advantages of mutually beneficial marketing relationships.

INTERNATIONAL COMMUNICATIONS AMONG SELECTED IRISH COMPANIES

For most Irish companies international communications falls into one of six categories: export commodity trading, sub-supply, branded trade marketing, single-market brand, multi-market brand or global brand (Figure 14.2). The export commodity trader represents an extreme position on this continuum. This stage is epitomised by Goodman International which sells raw material abroad, with little or no value-added processing.

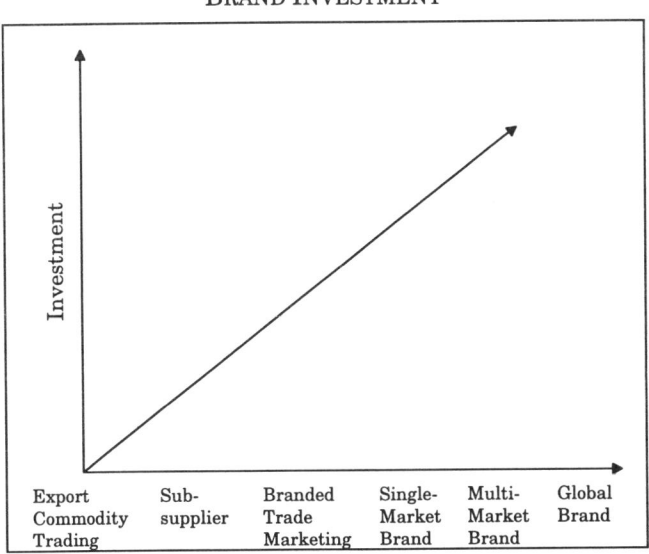

FIGURE 14.2: MODE OF INTERNATIONALISATION AND BRAND INVESTMENT

From Sub-Supply to Branded Trade Marketing

The next stage in this process is the "sub-supplier", who sells products under the customer's brand name. Kerry Foods has built its very significant US foods ingredients business in this way (Figure 14.2). Likewise, food manufacturers, such as the dairy companies, have substantial business as own-label suppliers to major UK and European supermarket chains. This route is favoured by many of those charged with improving the export performance of the Irish economy, precisely because it avoids the necessity for firms to incur the investment costs and risks associated with branding, many of which are related to the communications arena.

Where firms have chosen to adopt either of these routes, the role for formal communications is confined largely to trade marketing and customer relations, with the objective of consolidating trade-customer relationships. Most communications in this instance are conducted on a face-to-face basis, supported by trade advertising and direct marketing activity. However, when firms move beyond the sub-supply arena and begin to supply products bearing their own brand name in overseas markets, communications decisions become more complex.

The third point on the trading spectrum can be termed branded trade marketing (Figure 14.2). In this case, a company markets under its own brand name, using packaging, merchandising and point-of-purchase activity as the pillars of its programme of consumer communication. A high proportion of brand purchase decisions, particularly in low-involvement categories, are made at the point of sale. By way of illustration, Ballet Lingerie relies on brand trade marketing, and has carved out a premium, growing business, competing head to head with retail brands in Ireland and the UK. Irish Mist Liqueur was the subject of a worldwide re-launch in 1989, the focal point of which was the introduction of a new bottle and label design based on an ancient Celtic theme. Point-of-sale material, consumer and trade promotions, and limited, mainly duty-free, consumer advertising brought the new packaging to life.

In these cases, the communications objective is effective brand projection at the point of purchase. The key discipline is packaging design, both in physical and graphic terms. Many exporting companies, recognising the need to project a premium brand image, have turned to superior packaging as a cost-effective way of differentiating their brand. The success of this strategy depends on the competence of the firm, and its distributors, in merchandising, shelf-space management and retail promotional activity.

From Single Market Brand to Multi-Market Branding

The two most ambitious international brand-development strategies are distinguished by their breadth of operation — namely, single-market brand development and multi-market brand development. All brands in these categories set out to build brands with strong consumer franchises, with distinctive images and often tangible points of difference. In the case of Goodfellas Pizza, for example, a concerted effort is being made to establish the brand as a major consumer franchise in the UK market. This involves heavy consumer advertising and extensive promotional activity. Geographical concentration allows ambitious plans to be made without crippling expense. As a corollary, breadth of geographical operation, for most Irish companies, tends to mean more limited branding ambition, simply because of the organisational infrastructure and financial resources demanded by such a strategy (Figure 14.2).

Waterford Foods made Yoplait one of the success stories of the Irish grocery market. Franchising the brand from Sodema, a French company, Waterford Foods created a lucrative market overnight. So much so that, when it came to penetrating the UK market, the marketing and communications tasks were given to Waterford. A separate UK distribution arrangement was established by Waterford Foods, but within a relatively short period the franchise was transferred to Dairy Crest. Reasons for this change, cited by trade sources, revolved around market presence and "clout", Waterford's lack of heritage in the marketplace, and a lack of resources for promotional investment. In short, by opting for a very ambitious programme, aimed not merely at sales and distribution but also at the creation of a brand franchise, the company's lack of marketing infrastructure in an export context was cruelly exposed. Now, Waterford has successfully penetrated the UK market in its core product areas, notably milk and cheese. It has concentrated on trade marketing, and building sales through distribution advantage — for example, by acquiring dairies with doorstep-delivery networks (Figure 14.2).

The experience of Waterford Foods is not unique among Irish firms. Few companies, in the branded consumer goods arena at least, have made the leap from commodity production or sub-supply to genuine international brand marketing. Many Irish brands are made available abroad, but the majority are forced to be modest in their export ambitions, mainly because of financial constraints. The best illustration of this may be found in the "Irish Supermarket" in the centre of Moscow. Certainly any of the Irish brands available there (ranging from Galtee bacon rashers to Ballygowan spring water) can claim to be exporting to Russia, but they can hardly claim to be marketing their products there, given that the product and the packaging are identical to those produced for the Irish market, and there is no local promotional effort whatsoever.

BARRIERS TO IRISH GLOBAL BRANDS

While cognisant of the asset value delivered by strong brand franchise, many companies, particularly in Ireland, regard international brand building as a highly expensive exercise, difficult to quantify in tangible terms and better left to those multinational which can afford such intangible luxuries (Lambkin et al., 1994: 178–9).

Market Size and Cost of Marketing Communications

The explanation for the relatively under-developed state of Irish global consumer marketing may be found in the size and lack of competitiveness of the domestic market. Most Irish companies approach export marketing at a disadvantage, not merely in terms of local market knowledge, but also in terms of resource base and market experience. This influences their approach, and the relative priority attached to various elements of the marketing mix.

By way of contrast, well-known brands are supported by large investments in marketing communications, especially advertising budgets as can be seen from Table 14.2. Two points with respect to advertising expenditure of these well-known brands are informative in this regard. First, the figures quoted in Table 14.2 refer only to television advertising. They do not take into account all marketing communication expenditure. Secondly, the figure quoted for the No. 1 television advertised brand, Kellogg's, across the six key European markets was $208 million. This figure is approximately equal to two-thirds of the entire expenditure on all advertising on all media in Ireland for all products and services in the equivalent year (Lambkin et al., 1994: 181). The ability to exploit the branded route to internationalisation via heavy marketing communications expenditure is clearly a function of investment and financial capability.

Channels of Distribution

Distribution is the central variable as far as most export companies are concerned. A good distributor guarantees a critical mass of sales

TABLE 14.2: TELEVISION ADVERTISING EXPENDITURE FOR WELL-KNOWN BRANDS ACROSS MAJOR EUROPEAN MARKETS

Rank 1992	Brand	Product	Total $m	Germany $m	Spain $m	France $m	UK $m	Italy $m	Neth. $m
1	Kellogg	Breakfast Cereal	208	20	26	30	109	23	<1
2	Kinder	Confectionery	205	20	16	11	2	155	1
3	Renault	Cars	196	8	106	34	24	24	<1
4	Barilla	Baked Goods, Pasta	194	3	2	2	—	187	—
5	L'Oréal	Cosmetics	187	35	43	34	19	54	2
6	Fiat	Cars	186	7	25	4	7	142	1
7	Ariel	Detergent	181	35	59	19	47	15	6
8	Citroën	Cars	154	4	87	18	9	35	1
9	Ford	Cars	143	22	42	11	49	18	1
10	Peugeot	Cars	126	10	40	26	12	37	1
11	Opel	Cars	100	28	42	14	—	15	1
12	Danone	Dairy Products	95	7	54	20	3	11	<1
13	Dash	Detergents	89	9	19	8	—	52	1
14	Philips	Electronics	86	6	13	11	10	44	2
15	McDonald's	Fast Food	83	28	11	14	28	—	2
16	Nestlé	Confectionery	80	8	25	23	16	7	1
17	Coca-Cola	Soft Drinks	77	9	37	3	6	21	1
18	Persil**	Detergent	76	28	<1	3	43	—	2
19	Fairy	Dish Washing	76	20	76	20	14	—	—
20	Seat	Cars	76	2	42	3	1	28	<1

** Persil is marketed by Henkel in Germany, Spain and the Netherlands. Unilever markets Persil in the UK and France. A pan-European brand is defined as a product which is advertised on TV in three or more countries.

Source: Euromarketing (1993): "Top 100 Brands Boost Spend", in Euromarketing, 6(33).

quickly and ensures the viability of that market. Other tasks which become the jurisdiction of the distributor include resolving operational problems — that is, credit control — inventory management and organising promotional initiatives to the trade and customer. It is understandable then that, once having secured a good distributor and nurtured the relationship over time, Irish companies are loath to upset the status quo. In these cases, the distributor often takes total control of brand communications.

Short-Term Promotions

For a company in the "branded-trade marketing" mode, the approach to communications is very much a reactive one. The emphasis is on adapting material probably designed for use in the home market, and rarely is customised communication a feature of marketing support made available abroad. Most importantly, the issue of brand communication will come toward the bottom of the priority list, behind breadth of retail coverage, stock holding and trade promotion. Most of the activity takes place in promotions, since the entry cost is low, customers may be targeted efficiently, and the promotions can be produced and tailored locally at a relatively low cost. Often a salesperson will be pleasantly surprised to discover on their quarterly visit that such a promotion has taken place, that is until they are presented with a bill for a contribution to the cost!

The key communication issues for such a company, and they are many in the Irish context, is the provision of artwork for local adaptation, and the efficient channelling of successful ideas from market to market. The best the brand owner can generally do is to provide a common brand-communications theme, and a set of high quality photographic reproductions of products. In media terms, effort will often be focused on key points of sale, such as in-flight or duty-free magazines. This approach is particularly appropriate where brands sell in relatively small volumes across a large number of international markets. Cumulatively, this can deliver a big brand by Irish standards. Typical of this approach are brands such as Carolan's or Emmet's Cream Liqueurs, or indeed Irish Mist — all of which are highly successful international brands — without having to employ large-scale global consumer communication.

Impact of Market Focus

Conversely, brands with a heavy dependence on a particular market, such as Waterford Glass in the US or Murphy's Irish Stout in Britain, are often able to achieve ambitious brand-building programmes in those markets. Indeed, they may find themselves re-importing the positioning into the domestic market. Examples abound of brands using success in export markets as a selling point at home — for example, Jameson and Kerrygold Butter.

Irish brands grappling with international communications are the exception rather than the rule, therefore. Brands which have achieved the scale of operation and critical mass where a branded approach across a large number of export markets becomes a genuine choice include Bailey's Original Irish Cream Liqueur, Kerrygold, Bord Fáilte and An Bord Bia. Interestingly, with the notable exception of Bailey's, all the others represent cases where an umbrella brand is created to generate the breadth of international coverage and "critical" mass of sales necessary to justify and support an international communications effort. The key issues in such a campaign can be summarised as consisting of: communications objectives; brand positioning, implementation and management. A truly global approach demands common objectives, a single brand position and rigid control of implementation, centrally managed.

Impediments to Cultural Convergence and Market Homogenisation

The most successful exponents of the global approach to communications have been US companies. Having taken advantage of the near universality of aspects of US culture, and their domestic scale, many have chosen to generate a single brand image worldwide, created and nurtured by US agency networks. Levis, Mars, Coca-Cola and Marlboro are some notable examples of this approach in action. These brands, in turn, actively support the development of pan-national media with which to promote this single brand image.

Those in favour of a global approach argue that the essential elements of human nature apply across international boundaries, that the world's needs and desires have converged and have been irrevocably homogenised. Therefore, brands that encapsulate lifestyle positions, and the communications that bring these propositions to life, should travel effortlessly across borders, when suitable account is taken of linguistic and cultural differences. One basic advertising theme is seen to be desirable because similarities of product perception exist in different markets. One theme can promote the development of a consistent and universally recognised company image. The ultimate demonstration of faith in this approach is currently being carried out by US paper manufacturer Scotts, which is about to jettison Andrex, one of the UK's top ten brands in favour of the Scotts worldwide brand.

Opponents argue that international markets are fragmenting rather in the way that nation-states are disintegrating, particularly in Europe. They argue for a "Europe of the regions". They point to media fragmentation, to dwindling network television audiences, the increased use of the direct marketing and, most importantly, to the resurgence of local culture, dialect and nuance in many markets, as support for having different campaigns, which respond most effectively to cultural diversity.

The compromise view recognises local difference and cautions against the automatic use of standardisation. It holds that some degree of advertising uniformity is possible or even desirable. The challenge facing managers would appear to be to design global-marketing programmes that are based on meeting consumers' universal needs — foreign in image and local in usability, perhaps.

Country of Origin Effect

The experience of Irish brand-owners would seem to support the argument of a multi-local approach. Much of this has to do with the differing perceptions of what it means to be Irish across the developed world. The 44 million Americans who claim some Irish heritage represent a key audience for any Irish global brand, but their somewhat idealised perceptions of Ireland are far removed from the more realistic views of the British or French consumers. Bord Fáilte promotes Farmhouse Holidays to the new traditionalists of France and Italy, while offering ethnic tours to the Americans. Younger Europeans, in turn, see Ireland in a much more contemporary way. Dublin is now establishing a reputation as one of the fun capitals of Europe, where a vibrant pub and café scene combine to offer a superb entertainment experience for young people in particular.

While there is a fair degree of agreement in the major markets that Ireland possesses a rich, natural environment, a traditional way of life and friendly welcoming people, the relevance of these attributes varies dramatically from country to country. Kerrygold uses "die Grüne Insel" (the Green Island) imagery in the German market, where environmental concerns are paramount, and where an island "washed clean by Atlantic rain" is a worthy proposition. The platform in Britain and France is totally different, focusing much more on the product attributes than on the environment in which it is produced. A further example is Kerrygold Cheddar Cheese which is sold in north-western Europe on a theme of "lush pastures and free-range cows". In Greece, where Ireland's position as a dairying nation is almost subliminal, the appeal is straightforward brand awareness, with little or no product story.

In the UK lager market, product quality has tended to take a back seat to brand personality. Thus, while Harp was pursuing an Irish campaign emphasising its authenticity and product heritage, the UK ran a campaign entitled "Sharp Exit", which alluded only briefly to the brewing values that are so important in Ireland. Bord Bia has all but shied away from the idea of creating a "Food Ireland" brand for two main reasons — cost and difficulty in branding commodities such as meat and vegetables.

In all this, one brand — Bailey's Original Irish Cream Liqueur — stands out as an example of an Irish product that has matured into a genuine worldwide brand. As Bailey's has reached critical mass in markets throughout Europe and beyond, it has adopted a strict strategy in terms of protection of the brand integrity, as well as in terms of packaging and labelling, coupled with an increasingly integrated worldwide communications approach. But Bailey's is very much the exception. Ironically, international brands may be coming, through choice, to the stance on global branding which has been forced on Irish companies through circumstances, namely that the ideal scenario for international brands is to devise and implement multi-local communications plans.

The above analysis suggests that the companies, products and brands discussed may be placed on a continuum reflecting brand investment and level of internationalisation (Figure 14.3 below).

CONCLUSIONS

While core brand values do not vary from market to market, increased differences in consumer behaviour, market environment and media proliferation demand a flexibility which global campaigns cannot offer. If the days of the monolithic, one brand, one international advertising campaign are not quite over, there are signs that, for all but a small number of brands of genuine international scale and homogeneity, it is becoming ever less appropriate.

The implications for communications management are as follows: The communication objective should be to present a coherent brand image in each export market, in the way most appropriate for that market. Brand managers are likely to draw on the core value of the brand to create different positions in these different markets. Agencies are likely to be selected, less on their global strength and more on their ability to understand local market conditions. Implementation is likely to be on a multi-local basis, with local operations and distributors adapting international materials to the specific conditions facing them. Ongoing international communications management calls for flexibility and adaptability by protecting brand identity while preferably operating in multiple markets.

FIGURE 14.3: INTERNATIONALISATION AND BRAND INVESTMENT AMONG IRISH COMPANIES

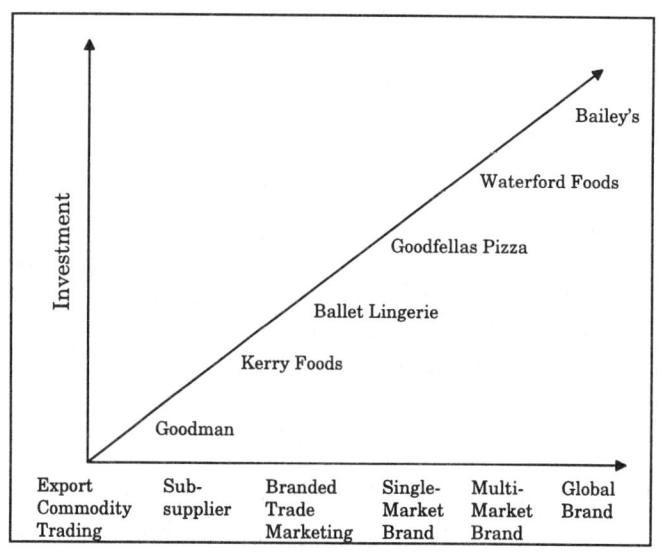

[Figure: Graph with Investment on y-axis and x-axis categories from left to right: Export Commodity Trading, Sub-supplier, Branded Trade Marketing, Single-Market Brand, Multi-Market Brand, Global Brand. Points plotted along an upward diagonal line: Goodman, Kerry Foods, Ballet Lingerie, Goodfellas Pizza, Waterford Foods, Bailey's.]

Realistically, because of the audience, budget and creativity factors discussed, few Irish companies have the option of building a global brand in the next decade. Most will ultimately decide between exporting to many markets, but with relatively limited ambitions, and creating lasting brand franchises in a more focused or differentiated way, addressing a limited number of key target markets. The choice made will have a critical impact on the role played by communications activity and in the nature of that activity.

REFERENCES

Bradley, F. (1995): *International Marketing Strategy*, 2nd Edition, Hemel Hempstead, UK: Prentice Hall.

Carpano, C. and Chrisman, J.J. (1995): "Performance Implications of International Product Strategies and the Integration of Marketing Activities", *Journal of International Marketing*, 3(1): 9–29.

Dunn, S.W., Barban, A.M., Krugman, D.M. and Reid, L.N., (1990): "Advertising — Its Role in Modern Marketing", 7th Edition, Orlando, FL: Dryden.

Euromarketing (1993): "Top 100 Brands Boost Spend 28%", 6(33).

Harris, G. (1994): "International Advertising Standardisation: What do the Multinationals Actually Standardise?", *Journal of International Marketing*, 2(4): 13–31.

Hill, J.S. and Shao, A.T. (1994): "Agency Participants in Multicountry Advertising: A Preliminary Examination of Affiliate Characteristics and Environments", *Journal of International Advertising*, 2(2): 29–39.

Jain, S.C. (1989): "Standardization of International Marketing Strategy: Some Research Hypotheses", *Journal of Marketing*, 53(1): 70–79.

Kapferer, J. (1992): *Strategic Brand Management — New Approaches to creating and Evaluating Brand Equity*, London: Kogan Page.

Krum, J.R. and Rau, P.A. (1993): "Organisational Responses of US Multinationals to EC — 1992: An Empirical Study", *Journal of International Marketing*, 2(2): 49–70.

Lambkin, M., Meenaghan, T., and O'Dwyer M.L. (1994): "International Brand Strategy : Its Relevance for Irish Marketing" in Lambkin, M. and Meenaghan, T. (eds.), *Perspectives on Marketing Management in Ireland*, Dublin, Oak Tree Press.

Levitt, T. (1983): "The Globalisation of Markets", *Harvard Business Review*, 83(3): 92–102.

Martenson, R. (1987): "Advertising Strategies and Information Content in American and Swedish Advertising", *International Journal of Advertising*, 6: 133–44.

Mueller, B. (1991): "An Analysis of Information Content in Standardised vs. Specialised Multinational Advertisements", *Journal of International Business Studies*, First Quarter: 23–39.

Porter, M.E., (1986): "The Strategic Role of International Marketing", *Journal of Consumer Marketing*, 3(2): 17–21.

Resnik, A. and Stern, B. (1977): "An Analysis of Information Content in Television Advertising" *Journal of Marketing*, January: 50–53.

Saimee, S. and Roth, K. (1992): "The Influence of Global Marketing Standardisation on Performance", *Journal of Marketing*, 56(2): 1–17.

Wind, Y. and Douglas, S.P. (1986): "The Myth of Globalisation", *Journal of Consumer Marketing*, 3(2): 23–6.

Part 3

Communication Strategy

15
Branding: Regaining the Initiative*

John Fanning

A product is something that is made in a factory, a brand is something that is bought by a consumer. A product can be copied by a competitor, a brand is unique. A product will be quickly outdated, a successful brand is timeless (Stephen King, *Developing New Brands*).

We have to do two things; push our top line growth through continuous innovation, and ensure our bottom line is enhanced by continuous attention to costs and capital efficiency (Neil Fitzgerald, Head of Detergent Division, Unilever).

We now see ourselves as the customer's manufacturing agent rather than the manufacturer's selling agent (Sainsbury).

A brand with a price advantage can simply undercut, a brand with a performance advantage can be outflanked by technological development, but a brand with an emotional difference can potentially command a premium forever (Don Cowley, *Understanding Brands*)

With technology eroding product differences and with the global mass media ever present, the era of branded marketing and the dominance of advertising is clearly over (Chiat Day).

The value of an established brand is in part due to the reality that it is more difficult to build brands today than it was only a few decades ago (David Aaker, Managing Brand Equity).

---

* This paper originally appeared in *Irish Marketing Review*, 1995, 8: pp. 21–31.

CHANGING BRAND FORTUNES

In 1988, Nestlé, the world's largest food manufacturer, paid £2.5 billion for Rowntree Mackintosh, a leading UK confectionery manufacturer. There was nothing remarkable about takeovers of this size at the end of a decade characterised by the triumph of free-market economics. In the same year, many similar deals were struck, including Philip Morris's $13 billion takeover of Kraft General Foods in the US and leveraged buyout specialists Kohlberg Kravis Roberts' $26 billion takeover of RJR Nabisco.

What was remarkable was the extraordinary premium prices paid in all these deals. Nestlé effectively paid five times the stock market value of Rowntree. The reasoning behind its decision was the power and reputation of the brands created and nurtured by Rowntree Mackintosh over the years, such as Kit-Kat, Polo, After Eight.

Business magazines around the world celebrated with features and articles on the power of branding, and the influential *Economist* magazine referred to 1988 as "the year of the brand". Within the space of five years the very same magazines were proclaiming "the death of the brand" and were running features and articles claiming the end of the long reign of the brand, with a new generation of consumers unwilling to pay a premium for manufacturer brands and settling instead for retailers' own brands. It would be too easy to dismiss this turnabout as another example of journalistic hyperbole, although there is undoubtedly some truth in this. The purpose of this article is to examine how such a dramatic change in the fortunes of brands took place between 1988 and 1993.

THE BRAND IN PERSPECTIVE
A Brief History of Branding

Although the word "brand" originated in Europe in the Middle Ages as a distinguishing mark or "burn" on craft products to distinguish one craftsman from another, modern usage dates from the turn of this century and the beginning of mass manufacturing. At that time, the dominant force in the distribution sector was the wholesaler, whose power base was a result of his ability to extract solid margins from weak manufacturers who had no direct access to consumers, and widely scattered small retailers with no bargaining power. A fortuitous coincidence of a number of key manufacturers who intrinsically understood the nature of brands, and the emergence of the mass media, tilted the balance of power. In 1881, Harley Procter, one of the founders of Procter and Gamble, ran the first ad for Ivory soap. Full of imagery and brand claims — "99.44 per cent pure" —the brand was an immediate success. Meanwhile in Britain, Sunlight soap was launched four years later by a company which ultimately evolved as Unilever. By establishing strong evocative brand names backed up by unique selling propositions, manufacturers eroded the power of wholesalers and became the dominant force in consumer markets for the next three-quarters of a century. However, in the mid-1960s and early 1970s the growing concentration of retailers changed the balance of power once again.

After the end of the Second World War, the emergence of retail power, which had been gathering force across Europe and the US, created the first "crisis in branding" during the early 1970s. The "crisis" was created mainly by retailers revelling in their new-found power and flexing their muscles in the form of belligerent demands to manufacturers for the "privilege" of obtaining shelf space. Manufacturers plundered their marketing and promotional budgets to cope with increasing demands for long-term agreements (LTAs), "hello" money and other forms of discount, with the result that brand franchise weakened and retailer demands became even more strident the next time round.

What is a Brand?

In recent years there have been almost as many different definitions as there are brands, an indication of the uncertainty and confusion which still surrounds the whole subject. One of the first was made in an article on the subject in 1955 in the *Harvard Business Review*:

> A brand name is more than a label employed to differentiate among the manufacturers of a product. It is a complex symbol that represents a variety of ideas and attributes. It tells the consumer many things, not only by the way it sounds (and its literal meaning, if it has one), but more important via the body of associations it has built up and acquired as a public object over a period of time. A net result is a public image, a character, or personality that may be more important for the overall status (and sales) of the brand than many technical facts about the product. (Gardner and Levy, 1955).

There is general agreement that, whereas a product consists only of the physical components that make up the sum of its parts, brands represent products plus a set of emotional associations which are built up over time in the minds of consumers through the brand name, packaging, advertising, PR, promotion and other methods of communication which are used to inform the public of its presence.

The addition of emotional values creates a complete personality, so that brands can often be perceived by consumers as real people. Although this aspect of branding is now much more clearly understood, there is still some confusion surrounding the roles that brands play in people's lives. This is partly because different brands play different roles, but also because the same brands can play different roles for consumers in different purchase or usage occasions. In general, brands are used by consumers to fulfil the following three functions:

- *Convenience*: Ease of decision-making — in many markets branding plays a low-level, but often crucial, role. Faced with a range of alternative products where some have had a degree of branding or added value from marketing communication and others have no provenance at all, consumers are not only likely to choose the brand which they have heard of but are likely to pay a little bit extra. Here the brand offers a solution to a familiar purchasing dilemma — how to decide between a variety of choices.

- *Guarantee*: Here branding operates at a slightly higher level of consciousness and offers a genuine bargain to consumers by a kind of unspoken guarantee — "as proof of the care and attention we took in making this product, we also took equal care and attention with the packaging, advertising and promotion". Consumers in many markets are forced into judging the book by the cover.

- *Personal Statement*: Branding operates at its highest level when the choosing of a particular brand in any market is also making a personal statement about the consumer. "Brands not only frame the environment in which I live but also enrobe me and by doing so help depict who I am".

The New Threat to Brands

Although it is too early to assess the full significance of anything that happened just two years ago, 2 April 1993 does appear to be a seminal date in the history of marketing. On that day one of the most famous and valuable brands in the world — Marlboro — was forced into the humiliating position of having to reduce prices by 20 per cent to cope with the growing threat from own-brand cigarettes. Over $13 billion was wiped off Philip Morris's stock market value. Leading fast-moving consumer goods companies also suffered significant reductions in market value:

> The fallout from Marlboro Friday spread far beyond the tobacco business triggering a worldwide slump in the shares of branded goods companies (Laurens and Alexander, 1994).

Marlboro Friday prompted a deluge of articles in newspapers, business magazines and academic business journals pronouncing the end of the line for brands, the end of an era of manufacturer dominance and the beginning of the rule of the retailer group. It would be easy to dismiss these reports as evidence of the growing "Murdochisation" of the business press — a search for the sensational at the expense of truth. The fact is that the vast majority of markets in all countries are still overwhelmingly dominated by manufacturer brands. However the decision by Philip Morris to reduce the price of Marlboro was not the only move from a leading manufacturer to combat the growing threat from retailer brands. During the same period, Procter and Gamble announced a major initiative across a range of brands to substitute what they referred to as "everyday low prices" for the myriad of individual promotions and coupon offers on different brands, which they claimed were confusing the consumer.

Obviously, some sea change in consumer behaviour was taking place. Various explanations were put forward. Manufacturers were too greedy and were overpricing their brands compared with the price of retailer brands. The quality of retailer brands was significantly improving. Mass-market advertising wasn't working as well as in the past because of the fragmentation of audiences. The materialistic, brand-flaunting consumer of the 1980s was giving way to the more discreet, caring consumer of the 1990s. Marketing departments and, in particular, brand managers, were often inept.

Like other changes in society, a single reason is rarely responsible but there is some truth in all of the reasons put forward. Essentially the crisis in branding can be attributed to one or a combination of three clusters of factors:

- The accelerating power of retailers and the growing sophistication of retailer brands

- Increased marketing literacy among consumers which weakened the power of traditional mass marketing techniques

- Weaknesses in the marketing departments of major companies.

THE NEW THREAT FROM RETAILERS
First Crisis in Early 1970s

The first crisis in branding during the early 1970s arose because the concentration of retailer power put pressure on the margins of manufacturers, who in turn raided their promotional budgets to buy-off this pressure. This meant that they had less funds to maintain the image of their brands in the minds of consumers. Soon manufacturers came to some kind of mutually acceptable relationship with the retail trade, and at the same time recognised the importance of maintaining the value of their brands by continuous dialogue with consumers. Retailer concentration continued, albeit at a much slower pace. With three to four retailers controlling anything between 40 per cent and 60 per cent of the grocery market in most developed countries, there were natural barriers to further growth:

- Monopolies Commission legislation

- The larger retail outlets could only operate with very large sites, thus ruling themselves out of less densely populated areas in any country.

- Smaller convenience retailers fought back by introducing a more focused product range and longer opening hours.

Therefore, to satisfy the voracious demands of the stock market (the majority of large European retailers are publicly-owned companies) and the equally voracious demands of executive compensation schemes for senior executives, the leading grocery retailers began to reassess their attitude towards own brands. Retailer own brands were traditionally regarded as cheap versions of the large manufacturer brands — usually of inferior quality and with poorly designed packaging which sometimes tried to reflect the colours and patterns of the brand leaders. Practice varied considerably among different retailers. In Ireland, Dunnes Stores, taking a cue from its highly successful drapery business, developed an extensive range of own brands under the St Bernard label. This range never attained a high-quality image, although the firm achieved substantial brand shares in some markets, mainly those where manufacturers were not supporting their brands. Neither of the other leading multiples, Quinnsworth or Superquinn, paid much attention to own brands.

In 1976 a leading French supermarket, Carrefour, introduced a different kind of retailer brand — "Produits Libres". The idea spread to the UK where it was referred to as generic own-brand when Fine

Fare introduced its Yellow Pack label. Generics were deliberately designed to appear even cheaper than retailer own brands, as evidenced by their most basic forms of packaging. Quinnsworth, a sister company of Fine Fare, introduced the Yellow Pack range in Ireland, while Superquinn introduced its own generic range — Thrift. Neither was particularly successful.

In the search for profits, many retailers then began to pay more attention to UK giants Marks & Spencer and Sainsbury — the two most consistently profitable UK retailers. Marks & Spencer not only pursued an exclusively own-brand policy under the St Michael label, but, instead of imitating manufacturer brands, often pursued its own product development programme. Sainsbury's own label had long been the most characteristic feature of its stores, accounting for over half of total sales, but unlike other retailers the quality of Sainsbury's own label often matched and sometimes surpassed that of manufacturer brands and its promotion and packaging were of a consistently high quality.

Second Crisis in Early 1990s

The second crisis of branding was partly a result of a combination of four parallel developments that occurred in the late 1980s and early 1990s. First, the price gap between manufacturer brands and retailer brands became too great. During the second half of the 1980s, some manufacturers, epitomising Gordon Gekko's epigram "greed is good", introduced regular price increases which took no account of the fact that inflation in most Western countries had been brought under control. Consumers, always closer to reality, did notice the widening gap between the price of manufacturer brands and retailer brands. Marlboro Friday was a direct result of this factor, with Marlboro selling at $2.10 a pack compared with discount brands as low as 69 cents. As a result, smokers' credulity was stretched to breaking point and premium sales started to slide.

Although one can never apply precise rules of thumb, it would appear that whenever manufacturer brand prices reach a 20–25 per cent gap over retailer brand prices, it tends to create a move towards retailer brands. In the Irish market for carbonated soft drinks, a gap of over 20 per cent emerged during the late 1980s — resulting in a significant increase in retailer brand share. Manufacturers reacted very quickly in this case to close the gap, and the situation was immediately reversed.

The second reason for the crisis was that retailer brands began to match manufacturer brands for quality. This trend was most notable in the UK, and it can be no coincidence that retailer brands have a higher share there than in other EU countries. Accompanying rising quality standards, retailers began to pay more attention to presentation and design. Sainsbury was again the most notable example but there are signs that other retailers are following suit. Consumers are far more attuned than many manufacturers assume to even small variations in quality.

Thirdly, retailers expanded their own brand range. The launch of Novon, Sainsbury's own-label washing powder, in 1991, was a particularly significant event in the history of retailer brands. There had always been a kind of unwritten acceptance that although certain markets were regarded by manufacturers as having been "lost" to retailers (paper products being the most notable example, with the exception of Andrex which has shown that even the most unpromising territory need not be abandoned prematurely to retailers), there are other market sectors where retail own brands would never be able to gain a foothold. Detergents would have fallen into this category — a market dominated by two of the world's most powerful and professional marketing companies, Unilever and Procter and Gamble. Both companies have a long history of brand management success, based on a combination of continuous technical innovation and superior brand management. However, Novon achieved an 8 per cent brand share within two years of launch. After that, nothing was sacred. "The last fence of the proprietary brands — perceived technical superiority — had been eroded" (Hazkins, 1994).

Fourthly, there was increasing manufacturer collaboration with retailers. Traditionally, most retailer brands were commissioned from often reluctant manufacturers. A number of manufacturers, most notably Kellogg, adamantly refused to go near own brands — "If it doesn't say Kellogg's on the box it isn't Kellogg's in the box". Kellogg now includes the following line on every single pack across the range — "We don't make cereals for anyone else".

One of the reasons why the perception of retailer brands' quality was poor was that consumers believed that they were either made by well-known manufacturers who "are not really trying" or by second-rate manufacturers of whom they had never heard. But technological advances in manufacturing have now made it possible to produce an equally high-quality alternative almost instantly:

> Make a better mouse trap and the possibility is that within a few weeks a cheaper version will appear next to yours having been

reverse engineered in Hong Kong and assembled in Guangded province (*The Economist*, 2 July 1994).

A new twist in the pressure on manufacturers occurred recently in the US when an obscure Canadian cola manufacturer, Cott, teamed up with a US also-ran, Royal Crown, to supply Cott with a higher quality concentrate. Up to then, Cott had sold cola in Canada without much success — hardly surprising given their slogan: "It's Cott to be good". With their higher-quality product, Cott introduced a new element into the development of retailer brands by creating different brands for different retailer groups.

- President's Choice — Loblaws
- President's Choice — D'Agostini
- Master's Choice — A & P
- Sam's American Choice — Wal-Mart.

In 1994, Cott appeared in Europe and caused consternation in the UK with a similar deal for Sainsbury's cola. Another complication was Cott's decision to design their own brand cola, making it look almost identical to Coca-Cola's packaging. This resulted in a series of high-profile court cases in the UK, followed by the House of Commons rejecting pleas from branded manufacturers to outlaw "lookalike" products. In response, leading brand manufacturers warned the UK government that they would reconsider investment plans unless curbs were put on supermarket lookalike products:

> The manufacturers are furious with the government decision not to amend the trademark bill to restrict the use of lookalikes. The warning was given by the British products and brand owners group in association with the major manufacturers. It was later reported that Sainsbury were changing the label of their lookalike cola (*Financial Times*, 3 May 1994).

The Threat from Consumers

The fact that the vast majority of markets are still dominated by brands suggests that they still fulfil a critical role for consumers. Nevertheless, many commentators on the subject argue that the "crass materialistic 1980s" represented the high point of branding and that in the more "sharing, caring 1990s" there would be a move away from ostentation of all kinds — including brands. This, in the view of this author, is mere journalistic hyperbole and, although tastes will obviously change from generation to generation, requiring in turn changes in the way in which brands are packaged and presented, it does not negate a continuing role for the fundamentals of branding.

However, a number of leading market researchers have been expressing concern for some time about increasing consumer scepticism towards brands. A research study carried out by an international agency found approximately two in every three consumers in a worldwide study believing that retailer brands were every bit as good as manufacturer brands. A more serious threat from consumers has been suggested by a leading UK qualitative researcher, Mary Goodyear, in a series of articles in different publications during the past few years. Goodyear believes that "there are clear indications that the absolute rule of the brand is over" (Goodyear, 1993). There has been a shift in focus among consumers from the core brand to the company brand — that is, closer to the manufacturer.

As consumers become more literate about business in general, partly as a result of the education system and partly because of a much increased level of media coverage, they are more likely to make the connection between the brand and the manufacturer. Some researchers have claimed that this shift in focus is occurring at the expense of the brand. As consumers become more knowledgeable about business, "they find it more difficult to divorce the brand from the profit motive and the general machinations of the company which makes it" (Goodyear, 1992). Goodyear goes on to argue that, as customers relate more closely to the manufacturer, they will begin to cut out the middle man — the brand. As a result, manufacturers will need to pay more attention to the company brand image and the company's wider social responsibilities, particularly in relation to the environment and local community.

Increasingly, marketing-literate consumers are playing back responses that manufacturers want to hear in consumer research, but behaving differently at the checkout. Goodyear pokes some legitimate fun at "new-age" qualitative researchers allowing consumers to sort out "files of faintly naughty pictures" into photo montages and brand managers basking in the reflected glory of the revelation that consumers rate their brand as "better in bed than brand X". Her point here is that consumers who go along with these games in qualitative research often behave quite differently at point-of-sale, where they may be more influenced by price and display than the imagery of the brand. But ever since Andrew Ehrenberg concluded over 30 years ago that most consumers have a repertoire of brands, belief in the existence of a totally brand-loyal consumer has been eroded (Bird and Eherenberg, 1966).

If we accept that all brands are made up of a combination of rational benefits (the physical characteristics of a product itself) and emotional benefits (the added value or personality that occurs through marketing communication), we might also have to admit that the combined weight of manufacturer marketing departments, advertising agencies and consumer-research organisations may have exaggerated the importance of emotional benefits, and consequently under-emphasised the importance of product attributes. Consumers may not act all the time from entirely rational reasons but this does not mean that decisions are based on emotions alone.

The Threat from Marketing: Brand Management

In May 1931, Neil McEllroy, a Procter and Gamble marketing executive in the US working on Camay, felt frustrated at the greater resources and importance that Procter and Gamble was giving to its brand leader, Ivory. He wrote a memo to top management which effectively outlined the idea of brand management — a system whereby each brand within a company's portfolio was assigned a manager or management team whose sole responsibility was the success of that brand. The idea quickly took root and spread to other companies selling a range of brands. Like many other US ideas it crossed the Atlantic in the wake of the Second World War, and was again associated with Procter and Gamble, prompting the famous quip "brand managers were invented in Newcastle (Procter and Gamble's UK headquarters) and invariably come in threes".

The system has remained more or less intact but has been the subject of fierce attacks in the past year, culminating in a lead story in *The Economist* (1994), titled "Death of the Brand Manager". To some extent, the problems now facing manufacturer brands are being blamed partly on the inadequacies of the brand-manager system, but there is also a feeling that the system itself has created a situation in which brand managers have become too divorced from both the consumer and the sources of real power within companies:

> Consumer product manufacturers tend to think that they are the font of all marketing wisdom but in reality they have been excruciatingly myopic and arrogant (*Financial Times*, 6 October 1993).

A recent report from management consultants McKinsey suggested that "creeping bureaucratisation" was the root cause of the problem and estimated that the typical marketing department spends 80 per cent of its time on routine administrative chores and only 20 per cent on product innovation strategy and ways of serving retailers and customers better. The most damning comment of all came from an important survey of 100 leading companies by Coopers and Lybrand, which reported that

> ... marketing as a discipline is more vital than ever — marketing as a department is increasingly failing to match up to expectations (Coopers and Lybrand, 1993).

Detailed findings from the Coopers and Lybrand study were even more scathing, with marketing departments accused of:

- Being responsible for an ill-defined mixture of activities
- Being over-indulged
- Rarely leading the drive to enhance business performance
- Being too short-sighted
- Being marginalised
- Over-estimating their own contribution.

The root of the problem would appear to be that, while the distinction between marketing as a business philosophy and marketing as a set of techniques appears to be much better understood, marketing departments are increasingly being marginalised from overall business strategy and left with responsibility for the techniques. An additional threat to the pre-eminent position that marketing departments achieved in the 1980s is the inexorable rise in the power and importance of the sales function and, in particular, the key accounts manager who deals with the powerful retailers.

> Marketing departments appear out of place in the more demanding business environment of the 90s. They are essentially a spending function. Caught in a period of cost savings and redundancies they have few roles that are uniquely their own or decisions which fall clearly within their remit (Coopers and Lybrand, 1993).

REGAINING THE INITIATIVE
Overcoming the Threat from Retailer Brands

The threat from retailer brands is by far the most serious problem facing manufacturers. For too long, manufacturers have adopted the classic business solution to the problem — the "if we do nothing about it, it might go away" solution. Initially, retailer brands were dismissed as being either irrational or an aberration that would go away once reason prevailed. When it became obvious that this would not happen, reaction changed to a more patronising approach which accepted their presence in the same way as accepting that the poor would always be with us. Even the evidence in some countries — that middle-class consumers showed a higher propensity to buy retailer brands — failed to produce a more realistic reaction. But trends that begin in middle-class areas have a habit of spreading throughout society.

Manufacturers' first response should be a more honest and realistic appraisal. We need new definitions of retailer brands and a greater understanding of how consumers react in each market. The following three strategies are proposed in a re-evaluation of retailer brands:

1) *Facing Reality*: retailer brands are brands in their own right. The marketing of brands is undertaken by both manufacturers and retailers.

2) *Understanding Diversity*: Retailer brands are commonly assumed to be homogeneous; they are not. At least the following four categories can be identified:

    ◊ Generic — simple packaging, no branding except retailer name

    ◊ Retailer price-led brands — carrying the retailer name but package design giving an overt signal of lower prices; product quality often below par

    ◊ Retailer quality-led brands — packaging designed to reflect product quality, which in turn is on a par (or even above) manufacturer brands

    ◊ Exclusive retailer brand — manufacturer-based but sold only through one retailer.

3) We need better definitions to reflect the new reality. The following three definitions are of interest (McWilliam and de Chernatony

1989). Note the close correlation between that for manufacturer brands and that for distributor brands:

- ◊ "A manufacturer brand is an added value entity conceived and primarily developed by a manufacturer for a specific group of customers and consumers which portrays a unique, relevant and distinctive personality through the support of product development, promotion, advertising and an appropriate pricing and distribution strategy."

- ◊ "A distributor brand is an added value entity produced by, or on behalf of a distributor, following the distributor's specifications. It is targeted at specific consumers and portrays a unique, relevant and distinctive personality which is clearly associated with the distributor and is backed by a coherent use of marketing resources."

- ◊ "Generic groceries are items presented in a commodity form, distinguishable by their basic packaging which is functional rather than aesthetic. No promotional support is given to generics which are characterised by their low prices."

Once we have come to terms with the reality of retailer brands we will be in a better position to take the next step in defence of manufacturer brands, which is to formulate a marketing plan for the brand, which takes account not only of competitive manufacturer brands, but also competitive retailer brands. To do this we need a deeper understanding of the role of manufacturer and retailer brands in the lives of consumers. In seeking this understanding, the following points should be taken into account.

First, the concept of a 100 per cent brand-loyal consumer is invariably the figment of a brand manager's wildly over-optimistic imagination. Most consumers operate from a fairly wide repertoire of brands in any given market. This has led to the use of the phrase "promiscuous consumer" in some marketing textbooks, as if the poor old consumer were somehow to blame for the problems of marketing management. A more realistic explanation is that consumers have different needs for the same product category and, therefore, vary purchase between different brands to fulfil these needs. So-called "need states" in the yogurt market could be:

- St Bernard own brand — frugal, responsible housewife
- Yoplait — caring mother

- Müller Fruit — indulgent mother
- Danone Bio — healthy, sophisticated woman (Gordon, 1994).

Second, the "cooking wine'" factor — the way that people use products — is important. In many food categories, such as staple items like rice and spaghetti, the price and the brand will only be known to the user who may feel that a cheaper retailer brand will suffice, unless a promotional campaign to the contrary is communicated. Similarly, a child who is prepared to tolerate and even enjoy a retailer-brand cola at home would invariably insist on Pepsi Cola with friends. The end result of all these complications is that manufacturers, if they are to face up to competition from retailer brands, will have to have a much greater understanding of the complexity of consumer choice in the markets in which they operate.

Third, there is no such thing as a retailer-brand shopper. People who buy premium-priced manufacturer-brand tea may buy retailer-brand coffee and vice versa. People who buy retailer-brand dogfood may buy the most expensive manufacturer-brand catfood and vice versa. It all depends on the level of interest and involvement in each particular market.

Facing up to the reality of retailer brands and gaining a deeper understanding of individual markets are essential steps in the battle to maintain brand profitability, but the only guarantee of success is constant attention to the functional and emotional elements of each brand — continuous product improvement and innovation and continuous high quality communication to develop the personality of the brand, while taking account of changing social circumstances:

> Real product innovation is one of the ways, perhaps the only way, manufacturers can hope to fight free from what are now a number of serious problems (Grender, 1994).

Finally, manufacturers need to examine their core strengths in relation to retailer brands — particularly their tradition and pride in making things. In the mid-1980s, faced with the threat of cheaper competitive imports in the Irish market, McConnell's Advertising created a range campaign for Irish Biscuits, the largest indigenous manufacturer, which included a jingle with the following words: "We baked our first last century and we're baking biscuits still". It was a powerful and incontrovertible claim and one that no retailer could ever begin to match.

Increasing Marketing Literacy among Consumers

The ability of today's consumer to deconstruct advertising strategies presents a more serious, but not insurmountable, challenge to brand management and ad-agency teams. At times, listening to consumers in group discussions can be like listening to senior management discussing marketing problems. Because of a natural tendency to be of assistance, respondents are also inclined to answer questions in both qualitative and quantitative research in a way they think will be helpful — to please the interviewer by giving the answer they think they're expected to give — but then to proceed in their daily lives to behave in very different ways.

This is not to suggest that we should reduce or abandon conventional market research. In fact, a central theme of this article is that now retailers are closer to consumers, research will be even more necessary to defend brands against the forces currently aligned against them. But we do need to take account of the tendency in consumers to second-guess when we are interpreting the results of some of the more innovative techniques currently being used, particularly in qualitative research. The high ground in brand management is understanding the consumer: we must never lose sight of the fact that brands exist in the minds of consumers. Manufacturers have legal ownership of their products, not their brands. The growth of scanning at checkouts — EPOS — and the development of retailer databases, mean that retailers can now justifiably claim to be closer to the consumer:

> Retailers have no clearer idea than brand managers how housewives will behave tomorrow, or why, but they know far more about what they bought yesterday thanks to the reams of data churned out by their point of sale systems (*The Economist*, 1994).

Manufacturers must not concede this area of control to retailers. Manufacturers should develop new observation-based techniques to add to their understanding of consumer behaviour. One of the earliest books about advertising, Martin Myers' *Madison Avenue,* profiled one of the founders of American advertising who used to devote three or four hours every Saturday morning to observing how consumers behaved by working in one of the checkouts in his local supermarket (Myers, 1961). He may well have had the right idea. It was recently reported that Maurice Tabaksblat, co-chairman of the giant Unilever company, first realised the potential of the Chinese ice-cream market when standing in a street in Guangzhou and watching two parents buy their son an ice-cream:

> The boy took one lick, made a face and threw it on the ground; the same thing happened with the second cone. Astonishingly, they bought him a third one from the same vendor. The child finally found it good enough to eat.

Tabaksblat drew two conclusions from this 1992 incident. First, the quality of Chinese-made ice-cream varies so wildly that even children often have trouble eating it. Second, China's one-child policy has produced a nation of indulgent parents willing to splurge on luxuries for their sole offspring (*Business Week*, 4 July 1994).

Soon Unilever was building one of the largest ice-cream factories in Beijing. Presumably the company carried out much more rigorous feasibility studies, but the importance of direct observation by senior management cannot be overlooked in understanding markets. Managers who are responsible for the fate of brands in manufacturing companies, advertising agencies and other promotional organisations should spend some time observing consumers in retail outlets. The current vogue among marketing executives for attending group discussions as observers is probably off-putting for the moderator and misleading for the executive — who would be better employed wandering around supermarkets observing consumers in action.

Reports that consumers are showing new interest in the company behind the brand have been put forward as further evidence of a decline in the importance of the brand. Certainly, the general public is showing increasing interest in business organisations. This writer believe that the reason for this is a growing suspicion that national governments are no longer able to deliver the goods as power moves to new international institutions, such as the EU, International Monetary Fund, and the boardrooms of big business. This, in effect, is where decisions affecting employment and subsequent prosperity are made. Consequently, the public is becoming more curious about these big business organisations — who they are, what type of people are in charge, what their plans are and how they behave in relation to the environment and the local community. Manufacturers can use this to their advantage by managing their companies as they would their brands. This will involve communicating with the public on a regular basis.

Overcoming the Weaknesses of the Brand-Management Function

The widely quoted Cooper and Lybrand study, *Marketing at the Crossroads*, presented a gloomy view of the performance of the marketing department. The report concluded that if the marketing department was to survive it would have to adopt the following four measures:

1) Have within its remit all the processes that contribute to managing the customer and customer interfaces.

2) Have clear and defined responsibility for these processes — in too many organisations marketing has only partial responsibility for too many tasks.

3) Focus on activities that demonstrably add value.

4) Be measured and judged against these measures.

Breaking down departmental barriers, interdisciplinary teams and teamwork in general are all part of the re-engineering movement that is currently occupying poll position in the business academic fashion stakes. But they're all relevant to the fact that brand management is too important to be left to a marketing department. The importance of brands to a company's profitability cannot be divorced from the concerns of senior management. All senior managers must take responsibility for the strategic development of the company's brands. In the more progressive companies this has always been the case, but there are still organisations where decisions on branding are assigned by default to a junior role. However, issues at the heart of branding — continuous innovation and continuous communication — require the co-operation and support of senior production and financial personnel.

Unless there is much greater integration at the top, and the marketing department is part of this integration, the true capability and energy of the marketing discipline will never be realised. There is evidence that these changes are taking place. A recent survey of US consumer goods firms found that 90 per cent of those surveyed had restructured their marketing departments (*The Economist*, 9 April 1994). Most of this restructuring involves the replacement of the old style marketing department, with its focus on the brand manager, with multidisciplinary teams based on product categories and customer-focused tasks. Each team involves people from sales, finance and production, as well as marketing.

CONCLUSIONS

The death of brands and the threat to brands have been greatly exaggerated but it would be foolish to ignore the reality of these threats, particularly from retailers. The growing quality and sophistication of retailer brands represents by far the most serious challenge to manufacturers. This is true both in large markets with economies of scale and in smaller regional economies. The Barbarians may not yet be at the gates but they are now visible on the horizon. Yet the central argument of this article is that the main threat of retailer brands can always be blunted by determined manufacturers. The classic Andrex case history in the UK has proven that, even in the most unpromising market circumstances, dedication to technical innovation and creative communication will keep retailer brands at bay. In understanding the issues facing brands and in regaining the initiative, the superior player should keep the following points in mind:

- Accept the fact that retailer and distributor brands are brands in their own right. The marketing of brands can be undertaken by both manufacturers and retailers.

- Retailer brands are not homogeneous. At least four categories can be identified from simple generic, to retailer price led and retailer quality led, to exclusive retailer brand. Each category has different competitive implications. In order to compete, manufacturer brands need to have a better understanding of the different "need states" that they fulfil in the minds of consumers. This type of information will be essential for the accurate targeting required in a more competitive situation.

- A potentially powerful defence of manufacturer brands is their company's manufacturing history — a history which no retailer can match. Consumers have always responded to messages about genuine pedigree and provenance.

- The interpretation of market-research results needs to take into account the growing marketing literacy of consumers.

- Being closer to the consumer means watching consumers in action, not just reading about them in pages of market-research reports. Senior management needs continuous exposure to real consumers in actual purchasing situations.

- The company behind the brand needs to be treated as a brand. This could potentially be used as a competitive advantage for manufacturer brands. Consequently, companies should communicate with their constituencies on a regular basis.

- The management of brands is the responsibility of senior management, not just brand managers.

REFERENCES

Bird, M. and Eherenberg, A. (1966): "Intention to Buy and Claimed Brand Usage", *Operational Research Quarterly*, 1.

Business Week (1994): "Unilever's Global Fight", 4 July: 40–45.

Coopers and Lybrand (1993): *Marketing at the Crossroads*, London: Coopers and Lybrand.

de Jonquieres, G. (1993): "A Rose by Any Other Name", *Financial Times*, 6 October.

Economist, The (1994): "Death of the Brand Manager", 331(7858): 71–2.

Gardner, B.D. and Levy, K. (1955): "The Product and the Brand", *Harvard Business Review*, March/April: 33–9.

Goodyear, M. (1993): "Reviewing the Concept of Brands and Branding", *Marketing & Research Today*, May.

Goodyear, M. (1992): "Devolution and the Brand", *Admap*, 27(10): 37–9.

Gordon, W. (1994): "Meeting the Challenge of Retailer Brands", *Admap*, 29(3): 20–24.

Grender, P. (1994), "Brands and the Innovation Option", *Admap*, 29(3): 15–9.

Hazkins, P. (1994): *The Independent on Sunday*, 20 February.

Laurens, A. and Alexander, S. (1994): "Brands Fight Back", *The Independent on Sunday*, 17 April.

McWilliam, G. and de Chernatony, L. (1989): "Branding Terminology — The Real Debate", *Marketing Intelligence and Planning*, 7(7/8): 29–32.

Myers, M. (1961): *Madison Avenue*, New York: Penguin Books.

Peston, R. and Rudd, R. (1994): "Anger at Brand Lookalikes Worries DTI", Financial Times, 3 May.

16
Advertising and the Development of Marketing Imagery

Tony Meenaghan

INTRODUCTION

In his seminal work on image and behaviour, Boulding (1956) suggested that, for the individual, image was truth:

> Image can only be compared to images. They can never be compared to any outside reality ... for any individual organism or organisation there are no such things as facts. There are only messages filtered through a changeable value system (154).

Nowhere is this more true than in the area of human relationships with business organisations — that is, the domain of marketing. Image and the determination of how people view corporations, retail outlets, product lines and brands have become critical issues in marketing today. This is particularly reflected in changes at the product/brand level where there has been a "shift in attention away from physical aspects and functional benefits of products to their symbolic associations, expressiveness" (Poiesz, 1989: 461).

The increased importance of image in marketing can be attributed to several factors

- The increasing role of consumer behaviour in explaining consumer decision-making

- A switch in emphasis in an affluent society from functional to symbolic values in products

- Continued convergence in many product categories towards product homogeneity, with image factors forced to carry the burden of differentiation

- The inability of technological advance to offer sustained competitive advantage, with a consequent shift to imagery in order to cement consumer/brand relationships (Wells, 1989; King, 1991; Parker, 1991).

The purpose of this paper is to outline the various forms of marketing imagery consumed by target markets, and to examine the role that advertising strategy has to play in the development of image in marketing.

TYPES OF MARKETING IMAGES

As a necessary ingredient of the relationships which businesses form with their various publics, a multitude of images is transmitted at each level of the corporate/consumer encounter. In general, three broad categories of image can be identified in marketing — corporate, retail and brand image — although increasingly these three image categories are being subsumed into the single, all-embracing, category of brand image (King, 1989; Levy, 1990; Grier, 1991).

Corporate image may be defined as "a composite of knowledge, feelings, ideals and beliefs associated with a company as a result of the totality of its activities" (Gunther, 1959: 62).

A variety of publics — such as customers, staff and the general public — form different impressions of the corporation as a result of receiving particular communications and experiencing different personal interactions. The second traditional level of marketing imagery is retail or store image, defined by Martineau (1958) as "the way in which the store is defined in the shopper's mind partly by its functional qualities and partly by an aura of psychological attribute" (47). This definition emphasises the two key strands of retail image formation: the cognitive approach (Mazursky and Jacoby, 1986) and the behavioural approach (Kunkel and Berry, 1968).

The third level of imagery in marketing is brand image. Brand image is variously defined as "the set of beliefs held about a particular brand" (Kotler, 1988: 197) or "a set of associations, usually organised in some meaningful way" (Aaker, 1992: 109–10). The *brand* is often regarded as separate from the functional product, with the brand being grafted on by advertising, thereby completing the transformation process from functional product to immortal brand. Kim (1990) suggests that:

> a product is a physical thing ... a brand has no tangible, physical, or functional properties.... Yet it is just as real as the product.

> Disembodied, abstract, ephemeral ... it exists like a myth in the imagination of the consumer (65).

This view sees the product as providing core functional benefits, with the brand being responsible for creating the magnetic human-style aura surrounding the actual product. In effect, the consumer is being sold at two levels of values — intrinsic values centring on perceived product quality, and extrinsic values focusing on the symbolic content of the brand. Intrinsic values derive from consumer beliefs about the product's capacity to satisfy functional desires, while extrinsic, or added, values largely derive from the brand imagery created by advertising. Where particular products/brands are seen as relatively homogeneous — for example, colas, lagers, etc. — heavy emphasis is placed upon adding symbolic values as the basis for product differentiation. The distinction between intrinsic and extrinsic values is evident in the following quotation:

> It is this symbolic or totemistic content to a brand which has given rise to the notion of brands having "personalities". These "personalities" are the sum of the emotional "added values" which the product carries, over and above its inherent quality and obvious functional purpose (McWilliam and De Chernatony, 1989: 30).

This distinction between "brand" and "product" is, however, largely inaccurate, as in reality both the mythical elements of the supposed *brand* and the functional elements of the supposed *product* are symbiotically related to form a single, total image in the mind of the consumer.

FROM IDENTITY TO IMAGE

Discussion on marketing imagery is awash with a confusing usage of basic terminology. It is important, however, for the purposes of this paper to distinguish between image and identity. Essentially, "identity means the sum of all the ways a company chooses to identify itself to all its publics ... image on the other hand, is the perception of the company by these publics" (Marguiles, 1977: 66). In seeking to manage the image development process, a company will focus on those elements that it can control — those constituting its identity. Image is ultimately formed in the mind of the receiver. It results from the interaction of two sets of ingredients, namely identity elements controlled by the brand owner, and factors such as competitive activity, media comment, the retail environment wherein the brand is carried as well as the consumer's own beliefs and predispositions. In summary, identity is sent, while image is received/perceived.

At each level at which it is attempting to manage the image-development process, an organisation has available a wide variety of elements of identity. At a corporate level, these include products, services, physical environment, information and staff behaviour (Olins, 1989). At the level of retail identity, Martineau (1958) defined four key dimensions: layout and architecture, colours and symbols, sales personnel, and advertising. At the product/brand level, the components of identity are in effect the elements of the marketing mix that combine to form the image of the brand in the mind of the consumer. While these elements constitute the components of brand identity, their importance can vary. Product features that deliver meaningful product benefits are generally central to the brand image-creation process, in that it is the ability of the product offering to satisfy buyer needs that is at the core of image formation. However, where there is little real, functional difference between competing product offerings, the weight of the image-creation task falls more heavily on other aspects of identity. In such circumstances, particular emphasis is placed on marketing communications in general, and advertising in particular, in order to provide the basis for consumer discrimination. With regard to brand image, the role of advertising is to communicate product benefits to consumers and to position the brand in the mind of the consumer by focusing on intrinsic, and by adding symbolic, values to the brand (Doyle, 1989).

THE CONCEPT OF BRANDING

Branding represents one of the central tenets of marketing. Various definitions of a brand appear in the literature. Kotler (1988) defines a brand as "a name, term, sign, symbol or design or combination of them, which is intended to identify the goods of one seller or group of sellers and to differentiate them from those of competitors" (463). This and similar type definitions fail to capture the essence of what branding involves or achieves. Inevitably couched in flat, abstract and lifeless language, such definitions focus primarily on the ingredients of brand identity, and as such fail to capture the essence of branding. The development of brand image involves the marketer in breathing life into an innate product, thereby endowing it with a distinct personality and human characteristics in the eyes of the consumer. Branding results in an invisible, yet magnetic, relationship between brand and consumer, which must, of necessity, involve the brand in the world of the consumer.

> In order to be successful, images and symbols must relate to, and indeed, exploit, the needs, values and life-styles of consumers in such a way that the meanings involved give added values, and differentiate the brand from other brands (Broadbent and Cooper, 1987: 3).

Within the marketing tradition, with its reliance on economic theory and related emphasis on rationality in buying behaviour, the recognition of products as having symbolic meaning for consumers co-incided with marketing's courtship of the behavioural sciences in the 1950s and 1960s. Gardner and Levy (1955) suggested that there was a need for a "greater awareness of the social and psychological nature of products" (34), while Levy (1959) captured the essence of symbolism when he suggested that "people buy things not only for what they can do, but also for what they mean" (118). The concept of brands as social signals is now well accepted, with congruence between brand and user self-image regarded as a key motivational factor in consumer choice. (Sirgy, 1982; Belk, 1983). Lannon and Cooper (1983: 205) suggest that:

> ... brands are used as a sort of language. Brands tell you a great deal about who you are, where you are in life, what you were and where you are going. Brand choices are as much a part of ourselves as the way we speak, the words we use, our dialect, dress, gestures and language. Brands are part of ourselves and we are part of our brands.

The marketing of the Volkswagen Beetle represents a prime example of the brand/consumer relationship and the brand as social statement. Conceived originally in 1938 as a "people's car" to suit the needs of the German mass-market, by the 1960s it came to represent a particular type of person and lifestyle.

> The Beetle owner was someone who was not into materialism and status symbols. Rather, he or she was willing to make a statement by driving an ugly, funky car, thereby demonstrating independence — a willingness to go against the grain, irreverence for convention, being young (or young in spirit) admitting to a sense of humour, and possessing a logical practical mind (Aaker, 1992: 183).

ADDING BRAND VALUES

Advertising represents a particularly potent element of identity, being central to the process of brand image development by informing consumers of inherent product benefits and positioning the brand in the mind of the consumer. While functional product qualities foster intrinsic brand values, advertising serves to transmit the existence of, and perhaps to embellish, beliefs regarding these product qualities, thus affecting a dimension of received brand image. At a more emotional/symbolic level, a prime function of advertising is to achieve for a brand a particular personality or character in the mind of the consumer market. This latter function is achieved by imbuing the brand with specific associations or values. A particular feature of all great brands is their association with specific values, both functional and symbolic. At the corporate level, IBM is regarded as owning "perception of bigness, computers and integrity" (Wells 1989: 100). In retailing, Marks and Spencer is associated with product quality and value for money. At the level of the product/brand, this feature of marketing activity is best observed, with notable brand names such as Marlboro, Coca-Cola, Doc Martins, etc. suggesting quite specific associations. Research into the Guinness brand showed two levels of values — "soft" values at the core or "yolk", such as nourishment, goodness, mystery, and elemental and "hard" values at the "shell" exterior, such as masculinity, individuality, maturity and control (Broadbent and Cooper, 1987).

The UK car industry represents a good example of brand personality and the addition of both functional and symbolic brand values.

> Car advertising has undergone a transformation. The aim seems to be to imbue both marques and individual brands with a personality and character through a more emotional pitch.... The shift has been towards adding brand values. The advertising is now appealing to the hearts as well as the heads of potential buyers. Cars are becoming more uniform and it is harder to make them stand out both in terms of product and style of advertising. Volvo has safety. Volkswagen has reliability.... All of BMW's advertising comes back to four main planks: performance, quality, technology and prestige.... Citroën is the quintessential French marque and its advertising reflects its quirky, Gallic nature (Spandler, 1987: 20–21).

ADVERTISING — ITS ROLE IN MARKETING IMAGERY

While advertising is identified as one of the principal components of image creation, the question of how advertising affects consumer behaviour is a particularly complex one. Two broad schools of thought regarding advertising effects and consumer behaviour, based on the cognitive and behavioural approaches to consumer decision-making, are generally suggested. However, it is obvious that the dichotomous views expressed by proponents of each school of thought can hardly be expected to explain the panorama of consumer decision-making situations.

The cognitive school views the consumer as a rational decision-maker, moving over a series of physical and mental steps towards the act of purchase. This school is represented by what might be termed the classical models of advertising effects, namely the STARCH (Starch, 1925) AIDA (Strong, 1925), DAGMAR (Colley, 1961) and Hierarchy of Effects (Lavidge and Steiner, 1961) models. These models, termed "linear sequential models" by de Groot (1980) and "hammer and nail, conversion and hierarchy of effects theories" by Lannon and Cooper (1983), could be described as left-hand-side-of-brain models, in that consumer behaviour is explained in analytical, rational terms. Their validity in representing the reality of consumer decision-making has long been challenged (Joyce, 1967, 1991; Lannon and Cooper, 1983; McDonald, 1992).

The second school, variously termed the "brand image school", (Ogilvy, 1963; Joyce, 1967), "humanistic advertising" (Lannon and Cooper, 1983) and "right-hand side of brain approach" (McDonald, 1992), has as its core a more symbolic, intuitive and emotional view of products and advertising in the scheme of consumer decision-making. According to this school, the primary function of advertising is to create the symbolism and imagery around the brand which will result in a relationship between the brand and the consumer. The consumer is seen as active, knowledgeable, sophisticated, and involved in the process of giving meaning to brands. Brand choice is based on emotional and intuitive feelings about brands, their images and meanings for consumers, and how these brands satisfy consumer needs and seem to fit into consumers' relationships with their world.

Drawing on these two broad approaches to consumer decision-making, two schools of explanation of how advertising works are generally proposed, with each having strong resonances of the rational/emotional motives debate. Durgee (1988: 21) suggests somewhat simplistically, "advertising has two purposes: to excite and to inform". Various labels are given to the two explanations of how advertising works. Johar and Sirgy (1991) distinguish between advertising based on value — expressive (image) or symbolic appeals, and utilitarian (functional) appeals. The image strategy involves endowing the brand with a humanesque personality. The utilitarian appeal involves informing consumers of the product benefits that are perceived to be highly functional and important to the consumer. Based on this classification, they suggest that there are two different routes to persuasion: self-congruity and functional congruity.

> The self-congruity route to persuasion can be viewed as a psychological process in which the audience focuses on source cues and matches these cues to their self-concept.... The greater the match of the source cues, the greater the probability of persuasion, and vice versa. Functional congruity, on the other hand, is defined as a match between the beliefs of product utilitarian attributes (performance-related) and the audience's referent attributes.... a self-congruity route to persuasion can be viewed as a form of peripheral processing, whereas the functional congruity route is likely to be a form of central processing" (Johar and Sirgy, 1991: 27).

The classification along expressive and functional grounds parallels the approach proposed by Rossiter and Percy (1987). Essentially, they subdivided advertising into informational and transformational advertising. They suggest that informational advertising is "reason why" style of advertising, in which the consumer is given information about brand benefits and helped to resolve consumption choice conflicts. With transformational, or "image" style of, advertising consumers perceive that they will be transformed intellectually or socially by using the brand. The classification of advertising along informational/transformational, think/feel lines is widely accepted in the advertising literature. (Vaughn, 1980; Aaker and Morris, 1982; Puto and Wells, 1984; Laskey, Day and Crask, 1989; Crask and Laskey, 1990; Rossiter, Percy and Donovan, 1991).

In reality, products and the buying situations involved are not likely to represent for the consumer either a purely rational or purely emotional/symbolic choice situation, but are likely to embody aspects of both simultaneously (Wicks, 1989). This view is supported by Rossiter, Percy and Donovan (1991) who suggest that *"think* and *feel* are cute summary labels that do not in any way do justice to the complexity of consumer purchase motivations" (15). While it might be convenient to represent all consumer purchasing on a commodity/ brand continuum, and related advertising on an informational/transformational spectrum, the reality is that consumer decision-making involves both the left-hand side (rational/analytical) and the right-hand side (emotional/intuitive) of the brain simultaneously, with variation in emphasis being related to characteristics of the decision and the decision-maker. Advertising strategy reflects this complexity, with advertising for certain product categories variously reliant on appeals to either rationality or emotion, or in certain instances embodying aspects of both strands of appeal into a single advertisement. This is evident from Figure 16.1 which shows that appeals to both rationality and emotion are possible, and that neither the cognitive nor the affective approach to explaining brand purchasing and related advertising should dominate, but that both have validity as explanations in different situations.

FIGURE 16.1: PRACTICAL AND SYMBOLIC ATTITUDES TO BUYING BRANDS

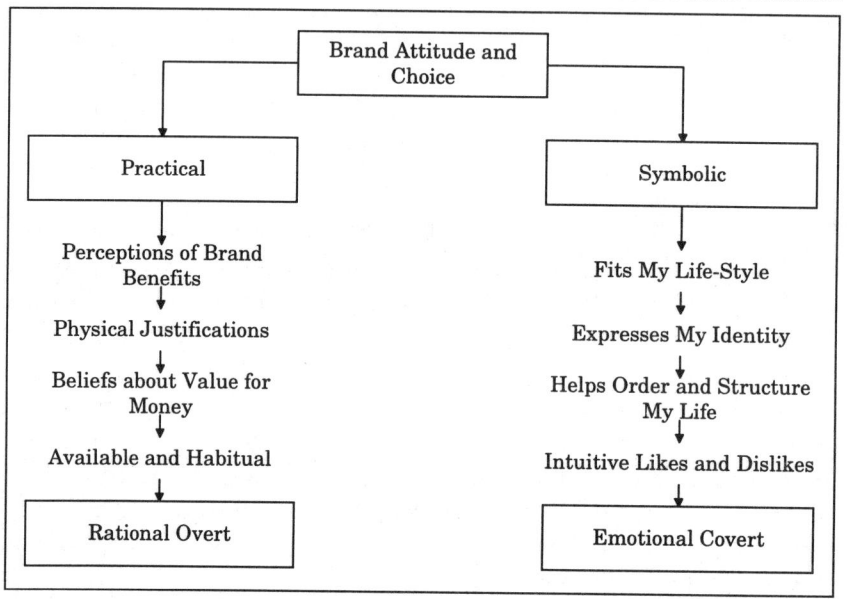

```
                    Brand Attitude and
                         Choice
         ┌───────────────┴───────────────┐
         ↓                               ↓
      Practical                       Symbolic
         ↓                               ↓
  Perceptions of Brand             Fits My Life-Style
      Benefits                           ↓
         ↓                        Expresses My Identity
  Physical Justifications                ↓
         ↓                      Helps Order and Structure
  Beliefs about Value for              My Life
        Money                           ↓
         ↓                     Intuitive Likes and Dislikes
  Available and Habitual               ↓
         ↓                        Emotional Covert
    Rational Overt
```

Source: Cooper, P. (1989): "Comparison Between the UK and US: The Qualitative Dimension", *Journal of Marketing Research Society*, 31(4): 515.

CREATING IMAGERY IN ADVERTISING

While sources other than advertising can contribute to the brand image-formation process — the product itself with its inherent benefits, the retail outlet, consumers themselves, and the producer's image (Cooper, 1980; Durgee, 1990) — advertising does represent a key method of endowing a brand with specific values. Two separate elements of an advertisement are involved in creating desired brand associations, namely, message content and media/media vehicle effect.

Message Content

The content of an advertisement which is controlled by the advertiser represents the principal method of communication with an audience, with message content being used to satisfy both informative and symbolic advertising intent. Where the purpose is to create a specific brand image, the advertiser seeks to draw meaning from the various elements in the context of the advertisement. The advertiser has available a wide variety of visual and verbal stimuli which combine to create the advertising context. Individual elements are carefully selected for their symbolic content, to be decoded by consumers who arrive at the intended impression regarding the brand being advertised. These can include the unfolding mini-drama of the advertisement, characters involved, lifestyle, activity pursued, colouring, music, tone, mood, location, as well as other elements depending on the medium chosen. Each of these elements can be seen at work in ads for brands such as Nescafé, Guinness and Yorkie, and in categories such as jeans, cars, lager, etc. In essence, creators of advertisements function as drama/film directors in that they are attempting to achieve rub-off or association effect to the brand from the context they create and the various associative stimuli within the advertisement which have particular meaning in the eyes of the targeted audience (Cooper and Kaye, 1987).

Advertising taps into the reservoirs of social and cultural knowledge maintained by audiences, and encodes this material into a message whereby specific values are transferred to the products. Leiss, Kline, and Jhally, (1986: 190) suggest that:

> The product becomes embedded or "situated" in a symbolic context that imparts meaning to the product beyond its constituent elements or benefits.... The symbolic association thus established brings the product into a meaningful relationship with abstract values and ideas signified by a natural or social setting such as a landscape, the workplace, the household, a cluster of artefacts of daily life, a historic moment, or a recognisable tradition or myth.... The fusion of product code and setting code, which formulates the basis of the product image, depends largely on narrative techniques like metaphor, implied use, allusion, allegory, story line, and simple juxtaposition to expand the symbolic dimension of the interpretation.

Advertising is seen as donating meaning or adding specific values to the brand. Noth (1988) suggests that much of advertising is about myth creation. Referring to advertisements in campaigns for Marlboro or Camel cigarettes, she suggests that:

> ... it is the narrative of a solitary hero in a successful struggle with the forces of nature, be it a lassoing cowboy who proves his command over a wild herd of cattle or the courageous discoverer who reaches unknown exotic shores in his primitive boat.... It is the myth of unbounded self-fulfilment in harmony with nature, which is the counter-image of real life within the confines of a polluted industrialised world (180).

Similarly, "McDonald's advertising has created a mythical world, a wondrous, magical place where everyone is welcome, safe, happy, loved, kind, caring, sharing and forever young or young at heart" (Randazzo, 1991: 4). The context for the brand Kerrygold as suggested in many international markets is a mythic Ireland of green fields, lush pastures, quaint rural villages and whitewashed, thatched cottages, populated by friendly, caring, rural folk, where time has its own meaning. The contextual values of care, nature, "green", unspoilt, clean and environmentally pure are, of necessity, absorbed by the brand.

METHODS OF CREATING BRAND IMAGERY IN ADVERTISING

Advertisers use a wide variety of approaches to creating images and imbuing brands with values. A number of these are now briefly examined to illustrate how advertising content is used in image development.

Metaphors and Symbols

A common method of imbuing a brand with specific values involves the use of metaphor. King (1991: 50) suggests that:

> ... a good communication idea for a company brand would be an original metaphor for the brand's personality. That is, the brand would borrow from the outside something with the same personality characteristics, which could be uniquely associated with it, could be reasonably long lasting, and in some way would illuminate and enhance the brand itself.

King offers the following examples of brands and related metaphors:

- Marlboro: The cowboy. The individual facing the elements
- Esso: The tiger. Graceful, powerful, aggressive
- Andrex: The puppy. Soft, durable, wholesome
- Persil: Mother love. Metaphor for taking care of clothes
- Mr Kipling: The voice. Metaphor for traditional craftsmanship and values.

A symbol can become the key differentiating factor in a brand, and as such become a reservoir of brand equity. Like the brand name, a symbol can become the lightening rod for consumer associations. The symbol, while communicating associations, can also underline specific attributes. Advertising for insurance companies will use an umbrella to suggest shelter and protection, while the bull-dog is often used to suggest Englishness and resolution. Symbols can be cartoon characters (Jolly Green Giant, Mickey Mouse), objects (umbrellas), logos, (Apple's apple), people (Rutger Hauer in Guinness commercials). An example of a symbol being combined with other message elements is provided by the case of the Volkswagen Beetle.

> The car's symbol was its distinctive shape. The symbol was, without question, an important part of the Beetle phenomenon. First, it represented a car design which was "ugly" in terms of the conventional wisdom of the day. It thus captured the irreverence for convention that was part of the image. The point was that no Beetle driver could possibly be concerned with fashionable appearance — economy and reliability had to be the ownership rationale. Second it was distinctive, for two decades, no competitor was willing to copy the shape. Third, the shape *was* the Beetle (Aaker, 1992: 185).

The Brand Name

The brand name performs two major tasks from an image point of view. It can become the anchor for all associations with the brand in the mind of the consumer. The very utterance of brand names such as Disney, Marlboro and Guinness all conjure up specific meanings and associations. Secondly, the brand name can, in certain instances, contribute to the image-formation process, by virtue of denotative and connotative values of the words for consumers. Obvious examples of brand names being utilised to articulate the functional values of the brand are Mr Sheen, Crisp 'n Dry, Brillo, Soft and Gentle, etc.

Slogans/Copy

While brand names and symbols are capable of communicating certain associations, the copy slogan chosen offers greater articulation and flexibility. It can be used to deliver core brand messages and assist in positioning the brand in the consumer's frame of reference. Examples of well-known slogans are "We try harder" (Avis), "The appliance of Science" (Zanussi), "Don't leave home without it" (American Express) and "Now, what can we do for you?" (Bank of Ireland).

Similarly, the advertising copy can convey potent images, as in the case of David Ogilvy's Rolls-Royce advertisement "At 60 miles an hour, the loudest noise in this new Rolls-Royce comes from the electric clock" or Fallon McElligott's campaign for the Episcopal Church in the US, "In a church started by a man with six wives, forgiveness goes without saying" (Collins, 1989). In an Irish context, advertising copy such as "This 30 seconds of darkness has been brought to you by Guinness" represents a highly effective exhortation to relax, thereby placing Guinness on the correct side in the "pace-of-life war".

MEDIA/MEDIA VEHICLE EFFECTS

The second major aspect of advertising that forms part of the image creation process is concerned with the effects wrought on an audience by placing an advertisement in a particular medium. Communication theory focuses on three key elements of such effects: source, medium and media vehicle. As used in advertising, source effect as a concept more properly belongs with message content, but it is briefly mentioned here as source, medium and media vehicle effect are generally discussed together.

Source effect is based on the belief that various characteristics of the perceived source of the communication have a beneficial effect on message receptivity (Hovland and Weiss, 1951; Hovland, Janis and Kelly, 1953; Kelman, 1961). Several source characteristics — credibility, attractiveness, power and visibility — are generally accepted as being important in bringing about attitude change (Percy and Rossiter, 1980). In local contexts such as Ireland, where source attributes are more easily understood by the consumer, such campaigns occur quite frequently. Individuals such as Jack Charlton, Dave Fanning and Darina Allen convey the source attributes of visibility, credibility, attractiveness, if not necessarily power, to emphasise particular messages targeted at different groups, with a view to encouraging specific buying behaviours.

Media Effect

Just as different methods of marketing communications differ in their effects on audience, the qualitative aspects of different media, such as television, radio and press, are also widely believed to affect audience reaction (Crane, 1970, 1972; Grass and Wallace, 1974). Joyce (1981), in analysing this issue of media values or rub-off effect from the medium to the message, suggests that inter-media comparisons are complex and that it is difficult to substantiate the different moods which they are supposed to induce based on suggested differences in terms of authority, climate, environment etc. In summary, he suggests that:

> ... the belief that an advertisement will act more effectively in one medium rather than in another is unconsciously built into most media planning, but few people would be able to justify their faith in it (609).

Media-Vehicle Effect

The third level at which the phenomenon of image association effect can be examined is at the individual media vehicle level. This level can encompass individual magazines, newspapers and individual radio and television channels, and, at a further level of analysis, the individual programmes occurring on these channels. Each particular media vehicle possesses its own individual characteristics as perceived by the recipient, and thereby induces a specific mood of receptivity that affects the impact of the persuasive communications. It is termed the media-option source effect by Aaker and Myers (1987), who suggest that it:

> ... is not a measure of a vehicle's capacity to attract readers ... nor is it the quality of the audience.... It is, rather, the differential impact that the advertisement exposure will have on the same audience member if the exposure occurs in one media option rather than another (473–4).

Central to this concept of image transfer and its effect on message receptivity is the belief that different media vehicles possess individual personalities A recent Irish study (Brennan, 1994) has shown that audiences do indeed see particular media vehicles as having distinct personalities. A multi-stage research study of third-level female students sought to determine their perceptions of two magazines available on the Irish market. The results revealed that these respondents perceived two distinct personalities for *Cosmopolitan* and *Woman's Own*. Some 38 different image dimensions of these magazines, unearthed in focus group research, were subsequently analysed in two follow-up research surveys. Figure 16.2 shows a selection of the key image dimensions on which respondents believed these magazines to differ.

FIGURE 16.2: PERSONALITY PROFILES OF *COSMOPOLITAN* AND *WOMAN'S OWN*

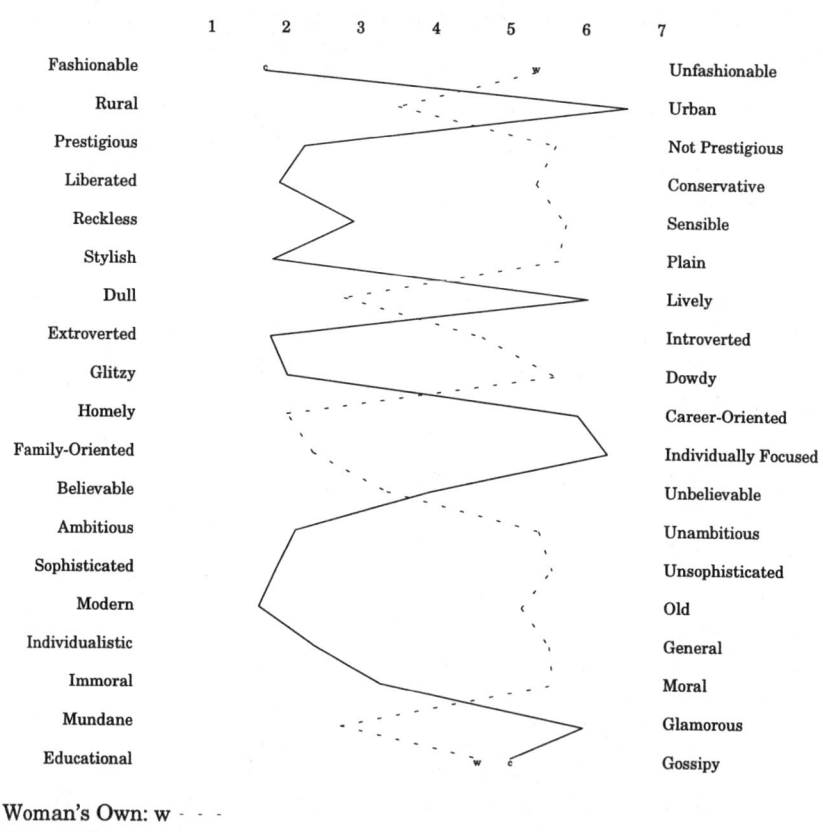

Fashionable	Unfashionable
Rural	Urban
Prestigious	Not Prestigious
Liberated	Conservative
Reckless	Sensible
Stylish	Plain
Dull	Lively
Extroverted	Introverted
Glitzy	Dowdy
Homely	Career-Oriented
Family-Oriented	Individually Focused
Believable	Unbelievable
Ambitious	Unambitious
Sophisticated	Unsophisticated
Modern	Old
Individualistic	General
Immoral	Moral
Mundane	Glamorous
Educational	Gossipy

Woman's Own: w - - -
Cosmopolitan: c ———

The research study further found that respondents believed that there was a congruence between particular product categories and the appropriateness of the magazine. Product categories with a highly symbolic content — such as perfume, cosmetics, lingerie, hair colorants and fashions — were appropriate for *Cosmopolitan*, while cleaning agents and food and beverages for the household were seen as appropriate for *Woman's Own*. The impact of the magazine's image on consumer perceptions of brand image was evident when the same ads for five products were inserted into a copy of each magazine and rated on the dimensions used to define the magazine's personality. These products appearing in *Woman's Own* were considered dull, homely, altruistic and practical. When the very same ads for the same products appeared in *Cosmopolitan*, the products were seen to be more extroverted, sophisticated, modern and stylish. Indeed the price of the same brands was perceived by the respondents as more expensive in *Cosmopolitan* than in *Woman's Own*.

While the implications of media-vehicle effect for brand image development are obvious, the reality is that alternative media vehicles in all markets, including Ireland, are rarely described according to the attributes outlined above. Media planners, intuitively aware of personality differences between vehicles, marry their own qualitative judgments in this regard with the more quantitative aspects of media selection.

CONCLUSION

Image creation has become a critically important aspect of modern marketing. The company seeking to form a particular image in the mind of the consumer has available a wide variety of ingredients of identity. However, other factors beyond the brand owner's control also serve to affect the image ultimately formed by the consumer. Of these company-controlled elements of identity, advertising represents a particularly potent method of image creation. It is capable of fostering consumer beliefs about particular product attributes and imbuing a brand with desired symbolic values. Where brand image objectives are sought, the content of the advertising message and the image rub-off from the carrying medium and media vehicle should be combined to foster the desired imagery.

REFERENCES

Aaker, D.A. (1992): *Managing Brand Equity: Capitalising on the Value of a Brand Name*, New York: The Free Press.

Aaker, D.A. and Myers, J.G. (1987): *Advertising Management*, 3rd Edition, Englewood Cliffs, NJ: Prentice Hall International Edition.

Aaker, D. and Morris, D. (1982): "Characteristics of TV Commercials Perceived as Informative", *Journal of Advertising Research*, 22(2): 22–34

Belk, R.W. (1983): *Explanations for Congruence Between Patron Stereotypes and Patron Self-Concepts, Proceeding of the American Psychological Association Conference*, Los Angeles, CA: American Psychological Association.

Boulding, K. (1956): *The Image — Knowledge in Life and Society*, Ann Arbor, MI: University of Michigan Press.

Brennan, M. (1994): "Establishing the Existence of the Media Vehicle Effect in Women's Magazines", (unpublished) MBS dissertation, University College Dublin.

Broadbent, K. and Cooper P. (1987), "Research is Good for You", *Marketing Intelligence and Planning*, 5(1): 3–9

Colley, R (1961): *Defining Goals for Measured Advertising Results*, London: Association of National Advertisers.

Collins, J.M. (1989): "Image and Advertising", *Harvard Business Review*, 67(1): 93–7.

Cooper, P. (1989): "Comparison Between the UK and US: The Qualitative Dimension", *Journal of the Marketing Research Society*, 31(4), October: 509–20.

Cooper, P. and Kaye, T. (1987): "The Art of Consuming", *Survey*, Autumn: 18–22.

Cooper, Peter (1980), "Symbiosis in Media: New Perspectives on Media Psychology", *Admap*, 16(6): 290–98.

Crane, E. (1972): *Marketing Communications — Decision Making as a Process of Interaction Between Buyer and Seller*, New York: John Wiley.

Crask, M.R. and Laskey, H.A. (1990): "A Positioning-based Decision Model for Selecting Advertising Messages", *Journal of Advertising Research*, 30(4): 32–8.

De Groot, G. (1980): *The Persuaders Exposed*, London: Associated Business Press.

Doyle, P. (1989): "Building Successful Brands: The Strategic Options", *Journal of Marketing Management*, 5(1): 77–95.

Durgee, J.F. (1988): "Understanding Brand Personality", *Journal of Consumer Marketing*, 5(3): 21–5.

Gardner, B.B. and Levy, S.J. (1955): "The Product and the Brand", *Harvard Business Review*, March/April: 33–9.

Grass, R.C. and Wallace, H. (1974): "Advertising Communication: Print vs TV", *Journal of Advertising Research*, 14(5): 19–23.

Grier, P. (1991): "The Corporation as Brand", *Chief Executive*, 66, April: 38–41.

Gunther, E.E. (1959): *Evaluating Corporate Image Measurement, Proceedings of the ARF (Advertising Research Foundation)*, New York: Advertising Research Foundation: 61–6.

Hovland, C.I. and Weiss, W. (1951): "The Influence of Source Credibility on Communication Effectiveness", *Public Opinion Quarterly*, 15, Winter: 635–50.

Hovland, C.I.,. Janis, I.J. and Kelly, H.H. (1953), *Communication and Persuasion*, New Haven: Yale University Press.

Johar, J.S. and Sirgy, M.J. (1991): "Value-Expressive versus Utilitarian Advertising Appeals: When and Why to Use Which Appeal", *Journal of Advertising*, 20(3): 23–33.

Joyce, T. (1967): What Do We Know About How Advertising Works?, ESOMAR Seminar, Noordurijk aan Zee, Holland.

Joyce, T. (1981): "Attitude Research as a Measure of Media Values", *Admap*, 17(12): 609–14.

Joyce, T. (1991): "Models of the Advertising Process", in *How Advertising Works and How Promotions Work, ESOMAR Seminar, 22–24 April 1991*, ESOMAR: Amsterdam: 267–81.

Kelman, H.C. (1961), "Processes of Opinion Change", *Public Opinion Quarterly*, 25: 57–78.

Kim, P. (1990): "A Perspective on Brands", *Journal of Consumer Marketing*, 7(3), 63–7.

King, S. (1989): "Marketing Thinkers — The Marketing Interview", *Marketing*, 16 March: 31.

King, Stephen (1991): "Brand-Building in the 1990's", *Journal of Consumer Marketing*, 8(4): 43–52.

Kotler, P. (1988): *Marketing Management: Analysis, Planning and Control*, Englewood Cliffs, NJ: Prentice Hall.

Kunkel, J.H. and. Berry, L.L. (1968): "A Behavioural Conception of Retail Image", *Journal of Marketing*, 32(4): 21–7.

Lannon, J. and. Cooper, P. (1983): "Humanistic Advertising — A Holistic Cultural Perspective", *International Journal of Advertising*, 2: 195–213.

Laskey, H.A., Day, E. and Crask, M.R. (1989): "Typology of Main Message Strategies for Television Commercials", *Journal of Advertising*, 18(1): 36–41.

Lavidge, R. and Steiner, G. (1961): "A Model for Predictive Measurements of Advertising Effectiveness", *Journal of Marketing*, 25(4): 59–62.

Leiss, W., Kline, S. and Jhaly, S. (1986): *Social Communication in Advertising: Persons, Products and Images of Well-Being*, London: Methuen.

Levy, L. (1990): "Brand Aid for Britain", *Management Today*, September: 101–4.

Levy, S.J. (1959): "Symbols for Sale", *Harvard Business Review*, July/August: 117–24.

Marguiles, W.P. (1977): "Make the Most of Your Corporate Identity", *Harvard Business Review*, 55(4): 61–77.

Martineau, P. (1958): "The Personality of the Retail Store", *Harvard Business Review*, 36(1): 47–55.

Mazursky, D. and Jacoby, J. (1986): "Exploring the Development of Store Image", *Journal of Retailing*, 50(2): 145–65.

McDonald, C. (1992): *How Advertising Works — A Review of Current Thinking*, Henley on Thames, Oxfordshire: NTC Publications Ltd, in association with the Advertising Association

McWilliam, G. and De Chernatony, L. (1989): "Branding Terminology — The Real Debate", *Marketing Intelligence and Planning*, 7(7/8): 29–32.

Noth, W. (1988): "The Language of Commodities: Groundwork for a Semiotics of Consumer Goods", *International Journal of Research in Marketing*, 4: 173–86.

Ogilvy, D. (1963): *Confessions of an Advertising Man*, New York, Ballantine Books.

Olins, W. (1989): *Corporate Identity: Making Business Strategy Visible Through Design*, London: Thames and Hudson.

Parker, K. (1991): "Sponsorship — The Research Contribution", *European Journal of Marketing*, 25(11): 22–30.

Percy, L. and Rossiter, J.R. (1980): *Advertising Strategy: A Communications Theory Approach*, New York: Praeger Publishing.

Poiesz, T. (1989): "The Image Concept: Its Place in Consumer Psychology", *Journal of Economic Psychology*, 10: 457–72.

Puto, C.P. and Wells, W.D. (1984): "Informational and Transformational Advertising: The Differential Effects of Time", in Kinnear, C. (ed.), *Advances in Consumer Research XI*, Thomas Provo, UT: Association for Consumer Research.

Randazzo, S. (1991): "Move Over Medusa, Here Comes Big Mac", *Marketing News*, 25(15), 4.

Rossiter, J.R. and Percy, L. (1987): *Advertising and Promotional Management*, New York: McGraw-Hill.

Rossiter, J.R., Percy, L. and Donovan, R.J. (1991): "A Better Advertising Planning Grid", *Journal of Advertising Research*, 31, October/November, 11–21.

Sirgy, J.M. (1982): "Self-Concept in Consumer Behaviour: A Critical Review", *Journal of Consumer Research*, 9: 287–300.

Spandler, R. (1987): "Making a Marque", *Marketing*, 30 July: 20–21.

Starch, D. (1925): *Principles of Advertising*, New York: Shaw.

Strong, E.K. (1925): *The Psychology of Selling*, New York, McGraw Hill

Vaughn, R. (1980): "How Advertising Works: A Planning Model", *Journal of Advertising Research*, 20(5): 27–33.

Wells, B. (1989): "Branding, (Part II), Order out of Chaos", *Marketing and Media Decisions*, 24(6): 99–100.

Wicks, A. (1989), "Advertising Research — An Eclectic View from the UK", *Journal of the Market Research Society*, 31(4): 527–35.

17
Strategic Corporate Identity and Corporate-Image Research in Ireland

John D. Byrne

INTRODUCTION

Corporate identity can have an extraordinarily powerful influence on the commercial position of a company. Some corporate identities give rise to imagery that is so well entrenched in consumers' minds, that they would find it almost impossible to accept familiar brand names on products with which they had no prior association:

> ... for example who would buy a bottle of "Maxol" milk or a can of "Esso" cola? (Burlingame, 1986: 17).

In a changing world, establishing a new or more appropriate identity may be no easy matter.

IMAGE AND IDENTITY

It may be helpful, at the outset, to differentiate between corporate identity and corporate image. Essentially, these are cause and effect, respectively. Corporate identity is "the articulation of what the organisation is, what it stands for and what it does" (Topalian, 1984: 55). Identity can be described in terms of products/services, environments, buildings, information-communications material and behaviour, and expressed in terms of names, symbols, logos, colours and rites of passage which the organisation uses to distinguish itself, its brands and its constituent companies (Olins, 1989). Figure 17.1 illustrates some likely constituents of this above model of corporate identity.

In the present dynamic environment, it is arguable, however, that statements of corporate identity must now contain a substantial subjunctive element — that is, what we want to be. A definition of corporate identity is especially a prerequisite for firms in transition: delaying commitment in this regard until changes have been accomplished is tantamount to saying to a company's public "We'll know where we are when we get there!" Corporate image, as opposed to corporate identity, is stated in terms of effect: "the perception of the company by its publics" (Margulies, 1977: 66) or "the impression of the overall corporation by its various publics" (Gray and Smeltzer, 1985: 73).

FIGURE 17.1: ELEMENTS OF CORPORATE IDENTITY

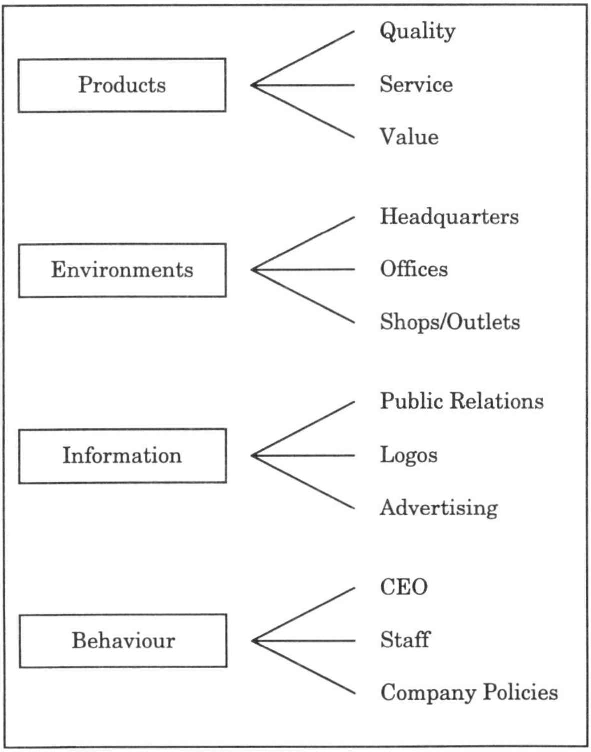

- Products
  - Quality
  - Service
  - Value
- Environments
  - Headquarters
  - Offices
  - Shops/Outlets
- Information
  - Public Relations
  - Logos
  - Advertising
- Behaviour
  - CEO
  - Staff
  - Company Policies

Source: Adapted from Olins, W. (1989): *Corporate Identity,* New York: Thames and Hudson.

MARKETING IMPLICATIONS OF CORPORATE IMAGE

Over the years, many well-known Irish companies and services, ranging from AIB and the Irish Permanent plc to Rehab, have implemented corporate-identity programmes, as part of their strategy to establish or rebuild equity — "to establish a strong presence in a particular market" (Decyk and McDonald, 1986: 37).

The marketplace demands that the fit between the corporation and the "brand" — product or service — be appropriate. This complex corporate/brand relationship can be rationalised into several basic categories, depending on the degree of dominance of either. This can range from the *single entity* nature of IIG-BOC — which produces a narrow and specialised product line or set of services (in the above case, gas products for industry). In other situations, the *brand image dominates* (exemplified by the relationship between Guinness plc and its well-known brands, such as Guinness itself and Harp/Celebration Brew or that between An Post and its branded service companies, such as SDS). In other situations, the *corporation's image dominates*, examples of which are provided by the Irish operations of multinationals such as IBM and Hewlett-Packard.

While by no means all corporate/brand relationships fit neatly into this classification, in the long-term, many will fit into one of the categories in the short-term. The marketing implications of corporate identity will vary, according to which of the above relationships is appropriate. The requirement for the correct linkage between corporate and brand identity is strong in the case of many production-based corporations, but it is likely to be even stronger in the intangible services market where, often, the corporate image provides one of the few indications to the customer of the service quality that can be expected.

Corporate identity may, therefore, be promoted in the marketplace for any (or possibly all) of the following reasons:

- To encourage favourable behaviour towards the company
- To effect the sale of the products
- To give products an additional advantage
- To attract shareholders
- To attract suitable employees
- To foster good relations with the community
- To aid good relations with government
- To influence attitudes
- To create favourability by creating familiarity
- To reflect the company positively

- To serve corporate objectives, specific or general
- To assist management decision-making.

Used in these ways, corporate identity functions, much like any other planned persuasive communication, to convince the public that the company is friendly, honest, keen to offer service (or whatever else it is that the company management wishes to convey). It also has secondary effects: for instance, it may have a strong bearing on the way in which employees act as salespersons externally on behalf of the company (Kennedy, 1977).

The Strategic Nature of Corporate Identity

> In the 1980s, corporate identity building activities attracted millions of pounds of investment — and enormous opprobrium from the media ... is it money wisely spent or the story of the emperor's new clothes? (Zentner, 1994: 117).

The search for corporate identity almost always starts — and all too often ends — with the search for a visual solution with often a consequent over-emphasis on the design function. It may be better to think in terms of strategic identity: the motor which drives the company and whose output — an increase in profitable business — can be measured. The strategic dimension of identity facilitates the important parties of the equation — customers, distributors, retailers, financial analysts, stockholders, government agencies, employees, suppliers, the general public — in coming to a rapid and accurate decision about where a company is going (Gray and Smeltzer, 1985). The perspective of strategic identity seems, thus, more appropriate to today's dynamic business environments than the static four-element model of corporate identity composed of "products/services, environments, information and behaviour." (Olins, 1989). It also encapsulates the subjunctive element more appropriately than models consisting of just the "physical, operational and human characteristics" (Topalian, 1984: 57). In effect, strategic identity implies a purposeful, holistic and future-oriented perspective.

The term "corporate identity" can therefore be used in a dynamic sense and it:

> ... lies in the company's approach — what it believes, how it conducts its business — and is expressed in everything the organisation does — its products and services, its communications, its buildings, its dealings with the outside world" (Sedgwick, 1990: 20).

However, identity must also be rooted firmly in achievable reality. One need only look across the water to the example of British Rail, which found, with its "We're getting there" image campaign, that:

> when the gap between dream and BR reality simply became too great, the best of design and creativity could not compensate for less-than-best reality (O'Connor, 1990: 20).

The carry-over of past, possibly negative, imagery associated with institutions such as public-transport systems often requires far-reaching measures to ensure a complete crossover to a new public perception. On this side of the Irish Sea, the strong linkage between the new operational transport systems — Iarnród Éireann, Bus Éireann and Dublin Bus — and their previous parent, CIE, seems to persist and is evidenced by corporate-image research carried out with the general public. This linkage is unlikely to be particularly supportive of their present ambitions and the imagery used to embody them.

Irrespective of the specific area of operation of a company (retail, production, services, etc.), its long-term business strategy — what it wishes, and feels it can achieve, over time — should determine its corporate identity. For example, in the services area, strategic commitment to demonstrating total quality translates just as easily into effective corporate branding as any logo or name does in the FMCG area.

It should also be remembered that corporate identity belongs on the equity side of the balance sheet and, as a long-term asset, it must be framed broadly enough to allow sufficient leeway for the timing and manner in which strategic objectives are achieved. Image is a long-term resource, communicating with institutions and the public in a unique way and, as such, its use as part of short-term PR programmes is questionable (Kennedy, 1977).

GLOBALISATION AND THE CHANGING ENVIRONMENT FOR IRISH CORPORATIONS

Even the most casual or disinterested observer of economic or business affairs can scarcely fail to have noticed the dramatic (or in some cases, traumatic) changes that have swept through the Irish corporate landscape in the 1990s. Institutions that have formed cornerstones of Ireland's business awakening over the past 30 years have suddenly been shown to have feet of clay.

A further consideration, of necessity, is the global development of business. Whether manifest in forcing the removal of protective barriers, or in deregulating industries, or simply in exposing native institutions to the rigorous fiscal requirements for conducting international business, this has been the root cause of almost all of the above sea-changes. The "clever coincidence of history" of the simultaneous rise to power of Thatcher, Reagan and Nagasome — all three strongly embracing a free-market economy, each at the centre of a trade bloc and all instrumental in forcing economic liberalisation on their respective nations — has constituted the powerhouse behind the unprecedented drive towards the internationalisation of business (Egan and McKiernan, 1993).

Failure of some of our native institutions to measure up in the new, increasingly open worldwide markets, even in the short term, has caused public confidence in many Irish corporations to be stirred, if not shaken. As an insurance policy against such loss of confidence, part of the strategic plan of any Irish firm must be to ensure that its corporate image among its various publics — customers, suppliers, employees, investors, government — is consistent with its competitive aims. On the global stage, if we do not trust, respect and understand our own institutions, how can we expect others to do so?

CORPORATE PUBLICS

If corporate image provides "a means of differentiation at both corporate and brand level", then corporate identity is "the glue that keeps these corporation from falling apart". Corporate identity, of necessity, incorporates strong demand-side (or customer-oriented) and supply-side (internally directed within the firm) aspects (Olins, 1979). Businesses are increasingly differentiating between demand-side, or customer-instigated, measures that affect the way they do business and supply-side, or internally instigated, processes, over which, they would claim at least, to have considerably more control.

Indeed, as the number of publics interacting with major corporations has grown dramatically, this inward- and outward-looking nature becomes increasingly important where corporate image facilitates or inhibits negotiations with suppliers, where the corporate identity has become inappropriate to the nature of the business, or to facilitate improved employee productivity, by boosting morale and efficiency. Corporate image frequently influences share price, and poor corporate image, may cause shareholder disquiet and may even influence the outcome of a flotation, as it did in the case of Guinness Peat Aviation (Cullen, 1994).

Ireland has a relatively small population size and a large services sector, and this proximity of supply and demand provides a considerable degree of feedback between those inside and those outside the corporation. The relatively open communications policies of some of the major service players in Ireland also serve to bring about a degree of convergence between the views of the internal and the external publics — namely, staff and customers.

COMMUNICATIONS IN CORPORATE-IDENTITY CREATION

Traditionally, when management is reconsidering its corporate identity, it turns immediately to a design consultancy:

> You go to a surgeon and the advice is "cut". You go to a designer and the advice is "design" (Zentner, 1990: 117).

However, creation of a corporate identity involves much more than the design of an eye-catching logo — it must represent a visual clarification of structural relationships and, ideally, reflect a company's personality. Communication of the identity is important, both within and outside the organisation. Within the company, the communications must be two-way — the potentially valuable contribution of employees can be unwittingly restricted by practising top-down communication only. In many cases, corporations in a state of change feel obliged to wait until those changes have been completed and the dust has settled on the new corporation, before unveiling their revised identity. By delaying in this way, and specifically, by failing to discuss in advance, outward signs of change with staff at various levels, using planned internal marketing, organisations in transition are inevitably missing out on valuable opportunities to bring employees down the road of the change process itself.

Specifically, in the design area, the visible image is:

> ...an appreciating asset which, tended with respect, can last for decades, working for 24 hours a day, 365 days a year (Sedgwick, 1990: 20).

The package and, particularly, the logo must be visible, must have a high visual-retention value and create a pleasant feeling. The fit between the identity "package" and the organisation's strategic direction must be exact if conflict is to be avoided. In today's competitive market, good examples of organisations in transition and cognisant of the need for fit between strategic direction and corporate identity is provided by financial institutions such as ACC, AIB and Irish Permanent plc.

PLANNING FOR CORPORATE-IMAGE DEVELOPMENT

Opinion research is the critical first step in planning a corporate-identity programme, since the gap between what a company thinks of itself and what its various publics think of it can be significant (Olins, 1989). While the strategic approach provides direction to the identity-creation or change process, considerable preliminary research, generally of a qualitative nature, may be required, to establish where the company is and to provide insights and pointers to future strategic directions. Customers — the larger public — as well as internal and external stakeholders, should be involved in this process.

Generally, a programme of individual depth interviews will be used to unearth the agenda for focus-group discussion. Techniques used will generally include word association, sentence or picture completion, construction of scenarios and various other projective methods. It is reasonable to suggest that a good deal of professional interpretation will be required to distil meaning from research findings and to draw the necessary inferences for the identity-creation process.

When one, or a even a number of, identity packages is finally produced, it (or they) should be pre-tested. Pre-testing of a package may be of a qualitative or quantitative nature. Readability and attractiveness of visual material may be tested by psychological measures such as eye-tracking or galvanometric tests. Focus-group discussions may also be included and, on the quantitative side, hall tests and ad hoc surveys may be carried out to explore the image dimensions in more detail. At this pre-launch stage, tracking survey instruments should also be prepared and fielded, to establish the status quo.

Introducing a new corporate identity requires much preparatory work within the firm or corporation. Ideally, the process will involve all or many of the following activities (Margulies, 1977):

- Preparation of the corporate-identity manual
- Formal meetings with managers and departmental heads
- Indoctrination of all divisional sales executives

- Discussion of the new communications philosophy with union leaders
- Addressing financial audiences to explain the new identity
- Communication to shareholders of the rationale behind the change
- Preparation of advertisements in media throughout the world
- Mailing announcement brochures to employees and letters to customers.

Tangible visual elements of the "old" image generally require immediate visual change. In launching a new corporate identity, almost every externally identifiable aspect must invariably take on a new look. These will include products, packaging, environments, graphics and visuals, publications and advertising.

The non-visual elements, crucial to achieving the unity of corporate purpose that will make the new identity a reality, must be addressed internally within the firm if the company is to follow through on the identity change process. The available evidence supports the view that as much energy as possible should be invested in the launching process. It is important, however, to ensure that elements such as public relations, sponsorship and advertising are completely consistent with strategic objectives of the identity change.

RESEARCHING CORPORATE IMAGE

Public perception of the new corporate identity can best be judged by quantitative longitudinal studies of image. In the dynamic market situation, this method provides the most accurate measures of the pre- and post-situation. Ad hoc measures tend to provide a snapshot of the current situation only, losing the valuable comparative, cause-and-effect dimension that tracking provides.

The broad nature of corporate image — "the sum total of what key constituencies know and think about (the firm)" (Gilfeather, 1986: 9) — makes public response to it notoriously difficult to research. Its strategic nature indicates that such response is best measured in terms of perceived progress towards the achievement of the stated objectives.

Under these circumstances, the following is a systematic approach to the problem:

1) Set out the individual, key goals of the corporation (both internal and external).

2) Identify those elements of corporate image which best indicate whether those goals are perceived to be attained (if such elements are difficult or impossible to identify, this in itself is likely to be a clear indication of deficiencies, mismatches or, simply, lost opportunities in the corporate-image portfolio itself).

3) Track movements in perception of each of these individual elements over time.

The main aspects of corporate image probed in tracking questionnaires are shown in Figure 17.2.

FIGURE 17.2: ASPECTS OF CORPORATE IMAGE PROBED IN FIELD RESEARCH QUESTIONNAIRES

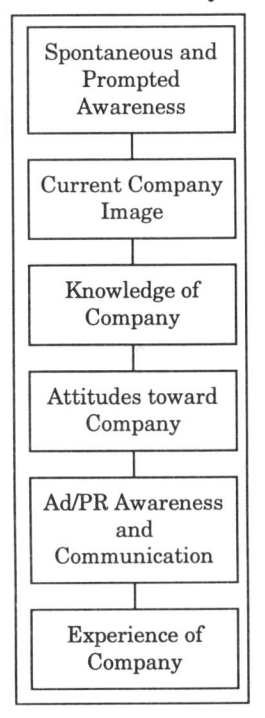

- Spontaneous and Prompted Awareness
- Current Company Image
- Knowledge of Company
- Attitudes toward Company
- Ad/PR Awareness and Communication
- Experience of Company

Corporate-image studies use a range of tools within the questionnaire format. Image Statement Grids — comparative statements applied to a comparative cross-section of similar or dissimilar companies — provide insight into ongoing perception of the company's direction in relative terms. Comparative Rating Scales — which compare companies in pairs or rank them against a particular semantic

— can disclose small but significant shifts in perception. Perhaps the most familiar devices are Attitude Scales, which consist primarily of semantic differential scales.

In Ireland, considerable difficulty is often encountered finding a range of corporations which facilitate like-for-like comparisons, particularly in the case of large bodies. However, this is partly compensated for by high levels of public awareness in respect of existing companies, which generally permits a more detailed line of questioning to be entered into than would otherwise be the case.

A case history in respect of ESB is provided in this paper to illustrate a number of these points. This case history uses original monitored tracking data, professionally collected and analysed. The research programme, from which the data is derived, is part of a large-scale, on-going tracking programme carried out on behalf of ESB, with a range of objectives, including the determination of the effect of its corporate policies on key dimensions of its corporate image, as perceived by customers. The case history focuses on ESB's corporate-change process and the elements of image investigated are chosen to reflect whether these goals are consistent with the way in which ESB's customers perceive that their present and future needs are being met and will continue to be met. They are also likely to reflect the extent to which the corporation is perceived to be approaching the attainment of its goals.

The desired outcome of the research process is therefore to ensure that customers continue to see ESB as a company that provides an appropriately high level of service, up to and including the completion of the corporate change process. Under these circumstances, it will assist in permitting a smooth and credible transition to the image appropriate to the transformed organisation, without loss of the high ground already occupied by the corporation.

At the same time, such feedback should also reinforce and provide direction to the change process itself. ESB staff are also members of the community that they serve. They are Irish people with a demonstrated pride in their work and their corporation. A strongly positive public perception of the corporation's change process would be very difficult for staff to ignore. Thus, while the customer-held view does not purport to represent the effectiveness of internal communications within the organisation, its very nature, as it has evolved over the past 65 years or so, is likely to ensure that such views will be taken into consideration by staff, in any deliberation of the organisational change process itself.

EVALUATING EFFECTIVENESS

The level of success of a corporate-identity programme is easiest to estimate along defined strategic dimensions, where the quantifiable measures, such as increasing sales or profits, attracting employees or encouraging shareholders, are relatively easy to evaluate. Less quantifiable are objectives stated in terms of improving community relations or influencing attitudes or behaviour towards the company. Experience and careful research-instrument design provide the only assurances that such objectives have been met.

A number of mathematical modelling techniques can be applied to on-going survey results, to ensure that the size and direction of trends are properly identified. In almost all cases, graphical techniques provide the most immediate method for linking cause and effect, as illustrated in the ESB case history. The more crucial aspects of corporate image should, however, be subjected to a fuller, yet linked, research, and inferences in respect of fundamental aspects of image, derived from graphical methods, should be backed up by this linked research.

Corporate-image research findings should be communicated at regular (at least quarterly) intervals to senior management, and highlights should be communicated to the boardroom at these times. General staff and other internal stakeholders may also be made aware, through internal communications systems, of important developments. This provides an important feedback mechanism, which may serve to fine-tune policy and response on specific corporate issues. A formal briefing approach, focusing on movements of key indices, generally facilitates optimal communication of information. Depending on the nature and size of the company or corporation, such briefing sessions will take between 20 and 45 minutes, and this will include adequate time for discussion of findings.

The strategic dimensions of the corporate image should provide the focus for analysis of data, as they represent a discrete set of objectives against which progress can be measured; in the age-old justification of evaluation — it is those things that get measured that ultimately get done!

ELECTRICITY SUPPLY BOARD (ESB) — A CASE STUDY

Introduction

Perceptions of the competitive structure of the services market in Ireland are virtually unique in Western Europe. The insular nature of the territory has encouraged the growth of native expertise and the process of "fending for ourselves" has put a peculiarly Irish flavour on our perceptions of most of our institutions. The origins of ESB are rooted in a time in post-independence Ireland when the creation of quasi-service corporations — a public corps — was required to function with a commercial remit, and yet to carry forward key parts of the mission of the state. For almost half a century, these corporations were perceived as providing particularly effective solutions to particularly intractable problems, associated primarily with lack of readily accessible sources of investment capital. Such circumstances must seem hardly credible to those who have grown up in dramatically more entrepreneurial times. Changed times have meant that such enterprises are today perceived as being insulated from the exigencies of operating in a truly competitive market.

The combination of our small population and our developing economy has resulted in state and semi-state enterprise playing, perhaps, a more pervasive role in our economy and occupying a more salient position in the hearts and minds of our citizens than in almost any other Western European nation. However, the potential for conflict in perceptions of the role and performance of such enterprise, in a changed era of extreme transnational competition, is now almost limitless.

Supply-Industry Restructuring

For ESB, the restructuring of the electricity supply industry to bring it into line with prevailing conditions in the EU over the next few years, will introduce unprecedented change in the competitive nature of the business in which the corporation has held a virtual monopoly position for so long. While it would be quite inaccurate to consider ESB as being unused to commercial pressure and lacking in the ability to compete — after all, its international subsidiary, ESBI, has operated very successfully in highly competitive international markets for many years now — new factors, such as the unbundling of its generation and distribution functions, exposure to competition in its home market, and the possibility of "out-of-state" supply to major customers — will certainly bring about changes in the way in which ESB conducts its business in Ireland. To compete in this new situation, ESB has initiated a strategic readjustment programme, which will require it to change the way that it perceives itself, and the way that others perceive it, in core areas of its business.

The corporate identity and corporate image of the company have a vital role to play in this dynamic process. While communication between corporate ESB and its publics — Government, consumers and staff — has functioned successfully throughout the change process, there is a need to communicate positively what its new strategic identity will be, in order to maintain the impetus of the process and to preserve the confidence of all parties.

ESB's Corporate-Reorganisation Programme

The present study focuses on events in the public domain that directly relate to corporate reorganisation and their effect on customers' perceptions of the organisation, as measured in ESB's Corporate Image tracking programme, over the period 1991–95. ESB first announced its intention to reorganise itself to meet future challenges in 1992. This announcement and subsequent progress reports on proposed changes received widespread attention in the national media. During the case-study period, therefore, a steady build-up in reporting of ESB's progress in its internal reorganisation process occurred in the period May, June and July of 1992. The cost and competitiveness review process (CCR) represented another high-profile event and commenced in December of 1993. The CCR was charged with the task of obtaining agreement on various radical change measures: the creation of strategic business units (SBUs), the requirement to control and, where possible, reduce costs, the general down-sizing of the organisation. Extensive media coverage was also given to that process in February–March of 1995.

Industrial action in 1991 had resulted in widespread power-cuts. There was, therefore, a heightened public awareness of proposed changes and the attendant risk of industrial-relations problems. Further media coverage of prospective price increases also occurred, particularly towards the end of the tracking period in question, in January through April 1994 and August through October 1994.

Corporate-Image-Tracking Research Carried Out by ESB

ESB introduced a formal research programme to track its corporate image and awareness in 1990. This programme now has two paymasters — ESB syndicated the research process in 1993 — and since its inception it has tracked perceptions of corporate profiles of five of the major Irish companies and corporations, in addition to those of ESB and its co-sponsor of the tracking study for comparative purposes. In this process, some 3,500 interviews are conducted by an independent market research agency annually among a sample of general domestic consumers. The sampling process is quota-based and structured around the spread of exposure to broadcasting media. The clusters so-derived are maintained, as far as possible, throughout the entire study period; different sets of respondents are of course interviewed in each survey cycle. The survey process is continuous and the whole geographical area of the country is covered in each four-week interview cycle. Interviews are carried out with heads of household and require about 25 minutes to complete. Analysis of survey questionnaire results is carried out on ESB's behalf by Millward Brown (UK) Ltd., a company with recognised expertise in this area.

The tracking approach employed by ESB in respect of corporate-image measurement provides both indirect and direct measures of corporate image equity. It investigates spontaneous awareness and recall of ESB, both as a corporation and as a fuel supplier, and uses a variety of qualitative techniques to suggest associations for the corporate image; it also tracks responses to real-world events affecting the corporation, and clearly illustrates the responses of consumers which affect one or more dimensions of corporate image over time. Overall, some 14,000 customer interviews were carried out on ESB's behalf in the four-year period in question as part of the ongoing survey process.

Dimensions of ESB's Corporate Image

In its initial section, ESB's corporate-image questionnaire requests respondents to identify 12 separate attitude statements with any, all, or none, of seven specified major enterprises — Aer Lingus, Bord Gáis Éireann, Bord na Móna, ESB, An Post, Telecom Éireann and CIE (Iarnród Éireann, Dublin Bus, Bus Éireann).

In analysing image changes in this way, it is possible to infer, with a high degree of confidence, cause-and-effect relationships between

Analysis of Results

Introduction

The tables presented in graphical form on the following pages are based on the findings of ESB's corporate-image-tracking process carried out over the period October 1990–March 1995. In this process, interviews are carried out among householders (16 years +), using a quota sampling technique which is designed to represent the national adult population on a demographic basis. The data has been weighted to compensate for any bias that might be introduced into the survey by the levels of recognition of the corporations in question or by the sampling process itself. It should also be noted that the results in the tables present a 16-week moving average of the parameter in question. This measure prevents spurious sampling effects from distorting the response function.

While the absolute level of response in respect of several of the parameters in question may appear low, it should be remembered that the survey relates to the complex issues of corporate image, rather than the consumption of count lines. As such, the salience level of some of the elements of its subject matter is relatively low. For this reason, much of the questionnaire format is comparative in nature. On all of the following parameters, ESB has been found to score consistently ahead of its nearest rival, in most cases, considerably so. This comparison with the next nearest competitor is shown in each of the accompanying tables. The figures accompanying the case study show the performance of ESB in terms of how it rated on each examined dimension by comparison to the nearest scoring company on that dimension. In addition, Millward Brown International, the research agency which processes and analyses the tracking survey results on ESB's behalf, is satisfied that the scores achieved by ESB are high, in comparison to those achieved by other corporations in parallel studies carried out in other developed markets.

ESB — Tracking Awareness and Image-Dimensions
Awareness

Two aspects of spontaneous company awareness are investigated in the survey process — awareness of ESB as a fuel supplier and awareness of ESB as a corporation. As might be expected, considering ESB's position in the energy market in Ireland, awareness of ESB as a fuel supplier as shown in Figure 17.4 is typically at a very high level (75–80 per cent) and appears relatively unaffected by reporting of the change process. Awareness of ESB as a corporation as indicated in Figure 17.3, however, appears to have undergone a substantial

FIGURE 17.3: SPONTANEOUS AWARENESS OF ESB AS A CORPORATION (ROLLING 16-WEEKLY DATA)

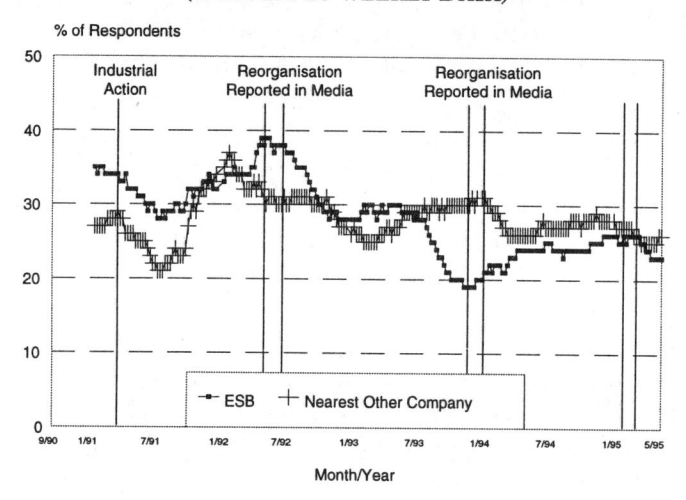

FIGURE 17.4: SPONTANEOUS AWARENESS OF ESB AS A FUEL SUPPLIER (ROLLING 16-WEEKLY DATA)

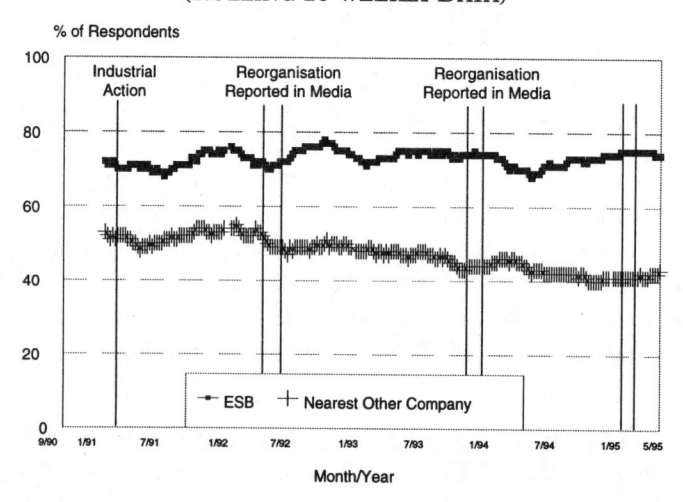

Source: ESB Customer Research, Customer Supply and Marketing.

change at the time of the initial announcement, reaching its highest level in June and July of 1992. After what appears to have been a decline in awareness in late 1993, this parameter underwent a steady build-up throughout 1994, continuing into 1995.

The inference of the foregoing result is that awareness of ESB as a corporation is moderately responsive to publication of the corporate-change process — both to the initial burst in 1992 and to the more gradual build up in 1994; such publicity has little effect on awareness of ESB as a supplier in the fuel or energy market. This evidence is supportive of remarks made earlier in this paper, concerning the ineffectiveness of corporate image as a short-term marketing or promotional tool.

Reliability

For a supply utility, perceived reliability is obviously a key parameter. The tracking study indicates that ESB's corporate image has recovered dramatically on the dimension of reliability since the strike of 1991. Not surprisingly, ESB's image as a reliable supplier had declined markedly as a result of widespread load-shedding which had occurred at this time. However, its recovery over the extremely short period, in corporate terms, of two years or so gives testimony to a high level of credibility which the corporation has established over its lifetime.

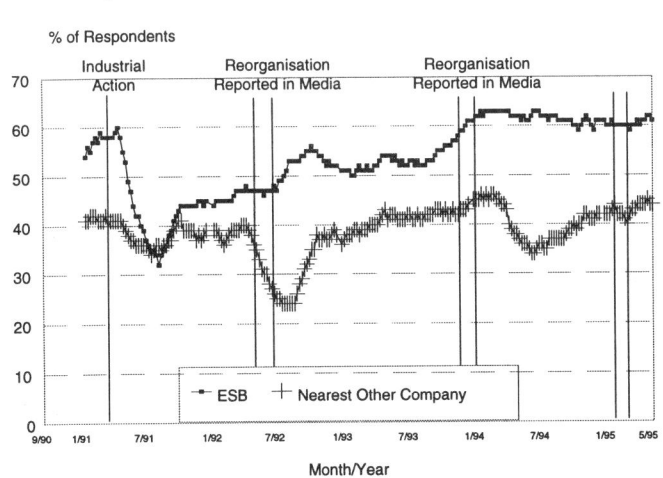

FIGURE 17.5: COMPANY IMAGE — RELIABILITY
(ROLLING 16–WEEKLY DATA WEIGHTED)

Source: ESB Customer Research, Customer Supply and Marketing.

ESB's score on the dimension of perceived reliability reached its highest level to date in the tracking process in mid-1995. This level exceeded that found in the period prior to the strike itself. Reporting of reorganisation coincided with marked increases in the perception of ESB as being reliable, effectively counteracting downturns caused by reporting of industrial relations in the period.

There is also evidence of a plateau effect for the reliability parameter, with little or no decay occurring in such perception in the absence of specific publicity in this regard. This "ratchet effect" points to reliability as one of the more stable of the corporate-image parameters, and would imply, particularly, that negative movements in perception of ESB as reliable should be the cause of grave concern.

"Moving with the Times"

The semantic "moving with the times" incorporates a number of perceived attributes, ranging from technological innovativeness to corporate competitiveness in current commercial conditions. The comparatively high levels of newspaper readership found in Ireland, and the overall quality of the news media, indicate a strong interest in public affairs among the adult population. Respondents to the survey process are therefore well equipped, by and large, to make accurate value judgments in respect of the current positions of large Irish corporations, and this currency has tended to make "moving with the times" one of the more volatile of the image parameters.

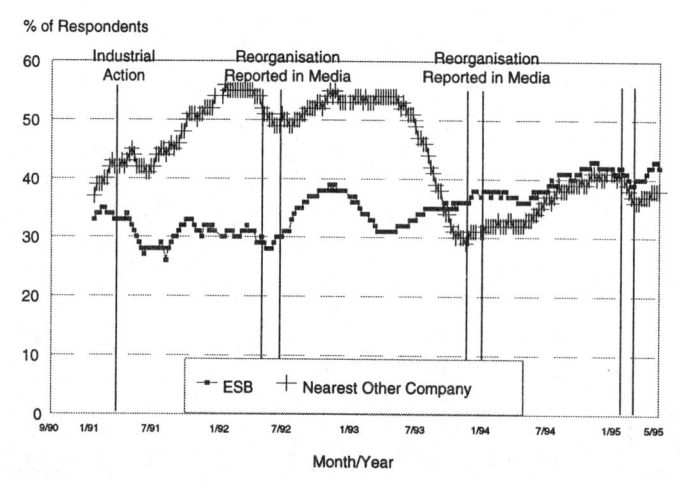

FIGURE 17.6: ESB MOVES WITH THE TIMES
(ROLLING 16-WEEKLY DATA WEIGHTED)

Source: ESB Customer Research, Customer Supply and Marketing.

As can be seen from Figure 17.6 perception of ESB as "moving with the times" had declined dramatically, following the strike in 1991. The first announcement of its corporate-change process was followed by a marked surge in the perception of ESB as "moving with the times". In early 1993, this immediate response decayed rapidly, in the face of negative publicity given, primarily, to aspects of industrial relations within the company.

Since 1993, there has been a steady rise in perception of ESB as a progressive company, corresponding to a build-up of media coverage of ESB's change process. In view of its volatility, however, the parameter of "moving with the times" continues to be monitored closely.

"Responsible Attitude Towards the Community"

The perception that it has a responsible attitude toward the community, most of whom are also its customers, is extremely important for a national utility such as ESB. Almost all of an electricity-supply utility's new works and developmental programmes have a high visibility and are a potential impact on the environment, either locally or on a wider scale. Even such areas as its pricing policy, the level and quality of service it provides and the measures it takes to control its internal cost-structures can be perceived as contributing to the utility "having a responsible attitude" to the (served) community. Information on this dimension is provided in Figure 17.7.

FIGURE 17.7: ESB HAS A RESPONSIBLE ATTITUDE TOWARDS THE COMMUNITY (ROLLING 16-WEEKLY DATA WEIGHTED)

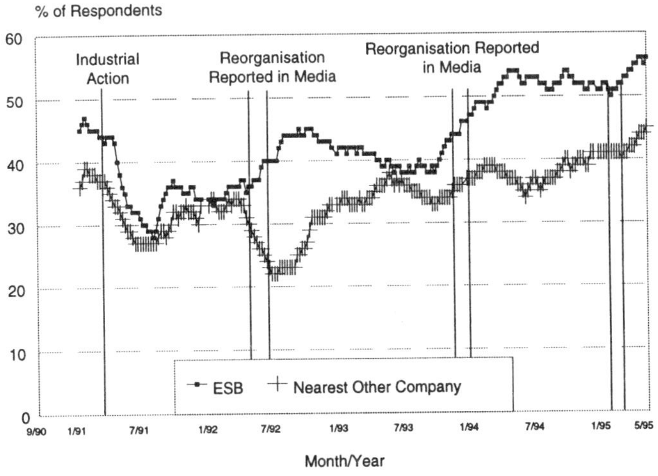

Source: ESB Customer Research, Customer Supply and Marketing.

Again, this parameter of ESB's corporate image has demonstrated itself to be relatively volatile and responsive to media coverage. In the case of ESB, it underwent a dramatic improvement since the strike in 1991. Its 1995 level is considerably higher than that achieved in the period preceding the strike. The response function is "stepped", the main changes corresponding to (a) the initial burst of publicity given to the start of the corporate change process, and (b) the more gradual build up of coverage given to that process in 1993 and 1994. Coverage of its reorganisation process has therefore enhanced perception of ESB as having a responsible attitude to the community and has contributed to raising this perception to an extremely high level, not only as a major corporation but, more particularly, as a national utility.

"Well-Managed Company"

The public's assessment of a corporation as being well-managed is, perhaps, the key indicator of its success (or failure) not only to formulate and implement strategies which are perceived to be in the best interests of all its stakeholders, but also to communicate them effectively. The generality of the term "well-managed" makes it one of the less volatile parameters of corporate image — holding this perception of an organisation appears to have a momentum or "carry-over" effect, which ignores minor or transient negative changes in its affairs.

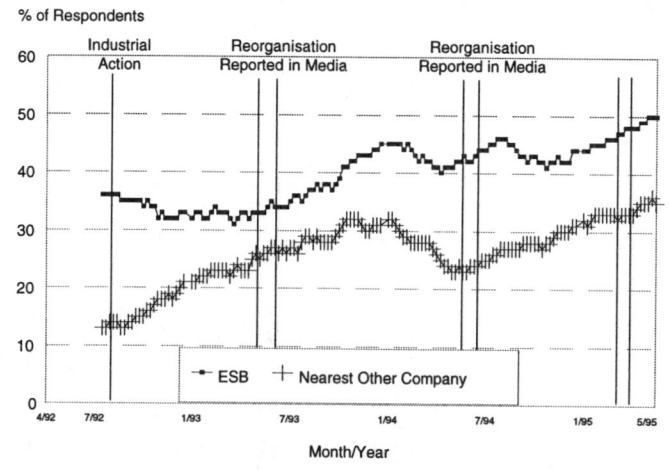

FIGURE 17.8: ESB IS WELL MANAGED
(ROLLING 16-WEEKLY DATA WEIGHTED)

Source: ESB Customer Research, Customer Supply and Marketing.

This semantic was first introduced into ESB's corporate image tracking questionnaire in mid-1992. As can be seen from Figure 17.8, the perception of ESB management was correlated positively with favourable coverage of the reorganisation process in 1993 and 1994.

CONCLUSIONS

Media coverage of ESB's reorganisation programme would appear to have had a strong positive effect on perception of its image as a corporation. This improvement has occurred against the background of an already exceptionally high level of public confidence in ESB as an institution, which has recovered quickly and completely from the strike in early 1991. ESB's dominant image is of a prominent and strong corporation, reorganising and renewing itself for the future. Its corporate image as a utility undergoing change has been successfully communicated. The very prominence of its public image is, however, a double-edged weapon: failure by ESB to meet public expectations in respect of its ability to compete in the future or to provide price- or service-quality benefit to the customer, resulting from increased organisational efficiency, would be unlikely to go unnoticed.

Internal communication of this changed image is implemented in two ways:

- Formal programmes have been established by ESB management for the purpose of explaining the process.
- Each member of ESB's large staff is also a customer and a member of the served public.

Congruence and synergy between its internal and external imagery and communication is vital to achieving and maintaining staff co-operation for the successful implementation of plans. From the level of indicated response, the public is keenly aware of the generalities and even the particulars of ESB's reorganisation programme, since its inception. Clearly, the onus on ESB, beyond 1995, is to provide tangible results of this process.

REFERENCES

Burlingame, H.W. (1986): "Consumers: Creating a New Image", in Simpson, M. (ed.), *Report from the Conference Board*, New York: Conference Board: 17–18.

Cullen, B. (1994): "GPA – The Global Floatation that Failed", Case Study, Department of Marketing, University College Dublin.

Decyk, R.J. and McDonald, J.D. (1986): "The Campaign as Case Study: Navistar", in Simpson, M. (ed.), *Report from The Conference Board*, New York: Conference Board: 37–9.

Egan, C. and McKiernan, P. (1993): *Inside Fortress Europe*, Reading MA: Addison-Wesley.

Gilfeather, J. (1986): "The Role of Research in Corporate Identity: Name, Image and Perception", in Simpson, M. (ed.), *Report from The Conference Board*, New York: Conference Board: 9.

Gray, E.R. and Smeltzer, L.R. (1985): "Corporate Image — An Integral Part of Strategy", *Sloan Management Review*, Summer: 73–8.

Kennedy, S. (1977): "Nurturing Corporate Images", *European Journal of Marketing*, 11(3): 120–59.

Margulies, W.P. (1977): "Make the Most of Your Corporate Identity", *Harvard Business Review*, July/August: 66–72.

O'Connor, M. (1990): "Marketing Image", *Management*: August: 20.

Olins, W. (1979): "What Corporate Identity Means", *Management Today*, April: 80–84.

Olins, W. (1989): *Corporate Identity*, New York: Thames and Hudson.

Sedgwick, L. (1990): "Design: Finding an Identity", *Management*, August: 20–23.

Topalian, A. (1984): "Corporate Identity: Beyond Visual Overstatement", *International Journal of Marketing*: 55–62.

Zentner, P. (1994): "The Dynamics of Strategic Identity" in Heller, R. (ed.), *Managing 1995 — The Global Perspective*, ABC Annuals, New York: Sterling Publications Group: 117–22.

18

Corporate Change: The Convergence of Internal and External Communications Strategies

Kevin Bourke

INTRODUCTION

In the mid-1970s, the AIB responded to the huge growth in the use of its services and in employee numbers in the previous decade by inserting a new middle-management role of Regional Manager. The long-standing and simple command style of head office and branch was no longer adequate or appropriate. The new managers were given extensive training and an explicit brief to be change agents and to represent forcefully the needs of staff and customers to head office and top management. In 1986, the newly-appointed chief executive, who had been one of those "change agents", and had been greatly influenced by his experience, set about the development and implementation of an accelerated change process.

Fundamental to the thinking of the new management team was the conviction that sustainable competitive advantage in financial services could only come from superior customer service. Product and technology innovation, while important, would provide only short-term advantage, as they would inevitably be copied. Furthermore, it was recognised that, uniquely, in banking the customer participated in the design and delivery of its services. That interaction of staff and customers is thus the key element in the achievement of success. Consequently, the quality of management at delivery level is critical to the achievement of the objective of superior customer service.

The customer's perception of service and value is the final arbiter of success, and in the banking context is illustrated by Figure 18.1, which traces the chain of influences on that perception and also shows the complexity and scope of the challenge to be addressed in a change programme.

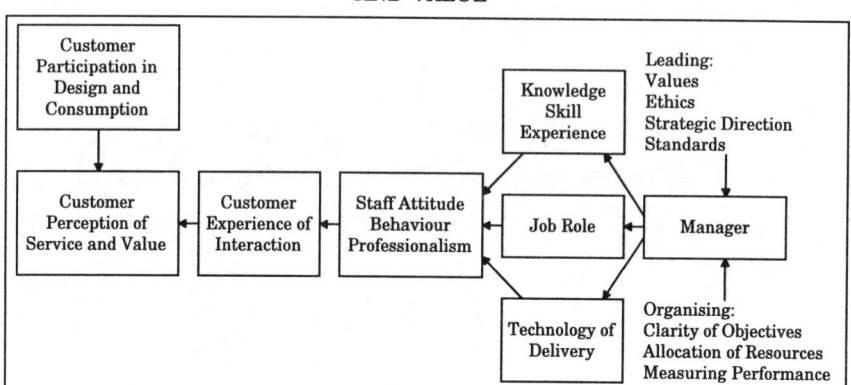

FIGURE 18.1: INFLUENCES ON CUSTOMER PERCEPTIONS OF SERVICE AND VALUE

```
Customer Participation in Design and Consumption
       ↓
Customer Perception of Service and Value ← Customer Experience of Interaction ← Staff Attitude Behaviour Professionalism ↔ Job Role ↔ Manager
                                                                                ↕
                                                                          Knowledge Skill Experience
                                                                          Technology of Delivery

Leading:
Values
Ethics
Strategic Direction
Standards

Organising:
Clarity of Objectives
Allocation of Resources
Measuring Performance
```

PLANNING AND DESIGN
Historical Background

AIB Group is the largest bank in Ireland and has substantial overseas operations. It has assets of over £20 billion and 14,500 employees operating in over 650 branches and representative offices worldwide. Allied Irish Banks (as it was known then) was formed with the merger of three long-established banks — Munster & Leinster Bank, the Provincial Bank and the Royal Bank (which continued to trade separately until 1968). At the time, it employed 2,600 people in Ireland. The name and corporate symbol reflected what it then essentially was — the coming together of three separate banks (see Figure 18.2).

FIGURE 18.2: ALLIED IRISH BANKS LOGO, 1966–90

⊕ Allied Irish Banks plc

The next two decades saw the new group grow dramatically and seek to come to terms with a number of major challenges posed by its internal and external environment. These included the implications of becoming a national organisation, rather than an essentially regional one, as the constituent banks had been. Furthermore, there was diversification into a much wider range of banking functions. What began purely as a clearing bank, has evolved, by the mid-1980s, into a broadly-based financial-services organisation, offering a multiplicity of services.

In parallel with this functional diversification, a geographical diversification was also taking place. AIB began developing significantly in Britain in the early 1970s, and eventually several of its businesses became highly active in this market. Entry to the US market took place in 1979, with the opening of a branch in New York, followed by the investment in (and eventual purchase of) a major regional bank in the State of Maryland. A network of other branch and representative offices in key markets throughout the financial world also grew up over this period.

At home, Ireland itself was undergoing a period of very rapid change, both economically and socially. Its entry into the EEC in 1973 necessitated an outward-looking industrial approach. This in turn contributed to major changes in the way in which business was done in Ireland. Within the banking world itself, changes in the financial-services sector contributed to an increasingly competitive situation.

As the newly merged bank sought to come to terms with all of this change, a major inhibiting factor was the culture that imbued the organisation. Though distinct in personality, the three constituent banks shared a culture born out of their history as clearing banks, which dated back to an era before the modern communications revolution. This culture was focused on the dominant objective of making the clearing system work in a uniform manner throughout the organisation. Remote offices, which had relatively little day-to-day contact with their head offices, had to perform in a standardised and predictable way within a national system of clearing payments.

This culture emphasised adherence to pre-ordained rules, with a rigid top-down management style leaving little scope for individual initiative, and career progress within the bank was strictly on the basis of seniority. Many people working within this framework regarded themselves as part of the "banking service" (sharing many of the characteristics of the civil service), rather than as part of a commercially driven entity. Customers were certainly not the centre of this world — it was a situation in which customers came to the bank seeking services, rather than one in which the bank sought to sell its services to customers. In summary, it was a classic clearing-bank culture, focused on system rather than customers.

This traditional culture lingered on, even though the conditions that had given rise to it had long since ceased to apply. In newer parts of AIB, a totally different culture obtained — one that was entrepreneurial and customer-focused. But these different approaches were cordoned off in subsidiary companies, with relatively little interplay between them and the main organisation. The need for root-and-branch organisational change moved centre stage with the change in the management team in 1986.

The Change Process

The first consideration in remoulding the company culture was an appropriate organisation structure — one that reflected customer needs rather than internal needs and historical contingencies. The key was to bring together business activities in units that addressed coherent markets. An example of how the structure had evolved up to then is provided by AIB's involvement in Britain. Several of the group's businesses had developed independently in that market, each with its own branch structure and each reporting separately to the management of its business unit in Dublin HQ. The result was, to say the least, a fragmented approach to the British market.

The new structure introduced in 1986 aimed to group together those activities that went naturally together from the customer's perspective, even though this meant mixing together in one division a variety of different cultures and practices.

The central theme underlining the communications strategy for this proposed change was a short and definitive expression by the Group chief executive of the principles guiding the proposed actions. These were a seminal influence on the subsequent development and momentum for change.

- Creating a unified organisation sensitive and responsive to customer needs

- Bringing together activities in units that are addressing the same market

- Creating a spirit of unity and professionalism among all our staff in our dealings with ourselves and our customers

- Making AIB a challenging, rewarding and secure place in which to work.

This restructuring immediately brought with it a need to create a guiding vision for the overall organisation. Up to then, the core organisation had been driven by its traditional view of itself as a clearing bank — each of the specialised subsidiaries had had its own rationale based on its business function. Now, deliberately, these reference points were removed. This created a need to replace them with an effective alternative to give meaning and focus to change. The heads of the new divisions had to communicate a common vision that would motivate their people within the new structure. The statement of principles clearly reflected the organisation's desire to put the market first, and also sketched a broad strategy for achieving marketplace success. Like the corporate structure, the mission statement needed further refinement during the change process (see Figure 18.3).

FIGURE 18.3: AIB GROUP'S MISSION STATEMENT, 1989

"Value and Service Are at the Heart of Our Business. We Aim to Provide Real Value to Every One of Our Customers and to Deliver the Highest Standard of Service in Banking and Financial Services"

If the new structure and the new vision formed the foundation for the cultural change, a third, and equally important, element was the approach that AIB developed in the task of achieving differentiation in the marketplace. How was AIB to be different? As part of the self-examination that produced the mission statement, top management became convinced that the only way to win successful differentiation in the financial-services market was by providing superior service and value as perceived by the customer. AIB could not hope to achieve sustainable competitive advantage through pricing or through product innovation alone. The reality was that it would provide services that were broadly similar to those provided by competitors. How it provided them would, therefore, be the basis of any advantage achieved in positioning. This was the key not only to future growth, but also to future profitability, as customers would be prepared to pay a premium for what they perceived as superior value and service.

There was a realisation that people throughout the organisation were central to achieving this differentiation in the marketplace. Because of the nature of AIB's business, superior service would be delivered to customers in an innovative and flexible way — relating to customers' needs on an individual basis. So, while a market-driven approach could be led from the top, it needed to be delivered at the customer interface. This meant that company-wide involvement and commitment were essential to making the new structure and the new vision work. If successful, however, this approach would have the benefit of creating a marketplace advantage that was sustainable, as it could not be copied overnight by competitors.

Long-Term Perspective

Adopting the approach outlined above was a recognition that the change needed in AIB was deep and fundamental, rather than cosmetic. For this reason, it was important that the intended change process be fully understood and communicated internally before any attempt was made to present it to the external marketplace. Selling the differentiation in the marketplace must, it was felt, be based on change that was already taking place, rather than on promises. Accepting this was an aspect of the long-term perspective that characterised the entire project from the beginning. The change programme was conceived from the outset as a multi-year project, rather than a quick fix, and the initial time-frame was viewed as a five-year process (1987–92) as shown in Figure 18.4. Making a heavy corporate investment in gradual change over such a long time-frame required a high level of conviction and commitment at the top echelons of the organisation, given that publicly-quoted companies in our Western business culture are under considerable pressure to achieve in the short term.

Marketing Action Programme (MAP)

The first step was to set down a framework that would map in broad terms the actions necessary to effect change. The task was to transform an organisation of people who considered themselves as "bankers" into people who also considered themselves to be "marketing professionals". It was necessary to alter the way that people thought about the job of banking, and then how they actually did the job. However, what was at issue was not simply sending people on marketing courses. What was needed was to develop within AIB a marketing ethos that would drive every action taken collectively and

Corporate Change

individually. The solution adopted had no fewer than six interlocking elements:

- First of all, the right marketing strategies were needed to satisfy client needs in a focused fashion.

- Fundamental to such strategic thinking were marketing information systems to provide detailed and sophisticated information continually about markets and customers.

FIGURE 18.4: PHASES OF MAP, 1986–91

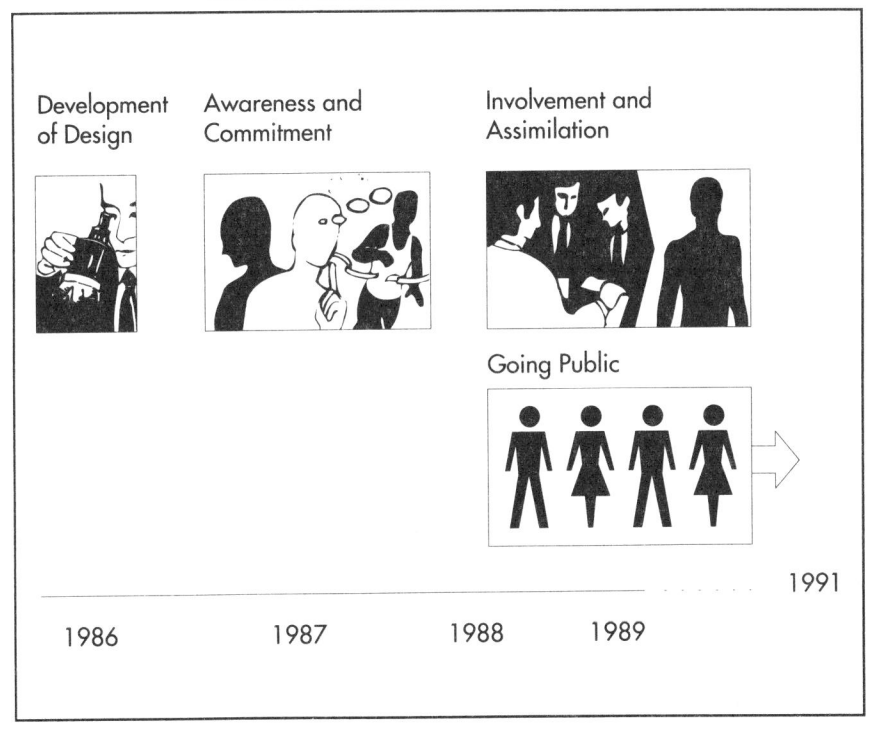

- Marketing strategy depended on good marketing leadership — management at all levels relentlessly communicating the message, displaying commitment and taking action.

- Leadership was reflected in commitment to high standards of marketing professionalism (not just banking professionalism per se, but real understanding of marketing principles and their application). This meant investment in the right skills and knowledge training.

- Marketing professionalism was dependent on the right structures. Job roles and structures which were not oriented towards the customer would quickly stifle any initiatives arising from training and development programmes.

- Marketing professionalism was also dependent on market-oriented technology — delivery systems, automated services, physical layout of branches, procedures, forms and so on. All these would have to be reshaped to the needs of various customer groups.

This conceptual framework is shown in Figure 18.5. Strategies, information systems, leadership, professionalism, job roles and structures, and technology were all fused together to represent a complex recipe. The complexity of this change recipe was one reason why it was decided to package the programme and even "brand" it internally as the "Marketing Action Programme" (MAP).

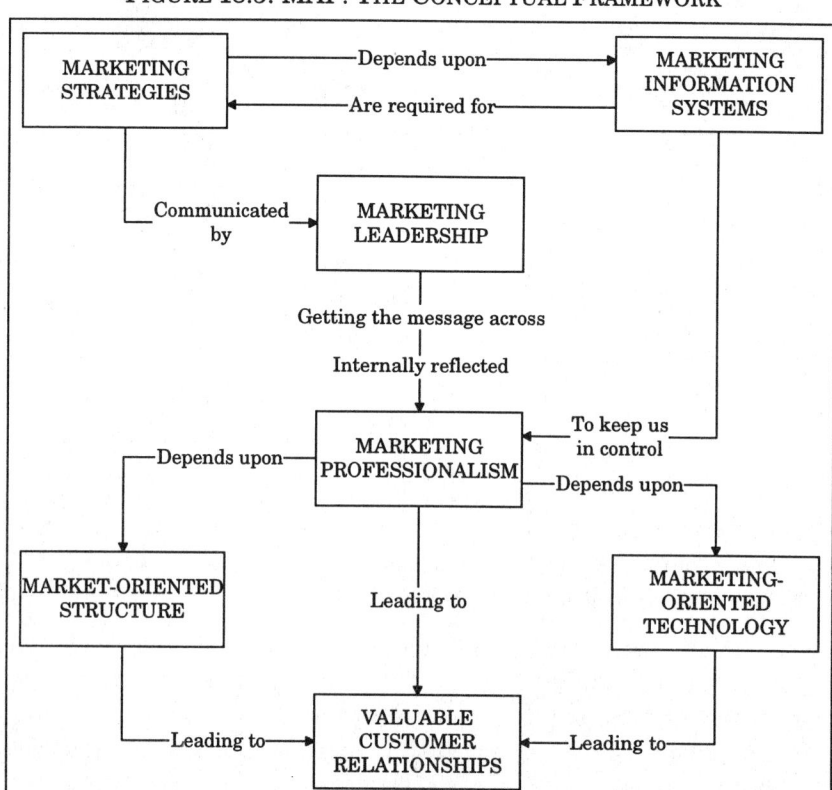

FIGURE 18.5: MAP: THE CONCEPTUAL FRAMEWORK

```
┌─────────────┐ ──Depends upon──→ ┌─────────────┐
│ MARKETING   │                   │ MARKETING   │
│ STRATEGIES  │ ←─Are required for│ INFORMATION │
│             │                   │ SYSTEMS     │
└─────────────┘                   └─────────────┘
       │ Communicated    ┌──────────────┐
       └──────by────────→│  MARKETING   │
                         │  LEADERSHIP  │
                         └──────────────┘
                              │
                  Getting the message across
                              │
                     Internally reflected
                              ↓
  ┌──Depends upon──┐  ┌──────────────┐  ← To keep us in control
  │                │  │  MARKETING   │
  ↓                └─→│ PROFESSIONAL-│←── Depends upon ──┐
┌─────────────┐       │     ISM      │                   │
│MARKET-      │       └──────────────┘          ┌────────────────┐
│ORIENTED     │          │ Leading to           │ MARKETING-     │
│STRUCTURE    │          ↓                      │ ORIENTED       │
└─────────────┘    ┌──────────────┐             │ TECHNOLOGY     │
      │            │   VALUABLE   │             └────────────────┘
      └─Leading to→│   CUSTOMER   │←─Leading to──────┘
                   │ RELATIONSHIPS│
                   └──────────────┘
```

INTERNAL MARKETING PROGRAMMES

Over the coming years, a series of Group-wide initiatives addressing key aspects of the conceptual framework were planned. These initiatives were to form an integrated dynamic for change driven by top management. However, because of the long time-scale (five years to 1992), there was a real danger that at lower levels of the organisation they would be seen as reactive and as separate "flavour of the month" initiatives. For this reason, the Group's advertising agency was engaged to develop a logo and an extensive branding design for all related internal communications under MAP.

What had happened up to this point was almost entirely at top-management level. In 1987, the task of taking the change programme to the wider organisation began. The first necessary phase in this was to create awareness of three things: the need for change; the direction in which the organisation needed to move (i.e., market-focused); and the need for the involvement and commitment of everyone in the organisation.

The programme required an unprecedented level of communication throughout the organisation. At the start of the programme, AIB employed 9,500 people in 500 locations in eight countries. This included no less than 1,200 managers. In early 1987, a series of mass meetings of managers was held at HQ in Dublin and at regional centres around the country. Staff throughout the group were reached through a combination of media — videos, print material and face-to-face briefings. The initial launch was consolidated by a series of week-long seminars for all executives from all parts of the group. These addressed the challenge of market focus and the implication for change of such a focus.

Involvement and Assimilation

The initial emphasis of the change programme was on the executive group — strategic-marketing workshops focused on strategic marketing and the management of change in large organisations at the middle-management level. These people were identified as central to the change process: if they did not accept it, there was little prospect of getting the overall staff to do so. But equally, it was recognised that the issue of how people were managed would be critical in ultimately delivering high-quality service to customers.

The main initiative in this area was called the "Management Effectiveness Programme". The approach was to discover, through internal research, the core management values appropriate to the new market-focused AIB, and to identify the management practices that would support those values. In turn, training and development would be provided to make possible the adoption of these practices. Thus, four core values were identified, together with 34 management practices to support them. The core values were:

- Concern for the individual
- Taking personal responsibility
- Developing open communication
- Commitment to goals and standards.

Every manager and assistant manager was given an opportunity to distribute a questionnaire on these practices to their staff. The completed forms were returned to a confidential database that was held outside AIB. Managers then attended a one-week training seminar to develop their understanding of the practices, and to receive feedback on the extent to which they used them (as perceived by their staff). The conclusion of the training seminar was the creation of the individual action plan relating to the 34 management practices. A feedback loop was provided by the offer to re-run the questionnaire process after a nine-month interval. An example of the kind of insight provided by this process was the discovery that while managers were saying repeatedly to their staff "the customer is king", the staff did not consider that the managers' actions always fully supported this statement. It is interesting to reflect that the core values, when applied to the interaction with customers, contain the key elements of value and service expected by customers in their dealings with the bank.

As a further element in creating awareness of the change process, the conclusions from the research were communicated to all staff in a booklet entitled *The Way We Work Together*. In effect, this spelled out what a staff member could expect from AIB, and what was expected in return. The Management Effectiveness Programme was large in scale and its execution extended over a period of two years. Though focused critically on the issue of managing staff, it did not directly involve non-managerial staff in the change process.

"Superthought"

Staff were, however, directly involved in a MAP initiative called "Superthought". This was a staff ideas programme that was carefully integrated into the change programme. One key element of the "Superthought" programme was that it involved team, rather than individual, activity. It was conceived and delivered on a massive scale, involving 98 per cent of the entire staff and management over a six-month period. This scale served to underline management's commitment to the initiative, and also helped to overcome the inevitable cynicism that is associated with such suggestion schemes. Some 1,200 ideas under three headings — customer service, income enhancement and cost saving — were implemented and rewarded. The scheme was highly successful, both in eliciting worthwhile ideas and, more importantly, in building commitment to the market-focused approach.

Making Marketing Effective

The next step undertaken in this phase was the "Marketing Effectiveness Programme". Having made considerable progress in raising awareness and commitment through the measures already outlined, it was necessary to address the critical task of making change happen in the way that AIB served the customer. Marketing effectiveness programmes were run in each of the business units. The objectives of the programme were to build an understanding of marketing principles and how to apply them. They focused on the specific changes necessary to do business and sought to define what the new customer-focused organisation should be at all levels.

The starting point for each of these programmes was a week-long marketing seminar, led by experts from outside the organisation. Following the seminar, teams of key managers applied the learning to project work related to their own work areas. That output was fed into local action plans, and upward into the strategy-creating process of the business unit. In this way, it interfaced directly with the on-going strategic planning for the organisation.

EXTERNALISNG THE MESSAGE

The thrust of AIB's change programme up to this point had been almost entirely internal. A number of years had been spent nurturing within the company a new set of values and attitudes about service and a commitment to customer needs. The time was now right to begin to introduce this commitment into the public arena — in effect, to externalise the change process. There were two elements to going public:

- "What we say" — the advertising and promotional programmes used to communicate with customers, and the corporate messages addressed to the many stakeholders in the organisation

- "How we look" — how AIB presented itself, its name, trading identities and the image offered at the point of sale.

In 1988, a corporate campaign was launched on television in the main market, Ireland. In contrast to competitive advertising at the time, this campaign did not seek to sell the group's services directly. Instead, it concentrated on getting over two central messages — that AIB was changing, and that the direction of change was towards a greater dedication to serving the customer. These messages were summed up by the slogan "You bring out the best in us".

This corporate campaign was remarkable in that it frankly admitted the need for change in AIB. Both this openness and the allegorical approach of the commercials themselves (which featured cartoon metamorphosis from caterpillar to butterfly, rather than actual people) ensured a very high awareness. Figure 18.6 below provides an example of a press advertisement.

Corporate Identity

A review of the group's corporate identity was the next major initiative under MAP, with the purpose of providing visible permanence to the changes and the new explicit values. This served to consolidate the changed mind-set internally and the success so far achieved, as well as providing a dynamic new beginning in the external presentation of the group. The first step in tackling the review of the existing corporate identity was to develop a brief, setting out key issues. Three design consultancies — each of which enjoyed a high reputation in the field of corporate identity and had experience of the huge logistical task of implementing such change in a large corporation — were asked to respond. Following submissions and presentations to a steering group under the chairmanship of a deputy chief executive, the contract was awarded in September 1988 to Wolf Olins, a UK-based consultancy of world reputation. The design consultants concluded at the outset that the way in which AIB was projecting itself did not fully reflect the changes that were occurring, nor did it communicate the company's ambitions and aspirations for the future. The design firm looked at three elements of corporate identity.

1) First of all, it researched the overall group identity, the name Allied Irish Banks plc., and its appropriateness now and into the future.
2) It considered the various and multiplying trading identities used in different markets.

FIGURE 18.6: PRESS ADVERTISEMENT, 1988

> # You bring out the best in us
>
> Understanding the needs of our customers, and responding to them, is what we at Allied Irish Bank aim to achieve.
>
> We know we have some way to go before we can really understand and respond to all our customers' needs. But we're working every day to continuously improve the service we provide for you.
>
> We aim to be the best not simply to satisfy our own ambitions, but to be the best in our customers eyes also. It's your needs that bring out the best in us.
>
> **Allied Irish Bank**
>
> **You bring out the best in us.**

3) Finally, it addressed how the company should present itself at the point of sale — a pressing need as it embarked on a radical development of its delivery systems.

The design consultants' work fell into three distinct stages. First, it developed recommendations for the name, the positioning of AIB in the marketplace, its personality and characteristics. Secondly, it recommended design concepts across a broad range of applications. Thirdly, it assisted in the implementation of these design concepts. These three stages of work took place between September 1988 and December 1990. The recommendations after the first stage covered two areas. The first was the issue of naming. It concluded that the existing, extended name, Allied Irish Banks, had outlived its usefulness, and was in fact causing confusion in certain markets. The recommendation was simply to use the initials AIB to prefix the Group or its operating parts — for example, AIB Group, AIB Bank or AIB Capital Markets. The second area was that of visual identity. The consultants suggested that the criteria for the new visual identity should be distinguishable and should reflect security as well as AIB's role with its various publics and its distinctive character. These recommendations followed after six months of interviews, desk research and design audits, and formed the creative brief for the second stage of the process.

Design

The recommendations from the second stage, essentially relating to design, followed after months of presentation and redevelopment. What eventually emerged as the final recommendation was the logo in use today (see Figure 18.7). This visual identity embraced the new corporate symbol and new colours. The corporate symbol, inspired by one of the earliest known Celtic images of the Ark, was representative of heritage, of security and of the many different communities that AIB served. The four colours incorporated into the logo expressed the warmth and friendliness of the Irish — an integral part of AIB's character. These design recommendations were presented to, and approved by, the board of directors in July 1989.

Further, it was decided to launch formally this new corporate identity within six months, and this actually occurred on 8 January 1990. This meant a relatively short period in which to design, approve, manufacture, print, communicate, and distribute all the items that customers normally come in contact with in their daily financial dealings. It was felt desirable to make the announcement of the new visual identity at the same time. This was then reflected in the most common items which customers use to do business, as well as in some external signage. To expedite this launch, the steering group set up a separate project team, the members of which were seconded from normal duties for the duration of the project. This team comprised a project executive, who reported directly to the steering group, and five other members.

FIGURE 18.7: AIB LOGO

Launch

The project team used classic project-management techniques to plan and structure the project, and to circumvent any bureaucratic tendencies that might have arisen. A range of communication initiatives were undertaken: internally, staff video, commemorative brochure, and briefing material were produced; externally, communication to shareholders, corporate clients and key customers took place. A media release was issued and media briefings were held for key journalists.

It was decided to launch the new corporate identity with a high-profile event held in AIB headquarters in Dublin, which, in a very innovative development, was televised live on national television. Some 500 guests — drawn from Government, shareholders, customers, staff, and the diplomatic corps — attended this launch. Simultaneously, each branch had a launch event to which customers were invited to mark the occasion.

Roll-out

A crucial phase in the corporate-identity project was the six months following the launch. Considerable time was invested co-ordinating the production of the remaining items and developing styles for literature. Improvements were made to some items following comments from customers. Briefings were made by the corporate identity consultants to advertising and design agencies, and they developed a set of guidelines to ensure that a sense of coherence and consistency would continue, and that any overzealous application of the identity would not occur.

As the roll-out period continued, each division took more ownership of the implementation of the identity in its area, and the project team was scaled down. A series of seminars was held to introduce interim corporate-identity manuals to staff and suppliers. The use of interim manuals indicated what needed to be added, amended or deleted before definitive manuals were introduced three months later.

INTERNAL RESEARCH AND CONCLUSION
Research

A major internal research programme was carried out during 1989. The research, which was carried out by an external firm, examined aspects of the staff's attitudes towards AIB and their own involvement in the organisation. In fulfilment of the commitment given to staff at the outset of the research, the detailed results were communicated back to the staff after completion.

The openness of the process, which demonstrated management's readiness to listen to frankly-expressed criticism from staff, made an important contribution to the ongoing process of change.

Some of the findings most closely relevant to this paper are summarised in the graphs in Figure 18.8.

- On the positive side, there was a remarkably high understanding of the overall direction in which the group was going and what the Marketing Action Programme was trying to achieve. There was even more widespread agreement that the Marketing Action Programme was beneficial to AIB's business.

- In addition, indications of where the programme needed to focus next were provided by other answers. For example, 50 per cent of the staff did not feel fully involved in the programme, while approximately one third felt it was not beneficial to their own career opportunities. A similar number felt that the programme had not changed the work process in their own work unit.

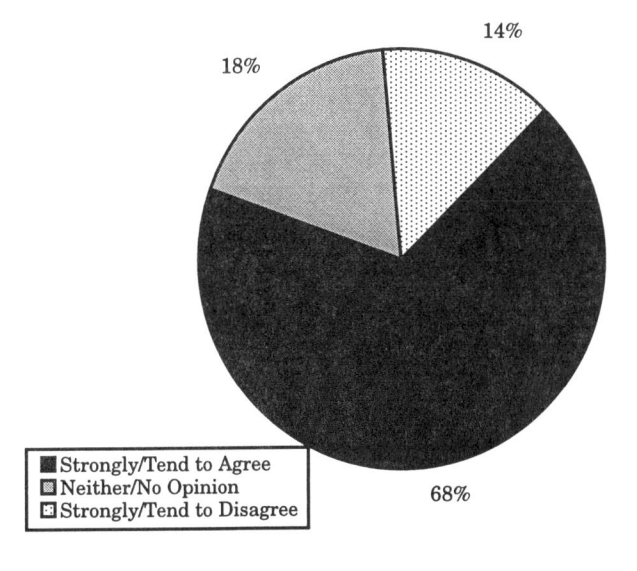

FIGURE 18.8: THE MAP RESEARCH INTO STAFF ATTITUDES

"I feel I understand the direction
in which AIB is going"

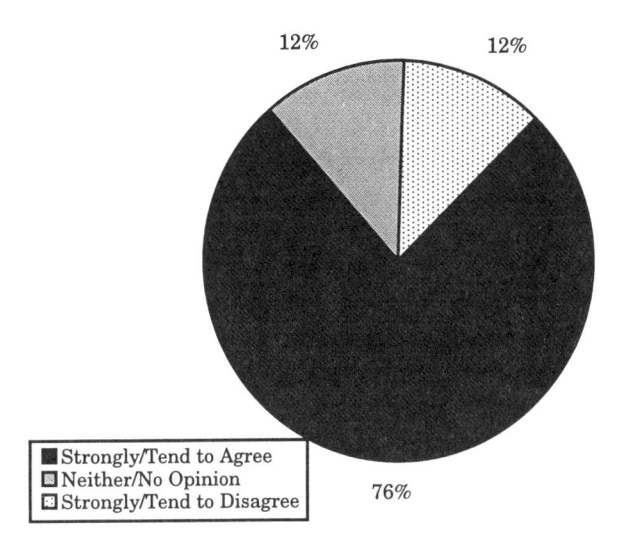

- Strongly/Tend to Agree: 76%
- Neither/No Opinion: 12%
- Strongly/Tend to Disagree: 12%

"I feel I understand what MAP
is trying to achieve"

- Strongly/Tend to Agree: 68%
- Neither/No Opinion: 18%
- Strongly/Tend to Disagree: 14%

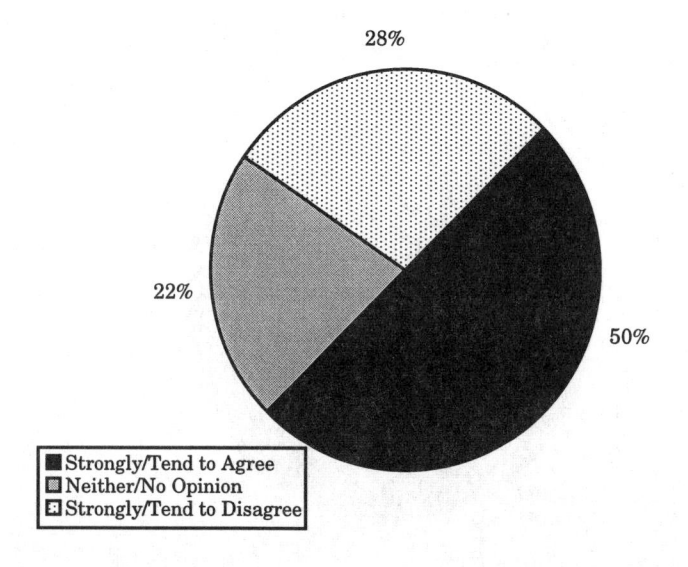

FIGURE 18.8: THE MAP RESEARCH INTO STAFF ATTITUDES (CONTD.)

"Its introduction is beneficial to AIB's business"

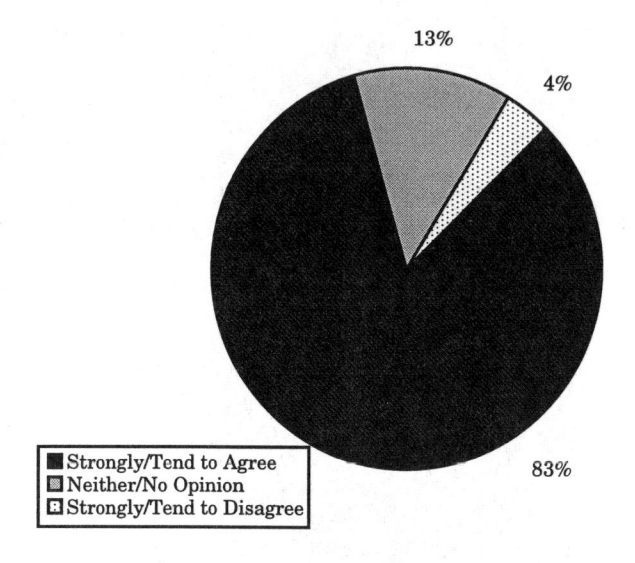

- Strongly/Tend to Agree: 83%
- Neither/No Opinion: 13%
- Strongly/Tend to Disagree: 4%

"I do not feel fully involved in the MAP"

- Strongly/Tend to Agree: 50%
- Neither/No Opinion: 22%
- Strongly/Tend to Disagree: 28%

Corporate Change

FIGURE 18.8: THE MAP RESEARCH INTO STAFF ATTITUDES (CONTD.)

"The MAP is beneficial for
my own career opportunities"

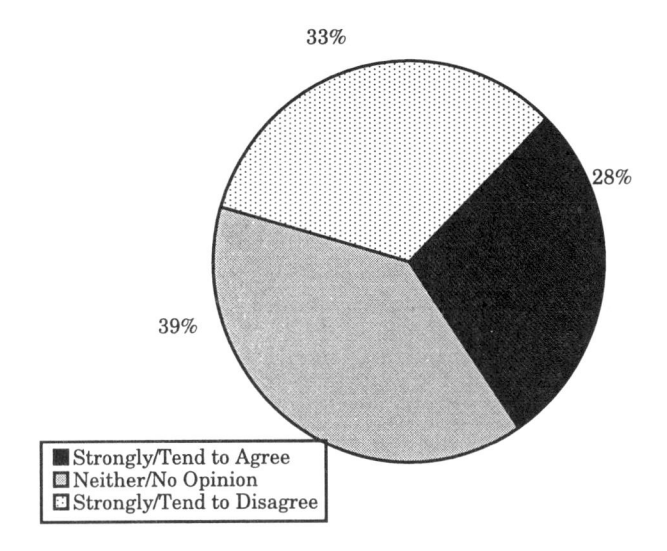

33%
28%
39%

■ Strongly/Tend to Agree
▨ Neither/No Opinion
▧ Strongly/Tend to Disagree

"The MAP has changed the way we
operate in our work unit"

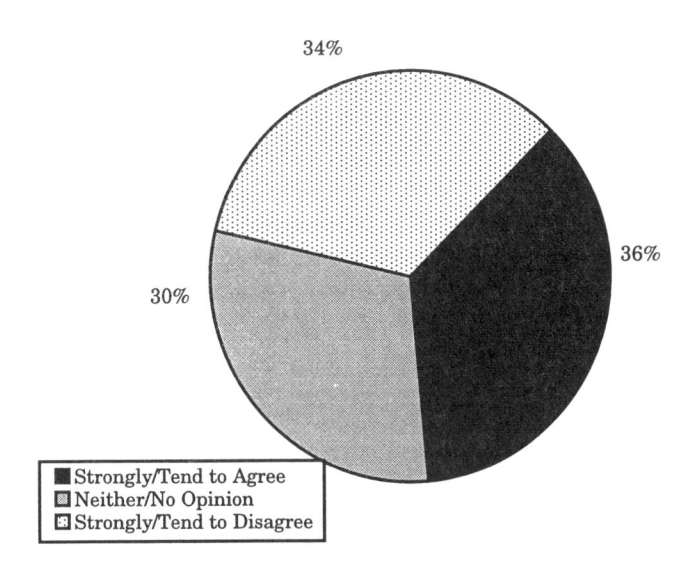

34%
36%
30%

■ Strongly/Tend to Agree
▨ Neither/No Opinion
▧ Strongly/Tend to Disagree

Responses to the questionnaire revealed that there was more work to be done in changing the management style to fit in with the new approach.

The results of this research provided an agenda for the continuation of the programme during the remainder of the initial period. The research initiative itself, and especially the communication of the results to staff, provided an opportunity for re-dedication to the aims and objectives of the programme at mid-point.

The Learning Organisation

The Marketing Action Programme set out to make radical changes in the internal attitudes and values of AIB staff. Its objective was to build a unified organisation, market-focused and responsive to customer needs. There was an awareness from the start that effecting change is a long-term process. From this has evolved the conviction that the process of change would be ongoing. AIB's change story has not finished. In late 1992, the results of an extensive review of AIB Group's direction for the rest of the decade was communicated to all staff. This aimed to consolidate the progress made under MAP by setting out a vision of the organisation in the year 2000, and the values that should characterise its operation, together with a clear view as to how stakeholder symmetry could be achieved. The appointment of a new chief executive during 1993 has enabled further fine-tuning of strategy and structure.

AIB recognises that the organisation of the future is one where learning is the axial principle and replaces control as the fundamental job of management. People must be empowered to learn and to take action about their work in ways that were inconceivable in a traditional setting. Only then can true market focus be achieved. This is particularly true in the area of financial services. Such thinking has profound implications for recruitment, enculturation, development, appraisal, communication and decision-making.

CONCLUSION

This paper set out to examine how the AIB Group developed a clear sense of purpose and how the role of corporate identity underpinned that process. Visual identity was only one in a series of initiatives in this development. Corporate identity, however, is a very important and public way of demonstrating and externalising this sense of purpose. It is vital that corporate identity be treated as an integral part,

Corporate Change

rather than a cosmetic adjunct, of the business; it cannot be addressed successfully without also considering business definition and direction as well as company culture and shared values. Successful marketing in the external competitive arena must go hand-in-hand with internal marketing. Furthermore, the establishment of a corporate identity requires not only first-rate design values but also, critically, ownership at board level, ongoing executive management and the a capacity to initiate continuously.

19

Fear Appeals: Segmentation is the Way to Go*

Valerie Quinn
Tony Meenaghan
Teresa Brannick

INTRODUCTION

Despite some initial reservations, it has long been accepted that the scope for the application of marketing principles extends beyond the traditional profit arena of goods and services. Within this expanded context, marketing principles have a particularly fertile application in the modification of health-related behaviour.

Much of the literature concerning the use of non-profit marketing has concentrated in the area of "social marketing", with the major approaches for producing social change being identified as legal, technological, economic and informational (Kotler and Zaltman, 1971). This latter informational approach has been used extensively by social marketers, with the advertising process being a central component in many social marketing campaigns.

Numerous models of the advertising process are cited in marketing literature but, essentially, advertising (whether on behalf of profit-making or non-profit-making organisations) is believed to have the objective of moving consumers through a staged behaviour modification/buying process, through the provision of information and persuasion.

In a health education campaign the process would be as depicted in Figure 19.1, where consumers' exposure to information increases their knowledge level, leading to an attitude change; and ultimately

---

* This paper originally appeared in the *International Journal of Advertising*, 1992, 11: 355–66.

to a change in their behaviour, resulting in better health.

In the more specific case of a smoking-cessation campaign, the intention will be to move different segments of the smoking population (in terms of their level of consumption of cigarettes) from a position of high consumption to reduced consumption levels, until the ultimate objective of non-consumption is attained. This is, in fact, the traditional marketing process of adoption in reverse, in that the objective is to reduce rather than to increase consumption of a product.

FIGURE 19.1: THE ATTITUDE-BEHAVIOUR HEALTH RELATIONSHIP

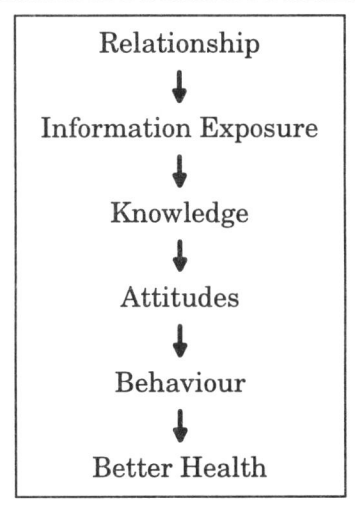

Relationship
↓
Information Exposure
↓
Knowledge
↓
Attitudes
↓
Behaviour
↓
Better Health

In developing a comprehensive advertising programme, five major decisions must be made (Kotler, 1988). These decisions (known as the five Ms) relate to "mission" (objectives), "money" (budget), "message", "media" and "measurement". This paper is concerned with the area of "message" and focuses on one specific element within "message", namely message content,. More specifically, it concentrates on fear appeals as a particular form of message content.

FEAR APPEALS IN ADVERTISING

In general, marketing communication attempts to inform consumers of the benefits of using a product. Advertising using fear appeals does the opposite: it informs consumers of the risks of using (e.g. cigarettes) or not using (e.g. deodorants) a particular product (Assael, 1987). Fear, being a powerful human motivation, can affect buyer behaviour. When credibility is high, fear appeal can enhance attitude change; however, the appropriate level of fear must be carefully determined. For certain audience sectors the appropriate amount of emotional tension may be achieved by means of negative appeals, while other sectors respond better to positive appeals (Wheatley and Oshikawa, 1970). The critical difference between fear appeals and positive appeals is that the former contain a deliberate attempt to arouse anxiety. While a positive appeal may also arouse anxiety, it is usually incidental to the main thrust of the message, which is a presentation of the product's want-satisfying attributes (Spence and Moinpour, 1972).

Research on fear-arousing appeals from 1953 to 1968 has yielded conflicting findings concerning the relative effectiveness of high versus low threat in persuasion. The belief that low threat is superior to high threat in persuasion is based mainly upon a study by Janis and Feshbach (1954). Since 1953, some studies have found no relationship between fear arousal and persuasion, while others have yielded mixed findings. For example, high fear has been found to affect attitude change without affecting behaviour change (Leventhal et al., 1965).

Those studies which have found that strong fear is more effective than weak fear appeals have involved such diverse topics as dental hygiene, smoking, and safe driving practices (Higbee, 1969). In other situations, a moderate level of fear might be most appropriate. This may occur because a weak appeal may not attract enough attention, whereas too strong a fear appeal may cause people to avoid the message, or to ignore the recommendations within the message as being inadequate to the task of eliminating the feared event (Ray and Wilkie, 1970). Research results would, therefore, seem to suggest that optimum efficiency occurs at intermediate levels where the amount of arousal is neither too weak nor too strong.

In general, recent studies in this area have found a positive relationship between fear and persuasion, suggesting that fear-evoking messages will continue to be used to effect persuasion (Sternthal and Craig, 1974).

INCONSISTENCIES IN THE RESEARCH

The mixed findings arising from the research may result from the concept of "threat" or "fear arousal" being viewed in so many different ways that the studies on fear-arousing communications have not actually been examining the same phenomenon. Differences in the nature of the fear (for example, anticipation fear, or inhibitory fear);

in the objects of the fear (for example, social disapproval or illness); topic differences (including knowledge of and importance to the individual); and diversity of respondents used (in age, education level, gender, personalities, and attitudes) may have also contributed to the inconsistency in the findings on the arousal of fear in persuasion.

Other attempts to reconcile the conflicting findings on threat appeals have lead to the suggestion of the existence of a curvilinear, rather than a linear, relationship between fear level and persuasion. This suggestion is implicit in Higbee's representation of the relationship between the level of fear arousal and the persuasive effectiveness of the communication.

FIGURE 19.2: POSTULATED CURVILINEAR RELATIONSHIP BETWEEN LEVEL OF FEAR AROUSAL AND PERSUASIVE EFFECTIVENESS OF THE COMMUNICATION

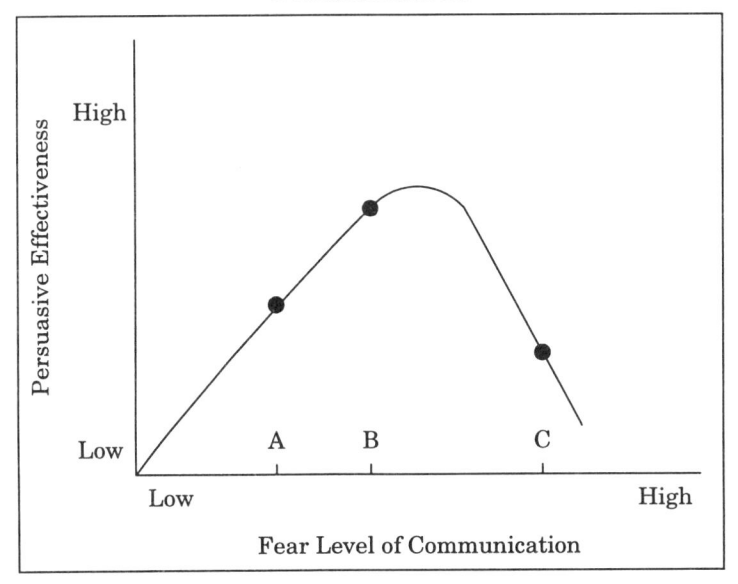

Source: Higbee, 1969: 440.

For example, if the low and high fear levels in one study were at A and B respectively, on the fear-level axis, then the results of that study would indicate a positive relationship between fear level and persuasion. However, if the low and high fear appeals in another study were at levels B and C, or A and C respectively, then the results of that study would show a negative relationship between fear level and persuasion (Figure 19.2). There is, however, no accurate way of determining the comparability of fear levels from one study to another. As fear has been described in many ways — weak, strong and neutral, for example — what may have been labelled "high fear" in one study may have been equivalent to "medium fear" in another (Higbee, 1969). It is therefore difficult to refute Higbee's assertions.

USING FEAR APPEALS — IMPORTANT CONSIDERATIONS

Where a communicator is contemplating the use of advertising involving fear appeals, then in addition to the normal considerations surrounding an advertising campaign, the following factors must be considered:

1) **The Level of Fear**: A key consideration is the appropriate level of fear for the specific situation. One of the great problems in using fear appeals in marketing is that which occurs with the use of any kind of appeal or motivation. It can only be applied in specific situations, and previous research may not indicate precisely the effect of fear in a new situation (Berkowitz and Cottingham, 1960).

2) **Source Credibility**: Hewgill and Miller (1965) showed that subjects exposed to a strong fear communication, attributed to a highly credible source, would demonstrate the greatest shift toward the position advocated in the persuasive communication.

3) **Type of Fear**: Fear research has examined topics that have dealt primarily with the physical consequences of action or inaction. Conversely, the commercial applications, such as mouthwash and deodorants, frequently describe the consequences of social disapproval resulting from performance of, or abstinence from, certain behaviours. However, it is not known whether the threat of social disapproval is a more effective means of motivation than the promise of social approval, as this relationship has only had limited examination (Powell and Miller, 1967). Powell and Miller's study found that social disapproval was substantially more effective in changing attitudes than was social approval.

4) **Interest Value of the Communication**: Communicators may not succeed in changing their audience's opinions if their message lacks sufficient interest, even though they may possess other prerequisites for successful influence, such as high credibility.

5) **Relevance**: Leventhal and Watts (1966) found in their study that people to whom a threat is relevant experience a greater personal involvement, and report more fear when confronted by the threat agent. It has therefore been suggested that a strong fear appeal could be more convincing than a weak one, when the communication is of low relevance to the actions of the audience.

6) **Ethics**: The most persistent ethical question concerns the use of fear appeals when the proposed solution to the feared condition is a product which does not satisfy the consumer's expectations. However, this difficulty also applies to positive appeals (Spence and Moinpour, 1972). Another ethical concern relates to the level of fear used in communication, but research has shown that the level of fear that is effective in marketing is not high enough to be even remotely unethical (Ray and Wilkie, 1970).

FEAR APPEALS AND MARKET SEGMENTATION

Market segmentation, one of the key concepts of marketing, has an obvious applicability in health education and, more particularly, in the area of cigarette smoking. Cigarette consumers, while obviously capable of being segmented on a volume-consumption basis, could also be expected to exhibit different sensitivities to alternate marketing strategies and advertising messages. The use of a market-segmentation approach in health education has been examined by Burnett and Wilkes (1980). Their study, involving a health-maintenance organisation, found that high fear arousal is more effective with certain consumer segments than with the total population.

Segmentation can be used to find groups of people for whom relatively high fear appeals are effective. In general, these seem to be people who do not see the product category in question as highly relevant to them, thus offering the possibility that fear appeals should be considered for opening new segments. Ray and Wilkie (1970) suggest that fear motivation should be most effective for those who have not seen themselves as part of the market for the recommended product or brand.

Thus, it may be surmised that stronger cancer fear appeals would be more effective for younger smokers than for older smokers. This is because younger smokers are less likely to see themselves as vulnerable to the cancer threat. If the anti-cigarette forces can further segment the market to find low anxiety, high self-esteem copers among the smokers, they will have segments for which extremely strong fear messages should be effective, if presented well (Ray and Wilkie, 1970). In a similar way, mouthwash advertisers might find that "fear appeals" work best with those who have not really considered the bad-breath problem.

RESEARCH METHODOLOGY

The purpose of the study outlined in this paper was to examine the applicability of a segmentation approach in the cigarette-smoking market, using fear appeals. A self-administered questionnaire, containing 14 statements regarding the health consequences of smoking, was distributed in Dublin to 225 male and female students at two school-going levels: secondary and postgraduate. A particular feature of university postgraduate education in Ireland is its bias towards the upper end of the social-class scale. Thus, in order to facilitate comparison between the two education cohorts, secondary level respondents were chosen from upper social backgrounds to match university respondents. While this sampling approach may not be representative of the entire cigarette-smoking population, it does provide an opportunity to test the hypothesis that fear appeals provide a meaningful basis for segmentation in the smoking market.

The specific objectives of this study were:

1) To obtain a profile of male and female smokers and non-smokers at different educational levels; and

2) To determine the impact of fear appeals on:

    ◊ Students at different educational (age) levels

    ◊ Male students compared to female students

    ◊ Smokers compared to non-smokers.

EMERGING RESULTS

Objective 1: To obtain a profile of male and female smokers and non-smokers at different (age) levels

The results revealed that the majority (62.7 per cent) of students were non-smokers. Of this 62.7 per cent, 18.4 per cent were ex-smokers, the majority of whom cited "health reasons" as the primary determinant in their decision to cease smoking. There was no significant difference (at $p < .05$) found between the number of male and female smokers at either educational level. This finding does not concur with the findings of the Grube and Morgan study (1986), which examined students' smoking habits. They found that among 13–16-year-old students, there was a higher percentage of male smokers compared to female, and that it was not until the late teens that the percentage of female smokers had caught up with that of their male counterparts. This present study has revealed that there was no significant difference (at $p < .05$) between the number of male and female smokers in the population at the age of 16 years. However, there was a significant difference in their consumption levels, with males at this age smoking more cigarettes per day than females. This study also revealed (in agreement with the Grube and Morgan study) that by the age of 24, there was no significant difference between male and female consumption levels.

A significant difference was found between the two student age groups regarding the average amount of cigarettes consumed per day. The majority of the second-level students smoked between one and five cigarettes a day, compared to 5 to 30 cigarettes consumed per day by postgraduate students. This is not considered to be a surprising result, as one would expect a student's level of consumption to increase over time (as the smoker passed from the level of experimentation to addiction).

In addition, there was a significant difference across the educational levels with regard to smokers' perceived difficulty in ceasing smoking. The majority of the second-level students believed that they could stop smoking with ease, in contrast to the majority of postgraduate students who stated that they would have difficulty in giving up smoking. This difference may be explained by the variation in the consumption and addiction levels across the two groups.

The above findings would indicate that fear appeals (or negative advertising) are more effective in encouraging the younger students to stop or not to start smoking, whereas additional measures (for example, the use of nicotine gum) may be necessary to help older students to cease smoking.

Objective 2

To determine the impact of fear appeals on:

- Students at different educational (age) levels
- Male students compared to female students
- Smokers compared to non-smokers.

When the questionnaire was constructed, the 14 statements were divided into four broad categories. The four categories grouping the statements were:

1) General Health Index
2) Socially-Related Index
3) Procreation-Related Index
4) Factual Health Index.

Statements were so grouped into these categories because it was believed that there was a relationship between the statements within each category. For example, if a male student stated that one general health statement induced a high level of fear in him, it was believed that this student would state that a high level of fear was also induced in him by the remaining general health statements. The research revealed that this correlation (between the statements in each category) did in fact exist.

Therefore, as there was a significant correlation between the statements in each category, it was possible to compare the average level of fear induced in all students for each category (Table 19.1), as well as the average level of fear induced in all students by each individual statement (Table 19.2).

TABLE 19.1: LEVEL OF FEAR INDUCED FOR EACH STATEMENT GROUP

	Level of Fear Induced					
	v. high/ high	moderate	low/ v. low	$\Sigma \bar{X}$	$\bar{X}$	R
Value:	1/2	3	4/5			
Index						
Gen (%)	53.3	38.3	8.4	10.4	2.6	3
Soc (%)	68.4	31.6	—	8.6	2.9	4
Pro (%)	77.8	22.2	—	7.1	2.4	2
Fac (%)	65.8	28.9	5.3	9.0	2.3	1

N = 225
$\Sigma \bar{X}$ = the aggregate mean for each group of statements.
$\bar{X}$ = the mean (average level of fear induced). The lower the mean value, the higher the level of fear induced.
R = Rank (from the highest to lowest fear induced).

Indices: Gen = the four general health statements grouped together.
Soc = the three socially-related statements grouped together.
Pro = the three procreation-related statements grouped together.
Fac = the four factual health statements grouped together.

TABLE 19.2: LEVEL OF FEAR INDUCED BY EACH STATEMENT

	Level of Fear Induced (%)						
	v. high	high	mod.	low	v. low		
Value:	1	2	3	4	5	X̄*	R**
(No.) Statements							
General Health							
(1) Smoking causes heart disease	16.4	48.0	17.3	14.2	4.0	2.41	5
(2) Smokers die younger	21.3	37.3	19.1	18.7	3.6	2.46	6
(3) Smoking seriously damages your health	23.1	41.8	13.3	19.6	2.2	2.36	3
(4) Smoking causes gangrene	18.2	23.1	10.2	22.2	26.2	3.15	11
Socially Related							
(5) Smoking is a dirty habit	17.8	29.3	16.4	22.2	14.2	2.86	9
(6) Smoking is socially unacceptable	12.9	23.1	19.1	31.1	13.8	3.10	10
(7) Smoking causes bad breath	26.2	28.4	12.9	20.9	11.6	2.63	8
Procreation-Related							
(8) Smoking increases the risk of miscarriage	30.2	35.6	9.8	16.4	8.0	2.36	3
(9) A smoker's baby is twice as likely to die during its first week of life	37.8	25.3	7.1	19.6	10.2	2.39	4
(10) Smoking increases the risk of stillbirths	33.8	28.9	10.2	18.2	8.9	2.39	4
Factual Health							
(11) 90 per cent of those who die from lung cancer are smokers	32.9	46.7	9.8	9.3	1.3	1.99	1
(12) 5,000 Irish people die every year because of smoking	28.4	40.9	9.8	18.7	2.2	2.25	2
(13) Tobacco kills four times as many people as the total killed by all known causes of accidental death put together	29.8	39.1	10.7	16.9	3.6	2.25	2
(14) Smoking kills 200 people a day in England and Wales	28.4	27.6	12.4	23.6	8.0	2.55	7

N = 225
Read: 16.4 per cent believed statement (1) "Smoking causes heart disease" to induce a high level of fear.
* X̄ = the mean (average) level of fear induced for each individual statement. the lower the mean value, the higher the level of fear induced.
** R = rank (from highest to lowest level of fear induced).

From Table 19.1 it can be seen that the group of factual health statements induced the greatest amount of fear in the students, and the socially-related statements induced the least amount of fear in students.

With regard to the level of fear induced by individual statements, the results set out in Table 19.2 underline the impact of highly dramatic numerical statements, with the most fear-inducing statement being "90 per cent of those who die from lung cancer are smokers". The statement "5,000 Irish people die every year because of smoking" was rated joint second. This numerical statement with reference to Ireland obviously had much more impact than the numerical statement (14) which referred to England and Wales. These results highlight the importance of providing dramatic messages which are meaningful to a particular audience. Bland statements, which perhaps lack dramatic assertion such as "Smoking is a dirty habit", "Smoking is socially unacceptable", and "Smoking causes bad breath" were deemed to have little impact.

The average level of fear induced by the statements was cross-tabulated by the students' educational levels, and smoking habits. The results (Table 19.3) show that there was a significant difference in the average amount of fear induced across each of these variables. (Significant differences are indicated by an asterisk).

Fear Induced and Respondent Educational Level

There was a significant difference between the two educational levels regarding the statement "Smoking causes gangrene", which induced a greater amount of fear among the second-level students than among the postgraduate students. The second-level students also experienced a significantly higher level of fear than the postgraduate students with the procreation-related statements and the factual-health statements.

Fear Induced and Respondent Gender

The female students, when compared to their male counterparts, experienced a significantly higher degree of fear concerning the statement "Smokers die younger" in the general-health statements. In addition, the level of fear aroused in females was significantly higher than males regarding all the statements within the "socially-related", "procreation-related" and "factual-health" statement groups.

TABLE 19.3: AVERAGE LEVEL OF FEAR INDUCED BY THE STATEMENTS

	Student:	Education		Sex		Smokers	Non-Smokers
		Secondary	Post-grad	M	F		
(No.) Statements							
General Health		2.3.	2.77*	2.70	2.49	2.85	2.45*
(1) Smoking causes heart disease		2.31	2.47	2.48	2.34	2.63	2.28
(2) Smokers die younger		2.37	2.51	2.64	2.27*	2.82	2.24*
(3) Smoking seriously damages your health		2.22	2.51	2.39	2.32	2.57	2.23*
(4) Smoking causes gangrene		2.36	3.64*	3.28	3.02	3.37	3.02*
Socially Related		2.89	2.84	3.13	2.59*	3.04	2.75
(5) Smoking is a dirty habit		2.91	2.83	3.13	2.58*	3.10	2.72*
(6) Smoking is socially unacceptable		3.15	3.06	3.39	2.79*	3.24	3.01
(7) Smoking causes bad breath		2.62	2.64	2.87	2.39*	2.80	2.53
Procreation-Related		1.97	2.64*	2.72	2.04*	2.57	2.27
(8) Smoking increases the risk of miscarriage		1.93	2.63*	2.70	2.02*	2.60	2.23*
(9) A smoker's baby is twice as likely to die during its first week of life		1.98	2.65*	2.71	2.06*	2.52	2.31
(10) Smoking increases the risk of stillbirths		1.99	2.65*	2.74	2.05*	2.58	2.28
Factual Health		2.11	2.36*	2.45	2.07*	2.51	2.12*
(11) 90 per cent of those who die from lung cancer are smokers		2.05	1.96	2.17	1.82*	2.23	1.86*
(12) 5,000 Irish people die every year because of smoking		2.05	2.38*	2.41	2.09*	2.46	2.13
(13) Tobacco kills four times as many people as the total killed by all known causes of accidental death put together		2.10	2.35	2.43	2.07*	2.51	2.10*
(14) Smoking kills 200 people a day in England and Wales		2.22	2.76	2.79	2.31	2.85	2.38*

*   Significant at p < .05 using f ratios
Note: Figures in Table 19.3 are in mean value form. As before, the lower the man value, the higher the level of fear induced.

Fear Induced and Smoking Status

On average, a significantly higher level of fear was stimulated in the non-smokers, compared to the smokers, by the general-health statements and the factual-health statements. No significant difference was found between smokers and non smokers with respect to the "socially-related" and "procreation-related" categories. However, there was a significant difference concerning the statement "Smoking is a dirty habit" within the "socially-related" statement group, and concerning the statement "Smoking increases the risk of miscarriage", within the "procreation-related" statements group. Both statements induced a significantly higher level of fear among non-smokers.

A multivariate analysis of variance (MANOVA) was used to test for the effect of fear level on the students' responses to the four indices.

- **The General-Health Index**: For this index educational level and smoking habits had the greatest impact on the students' responses, with educational level having a slightly greater impact than students' smoking habits.

- **The Socially-Related Index**: For this index both students' gender and smoking habits had the greatest impact on responses, with the gender having by far the greatest impact.

- **The Procreation-Related Index**: Here, the students' gender and educational level had the greatest impact on their responses, with the gender having a slightly greater impact.

- **The Factual-Health Index**: All three variables, students' gender, smoking habits and educational level, had a significant impact on the students' responses, with smoking habits having the greatest impact overall.

To conclude therefore: students' gender, educational level and smoking habits each had an impact on the students' responses for the four indices (though the indices affected were different in each case).

COMMENTARY

The Impact of Fear Appeals on Students at Different Educational Levels

A significantly higher level of fear was induced in the second-level students by all (except the socially-related) statements. This may be because older postgraduate students are more critical and questioning regarding the validity of certain information, whereas the younger students may be more impressionable and susceptible to the same information, without questioning its validity. Thus, the younger students experienced a higher level of fear. This would imply that younger age groups should be exposed to fear appeals relating to smoking as early as possible, as they appear to be most impressionable at this stage.

The Impact of Fear Appeals on Male Students Compared to Female Students

A significantly higher degree of fear was aroused in the female (compared to the male) students regarding all (except the general-health) statements. This could be accounted for by the fact that males, because of "bravery" or "machismo", believe that they are not vulnerable. Alternatively, females are positively more emotionally responsive. Therefore, in order for a fear-related anti-smoking campaign to have the same impact on males and females, a segmentation approach is required, involving a stronger appeal targeted at the male segment.

The Impact of Fear Appeals on Smokers Compared to Non-Smokers

No significant difference was found (at $p < .05$) between the level of fear induced in smokers and that induced in non-smokers, regarding the socially-related and procreation-related statements. However, a higher level of fear was aroused in non-smokers with respect to the general-health and factual-health statements. As non-smokers are more fearful than smokers of the health consequences of smoking, this may explain why these students have not taken up the smoking habit. This would indicate the exposure to the health consequences of smoking may be effective deterrent to smoking commencement.

CONCLUSION

The results of this survey revealed that a higher level of fear was aroused in the non-smokers, female students and second-level students, when compared to other student groups. The results accord with the evidence of Burnett and Wilkes (1980) that fear appeals are a potent form of advertising, particularly when the message strategy and content are targeted according to the identified market segments.

REFERENCES

Assael, H. (1987): *Consumer Behaviour and Marketing Action*, Third ed. Boston: Wadsworth Inc.

Berkowitz, L. and Cottingham, D.R. (1960): "The Interest Value and Relevance of Fear Arousing Communications", *Journal of Abnormal and Social Psychology*, 60(1): 37–43.

Burnett, J.J. and Wilkes, R.E. (1980): "Fear Appeals to Segments Only", *Journal of Advertising Research*, 20, October: 21–4.

Grube, J.W. and Morgan, M. (1986): *Smoking, Drinking and Other Drug Use Among Dublin Post Primary School Pupils*, ESRI Report, Paper No. 132, Dublin: The Economic and Social Research Institute, (ESRI).

Higbee, K.L. (1969): "Fifteen Years of Fear Arousal: Research in Threat Appeals 1953–1968", *Psychological Bulletin*, 72(b): 426–44.

Hewgill, M.A. and Miller, G.R. (1965): "Source Credibility and Response to Fear Arousing Communications", *Speech Monograph*, 32: 95–101.

Janis, I.L. and Feshbach, S. (1954): "Personality Differences Associated with Responsiveness to Fear-Arousing Communications", *Journal of Personality*, 23: 154–66.

Kotler, P. (1988): *Marketing Management-Analysis, Planning, Implementation, and Control*, Sixth ed., Englewood Cliffs, NJ: Prentice Hall.

Kotler, P. and Zaltman, G. (1971): "Social Marketing: An Approach to Planned Social Change", *Journal of Marketing*, 35, July: 3–12.

Leventhal, H., Singer R. and Jones, S. (1965): "Effects of Fear and Specificity of Recommendations upon Attitudes and Behaviour", *Journal of Personality and Social Psychology*, 2: 20–29.

Leventhal, H. and Watts, J.C. (1966): "Sources of Resistance to Fear-Arousing Communications on Smoking and Lung Cancer", *Journal of Personality*, 34: 155–75.

Powell, F.A. and Miller, G.R. (1967): "Social Approval and Disapproval Cues in Anxiety-Arousing Communication", *Speech Monograph*, 34(2): 152–9.

Ray, M.L. and Wilkie, W.L. (1970): "Fear: The Potential of an Appeal Neglected by Marketing", *Journal of Marketing*, 34, January: 54–62.

Spence, H.E. and Moinpour, R. (1972): "Fear Appeals in Marketing — A Social Perspective", *Journal of Marketing*, 36, July: 39–43.

Sternthal, B. and Craig, C.S. (1974): "Fear Appeals: Revised and Revisited", *Journal of Consumer Research*, 1, December: 22–34.

Wheatley, J. and Oshikawa, S. (1970): "The Relationship Between Anxiety and Positive and Negative Advertising Appeals", *Journal of Marketing Research*, 7, February: 85–89.

20
Advertising and the Senior Market

Darach Turley

INTRODUCTION

According to the latest census data for the Irish Republic, the over-55 age group comprises 671,549 persons or 19 per cent of the entire population. Almost one in five consumers in Ireland is currently 55 years or over. This demographic trend is set to continue particularly in the first decade of the coming millennium as the post-war baby boomers come of age. Younger students of marketing communications often overlook the fact that this generation and marketing grew up together. Virtually all world-class consumer brands have achieved this status simply because they appealed to, and were purchased by, this consumer cohort. To this extent, they have exercised a form of consumer veto over much of their life span. Their number and spending power have had no demographic equal to date. Weaned on and wooed by a continuous diet of ever more sophisticated advertising and marketing communications, they are unlikely to modify their expectations, suspend their critical powers, and move to a lower consumer gear simply because their first fifty-fifth birthday card drops through the letterbox. Mainstream consumer brands may have ignored the senior market segment up until now, and survived; over the coming decade, such an oversight may well spell disaster.

There is still considerable dispute over what exactly makes a consumer a "senior consumer" (Turley, 1994). At one level, many writers feel that it is the consumer's subjective, cognitive age that counts (Barak and Schiffman, 1981). People respond to advertisements and purchase according to the age that they *feel* and not according to their chronological age. For this reason, calendar age could be profitably replaced by subjective age. At another level, some authors are prepared to make do with chronological age — it is a cut-

and-dry means of segmenting consumers — but disagree on which age cut-off to employ. The majority opt for 65 since it has traditionally marked the onset of old age and the normal age for retirement. Nonetheless, there are compelling reasons for considering 55 years as an alternative cut-off.

- Early and staggered retirement are set to become permanent features of the employment landscape in years to come. The consumer's working life may begin to taper off sooner than it does at present.

- While financial data for discrete consumer groups in Ireland are not available, the figures for UK over-55s are quite staggering; estimates of their share of the nation's savings range between 50 and 67 per cent (Kiernan, 1986; Buck, 1990). In this sense, the over-55s are a financially promising segment.

- Events are likely to have happened by the age of 55 which will either occasion or coincide with changes in spending patterns, events such as the departure of offspring from the family home, high levels of disposable income, and inheritance from the preceding generation.

For these reasons and the fact that much data on Irish senior media consumption is based on a 55-year cut-off, this paper will take "seniors" to mean the over-55s, unless otherwise stated.

A final point for all students of the senior market concerns heterogeneity. The senior market is conceivably more varied than any other age segment. Ageist stereotypes of lonely, frail, and financially stretched seniors can often blur this fact. It is worth remembering that this segment includes government ministers, millionaires, media celebrities and business managers as well as their less prominent counterparts. Senior-market literature suggests that the real question which marketing communicators have to address is not whether to segment the senior market, but rather which segmentation basis to use (Bone, 1991).

SENIORS AND THE MEDIA.

Fundamental to any discussion on marketing communications is the question of media behaviour. Mass media are the vehicle for much of this communication. However, in the case of seniors this is doubly important. Mass media may be viewed as a service, commercial or otherwise, which seniors consume. Indeed, in terms of the time allocated to them, the media are *the* principal service that older people consume. Media consumption of seniors differs significantly from that of other age groups with regard to time expended, media/programme preferences, and viewing motivation.

Senior mass-media research has increasingly become synonymous with senior television research: television has become the leading medium for seniors (Bell, 1992). The weight of empirical evidence supporting this view has been both comprehensive and consistent. Television has been shown to be the most talked-about subject among seniors (Bennett, 1989), to be their principal leisure activity (Rubin and Rubin, 1982), and to have more time devoted to it than any other mass medium (French and Crask, 1977; Davis and Davis, 1985; Moschis, 1987). Indeed, more time is devoted to television than to any other senior activity, with the exception of sleeping (Moss and Lawton, 1982; Fouts, 1989). A large senior sample in San Diego spent more time watching television than even young children from the same city (Real, Anderson and Harrington, 1980), and in the UK older viewers spent 50 per cent more time in front of their sets than the average viewer (Hemming, 1988; Bennett, 1989). The import of this research is all the more remarkable when it is borne in mind that most of the senior subjects in the studies cited would have been in middle age when they first encountered the television medium, and thus would not have been socialised into any viewing patterns: television was "new" for this cohort.

The centrality of television in the lives of senior consumers has been reinforced by specific research to gauge the exact amount of time devoted to television-watching. Estimates of the average amount of daily viewing time in the US vary between three-and-a-half hours (Moss and Lawton, 1982) and five hours (Davis and Davis, 1985). Variations such as these may stem from the use of different research instruments. Television meters, time-budget diaries kept by the senior viewer, and recall questionnaires are all likely to register different amounts of daily viewing time.

Other authors have sought to determine those times during the day when viewing by seniors was at its highest. Most have reported that viewing peaks during what is termed "prime-time" (7–10 p.m.) (Korzenny and Neuendorf, 1980; Rubin and Rubin, 1982; Fouts, 1989). Viewership declines after 10 p.m. (Bernhardt and Kinnear, 1975) and despite availability, few seniors appear to watch morning programming (Davis, 1971; Schreiber and Boyd, 1980). Nonetheless, overall reach for older viewers during daytime television is much higher than for the general population (Durand, Klemmack, Roff and Taylor, 1980). Figure 20.1 below looks at viewing times for Irish seniors.

FIGURE 20.1: AVERAGE VIEWERSHIP OF TV X TIME OF DAY, JANUARY–JUNE 1995

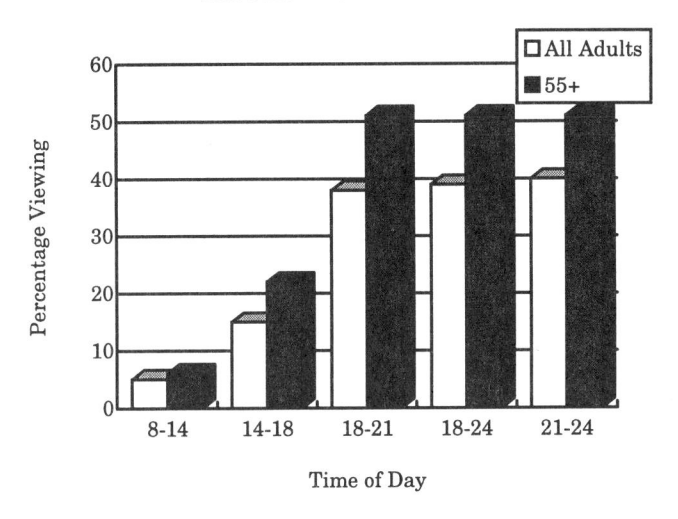

Note: All adults = All viewers over 15.
Source: AGB TAM, 1995.

Figure 20.1 shows a number of similarities between Irish and US senior viewers. First, morning television offerings do not seem to be all that enticing to seniors. Second, the proportion of older people viewing exceeds the proportion of all adults viewing over all transmission periods during the day. Third, the number of seniors viewing peaks in the early evening. However, unlike the US, this peak does not taper off later in the evening in Ireland.

Comparative analyses of times and amount of viewing should be treated with some caution. In this case any comparison between the US and Ireland should take a number of crucial variables into account, such as programme assortment, number of channels, length of daily transmission climatic and seasonal variation. As if to accentuate this point, Figure 20.2 below shows how there is a downward trend in senior Irish viewership for all daytime viewing periods as one moves from winter, through spring to summer. Though not shown in Figure 20.2, a similar downward trend is also evident from data for the general adult population.

FIGURE 20.2: PERCENTAGE VIEWERSHIP OF TV BY IRISH 55+ X TIME OF DAY, JANUARY–JUNE 1995

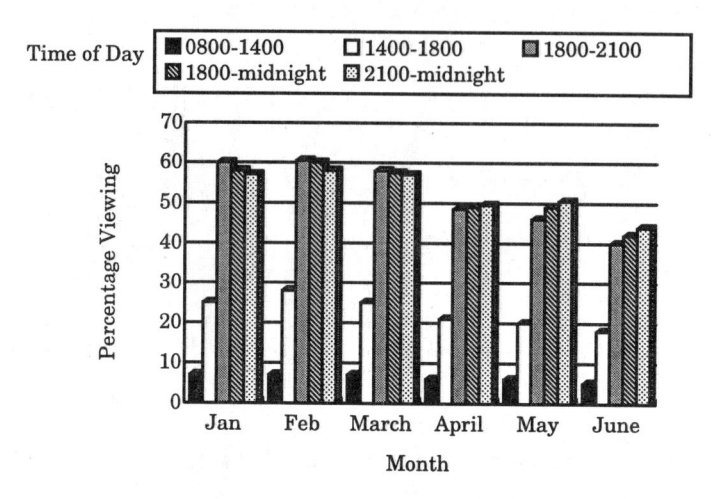

Time of Day: ■ 0800-1400 □ 1400-1800 ▨ 1800-2100 ▧ 1800-midnight ▥ 2100-midnight

Source: AGB TAM, 1995.

PROGRAMME PREFERENCES

From a marketing-communications perspective, any analysis of the amount of television viewed by seniors is secondary to the question of what specific types of television programme are watched and preferred (Durand, Klemmack, Roff and Taylor, 1980). Most of the research on this topic has addressed this question by seeking to ascertain respondents' favourite programme type — documentary or feature film, for example. It should be noted that this is not quite the same as asking what precise programmes are watched, or "what is your favourite show?"

If authors concur on the centrality of television in senior lifestyles, they are equally at one on the type of programming that older viewers enjoy most. Advancing age occasions a shift from entertainment-centred to non-fictional, information-centred viewing patterns (Wenner, 1976; Gelb, 1982; Rubin and Rubin, 1982; Kaiser and Chandler, 1985). Specifically, news/public affairs programmes have been consistently rated the most widely watched and enjoyed (Bartos, 1980; Real, Anderson and Harrington, 1980; Daly and O'Connor,

1984; Goodman, 1990). Fouts (1989: 573) summarised the situation as follows:

> Although researchers occasionally categorise some programs differently and use a variety of assessment techniques, the appetite for news and information is the most documented finding in the literature involving television and the elderly.

This predilection for television news, especially local news, has been echoed in numerous studies which have offered older respondents a selection of programming choices. While news is invariably the first choice, there is less than total unanimity on the subsequent rankings. Among the contenders for second-favourite programme type are documentaries/current affairs (Davis and Westbrook, 1985; Goodman, 1990), soaps/serials (Hemming, 1988) and game shows (Davis et al., 1976). Subsequent preferences after news programming and their respective rankings are of lesser moment. In fact, many apparent inconsistencies across studies on these rankings may simply result from the fact that there is a lack of agreement on the appropriate programme-classification system; "documentaries" may be a separate category in one study and subsumed under "educational" in another. Table 20.1 below affords some insight into current programme preferences of senior viewers in Ireland.

TABLE 20.1: TOP TEN 55+ PROGRAMMES (1 JANUARY–30 JUNE 1995)

Title	% of 55+ Viewing
Glenroe	62
Late Late Show*	61
Budget Broadcast	55
Eurovision Song Contest*	54
Crimeline*	53
Winning Streak	53
Kenny Live	53
Fair City	50
Where in the World?	49
Visit of Prince Charles	46

* Also appears in Top Ten list for all adults though not necessarily in the same place.
Source: AGB TAM, 1995.

Some caution is necessary in interpreting Table 20.1 above. In the first place, the listing is based on the proportion of over 55s watching a particular programme on a particular day. For example, *Glenroe* achieved its highest over-55 viewership on 12 February 1995. *Glenroe* was automatically eliminated from any further place in the rankings even though other editions of the same serial achieved higher viewership rates than other Top Ten programmes. Also, the fact that only three out of the 55+ Top Ten coincided with the Top Ten for all adults suggests a characteristic programme assortment for older viewers in Ireland. But perhaps the most noticeable feature of Table 20.1 is the absence of any listing for news programmes. TAM in Ireland has found the levels of news viewership to be so high that it is left out of lists such as Table 20.1 in order to allow other kinds of programming to feature more prominently. The absence of any news classification in Table 20.1 thus adds weight to, rather than contradicts, the findings from US research discussed above. Finally, it is worth noting that the more common second preferences noted in the senior literature — such as current affairs, soaps, and game shows — are well represented in the Irish Top Ten list.

It should be borne in mind that metered viewership such as TAM does not ask seniors the *type* of programme they prefer. For example, if those in a sample of Irish seniors were asked their favourite programme type, they might choose "music/variety", meaning that, while *Glenroe* is their favourite programme, they dislike most of the other soaps on offer and prefer music/variety as their most preferred *type* of programme. Some light has been thrown on this question in recent research (Turley, 1993). This research involved asking a random sample of Irish widows (n = 194) over 60 to list their three favourite television programmes. Classification of programmes involved a modified version of the list proposed by Rubin and Rubin (1982). Results are reproduced in Table 20.2 below.

A number of features in Table 20.2 are worthy of mention. First, the self-report instrument used here has produced broadly the same spectrum of preferences as the behavioural instrument employed by TAM in Table 20.1. So, in answer to the question posed above, it would appear that individual soaps are the most preferred programmes and that soaps in general are the favourite programme type. The relatively low rating accorded news programmes was not that surprising as an open question was used to elicit preferences: most respondents did not regard news bulletins as programmes proper. Had news been included on a checklist with other types of programmes, soaps would doubtless have come second.

If news is the clearly preferred programme genre, older viewers exhibit an equally definite antipathy towards other programme genres. Rubin and Rubin (1982) and Samli and Palubinskas (1972) reported a strong dislike for any shows or films featuring violence or promiscuity. Davis (1971) ventured the possibility that senior antipathy in this area may be partly the result of a feeling that one "should" be against such genres. He further detected little responsiveness to such youthful themes as romantic love and adventure thrillers. Another possibility adverted to by Fouts (1989) is that dislike for some programmes is linked to sensory decline. If one third of the light reaching the retina of a ten-year-old reaches the retina of a 60-year-old, then it should come as no surprise that mysteries and thrillers which carry a considerable complement of dark, fast-action footage with loud background music are less than enthusiastically received.

TABLE 20.2: PROGRAMME PREFERENCES OF IRISH 60+ WIDOWS

Programme Type	% First Preferences	% Second Preferences	% Third Preferences	% of all 3 Preferences
News	8.0	7.0	13.3	9.0*
Current Affairs	10.7	8.6	9.2	9.5
Soaps/Serials	51.0	46.0	36.0	44.0
Game Shows[†]				
Variety/Music[†]				
Chat Shows	18.0	21.0	19.0	19.0
Films[†]				
Other[†]				

* 9 per cent of all first, second and third preferences combined were for news programmes.
† Percentages for game shows, variety, films and "other" were uniformly low. They are omitted to ease interpretation.
Source: Turley, 1993.

VIEWING MOTIVATION

The considerable amounts of time allocated by the elderly to watching television, and their distinctive programme preferences, have lead several media researchers to investigate the motives that underpin their viewing behaviour. At a fundamental level, most seniors, because of altered life circumstances, have more leisure time available and an increasing impetus to maintain contact with a world which may be imperceptibly distancing itself from them (Doolittle, 1979). To this extent, there is a natural logic to senior viewing behaviour. When older viewers are questioned as to what motivates their television watching, replies tend to gravitate towards one or other end of the information–entertainment spectrum.

Those studies which have examined viewing motivation in a thorough fashion have uncovered a rich motivational texture. The idea that television provides seniors with a "window on the world" has been suggested by several authors (Rubin and Rubin, 1981; Davis and Davis, 1985). According to this view, the benefit of television lies in its ability to enable seniors to "share the same facts" as the rest of the population at a time when their sphere of social interaction may be shrinking. A further benefit suggested is the way in which television can divide up the day: certain programmes can act as markers signalling that particular activities — such as eating, getting dressed, or going shopping — should be initiated (Davis, 1971). A further motive suggested in the literature is the desire for companionship. Seen in this light, the older viewer is endeavouring to maintain contact with the world, albeit at one remove, and thereby to experience it vicariously. So, far from being a medium of withdrawal, television is desired as a means of social engagement (Doolittle, 1979; Real, Anderson and Harrington, 1980).

The most probing and recondite study of elderly viewing motivation has been carried out by Fouts (1989). He advances eight possible motives in all underlying senior television viewership; as they encompass all the motives mentioned in the literature, they bear repetition:

1) Information acquisition

2) Entertainment

3) Provides topics for conversation

4) Helps schedule activities — Going shopping after the news at lunch-time

5) Substitute companion — Celebrity/newsreader is seen as a personal friend

6) Relaxation

7) Arousal

8) A cross-generational activity — watching television with grandchildren, for example.

While these motives are not mutually exclusive, Fouts (1989) suggests that the first two are particularly salient for older viewers. This suggestion was corroborated in Turley's (1993) research on senior Irish widows, which is summarised in Table 20.3 below.

TABLE 20.3: TELEVISION VIEWING MOTIVES OF SENIOR IRISH WIDOWS

Viewing Motivation	% of Mentions*
Divides up the day for me	6
Helps me relax	18
Helps pass the time	13
Entertains me	23
Keeps me in touch	20
Keeps me company	20

* Widows were asked to choose their three most important motivations out of the six listed above. "Divides up the day for me" received 6 per cent of all first, second, and third preferences combined.
Source: Turley, 1993.

As postulated by Fouts (1989), the entertainment and information (Keeps me in touch) motivations were significantly endorsed. The 20 per cent mention level for "Keeps me company" may well be because of the particular circumstances and needs of widows.

ADVERTISING AND THE SENIOR MARKET.

The literature on marketing communications and seniors has focused primarily on above-the-line advertising. Readers wishing to investigate below-the-line promotion and the grey market can profitably consult Lumpkin, Caballero, and Chonko (1989) and Davis and French (1991). Specifically this section will examine five key topics relating to advertising and seniors.

1) The manner in which older people are portrayed in advertisements

2) The appeals that such advertisements make

3) The attitudes of older audiences to such appeals

4) The impact of advertising on seniors

5) The models featured in advertisements aimed at seniors.

The Portrayal of Older People in Advertisements

Both the extent and quality of portrayal of the elderly in advertising is of more than academic interest. The amount and type of advertising they are exposed to can have significant effects on their own self-esteem and on their perception of the elderly in general (Smith, Moschis and Moore, 1984; Moschis, 1987).

A point that should be made at the outset is that the majority of older models appear in advertisements for products that are not specifically aimed at the senior market. Most appear with models of other ages for products as diverse as ice-cream and facial tissues, and thus their portrayal is formative both of the general public's image of the elderly and of the elderly's own image of how they should relate to other consumer groups.

The portrayal of older people specifically in advertisements has received considerable attention in the literature. As with their portrayal in the mass media, conclusions are mixed although studies suggesting a generalised negative portrayal outnumber those suggesting a positive portrayal (Whetton, 1990) and point to two features of senior advertisements in support of this view.

First, the number of advertisements featuring any older model, the number of older models compared with non-elderly models, and the proportion of older to non-old models relative to their numbers in the population are disproportionately low (Greenberg, Korzenny and Atkin, 1979; Langmeyer, 1983; Patel, 1988; Bramlett-Solomon and Wilson, 1989; Milliman and Erffmeyer, 1989; Bennett, 1989; Zhou and Chen, 1992). While there are signs that this underrepresentation is ameliorating (Mandese, 1989; Milliman and Erffmeyer, 1989), this omission has engendered a feeling of lack of importance among some older consumers (Minkler, 1989) and may help to explain why they often register poor advertising-recognition scores — if they fail to feature in many advertisements, it should come as no surprise that they find few advertisements to be memorable (Bennett, 1989).

The second reason why these studies find senior advertising portrayal less than complimentary concerns the manner or role in which senior models are cast. Clearly, claims concerning the manner of portrayal are bound to be more subjective than claims of underrepresentation. A small Long Beach senior sample said that the portrayal of older people in television advertisements was "unsatisfactory" (Davis, 1971). Older models are also likely to appear less healthy in advertisements than they are in reality (Davis and Davis, 1985). A UK content analysis of advertisements shown on television over a typical weekend found that most older models were cast in a humorous role (Bennett, 1989), while another US content analysis of magazine advertisements found that older models were twice as likely to appear accompanied by a younger model as to appear alone, and that they often endorsed unflattering products (Bramlett-Solomon and Wilson, 1989). Fifty-nine per cent of a large US elderly sample felt that they were honestly represented on television drama — the figure for advertisements was 40 per cent (Davis and Westbrook, 1985).

Noting this generalised negativity, Milliman and Erffmeyer (1989) attribute it to a combination of three factors:

1) The ageist attitudes of younger people

2) The way in which older models allegedly make for "poor copy" with negative overtones

3) The possibility that older models may adversely affect the credibility of the advertised message.

As regards gender, older males tend to receive a more complimentary coverage in advertising than females (Langmeyer, 1983; Patel, 1988) and to have role models on television who are more fashionable and less stereotypically portrayed (Kaiser and Chandler, 1985).

However, despite majority support for negative portrayal, a small number of authors have disputed that the elderly fare poorly in advertising or, at least, that they feature more benignly than heretofore (Schreiber and Boyd, 1980; Langmeyer, 1993). All that can be said at present is that much of this discordance stems from selecting different advertising media, directed at different audiences and subsequently using different research instruments to analyse the partiality of this portrayal. It is also clear that results will be moderated by the sensitivity of older audiences to stereotypical portrayals and the degree to which this sensitivity has been lowered by previous exposure to unflattering advertising.

Appeals in Senior Advertising

This section progresses from the representation and portrayal of older people in advertisements to the appeals most appropriate for marketing communications aimed directly or collaterally at the mature market. One overriding injunction in the literature is not to focus on the question of age (Moschis, 1987). For store advertising, this entails valuing older customers not because they are old and *should be* valued, but rather because of their long-term patronage over the years (Gelb, 1982). With fast-moving consumer goods, a link should be forged in the advertising copy between the product and some need characteristic of older shoppers, rather than highlighting them explicitly as different or deserving. Hartmann (1988) instanced "a cereal that lowers cholesterol" rather than "a cereal for seniors" as an example of such a link. This policy should also colour need driven product-line extensions (Radding, 1989). Such extensions should be marketed for specific need patterns characteristic of older shoppers — "smaller portions for those who dislike waste" — rather than "special models and sizes for the elderly" (Miaoulis and Cooper, 1987).

> The message of the "pioneers" of the older market is that age-based strategies are inappropriate ... it is usually a mistake to sell products to older people by telling them that the product is specially designed for them. A more effective strategy is to sell them the product by telling them how appropriate it is to their interests and aspirations (Wolfe, 1987: 28).

In a similar vein, UK holiday operators advertising to older customers have discovered that presenting an appropriate and tailored product mix is pivotal. If this can be achieved, there is less need for concern over the amount and manner in which seniors are portrayed (Stacey, 1987). The central admonition is not to single out older clients or customers (Schneidman, 1988) but to generate advertising appeals, seemingly directed at all, but which "happen" to meet their precise needs (Visvabharathy and Rink, 1984).

A second theme to emerge in the literature is the use of trans-generational advertising appeals (French and Fox, 1985; Mertz and Stephens, 1986). Advertisements using this technique typically portray an elderly model using the product either with, or in the company of, a model or models belonging to a younger age cohort; it is not uncommon in practice for this younger model to be depicted as the senior's grandchild. Recent examples on Irish television of this technique include advertisements for a well-known brand of tissue and a brand of ice-cream. Apart from the strong emotional appeal which grandchildren naturally engender, these advertisements are thought to bolster the older viewer's self-esteem; they are also thought to be highly persuasive.

A more recent advertising innovation alluded to in the literature is that of reverse stereotyping (Davis and Davis, 1985; Gabriel, 1990).

This technique invariably involves a stereotypical older model engaged in some pursuit typical of some younger, more active, cohort. A recent example on Irish television screens involves two elderly ladies manually lifting an incorrectly parked car, for which they are rewarded with a well-known brand of chocolate. No definitive findings on the impact of this technique have been proffered. At one level, this approach may well leave older viewers feeling somewhat chuffed at their seemingly long-lived vitality; at another, it may insult them by portraying the elderly model as one pole in an uncomplimentary bi-polar contrast, all in the interests of creating a humorous impact. One possibility that has not yet been explored in the literature, is that reverse stereotyping may have its primary focus and impact on the 50–60-year age group. Anxious over impending retirement and the onset of old age, such advertisements may well reassure them that the active lifestyle they now enjoy will persist over coming decades.

Apart from thematic suggestions, a small corpus of writers has presented a number of pragmatic rules of thumb to the advertising community based on their research on older viewers. Greco (1987) advocated the use of simple language and appeals, employing a message that links up with some event in the senior's earlier life, and portraying the older model as useful, competent, and coping. Similar directions are given by Moundlic (1990) who suggests concrete rational arguments, featuring models 40–50 years of age who exude what he terms "soft dynamism" — that is, sober activity levels consistent with their age. Interestingly, this advice echoes the stated guidelines of the American Association of Retired Persons for advertisers: honesty, a clear statement of value, and the absence of hyperbole (Wolfe, 1988).

Attitudes of Seniors towards Advertising

Research on the attitudes of older viewers/readers towards advertising per se has been rather scant. French and Crask (1977) found that their small sample saw no difference in the credibility of advertisements across the different media. Credibility levels were quite high — 64 per cent for advertising in the media in general. Later, in a comparative study across four countries, French et al. (1983) reported that seniors in the respective countries held advertising in low esteem, although the American respondents were less critical than those from the UK, Israel, and Norway. An increasing distrust and scepticism towards advertising by older people is predicted by

Dychtwald and Gable (1990) who claim that the current literate and highly-educated baby-boomer cohort will continue to exercise their critical powers on what advertisers have to say in succeeding decades.

The most rigorous, and perhaps most promising, piece of research conducted on senior attitudes to advertising is that of Davis and French (1989). While their sample was not a representative one and featured females alone, they did find it possible to uncover three distinct senior segments, based solely on the attitudes of respondents towards advertising. Distinctive profiles and media behaviours were subsequently isolated. To date, they are the only authors to advance the view that senior attitudes towards advertising are sufficiently salient to provide a possible basis for segmenting the mature market.

Impact of Advertising on Seniors

Perhaps more fundamental than senior attitudes to advertising is the question of the effects of mass-media advertising on the elderly. The overwhelming consensus in the literature is that these effects are primarily negative. Smith, Moschis, and Moore (1984) found that the amount of mass-media advertising to which older viewers were exposed was negatively related to their perceptions of old age, to their own sense of self-esteem, and to their views of how older people were portrayed in advertisements. In other words, seniors who watched greater amounts of mass-media advertising developed a poorer image of what it means to be old, enjoyed lower self-esteem, and felt that older people fared badly in advertisements. In a similar negative vein, Smith and Baker (1986) suggest a deleterious effect by mass media advertising on senior dietary intake, as most of the foodstuffs promoted in the media are high in ingredients unsuited to the older digestive system. A further, if less than surprising, negative consequence of watching mass-media advertising is a reported diminution in the ability to filter puffery (Moschis, 1987). Among the less damaging outcomes of advertising exposure suggested, are the likelihood of a more economical shopping style, the usage of a larger number of salient evaluative criteria, and a higher propensity to switch brands (Moschis, 1987).

Models in Senior Advertising

The received wisdom in the advertising literature suggests using senior models for the senior market (Gronhaug and Rostveig, 1978). The use of such models is unlikely to antagonise the general population, according to the work of Radding (1989) where 77 per cent of all US adults reacted positively to advertisements featuring older models. It is likely that older consumers themselves bear no antipathy towards older models. However, this leaves open the question as to whether an older model has a more persuasive impact on the older person than a model from another age group. Early research by Klock and Traylor (1983) concluded that model age had no effect on the purchase intentions of a small convenience sample.

The suitability or not of using older models should not be viewed unidimensionally. There is evidence to suggest that the model's perceived age is what is most crucial and that a variety of factors can influence this. Barak and Gould (1985) discovered that older models who appeared with their own children in advertisements were perceived as younger than other models of the same age who had no progeny present.

A case has also been made for distinguishing between the impact of an older model on liking for an advertisement and their impact on the advertisement's credibility. When a large sample of Florida seniors was presented with the same advertisement featuring models of three different ages, it emerged that the model's age had no impact on *liking* for the advertisement itself. However, the senior and middle-aged models had a considerably higher impact on the *credibility* of the advertisement, than had the younger models (Milliman and Erffmeyer, 1989).

A more sophisticated approach to model selection was initiated by Rotfeld, Reid and Wilcox (1982). Using a youth-oriented product (toothpaste) and an elderly-oriented product (denture cream), they produced six advertisements, using three different model age types for each of the two products. When these six advertisements were shown to a sample of housewives, it emerged that evaluations of the advertisement itself, of its sponsor, and of the product advertised, were not a function of the model's age but of the perceived "fit" between the model's age and the product's orientation — elderly models per se were not an issue.

Indirect support for this concept of perceived fit was found in recent research by Greco and Swayne (1992). Using an "age neutral" product — coffee — they discovered that purchases by older shoppers were unaffected by the age of models featured in point-of-purchase displays. A similar conclusion was reached by Greco (1988) in a survey of advertising executives. Their estimation of the usefulness of older models was predicated on the compatibility between the age of the model and the product's orientation. Healthcare, travel, and financial services had orientations suited to older models; cars, cosmetics and sports goods did not, and so they considered that advertisements for these ought not to feature older models, even when directed at an elderly audience.

CONCLUSIONS

The earlier review of the media behaviour of older people supports their being regarded as a distinct consumer segment. They were shown to have a strong predilection for one medium in particular, television, devoting more time to it than any other age group in the population — this despite a number of adverse effects on their psychological well-being. Within this medium, they exhibit distinctive programme preferences, preferences consistent with a group of viewers who have more time, increasing psychological decrements, and a feeling of being distanced from society at large.

The above considerations should not obscure the fact that, although seniors are avid viewers, much of what they see is irrelevant to them: many programmes are *endured* rather than enjoyed (Davis, 1971). However, in the final analysis, television would be preferred to no television at all. It is also important to bear in mind that, while older viewers have distinctive programme preferences and viewing motivation, few programmes have a viewing profile skewed by age. Seniors are still a fraction of the population and often watch what they do not particularly like (Buck, 1990). The effects that exposure to mass-media advertising have on older viewers lends some support to those who detect an unfavourable bias in the way that advertisements depict older people. Seniors who see and hear more mass-media advertising enjoy lower levels of self-esteem and a less flattering image of older people in general.

The question of which model age and advertising theme has the greatest persuasive impact on older consumers has also been examined. While the current advertising practice is to employ models 15–20 years younger than the target audience, it now appears that an appropriate "fit" between the advertised product's orientation and the perceived age of the model is more crucial than the model's age alone. On the question of appropriate advertising appeals, older consumers share many of the same needs and wants as the population at large. To this extent there are no distinctive advertising appeals exclusive to older audiences, although they do exhibit characteristic sensitivities.

Indeed, the likelihood is that the coming cohort of over 55s will insist on being addressed and portrayed as consumers in the mainstream and will exercise their considerable purchase power to remind marketing communicators of this fact.

REFERENCES

AGB, TAM (1995): Attwood Research, Dublin.

Barak, B. and Gould, S. (1985): "Alternative Age Measures: A Research Agenda" in Hirschman, E. and Holbrook, M.B. (eds.), *Advances in Consumer Research*, 12, Provo, UT: Association for Consumer Research: 53–8.

Barak, B. and Schiffman, L. (1981): "Cognitive Age: A Non-chronological Age Variable" in Monroe, K. (ed.), *Advances in Consumer Research*, 8, Ann Arbor, MI: Association for Consumer Research: 602–6.

Bartos, R. (1980): "Over 49: The Invisible Consumer Market", *Harvard Business Review*, January/February: 140–47.

Bell, J. (1992): "In Search of a Discourse on Ageing: The Elderly on Television", *The Gerontologist*, 32(3): 305–11.

Bennett, B. (1989): "Television — A Captive Audience of Grampies?", *L.W.T. Marketing Review*, 79, February: 2–4.

Bernhardt, K. and Kinnear T. (1975): "Profiling the Senior Citizen Market", in Anderson, B. (ed.), *Advances in Consumer Research*, 3, Ann Arbor, MI: Association for Consumer Research: 449–52.

Bone, P. (1991): "Identifying Mature Consumer Segments", *Journal of Consumer Marketing*, 18(4): 19–32.

Bramlett-Solomon, S. and Wilson, V. (1989): "Images of the Elderly in *Life* and *Ebony*, 1978–1987", *Journalism Quarterly*, 66(1): 185–8.

Buck, S. (1990): "Turning an Old Problem into a New Opportunity", *Admap*, 25(3): 20–22.

Daly, M. and O'Connor, J. (1984): *The World of the Elderly: The Rural Experience*, Dublin: National Council for the Aged.

Davis, B. and French, W. (1989): "Exploring Advertising Usage Segments Among The Aged", *Journal of Advertising Research*, 29(1): 22–9.

Davis, B. and French, W. (1991): "Another View of Older Consumers and Catalogue Shopping", *Journal of Direct Marketing*, 5(3): 29–38.

Davis, R. (1971): "Television and the Older Adult", *Journal of Broadcasting*, 15(2): 153–9.

Davis, R. and Davis, J. (1985): *The Television Image of America's Elderly*, Lexington, MA: Lexington Books.

Davis, R., Edwards, A., Bartel, D. and Martin D. (1976): "Assessing Television Viewing Behaviour of Older Adults", *Journal of Broadcasting*, 20(1): 69–76.

Davis, R. and Westbrook, G. (1985): "Television in the Lives of the Elderly: Attitudes and Opinions", *Journal of Broadcasting and Electronic Media*, 29(2): 209–14.

Doolittle, J. (1979): "News Media Use by Older Adults", *Journalism Quarterly*, 56(2): 311–17.

Durand, R., Klemmack, D., Roff, L. and Taylor, J. (1980): "Communicating with the Elderly: Reach of Television and Magazines", *Psychological Reports*, 46: 1235–42.

Dychtwald, K. and Gable, G. (1990): "Portrait of a Changing Consumer", *Business Horizons*, 33: 62–73.

French, W., Barksdale, H., Perreault, W., Arndt, J. and Zif, J. (1983): "The Problems of Older Consumers: A Comparison of England, Israel, Norway, and the United States" in Murphy, P. et al. (eds.), *American Marketing Association Educators Proceedings*, Chicago, Illinois: American Marketing Association: 390–95.

French, W. and Crask, M. (1977): "The Credibility of Media Advertising for the Elderly", in Greenberg, B. et al. (eds.), *American Marketing Association Educators Proceedings*, Chicago, Illinois: American Marketing Association: 74–7.

French, W. and Fox, R. (1985): "Segmenting the Senior Citizen Market", *Journal of Consumer Marketing*, 2(1): 61–74.

Fouts, G. (1989): "Television Use by the Elderly", *Canadian Psychology*, 30(3): 568–77.

Gabriel, J. (1990): "The Size and Nature of the Ageing Population" in Buck, Stephan (ed.), *The 55+ Market*, London: McGraw Hill.

Gelb, B. (1982): "Discovering the 65+ Consumer", *Business Horizons*, May/June: 42–6.

Goodman, R. (1990): "Television News Viewing by Older Adults", *Journalism Quarterly*, 67(1): 137–41.

Greco, A. (1987): "Linking Dimensions of the Elderly Market to Market Planning", *Journal of Consumer Marketing*, 4(2): 47–55.

Greco, A. (1988): "The Elderly as Communicators: Perceptions of Advertising Practitioners", *Journal of Advertising Research*, 28(3): 39–46.

Greco, A. and Swayne, L. (1992): "Sales Response of Elderly Consumers to Point-of-Purchase Advertising", *Journal of Advertising Research*, September/October: 43–53.

Greenberg, B., Korzenny, F. and Atkin, C. (1979): "The Portrayal of the Ageing: Trends on Commercial Television", *Research on Ageing*, 1: 319–34.

Gronhaug, K. and Rostvig, L. (1978): "Target Groups and Advertising Messages", *Journal of Advertising Research*, 18(2): 23–8.

Hemming, A. (1988): "Elderly People's Use of Broadcast Media", *Annual Review of BBC Broadcasting Research Findings*, 14: 35–44.

Hartmann, C. (1988): "Redesigning America", *Inc.*, 10(6), June: 58–74.

Kaiser, S. and Chandler, J. (1985): "Older Consumers' Use of Media for Fashion Information", *Journal of Broadcasting and Electronic Media*, 29(2): 201–7.

Kiernan, P. (1986): "Why an Older Market?", *Marketing Week*, December: 38–42.

Klock, S. and Traylor, M. (1983): "Older and Younger Models in Advertising to Older Consumers: An Advertising Effectiveness Experiment", *Akron Business and Economic Review*, 14(4): 48–52.

Korzenny, F. and Neuendorf, K. (1980): "Television Viewing and Self-Concept of the Elderly", *Journal of Communication*, 30(1): 71–80.

Langmeyer, L. (1983): "Age Role Portrayals in Magazine Advertisements: A Content Analysis", *Proceedings*, Southern Marketing Association: 286–9.

Langmeyer, L. (1993): "Advertising Images of Mature Adults: An Update", *Journal of Current Issues and Research in Advertising*, 15(2): 81–91.

Lumpkin, J., Caballero, M. and Chonko, L. (1989): *Direct Marketing, Direct Selling, and the Mature Consumer: A Research Study*, New York: Quorum Books.

Mandese, J. (1989): "The New Old", *Marketing and Media Decisions*, 24(4), 32–40.

Mertz, B. and Stephens, N. (1986): "Marketing to Older American Consumers", *International Journal of Ageing and Human Development*, 23(1), 47–58.

Miaoulis, G. and Cooper, P. (1987): "The Grey Market Lights Up: The Satisfaction Syndrome", *Marketing Communications*, 12(3): 36–42.

Milliman, R. and Erffmeyer, R. (1989): "Improving Advertising Aimed at Seniors", *Journal of Advertising Research*, December/January: 31–6.

Minkler, M. (1989): "Gold in Gray: Reflections on Business's Discovery of the Elderly Market", *The Gerontologist*, 29(1): 17–23.

Moschis, G. (1987): *Consumer Socialisation: A Life Cycle Perspective*, Lexington, MA: Lexington Books.

Moss, M. and Lawton, M. (1982): "Time Budgets of Older People: A Window on Four Lifestyles", *Journal of Gerontology*, 37(1): 115–23.

Moundlic, A. (1990): "Communication with Senior Citizens", *Admap*, March: 33–5.

Patel, S. (1988): "Taking Care of the Elderly", *L.W.T. Marketing Review*, 77: 18–19.

Radding, A. (1989): "You Don't Turn 50 and Change what You Read", *Advertising Age*, 22 May: S4–S6.

Real, M., Anderson, H. and Harrington, M. (1980): "Television Access for Older Adults", *Journal of Communication*, 30(10): 81–9.

Rotfeld, H., Reid, L. and Wilcox, G. (1982): "Effect of Age of Models in Print Ads on Evaluation of Product and Sponsor", *Journalism Quarterly*, 59(3): 374–81.

Rubin, A. and Rubin, R. (1981): "Age, Context, and Television Use", *Journal of Broadcasting*, 25(1): 1–13.

Rubin, A. and Rubin, R. (1982): "Older Persons' TV Patterns and Motivations", *Communication Research*, 9: 287–313.

Samli, A. and Palubinskas, F. (1972): "Some Lesser Known Aspects of the Senior Citizen Market: A California Study", *Akron Business and Economic Review*, Winter: 47–55.

Schneidman, D. (1988): "Older Consumers Adopt Baby Boomer Buyer Behaviour: Consumers over Age 50 Pose Marketing Challenge", *Marketing News*, 22(4): 8–17.

Schreiber, E. and Boyd, D. (1980): "How the Elderly Perceive Television Commercials", *Journal of Communications*, 30(1): 61–70.

Smith, R. and Baker, G. (1986): "The Elderly Consumer: A Perspective on Present and Potential Sources of Consumerism Activity", in Bloom, P. and Belk, R. (eds.), *The Future of Consumerism*, Lexington, MA: Lexington Books.

Smith, R., Moschis, G. and Moore, R. (1984): "Effects of Advertising on the Elderly Consumer: An Investigation of Social Breakdown Theory", in Belk, R. and Peterson, R. (eds.), *American Marketing Association Summer Educators Proceedings*, Chicago, IL: American Marketing Association: 1–5.

Stacey, C. (1987): "Catering for the Over 60's", *Hospitality*, September: 10–12.

Turley, D. (1993): "An Exploratory Investigation of the Impact of Conjugal Bereavement on Selected Consumer Behaviour and Lifestyle Dimensions of Women Over 60 in Ireland", unpublished PhD thesis, Dublin City University.

Turley, D. (1994): "The Senior Market: Opportunity or Oxymoron?", *Irish Marketing Review*, 7:16–30.

Visvabharathy, G. and Rink, G. (1984): "The Elderly: Neglected Business Opportunities", *Journal of Consumer Marketing*, 1(4): 35–46.

Wenner, L. (1976): "Functional Analysis of TV Viewing for Older Adults", *Journal of Broadcasting*, 20(1): 77–88.

Whetton, S. (1990): "Is an Older Age Profile a Media Disadvantage?", *Admap*, 25(3): 30–32.

Wolfe, D. (1987): "The Ageless Market", *American Demographics*, 9(7): 26–9, 55–6.

Wolfe, D. (1988): "Learning to Speak the Language of the New Senior", *Marketing Communications*, 13(3): 47–52.

Zhou, N. and Chen, M. (1992): "Marginal Life after 49: A Preliminary Study of the Portrayal of Older People in Canadian Consumer Magazine Advertising", *International Journal of Advertising*, 11: 343–54.

21
Disturbing the Stability of Purchasing Patterns: The Key to Successful Launching of FMCG Brands

Cathal Brugha
Kevin Donnelly

THE NATURE OF FMCG PURCHASING

To develop a communications strategy for the launch of a new fast-moving consumer good (FMCG) it is necessary, first of all, to explore the mind of the consumer and, more particularly, of the purchaser. FMCGs are typically frequently-used low-price items such as tins of beans, peas, packets of washing powder, breakfast cereals, etc. They are purchased frequently, in many cases as part of the weekly supermarket shopping. FMCG brands are usually associated with a low-involvement purchase decision, in that little evaluation goes into the decision. The FMCG purchase decision is usually routine, and loyalty can be quite low, as the purchaser may not have well-thought-out reasons for purchasing a particular brand continually. This does not mean that purchasers do not have reasons for purchasing one brand rather than another. They do have reasons. In some cases, purchasers may even have strong reasons for purchasing a brand — for example, preferring a low-fat milk brand for health reasons. But this, in itself, may not mean loyalty to a specific brand, but just to the requirement of a specific product characteristic.

If asked at the point of purchase why they bought a particular brand, purchasers will certainly be able to give reasons. They may not be able to recall those reasons if interviewed at home some evening three days later. The reasons that purchasers may give at a point of purchase may not fit traditional high-involvement loyalty theory. They could be very general and not specific to the brand such as "I prefer to buy Irish unless I think it is bad value" or "The children will only eat brown bread if it is sliced". When developing a communications strategy for an FMCG it is a mistake to assume automatically that the FMCG decision is not preceded by a hierarchy of effects normally associated with more complex high-involvement decisions. The real distinguishing feature of FMCG decision-making is not the absence of evaluation prior to purchase, but rather the amount of time spent on the decision, which is often only a few seconds. It is possible, even, for a purchaser to be intensely involved in the decision to buy an FMCG brand, even though this involvement may happen over a very short time span. High involvement is often misunderstood. It can have at least the following dimensions:

- Length of time: a lot in the case of buying cars, very little for FMCGs

- Intensity: a lot for snacks for an adults' party, less for a children's party

- Hierarchy of needs: the unique selling point of FMCGs is often at the physical level, literally bread and butter issues, but an ice cream focuses more on the emotional level. It is assumed that the purchase of a car is "high-level"; however, many car purchases are made to satisfy specific technical needs (physical level) within a limited budget (economic level).

The communications strategy for an FMCG should not be devised without reference to how the product might add value to the purchaser, and to the process whereby customers will come to realise this and convert it into a buying decision.

REPERTOIRE BUYING

With FMCG markets, it is quite rare to encounter households that are exclusively loyal to one brand, particularly over a period covering multiple-purchase occasions. Ehrenberg (1988) has identified and empirically established a phenomenon which he terms "partial loyalty" for FMCG brands. "Loyal" consumers of a particular brand are defined as consumers of other brands in the product category who occasionally (though more than any other single brand) purchase the brand under discussion.

There is a variety of reasons why a household would purchase from a repertoire of FMCG brands. These include variety-seeking behaviour, out-of-stocks (where the preferred brand is not available), different usage occasions (even in markets like toilet tissue there can be a shift from economy to premium brands at Christmas, to "impress" visitors), purchasing for different members of the household (e.g. where a housewife purchases cola for the children and a lemon/lime brand for the adults). Other reasons for repertoire buying can be directly linked to the collective actions of manufacturers and retailers. Promotional activity, both in-store and door-to-door, ensures more temptation for brand switching at every purchase occasion. Well-stocked and strongly-displayed private-label offerings are also triggers for widening purchase repertoires. Proliferation of stock-keeping units through range extension (different sizes, varieties and packaging types) has also contributed to widening repertoires. For example, in the washing powder market there have been over 150 new product variations (stock-keeping units) introduced in the past 10 years.

A household's evoked set is the range of alternative brands in a market that the household finds acceptable. A simple measure of this is the number of different brands in a market actually bought by purchasers from a household. Evidence from the Attwood Household Consumer Panel (see Table 21.1) suggests an increase in evoked set size over the past three years.

TABLE 21.1: AVERAGE NUMBER OF BRANDS OR VARIETIES PURCHASED BY HOUSEHOLDS WHEN BUYING OVER 48 WEEKS

Product	1993	1994
Washing Powders	4.7	8.6
Tea	2.9	4.2
Milk from shops	5.5	7.7

Source: AGB Attwood (1995).

A further factor driving repertoire size is the convergence in perceived quality in FMCG brands. Consumers accept that most, if not all, brands and private-label products deliver a minimum acceptable level of quality. The increasing concentration of the grocery trade, and the fact that a brand is stocked by a major retailer, endorses perceived quality of the range of options stocked. The existence of regulating bodies and the increasing tendency of people to complain publicly about faulty products, and even to take companies to court, leads people to assume that if they have not heard anything bad about a product, they can assume that it is, at least, safe and achieves what it purports to. The absence of negative, comparative advertising in many FMCG categories also supports a perception that many brands can deliver a minimum quality level. Added to this is the increasing repertoire itself, which is making people more comfortable with brand switching. The variety of shopping alternatives (supermarket, local shop, shop near work, etc.) and the consequent necessity to accept different brands instead of their usual brands has also led to a greater experience of multiple brands, and a consequent increase in trust of other brands. High repertoire size, especially for FMCGs, is here to stay.

CONSUMER FLOWS

Repertoire-buying means that for FMCG markets there is continuous and considerable movement of households in and out of a brand. A company, or brand, does not own a discrete franchise of consumers in an absolute sense as used to be thought. There are flows of consumers which brand managers seek to influence towards their particular brand. Lipstein (1970: 3) observed that:

> A set of stable brand shares conceals this dynamic movement of consumers that occurs below the surface.

Thus, even in the steady-state share situation there are flows of consumers in and out of brands. However, this exchange of consumers between brands is occurring at a fairly constant rate which keeps the market in equilibrium. It is the rate of consumer flows, and not the brand-share patterns, that lies at the heart of markets. The evidence of widening repertoires cited earlier suggests an increase in the rate of consumer flows across most FMCG markets; these markets have become inherently more unstable, even though the brand shares may not fully reflect that. Even in the steady-state share situation, widening repertoires suggest an increase in the amplitude of consumer flows in and out of brands.

In order to cause a change in brand shares, a brand manager must dislocate the underlying flow of consumers in a market and then attract a share of the dislocated consumers or, more strictly, those who purchase on their behalf. Perhaps the most dramatic way of dislocating established purchasing patterns is through new-brand launches. Though never empirically established, it is assumed that the more effective the new-brand launch, the greater the dislocation of the market equilibrium, and the higher the settled-down market share of the new brand. However, what has been established is that once a new brand has been launched and has reached critical mass share, the new brand adopts the characteristics of a mature brand in terms of purchasing dynamics with, in general, large brands not only being bought by more consumers, but purchased more frequently than smaller brands. Wellan and Ehrenberg (1988: 36), have concluded that after a new-brand entry, a market does not remain in a perturbed state indefinitely and that forces within the market tend to move it back to a state of equilibrium.

Any brand manager launching a new FMCG brand must realise that the process moves the market from a state of equilibrium to disequilibrium followed by a settling-down period.

THE STABILITY INDEX

The Stability Index, introduced by Brugha and Turley (1987), is a single numerical score running between zero and one, which measures the stability of a purchaser's choice of products within a market over a period of time. If a purchaser stayed with one brand, the score would be one. Evenly switching between three brands would give a score of one third. Generally buying one brand, and very occasionally switching to two others, would leave the score near to one — that is, it takes frequency of purchase into account.

The index captures in one synthesised score the four elements of aggregate market response to any marketing variable, namely: trial, first repeat, depth of repeat and purchase frequency. It can be applied to purchase sequences by individual households as recorded on a consumer panel, and can be aggregated across households (even those with different purchase frequencies and hence sequence lengths) on a total-market basis or on any standard or purchase-based demographic groupings such as ABC1 consumers or only purchasers of brand X. The Stability Index taps into the rates of consumer flows between brands in an FMCG market. It takes the brand manager beyond market-share data to represent graphically the underlying market structure.

THE EFFECT OF NEW BRAND LAUNCH ON MARKET STABILITY

The Stability Index was empirically tested by Donnelly (1988) on Attwood Consumer Panel data for the Yellow Fats Market, which comprises butter, margarine, baking fats and dairy spreads. The analysis period covered four new brand launches into the dairy spread sector.

The research addressed three hypotheses:

1) That for a new-brand launch, dislocating market stability, as measured by the Index, is a determinant of settled-down market share

2) That a market tends to move back to equilibrium following a new brand launch

3) That the immediate effect of several brand launches over time reduces market stability.

An illustration of the Stability Index scores for the Irish Yellow Fats market over the 89 weeks during 1987–88 is indicated in Figure 21.1. Four new brands were launched over the period. These are shown as Launch Disturbances (LD) 1 to 4. More successful launches appeared to cause a greater trough in the graph — a deeper destabilisation of purchasing patterns in the market. That is, more purchasers tried other brands after the launch of the new brand. High correlation was recorded between the depth of destabilisation, caused by new brand entry, as measured by the Stability Index, and the eventual settled-

FIGURE 21.1: STABILITY INDEX SCORES FOR YELLOW FATS MARKET

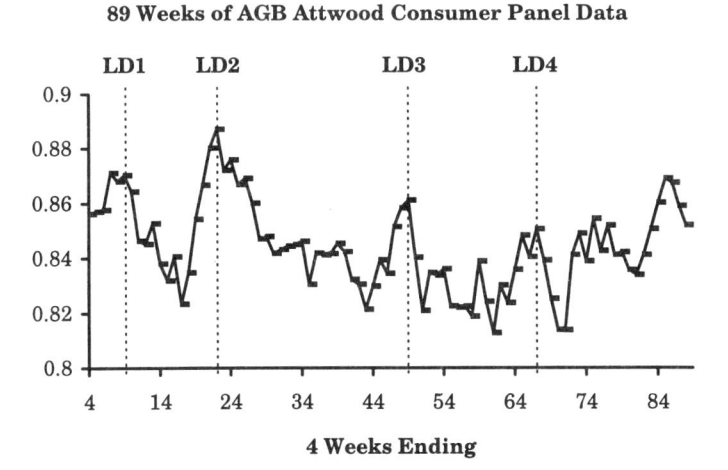

89 Weeks of AGB Attwood Consumer Panel Data

Source: Donnelly (1988).

down market share of the new brand adjusted for subsequent entries. While the overall level of stability was quite erratic over the 89-week period, this is hardly surprising. The overall market was expanding rapidly as the new dairy-spread sector emerged. Towards the end of the analysis period there is an indication of the market seeking to re-establish higher levels of stability, though at a lower average level of stability than during the period before the new-brand launches. This reflects the establishment of several new brands, and the inevitable widening of purchase repertoires that accompany the process. Stability is lower, and rates of consumer flows are higher, as there are now more brands to switch to.

The tendency for a market to move back to equilibrium suggests that a new brand must make its entry as dramatic as possible, as early as possible. This has significant consequences for the investment in communication. Given the fleeting nature of the FMCG purchase decision, much that a brand manager might seek to do will go unnoticed, particularly brand refinements. Advertising or even price changes may not gain instant attention. For example, surveys of recall of television and cinema advertising for FMCG products indicate many cases of uncertainty about which brand was advertised. Another example is the price of petrol. The rise in the price of petrol in the 1970s and the switch from gallons to litres broke the habit that people had of checking petrol price and car performance in miles per gallon. Price has only come back recently in a significant way with the Jet policy of lowest price in the area and the competing policy of 20p off per litre for unleaded petrol. One wonders how aware consumers are of price differences between FMCG products.

ACHIEVING PRODUCT TRIAL

It is quite possible for many purchasers to have little or no knowledge of any competitor brand. The main reason why they purchase their brand may be habit. Hence, an initial aim of the manager of a new FMCG brand may be to try to get purchasers, and consequently consumers, to break their habit and to try their new brand. A simple, effective, and often inexpensive, tactic is the use of free samples — either delivered door-to-door or offered in the supermarket. Of course, there are many cases where purchasers are well aware of the characteristics of the main brands, or they do not care about the difference. They will happily accept the little plastic tumbler of wine offered to them in a supermarket and not purchase a bottle. Or they will use the money-off coupon to buy the product once but not change their habit. The extreme is where someone will never order a home-delivered pizza if they do not have a discount coupon. So, while the simplest underlying plan may be to get as many people as possible to try the product, it is not as simple as it seems. Old habits die hard. One may succeed in getting someone to try the product once or twice; it may be a different matter to get them to form the habit of buying your product. This has significant consequences for the nature of the communication. The experience of the first trial should confirm the message in the advertising, and both must provide a sufficient hook (added value to the consumer) to make consumers want to switch on a more permanent basis.

It is easy to fall into the trap of thinking that an FMCG follows rules which are totally different from those for high-involvement or high-loyalty products. In some senses, the high-involvement situation is simpler. It is possible to carry out qualitative research and in-depth interviews with purchasers of BMW and Porsche cars and develop cognitive maps of their evaluative processes. It is not so easy to do that for dairy spreads — and yet purchasers make real choices when they decide to switch brands habitually. And, if there is a randomness to what they choose, this is only partial. FMCG purchasers make their decisions very frequently and so may have ideas about at least some reasons why they choose some brands and not others. The essential difference may be in the short attention span that they are willing to give to such a proposed purchase decision to change brands. As indicated above, the easiest reason to use to prefer one FMCG brand over another is probably a product difference. If a brand manager genuinely believes that their brand performs discernibly better on a relevant and motivating dimension, then sampling and maximising trial is central. However, given the costs of launching, distributing, stocking, advertising and promoting the product, the brand manager probably does not have any more than a small window of opportunity in terms of money and time to make a mark. At the time of the trial, the consumers, presumably (or so it is hoped), will experience some reason to purchase this product in the future. The aim of the communication, subsequently (but also beforehand in the form of a promise of benefits) should be to remind and confirm those benefits that are genuinely associated with the product. To make things worse for the manager launching a new brand, frequently in FMCG markets the brand leader, who usually was first in, has an enormous market advantage. If a product has a negligible difference in comparison with the leader, the brand manager may not have any option other than simply to try to shift some of this market in their product's favour.

COMMUNICATION STRATEGY: CREATING UNCERTAINTY

Whatever the basis for an FMCG launch, anyone who wants to establish their product will have to create a sense of uncertainty in the mind of the purchaser, if at all possible, about the value of not buying the new product. FMCGs, by their nature, mean low uncertainty. With FMCGs there is a tendency to try to create uncertainty based on product differences, and given the strict rules on advertising copy claims, we often see "new improved brand X", where the comparison is made not against a competitor, but rather against the previous version of the product which has been replaced. The objective is to convey to purchasers that there has been a significant change in the market which they should take account of for fear of losing out. Of course, if the change is spurious, this could be damaging to the corporate image and disastrous for the product. But if the effect of creating the appearance of change is somewhat credible, some purchasers are likely to change and forget to move back.

The key message that FMCG new-brand managers wish to communicate is that they are proposing something new and different. They also want to create a feeling of uncertainty about product differences between their new brand and other brands and about the risk of loss of opportunity caused by not trying the new brand. Essentially it is to create a fear in the mind of the purchaser that leads them to consider changing their purchasing pattern. This need not be a very conscious act: it might be considered successful if one in every three purchasers in a supermarket recalls or feels this uncertainty when they are at the point of choosing from the particular product category. Once this point is reached, the purchaser may carry out a "real" evaluation such as, for instance, trying to read the prices from the supermarket shelf. A barrier to changing FMCG brands is often a failure to provide purchasers with key assistance, usually information, at the time when they most need it. While the product may be only an FMCG, the uncertainty that a purchaser feels is very real. Lack of appropriate information about product characteristics (E-numbers, ingredients, biodegradability, etc.) or about value (weights in pounds, grammes and price per equivalent weight) can create intense annoyance. In the case of an FMCG product the purchaser may not be prepared to handle such uncertainty and annoyance, even embarrassment, by being seen trying to calculate pounds to kilogrammes conversions in a supermarket, and thus the opportunity to get a genuine new trier may be lost. So, the importance is strongly emphasised of communication in that small window of opportunity when a purchaser decides about an FMCG product.

The purchaser must be facilitated in the process of change and towards genuinely considering the new product. Central to this is proper communication of the information that the purchaser needs at the time of purchase, and in the form desired. This process of evaluation may be simple and objective. In this situation, the purchaser acts as an agent for the consumers, which may include that purchaser. The purchaser typically firstly evaluates the product characteristics of the brands being compared; then, secondly, rates these against their prices; thirdly considers any other factors which might influence what the consumers would prefer; and finally makes the change, being prepared if necessary to convince the consumer of the benefit of the change. The FMCG brand manager should presume that the purchaser follows this logic and is intelligent. For example, petrol is frequently sold at a premium price with some performance-enhancing additives included. If customers can be convinced that the product difference is important, then a customer segment can be identified. However, for many people (including some experts) the additives make no difference — consequently, the only real differentiating factor is price. Whether or not many consumers are right in having this perception that price is the most important factor, it may be hard to switch them from their view which is based on the belief that petrol is a simple commodity product. A further segment might be influenced by differences in customer service — for instance, an elderly person might like to have a petrol attendant available. Again, this is a simple and objectively measurable benefit.

TYPES OF UNCERTAINTY

This process of evaluation described above may not always be simple and objective, even for FMCGs which are looked upon as simple. The purchaser is probably also a consumer, if only jointly with others. The feeling of uncertainty that they have received about the products that are on offer can carry itself over into a feeling of uncertainty about what they themselves want. From the point of view of the FMCG new-brand manager, this can provide an opportunity to get purchasers/consumers to reconsider their purchasing patterns. Take for instance, the launch of a new brand in a developing FMCG sector. The purchaser may be developing ideas about the appropriate attributes for such products. The brand manager can use this uncertainty in a different way. It may be possible to create doubt in customers' minds that their needs are being met by existing brands; indeed, there might be different dimensions of product characteristics of which they are unaware. The first such focus is on confusion particularly about the technical aspects — for instance, harmful preservatives and colorants in food and powerful cleaning agents that are damaging to clothes, skin or the environment. Because of the low level of involvement in such products, it can be particularly easy to create these doubts. However, again, it is dangerous to manipulate this idea falsely or to presume that the consumer is not intelligent. Unjustified allegations or hints can be exposed by competitors, in the media, and by word of mouth amongst consumers, and can lead to a long-term loss of credibility. Product enhancements or communications that address these uncertainties are probably the most effective.

The next area of uncertainty for a purchaser relates to the acceptability of the product to the other consumers (presumably) at home. Some FMCG advertising is aimed specifically at children as consumers. The idea is that if there are no great physical differences between the products — for example, breakfast cereals — then the purchaser may have no sense of certainty about how to select one. In this situation they may be amenable to the suggestion that some products are more acceptable than others. So, in one family, a mother may insist on porridge because "it is good for you". In another, she may not have made such an evaluation at all and may go for Frosties or "whatever I can get them to eat".

A third form of uncertainty relates to the appropriateness of the product for particular situations. Brown bread may be the most healthy, sliced white bread may be the only sort the children will accept in their school lunches, but French bread might be the most appropriate for special occasions. Purchasers of FMCG products commonly buy more than one brand depending on whether it is the place they buy in or the purpose for which it is intended. Someone might check the price very carefully for the standard sliced pan and yet not check the price of freshly-baked French bread in the local delicatessen. In this case, price may be less of an issue because the value that they are seeking is measured differently — that is, in terms of the situation. Why ruin an important dinner party for the sake of £2 or £3 spent on nice bread for the soup or the cheese afterwards? The purchaser has a sense of uncertainty here because it is impossible to know what the guests will like. Consequently, they may be open to suggestion that a new brand may be just the thing to "make the meal".

INCUMBENT REACTION TO NEW-BRAND CHALLENGES

The focus to date has been on uncertainty in the minds of purchasers. The idea is that FMCG brand managers need to understand the different forms of uncertainty so that they can match them with the characteristics of the market and in particular with the benefits of their own brand. For low-involvement products, the significant obstacle that has to be overcome is to get enough people to try the product seriously — in other words, to destabilise the purchasing of other brands. If the new or relaunched brand has merit, it will hold some significant fraction of the new customers. But if it cannot break into more than 10 per cent of the market, there is little hope that there will be sufficient economies of scale to justify the logistical overheads.

In a mature, stable market where no new brands have been launched to threaten the status quo, established brand positions are usually maintained on the basis of brand image. For years, the tea market was dominated by Lyons and Barry's, competing on the plane of higher-level needs, as shown by the Barry's "Golden Moments" campaign. The arrival of Lipton in 1994 and the resurgence of Bewley's and Punjana created a discontinuity in the hitherto stable tea market. This led to uncertainty in the minds of many consumers, causing a reassessment of the established brands and of their own requirements with regard to tea. With the retailers seeking to maximise returns from their shelf space, the window granted to consideration of a new brand to prove itself could be as short as six months. This, coupled with the need to dislocate established purchasing habits by creating uncertainty in the mind of the consumer, forces the brand manager to base the launch or relaunch proposition and support package on tangible added-value, such as "bigger leaves", "40 bags free", etc. This moves the focus of the market down from the higher-level needs established in the stable, mature market to lower-level needs. In tea, this has manifested itself in a search for value, and a general trading down. So, while the new brand may not significantly erode the share of the brand leaders, it can cause a general consumer reappraisal of the category and change the nature of decision-making in the market. The brand leaders in tea can no longer rely on brand imagery alone and must integrate the tangible elements of price, value and taste into their approaches.

Even brands with very secure market positions cannot ignore the potentially destabilising effects of new challengers focusing on tangibility. The leader must understand the nature of the attack, and act swiftly and decisively to minimise the dislocation of purchasing patterns. Kellogg's response to the twin threats of Nestlé and St Bernard Corn Flakes is a good example of this. The new entrants targeted the purchaser (mother) and not the consumer (children) with promises of more vitamins and lower prices. Kellogg's, too, shifted its emphasis, launching a better-value larger pack size which locks its consumers into the brand for longer, providing immunity against brand-switching. This was supplemented by on-pack coupons delivering value across a range of well-known brands — again appealing to the mother. Therefore, even a brand as strong as Kellogg's Corn Flakes cannot ignore a focused competitive threat based on tangibility: it must respond physically and not just rely on superior image and heritage. Here was an example of an established company rapidly changing its brand strategy in response to a competitor's advertising.

SUMMARY

FMCG purchase decisions are usually routine with little evaluation prior to purchase. However, some FMCG decisions, depending on the needs of the purchaser and the characteristics of the category and brands, can be highly involving, albeit for a very short time-span. Consumers purchase from a repertoire of brands, and there is evidence that these repertoires are widening, suggesting that the rate of consumer flows between brands, endemic to FMCG markets, has accelerated. A new brand competes for its share of a consumer's purchasing rather than for the establishment of an exclusively loyal franchise.

Results from the Stability Index, which quantifies the degree of market stability and captures the underlying rate of consumer flows in the market, suggest that disturbing purchasing patterns in a market are a key determinant of success for a new brand launch. The greater the dislocation of existing patterns caused by new-brand entry, the higher the eventual settled market share for that new brand. The Stability Index also confirms that FMCG markets seek to re-establish stability after the disturbance of a new-brand launch.

There is a window of opportunity within which the new brand must optimise its impact, suggesting a front-loaded launch-support package.

In order to dislocate purchasing patterns and hence to maximise eventual market share, the new brand must create uncertainty in the minds of consumers. The brand proposition and communication approach must appeal at both the tangible and intangible level. They must offer something real and genuine to induce a brand switch, and the product must perform relative to the expectations aroused by such a focused approach, to provide the opportunity of commanding a material ongoing share of consumer repertoires. Emphasis on tangible benefits only will allow the established brands to respond in kind — brands which through economies of scale can respond effectively and with heavyweight investment.

Leading brands must realise, even in situations where new entrants fail really to threaten their share, that the nature of their attack, invariably focusing on tangible factors such as price, value etc., can cause consumer reassessment of the leading brands and of their own requirements of the category. This must be taken into account when managing the communications strategy of an established brand in a market experiencing new entrants.

REFERENCES

Brugha, C.M. and Turley, D. (1987): "A Low Involvement Choice Model For Consumer Panel Data", *Irish Marketing Review*, 2: 51–60.

Donnelly K. (1988): "Empirically Testing the Stability Index", unpublished thesis, College of Marketing and Design, Dublin.

Ehrenberg, A.S.C. (1988): "New Brands and the Existing Market", CMAC (Centre for Marketing Communications) Working Paper : London Business School: 7.

Lipstein, B. (1970): "Modeling and New Product Birth", *Journal of Advertising Research*, 10(5): 3–11.

Wellan, D.M. and Ehrenberg, A.S.C. (1988):"A Successful New Brand: Shield", *Journal of the Market Research Society*, 30(1): 36.

Part 4

Marketing Communications — Beyond the Line

22

Sales Promotion — An Irish Perspective

Laura Cuddihy
Kate Uí Ghallachóir
Fred Hayden

INTRODUCTION

Sales-promotion activity would appear to have come into greater prominence as a marketing-communications-mix element in Ireland in recent years, but parallel with this there is perhaps less certainty about the range of activities which the term is understood to embrace.

Definitions of sales promotions proliferate. For example:

> [Sales promotion consists of a] diverse collection of incentive tools, mostly short term, designed to stimulate quicker and/or greater purchase of particular products/services by consumers or the trade (Kotler, 1994: 664).

> Sales promotions are incentives to consumers or to the trade that are designed to stimulate purchase (Jobber, 1995: 428).

However, the following definition captures the essence of the strategic and tactical nature of sales promotion:

> Sales promotion comprises a range of tactical marketing techniques designed within a strategic marketing framework to add value to a product or service in order to achieve specific sales and marketing objectives (Chapman, 1994: 12).

Sales promotion is a key component of the communication strategy of products and services. As an integral part of the product and/or brand communication strategy, sales-promotional activity may be aimed at the trade, the consumer or the sales force. Figure 22.1 indicates the main sales promotion techniques. Rebates and long-term agreements

(LTAs) are examples of volume-related discounts paid by suppliers to retailers. The aim of these discounts is to encourage retailers to increase purchasing. They are generally not included in the definition of sales promotions.

FIGURE 22.1 TAXONOMY OF CONSUMERS, TRADE AND SALES-FORCE PROMOTIONS

PULL STRATEGY	PUSH STRATEGY
CONSUMER	**SALES FORCE**
Money Off	Contests
Premiums	Meetings
Coupons	Sales Brochures
Bonus Packs	Trade Shows
Free Samples	Exhibitions
Prize Promotions	Bonuses
	TRADE
	Price Discounts
	Competitions
	Allowances
	Free Goods

Sales promotions are usually categorised as below-the-line or non-media activity, while advertising and public relations are considered above-the-line. Wilmshurst (1993) declares that the concept of the "line" grew from a purely administrative convenience. It arose from the once customary advertising agency practice of invoicing clients by first itemising all advertising booked on their behalf in the main media (press, cinema, posters, radio and television). On these activities the agency drew a commission from the media owners, which paid for its services. At this point, a line was drawn on the invoice so that the amount of commission due could be recorded. Then the other expenditure below the line followed — point of sale material, sales literature and so on. On these, the agency did not draw a commission from suppliers, and therefore usually charged a service fee for this part of the work.

Often the distinction between above-the-line and below-the-line activity leads to confusion rather than increased clarity — definitions of sales promotion and direct marketing are becoming increasingly blurred. For example Superquinn's Superclub, a transactional database, integrates advertising, direct marketing and sales promotions.

Such demarcation is becoming increasingly irrelevant in the rapidly changing environment of the marketing-communications field. There are currently unprecedented levels of change in the marketing-communications process and we are seeing the reconfiguration of a once stable traditional marketing-communications system. The causes of this reconfiguration are well documented and include:

- The impact of technology. Electronic information is now changing the "rules of the game" in marketing. Technology now exists to manage customer relationships — initiate them, nurture them and defend them — on the scale of mass marketing but with the flexibility of individual marketing. In a word, this is the technology of addressability (Deighton et al., 1994: 63).

- The emergence of "new" media forms. Transactional databases are a new communication medium set to challenge television and print as ways to reach customers. They generate volumes of behavioural data that can be used to design sales promotions tailor-made for the individual consumer, as well as to track and evaluate how well these promotions are working. Again, Superquinn's Superclub is an outstanding Irish example of this process in practice.

- The fragmentation of the media (Shergill, 1993: 102).

- The increase in retailer power, primarily because of the ownership of consumer information at retail level.

- New forms of shopping (especially non-store shopping) and increasing consumer sophistication.

Greater integration has been the response of many in the marketing-communications business to this changing environment. As Deighton (1994: 94) points out:

> Whenever a once-stable system wrestles with change, the mantra of "integration" holds some redemptive appeal to its participants.

This increased integration is evident in the range of services provided by promotion agencies. Sales-promotion campaigns are being more fully integrated into marketing and brand strategies. Increasingly, agencies — both advertising and promotion — are offering clients a fully integrated service and are producing integrated campaigns.

ROLE OF SALES PROMOTION IN MARKETING STRATEGY

Sales promotion should be an integral part of the communications mix for a brand or product and must be carefully planned to support and enhance the brand or product strategy. The role of sales promotions will vary according to the stage of the life cycle and competitive conditions. Figure 22.2 indicates possible roles of sales promotion over the life cycle of a product.

FIGURE 22.2: SALES PROMOTION AND THE PRODUCT LIFE CYCLE

Life-Cycle Stage	Product Objectives	Sales-Promotion Methods
Introduction	• Consumer Trial • Distribution	• Product Sampling • In-store Demonstrations • Banded Offers • Coupons
Growth	• Stimulate Demand for Product/Brand • Continued Brand Preference	• Sampling • Coupons • Premiums
Maturity	• Encourage Dealer Loyalty • Encourage Switching to the Brand • Increased Usage • Encourage Retrial by Lapsed Users	• Competitions • Money off next purchase • Self-Liquidating Offers • Companion Brand Offers
Decline	• To Maintain Distribution	• Trade Promotion • Allowances and Discounts

In practice, however, many companies continue to use sales promotions only as a short-term tactical tool to support what they term as the more strategic element of the communication mix, namely advertising. Often sales promotion begins and ends in-store or on the pack and is used to build volume only. Many marketers have not included sales promotion in the marketing mix aimed at building brand imagery and differentiating their product. This under-use of sales promotion has resulted in the proliferation of inappropriate, poorly conceived and badly executed sales-promotions campaigns.

Smith (1993) suggests possible reasons for this short-term perspective:

- Management pressure to boost quarterly sales
- The shortening of the product life cycle
- Increased competition and increased new product introductions increases the need for tactical, defensive sales promotion
- Sales promotions often lend themselves to the speedy response required to handle business problems when they arise
- Full service agencies may try to sell the client additional services such as sales promotion on an *ad hoc* "add on" tactical basis. (Adapted from Smith, P.R., 1993: 230.)

There is some dispute as to the role of sales promotions in the marketing of brands. Many assert that sales promotion, as it is intrinsically tactical and short-term, cannot enhance brand values and build the consumer franchise, as these quotes illustrate:

> ... we have seen more brand damaging sales promotion than brand damaging advertising in recent years. This I believe is partially due to the lack of priority given to the area of sales promotion by senior management in brand owning companies (Carey, 1995: 7).

> ... another disadvantage of promotions is that unlike advertising, they almost never have a positive long term effect on established brands (Abraham and Lodish, 1990: 56).

Jones (1990) warns of the "double jeopardy" of sales promotions — that is to say, sales promotions may increase sales in the short term, but the long-term result could be the destruction of the brand. Jones concludes that promotions can never improve a brand image or help the stability of the consumer franchise, hence the phrase "promotion, commotion and demotion" of the brand.

However, the marketing of a brand requires both tactical and strategic measures. Sales promotion must be an integral part of the longer-term brand/product and company strategies. Sales promotion has a strategic role to play in communicating the benefits of the product/brand. It can contribute to the creation, defence and maintenance of brands. Branding, in turn, when used strategically, builds on a company's marketing and innovation functions so that the survival needs of the company are continuously addressed (Macrae et al., 1995: 16).

Brands can either be built or damaged by sales promotion. Poorly conceived and executed sales promotions damage both brand and corporate image. Continuous value-added sales promotions, such as price off or extra free product on a particular brand, are indicative of poor strategic planning. Giving sales promotion a low priority in the management of brands and products will ensure that this situation continues.[1]

Creative, well-planned and well-executed sales promotions that are an integral part of the product's communication plan can enhance brand values and build consumer franchise. Dove Soap (Figure 22.3) offers one such example.

FIGURE 22.3: LEVER BROS. INTEGRATIVE APPROACH

DOVE SOAP
Lever Bros. used a creative combination of sales promotion and direct marketing in the launch and marketing of Dove. **Brand Proposition** • Dove doesn't dry the skin like ordinary soaps • It is different from other soaps • It is a beauty treatment — a moisturiser in a bar. Given this positioning, Dove could not be marketed like other soaps with extensive discounting — two for the price of one, multi packs etc. **Aim** To get General Practitioners (GPs) to recommend Dove to all patients, not just those with skin complaints. This approach capitalised on their role as opinion leaders. GPs are not often used as the vehicle for promoting FMCGs. **Method** Three rounds of direct mail personalised letters were sent to all GPs. The letter included a product sample, high-quality literature and display material, for the surgery and waiting room, and a request card. The request card was to be given to the patients so that they could send for more samples, known as marketing by referral.

---

[1] For a fuller discussion of the challenges facing brands in the 1990s, see Chapter 15: Branding: Regaining the Initiative, by John Fanning.

The role of sales promotion in marketing strategy is changing in line with overall changes in the communications industry. The full potential of sales promotion has yet to be realised in this age of the addressable consumer. Figure 22.4 shows the changing face of sales promotion over time.

FIGURE 22.4 CHANGING VIEWS OF SALES PROMOTION

Traditional View	Current View	Future Direction of Sales Promotion
• Techniques driven • Instant results-sales • Tactical with short lead time and evaluation only in terms of sales • Delegated to most junior marketing staff • Reactive to market conditions	• Greater integration with other communication elements • More strategic orientation with longer lead time in developing campaigns and a broadening of the view of the role of SP in brand and product management • Sales promotion follows the lead of advertising — extends and develops the themes created by advertising campaign • Greater spend on sales promotions as proportion of the overall communications budget • Powerful retailers dictating and managing sales promotion and consumer data • Clients expect strategic input from their agencies	• Sales promotion has a strategic role in data capture and transactional data management • Sales promotions becoming more addressable as part of the marketer's ongoing dialogue with the consumer • Greater involvement of senior management in the sales promotion • Brand value benefits not just sales and short-term stocking objectives • Sales promotion becoming more sophisticated, controlled and accountable • Continued integration of marketing communication methods, particularly sales promotion and direct marketing

STRUCTURE OF SALES-PROMOTION INDUSTRY IN IRELAND

A report entitled "The Extent and Trends of Non-Media Advertising (NMA) in Ireland" prepared for the Association of Advertisers in Ireland in 1993 stated that 38 per cent (IR£117 million) of total advertising budgets was spent by Irish advertisers on NMA, and forecast that the percentage would rise to 41 per cent in 1994 (AAI/MDP, 1993).

There is some debate regarding the inclusion of direct mail as a non-media activity. Many direct marketing practitioners would claim that direct marketing is a separate strategic discipline rather than a sales promotion activity. The value of non-media activities in Ireland in 1992 is shown in Table 22.1.

TABLE 22.1: VALUES FOR NMA ACTIVITIES, 1992

Non-Media Activity	1992 Expenditure (IR£ m)
Point of Sale	34
Direct Mail	19
Exhibitions	18
Competitions	15
Added Extra	10
Extra Product/Money Off	8
Demonstrations	7
Sampling	6

Source: AAI/MDP Report (1993),

Overall non-media advertising spend allocation in 1992 was 62.0 per cent to the consumer sector and 38 per cent to the trade.

Table 22.2 illustrates the sectoral use of non-media advertising.

TABLE 22.2: SECTORAL USE OF NON-MEDIA ADVERTISING BUDGET

Industry Sector	Percentage of Budget Allocated to Trade	Percentage of Budget Allocated to Customer
Food	23.0	77.0
Household	48.8	51.2
Industrial	39.8	60.2
Finance	43.5*	56.5
Other	36.6	63.4
Overall	38.0	62.0

* The financial sector allocates a high proportion of its NMA promotions to brokers.
Source: AAI/MDP study (1993).

The percentage of budget allocated to consumers is broadly illustrative of the presence of a pull strategy. This strategy is most extensively used in the food sector for a variety of purposes, such as stimulating purchase, holding shelf space and diluting the effectiveness of competitors' promotional activities.

To date, there are approximately 10 dedicated sales-promotion consultancies in Ireland employing more than three people. The 1995 *Irish Marketing Journal* guide to Direct Marketing and Sales Promotion Consultants lists another 30 companies that claim a specialism in sales-promotion consultancy. The major players established the Irish Institute of Sales Promotion Consultants in January 1993 to promote the professional development of the discipline and to serve the needs of both users and practitioners.

FIGURE 22.5: NON-MEDIA ACTIVITIES CARRIED OUT USING AN OUTSIDE PROMOTIONS AGENCY

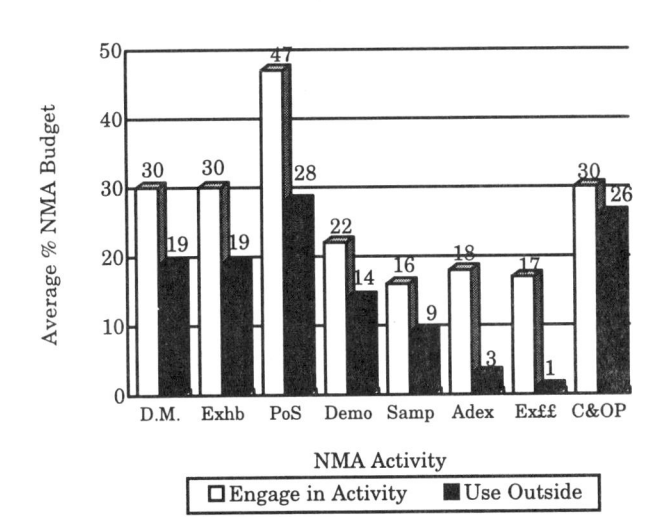

NMA Activity	Engage in Activity	Use Outside
D.M.	30	19
Exhb	30	19
PoS	47	28
Demo	22	14
Samp	16	9
Adex	18	3
Ex££	17	1
C&OP	30	26

Key:
- D.M. — Direct Mail
- Exhb — Exhibitions/Trade Fairs
- PoS — Point-of-Sale Display/Merchandising
- Demo — Demonstration/Tastings
- Samp — Sampling
- Adex — Added Extra Promotion
- Ex££ — Extra Product — Money Off
- C&OP — Competitors and Other Promotions.

Eighty-seven per cent of companies use outside agencies when carrying out competitions and other promotions, whereas the majority of companies carry out added extra and extra-product/money-off promotions in-house. For all other activities, outside agencies are used approximately 60 per cent of the time.

COMPANIES' ALLOCATION TO NON-MEDIA ADVERTISING

The increasing importance of sales promotions in marketing is reflected in a greater allocation of communications budgets to non-media advertising (NMA).

> Advertisers have been spending an increasing proportion of their marketing budget on consumer and trade promotions (Shergill, 1993: 96).

> Consumer and trade promotions are now estimated to account for more than 7 out of 10 dollars spent by packaged goods marketers in the US (Donnelley, quoted in Shergill, 1993: 96).

> For more than a decade, sales promotions have grown in importance, becoming the most popular tool in the marketers kit (Jones, 1990: 145).

This trend towards greater spending on non-media expenditure is also evident in the Irish context.

TABLE 22.3: OVERALL MOVEMENTS IN NMA EXPENDITURE, 1991–92 AND 1992–93

	1991–92	1992–3
Increased NMA Expenditure	49.1%	38.2%
Decreased NMA Expenditure	3.6%	10.9%
Maintained	47.3%	50.9%

Source: AAI/MDP study (1993).

Table 22.3 illustrates the trends in NMA expenditure in the periods 1991–92 and 1992–93 respectively. The majority of companies either increased or maintained their NMA expenditure, with the greatest increase in the food and industrial sectors (see Table 22.4).

TABLE 22.4: SECTORAL BREAKDOWN OF TRENDS IN NON-MEDIA EXPENDITURE, 1992–93

Sector	Increasing NMA Expenditure	Decreasing NMA Expenditure	Maintaining NMA Expenditure
Food	43.0	—	57.0
Household	25.0	12.5	62.5
Industrial	64.0	23.0	23.0
Finance	22.0	11.0	67.0
Other	36.0	9.0	55.0

Source: AAI/MDP study (1993).

The reasons underlying these trends relate to the accountable and targeted nature of sales-promotions activities. The ability to target customers was perceived by all except the food sector as the most important benefit of NMA. In the food sector, short-term sales gain was considered to be the most important benefit of NMA, but was regarded by all other sectors as of little significance.

Reasons for increasing NMA spend included:

- Better targeting
- More measurable
- More cost-effective
- Effective for increasing brand awareness
- Influences opinion leaders
- Increases awareness
- Increased competition in the marketplace
- Expected increase in consumer demand for below the line
- Important to support larger brands with in-store promotional activity (AAI/MDP study, 1993).

CONSUMER PROMOTIONS

The major types of consumer promotions are as follows:

- *Money-off Promotions* offer savings on the regular price of the product. These are usually flagged on the package or label. Money-off promotions offer a direct value to the consumer and are effective at stimulating short-term sales. Money-off promotions are easily imitated, and if used too frequently may devalue the brand image.

- *Reduced-Price* pack is a single package sold at a reduced price — for example, two for the price of one.

- *Banded Pack* is where two related products are banded together. This form of promotion is especially useful in encouraging trial of a new product. For example Procter and Gamble banded Fairy Excel to Ariel liquid to encourage the trial of the new Excel product.

- *Bonus Packs* give added value by giving extra quantity — for example, "20% free" at no additional cost. Bonus packs are less likely to devalue the brand image as the price is not lowered. This form of promotion is well received by both the consumer and the trade, though the sales-promotion agencies feel that it is somewhat uncreative.

- *Premiums* are any merchandise offered free or at low cost as an incentive to purchase a brand. There are three major forms:

    ◊ *Free in/on-pack gifts.* Gifts may be given away free and the offer flashed on the outer package of the branded product. Examples include the following: Kellogg's gave cards of GAA football stars free *in pack*, Goodfellas gave a free pizza cutter *on pack*. Cereal manufacturers often include a free toy in the cereal pack, targeted at children, who are major influencers in the purchase of cereals. The ASAI Code of Sales Promotion Practice includes regulations governing the inclusion of such *in-pack* offers.

    ◊ *Free-in-the-mail offer* involves the collection of packet tops or labels which are sent by post as proof of purchase, in order to claim a free gift or money voucher. The main purpose of this form of promotion is to build loyalty by encouraging repeat purchase on a regular basis. Free-in-the-mail offers are also valuable as a means of data building. An example is Batchelors' offer of free audio books on their Sqeez orange juice packs.

    ◊ *Self-liquidating offers* are similar to free-in-the-mail offers, except that consumers are asked to pay a sum of money to cover costs of the merchandise plus administration and postage charges. The consumer benefits by getting the merchandise at below normal cost because the manufacturer passes on the advantage of bulk buying and prices at cost. Examples include: Robert Roberts' offer of a six-cup cafetière for £6.99 plus proof of purchase; Beechams and Smith and Nephew jointly offered an Elastoplast first-aid kit for £2.50 flashed on Lucozade bottles. This joint promotion yielded a 6 per cent redemption rate where 0.5 per cent or 1.0 per cent would be an acceptable industry norm.

- *Free Samples/Trials* offer a free amount of a product. Samples/trials may be on-pack, given out in-store, or delivered direct. For new brands/products or brand extensions, this form of promotion is an effective means of getting consumers to try the product. Sampling, while effective at achieving awareness and trial, is the most expensive form of promotion and is usually only used when the company has great confidence in the superior quality of the product.

- *Coupons* are certificates entitling the bearer to a stated saving on the purchase of a specific product. Coupons can be delivered directly to the home, via print media such as magazines and newspapers, or on packs. Coupons can be effective in stimulating sales of a mature brand and inducing early trial of a new brand.

- *Prize Promotions* include competition, games and sweepstakes. Unlike other promotions, the cost can be established in advance and does not depend on the number of participants.

- *Competitions* require participants to exercise a certain degree of skill and judgment. Entry is usually dependent on at least one purchase. Compared to premiums and money off, competitions offer a less immediate incentive to buy, and one that requires time and effort on the part of entrants.

- *Draws or Sweepstakes* make no demands on skill or judgment as the result depends on chance. Entrants fill in their name and address on an entry card and on a certain day a draw is made.

- *Game Promotion* is where, for example, a newspaper encloses a series of bingo cards, and customers are told that over a period of time sets of bingo numbers will be published. If these numbers form a line or full house on a bingo card, a prize is won. Such a game encourages repeat purchase of the newspaper.

- *Tie-in Promotions* involve two or more brands or companies that team up on coupons, refunds, and contests to increase their pulling power. Companies pool funds with the hope of broader exposure, as their combined salesforces can push these promotions to retailers, giving them a better shot at extra display and advertising space.

- *Cross-Promotions* involve using one brand to advertise another non-competing brand.

- *Point-of-Purchase (POP) Display and Demonstrations* take place at the point of purchase or sale and are aimed at drawing attention to the product and encouraging impulse purchase.

- *Continuities* or patronage awards are values in cash or in other forms that are proportional to one's patronage of a certain vendor or group of vendors. Superquinn's Superclub is an example of a continuity promotion where patrons are rewarded for their patronage by points that can be exchanged for a range of products and services in the Superclub catalogue. Such promotions are aimed at encouraging loyalty to the outlet and are extremely valuable as a means of database building.

ORDER FULFILMENT AND PROMOTIONS-HANDLING PROCESS

Order fulfilment and promotions handling include opening and sorting mail, checking that competition responses are correct and sending respondents the gift, coupon or merchandise that the promotions entailed. Promotions Handling Service (PHS) is the largest promotions-handling company in Ireland, with on average 120 clients in-house at any one time. PHS would argue that they offer much more than promotion handling. Their services include advising clients on the promotion, designing the promotion, opening and sorting mail, data capture and analysis, physical handling and fulfilment of the promotion (i.e., packing and dispatching), and finally the production of a marketing report for the client, analysing the promotion (see Figure 22.6). Data capture and information processing are becoming an increasingly important aspect of promotions handling.

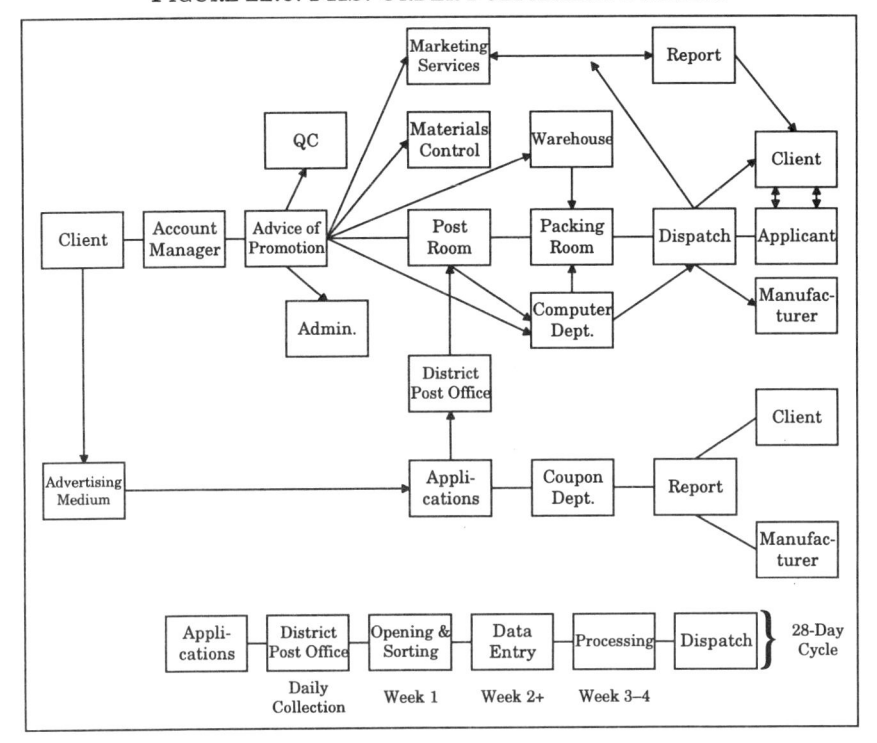

FIGURE 22.6: PHS: ORDER FULFILMENT PROCESS

TRADE PROMOTIONS

As Ireland has a strong retailer concentration, suppliers need the co-operation of the trade, particularly in terms of stocking, display space and adequate facings for their products. Promotions aimed at the trade to achieve these objectives are therefore commonplace.

One such trade promotion is the 1993 trade launch of the Green Isle Foods Ltd. product, Goodfellas Pizza, a classic example of a creative and well-executed promotion.

Green Isle's *target audience* was the Managing Directors, Marketing/Commercial Directors and Buyers of Ireland's top multiple and symbol group stores. This audience accounts for 90 per cent of total frozen pizza sales. Green Isle's *objective* was the attendance of these key decision-makers and buyers at a themed launch of Goodfellas Pizza. This is a much solicited group, as on average one new product is launched daily on the Irish market.

The *strategy* was the use of a highly impactful invitation, which would create excitement and awareness of the launch event. This invitation/package was hand delivered to the key decision-makers for each of the eight target retailing groups. The package contained a personalised director's chair and, using the "A Star is Born" theme, had teasing graphics and copy to whet the appetite of the recipient.

The company used a Call-Mail-Call strategy, the initial call confirming the availability of the target to receive the package prior to the sending of the mailing itself; the hand delivering of the mailing package; and a follow-up call organising the time and pick-up location for a limousine drive to the launch.

At the launch venue, Windmill Lane Studios in Dublin, a "première" effect had been created. Each attendee had a personalised director's chair awaiting them on arrival, and was lavishly entertained. The event climaxed with the presentation of the new product.

A *budget* of IR£16,500 had been allocated to the campaign, and a £103 cost per response was incurred.

Subsequent *evaluation* showed this launch to have been the most successful ever in Ireland, with each company asking to bring several executives. Goodfellas captured 60 per cent market share of this intensely competitive and crowded market in the first six months.

Another recent Irish promotion was the Guinness Harp Celebration Brew Classic Car Competition aimed at the licensed trade. This promotion used a combination of media and non-media, targeted at the trade, to support and enhance brand values, gain awareness and knowledge, and increase sales.

The campaign began with a direct mailshot, which was a cleverly worded teaser postcard to the trade informing them of the promotion and alerting them to the forthcoming infomercial. Ten days later two 10-minute infomercials were transmitted on RTE Network 2 at 12.35 a.m. The time was chosen to suit the audience, as most publicans would still be on the premises clearing up. The infomercial gave the product and brand information needed to answer the competition questions. A follow-up mail pack gave the mechanics for entering the competition, namely the questions and entry forms.

PLANNING A CAMPAIGN

As in all marketing-communication campaigns, the planning of a sales-promotion campaign requires a rigorous approach. A proposed planning process is illustrated in Figure 22.7.

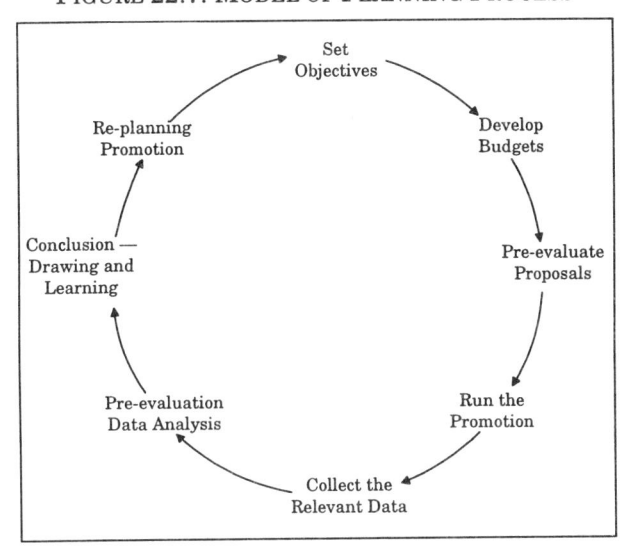

FIGURE 22.7: MODEL OF PLANNING PROCESS

Cycle diagram with the following stages (clockwise):
- Set Objectives
- Develop Budgets
- Pre-evaluate Proposals
- Run the Promotion
- Collect the Relevant Data
- Pre-evaluation Data Analysis
- Conclusion — Drawing and Learning
- Re-planning Promotion

The above model is a framework which may help the practitioner in planning a campaign. Quite clearly, different types of sales-promotion campaigns will require some variations in the planning stages. However, all should start with clearly identified, quantitative objectives, tied into a realistic time frame, which in turn will help to determine the required budget, and ultimately, evaluation of the success or otherwise of the promotion.

When planning sales-promotion campaigns, Irish companies variously develop in-house resources or use an outside agency as illustrated in Figure 22.8.

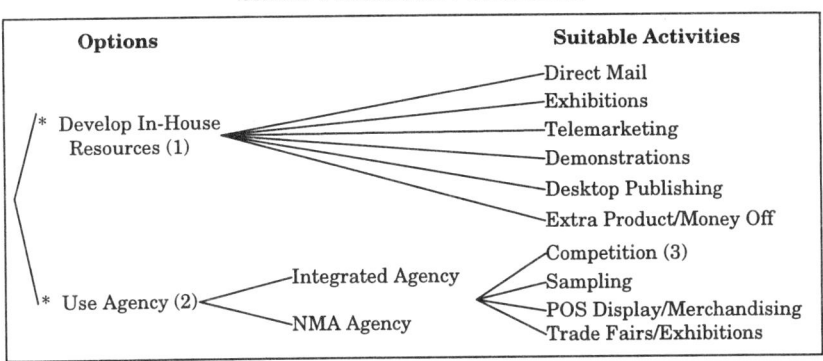

FIGURE 22.8: PLANNING —HOW TO RUN A SALES-PROMOTION CAMPAIGN

Options

* Develop In-House Resources (1)
* Use Agency (2)
  - Integrated Agency
  - NMA Agency

Suitable Activities

- Direct Mail
- Exhibitions
- Telemarketing
- Demonstrations
- Desktop Publishing
- Extra Product/Money Off
- Competition (3)
- Sampling
- POS Display/Merchandising
- Trade Fairs/Exhibitions

BUDGETING FOR SALES PROMOTION

An essential part of a sales promotion is the creation of a budget and subsequent adherence to it. When a company takes the decision to use the services of an agency in the development and execution of a sales-promotion campaign, an agreement is necessary as to which elements of the cost will be the client's responsibility and which will be covered by the agency.

The breakdown obviously varies depending on the promotion, but a possible structure for the appropriation of costs could be as illustrated in Figure 22.9.

FIGURE 22.9: POSSIBLE BREAKDOWN OF SALES-PROMOTION COSTS

Agency Budget Responsibilities	Client Budget Responsibilities
Artwork	Product
Copy	Promotional Packaging
Print	Price Discounts
Prize Fund/Gift Item	Promotion Placing
Personnel	Advertising/PR Support
Technical Equipment	
Fulfilment Houses	
Couriers/Post/Packaging	
Merchandising	
Legal	

Source: Seymour (1994): 17.

Seymour (1994) offers some simple guidelines to facilitate the budgeting process:

1) Break costs into groups (artwork, printing, sales support, media support, redemption costs etc.); subtotal them; and finally total them all to arrive at a projected spend. If the draft total is bigger than the allocated amount available, identify alternatives — for example, substitution of cheaper prizes, reduction in the number of participating stores. In this process, do not compromise quality, otherwise objectives may not be achieved and brand equity may be damaged.

2) During the production of the campaign watch out for additional costs, such as late amendments to the promotion that may make the project untenable.

3) At all stages, time cash-flow requirements — for example, payment of personnel weekly/daily, upfront cash payments for merchandise etc.

4) Document and date all drafts of the budgetary process to facilitate tracking and checking at a later date.

EVALUATION OF SALES PROMOTIONS

Evaluation involves measuring promotional effectiveness. Unfortunately, in the past, marketers have not had a good record in this critical control area. However, increasingly, both clients and agencies are making concerted efforts to evaluate the effectiveness of campaigns, both as a short-term process and as an integrative tool, in order to develop even more effective ones next time around. This process has been greatly facilitated by developments in information technology.

Quite clearly, evaluation cannot occur in the absence of pre-stated objectives. These also serve to help develop the budget for the proposed campaign. Many authors favour the use of pre-evaluation techniques. Grove (1992) says "pre-evaluation can assess the realism of the promotion and its potential risks before committing to a definitive budget" (29). His preferred method of pre-evaluation is a store test with real purchasers and real in-store competition. Jobber (1995) includes *group discussions* with target consumers and *hall tests* as alternatives to the *experimentation* methods.

Data capture for analysis will include both quantitative and qualitative elements. Marsden (1994) gives examples of both types of measurement approach. In the quantitative arena, he includes the standard cost/benefit analysis — that is, the investment per unit against gross margin made from that unit. He also includes analysis of trade relationships, such as trade-distribution changes, forward stocks and displays, and rate-of-sale changes.

In the qualitative measurement area, he suggests analysis examining the linkage of the promotion with the overall brand objectives and strategy. Did it add value to the existing brand franchise? Was it strategically correct for the brand? Did it add value to the retailer relationship? Did it fit into the retailer's systems smoothly?

Answers to these and other pertinent questions assist the agency and/or the client's sales and marketing personnel in drawing conclusions and in learning from the campaign. This experience and knowledge is then used in the replanning of subsequent campaigns.

LEGAL ISSUES IN SALES PROMOTION IN IRELAND

Across Europe, there are widely differing laws governing promotion activities. In Ireland, the sales-promotion industry is self-regulatory (governed by the ASAI Code of Practice) and offers one of the most liberal legal environments in Europe for sales promotional activities. Germany and Norway, at the opposite extreme, have a very restrictive legal environment.[2]

In the move towards European harmonisation of laws governing sales-promotion activities, countries with a liberal legal environment, such as Ireland and the UK, fear losing their autonomy and urge the adoption of self-regulation as the European model. The Irish Institute of Sales Promotion Consultants (IISPC) retains a lobbyist in Brussels to ensure that it is aware of any proposals likely to affect sales promotions.

Certain sales-promotion activities in Ireland are governed by the Gaming and Lotteries Act, 1956. As Lee (1994) points out, this Act was not designed specifically to govern sales-promotion activities, and its application to sales promotion is through case law. The finding of the Supreme Court in the case known as *Flynn v. Denieffe, Independent Newspapers and Easons*, concerning a newspaper bingo promotion, held that if a "consideration" of any kind — for instance, a purchase — was involved, then the promotion could be termed a lottery, and consequently illegal under the Act.

In a factually similar situation in the UK (*Express Newspapers case*), such promotions were found to be legal. Because of the geographic proximity of the Irish and UK markets this has caused confusion as to what is and is not legal regarding sales promotions. The reality is that UK promoters can operate sales promotions in Ireland that are illegal for Irish promoters. A pending case, *Perri Crisps v. the DPP*, concerning the legality of instant wins, will further clarify the legal situation for promoters.

---

[2] For a fuller explanation of the legality of promotions in European countries, see: IMP Europe (1992): *Guidelines to Sales Promotions Regulations*.

REFERENCES

Abraham, M.M. and Lodish, L.M. (1990): "Getting The Most Out of Advertising and Promotion", *Harvard Business Review*, May/June: 50–60.

Advertising Standards Authority for Ireland (1995): *Code of Advertising Standards for Ireland*, 4th edition, and *Code of Sales Promotion Practice*, 2nd edition, Dublin: ASAI.

Association of Advertisers in Ireland Ltd. (AAI) (1993): *A Report on the Extent and Trends of Non-Media Advertising in Ireland*, Marketing Development Programme (MDP), University College Dublin.

Carey, M. (1995): "Government Health Warning: Sales Promotion Can Seriously Damage Your Brand" Proceedings of the 2nd Annual Conference of the Irish Institute of Sales Promotion Consultants.

Chapman, A., Lawton, K. and Lee, K. (1994): "Sales Promotion ... Getting Started!", *Promotions*, Dublin: Ryan Media: 12–14.

Deighton, J. (1994): "The Future of the Marketing Communications Industry: Implications of Integration and Interactivity", Conference Proceedings, Marketing Science Institute Conference, Boston, MA, February: 94–109.

Deighton, J., Peppers, D. and Rogers, M. (1994): "Consumer Transaction Databases: Present Status and Prospects" in Blattberg, R.C., Glazer, R. and Little, J.D.C. (eds.), *The Marketing Information Revolution*, Boston, MA: Harvard Business School Press.

Donnelley Marketing, Inc. (1992): "Fourteenth Annual Survey of Promotional Practices" quoted in Jones, J.P. (1990): "The Double Jeopardy of Sales Promotions" *Harvard Business Review*, September/October: 145–52.

Donnelley Marketing, Inc. (1992) cited in Shergill, S. (1993): "The Changing US Media and Marketing Environment: Implications for Media Advertising Expenditures in the 1990's", *International Journal of Advertising*, 12: 95–115.

Grove, D. (1992): "Evaluation", *Promotions and Incentives*, June: 25–30.

IMP Europe (1992): *Guidelines to Sales Promotion in Europe*, London: IMP Europe.

Jobber, D. (1995): *Principles and Practice of Marketing*, London: McGraw Hill.

Jones, J.P. (1990): "The Double Jeopardy of Sales Promotions" *Harvard Business Review*, September/October: 145–52.

Kotler, P. (1994): *Marketing Management-Analysis Planning and Control*, 8th edition, Englewood Cliffs, NJ: Prentice Hall.

Lee, P. (1994): "The Legal Issues in Sales Promotion", Paper presented to the Annual Conference of the Irish Institute of Sales Promotion Consultants, Dublin, 31 March.

Macrae, C., Parkinson, S. and Sheerman, J. (1995): "Managing Marketing's DNA: The Role of Branding", *Irish Marketing Review*, 8: 13–20.

Marsden, A. (1994): "The Cost-Effectiveness of Sales Promotions", *Admap*, October: 19–21.

Seymour, H. (1994): "Money's Too Tight to Mention", *Promotions*, Dublin: Ryan Media: 16–17.

Shergill, S. (1993): "The Changing US Media and Marketing Environment: Implications for Media Advertising Expenditures in the 1990's", *International Journal of Advertising*, 12: 95–115.

Smith, P.R. (1993): *Marketing Communications, An Integrated Approach*, London: Kogan Page.

Wilmshurst, J. (1993): *Below the Line Promotion*, Oxford: Butterworth-Heinemann Ltd.

23
Couponing and Coupon Redemption: Problems and Perspectives*

Marie Louise O'Dwyer
Mary Lambkin

For more than a decade, sales promotion has grown in importance, becoming the most popular tool in the marketer's kit. Most of this growth has been at the expense of advertising. In 1978, advertising in the US accounted for 42 per cent of consumer packaged-good companies' marketing budgets, and sales promotion accounted for 58 per cent. By 1988, advertising spend had slipped to 31 per cent, against 69 per cent for promotion (Buzzell et al., 1990). A similar picture exists in Europe, where there has been a greater movement towards the use of sales promotional techniques in recent years, largely because of the focus of business on short-term profits and value and the perceived need for promotional strategies that produce short-term sales boosts (Dibb et al., 1991).

Despite the growth in spending on sales promotion, little research has been done to assess the performance and consider the usefulness of such expenditure. In comparison to advertising, the literature on sales promotion is underdeveloped and it is an area which requires more managerial attention. Studies are beginning to emerge such as those conducted by the Marketing Development Programme (MDP), UCD, in association with the Association of Advertisers in Ireland. A 1989 study by the MDP, estimated that well over £100 million is spent annually on sales promotion. In the area of couponing alone, the MDP studies maintained that at least 7 million coupons were redeemed in 1991. This figure is very likely to be an understatement (MDP, 1989; MDP, 1993).

In this paper, international research evidence on coupon redemption is reviewed, which focuses specifically on coupon redemption and

---

* This paper originally appeared in *Irish Marketing Review*, 1994, 7: 65–76.

on the various factors influencing the coupon-redemption rate. This is supplemented by information on couponing and coupon redemption in Ireland. Experts in the area of coupon redemption were interviewed for their insights into this topic. The research highlights a number of issues which ought to be noted by those companies engaging in couponing activity.

The first section of the paper discusses the use of couponing and its growth in recent years. Research evidence related to the many aspects of couponing and coupon redemption is then outlined. Various factors influencing the coupon-redemption rate — coupon value, method of distribution, and couponing effort and timing — are also examined. Finally, a number of conclusions drawn from the research are outlined and future research possibilities in the area are noted.

TYPES OF SALES PROMOTION

Most sales-promotion methods can be grouped into the categories of consumer sales promotions and trade sales promotions. Consumer sales-promotion techniques encourage or stimulate consumers to patronise a specific retail store or to try a particular product. Trade sales-promotion methods stimulate wholesalers and retailers to carry a producer's product and to market these products aggressively. There are several forms of sales-promotional techniques from which a marketer can choose (Robinson, 1977). These are outlined in Table 23.1. Marketers must consider a number of factors before deciding which of these sales-promotion techniques to use. They must take into account both product characteristics and target market characteristics. How the product is distributed and the number and types of resellers may determine the type of method used. The competitive and legal environment may also influence the choice.

As one of the sales-promotion techniques used by marketers, couponing has received a greater proportion of marketing spending in recent years. The vast majority of consumer promotions — 76 per cent — are coupons, which offer a discount off the regular retail price of a brand in order to encourage non-users to try a product or existing users to buy more frequently. A 1990 US study suggests that coupons have more impact on consumer purchase behaviour than other promotional methods. More than 70 per cent of respondents said that they bought a product they had never tried before because of a coupon, and more than 75 per cent said that because of a coupon they purchased a different brand from the one they regularly used (Assael,

1990). For these reasons, the subject of couponing and coupon redemption merits investigation and review.

TABLE 23.1: THE 12 SALES-PROMOTION TECHNIQUES

	1.	Sampling
	2.	Coupons: Consumer Direct Mail/ Consumer Retail Advertisements
	3.	Trade Coupons
	4.	Trade Allowances/Deals
	5.	Price-offs
	6.	In-, On- and Near Packs (and reusable containers)
	7.	Free In-the-Mail Premiums
	8.	Self-Liquidating Premiums
	9.	Contests and Sweepstakes
	10.	Refund Offers/Money-Back Offers
	11.	Bonus Packs (twin packs, branded packs)
	12.	Stamp Plans and Continuity Premiums

Source: Robinson, W.A. (1977): "12 Basic Promotion Techniques: Their Advantages and Pitfalls", *Advertising Age*, 10 January.

COUPON USE AND GROWTH

Retail coupons, those small cards or slips of paper that offer the supermarket shopper a few cents-off on this product or that have come of age. They are no longer a nickel-and-dime business. Billions of them are distributed each year by grocery product manufacturers, millions of dollars worth are redeemed too, sometimes with tremendous impact on a manufacturer's marketing programme (Nielsen, 1965).

As this quotation from Nielsen suggests, even in 1965 couponing had an important role to play in marketers' promotional strategies. In the years since then, we have witnessed a massive increase in the number of coupons being distributed by manufacturers. Strang (1981) states that in 1980 US marketers distributed fewer than 17 billion coupons. By 1983, they distributed nearly 143 billion and in 1987 this figure reached over 215 billion (Strang, 1981). According to an annual review of the coupon market by NCH Promotion Services in the UK, the number of coupons distributed in 1984 reached almost 3,045 million (Dibb et al., 1991). A more recent study by the same promotions company states that the number of coupons distributed has risen by 213 per cent since 1984 (Gofton, 1992). The massive increase in the number of coupons distributed reflects the growing importance of couponing to marketers, especially packaged-good companies, and the growing number of marketers using coupons as an integral part of their promotional activities.

It has been suggested that coupon growth will continue in the future, because of the current recession and poor economic circumstances which place increasing pressure on consumers to save money through coupon use. In recent years, developments have taken place which help to ensure the future growth in coupon use. One such advance has been in the area of electronic couponing. Electronic couponing refers to frequent-shopper cards or "smart cards" that automatically credit cardholders with coupon discounts when they check out. When combined with a touch-sensitive video screen, computer graphics, printer and laser video-disc player, cardholders can take advantage of a variety of retailer and manufacturer promotions by simply touching the video screen.

The growth in coupon offers has not occurred without criticism (Schimp, 1990). Schimp argues that the issue of coupons can prove expensive. In order to illustrate how costly a coupon issue can be for a firm, Schimp adapted the work of Haugh (1981) which was concerned with the measurement of the full coupon cost per redeemed coupon. Schimp considers the case of a hypothetical cake-mix product that offers a 25-cents-off coupon to customers. Table 23.2 details the actual full cost per coupon of 56 cents, indicating that coupon activity requires substantial investment to accomplish desired objectives. Adapting this to reflect the cost to Irish marketers shows that a 20p coupon can actually cost as much as 43p.

However, the opinion of those operating in Ireland's major clearing-house (PHS Promotions) would seem to suggest that this cost can be even greater than the table suggests. Without taking misredemption into consideration, the cost of a redeemed coupon is seen to range from a low of 45p to a high of £1.25. This coupon cost is comprised of a number of fixed and variable costs. Fixed costs include the face value of the coupon itself, the store bonus given to retailers and handling charges. Variable costs include the cost of distributing the coupon, cheque costs, postage in and out and envelopes and stationery. Variable costs are dependent on the number of coupons issued and redeemed and as such can have a substantial impact on the final cost per redeemed coupon.

TABLE 23.2: FULL COUPON COST PER REDEEMED COUPON

		$	£
1.	Distribution Cost 10,000,000 Coupons Circulated @ $5/$3.50 per Thousand	50,000	35,700
2.	Redemption Rate (3.5%)	350,000 redeemed coupons	350,000 redeemed coupons
3.	Redemption Cost 350,000 Redemptions @ 25c/20p face value	87,500	70,000
4.	Handling Cost 350,000 Coupons @ 8c/6p each	28,000	21,000
5.	Total Programme Cost (1+3+4)	165,500	126,700
6.	Cost per Redeemed Coupon ($165,500/£126,700)/350,000	47.3 cents	36p
7.	Actual Product Sold on Redemption with Misredemption Estimated @ 15 %	297,500 coupons	297,500 coupons
8.	Actual Cost per Redeemed Coupon	55.6 cents	43p

COUPON REDEMPTION

Recent years have seen not only an increase in the number of coupons being distributed by manufacturers, but also an increase in coupon redemption. Coupon redemption refers to the return of coupons from the retailer or consumer to the manufacturer for reimbursement. NCH Promotional Services in the UK estimates that the number of coupons redeemed in the UK in 1984 was 274 million. Subsequent studies by NCH show that the number of coupons redeemed has increased by 65 per cent between 1984 and 1992. Mr John Keane, director of PHS Promotions states that coupon redemption per capita in Ireland has increased by over 600 per cent in the past four to five years. He states that four to five years ago, 2.4 million coupons were redeemed. By 1992, this figure had reached 14 million and it is estimated that by 1995, the figure will be in the region of 25 million coupons per annum. Mr Keane is of the opinion that 75–80 per cent of this increase in redemption is because of increased redemption per coupon drop. The remainder is a result of the increase in the number of coupons being issued. Having said this, the increase in redemption is in some part a result of the movement towards in-store, point-of-purchase coupons which facilitate greater redemption by the consumer.

Expert opinion in the area would seem to suggest that the average coupon redemption rate is between 1.5 and 5 per cent of the coupons issued. The mythical redemption rate of 2.5 per cent, frequently cited by manufacturers and marketing practitioners alike, does not necessarily hold. Coupon redemption is, in fact, company and product specific and depends to a great extent on the couponing strategy employed by the manufacturer in question. The coupon issue should be seen as part of the whole picture and should fall easily into the overall promotional strategy of the company. A sound promotional strategy and the tactical use of coupons is seen as an important prerequisite to couponing success.

THE COUPON-REDEMPTION PROCESS

Schimp (1990) outlines the typical redemption process faced by many firms. The process begins when a shopper presents the checkout clerk with coupons that are then subtracted from the total bill. Retailers redeem the coupons they have received in order to obtain reimbursement from the manufacturers who sponsored the coupons. Retailers, particularly in the US, may hire another company called a clearing-house, to sort and redeem the coupons for a fee. Clearing-houses, acting on behalf of a number of retail clients, consolidate coupons by redemption address before forwarding them. Clearing-houses forward the coupons to redemption centres which serve as agents of the manufacturers who issue the coupons. The redemption centre pays off on all properly redeemed coupons (Schimp, 1990). The system is not quite as clear cut as it might appear from the description. Some retailers act as their own clearing-houses, some large manufacturers act as their own redemption centres, and some independent firms, such as AC Nielsen and PHS Promotions (Ireland), offer both clearing-house and redemption-centre services.

Retailers, many of whom belong to multiple groups, send their coupons for redemption typically on a weekly or two-weekly basis, with a claims form attached seeking the amount in question. Once received by the clearing-house, such coupons are separated into manufacturer groups, and counted using a barcode-scanner computer system. Once this task has been completed, an invoice or claims form is filled out seeking reimbursement for the coupons being redeemed by the retailer. Such money is collected from the manufacturer and returned to the retailer in question. In the case of independent firms, such as PHS Promotions, which act as both clearing-houses and redemption centres combined, the company itself will raise a cheque to reimburse the retailer and will be refunded when paid for its services by the manufacturer at a later date. This cheque reimbursing the retailer will cover not only the face value of the coupon being redeemed, but also postage, VAT and a handling charge of approximately 10 per cent, levied by the retailer for dealing with the manufacturers' coupons.

Redemption centres usually report monthly to manufacturers, informing them of the number of coupons being redeemed and their progress in this regard. Such reports will typically contain the following:

- Fiscal Summary

- A Retailer Breakdown, which shows the number of coupons redeemed by particular retailers and the value of the claims being made

- A Coupon Breakdown, which states the number of coupons redeemed and the cost of such redemption.

Redemption centres are paid for the work they perform, based on a 1,000-coupon rate. This rate can vary from a low of 20 per cent to a high of 40 per cent, depending on the type of coupon in question and whether or not it is barcoded, allowing for easier handling and less paperwork.

Misredemption is a form of couponing abuse which may represent a problem for many companies issuing coupons. Misredemption includes retailer fraud, redemption for a different size of the brand than indicated on the coupon, or even for a competitive brand in the case of stockouts. Evidence from the UK would suggest that misredemptions have been running at an average rate of 27 per cent of the coupons issued (Cobb, 1993). One thousand such misredeemed coupons, even at face value, are worth a sizeable amount of money! Barcoding of coupons is seen as one means of reducing misredemption. In the US, some 94 per cent of coupons are barcoded and the reliability of barcoding has improved to an accuracy of 96 per cent. There has also been an increase in the number of stores scanning coupons (*Chain Store Age Executive*, 1992)

RESEARCH ON COUPONING

Changing perspectives and attitudes towards couponing and coupon redemption are evident from a review of the relevant literature published over the past number of decades. The majority of this research can be divided into two stages: the first looking at the degree of deal-proneness, and the second at what consumers do and the different factors affecting the coupon-redemption rate.

Deal-Proneness

Coupons give consumers opportunities to obtain promoted products at reduced prices. Because these reduced prices are in the form of a coupon, individuals who respond to coupon offers have been referred to as "coupon-prone" consumers, or more generally "deal-prone" consumers" (Lichtenstein et al., 1990).

Over the past number of decades, most academic research has been concerned with the consumer's or the household's response to couponing, and attempts have been made to discover whether a deal-prone or coupon-prone consumer exists. Webster (1965) and Montgomery (1971) both tried to identify the deal-prone consumer by establishing an association between demographic, socioeconomic and/or personality characteristics and deal-proneness. However, the research conducted by both these authors lacks a theory that would identify the variables which should and should not indicate deal-proneness and, as a result, the usefulness of their research must be questioned (Montgomery, 1971; Webster, 1965).

In 1978, Blattberg et al. developed a model of household purchasing behaviour, in an attempt to identify variables which should affect deal-proneness. They predicted that deal-proneness would be lower for households with children under six, no car, higher income, working wives and a rented home. However, the observed associations between demographic factors and deal purchase were not totally consistent with the model (Blattberg et al., 1978).

Further research studies in this area were also carried out by Bawa and Shoemaker in 1987, who examined whether households are consistently coupon-prone when buying in different product classes. Their results indicate that information about one product class can be used to predict responses to coupons in other product classes. Bawa and Shoemaker (1987), Levedahl (1989) and Lichtenstein, Netemeyer and Burton (1990) have also made useful contributions to this area. The latter suggest that previous research in the area of coupon-proneness has measured coupon-proneness in behavioural terms — consumers who are more responsive to coupon promotions are coupon-prone. They suggest that one or other psychological construct — value consciousness — also underlies the behaviour of redeeming coupons. Value consciousness is seen as the concern for paying low prices, subject to some quality constraint. Coupon-responsive behaviour is seen to be a manifestation of both value consciousness and coupon-proneness. Hence the authors' argument that coupon-proneness should not be seen as isomorphic with coupon-responsive behaviour, but rather should be seen as only one construct that affects the behaviour of coupon redemption (Lichtenstein et al., 1990).

In general, such studies have not clearly identified the factors that distinguish deal-prone or coupon-prone consumers from other consumers, and therefore one has to question the existence of the deal-prone consumer. Researchers such as Webster (1965) and Montgomery (1971) have argued that research on coupon-proneness can aid marketers in identifying to whom promotions must be targeted. However, such research does not guide marketers when deciding how to design coupon promotions. This is the less researched area of coupon promotions.

Factors Influencing the Coupon-Redemption Rate

The second aspect of coupon promotions which has been the focus of research, though at a less intensive level, refers to the factors that influence coupon-redemption rates among consumers. This area of research is much more concerned with deciding how to design coupon promotions in order to achieve the most effective results, than with deciding at whom the promotion should be targeted, which has tended to be the focus of previous studies. Nielsen (1965) identifies a number of marketing factors which influence coupon redemption. He states that the type and size of the product have a significant influence on the redemption rate. The measurable factors which Nielsen cites as exercising the greatest influence on coupon-redemption rates are the following (Nielsen, 1965):

- Method used to distribute the coupons
- Size of the product class
- Rate of discount
- Face value of coupon
- Brand distribution

In their 1978 article, Ward and Davis examine the use of coupons as a sales-promotional technique. The paper examines an econometric coupon-redemption model that provides empirical estimates for evaluating coupon redemptions. The model relates redemption to the total couponing effort, the distribution media, the coupon value and the amount of time since the initial coupon drop. Another study carried out in this area was by Reibstein and Traver, who in 1982 proposed to examine the impact of a number of factors on the coupon-redemption rate. All previous studies in this area focused on product-specific models. Reibstein and Traver (1982), however, developed a model that was specific to the brand being examined. The model chose a number of independent variables, such as the method of distribution, the face value of the coupon, the size of the coupon drop and the brand's consumer franchise, and estimated the redemption based on these independent variables. A list of the various influences on the coupon-redemption decision, as highlighted by these authors, is to be seen in Figure 23.1 (Reibstein and Traver, 1982). All of these factors are seen to influence the coupon-redemption rate to a varying extent. The specific findings and conclusions will be explained in subsequent sections of this paper.

METHOD OF COUPON DISTRIBUTION

Many different types of media are available to the manager when issuing coupons. These distribution methods may be identified by making reference to the work of Reibstein and Traver (1982), who outline various couponing media available (see Table 23.3). In 1966, Schwartz attempted to shed some light on the comparative effectiveness of couponing media. While only recognising three media (direct mail, magazines and newspapers), Schwartz maintained that direct mail obtained the highest rate of redemption because it achieved a primary level of attention from all consumers, as it is perceived at a fixed time pre-determined by the advertiser (Schwartz, 1966).

In their 1978 work, Ward and Davis confirmed Schwartz's findings when their research showed coupons distributed by direct mail far exceeding other methods in terms of redemption. The actual use of different media relative to the actual drop is included in Table 23.4 in order to highlight the most effective media. This demonstrates that, in general, when all other media are expressed relative to direct mail, redemption through all other media is no more than 37 per cent as large as that through direct mail. Coupons distributed by direct mail are most effective, while on-package coupons are the least effective.

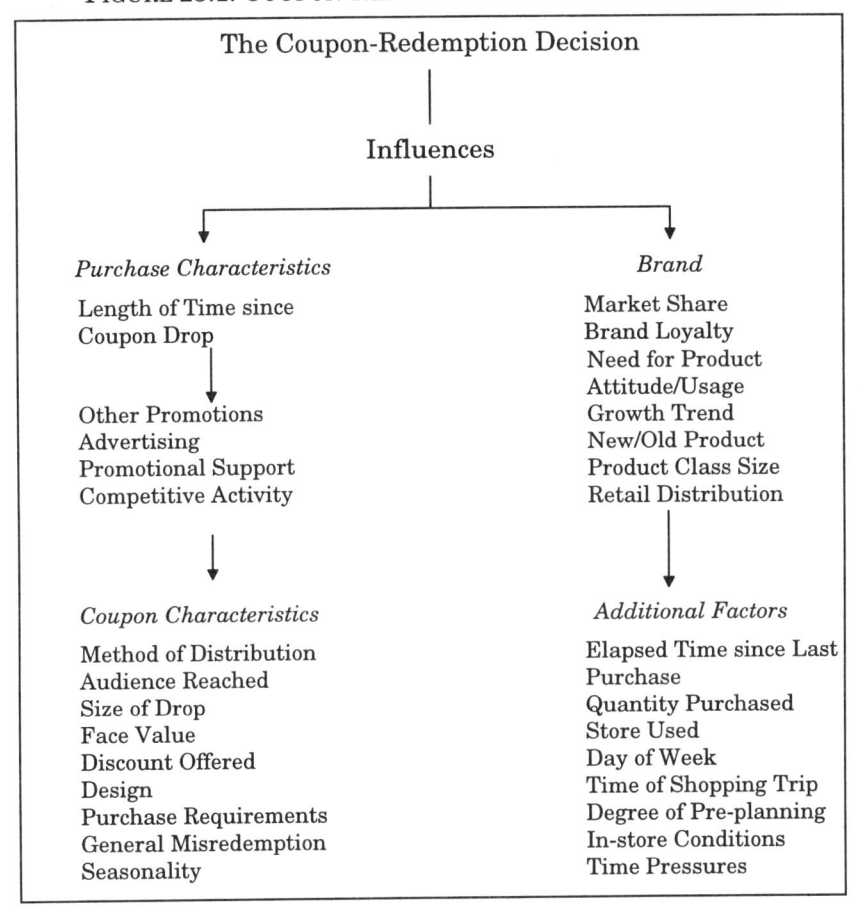

FIGURE 23.1: COUPON-REDEMPTION DECISION INFLUENCES

The Coupon-Redemption Decision
|
Influences

Purchase Characteristics

Length of Time since
Coupon Drop

Other Promotions
Advertising
Promotional Support
Competitive Activity

Coupon Characteristics

Method of Distribution
Audience Reached
Size of Drop
Face Value
Discount Offered
Design
Purchase Requirements
General Misredemption
Seasonality

Brand

Market Share
Brand Loyalty
Need for Product
Attitude/Usage
Growth Trend
New/Old Product
Product Class Size
Retail Distribution

Additional Factors

Elapsed Time since Last Purchase
Quantity Purchased
Store Used
Day of Week
Time of Shopping Trip
Degree of Pre-planning
In-store Conditions
Time Pressures

Source: Adapted from Reibstein and Traver (1982): "Factors Affecting Coupon Redemption Rates", *Journal of Marketing*, 46, Fall: 102–13.

The opinions of both marketing practitioners and promotion agencies in Ireland would suggest that in recent years point-of-purchase coupons seem to be taking over from direct-mail coupons in terms of redemption. The growth in this distribution method is seen to result from the fact that companies prefer to access their customers as closely as possible to the point of sale, thus ensuring greater redemption. In-store distribution of coupons, while offering instant rewards to the consumer, also allows marketers the opportunity to display and sample their products, an added merchandising benefit. Coupon-handling agencies in Ireland estimate that redemption rates for such instant, point-of-sale coupons range between 20 and 40 per cent, whereas the use of a door-to-door coupon book will only produce a redemption rate of between 5 and 10 per cent.

TABLE 23.3: DESCRIPTION OF COUPONING MEDIA

Newspaper	Manufacturers' coupons included in the ROP (rip-off-page)
Sunday Supplement	Syndicated independent magazine sections circulated with Sunday papers
FSI	Pre-printed sheets containing multiple coupons and advertising copy, generally printed on heavier stock, inserted in the Sunday paper
Magazine On-page	Manufacturers' coupons printed on page as part of the advertisement
Magazine	Tip-in coupon, generally of heavier stock, bound into magazine separately, normally facing an on-page advertisement
Direct Mail	A package or envelope containing coupons sent by mail to individual consumer households, usually in a co-operative programme
In/On-Package	Coupons inserted in, or imprinted on, product packages, redeemable on subsequent purchase

Source: Reibstein and Traver (1982): "Factors Affecting Coupon Redemption Rates", *Journal of Marketing*, 40, Fall: 102–13.

Nestlé

A 1994 couponing programme recently undertaken by Nestlé (Ireland) is useful in illustrating the effectiveness of point-of-purchase couponing efforts. Nestlé ran a coupon promotion on one of its products — Cross & Blackwell Simply Mix, a dehydrated cook-in sauce. The coupon programme ran in four stores per week for a four-week period, and 500 coupons per store were issued.

Based on past programme results, Claire Montgomery, product manager at Nestlé, expected the couponing programme to yield a redemption level of about 75 per cent. This redemption level may appear quite high, but Ms Montgomery stresses that such redemption levels are made possible through the use of point-of-purchase coupons in-store. The company distributed the 500 coupons per store, with a face value of 15p, by means of an in-store demonstrator. The demonstrator is typically located at the point of product purchase and will be there to offer the consumers an incentive to purchase. Nestlé has found such coupon promotions most effective as they facilitate greater redemption than any other distribution method and lead to increased product purchase, which is one of the primary aims of its couponing programmes.

COUPON VALUE

One of the questions which management need to ask when using couponing as a promotional tool is: what value should be offered by the coupon? In their 1978 study, Ward and Davis noted a significant response to the use of 15-cents coupons versus 10-cents coupons (see Table 23.4). All elasticities were increased by a factor of +.023 with the use of 15-cents coupons over 10-cents coupons. Ward and Davis therefore suggest that generally the redemption level of 15-cents coupons can be expected to be 25 per cent greater than for 10-cents coupons. This suggests that the relationship between coupon value and redemption is non-linear. In this case, for example, a 50 per cent increase in coupon value provides a 25 per cent increase in redemption.

TABLE 23.4: RANKING OF REDEMPTION LEVELS OF MEDIA

	Relative Effectiveness to that of Direct Mail	Actual Share of Drops %
Direct Mail	1.000	9
Magazine Pop-up	0.370	3
Sunday Supplement	0.269	19
Magazine On-page	0.216	29
Newspapers	0.211	18
On-Package	0.130	22

Source: Ward and Davis (1978): "Coupon Redemption", *Journal of Advertising*, August: 51–8.

A study by Nielsen (1965) showed that while the housewife was seen to be impressed by a high-face-value coupon, she was also impressed by the rate of discount represented by the value of the coupon in comparison with the normal retail selling price of the product offered (Nielsen, 1965). Numerous authors have suggested that a positive relationship exists between incremental sales and coupon face values. This would suggest that a higher face value yields higher incremental sales (Irons et al., 1983; Shoemaker and Tibrewala, 1985; Bawa and Shoemaker, 1989).

However, in a 1989 study, Quelch recommended that product managers consider a number of factors when setting a discount rate. These factors included consumer involvement, inventory risk and franchise strength. His research would suggest that higher discount rates should be offered on low involvement, high-inventory-risk products with weak brand franchises (Quelch, 1989).

It may be argued that too many coupons offer consumers a 20p discount on the products purchased, and not enough companies are offering consumers more favourable discounts, which would increase the likelihood of redemption. Expert opinion in the area shows that coupon values that offer a consumer a 15–20 per cent discount on the product being purchased are meaningful. However, if a marketer issues 10p coupons, even if they represent a 25 per cent discount on the product price, the redemption rate will fall rapidly, as consumers see little perceived value in using the coupon. Procter and Gamble has been known to issue coupons to the value of 70p or more here in Ireland. For example, L'Oréal recently offered (1994) a £2 cashback on its hair colorant product, Casting, which has a retail price of £3.50. This coupon value may seem quite large, but such an offer was made in an attempt to increase redemption and simultaneously build up a useful consumer database of current users of the product.

COUPONING EFFORT AND TIMING

Ward and Davis's (1978) coupon-redemption model implies that increases in couponing effort (i.e., the size of the coupon drop) will not lead to proportional increases in coupon redemption. The fact that all elasticities in Table 23.5 are less than 1.0, suggests that for all media, increases in effort cannot be expected to lead to proportional increases in redemption. Therefore, the ratio of redemption to effort must always decline with increased effort — that is, diminishing returns to coupon drops are prevalent for all media. Redemption centres deal with coupon programmes over all levels of effort. For example, Procter and Gamble, a major coupon user, has issued coupons ranging from 1,000 to 1 million plus in Ireland alone.

Ward and Davis (1978) also demonstrate the significance of time on the level of coupon redemption. A measure of the delayed response to an initial coupon drop is seen to give both an indication of the total expected redemption level over time, as well as the point in time where the maximum redemption rate is expected. Their model indicates that the maximum rate can be expected during the second month following the initial coupon drop. The authors state that during the first month, less than 3 per cent of total estimated redemption is expected to occur. By the third month, over 30 per cent of the redemption will have occurred and nearly 50 per cent of redemption is realised by the fifth month.

TABLE 23.5: REDEMPTION RATES AND COUPON FACE VALUES

	Redemption Elasticity	
	10 cents	15 cents
Direct Mail	0.8346**	0.8579**
Magazine Pop-up	0.7381	0.7614
Sunday Supplement	0.7074	0.7307
Magazine On-page	0.6857	0.7090
Newspapers	0.6853	0.7087
On-package	0.6365	0.6598

* A 1 per cent increase in couponing effort for a 10-cents direct mail coupon would lead to a 0.8346 per cent increase in redemption.
** A 1 per cent increase in couponing effort for a 15-cents direct mail coupon would lead to a 0.8579 per cent increase in redemption.
Source: Ward and Davis (1978): "Coupon Redemption", *Journal of Advertising*, August: 51–8.

Irish marketing experts estimate that 80 per cent of all coupons redeemed are usually redeemed in the two months following the initial coupon drop. Redemption will continue to decrease after the second month, when the remaining 20 per cent will gradually be sent for redemption. However, often increases in redemption are experienced in the weeks prior to the closing date, when a general rush to redeem the coupons is common. Most companies place a closing date of four to five months on their coupon programmes. However, if a coupon programme has been targeted to a specific group of individuals, then a closing date two to three weeks from the date of issue would be most appropriate. The maximum rate of redemption may not always take place during the second month following the initial coupon drop, especially in the case of more short-term coupon promotions, which often only last for a period of six to eight weeks.

THE IMPACT OF COUPON USE ON SALES

The redemption of manufacturers' coupons will have an impact on company sales. There is a need to evaluate any coupon promotion in order to assess its managerial implications. This evaluation is made possible by examining the effects of a coupon promotion on brand loyalty, market share, redemption rates and incremental sales. Coupons are often viewed as price-discrimination devices which allow a manufacturer to engage in differential pricing. This allows a firm to maximise its revenue and profit by adapting its prices to each consumer's willingness to pay (Narasimhan, 1984). The ability to maximise revenue by the use of coupons has led to widespread coupon use among manufacturers. This coupon use, in turn, has had an effect on sales, and some say, a detrimental effect on brand loyalty, as consumers readily switch to buy whatever brand is offered on a deal basis (Cotton and Emerson, 1978).

Consumer brand-choice behaviour will be influenced by coupon availability, but whether or not the deal brand will continue to be purchased once the coupon programme has terminated is questionable. More likely, consumers will engage in brand-switching, switching in favour of those brands offering deals. As a result, manufacturers have been forced to use coupons on a regular basis. At one time, coupons were mainly used to aid a new brand during its introduction. Now, however, they are continually being used by existing brands to defend their market share from competitors (Dodson et al., 1978; Cotton and Emerson, 1978). Rothschild looks at the issue in behavioural terms (see Figure 23.2). The stimulus of the coupon is seen to lead to the response of awareness of the coupon. This is cognitive learning. Later, the response of purchase (aided by the coupon) is reinforced by the stimulus of the product (at a lower price). This is behavioural learning and is repeated often across many product classes. There are at least two possible long-run outcomes. One is that consumers will learn to look for deals. The other outcome is that brand loyalty towards the new brand emerges. This will only really occur if some other benefit is more salient than price and no better deal emerges to interfere with this new loyalty (Rothschild, 1987).

Marketers face the risk that their continued emphasis on sales-promotional techniques, such as couponing, may condition consumers to expect constant price cuts. Since many consumers see little difference between brands, when a promotion on a given brand ends, they will simply switch to another brand being promoted. As a result, many marketers will be forced continually to use sales promotions to keep their market share from eroding (Assael, 1990). In addition, intense competition for retail shelf space and the desire on the part of brand managers to show quick gain in market share has had a snowball effect on promotional campaigns. Companies keep offering more coupons, bigger rebates and more reliable sweepstake prizes in an effort to draw customers from competitors. This marketing approach neglects the brand images that some manufacturers have spent decades developing through advertising. Companies fear that heavy couponing, which represents a significant proportion of all sales promotion, is evaporating brand loyalty and turning retail brands into commodities (Engel et al., 1991).

FIGURE 23.2: A BEHAVIOURAL VIEW OF PROMOTIONS

```
Coupon ─────────────→ Awareness of Coupon
                       Cognitive Learning
                              │
More Price Sensitivity ←─┐    │    ┌─→ Cost/Benefit Relation
                         │    ↓    │
                         │ Purchase with Coupon
                         │         ├─→ More Coupon Usage
                         │ Behavioural Learning
                         │              │
More Brand Switching ←───┘              └─→ More Brand Loyalty
```

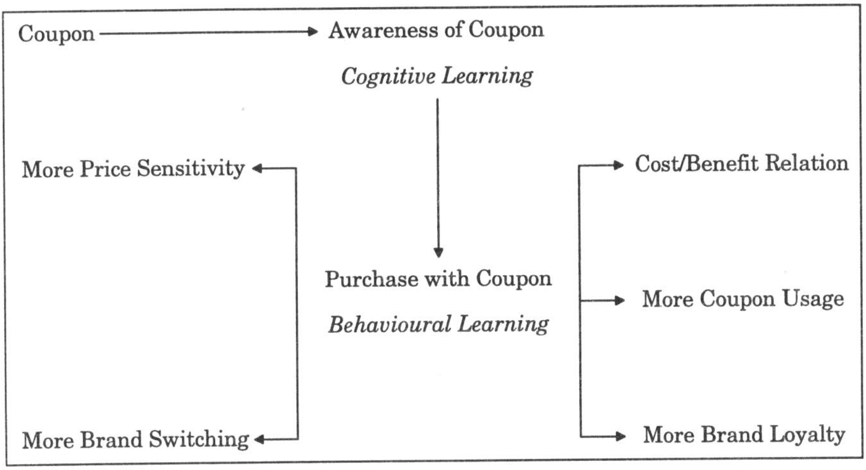

Source: Adapted from Rothschild, M.L. (1987): "A Behavioural View of Promotions Effects on Brand Loyalty", *Advances in Consumer Research*, 14: 119–20.

In an attempt to overcome brand-switching problems, Irish marketing consultants recommend the establishment of database building and frequent-buyer programmes. The aim of such programmes is to bring back loyalty while collecting data that can be used to target promotions more effectively at consumers and to create customised couponing. Agencies continually encourage clients to build databases and increasingly are incorporating a database-building mechanism into sales promotion. The lack of precise and relevant databases means that sales-promotion techniques serve two purposes: the campaign objective and database building. The use of coupons in such a strategic manner is seen by those at the forefront in this area to be the key to maintaining brand-loyal consumers and increasing market share.

Cow & Gate

Cow & Gate (Ireland) is a company that has become involved in database building on an on-going basis. With the introduction onto the Irish market of Olvorite baby food, the company initiated a couponing programme whereby a list of Irish mothers was purchased and coupons were made available to these mothers for their subsequent use. Coupons giving 15p off were sent to Irish mothers by means of direct mail, and 20p coupons were issued in-store.

The company engages in regular assessment of this coupon programme's effectiveness. Since this is an on-going programme, a group of new mothers is targeted each month — that is, mothers with babies aged two months. Consequently, the company regularly assesses the effectiveness of the mailing-coupon programme by calculating the level of responses each month. Furthermore, because each coupon issued has a specific code to each contact, follow-up tele-research on an ad-hoc basis has revealed how effective this couponing programme has been in establishing loyalty.

According to Donal Quinn, marketing director of Cow & Gate (Ireland), this couponing programme has proven its effectiveness as once a mailing is sent out, an increase in sales is evident. In-store coupons issued also resulted in an increase in sales of up to three or four times the average. This is an example of specific targeting of baby-food users which has helped to avoid wastage and has increased efficiency. More accurate targeting may seem an expensive proposition, but the resultant savings tend to outweigh by far the costs involved. Because of the use of such a focused approach, redemption levels for these coupons issued reached a high of 45 per cent.

Redemption rates are frequently used to assess a couponing programme's effectiveness, and many researchers over the years have highlighted several factors seen to influence the coupon-redemption rate. However, the redemption rate is seen to ignore profitability and is only one of several variables relevant to the effectiveness of a couponing effort. Incremental sales, or the additional sales generated by a promotion, have a direct influence on the profitability of a coupon promotion and can be a useful coupon-evaluation technique. However, because of the difficulty in assessing incremental sales from a couponing programme, redemption rates are commonly used, because of the relative ease in collecting information. It may be said that it is neither redemption rates nor incremental sales that should be used by managers as evaluation techniques. Rather, the two should be used together to obtain a more complete couponing evaluation.

FUTURE RESEARCH

Future research into coupon redemption is needed. Over the past two decades, much attention has been paid to identifying the characteristics and behaviour patterns of coupon-users. Very little research has been undertaken to help marketers when using coupon promotions, to help to guide their decision making or to highlight the problems and pitfalls of these activities. Understanding the redemption properties of coupon programmes is vital to the planning and implementation of coupon distributions.

This study provides a situation analysis of coupon redemption. Because of the lack of historical data in this field of interest, no longitudinal comparisons could be made. However, it is hoped that in the future as more and more companies begin to keep records of the redemption of their coupons issued, and as more research by vested interests and organisations becomes available, patterns and trends in coupon redemption can be identified and more can be learned about this area.

Two recent happenings have been instrumental in ensuring the future recording and assessment of coupon-redemption rates. The first of these has been the introduction by many companies of computerised systems which record all details of coupons redeemed through the promotions company. Such an approach to coupon redemption will have an important role to play in the accurate calculation of redemption rates for different products and product classes.

The second factor has been the establishment of sales-promotion regulating bodies such as the Irish Institute of Sales Promotion Consultants (IISPC) which came into being in early 1993. Although the Institute is now just in the early stages of operation, one aim of the IISPC will be to conduct research into the whole area of coupon redemption rates for a variety of product classes. This should prove beneficial for all sales-promotion consultancies involved, allowing them to predict accurately redemption rates for their clients.

CONCLUSIONS AND IMPLICATIONS

As highlighted at the beginning of this paper, coupon redemption is a topic which has not received much academic interest, despite the recent growth in the use of couponing and its ability to influence company sales positively and to displace the role of traditional advertising. The research reviewed in this paper has yielded a number of insights which ought to be noted by companies engaging in couponing activity.

In the first instance, the redemption of coupons issued by any company will be influenced to a great extent by a variety of factors, including the company's promotional strategy, the method of coupon distribution used, the value of the coupon and the effort and timing of the coupon drop. Companies must view a sound promotional strategy as a prerequisite to couponing success. Without adequate pre-planning, a long-term view and regular couponing assessment, the issue of coupons may represent a loss-making activity of the firm. Too often, coupons are issued simply because competitors do so and little follow-up or coupon-programme assessment takes place.

Previous research and the views of those knowledgeable in the area have identified instant point-of-purchase coupons as being the most suitable and obtaining higher redemption rates when compared to other media. Taking cognisance of this fact can save on inefficient spending. Marketers must beware of offering consumers coupons at values which will be too small to encourage redemption. This may lead to poor redemption rates and subsequently inefficient and ineffective allocation of the promotional budget. Ideally, coupons should offer consumers a discount of 15–20 per cent on the value of the product if consumers are to consider them for redemption. In terms of couponing timing, it has also been suggested that the maximum rate of coupon redemption is likely to be experienced during the second month following the initial coupon drop. This information may prove useful to marketers when planning any couponing programme.

Finally, the necessity for further research on this important topic area needs to be highlighted. This study represents a starting point rather than a conclusive review, and it is hoped that other researchers and organisations may be interested in exploring in greater detail various dimensions touched upon here.

REFERENCES

Assael, H. (1990): *Marketing: Principles and Strategy*, Orlando: The Dryden Press.

Bawa, K. and Shoemaker, R.W. (1987): "The Coupon Prone Consumer: Some Findings Based on Purchase Behaviour Across Product Classes", *Journal of Marketing*, October: 99–110.

Bawa, K. and Shoemaker, R.W. (1989): "Analysing Incremental Sales from a Direct Mail Coupon Promotion", *Journal of Marketing*, July: 66–78.

Blattberg, R., Buesing, T., Peacock, P. and Sen, S. (1978): "Identifying the Deal-Prone Segment", *Journal of Marketing*, August: 369–77.

Buzzell, R.D., Quelch, J.A. and Salmon, W.J. (1990): "The Costly Bargain of Trade Promotion", *Harvard Business Review*, March/April: 141–9.

Chain Store Age Executive (1992): "Coupons Get Serious: Scanning Reduces Misredemption", 67(10): 68.

Cobb, R. (1993): "Counting on Coupons", *Marketing*, 8 April: 25–7.

Cotton, B.C. and Emerson, M.B. (1978): "Consumer Response to Promotional Deals", *Journal of Marketing*, July: 109–13.

Dibb, S., Simken, L., Pride, W. and Ferrell, O.C. (1991): *Marketing*, European ed., Boston: Houghton Mifflin: 477–87.

Dodson, J.A., Tybout, A.M. and Sternthal, B. (1978): "Impact of Deals and Deal Retraction on Brand Switching", *Journal of Marketing Research*, February: 72–83.

Engel, J.F., Warshaw, M.R. and Kinnear, T.C. (1991): *Promotional Strategy: Managing the Marketing Communications Process*, Boston: Irwin.

Gofton, K. (1992): "Seeking Redemption", *Marketing*, 12 March: 25–6.

Haugh, L. J. (1981): "How Consumers Measure Up", *Advertising Age*, June: 58.

Irons, K.W., Little, J.D.C. and Klein, R.L. (1983): "Determinants of Coupon Effectiveness", *Advances and Practices of Marketing Science*, Proceedings of the 1983 ORSA/TIMS Marketing Science Conference, March: 157–64.

Levedahl, W.J. (1989): "Coupon Redeemers: Are They Better Shoppers?", *Journal of Consumer Affairs*, 22(2): 264–83.

Lichtenstein, D.R., Netemeyer, R.G. and Burton, S. (1990): "Distinguishing Coupon-Proneness from Value Consciousness: An Acquisition-Transaction Utility Theory Perspective", *Journal of Marketing*, July: 54–67.

Marketing Development Programme (MDP) (1989): Report on the Investigation of Non-Media Advertising in Ireland 1989, University College Dublin.

Marketing Development Study (MDP) (1993): *Report on the Investigation of Non-Media Advertising in Ireland 1993*, University College Dublin.

Montgomery, D.B. (1971): "Consumer Characteristics Associated with Dealing: An Empirical Example", *Journal of Marketing Research*, February: 118–20.

Narasimhan, C. (1984): "A Price Discrimination Theory of Coupons", *Marketing Science*, 3(2), Spring: 128–47.

Nielsen, A.C. Jr. (1965): "The Impact of Retail Coupons", *Journal of Marketing*, October: 11–15.

Quelch, J.A. (1989): *Sales Promotion Management*, New Jersey: Prentice Hall.

Reibstein, D.J. and Traver P.A. (1982): "Factors Affecting Coupon Redemption Rates", *Journal of Marketing*, Fall: 102–13.

Robinson, W.A. (1977): "12 Basic Promotion Techniques: Their Advantages and Pitfalls", *Advertising Age*, 10 January.

Rothschild, M.L. (1987): "A Behavioural View of Promotions Effects on Brand Loyalty", Advances in Consumer Research, 14: 119–120.

Schimp, T.A. (1990): *Promotion Management and Marketing Communications*, Orlando: The Dryden Press.

Schwartz, A. (1966): "The Influence of Media Characteristics on Coupon Redemption", *Journal of Marketing*, January: 41–6.

Shoemaker, R.W. and Tibrewala, V. (1985): "Relating Coupon Redemption Rates to Past Purchasing of the Brand", *Journal of Advertising Research*, October/November: 40–47.

Strang, R.A. (1981): "Sales Promotion — Fast Growth, Faulty Management", *Harvard Business Review*, July/August: 115–24.

Ward, R.W. and Davis, J.E. (1978): "Coupon Redemption", *Journal of Advertising*, August: 51–8.

Webster, F.E. Jr. (1965): "The Deal-Prone Consumer", *Journal of Marketing Research*, May: 186–9.

24
Public Relations and Publicity

Francis Xavier Carty

Many people, including some who work in public relations, confuse public relations with publicity. There can, however, be excellent public relations without any publicity, nor any need for publicity. On its own, publicity is rarely effective without the underpinning of planned public relations: publicity without public relations is like seed thrown on cement.

When residents' associations, sports clubs and similar organisations choose a "PRO" it is usually a person to look after publicity rather than public relations. When a staff member is given responsibility, especially at a relatively junior level, for "marketing, advertising and public relations", one can assume that the public relations content will be minimal, and it will almost exclusively be publicity.

This confusion is not new. Harlow (1952: 283) saw it as the

> ... bête noir of the public relations worker. It keeps him in constant hot water — first, because too many of those for and with whom he works expect his public relations efforts to produce spectacular publicity results; and second, because publicity so dominates public relations practices and procedures that much of the public relations workers' efforts are forced into this channel.

Because of its chequered early history, in the days of sleazy American press agentry, public relations acquired a dubious reputation, so that those who are not properly informed are still suspicious — not wholly convinced that it is concerned with the truth. Such people unwittingly create a man of straw which they call public relations. They then judge public relations and public relations people by that false model.

Most of the confused ideas that exist about public relations spring from the fact that it is both an advisory and an executive function. Black (1989: 11) writes:

Sometimes "public relations" is used to describe the advisory aspect, and "publicity" the actual execution of it. It is preferable to use "public relations" to describe the whole field. Again, "publicity", is sometimes used to describe paid-for activities such as exhibitions, films, publications, etc., while "public relations" is reserved for actions which do not incur direct expenditure. This distinction is quite artificial and of little practical value. Public relations is everything from an attitude of mind to a minute detail in the successful implementation of a programme. As with many activities, it is possible to pick out individual acts for criticism or ridicule, but any serious assessment of public relations must take into account its full ambit.

There are public relations people and companies who confine their work to publicity and media coverage for products. This is what causes suspicion among journalists who see them as "flacks". Cutlip, Center and Broom (1985: 430) quote from the Associated Press Managing Editors' Manual, *APME Guidelines*:

> A flack is a person who makes all or part of his income by obtaining space in newspapers without cost to himself or his clients. Usually a professional ... they are known formally as public relations men. The flack is the modern equivalent of the cavalier highwayman of old.... A flack is a flack. His job is to say kind things about his client. He will not lie very often, but much of the time he tells less than the whole story. You do not owe the PR man anything. The owner of the newspaper, not the flack, pays your salary. Your job is to serve the readers, not the man who would raid your columns.

DEFINING PUBLIC RELATIONS

Harlow (1976: 36) found 472 separate definitions of public relations. Some are descriptions of what public relations professionals do rather than strict definitions. Public relations developed as an organised profession in the twentieth century, but public-relations-like activities have always been practised. For an early American pioneer like Ivy Ledbetter Lee, public relations was an art, but the first public relations intellectual was Edward Bernays who died on 8 March 1995 at the age of 103. For Bernays (1972: 29):

> Public relations is a profession, an art applied to a science (social science). The public interest, rather than pecuniary motivation is the primary consideration.

Others have variously looked upon public relations as a craft, an industry, a business, a profession, a mind-set, a philosophy. Among the many definitions, the best will usually incorporate three basic notions — relationships, communication and reputation.

For Bernays (1972: 29):

> Public relations concerns itself with the relations of an organisation or individual with the publics on which it depends for viability.

Grunig and Hunt (1984: 6) settle for the following as a definition:

> The management of communication between an organisation and its publics.

The Institute of Public Relations (UK) (1993) has formulated a new definition that it judges to be more "user-friendly", accessible to people other than public relations practitioners. It has adopted this definition as a supplement to its older definition that:

> Public relations is the planned and sustained effort to establish and maintain good will and mutual understanding between an organisation and its publics.

The new definition says simply:

> Public relations is about reputation: the result of what you do, what you say and what others say about you. Public relations practice is the discipline that looks after reputation — with the aim of earning understanding and support, and influencing opinion and behaviour.

The difference between public relations and other disciplines associated with communication is that for real public relations there has to be dialogue, two-way communication.

Traverse-Healy (1995: 7) says:

> I want to assert that we are not advertising practitioners, we are not publicists and we are not simply communicators. We are not press agents, we are not sales promoters and we are not propagandists. We practise public relations which differs from, say, publicity on the one hand or propaganda on the other in that three ingredients need always to be present in our endeavours — truth, concern for the public interest and dialogue. Of course, the first two of these ingredients, truth and concern for the public interest, are invariables, but nevertheless they need to be weighed, argued and adopted. However, the third ingredient, dialogue, is either

taking place or it is not. Indeed dialogue is measurable and if it is not happening in the process then although communications "at" rather than "with" may be being practised, clearly public relations is not.

When public relations states its concern for the truth, it does not claim that other disciplines are not equally concerned. However, public relations in particular has to be the conscience of the organisation, concerned that it behave well and act in the interests of its publics.

Increased social awareness and greater emphasis on ethical and environmental issues, have enhanced the importance of the public relations function. If the organisation is not behaving itself, it is the duty of public relations to ensure that it changes — otherwise reputation will be lost, possibly never to be regained. People are reluctant to do business with organisations that do not behave. There is now a social bottom line, in addition to the economic bottom line. Public relations has to look to the social bottom line, persuading the organisation to behave in a way that is acceptable to its publics.

The publics of an organisation are more than its customers: they are its employees, the local community, suppliers, distributors, politicians, the financial community, opinion leaders. Public relations has to deal with all of these publics and has to ensure mutual understanding and support. An organisation should never alienate its publics. Note that in public relations there is no such thing as the general public, but groups who are of consequence to the organisation and vice versa. In a dynamic environment, these groups change and there is regrouping as issues develop and are resolved.

According to Carty (1992: v):

> Real public relations is far from the pestering of journalists with trivial and totally uninteresting stories. That is joke public relations, the public relations of yesterday. Public relations, concerned with the effect of company behaviour upon reputation, is trying to move to a higher moral ground as guardian of the corporate conscience.

Public relations people tend to be over-anxious that their role is not properly appreciated. They take to heart what their critics say, but do not respond very well in their own defence. If the public-relations profession were as good at advising itself as it is at advising its clients, popular perceptions would be very different.

Healy (1995: 9) adds:

> We should not be self-conscious of, or defensive about, being public relations practitioners, because, if we did not exist as a group, then society would have had to have invented us. And if we are performing responsibly and effectively, then we should be proud of the job we do.

PROBLEMS AND PERSPECTIVES

At one time, public relations was confused with advertising. Consultancies often grew from departments within advertising agencies. There was a tendency to see public relations — often no more than publicity and promotions — as a free extra service to an advertising client. Then marketing came of age and public relations was seen by many as part of that, again confusing it with publicity and promotions.

One reason for the close association in practice between public relations and marketing is that the knowledge and skills that good public relations people have can be applied very effectively to marketing communications and to helping to make better known a product or service. Public relations, marketing and advertising are brothers and sisters, but that does not mean that they should automatically merge and become one. If you love your sister and share many interests with her, that does not mean that you become your sister.

However, both public relations and marketing are changing and will continue to change as they are taking on some of the virtues of each other. Marketing is looking to relationships; public relations is dealing with segmentation and niche activities. Traverse Healy (1995) asks whether in the future there will not be a merger at strategic level while each retains its specific objectives.

For Ehling, White and Grunig (1992: 368), the problem in associating public relations too narrowly as publicity within a marketing framework is that the activity is regarded as:

> ... made up solely of tactics and techniques. Nothing is said of strategies or strategical planning *vis-à-vis* public relations.

This is a depressing situation for those who have sought for many years to advance public relations professionalism and strengthen public relations education.

Ehling (1992: 462) writes:

> If publicity is to be taken as the be-all and end-all of public

relations, then there is no basis for professionalism and no reason for education.

Those who see their practice of public relations as only publicity become communication technicians, but never managers. Career-wise they miss out, and others — whether they be legal, financial, personnel or marketing people — who have neither experience nor expertise in public relations, are appointed over them.

Public relations people have to be good communicators and good publicists, but if they are to get to the top of their profession, they must be agents of change in an organisation, able to analyse issues, plan strategies, solve problems and resolve conflict.

GRUNIG'S FOUR MODELS OF PUBLIC RELATIONS

Management of relationships, communication and reputation does not just come naturally. Situations have to be analysed, issues identified, messages developed, strategies planned, tactics adopted and so on. What suits one organisation will not necessarily suit another organisation, nor the same organisation at another time.

For Grunig (1984: 21–44) there are four models of public relations:

- Press Agentry/Publicity
- Public Information
- Two-Way Asymmetric
- Two-Way Symmetric.

The press agentry/publicity model is the oldest, in reality, that which gave a bad name to public relations. It was the predominant model in the United States from 1850 to 1900. It is still prevalent: there will always be need for some of it. This is the predominant model that companies have in mind when they bring in the public relations people to help them to get media coverage, or to aid their marketing communications.

The purpose of this model is propaganda, using the word in a neutral rather than pejorative sense. It is the spreading of a message where the communication is essentially one-way. Truth is essential, but not necessarily the complete truth. Communication moves from source to receiver without either side being affected or changed. There is little research, possibly no more than the counting of column inches in the media.

The press agentry/publicity model is most widely practised in the areas of sport, theatre and entertainment and in product promotion. It is what many clients are looking for when they call in the PR people. It is where publicity has its largest contribution to a public relations programme.

The public-information model goes a bit further. The purpose is not propaganda, but the dissemination of information that will be of some value to the receiver. The communication is still one-way. Again, apart from some examination of the media and tests on readability and readership, there will be little research. Health promotions and political campaigns come into this model. As in press agentry, there is a high role for publicity, but it is far from being the only tool used.

The two-way asymmetric model brings in some element of two-way communication, but it is unbalanced. The purpose is scientific persuasion, which can lead to accusation of manipulation. The organisation is more concerned with maintaining its position than with providing information that is for the good of its publics. There is some research of a formative nature with evaluation of attitudes.

The purpose of the two-way symmetric model is mutual understanding. There is two-way balanced communication. Not only is the receiver of the message affected and, it is hoped, improved, but so is the sender. The company that engages in this form of public relations is open to its environment, aware of changes, prepared to change itself in response to the feedback it obtains. It responds creatively to issues. There is emphasis on research, with evaluation of understanding as well as of attitudes. Awareness of two-way symmetric public relations has developed only in the past 30 years, and many practitioners have not adopted it. Grunig (1992) agrees that it explains more what should take place than what usually happens.

Grunig recognises a continuing role for all four models, but sees the two-way symmetric model as the pinnacle, the most perfect practice of public relations. Here is public relations that creates change and improvement not only in the surrounding environment of a business, but in the business itself.

The skill of public relations management is to know which model, or combination of models, fits a particular organisation at a given time. When the priority is media relations or marketing support, there will be an emphasis on the first two models. The wrong choice of model can lead to public relations being seen only as publicity, gimmicks and stunts, and its contribution to the success of the organisation is undervalued. Alternatively, the wrong fit of two-way symmetric public relations could give the impression that it is vague and commercially insignificant. The professional needs to understand all models and know when each is the correct prescription.

Grunig and Hunt (1984: 97) hold that organisations in a static environment will generally use the first two models, while those in a dynamic environment will need to look to the other two as well.

It would be impossible to calculate how much of public relations practice today consists of each of the four models. Grunig and Hunt (1984: 22) estimated that, in the United States, the percentage of organisations practising model one was 15 per cent, model two 50 per cent, model three 20 per cent and model four 15 per cent. There has been no research in Ireland or the UK to give a similar breakdown. It seems that many organisations still confine themselves to the first two models.

Public relations has to educate employers and clients if it is to play its complete role in business. O'Flynn (1989) writes:

> The most important factor influencing the effectiveness of the in-house public relations department is the role which public relations has in the area of policy making. Without a role in policy making the department cannot give, and the company cannot expect, really effective public relations management. Without a policy making role the public relations manager becomes, in effect, a technician rather than an executive.

Stressing the role of public relations in top management and the fact that everything a company says or does can have a public-relations impact, he says that too often the public relations manager is seen as "the company exorcist" and is called in to make the best of a bad job:

> In many cases the chief executive would no more consult with public relations about a major policy matter than ask his barber for stock market investment advice.

PUBLICITY

Publicity is a feature of all four of Grunig's models, though it is more dominant in the first two. The purpose of the publicity can, however, differ, ranging from propaganda to dissemination of information, to scientific persuasion and to mutual understanding.

Publicity resulting from public relations activity is usually "unpaid for" as distinct from advertising that is "paid for". However, good public relations cannot ignore the power of advertising: at times the most effective way to get a message across to a particular group of people is advertising, even when the purpose is not directly to sell the product. Public relations programmes frequently include corporate advertising. When there are power cuts, for example, the electricity company will not just issue press releases but will also take out advertising to state when the power will be cut off in each part of the country.

Some publicity is sought and it endeavours to achieve specific objectives and influence attitudes and behaviour. In seeking publicity, one has to be systematic, asking the questions who, where, what, when, why and how. What is the specific message that one wishes to communicate through the publicity? To whom is it addressed? Where will the communication take place? How, or through which media? When is the most appropriate time and place to achieve the communication? And finally, why is the publicity sought and can one be sure what it will achieve?

Those who seek publicity, whether by a planted "leak", a press release or a special event, must be ready for the consequences and for the follow-up. Therefore, strategies and tactics must be planned so as to gain the most from the opportunity and not turn it into a banana-skin. Don't step into the kitchen unless you are prepared for the heat!

Always in dealing with the media, the PR person must remember that news is what the journalist wants and news is what interests the reader. Organisations can be short-sighted and think that all those minor details about their product are of interest. Put oneself in the mind of the readers: what do they want to know about the company or the product? Looking for editorial space is different from advertising where there is total control of the message and how it is presented. For editorial coverage, it is necessary to go through the journalist who has no reason to see the organisation as it sees itself. The journalist thinks for the reader, so does not want commercial plugs or boastful statements. The journalist wants facts, wants news, something that is new, that the reader does not already know. Some say that news is what makes the reader jump up and say "Oh Gosh!"

There is, however, bad publicity, that can be damaging to the reputation of the organisation or its products and services. Such publicity is not sought and public relations seeks to minimise, or at least to control it. Frequently, the success of public relations will be not in the number of column inches, but in what was not covered, the success in cooling down a difficult story.

Phineas T. Barnum (of circus fame) did not care if the newspapers attacked him, as long as they spelt his name correctly — all publicity was good publicity. A modern-day counterpart is Max Clifford, the British publicist, who represents various celebrities and plants stories about them in the tabloid newspapers, admitting that they are not always true. He feels that a spoof is acceptable if it gets coverage for his client and does not hurt anybody.

THE PRESS RELEASE

The press release, a common way to seek publicity, is the most overused tool in public relations. Estimates range up to 95 per cent for the number of press releases that are dumped unread into the journalist's bin. Too often they are badly written, full of hype, lack news, are sent to the wrong paper, use advertising language, are heavy on jargon, omit relevant information, are incomplete, are vague, make unsubstantiated claims, include vacuous quotes from company executives, and so on. The press release is an initiative taken by the organisation. It is, in a sense, forced upon the journalist. The journalist is under no obligation to read or to act upon it, and must be convinced within seconds that it is news for the readers. It must be written in language that the journalist appreciates, the language of the newspaper, the language of the readers.

Before issuing a press release, it is always necessary to ask why it is being sent and what it is intended to achieve. According to Van Zanten (1992), the business editor of the London *Evening Standard* in one week receives 800 press releases. Many others are sent to the newsdesk and other departments of the newspaper. Of those, he used only two, and these indirectly. The reason for this wastage is that too many PR people, too many organisations, do not realise that publicity needs a professional approach: it is not something that the amateur can learn in an afternoon.

In planning publicity, it is realised that the PR professional knows the media, not just who works in the media, but the effect of each element in the media, who reads what and how they are influenced. Media relations is not a scatter-gun job where flak is fired in all directions hoping that something will stick.

A PR person should never expect too much from media coverage. People are surrounded by messages from the media and elsewhere. It is just not possible to comprehend it all. The reader of the targeted morning newspaper may be the ideal person for the message, but don't assume that that person will have time to read the message in the paper on that day.

Some think that when they have obtained media coverage, they have succeeded in their public relations objectives. This may not be so. Public relations needs to research whether the message reached its target and whether the target responded as desired. Ideally, for two-way symmetric public relations, there must be change. Was the receiver of the message improved? Was the organisation improved as a result of the communication? There is still too little of this type of research.

Prominent coverage on, say, the business page of *The Irish Times* is an indication not necessarily of public relations success but of effort: it means that a publication that is interested in the story has been targeted and that the PR person has completed the technical processes efficiently. It does not automatically mean that any change has been achieved, any improvement in public relations, any enhancement of reputation. Very few go on to investigate what really has changed. Too often, if the client is happy, the PR person is happy.

HANDLING THE BAD NEWS

It is relatively easy to create good publicity and deal with it. How many ministers are seen at the opening of a new factory? How many are seen when it is closing? The professionalism of public relations is more in demand when the news is bad: the media respect the PR professional who is straight with them when the news is bad.

McMahon (1994) has developed a series of guidelines for coping with bad publicity:

- Be prepared for bad news.
- Realise that it is inevitable at some time.
- Make media friends beforehand and keep them briefed.
- Prepare lists of all that could go wrong.
- Prepare factual materials such as press packs, video clips etc.

Then, when the news breaks:

- Ascertain the "6Ws", as any good journalist would — who, where, what, when, why and how?
- Brief staff who need to know, including the telephonist.
- Appoint a spokesperson.
- Write out facts and copy them to relevant people.

Finally, when the journalists phone, or arrive on the doorstep:

- Stall, play for time if not ready.
- Take their names, the name of their journal, phone number and deadline time for phone back.
- Have an area designated for journalists.
- Try to discover what the journalist knows already.
- Stick to facts, don't speculate.
- Correct inaccuracies.
- Have background materials ready to give out.

In a crisis, the first 72 hours are crucial. If the organisation does not get control of the communication in that time, the battle is lost.

McMahon's experience is based on some high-profile Irish crises, like the explosion of the Betelgeuse oil tanker at Whiddy Island in 1979, as described by O'Shea (1995), but the principles he outlines apply, admittedly in lesser proportion, to all crises, even minor ones.

EVALUATING MEDIA COVERAGE

How does one evaluate media coverage? The obvious mistake is to count up the column inches and compare that to the cost of advertising. Too often people say that they got, for example, £400,000 worth of coverage. This is nonsense and in no way related to proper evaluation. In a respectable publication, advertising has a price, but editorial is priceless.

Quantity of coverage can never be the criterion: quality is what matters. Ten lines in a publication that is respected and that will be read by all of the target audience is infinitely more valuable than a page in another publication that is held in low regard and not read by the target audience. In what position of the paper or at what point in the news bulletin was it covered? Small on page one is better than big on page 16 because there is more chance that it will be read and, it is hoped, acted upon.

The content of the coverage is also important. If a person seeks publicity, does that person have a message to give? Did the coverage give that message, or did it ramble into other irrelevant details?

Finally, what systems are in place to determine whether the coverage achieved the purpose that it was intended to achieve. Was mere coverage the purpose?

CONCLUSIONS

Public relations has now come of age. The new century will see it grow into a confident adult, no longer shy towards, nor over-awed by, the other members of its family. Technology will have an immense effect on the way in which everything is done. One significant change will be the final maturing of professionals who have been educated in public relations. They will not be content to remain as technicians. They will want to be in the boardroom where the decisions are taken, decisions that have a vital impact upon public relations and upon reputation. If public relations is not there to influence these decisions, how can it be an agent of change, a solution to problems, a means towards the resolution of conflict?

REFERENCES

Bernays, E. (1972): Lecture to Rotary Club of New York, Reprinted in *International Public Relations Review*, 1995: 18(2): 29.

Black, S. (1989): *Introduction to Public Relations*, London: The Modino Press Ltd.

Carty, F.X. (1992): *Farewell to Hype — The Emergence of Real Public Relations*, Dublin: Able Press.

Carty, F.X. (ed.) (1995): *From John Paul to Saint Jack — Public Relations in Ireland*, Dublin: Able Press.

Cutlip, S.E., Center, A.H. and Broom, G.M., (1985): *Effective Public Relations*, Englewood, NJ: Prentice Hall.

Ehling, W.P., White, J. and Grunig, J.E. (1992): "Public Relations and Marketing Practices, in Grunig", J.E. (ed.), *Excellence in Public Relations and Communication Management*, New Jersey: Lawrence Erlbaum and Associates.

Ehling, W.P. (1992), Public Relations Education and Professionalism, in Grunig, J.E. (ed.), *Excellence in Public Relations and Communication Management*, New Jersey: Lawrence Erlbaum and Associates.

Grunig, J.E. and Hunt, T. (1984): *Managing Public Relations*, New York: Holt, Rinehart and Winston.

Grunig, J.E. (ed.) (1992), *Excellence in Public Relations and Communication Management*, New Jersey: Lawrence Erlbaum and Associates.

Harlow, R.F. and Black, M. (1952): *Practical Public Relations*, New York: Harper and Bros.

Harlow, R. (1976): "Building a Public Relations Definition", *Public Relations Review*, 2: 36.

McMahon, J. (1994): "Crisis Management" Lecture to Dublin Institute of Technology, 13 February.

Newman, W. (1993): "New Words for What We Do", *The Institute of Public Relations Journal*, 12(4).

O'Flynn, N. (1989): "The In-House Public Relations Department at Work", Lecture to Public Relations Institute of Ireland, Dublin.

O'Shea, P. (1995): "God Gave Us Bantry — We Gave it to Gulf Oil", in Carty, F.X. (ed.), *From John Paul to Saint Jack — Public Relations in Ireland*, Dublin: Able Press: 143–9

Traverse-Healy, T. (1995): "40th Anniversary of IPRA — Societal Value and Professional Values", *International Public Relations Review*, 18(2).

Van Zanten, N. (1992): *How to Write a Press Release*, audio cassette recording of conference, London: Communications Training plc.

25
Managing Sponsorship Effectively

Tony Meenaghan

INTRODUCTION

Commercial sponsorship represents one of the most rapidly growing areas of marketing communication, having out-performed media advertising in terms of year-on-year growth in most developed economies over the past decade. Its success as a marketing communications medium can be attributed to its flexibility and cost-efficiency in achieving objectives laid down by marketing management. While it is generally classified alongside direct marketing and promotions as a below-the-line medium, the reality is that sponsorship might more appropriately be compared with traditional media advertising, in that its primary communications capabilities are in awareness generation and image enhancement. The purpose of this paper is to analyse the phenomenon that is commercial sponsorship and to examine the management of this marketing communications medium.

BACKGROUND

While sponsorship with a philanthropic orientation has long been a feature of civilised society, the past 25 years have seen the emergence of sponsorship as a commercially-driven corporate communications medium. The extent of this development can be seen from the fact that expenditure on sponsorship in the UK grew from £4 million in 1970 (Buckley, 1980) to £450 million in 1993 (Mintel, 1994). Pro-rata expenditure in 1993 on sponsorship in the Republic of Ireland is of the order of £20–£25 million. The ability of sponsorship to transcend language and cultural barriers has led to the emergence of sponsorship as a global communications medium. The worldwide sponsorship market has grown from $2 billion in 1984 to $10.8 billion in 1993 (Sponsorship Research International, 1994), with the US and Europe accounting for 34 per cent and 35 per cent respectively of worldwide expenditure. Continued strong growth is expected with an 11 per cent increase in sponsorship expenditure being forecast for the US market in 1995 (IEG Sponsorship Report, 1994). These estimates of expenditure include only the costs of securing the sponsorship property rights — that is, the rights to sponsor the event. To ensure effective sponsorship, it is generally agreed that a sum equivalent to these direct costs must be expended in leveraging/exploiting the initial investment.

Limited-scale commercial sponsorship activity has been evident since the early decades of this century. A particularly well-known example, Texaco's "Live from the Met" Series, continues to this day, having been established in the 1920s in New York. Sponsored programming began on Radio Éireann soon after the establishment of the station in 1926, with sponsored programmes by companies such as Waltons, the Irish Hospital Sweepstakes and Fry's Cadbury — of *The Kennedys of Castleross* fame — forming an important backdrop to the development of Irish society, until this approach was gradually abandoned in favour of spot advertising in 1981 (RTE Press Office, 1995). More recently, sponsored radio programmes have again begun to appear in RTE schedules, as in the case of the *Levis Hour* on Dave Fanning's evening show and Irish Ferries' sponsorship of the *Both Sides Now* programme.

The major upsurge in sponsorship expenditure in developed economies can be dated to the early 1970s, with restrictive government policy on tobacco advertising, and later alcohol advertising, providing the initial impetus for the development of this medium. Other contributory factors have been the increased social prominence and related media coverage of sports, arts and other leisure-oriented pursuits. The factors which have led to client disillusionment with traditional advertising approaches, such as escalating media and production costs, audience fragmentation and consumer literacy and cynicism, have also encouraged the increased adoption of sponsorship as a corporate and marketing medium.

SPONSORSHIP — AN INDUSTRY IN TRANSITION

Marketing communications in general are currently undergoing fundamental change, and sponsorship as a medium has also been the subject of considerable turbulence over its relatively brief history. Certain patterns of change can be identified as occurring in the global sponsorship market, with similar changes also taking place in an Irish context.

Developing Range of Sponsorship Media

In most markets, sports and, to a lesser extent, the arts, have been the major recipients of sponsorship investment. In 1993, sports sponsorship accounted for 61 per cent of total UK sponsorship expenditure (Mintel, 1994) and 66 per cent of total US expenditure (IEG Sponsorship Report, 1994). Arts sponsorship, traditionally the second major beneficiary, accounted for 16 per cent of total UK expenditure in 1993 (Mintel, 1994).

In more recent times, a range of newer sponsorship media has begun to develop. The most significant is broadcast/programme sponsorship, which has grown substantially in recent years because of the increasing number of stations available in Europe and the liberalisation of funding guidelines for broadcast media. Sponsorship in this category in the UK grew from £7 million in 1990 to £70 million in 1993 (Mintel, 1994). As a source of revenue, broadcast sponsorship is reasonably important to satellite stations (Ward, 1995). However, despite some high profile examples of similar sponsorship in Ireland, broadcast sponsorship currently only contributes 1 per cent of total RTE income — that is, licence fee and advertising revenue combined (Mulligan, 1995).

While arts sponsorship generally has long been a much utilised medium for corporate sponsors, the sponsorship of popular music, with its appeal and access to the youth market, is more recently growing in popularity worldwide. In the US market, some $425 million or 10 per cent of total 1994 sponsorship expenditure, was invested in popular-music sponsorship (IEG Sponsorship Report, 1994). Well-known examples under this heading have included Philips and Dire Straits, Pepsi and Michael Jackson, Sears Roebuck and Phil Collins, and 7Up and Bon Jovi.

Another developing sponsorship medium is cause-related marketing, which involves the corporate sponsorship of social/charitable causes. This commercialised version of corporate philanthropy is used by sponsors to portray a more caring, concerned and benevolent image. Cause-related marketing is particularly important in the US market where it accounted for $340 million or 8 per cent of total sponsorship expenditure in 1994 (IEG Sponsorship Report, 1994). Though less important in Europe, cause-related marketing programmes are run in Ireland by companies such as Bord Telecom, AIB and McDonald's.

Other sponsorship media include community programmes and educational sponsorship, although major markets permit the exploitation of less obvious sponsorship opportunities such as venue sponsorship — Fosters' sponsorship of the Oval, for example. There have even been suggestions in both the UK and France that aspects of the Health Services be sponsored, while the United Nations is currently attempting to generate revenue through sponsorship. A classification of sponsorship opportunities and relevant Irish examples is indicated in Figure 25.1.

One of the more worrying aspects of the developing range of opportunities is the increasing level of clutter surrounding major events, such as the World Cup in 1994. Increased clutter makes it difficult for sponsors to "stand out" in terms of getting their message through and can lead to consumer cynicism.

Changing Perceptions of Sponsorship

It would be true to say that sponsorship in the 1960s and early 1970s was not generally regarded in strictly commercial terms. In many corporations, sponsorship frequently overlapped with corporate donations and a "donations mentality" pervaded the thinking of both recipients and sponsors. The following definition is of its time and reflects this perception:

> Sponsorship is the donation or loan of resources (people, money, materials, etc.) by private individuals or organisations to other individuals or organisations engaged in the provision of those public goods and services designed to improve the quality of life (Royal Philharmonic Orchestra (RPO), 1974).

However, as expenditure on sponsorship escalated, major corporations applied a stringent commercial rationale to their sponsorship programmes. The era of the "chairman's choice" syndrome, whereby senior executive personnel indulged their personal whims and fantasies, has largely disappeared. Increasingly, sponsorship is seen as a commercial investment intended to achieve corporate/marketing objectives on behalf of sponsors. This more hard-nosed view of sponsorship is implicit in the following more contemporary definition:

> Commercial sponsorship is an investment, in cash or in kind, in an activity, in return for access to the exploitable commercial potential associated with that activity (Meenaghan, 1991: 36).

It is possible to regard such a definition as overly emphatic of the needs of the sponsor and it is arguably more appropriate to place emphasis on the relationship aspect of the transaction between sponsor and sponsored, which is critical to the successful implementation of a sponsorship programme.

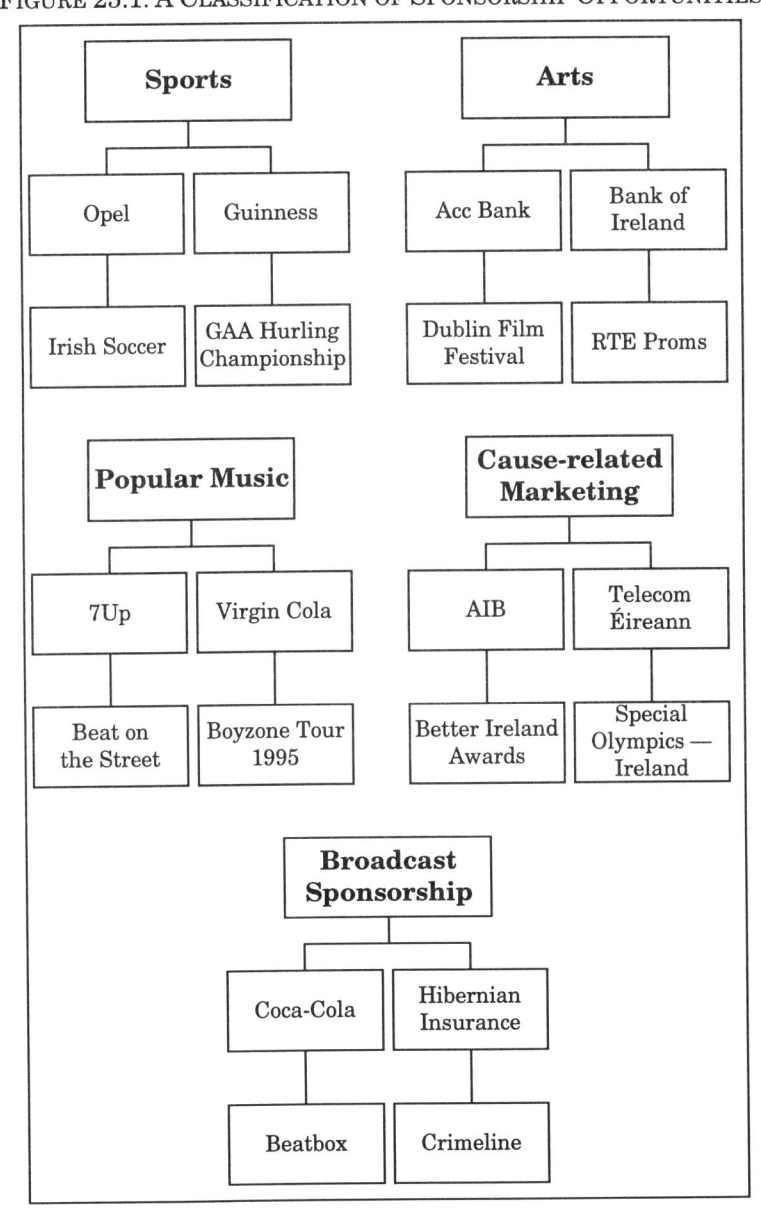

FIGURE 25.1: A CLASSIFICATION OF SPONSORSHIP OPPORTUNITIES

Sports
- Opel — Irish Soccer
- Guinness — GAA Hurling Championship

Arts
- Acc Bank — Dublin Film Festival
- Bank of Ireland — RTE Proms

Popular Music
- 7Up — Beat on the Street
- Virgin Cola — Boyzone Tour 1995

Cause-related Marketing
- AIB — Better Ireland Awards
- Telecom Éireann — Special Olympics — Ireland

Broadcast Sponsorship
- Coca-Cola — Beatbox
- Hibernian Insurance — Crimeline

Increased Sophistication of Management Practice

The early days of sponsorship were marked by low levels of corporate knowledge of this new medium. Sponsorship was regarded as "something different", not amenable to conventional management principles. The result was poor decision-making and often unprofitable investment. Over recent years, corporate understanding arising from cumulative experience has led to increased sophistication in all aspects of sponsorship management. Confused rationales for involvement have been replaced by strictly-stated objectives. Many major sponsors now have in place sophisticated selection models to guide their choices — a considerable improvement on the quick checklists of the not-too-distant past. Integration and exploitation of sponsorship programmes, often overlooked in the past, are now essential components of the overall marketing plan. Rigorous approaches to evaluation have replaced the "gut-feel" factor of yesteryear.

It can be argued that this paints too rosy a picture of current management practice, in that there are admittedly still many naïve and unsophisticated users of the medium. However, there can be little doubt about the distance travelled by many major sponsors in terms of sophistication in usage. Although in general terms understanding and sophistication in use may still be considerably short of those attained in advertising, the sponsorship industry, while still having much to learn, has made considerable strides over its 25-year history.

Developing Sponsorship-Support Industry

Increased scale of investments, allied to increased understanding of sponsorship and sophistication in its use, has placed demands on sponsorship-support services. This has generated an expanding subsidiary industry worldwide. Sponsorship consultants have increased in numbers and become more professional and have begun to specialise by sector, such as popular music, broadcasting and the Internet. Advertising agencies, while initially hostile, are now responding to client pressures to utilise the sponsorship medium. This has forced the traditional agency either to develop skills in this area or to seek alliances with sponsorship-consultancy groups. Sophisticated users of sponsorship seek to use research to inform all aspects of sponsorship management and, in particular, to aid programme selection (Brown, 1995; Jones and Dearsley, 1995) and final evaluation (Kohl and Otker, 1995). The demands of sponsors, allied to those of sponsorship seekers who base their proposals on market information, have given a substantial impetus to the developing sponsorship-research industry.

THE SPONSORSHIP-MANAGEMENT PROCESS

Like all other elements of the marketing communications mix, sponsorship must be managed for maximum effect. Figure 25.2 shows how sponsorship links to overall marketing strategy, and outlines the sequential process involved in ensuring the proper management of sponsorship activities.

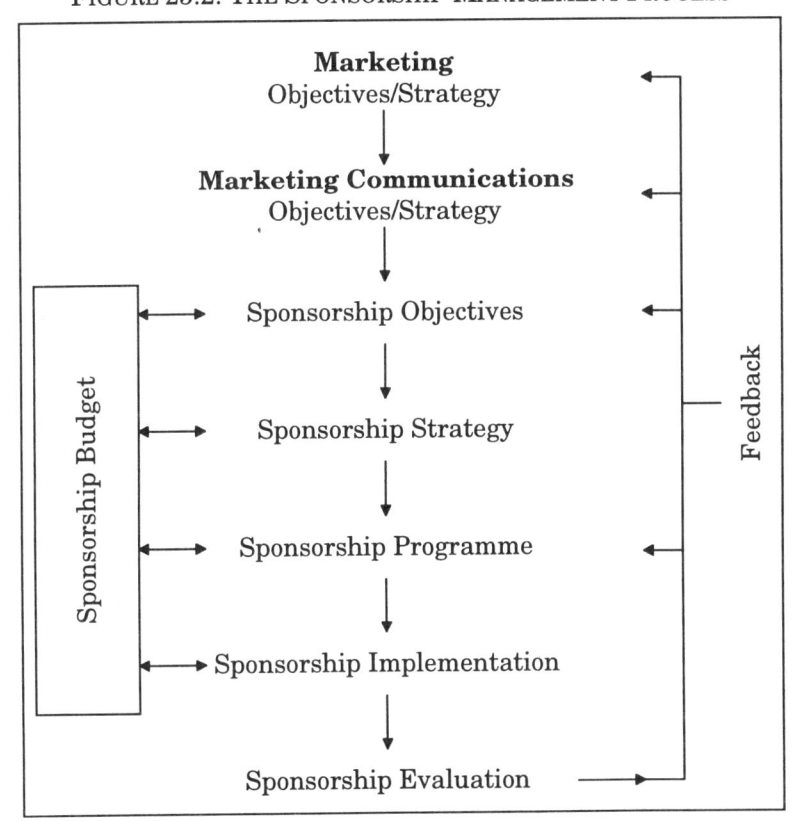

FIGURE 25.2: THE SPONSORSHIP-MANAGEMENT PROCESS

```
                    Marketing
               Objectives/Strategy
                        ↓
            Marketing Communications
                Objectives/Strategy
                        ↓
  Sponsorship        Sponsorship Objectives
   Budget                  ↓
              ↔    Sponsorship Strategy          Feedback
                        ↓
              ↔    Sponsorship Programme
                        ↓
              ←    Sponsorship Implementation
                        ↓
                   Sponsorship Evaluation  →
```

Marketing and Marketing Communications Strategy

Having evaluated its own position relative to competition and other environmental forces, the company will specify achievable marketing objectives and the strategy deemed appropriate to attain them. The marketing strategy will specify the intended target market and the broad thrust of the marketing programme required. Within the overall marketing programme, particular objectives for marketing communications and the strategy to ensure their fulfilment are specified. In turn, in the overall marketing communications framework, specific objectives for sponsorship are suggested, which reflect management's beliefs and expectations about this particular medium. In effect, sponsorship objectives and subsequent programmes ought to derive from overall corporate direction.

Objective-Setting in Sponsorship

In analysing objectives in a sponsorship context, it is important to realise that this represents an area of activity distinct from other elements of marketing communications. Firstly, sponsorship is a medium in which it is possible for corporate executives to realise considerable personal objectives in terms of status and other personal rewards. Secondly, it is possible to target several diverse corporate publics in the context of a single campaign, and while this is also possible with other elements of marketing communication, it is particularly so in the case with sponsorship. Thirdly, objectives in sponsorship can sometimes simultaneously represent both the philanthropic and the commercial motivations of the corporation, as in the case of cause-related marketing.

The targets for sponsored programmes can embrace a wide variety of corporate publics including the company's own staff, its various target markets, influence groups such as the media, government figures and other regulators, as well as business decision-makers — intermediaries, financial institutions and the company's own suppliers and shareholders.

In general, two broad types of sponsorship objectives can be identified. These are a) corporate and b) brand objectives. At the corporate level, the company may wish:

1) **To Increase Public Awareness of the Company**: This is an objective for which sponsorship appears particularly appropriate, as witnessed in international campaigns on the global stage such as Visa and the Olympics (Prazmark, 1995) and Mastercard and the World Cup Soccer (Jones, 1995). Cornhill Insurance and cricket (Dinmore, 1980) and Canon Electronics and soccer (Bridgewater, 1991) achieved equally impressive results in an English context, as did Nissan and Opel in the Irish market.

2) **To Change the Corporate Image**: The desire to alter the public's perception of a corporation is often a key objective of sponsorship. Indeed, sponsorship is often used by multinational

organisations to "root" in a particular country — to make the company appear less foreign and more local, e.g. Opel in Ireland (soccer) and Gillette in England (cricket sponsorship). Sponsoring a particular programme can emphasise specific corporate values for a company. This is the case with the Bank of Ireland and the GAA on the dimension of Irishness. This has helped position the Bank of Ireland close to the accepted core values of Irish society.

At a Brand level, a company may wish:

1) **To Increase Public Awareness of the Brand**: Sponsorship is widely used to increase the public profile of the brand. Examples of this in the Irish market are Murphy's sponsorship of the Irish Open Golf Championships and Budweiser's sponsorship of the Irish Derby.

2) **To Change/Reinforce the Brand Image**: Sponsorship is a particularly effective method of developing the brand image. Examples in an international context are Dire Straits and Philips CD (Kohl and Otker, 1995), Intel and the World Chess Championships (Couzens, 1995), Timberland and the Iditerod sleigh race in Alaska (*Business Week*, 1987). In an Irish context, the sponsorship of events such as the Cork Jazz Festival and the Temple Bar Blues Festival has been particularly important in the positioning of Guinness. Similarly, Bailey's has undertaken a five-year sponsorship programme of ice skating and speed skating in the European and World Championships, to tie in with the "Bailey's on Ice" theme.

Table 25.1 shows the objectives pursued by Irish sponsors in utilising sponsorship. While a variety of objectives are sought, they largely fit into the general pattern of corporate and brand awareness and image objectives with various corporate publics, though sales objectives are sometimes specified.

SPONSORSHIP SELECTION

Once the role of sponsorship in the overall marketing communications programme has been identified, the next logical aspect of sponsorship management is that of sponsorship selection. Establishing a formalised sponsorship policy will provide guiding parameters for all sponsorship-management decisions, as well as assisting the sponsor in sorting through the numerous sponsorship requests received.

TABLE 25.1: SPONSORSHIP OBJECTIVES PURSUED BY IRISH COMPANIES

Ranking*	Mean
1. Corporate Image Improvement	2.9
2. Increased Brand-Awareness	2.2
3. Long-Term Sales Increase	2.03
4. Making of Business Contacts	1.51
5. Entertainment of Clients	1.48
6. Employee-Relations Improvement	1.15
7. Meeting of Client Requests for Sponsorship	1.01
8. Short-Term Sales Increase	0.98
9. Creation of Outlet for Free Sample or Product Demonstration	0.7
10. Creation of Outlet for Selling Product at the Event	0.6

* Objectives ranked in order of importance by mean scores.
Source: O'Donoghue, B. (1989): *Irish Sponsorship — Market Characteristics and Management Practice*, unpublished MBS Thesis, UCD: 143.

A sponsorship policy must, by its nature, be company-specific and will reflect the company's view of itself and its products and how it wishes to be seen by its many publics. A basic feature of a sponsorship policy will be an articulation of what the company regards as acceptable and unacceptable activities, in the light of its own ethical perspective. Controversial activities such as blood sports, politically associated events and the sponsorship of individuals are regularly deemed unacceptable by sponsors.

Methodologies for selection have improved as sponsorship has developed, but these tend to vary according to the experience and scale of investment of the sponsor. Multinational sponsors such as Coca-Cola, Mars, Visa, have developed their own advanced selection models. Inevitably, a range of approaches is currently being employed, the most basic form of which is the use of a selection checklist. One such checklist is that proposed by Sedgewick (1984):

1. Does the sponsorship fulfil the company's policy (if one exists)?
2. Is the sponsorship unique? If not, can it be given a personality to "differentiate" it from the rest?

3. Is it appropriate to the sponsoring company?
4. Has it repeat or build-up value?
5. Can it be cost-effective?
6. Can it be exploited?

A somewhat more thorough approach is the development of a list of criteria against which proposals are examined. One such example of a highly developed list of selection criteria is that employed by Hewlett Packard and shown in Table 25.2 below.

Elsewhere it is suggested that potential sponsorship programmes be evaluated against the following key criteria (Meenaghan, 1991).

1) The ability of the programme to fulfil the objectives stated for involvement. This can include awareness and image objectives on behalf of the corporation or the brand, and can be directed at various target groups, such as consumers, own staff and business decision-makers.

2) The extent to which the proposed activity reaches the defined target market. In effect, this involves comparing the audience for the arts or sports activity with the company's defined target market and examining the extent to which these match. This matching process can be done on a demographic, geographic or life-style basis.

3) The extent of media exposure associated with the proposed activity. This factor will determine the level of publicity which the activity generates and it can also be used to indicate the extent to which the sponsor must provide leverage for the sponsorship with support promotions.

4) The costs associated with the programme. This must involve the total cost of the programme to the sponsor, including both direct costs (rights fee) and indirect costs (leveraging costs). The value of the programme is then judged against the totality of benefits accruing, resulting in a selection decision.

While other criteria can be utilised in the selection decision, such as the potential for guest hospitality and the commercial realism of the sponsored body, each company must specify its own criterion list and the relative importance of each criterion in arriving at a selection decision.

TABLE 25.2: HEWLETT PACKARD'S SPONSORSHIP SELECTION CRITERIA

1. *Visibility*: How much innate visibility is associated with this activity? Is press interest assured? TV? Radio? To what degree does the activity allow HP to expose the logo to public view?

2. *Major Message Delivery*: To what degree does the SM vehicle allow me to deliver major messages that support my overall positioning? How many major messages? How clearly and credibly stated? Are overall positioning messages subject to change in the near future?

3. *Target Audience Analysis*: Exactly who am I reaching through this programme? How closely does the audience profile parallel my target audience?

4. *Linkage to Products*: Does the programme provide ample opportunity to showcase my products? Is the link between product and programme *explicit* and *functional*?

5. *International Coverage*: Does the programme offer opportunities for international visibility? How many countries? Does participation in any one country cause problems in another?

6. *Cost-effectiveness*: What is the relative cost to deliver major messages to the target audience? How does this compare with other communication options?

7. *Public Image*: Does H.P.'s association with this activity contribute to a positive, progressive public image? Could it result in association with a "loser"?

8. *Risk/Controversy Index*: Does the activity pose any unusual risks to human life, the environment, local or international relations, or other areas of controversy? If so, are there off-setting benefits to taking such risks?

9. *Customer Involvement*: Does the programme provide a venue for high-level customer interaction in an appropriate setting? Can it be used for other promotional purposes?

10. *Exclusivity*: Can HP "own" the programme to the exclusion of all competitors or other corporations? What assurances do we have of this? At what cost? If co-ownership is required, can this be turned into a positive opportunity? What are the "control" implications?

11. *Compatibility with Other Programmes*: Does the activity complement and reinforce other communication activities? Could it be perceived as contradictory in any way?

12. *Sustainability*: Does HP have the resources to sustain its commitment to the SM programme? Does this programme itself offer long-term opportunity? Is it regular and continuous, or more sporadic and unpredictable? How viable is the sports entity/activity itself?

Source: Bandle, A. (1989): "Selection Process of the Sponsors and the Objectives to Reach through Them", Strategic Sponsorship Management Conference, 16–17 November, Montreux, Switzerland.

SPONSORSHIP BUDGET

Budgeting in a sponsorship context is difficult for several reasons. Firstly, most sponsors respond to sponsorship requests, in effect operating in a reactive, rather than proactive, manner. This results in companies attempting to assemble budgets to buy the particular property, often pulling resources from other areas of marketing communications. Secondly, sponsorship, unlike advertising, is not bought in a collection of units — as is the case with spot advertising. Purchasing sponsorship usually involves a single, large commitment of resources, with some discretion over the level of funding made available to leverage the sponsorship. While many of the problems with sponsorship budgeting could be overcome were the sponsor to have both a clear view of the task which sponsorship is being asked to achieve and a determination of how much the achievement of the task is worth, the reality is that sponsorship management is rarely undertaken in such a proactive manner. In practice, budgeting decisions continue throughout the sponsorship programme, with funds being sought and made available to leverage the campaign as it progresses. The result is that in many instances funds are found to purchase the title rights, but inadequate resources are made available to exploit the initial investment properly.

SPONSORSHIP EXPLOITATION, IMPLEMENTATION AND INTEGRATION

Once a particular sponsorship programme has been selected, time and effort must be expended on planning the various activities which will be associated with its implementation. A critical first step is to determine how the sponsor's involvement can be exploited in a manner which does not offend the sensitivities of the sponsored body, yet still allows the sponsor to achieve their objectives. This aspect of a sponsorship can best be termed exploitation. It is concerned with enhancing a sponsor's involvement above and beyond the basic terms of the contract. It is different from implementation in that implementation is concerned with executing those activities which arise from decisions regarding selection and exploitation. Exploitation, however, is not a licence for publicity overkill, but a recognition that sponsorship involvement provides a considerable promotional opportunity for the investor (Otker, 1988). It is therefore concerned with decisions as to how the profile of an event can be enhanced and can thus work in the interests of both sponsor and sponsored activity.

Observation of practice suggests that a common mistake made by early sponsorship users was that they treated sponsorship as if it were a traditional media purchase. In effect, they did nothing to support and exploit their sponsorship investment, with inevitably disappointing consequences. Such outcomes caused many early sponsors to question the effectiveness of sponsorship as a marketing tool. The reality, as was soon learned by successful users, is that buying the right to a specific sponsorship property will not of itself guarantee results. Exposure in sponsorship, unlike advertising, results from additional support and exploitation. Purchasing the sponsorship property rights merely gives the sponsor an opportunity to exploit the initial investment.

Experienced sponsors now fully recognise the importance of providing adequate funds to leverage their sponsorships, and that related costs must be built into the overall cost of the programme. Leveraging has been defined as:

> ... the additional effort, largely promotional, which must be invested by the sponsor in order to properly exploit the opportunity provided as a result of securing particular sponsorship rights (Meenaghan, 1991: 43).

The costs of leveraging the profile of the sponsorship can involve both financial and human investment. In 1995, the marketing budget to support the Murphy's Irish Open was £500,000 (Coleman, 1995).

From a position where many earlier sponsors spent very small sums on exploitation, the accepted industry norm today is that it is necessary to spend £1 on leveraging for every £1 spent on securing the sponsorship rights. More successful sponsors do, however, spend sums far in excess of this — for example, Philips spent a ratio of ten to one in supporting its investment on the Dire Straits sponsorship (Kohl and Otker, 1995). Similarly, Gross, Traylor and Schuman (1987) report that one of the major sponsoring companies worldwide, Anheuser-Busch, spends three dollars on leveraging for each dollar of fee sponsorship.

One of the key requirements of sponsorship management is to integrate the sponsorship programme into the company's overall marketing activities, rather than to isolate sponsorship as if it were "something different". The mistake, again often made by less experienced sponsors, is to undertake the sponsorship programme in glorious isolation, and thereby fail to capitalise on the natural synergies to be gained from operating an integrated approach to marketing communications.

MEASURING SPONSORSHIP RESULTS

A wide variety of objectives, involving multiple publics, is pursued via sponsorship involvement, and sponsors resort to varied methods of evaluating the effectiveness of their sponsorship investments (Meenaghan, 1983). Some widely-used methods of evaluation are discussed below.

Measuring the Level of Media Coverage Gained

The level of media coverage gained as a result of sponsorship involvement is frequently used by sponsors as an indicator of performance. Such evaluation involves measuring:

- The duration of television coverage
- Monitored radio coverage
- The extent of press coverage in terms of single column inches.

The monitoring of media coverage, effectively confined to indications of gross impressions and opportunities to see (OTS), is widely used as a proxy measure of sponsorship effectiveness, essentially because it is practicable. It provides the sponsor with tangible and comforting evidence of its publicity effects. However, the level of media coverage will only indicate the extent of publicity resulting from the sponsorship, and as such it is basically similar to indicating the level of advertising time or space bought. This measure on its own is not concerned with the audience reached and does not evaluate the effectiveness of the exposure gained.

Measuring Communications Effects in Sponsorship

As the communication objectives of awareness and image are widely sought in sponsorship programmes, subsequent evaluation focuses on the achievement of these objectives. In the case of awareness at either the corporate or brand level, various approaches to evaluation can be established. One such measure is the spontaneous/prompted awareness of the company or the brand, and while this is not a direct measure of sponsorship per se, it is often undertaken alongside dedicated sponsorship awareness studies as a proxy measure of success. Measuring spontaneous or prompted association of the sponsor with an activity is also a widely-used approach. An example of this form of research is shown in Table 25.3. This research, conducted by AGB Adelaide as part of its Sponsorcheck survey, shows which sponsors dominated particular categories of sponsorship over the year 1994 (AGB Sponsorcheck, 1995). The results provide an indication of

TABLE 25.3: TOP 15 BRANDS ASSOCIATED WITH SPONSORSHIP IN IRELAND

Sport	Company	All Adults %
Snooker	Benson & Hedges	54
Soccer	Opel	49
Golf	Carrolls	37
Horse racing	Budweiser	33
Olympics	Mars	26
Gaelic Football	Bank of Ireland	25
Pop/Rock Music	Coca-Cola	23
Cycling	Raleigh	22
Rock/Pop	2FM	21
Olympics	Coca-Cola	19
Golf	Murphy's	19
Equestrian	Kerrygold	19
Hurling	Bank of Ireland	17
Horse racing	Guinness	17
Athletics	Adidas	15
Tennis	Robinsons	14
Soccer	Mars	14
Athletics	Nike	12
Gaelic Football	Arnotts	12
Snooker	Carrolls	12
Classical Music	RTE	12
Soccer	Coca-Cola	11
Athletics	Lucozade	11

Source: Sponsorcheck, AGB Adelaide, January 1994–January 1995.

the sponsor's progress in exploiting a sponsorship programme and the threat posed by rival sponsors in the category, and thus are a most useful mechanism for tracking progress year by year in a sponsorship category over the life of a sponsorship programme. The results in Table 25.3 on their own do not, however, indicate the extent to which an activity (e.g. snooker), intrudes upon social consciousness, or the degree to which it does so relative to another activity (e.g. GAA Games). Other sections of the Sponsorcheck survey enable the sponsor to determine the popularity of an activity, based on participation rates for each activity, and also to relate the research results to information on respondents such as customer loyalty status and product usage.

Sponsorship image effects are achieved by ensuring high levels of association between a sponsor and an activity, a feature indicated on AGB Sponsorcheck's survey. The measurement of sponsorship image can be undertaken using either quantitative or qualitative research. One widely-used quantitative measurement approach is favourability scales, which indicate the degree to which consumers feel disposed towards a company or brand. Alternatively, sponsors use corporate or brand image research to indicate movement on desired dimensions of image. Qualitative research is less used in measuring image effects but can be particularly useful in indicating the image inherent in an activity, and can consequently be transferred to the sponsor in a sponsorship relationship.

Measuring the Sales Effects of Sponsorship

With specific methods of marketing communication, such as advertising or sponsorship, the task of attributing particular sales results to specific inputs is highly problematic. Clear lines of attribution are generally not possible because of the effects of external variables such as competitor activity and changing trading conditions, and company-controlled variables such as other marketing-mix inputs and the simultaneous usage of several communication methods in an orchestrated campaign. In certain instances, sales and sales-related effects can be sought and achieved. Bailey's Cream Liqueur's sponsorship of the Stately English Homes programme presented an ideal opportunity to provide 50,000 product tastings in appropriate surroundings (EIU, 1990). Similarly, sales results can be easily identified where an ethnic or neighbourhood festival provides an exclusive sponsorship opportunity. This is particularly true in the US where food companies such as Kentucky Fried Chicken sponsor such festivals. A local equivalent is provided where a company such as Guinness sponsors a festival or where Murphy's sponsors the Irish Open Golf Championship. Sales of the Murphy's brand have increased by 8–10 per cent over 1994 figures, achieving 5 per cent of the Irish stout market. Export sales rose by 24 per cent in 1994, with expected growth in 1995 of 60 per cent. These results follow a campaign in which sponsorship was a central feature, and they were obviously assisted by the relaying of the Irish Open to 170 countries on 10 television networks (Coleman, 1995). Another type of sales evaluation is used by a US telecommunications company that sponsors 400 local festivals and events in Southern California. Each event is analysed for sales leads and subsequent line activations. One such event led to 730 leads, resulting in 300 line activations, on which the profit per customer is calculated over a five-year period, giving the company a seven-fold return on its investment (Maischoff, 1995).

Other methods of sponsorship evaluation can include the monitoring of feedback from corporate guests and the collective wisdom of senior management. Indeed, many methods may be utilised simultaneously, given the range of objectives sought and publics targeted in the context of a single sponsorship campaign. Table 25.4 indicates the extent to which Irish sponsorship companies employ different methods of sponsorship evaluation.

TABLE 25.4: METHODS OF SPONSORSHIP EVALUATION USED BY IRISH SPONSORS

What methods do you use to measure the effectiveness of sponsorship afterwards?	
Method Used to Evaluate	**Percentage**
Degree of Media Coverage	64.1
Testing Awareness Before and After the Sponsorship	12.8
Sales Increase	33.3
Customer Feedback	69.2
Other	10.3

Source: O'Donoghue, B. (1989) Irish Sponsorship — Market Characteristics and Management Practice, unpublished MBS Thesis, UCD.

CONCLUSIONS

Commercial sponsorship represents a particularly potent marketing-communications medium. While its spectacular growth pattern can be attributed to a variety of external factors, such as government regulation and changing leisure trends, the development of the medium is testimony to the strength of corporate faith in its ability to achieve marketing objectives.

In order to maximise the efficiency of sponsorship, those charged with its management must have a clear vision of the role which it is intended to serve, and its capabilities relative to other methods of communication. Sponsorship must be subjected to rational patterns of management, involving specified objectives, vehicle selection against pre-determined criteria, creative exploitation and integration, and ongoing evaluation, in order to maximise the benefits clearly available from this flexible marketing-communications option.

REFERENCES

Bandle, A. (1989), "Selection Process of the Sponsors and the Objectives to Reach through Them", Strategic Sponsorship Management Conference, 16–17 November Montreux, Switzerland,.

Bridgewater, G. (1991): "Sports Case History 1 — The Canon League", *Sponsorship '91*, London: CSS International: 6–7.

Brown, A. (1995): "TGI Sponsortrack — A Practical Guide to the Evaluation of Sponsorship Opportunities", in Meenaghan, T. (ed.), *Researching Commercial Sponsorship*, Amsterdam: ESOMAR: 11–24.

Buckley, D. (1980): "Who Pays the Piper?", *Practice Review*, Spring 1980: 10–14.

Business Week (1987): "Nothing Sells Like Sport", 31 August: 42–7.

Coleman, S. (1995): "Taking a Sporting Swing to Sell Murphy's" *Irish Independent*, 6 July: 5 (Business Supplement).

Couzens, M. (1995): "Inside Intel! How Market Research showed Sponsorship's Potential to a First-time Sponsor", I.E.G. Event, Marketing Conference No. 12, 26–29 March, Chicago, IL.

Dinmore, F. (1980): "Cricket Sponsorship", *The Business Graduate*, (UK), Autumn: 68–72.

Economist Intelligence Unit (EIU) (1990): *Sponsoring the Arts: Strategies for the '90's*, EIU: London.

Gross, A., Traylor M.B. and Schuman P., (1987): "Corporate Sponsorship of Arts and Sports Events in North America", 40th ESOMAR Marketing Research Congress, Montreux, Switzerland, 13–17 November, Conference Proceeding, General Sessions.

IEG Sponsorship Report (1994): 13(24), December, Chicago: International Event Group.

Jones, M. and Dearsley, T. (1993): "Understanding Sponsorship", in Meenaghan T. (Ed.) *Researching Commercial Sponsorship*, Amsterdam: ESOMAR: 41–54.

Jones, R. (1995): "Mastercard Welcoming the World to the US: A Case Study of the World Cup Sponsorship", Paper presented at Sponsorship Europe '95 Conference, 6–7 April, Conrad Hilton, Brussels, Belgium.

Kohl, F. and Otker, T. (1995): "Sponsorship — Some Practical Experiences in Philips Consumer Electronics", in Meenaghan T. (Ed.), *Researching Commercial Sponsorship*, Amsterdam: ESOMAR: 55–74.

Maischoff, D. (1995): How L.A. Cellular Reaps a Seven-to-one Return on its Sponsorship Investment, I.E.G Event, Marketing Conference No. 12, 26–29 March, Chicago, IL.

Meenaghan, J.A., (1983): "Commercial Sponsorship", *European Journal of Marketing*, 17(7): 1–74.

Meenaghan, T. (1991), "Sponsorship — Its Role in the Marketing Communications Mix", *International Journal of Advertising*, 10: 35–47.

Mintel (1994): *Special Report on Sponsorship*, London: Mintel Publications.

Mulligan, P. (1995) RTE, Personal Discussion, July, Dublin.

O'Donoghue, B. (1989): *Irish Sponsorship — Market Characteristics and Management Practice*, unpublished MBS Thesis, University College Dublin

Otker, T. (1988): "Exploitation: The Key to Sponsorship Success", *European Research*, 16(2): 77–86.

Prazmark R. (1995): "Olympic Games — The Thrill of Victory and the Agony of Defeat", Paper presented at Sponsorship Europe '95 Conference, 6–7 April, Conrad Hilton, Brussels, Belgium.

Royal Philharmonic Orchestra (1974): *The Case for Sponsorship*, London: Royal Philharmonic Orchestra.

RTE (1995): Press office, Personal Discussion, Dublin.

Sedgwick, A. (1984): "Measuring the Value For Money of Sponsorship", Paper presented at Sponsorship in Sport, Arts and Leisure Conference, 6 November, RICS Westminster Centre, London, *European Study Conferences Ltd.*, 535–61.

Sponsorcheck, AGB Adelaide, Blackrock, Co. Dublin.

Sponsorship Research International (1994): Annual Estimates of Sponsorship Expenditure, London: SRI.

Ward, M. (1995): "Selling Change-Broadcast Sponsorship in a Multimedia World", Sponsorship Europe '95 Conference, 6–7 April Conrad Hilton Hotel, Brussels.

Young, D. (1984), "Developing a Sponsorship Strategy and Making it Work", Using Sponsorship Effectively Conference, Organised by Business Research International, 12–13 November, Café Royal, London.

26

Exhibiting Planning and Practice

David Shipley

INTRODUCTION

Exhibiting at trade shows is an important, exciting and growing communications medium. Managed effectively, it can provide numerous potent advantages. Prominent among these is that exhibiting enables suppliers to meet, strengthen relationships with, and promote products to, tightly targeted and keenly interested visitors, consisting of buyers and important purchasing influencers from the trade and both industrial and consumer audiences (Dudley, 1990; Shipley and Wong, 1993). Other important benefits are that exhibiting provides opportunities to conduct customer and competitor research, launch new products, rekindle interest in flagging products, build company and brand image, build staff morale and strengthen competitive status (Banting and Blenkhorn, 1974; Bello, 1992; Bonoma, 1983; Cavanaugh, 1976: Konikow, 1983; Tanner and Chonko, 1995; Shipley and Wong, 1993). Pursuit of these kinds of advantages has induced much participation in exhibiting among Irish companies. A recent survey by the Marketing Development Programme at UCD, on behalf of the Association of Advertisers in Ireland, found that 93 per cent of the Irish firms studied engage in exhibiting, 72 per cent had done so for over five years, and 76 per cent of them had increased their exhibiting expenditures during the past five years. Moreover, only 20 per cent of the participants experienced general dissatisfaction with exhibiting as a mode of promotion (AAI/MDP, 1995).

Consumers and small specialist retailers often visit exhibitions on buying trips. Hence, considerable volumes of products, such as furniture, antiques, jewellery, pottery and gift items, are sold at shows. Exhibiting is also a particularly important medium for accessing large audiences economically in overseas markets (Albaum et al., 1989; Jeannet and Hennessey, 1988; Paliwoda, 1993). However, exhibiting is a particularly effective promotions medium in industrial markets, where its influence on buying decisions is exceeded only by customer recommendation and personal selling (Parasuraman, 1981).

A principal advantage of exhibiting is that the visitors to shows are both interested and attentive. Whereas many consumers and small retailers attend shows to make purchases, industrial visitors seek to gain new ideas, product and technical information, to assess products and innovations, and to meet, interact with, and compare, potential vendors (Bello, 1992; Dudley, 1990). Alternatively, the objectives of exhibitors include meeting, nurturing, and ultimately converting, customers. Hence, the motives of exhibitors and visitors at shows strongly coincide. Moreover, while exhibiting can be costly in absolute terms, it can also be considerably more efficient than personal selling at generating leads (Browning and Adams, 1988; Hutt and Speh, 1992). For example, whereas in an average day, industrial salespersons may make around six calls, exhibiting can result in up to fifty leads (Hart, 1988).

Arguably the most important advantage of exhibiting, however, concerns audience composition. Very high proportions of exhibition visitors are not buyers but other key role players in the purchasing decision. Among larger retailers these include merchandisers and marketing managers, while among industrial customers they include engineers, quality managers and finance specialists. These types of personnel occupy key roles in the organisational buying process, particularly at the needs recognition, product-specification and supplier-evaluation stages. Indeed, 80 per cent, or more, of visitors are buying influencers (Trade Show Bureau, 1991). It is known that these key decision influencers do visit exhibitions as part of their information-search activity (Moriarty and Spekman, 1984). Moreover, elsewhere, potential suppliers often have major difficulties in identifying or gaining access to them, despite the obvious need to do so (Browning and Adams, 1988). Thus, a prime advantage of exhibiting is that it provides suppliers with opportunities to meet and display products to major and elusive purchasing-decision influencers (Bello and Lohtia, 1993; Williams et al., 1993).

In spite of the considerable and growing involvement with exhibiting by indigenous firms, very limited attention has been given to the subject by academics in Ireland. There is a considerable prescriptive literature and there is a modest empirical literature, but these have been largely focused on the US market. One researcher posited that exhibitors pursue a range of quantitative and qualitative objectives (Bonoma, 1983). This was verified in another study which also reported that firms set both selling and non-selling objectives (Kerin and Cron, 1987). A different investigation identified findings on objective-setting for exhibitions, show-selection influences and budget determination (Browning and Adams, 1988). Other researchers emphasised the need to tailor exhibiting tactics to fit objectives and phases in the customers' buying cycle (Bellizzi and Lipps, 1984). Important advice concerning exhibition evaluation was also provided (Lilien, 1983). This was augmented by later authors who provided a valuable set of exhibiting-performance measurement criteria (Herbig et al., 1994). A rare British study among domestic and export exhibitors identified findings about objectives, show-selection criteria, staff-selection criteria and budgeting methods (Shipley and Wong, 1993).

The insights provided in these earlier studies have helped to clarify understanding of exhibiting planning and practices. Nevertheless, large gaps in knowledge remain, especially about exhibiting in Ireland. This paper provides a planning framework to guide exhibiting decision-making, and it provides recent findings about exhibiting practice from Irish and British firms.

AN EXHIBITING PLANNING FRAMEWORK

Figure 26.1 illustrates the planning and implementation stages involved in effective exhibiting. Stage 1 is the specification of objectives, based on the role of exhibiting in the more general market and communications strategies. This is a crucial stage, since objectives communicate what is expected from the exhibiting programme, convey direction for the personnel involved, and set standards for evaluation and control.

Exhibiting objectives should be set for both selling and non-selling accomplishments (Bonoma, 1983, Kerin and Cron, 1987). The former relate directly to sales volume and revenue and may be short-term and/or long-term focused (Shipley and Wong, 1993). Examples of longer-term sales objectives concern numbers of leads generated or contacts established, whereas short-term selling objectives include numbers of sales presentations and orders sealed.

Astute managers also specify a complementary set of qualitative and quantitative non-selling objectives. Among the qualitative factors are requirements for image-building, matching rivals' show presence,

Exhibiting Planning and Practice

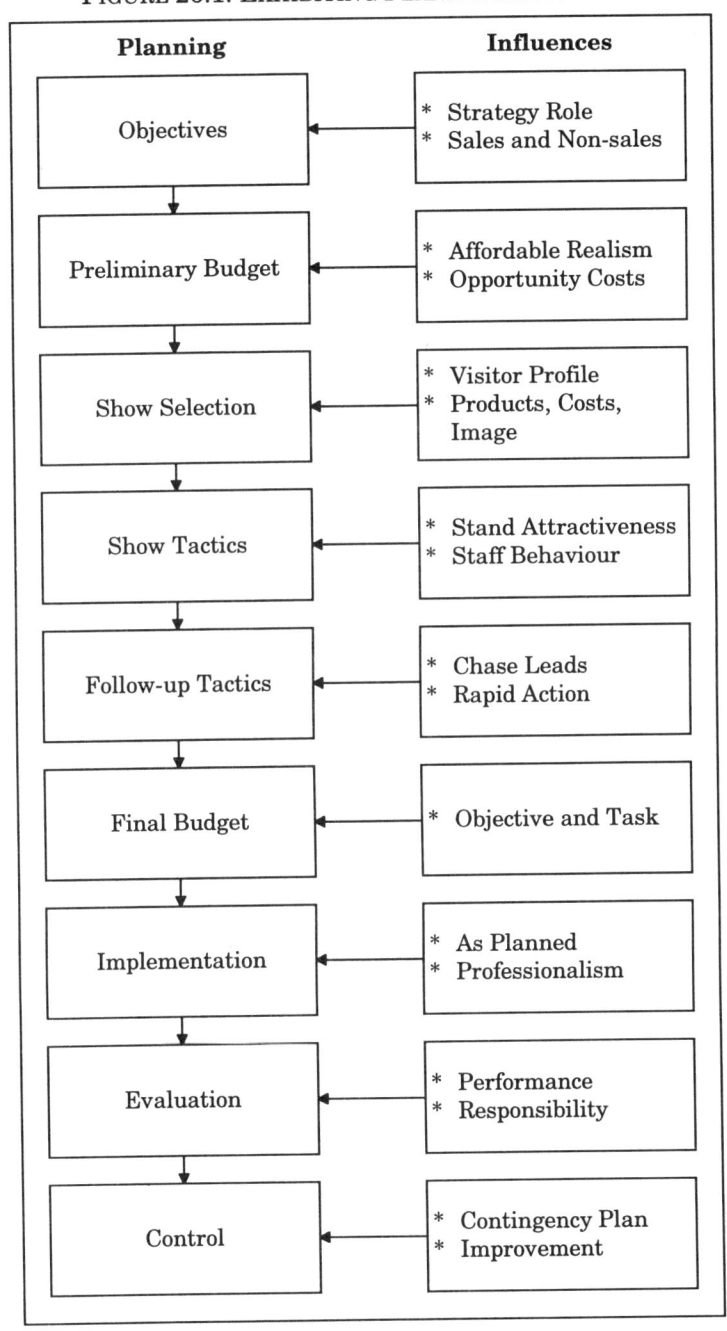

FIGURE 26.1: EXHIBITING PLANNING ACTIVITIES

Planning	Influences
Objectives	* Strategy Role * Sales and Non-sales
Preliminary Budget	* Affordable Realism * Opportunity Costs
Show Selection	* Visitor Profile * Products, Costs, Image
Show Tactics	* Stand Attractiveness * Staff Behaviour
Follow-up Tactics	* Chase Leads * Rapid Action
Final Budget	* Objective and Task
Implementation	* As Planned * Professionalism
Evaluation	* Performance * Responsibility
Control	* Contingency Plan * Improvement

Source: Shipley, D. and Wong, K. (1993): "Exhibiting Strategy and Implementation", *International Journal of Advertising*, 12: 119.

and conducting customer research. Quantitative non-selling objectives can include cost-control measures and measures of customer response to new products being launched at the show.

The second stage in the exhibiting planning process is the determination of the preliminary budget. The final budget cannot be estimated until most of the plan has been formed. The purpose of the preliminary budget is to guide the scope of the exhibition programme within the constraints of what resources can realistically be afforded. The costs of specific exhibitions vary enormously depending on products involved, show location, display and promotion activities, staff numbers involved, whether the show is an open one or private, whether it is regional, domestic or international, etc. Exhibiting costs also vary greatly with the scale of transportation involved, the amount and location of space rented, the scale of stand-design elaboration, the level of pre-promotion activity, staff travel and accommodation arrangements, and the scale of visitor entertainment provided. A matter of prime consideration is the opportunity costs of the time of personnel spent away from regular activities.

The monetary costs of exhibiting at an individual show in Ireland typically vary between £2,000 and £50,000 (AAI/MDP, 1995). However, costs incurred in attending some of the highly prestigious shows overseas in locations such as Cologne, Milan, Chicago, or Beijing can extend to £250,000 or more (Shipley and Wong, 1993) Hence, enormous care should be exercised when setting the preliminary budget, and the key determining factors should include the resources available and the objectives sought.

Stage 3 in exhibition planning is the selection of shows at which to be present. First, it is necessary to identify all of the various exhibitions that can be expected to satisfy the predefined objectives. This can be facilitated by obtaining and examining relevant directories and catalogues, exhibition-promotion literature, audit results from previous years, and so on. Second, since there are usually more potential shows than can be afforded on available budgets, and since it is necessary to select the most effective shows, it is necessary to assemble and apply a range of selection criteria. A wide range of sensible criteria has been identified (Dickinson and Faris, 1985; Kijewski et al., 1993; Shipley and Wong, 1993). However, particular attention needs to be given to the types of products exhibited at the show, the number and composition of visitors and exhibitors, the promotion done by the organisers, and the facilities, costs, prestige and location of the show.

The criteria can be used to compile a shortlist of potential exhibitions. The quality of the final decision can then be substantially enhanced by gaining deeper knowledge of the candidate exhibitions. Many managers attend a show as a visitor to assess its attributes before selecting it. Other managers ask searching questions among previous visitors and exhibitors. Insights gained in these ways can then be deepened by requiring exhibition organisers to provide evidence of the quantity and composition of visitors in previous years, and accurate information about which exhibitors have already made firm reservations for attending the upcoming show.

Stage 4 is the planning of tactics for the show selected. Among the many issues that require attention are the design and site location of the exhibiting stand, personnel selection and activities, customer-interaction techniques, and the market-research activity to be conducted at the show. Stand design is a major determinant in successfully attracting visitors to the stand. Appropriate tactics include ensuring that the stand has an extensive frontal spread; is comfortable and uncluttered; is made to be distinctive with striking colour schemes and slogans, moving objects, flashing lights, etc.; advertising the attendance of a popular celebrity; and offering generous hospitality — although care needs to be taken to avoid diverting attention away from the products and benefits exhibited. Stand design can be enhanced by recruiting the services of specialist consultants, although this can adversely affect costs (Dudley, 1988).

Stand location is also an important determinant of the number of visitors to a particular stand or booth. It can be advantageous to select sites in high-traffic locations, such as those on major thoroughfares or intersections, close to refreshment facilities, or adjacent to the market leader's stand. The best locations usually command higher costs, although these may be bargained down by confirming an early booking. Nevertheless, it is necessary to make a cost versus site-size and location trade-off.

Another key determinant of exhibiting success is the number, composition and experience of personnel deployed on the stand. Selling or relationship-building efforts can be threatened at exhibitions since salespeople, trained and experienced in the field, sometimes encounter problems in adapting to the show environment (Bello and Lohtia, 1993). Hence, safeguards need to be established. To begin with, staff should be specifically trained for exhibition work. Also, as exhibition visitors are drawn from multiple functional specialisations, the stand team should include not just salespeople, but specialist finance, technical and other experts who are used to conversing in the specialist language of multifunctional visitors. Another aid to effectiveness is to keep staff fresh and alert by ensuring that they take frequent breaks in rotation, so as to relieve them from what is often tedious and exhausting work. Personnel should be encouraged to keep a register of all contacts established, and to exchange business cards with all visitors. Many visitors leave or discard much of the literature they collect at the exhibition. To counter this, cards and literature should be dispatched to visitors' addresses from the show, and timed to be there upon the visitors return to work.

The fifth planning stage is the determination of effective follow-up tactics to exploit fully opportunities created at the event. Leads need to be pursued rapidly before the interest of visitors wanes, and to preempt rivals. Contacts may be telephoned or visited, and brochures, samples and so on should be dispatched to augment literature provided at the exhibition. Other relevant opportunities should also be used to advantage. Examples would include publicising a major sale, reporting sales to a new country or describing the role played by a major celebrity.

Stage 6 is budget finalisation. Various techniques are available for this, although the most effective is the "objective and task" approach. Other approaches are quicker, simpler and cheaper, but the objective and task technique is the only approach that systematically accounts for objectives, the costs of the exhibition programme and relevant conditions (Jobber, 1995). By this method, the final budget is set at the level of the aggregate estimated costs of the exhibiting tasks planned to achieve the objectives.

The seventh stage of the process is implementation. This should follow the planned programme as closely as possible, although some flexibility may be required to cater for contingencies arising. Painstaking thoroughness is required at this stage, as is complete professionalism.

The penultimate stage is the important task of evaluating each exhibition attended and the overall annual programme. Effective evaluation involves forming comparisons of performance against objectives, costs and conditions in the market and at each show. Important quantitative measures include numbers of stand visitors, numbers of leads and enquiries, costs per head and enquiry, numbers and values of orders taken, and costs per order. Qualitative criteria include the cultivation of new or existing relationships, the worth of competitor intelligence, and reactions to new products (Jobber, 1995).

Efforts must be made to identify the causes of any gaps between the measures applied and performance attained. Problems might be a result of market developments or of planning or implementation mistakes. Steps must be taken to uncover what went wrong, the reasons why and who was responsible. If an agency was used, action should be taken to identify which party was responsible.

Finally, corrective control action may be required to avoid future repetition of errors and to build effectiveness. Control may be confined to improving individual parts of the programme, or the entire strategy may need to be modified. Common problems are over-ambitious objectives-setting or an absence of objectives entirely (Herbig et al., 1994). When an implementation error has occurred, it may be necessary to change the staff involved or to provide tailored training to enhance effectiveness.

RECENT RESEARCH FINDINGS

This section provides insights on exhibiting and exhibiting management provided by Irish and British managers. The two sets of findings are not strictly comparable, because of differences in the research methods employed, the questions examined, and the samples studied. Nevertheless, strikingly similar results emerged from the two projects and, given the sparseness of other results, they can be considered broadly representative of exhibiting management practices in the two countries. In some cases, data are given for only one of the samples. This is because corresponding data were not sought in the other survey. The Irish data were collected in 42 in-depth interviews with Irish exhibitors. These were from firms in a range of industries. As an indicator of firms size, 64 per cent of the respondents had fewer than 50 employees, 22 per cent had between 50 and 199 workers, while 14 per cent had more than 200 employees. For further information see AAI/MDP (1995). The British findings were gathered in a postal survey of 124 domestic exhibitors in a range of engineering industries. By number of employees, 22 per cent had fewer than 50, 24 per cent had between 50 and 199, while 54 per cent had 200 or more. Further information on methodology and sample composition was presented in Shipley and Wong (1993). Table 26.1 presents the main reasons why the Irish respondents engage in exhibiting as a mode of communication. These factors clearly indicate a blend of selling and non-selling motives.

Table 26.2 presents the set of exhibiting objectives specified by the British sample. Although this list is longer than that shown in Table

26.1, the first five ranked factors are the same in both instances. The British results also include a mix of selling and non-selling factors. Interestingly, however, taking orders is ranked twelfth out of thirteen objectives, supporting the general consensus that sales are rarely made at industrial exhibitions.

TABLE 26.1: REASONS WHY IRISH COMPANIES ENGAGE IN EXHIBITING

	Rank by Frequency
Meet New Customers	1
Promote Existing Products	2
Enhance Company Image	3
Launch New Products	4 Joint
Interact with Customers	4 Joint

Note: n = 42.

TABLE 26.2: EXHIBITING OBJECTIVES OF BRITISH COMPANIES

	Rank by Importance
Meet New Customers	1
Enhance Company Image	2
Interact with Customers	3
Promote Existing Products	4
Launch New Products	5
Gain Competitor Intelligence	6
Gain Edge on Non-Exhibitors	7
Keep Up with Competitors	8
Enhance Personnel Morale	9
Interact with Distributors	10
General Market Research	11
Take Sales Orders	12
Meet New Distributors	13

Note: n = 124.

Table 26.3 displays the main criteria used to select particular exhibitions by both samples of firms. The two sets of criteria are of different length because of research methodology differences. However, they do contain considerable similarity. Both samples apply multiple criteria and both samples support the findings in Tables 26.1 and 26.2 which show that both selling and non-selling considerations are characteristic of exhibiting planning. Short-term sales was not a prime consideration in either sample, while non-selling criteria were ranked highly by both sets of firms. Both assigned some importance to types and numbers of visitors and exhibitors, estimated costs and organiser's promotion activity, while the British firms particularly were concerned with characteristics of the show such as location, timing and duration.

TABLE 26.3: EXHIBITION-SELECTION CRITERIA OF IRISH AND BRITISH COMPANIES

Irish Firms n = 42	Rank by Frequency	British Firms n = 124	Rank by Frequency
Number and Profile of Attendees	1	Types of Visitors	1
		Types of Products Exhibited	2
Cost of Exhibiting	2	Estimated Number of Leads	3
Reputation of Exhibition or Our Past Experience	3	Estimated Number of Visitors	4
		Estimated Costs Involved	5
Other Exhibitors Attending	4	Estimated Exhibitors' Publicity	6
		Types of Exhibitors	7
Level of Organiser's Promotion	5	Prestige of Event	8
Space Available at Exhibition	6	Exhibition Location	9
		Numbers of Exhibitors	10
Industry Relevance of Exhibition	7	Estimated Sales at Venue	11
		Facilities at Venue	12
		Frequency of Event	13
		Duration of Event	14
		Date of Event	15
		Organiser's Reputation	16

The Irish companies were asked to comment on the types of information required to facilitate successful exhibiting participation. Table 26.4 presents the results which underscore the importance of obtaining knowledge about audience size and the mix of exhibitors. The former clearly influences the in-show promotional research of potential exhibitors, while the latter has clear implications concerning the competitive impact of attending.

TABLE 26.4: IRISH COMPANY PERCEPTIONS OF INFORMATION REQUIREMENTS FOR SUCCESSFUL EXHIBITING

	Rank by Frequency
Anticipated Attendance Numbers	1
Other Confirmed Exhibitors	2
Pre-exhibition Promotion Schedule	3
Venue and Facilities Details	4
Calendar of All Exhibitions for the Year	5
Analysis of Exhibiting Costs	6

Note: n = 42.

Information concerning exhibiting-staff selection criteria was provided by the British respondents. The data shown in Table 26.5 emphasise the importance of general sales experience and the need for personnel to have established customer networks. The former can

TABLE 26.5: EXHIBITION-STAFF SELECTION CRITERIA OF BRITISH COMPANIES

	Rank by Importance
Sales Experience	1
Established Customer Contacts	2
Technical Know-how	3
Other Functions Know-how	4
Personal Characteristics	5
Exhibiting Experience	6
Marketing Experience	7
General Knowledge	8
Foreign Language	9

Note: n = 124.

help with stand work with visitors, whereas the latter may play an important role in customer entertainment. However, the results also underline the points made earlier about the necessity for exhibiting experience and multifunctional staff participation.

The British respondents were also asked about their exhibiting budget determination. The findings in Table 26.6 reveal that the objective and task method is the most commonly used method. This is sensible as it requires consideration of all relevant factors. Conversely, all of the other methods cited risk ignoring exhibiting objectives, market conditions and/or competitive conditions.

TABLE 26.6: EXHIBITING BUDGET ALLOCATION METHODS OF BRITISH COMPANIES

	Rank by Frequency
Objective and Task	1
What We Can Afford	2
Last Year's Budget plus Inflation Premium	3
Percentage of Sales	4
Match Competitors	5
Same as Last Year	6

Note: n = 124.

Finally, the Irish sample was asked to indicate what advice they would offer to newcomers exhibiting. The answers given may indicate some of the pitfalls encountered by the respondents, as well as being of value to newcomers. The insightful comments provided (in some cases abridged by the author) are listed below:

- "Ensure a good position in the exhibition hall"
- "You may need to negotiate floor space"
- "Be aware of organisers who promise one thing and don't deliver"
- "Ensure the exhibition organiser has a good reputation"
- "Ensure the exhibition is relevant to your company"
- "Make sure you need to exhibit and that you couldn't use another promotional medium"
- "Ensure that the exhibition is included in the overall marketing strategy"

- "Evaluate the full costs involved in the exhibition including opportunity costs"

- "Be professional, ensure that staff are properly briefed and trained for the exhibition"

- "Know who your target market is"

- "Ensure that you have insurance cover"

- "Ensure that proper security is available for your equipment"

- "Beware of arrogant organisers insisting that you pay twelve months in advance"

- "Ensure that good lighting and electrical facilities are available"

- "Use large photographs"

- "Ensure that you have an exhibition plan and keep to the objectives".

SUMMARY AND CONCLUSIONS

Exhibiting is an important and effective means of communicating with buyers and buying influencers in distribution channels and a wide range of consumer and industrial markets. It provides powerful benefits for participants, and its incidence in most countries, including Ireland, is in *long*-term growth. A planning framework to guide exhibiting practice was provided in the second section of this paper, while the third section reported some of the exhibiting practices of Irish and British participants. Where relevant comparisons of the research findings were attempted, there was considerable commonality in the results. Moreover, there was also as much overlap with findings reported in studies in the US. The findings presented are also in broad accord with prescriptions concerning effective exhibiting practice in the relevant literature. A tentative conclusion is that astute planning is characteristic of exhibiting internationally.

Sound pragmatic advice for exhibiting practices as given by Irish participants was presented above. A few additional suggestions are offered by the author:

- Decide the most effective role for exhibiting within the broader marketing and communications plans.

- Evaluate all of the opportunity costs of exhibiting.

- Set and adhere to exhibiting objectives.

- Set selling and non-selling objectives, both quantitative and qualitative.

- Set a realistic preliminary budget to guide the exhibiting programme.

- Decide and conform to a set of criteria for selecting the most productive exhibitions.

- Be meticulous in tactical planning for exhibiting, especially with regard to stand location, design and promotion, and to personnel attributes and behaviour.

- Act quickly for effective follow-up, chase leads and maximise publicity.

- Implement the programme in accordance with the plan, but leave scope to meet contingencies flexibly.

- Set the final budget by the objective and task method.

- Evaluate performance against objectives, costs and the conditions encountered.

- Learn from experience and improve for the future.

Finally, as well as being potentially costly, gruelling and tedious, exhibiting does provide opportunities for fun. It is also a major aid to selling effectiveness, especially in the longer term.

REFERENCES

Association of Advertisers in Ireland, (1995): *Report on Exhibitors' Satisfaction with Irish Trade Shows and Exhibitions and Guidelines for Successful Exhibition Participation*, prepared by the Marketing Development Programme, UCD.

Albaum, G., Strandskov, J., Duerr, E. and Dowd, L. (1989): *International Marketing and Export Management*, Wokingham: Addison-Wesley.

Banting, P. and Blenkhorn, D. (1974): "The Role of Industrial Trade

Shows", *Industrial Marketing Management*, 3: 285–95.

Bellizzi, J. and Lipps, D. (1984): "Managerial Guidelines for Trade Show Effectiveness", *Industrial Marketing Management*, 13: 49–52.

Bello, D. (1992): "Industrial Buyer Behaviour at Trade Shows", *Journal of Business Research*, 25: 59–80.

Bello, D. and Lohtia, R. (1993): "Improving Trade Show Effectiveness by Analysing Attendees", *Industrial Marketing Management*, 22: 311–18.

Bonoma, T. (1983): "Get More Out of Your Trade Shows", *Harvard Business Review*, 61: 75–83.

Browning, J. and Adams, R. (1988): "Trade Shows: An Effective Promotional Tool for the Small Industrial Business", *Journal of Small Business Management*, 26(4): 31–6.

Cavanaugh, S. (1976): "Setting Objectives and Evaluating the Effectiveness of Trade Show Exhibits", *Journal of Marketing*, 40: 100–103.

Dickinson, J. and Faris, A. (1985): "Firms with Large Market Shares and Product Lines Rate Shows Highly", *Marketing News*, 10 May: 14.

Dudley, J. (1988): *How to Promote Your Own Business*, London: Kogan Page.

Dudley, J. (1990): *Successful Exhibiting*, London: Kogan Page.

Hart, N. (1988): *Practical Advertising and Publicity*, Maidenhead: McGraw Hill.

Herbig, P., O'Hara, B. and Palumbo, F. (1994): "Measuring Trade Show Effectiveness: An Effective Exercise" *Industrial Marketing Management*, 23: 165–70.

Hutt, M. and Spek T, (1992): *Business Marketing Management*, Orlando, FL: Dryden.

Jeannet, J. and Hennessey, H. (1988): *International Marketing Management: Strategies and Cases*, Boston, MA: Houghton Mifflin.

Jobber, D. (1995): *Principles and Practice of Marketing*, London: McGraw-Hill.

Kerin, R. and Cron, W. (1987): "Assessing Trade Show Functions and Performance: An Exploratory Study", *Journal of Marketing*, 51: 87–94.

Kijewski, V., Yoon, E. and Young, G. (1993): "How Exhibitors Select

Trade Shows", *Industrial Marketing Management*, 22: 287–98.

Konikow, R. (1983): *How to Participate Profitably in Trade Shows*, Chicago, IL: Dartnell.

Lilien, G. (1983): "A Descriptive Model of the Trade Show Budgeting Process", *Industrial Marketing Management*, 12: 25–9.

Moriarty, R. and Spekman, R. (1984): "An Empirical Investigation of the Information Sources Used during the Industrial Buying Process", *Journal of Marketing Research*, 21: 137–47.

Paliwoda, S. (1993): *International Marketing*, Oxford: Butterworth-Heinemann.

Parasuraman, A. (1981): "The Relative Importance of Industrial Promotions Tools", *Industrial Marketing Management*, 10: 277–81.

Shipley, D. and Wong, K. (1993): "Exhibiting Strategy and Implementation", *International Journal of Advertising*, 12: 117–30.

Tanner, J. and Chonko, L. (1995): "Trade Show Objectives — Management and Staffing Practices", *Industrial Marketing Management*, 24(4): 257–64.

Trade Show Bureau (1991): *Trade Show Success Indicators: Audience Quality, 1984–89*, Research Report No, AC/22, Denver: Trade Show Bureau.

Williams, J., Gopalakrishna, S. and Cox, J. (1993): "Trade Show Guidelines for Smaller Firms", *Industrial Marketing Management*, 22: 265–76.

27
Direct Marketing — Irish Perspectives

Michael McGowan

Direct marketing is gradually becoming established as a routine part of promotional and marketing activity in Ireland. Its development in Ireland, while relatively late by international standards, has largely mirrored the patterns evident in the main centres of direct marketing activity abroad: strong growth in usage by the financial services sector, and then slower diffusion into other sectors such as transport, travel, leisure and the packaged-goods sector. Ireland however, unlike the UK and the US, has a weak mail-order tradition and this would have somewhat constrained the growth of direct marketing in the 1960s through to the 1980s.

The main period of growth has been the first half of the 1990s, with an active direct-marketing agency sector emerging, as well as the adoption of direct marketing in the retailing sector, and the diffusion of database marketing techniques into the consumer services and business-to-business sector. This paper examines the factors that have led to the growth of direct marketing in Ireland, and assesses its likely future development. In all probability, the future of direct marketing in Ireland will be tied closely to its development internationally, and particularly to the electronic and on-line media revolutions that are taking place. Firstly, it is important to examine the nature of direct marketing in terms of its varying definitions, its distinguishing characteristics, and the media that combine to make direct-marketing communications possible.

THE CHALLENGE OF DEFINITION

While it is useful to examine the definition of a subject, in the case of direct marketing, one finds that there is no single, agreed, all-encompassing definition which is generally accepted. Broadly, one can discern two approaches to defining direct marketing. The first, which might be called the media-oriented approach, attempts to explain direct marketing in terms of the media deployed, the ensuing interaction with customers and the all important response. Typical of this approach are the following definitions:

> Direct marketing is a generic term for the use to which all media can be put in order to generate a direct communication with a potential, or existing customer (Rowney, 1995: 19).

> An interactive system of marketing which uses one or more advertising media to effect a measurable response at any location (Jenkins, 1989: 4).

These definitions present direct marketing primarily as a set of media options that create a path to the customer and bring back a response: a two-way communication channel that delivers tactical promotional or communication results. This view of direct marketing has meant that in practice it will be used for short-term purposes and may not be seen to offer a long-term strategic approach to managing customers and markets. While these definitions might reflect the way in which direct marketing is applied in practice, they do not represent the overall philosophy of the direct marketing system.

An alternative approach that is more conceptually oriented explains direct marketing as a way of delivering customer satisfaction, and is altogether more holistic than the approach detailed above. Two examples of definitions that attempt to give direct marketing a conceptual basis (even perhaps a direct-marketing philosophy) are offered:

> Any activity which creates and exploits a direct relationship with the customer (Bird, 1989: 8).

> Recognition of customers as individuals, with careful attention to personal likes and dislikes is of course, the ultimate goal of direct marketing (McCorkell, 1992: 6).

These definitions, while not altogether explicit, do imply that direct marketing has a strategic role to play in delivering customer satisfaction, and is more than the sum of the various media used. At best, the definitions recognise more the goals than the substance of direct marketing. The differences between the two definitional stances are worth recognising, in that they imply that individual direct marketers may be likely to view the content, role and value of direct marketing quite differently — namely, either as a range of media or as a complete marketing system.

THE DEFINING CHARACTERISTICS OF DIRECT MARKETING

Definitions are a limited basis through which to get insights into any subject, and this is certainly the case with direct marketing. It is therefore better to examine the "hallmarks" or characteristics of direct marketing, where one can begin to recognise the foundations of a very powerful discipline. A useful classification of such characteristics was produced by McCorkell (1992) and it is broadly followed in the discussion which ensues. Any classification must seek to determine what constitutes direct-marketing activity and what a direct-marketing system should look like. The four characteristics presented below are likely to be found in any direct-marketing activity or system. See Figure 27.1 for further elaboration.

1) *Targeting* — A term often misused by direct marketers but which refers to the objective of communicating with, and serving, customers using group or individual-specific information. Theoretically, this means that marketers can tailor offerings and communications to the marketplace, avoiding wastage and maximising customer satisfaction.

2) *Interaction and Feedback* — Direct-marketing activity should involve the receiver (or the customer/prospect) actively interacting with both the communications received and with the sender (or the seller) as the source of this communication. This is a crucial aspect of direct-marketing promotional communications in terms of getting a response, and distinguishes the activity from most other communications. It is by identifying this characteristic that one can recognise that the emerging electronic-communications media are pure direct media, providing enormous scope for interaction and real-time feedback.

3) *Control and Measurement* — This refers to a scientific approach to developing direct communications, and offers the potential for subsequent tracking and measurement of results and productivity. This aspect of direct marketing has also given rise to the formulaic approach to developing direct-marketing communications.

4) *Continuity* — The strategic aspect of direct marketing that focuses on the need to develop long-term or lifetime relationships with

customers, supported by current and historical data and continuous communication. This characteristic now finds practical expression through the development of customer retention and loyalty programmes, aided by database marketing techniques. (There should of course be an intent to create a direct relationship with the customer).

FIGURE 27.1: THE CHARACTERISTICS OF DIRECT MARKETING

Targeting	Communicating with identifiable individuals or locations
	Data and information about individuals and locations is collected, recorded, and stored
	Messages and product/service offerings can be tailored to suit subgroups and individuals and this process should improve as more data is collected
	A wide range of customer contact points is used
Interaction and Feedback	The Receiver actively participates in a communication/transaction
	The objective of the Sender is almost always to receive a response, e.g. an enquiry, a referral, the provision of information
Control and Measurement	A scientific approach is used to generate response
	Responses are subjected to counting, tracking (often using "source codes")
	Response levels affect cost and efficiency levels
	Detailed response analysis is used to segment audiences
	Predictive analysis using historical data is used to improve customisation and to increase marketing expenditure planning
Continuity	The objective is to win long-term customer loyalty through developing a one-to-one relationship with the customer. (Alternatively expressed as maximising the "lifetime" value of the customer). Data gathering that facilitates relationship building is ongoing

These characteristics are not present in every direct marketing activity or system — probably far from it. However, they represent an ideal to work towards, notwithstanding individual market and industry contexts. By examining the characteristics, it soon becomes obvious that direct marketing is more than the sum of the many promotional-type communications that form the direct-marketing media mix.

THE MEDIA OF DIRECT MARKETING

As this discussion cannot possibly examine in detail the range of individual media used in direct marketing, it is therefore proposed to focus on the main types of media employed. It is now possible to argue that all media can be classified as direct-marketing media including even the mass-marketing mainstay of broadcast television. In determining the likely number of direct media, it is not so much a question of whether a medium is first and foremost a direct marketing medium, but the extent to which it accommodates the techniques of direct-marketing communication. What is interesting about the listing in Figure 27.2 is the number and type of electronic media that can now be regarded as direct media.

FIGURE 27.2: THE MEDIA OF DIRECT MARKETING

Print Media	Electronic Media	Distribution Media*
• Direct Mail (addressed and unaddressed)	• Telephone (and associated technologies)	• Lists
• Press (Direct Response Advertising)	• Facsimile	• Door-to-Door
• Leaflets/Inserts/Flyers/ Bangtails	• Television	• Referral Systems
• Posters	• Radio	• Electronic Networks
• Catalogues	• Electronic Catalogues	• On-pack or via physical products
• On-pack	• Computer-Diskettes/ CD-ROM	
	• Computer On-line Marketplaces	
	• Electronic Kiosks	

* The traditional dichotomy of print and electronic leads to the exclusion of other "media" which may essentially be described as "distribution" media.

In reality, there are many direct-marketing media, some of them specific to particular industries. For example, an insert (print medium) can be distributed at counter-tops (i.e. "take-ones"), or placed in or on the product (i.e. on-pack). One of the challenges facing the direct marketer is to find the distribution channels and contact points which will deliver a message directly to a prospect or customer. The new emerging electronic media, and in particular, on-line computer-to-computer communications, present many new media options.

TRENDS IN DIRECT MARKETING MEDIA

Direct mail still remains the primary direct marketing medium in Ireland and is set to grow substantially as list availability improves. The business-to-business list infrastructure in Ireland would be considered good, while the complete opposite is the case regarding consumer lists. If one uses direct mail volume as the primary yardstick to indicate the scale of direct marketing activity, the conclusion at present would be that development in Ireland is slow by international standards, as can be see in Table 27.1.

TABLE 27.1: ADDRESSED DIRECT-MAIL MARKET — ADDRESSED MAIL VOLUME PER HEAD OF POPULATION, 1993

Market	Volume per Head of Population
Switzerland	105
Belgium	86
Germany	67
France	64
Sweden	62
Denmark	51
Norway	49
Finland	44
UK	42
Spain	34
Ireland	16
Portugal	11

Source: Association of European Postal Administrations (1994): *Postal Direct Marketing Services Survey*, Dublin: General Post Office.

Telemarketing as a direct marketing medium is showing strong growth in Ireland, with significant developments in specific areas of business activity. In particular, it is used by organisations in a range of industries, for both in-bound and out-bound lead generation, customer servicing and information gathering. There is also an increasing use of the telephone for selling and order-taking, with many business-to-business marketers setting up a dedicated sales desk as a cost-effective, service-efficient alternative to traditional sales rep activity. More recently, the Irish economy has seen the establishment of (wholly) telephone-based marketing systems in the financial services and computer software industries. The growing sophistication of Ireland's digital fibre-optic telecommunications system has led to the establishment of significant numbers of telemarketing operations by international companies (Glover, 1994). A further expression of the potential offered by direct marketing lies in the continuing application of interactive telephone technology to enquiry and ordering transactions as is illustrated in part in Table 27.2.

TABLE 27.2: GROWTH IN FREEPHONE USAGE — REPUBLIC OF IRELAND

	Freephone Usage Trends in Republic of Ireland	
	Numbers in Service	Traffic Volume
1990/1991	380	1.0m
1991/1992	594	1.9m
1992/1993	770	2.9m
1993/1994	1,032	4.4m
1994/1995	1,418	6.6m

Source: Telecom Éireann Freephone, 1995.

FACTORS THAT HAVE INFLUENCED THE GROWTH OF DIRECT MARKETING IN IRELAND

A variety of factors that have influenced the growth of direct marketing in Ireland can be identified, both within the industry and outside it. The factors that influence the emergence and growth of an entire industry will be many and will be complex in terms of their interactions. The industry itself has made significant efforts to promote direct marketing. The task of increasing Irish businesses' use of direct marketing at both tactical and strategic levels has been an onerous one. This can be attributed partly to the restricted list availability, but particularly to the high traditional fixed cost of production in the print media, to a lack of professional direct marketing expertise at individual-company level and to a slowness in adopting database marketing technologies. At the consumer level, it could be argued that there is an unwillingness on the part of marketers to inflict volumes of direct mail or intrusive telemarketing on a conservative and discerning Irish public. The industry itself actively promotes direct marketing through the Irish Direct Marketing Association (IDMA), and is probably unique in Europe in its willingness to adopt strict codes of behaviour for its members. A well-regulated industry will therefore grow more gradually, but on a sounder footing, and will ultimately earn greater respect from business and from the end markets.

The direct-marketing industry in Ireland, like its counterparts around the world, has had many external influences. These are general trends, which are not specific to Ireland, and which facilitate the promotion and justify the adoption of direct-marketing techniques, media and systems. In the consumer sector, rising media costs caused many marketers and their advertising agencies to consider alternatives to the traditional mass media. A result of this has been the increasing use of direct-response print advertisements, "double duty" advertising and combined sales-promotion and direct-marketing campaigns.

Direct marketing offers a more accountable way of spending marketing budgets than does traditional above-the-line advertising activity; hence it has become an attractive option for managers. It should be recognised, of course, that the fact that direct expenditure is more accountable does not automatically mean that it leads to superior results, a point often overlooked by direct marketing zealots. Direct-marketing media generally are less inflationary than the traditional mass media of print and television. For example, postage costs in Ireland have remained relatively stable over the past five years, telephone costs continue to fall, and the cost of printing and the associated (re)production activities have fallen quite dramatically during the first half of the 1990s. A further important influence on the growth of direct marketing has been the emergence of service-based industries and an increasing emphasis on the service aspects of industries that market physical products. Typical of the former are the direct-marketing systems associated with the leisure/travel, financial services, local services and business service industries. Examples of the latter include the growing acceptance by consumers of direct selling of computer hardware and software.

TECHNOLOGY DEVELOPMENTS

The influence of technology on direct marketing has been, and continues to be, profound. Of all the possible influences on the direct-marketing industry, technology developments will probably be greatest as we move into the twenty-first century. It is becoming progressively more cost-effective to store, analyse and transmit large volumes of data using computer database technology. This will enable companies in the consumer goods and services sectors (where data volume can be enormous) to make more use of databases, and will in turn lead to increases in direct-mail and telemarketing activity. Another effect will be that organisations will, in time, be able to analyse and segment large customer databases cheaply and quickly, using, for example, techniques such as Massive Parallel Processing.[1]

There is also increasing use being made of databases by organisations in the business-to-business sector. Typical is the use of contact management systems by the salesforce, which in turn generates demand for lists, and subsequently direct mail. As database software prices fall, the adoption rate will increase, which in turn will lead to increases in direct-marketing activity. The ability to centralise data, while retaining the capability to distribute it quickly and accurately within and outside the organisation using computer and telecommunications networks, is also assisting the growth of direct marketing. The nature of computer and telecommunications network technology is such that it allows an organisation to control customer data centrally, yet ensure that it is kept up-to-date and is available at all points of customer contact. This provides an important and useful infrastructural foundation for an organisation to manage its customer base using direct-marketing principles.

Another technology development, which is influencing both the rate and direction of growth in direct marketing, relates broadly to the print and publishing area. Because of the diffusion of new printing methods it has become cheaper to produce both large (and — importantly — small) volumes of printed material, thereby encouraging organisations to consider using direct mail more frequently. Generally, promotional design processes are becoming more flexible and are available to a widening audience. It is now possible for small and medium-sized companies to manage well-targeted print communications partially, if not wholly, in-house. This makes direct marketing, particularly in the form of direct mail and direct response advertising, a reality for organisations that would traditionally have shunned it.

---

[1] Massive Parallel Processing (MPP): A process whereby a computer can process data in parallel — i.e. a number of processors can work on a problem simultaneously. The system can involve multiple processors in a single computer or a parallel networking technique that is, computers (e.g. PCs) can be linked to work in parallel. MPP's advantage is that it facilitates very rapid retrieval and analysis of large amounts of data and will make it possible to deal with very complex database analyses quickly and cost-effectively.

THE BENEFITS ASSOCIATED WITH USING DIRECT MARKETING

Regardless of the external influences or the technology developments that are impacting on the growth of direct marketing, it was only when particular benefits were recognised and experienced by potential users that the sector began to show strong and reliable growth in Ireland. Some of the benefits that can be associated with the successful implementation of a direct marketing programme or system are listed below:

- Improved accountability for advertising and promotional expenditure.

- Communications expenditure wastage is reduced through better targeting.

- Direct marketing media have tended to remain relatively less inflationary than the traditional mass-media mix, and therefore deliver more cost-effective communications.

- Profitability can be improved through adhering to the "lifetime" value principle (and focusing on customer loyalty).

- Direct marketing media are usually inherently flexible and suit short-horizon selling environments. For example, telemarketing activity can be increased at very short notice, or a direct-mail campaign developed quickly to take advantage of a short-term opportunity. This aspect will appeal, in particular, to small companies that require fast response with maximum results at relatively low cost.

- The value of the information that direct-marketing activity generates can be enormous in terms of identifying commercial opportunities and prospect and customer needs. Also, the organisation of data, made possible by the use of marketing databases, can greatly enhance a company's relationship with its customers in terms of the quality and frequency of contact.

THE FUTURE FOR DIRECT MARKETING

A number of key pointers to the future of direct marketing can be identified:

- Interactive (electronic) marketing media
- Customer loyalty
- Telephony-based direct marketing.

Interactive (Electronic) Marketing Media

The term "interactive marketing" is one that is likely to become commonplace in the near future and firmly belongs in the direct-marketing area. Broadly, it refers to two marketing activities:

1) The promotion of products/services and the transmission of product/service information using media that permit interaction between buyer and seller. A current example would be the use of on-line enquiry and ordering services offered on the Internet or by kiosks placed at customer-contact points. These media facilitate the gathering of prospect/customer data, allow the end-user to interact extensively with the information being provided, and in many instances will enable the marketer to monitor response rates in minute time segments.

2) The second activity that is set to become an important form of interactive marketing is the delivery of services per se in electronic form, and the *informationalising* of physical products. An example of the former will be the delivery of banking services via personal computers or, in the business-to-business sector, the delivery of lists on-line between seller and client. It is also increasingly becoming the case that physical products are marketed using far greater information content.

Both of the above developments are facilitated by the diffusion of information technologies and, in particular, computer-to-computer communication and multimedia presentation. This means that marketing is increasingly becoming direct-orientated, not just tactically but infrastructurally. The claim that in time all marketing will be direct marketing is beginning to have more substance as we approach the end of the twentieth century. Libey (1994) has alluded to this notion indirectly in his assertion that "marketing is destined to be the science of delivering the individual choice" (178). This idea has alternatively been expressed as "all businesses must informationalise" (Rapp and Collins, 1994: 4).

Customer Loyalty

Direct marketing activity has traditionally concentrated on customer acquisition, with customer retention and loyalty-building being considered an optional, secondary activity. This is now changing, with relatively more attention (and budgets) being given to the latter. In Ireland, several agencies servicing the Irish direct-marketing industry are now increasingly focusing on retention work for clients, while several UK agencies now have whole departments or units that focus exclusively on retention work. The practical implementation of retention activity will take the form of affinity and post-sales servicing programmes, club schemes, and attempts to individualise information output and even services and products. The Superquinn Superclub represents a highly sophisticated and apparently successful application of a comprehensive customer retention programme.

Telephony-Based Direct Marketing

> Research suggests that Europe is now ready for US-style telemarketing. But I don't believe that the US experience of at least 6 calls interrupting the family dinner ... is going to be repeated here (Tutton, 1995: 12).

The deregulation of the telephone-services market, coupled with the diffusion of a range of telephony technologies, is set to make the telephone an important part of direct-marketing activity, and to provide a major boost to the growth of direct marketing. Mobile communications will facilitate improved direct customer contact on a day-to-day basis, while the key tasks of selling and information gathering will increasingly be carried out by telephone.

FACTORS THAT WILL INFLUENCE THE GROWTH OF DIRECT MARKETING IN IRELAND, 1995–2000

- The availability of consumer lists will have an enormous influence on the overall size of the Irish direct sector. If the present paucity of lists remains, the sector's growth will never even remotely mirror international levels.

- The widespread adoption by the packaged goods, hardware and retail sectors of direct marketing (possibly combined with sales promotion activities) would also significantly bolster activity in Ireland. While a small number of such companies currently use direct programmes, their use tends to be limited and tactical. Only when direct marketing is strategically implemented by big-budget clients will significant new growth be realised.

- An important, and as yet largely overlooked, development is the introduction of marketing databases by organisations. The availability of low cost, off-the-shelf database software, such as Contact Management packages and relational databases, is enabling more organisations to collect and store prospect and client data, and subsequently to develop customer-contact programmes using direct mail and telemarketing. The key strategic-development requirement that will fuel the growth of direct marketing will be the development of marketing databases that have the dual functions of customer-information systems/contact-management systems and promotional management/customer analysis and profiling. The business-to-business sector is already moving in this direction and is likely to do so more rapidly in the latter half of the 1990s.

- Desk-top direct marketing has been made possible by two developments. Firstly, the availability of publishing software that enables individual companies to design print communications (and deliver electronically to media intermediaries), which traditionally would have involved substantial third-party input and costs. The reduced cost of design, production and printing will lead to increased levels of promotion and customer contact. Furthermore, the adoption of customer-information systems, marketing data-bases and executive information systems delivered at desk-top PC level, will lead to more rigorous and frequent market analysis, which in turn will lead to increased customer contact, frequently employing a combination of direct mail and telemarketing.

- The agency sector that services Irish clients has an important role to play in the growth of direct marketing in Ireland. It is no longer the case that solutions to clients' marketing and promotion problems rest exclusively in one particular discipline or can be solved effectively by drawing on practices and techniques based on a single model — the mass advertising model versus the pure direct media model, for example. Direct marketing will grow in terms of usage and budget allocation if presented as a method of managing prospects and customers cost-effectively and with long-term value added, rather than as a stand-alone approach to marketing. This means that traditional selling, branding and mass communication will work together as part of the marketing mix and the communications mix to help organisations to manage their markets. Otherwise, positioned as a single panacea, too much will be expected from investment in direct marketing, with the result that the rewards will not appear to follow, and many potentially large users of direct techniques and strategies will either abandon the approach or largely ignore it.

REFERENCES

Bird, D. (1989): *Commonsense Direct Marketing*, London: Kogan Page.

Collins, T.L. and Rapp, S. (1994): *Beyond Maximarketing*, New York: McGraw Hill.

Glover, T. (1995): "What Is Direct Marketing?", *Direct Response*, March: 19–26.

Jenkins, V. (1989): "Understanding Direct Marketing Concept is Vitally Important" in Brown, H.E. and Burkins, B. (eds.), *Readings and Cases in Direct Marketing*, Chicago, IL: NTC Publishing.

Libey, D.R. (1994): "Business to Business Direct Marketing" in Reitman, J.I. (ed.), *Beyond 2000, The Future of Direct Marketing*, Chicago, IL: NTC Business Books: 178.

McCorkell, G. (1992): *Direct Marketing — A New Industry or a New Idea, The Practitioner's Guide to Direct Marketing*, London: The Direct Marketing Centre.

Tutton, M. (1995): Keynote Speech at the European Direct Marketing Association Forum, reprinted in *EDMA GRAM, Newsletter of the European Direct Marketing Association*, 2(12),(19) June/July.

Rowney, P. (1995): "What is Direct Marketing?", *Direct Response*, March: 19–26.

28

Store Atmospherics and the Rituals of Consumption

Paul O'Sullivan
Donald C. McFetridge

In an authoritative article entitled "Atmospherics as a Marketing Tool" (1973), Kotler defined atmospherics as "...the effort to design buying environments to produce specific emotional effects in the buyer that enhance his purchase probability" (50). Since the publication of that article, some attention has been duly paid to the topic, albeit intermittently and often inconsistently, but it still remains a largely neglected area of marketing-communications activity. The existing research literature in this area lacks cohesion, uniformity and consistency, and there is, as yet, no general consensus of opinion or agreement as to the effects of environmental atmospheric factors on consumer buying behaviour in even one particular type of retail environment.

Much of the popular commentary has been concerned with an exaggerated view of what atmospherics as an instrument of retail strategy, can actually achieve. One school of thought can be traced to Vance Packard's sensationalist 1957 bestseller, *The Hidden Persuaders*, which proposed that consumers are essentially the victims of omnipotent marketers who employ a battery of psychologically grounded techniques to influence, to manipulate and finally to control the target public. Such a study was very much of its time, coming in the first decade of the consumer boom, and at a period when awareness of consumer psychology as a new, and perhaps suspect, discipline was beginning to grow. It echoes the note of cold-war paranoia then prevalent in American public life, with fears of political brainwashing techniques a regular subject of debate. In *Store Atmosphere: An Environmental Psychology Approach,* Donovan and Rossiter (1982) point out that even much of the research work that has been carried out on store atmospherics has been purely anecdotal in nature.

This is not to suggest that in the areas of retail management, retail design and atmosphere creation, practitioners are not skilled and sophisticated. In fact, there is considerable evidence to suggest that the front-line practitioners are significantly ahead of the academic theorists in the understanding and application of the relevant techniques.

The principal purpose of this paper is to examine the current understanding of store atmospherics through a review of the existing literature, to evaluate critically the somewhat melodramatic claims that are frequently made about atmospherics by popular commentators, and to suggest possible routes forward for future research.

RETAIL CHANGE

There is a fundamental truth in the often repeated cliché that the only constant in retailing is change, and in the complex operating environment of the 1990s, the dynamic of change is throwing up new challenges to the retail manager. However, the essence of retail strategy remains essentially focused on building retail patronage and promoting purchase within the store. As Baker, Grewal and Levy (1992) point out, several factors have been shown to affect the retail patronage decision, among them location, service level, pricing polices and merchandise assortment and store environment. They argue that store patronage is influenced, at least to a degree, by the store environment, particularly where consumers are choosing between stores of the same type, rather than stores in different categories. They further point out that the literature supports the idea that store image is an important element in store choice, and that the physical environment, in turn, is an important element in creating store image. Thus, the environment within the store is a key element of the image that is communicated to the consuming public, and a significant reason why customers choose to come to that particular store.

The behaviour of the consumer within the store will, at least in theory, be modified to "enhance his purchase probability" (Kotler, 1973: 50). It is in this area, perhaps, that atmospherics makes its major contribution to retail performance, a view strongly expressed by Donovan and Rossiter (1982):

> ... we would argue that, whereas emotional responses to the in-store atmosphere certainly contribute to store patronage, albeit

not always at a conscious level, atmosphere effects are far more influential on behaviour within the store (36).

They note that a number of other writers appear to "agree with this subtle, preconscious, emotional conceptualisation of store atmosphere" (36).

It is not surprising then to find that the atmospheres created in retail outlets are constantly changing and being regularly updated to accommodate changes in consumer patterns, and to achieve positioning shifts in terms of the overall store image. Solomon (1992) has stated that, in the 1990s, "... retailers must offer something extra to lure shoppers, whether that something is excitement or just plain bargains". In a similar vein, Walters and White (1989) have indicated that, in the 1990s, there is a much more discerning, more sophisticated, better-educated, more widely-travelled type of consumer and that these consumers are simply not prepared to accept second-best or second-rate retail environments. A.J. Parker (1990/91), in the *Irish Marketing Review*, has noted that, in the early 1990s, consumers are cash-rich but time-poor; they demand and expect to find the best and most attractive retail environments on every high street throughout the world.

ATMOSPHERICS

Kotler (1973) predicted that marketing planners in the future "will use s*patial aesthetics* as consciously and skilfully as they now use price, advertising, personal selling, public relations and other tools of marketing" (50). He defines atmospherics as

> ... the conscious designing of space to create certain effects in buyers. More specifically, *atmospherics* is the effort to design buying environments to produce specific emotional effects in the buyer that enhance his purchase probability (Kotler, 1973: 50).

While technically atmosphere is "the air surrounding a sphere", Kotler notes that the term is used colloquially to describe "the *quality* of the surroundings" (50). He goes even further by pointing out that in "some cases, the atmosphere is the primary product" (48) — a lesson many retailers would do well to remember. He notes that people describe a restaurant as "having atmosphere", though that atmosphere can of course be categorised in negative as well as positive terms.

In all of this, he is discerning a basic truth about the way in which people apprehend experience. In a real sense, individuals are not just consumers, but rather connoisseurs of atmosphere. People speak of the atmosphere of a pub or club, a one-off music event, a religious ceremony, a sports gathering or a restaurant. In doing so, they are encompassing three important dimensions of experience — namely, the sensory apprehension of surroundings, the heightened receptivity or emotional state associated with the experience, and an evaluation of the quality of the human interactions involved. Belk (1975) has stressed the importance of this latter issue, arguing that social surroundings are a key factor to be considered in store atmospherics. Irish consumers will readily identify the quality of personal service experienced in Superquinn, for instance, as a key component of the atmosphere of the store. The Superquinn chain features the experience of customer friendliness as a main theme in its advertising and public-relations campaigns. Spar, Centra and Quinnsworth use similar strategies. Thus, there may be scope for a fruitful convergence of atmospherics research with the ongoing body of research into the service encounter.

A further important dimension is the tendency to evaluate the experience of the atmosphere in hedonistic terms, that is, according to an intrinsic pleasure principle. The emerging literature on hedonistic consumption suggests another useful framework for the discussion of retail atmospherics and for the design of research investigations.

Atmospherics or atmospheres are a silent language, and the grammar, punctuation, syntax and vocabulary of individual atmospheres vary from retailer to retailer, but it is always present whether intended or perceived — a distinction highlighted by Kotler. The manipulation of atmospheric elements is a matter of everyday management routine for many retailers, as is evidenced by the following extract from a trade journal:

> The practice of perfumery dates back to at least 6,000 BC and customers' sense of smell, which is ten thousand times more sensitive than that of taste, can be played on by retailers each time they go shopping. Smell is capable of influencing mood and emotion. The smell of fresh bread produces a feeling of well-being, making us feel secure, and it is just one of the many smells used to entice shoppers to make purchases....
>
> ... Around the Christmas season last year a top London store had the aroma of brandy and Christmas puddings filtered through the air conditioning system. Sales were found to be up by about 30 per cent.

At Easter, some bakers sprinkle cinnamon on the pavement outside their premises. People walking by rub their feet in it and set off the smell, thereby luring themselves and others into the bakery.

Micro-encapsulation, a more sophisticated version of the baker's trick, is currently being researched. For example, as a customer's hand brushes off a jar of coffee, capsules that emit the same smell are broken. The capsules can also be triggered by heat.

The smell of fresh food makes people hungry, and a lot of people find themselves buying much more than was on their shopping list. Consumers are always being advised to shop on a full stomach. When you have eaten, your blood-sugar levels rise and you are less likely to be influenced by smell.

As well as using consumers' sense of smell to their advantage, retailers can also play on the senses of hearing and touch.

It is quite likely that if you go to a jewellery shop strains of classical music will be playing quietly in the background. The type of music adds quality to the outlet and the tempo gently persuades you to linger.

The same principle applies to all types of shops, enhancing the personality of the product they sell.

Supermarkets are no exception. Slower "elevator" music played at off-peak times, helps to relax customers so that they wander aimlessly around the aisles, probably purchasing more than they set out to. At busier times faster music is played, the idea being to get shoppers to make their purchases and leave quickly.

Another way that stores can seduce shoppers is through customers' tactile sense with temperature.

The ideal temperature for a supermarket — one which makes the customer feel most relaxed and comfortable is said to be between 70 and 73 degrees Fahrenheit.

Anything below that leaves shoppers cold and makes them want to leave more quickly, and anything above that is too warm and either makes them so hot they want to leave, or stay too long to enjoy the balmy conditions (O'Dowd, 1995).

Kotler's 1973 article sought to raise the issue as to why atmospherics has continued to be a relatively neglected tool in the marketing communication mix of most firms? While his article has been subject to a degree of criticism by subsequent commentators, it must be borne in mind that his purpose was to make an initial map of the territory and suggest an agenda for future research. Some of the questions to be addressed in his view relate to the comparative state of atmospheric planning in different industries, the social and ethical implications of atmosphere creation, the buyers defence mechanisms and a number of other issues including the following:

- How do different atmospheric elements work? What messages are communicated in our society by particular colours, sounds, odours and textures?
- What values are customers seeking in different common buying and consuming situations?

Some of the researchers who took up Kotler's challenge examined these questions and their findings are briefly examined below.

Atmospheric Elements

Research into the elements which may be viewed as constituting a store atmosphere has largely focused on the issues of *music* and *colour* in retail settings, for a variety of reasons, not least the opportunity for cross-fertilisation with a range of other disciplines.

Music

Music would appear to be one of the more easily manipulated elements of store atmosphere. A number of studies (Langreher, 1991; Milliman, 1982) have established that music can be an important component of retail atmosphere and Baker, Grewal and Levy (1992) have shown that background music may influence choice between stores of the same type. It would appear that retailers can use background music to influence consumers by manipulating tempo (Milliman, 1982, 1986) and volume (Smith and Curnow, 1966). Yalch and Spangenberg (1990) found that the use of different types of music created different emotional responses in customers within the store, and the right type of music may influence consumers to purchase more goods.

Milliman (1982) and Smith and Curnow (1966) suggest that individuals adjust their walking pace in response to the tempo of music and will walk faster in the presence of loud music. Background music has also been found to influence mood (Bruner, 1990), which Gardner (1985) has suggested is an important means of moderating consumer behaviour at the point of purchase. Furthermore, background music can reduce the stress associated with queuing, and supermarket shoppers feel that background music makes shopping more relaxing, leading to more time being spent in the store (Keenan and Boisi, 1989).

The experience of human interaction in the service encounter is an important component of perceived atmosphere quality. Background music would appear to influence positively the performance of store employees (Shrimp and Rose, 1993) and Herrington and Capella (1994) suggest that "retailers may be able to enhance employee–customer relationships through the proper use of background music" (54).

Herrington and Capella (1994) offer a structural framework for the examination of music within a retail environment (Figure 28.1).

FIGURE 28.1: STRUCTURAL FRAMEWORK FOR RELATIONSHIP OF MUSIC TO A RETAIL ENVIRONMENT

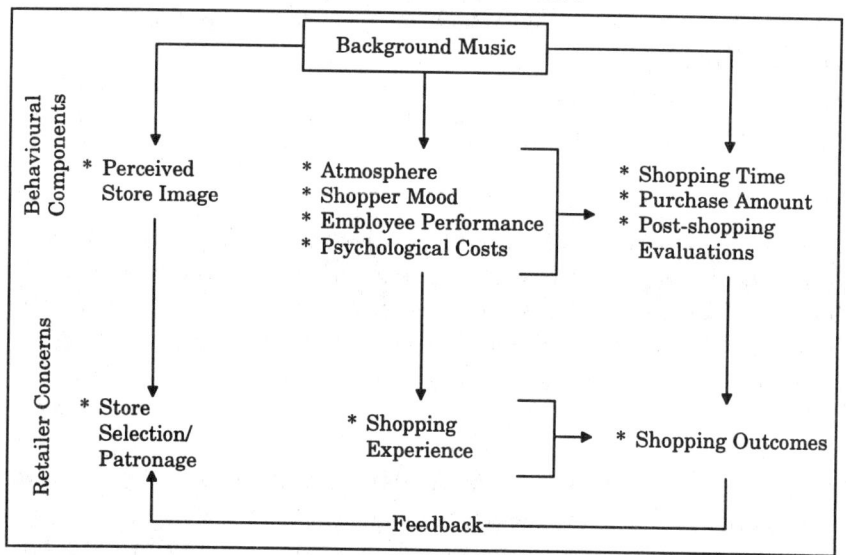

```
                        ┌──────────────────┐
                        │ Background Music │
                        └──────────────────┘
  Behavioural
  Components
        * Perceived         * Atmosphere            * Shopping Time
          Store Image       * Shopper Mood          * Purchase Amount
                            * Employee Performance  * Post-shopping
                            * Psychological Costs     Evaluations

  Retailer Concerns
        * Store
          Selection/        * Shopping              * Shopping Outcomes
          Patronage           Experience

                        ─── Feedback ───
```

Source: Herrington and Capella (1994).

This framework sees the retail selection decision as influenced by knowledge of the retailer and previous experience with the retail outlet. Background music influences the customer through variables such as atmospheric mood and employee performance (which in turn influence time spent and purchase amount), as well as the shopper's evaluation of the shopping experience. All of these outcomes serve as inputs for future retail selection.

An Irish study conducted amongst retail customers in supermarkets by O'Shea and O'Shea (1993) found that 92.5 per cent of respondents claimed that they liked to hear background music in stores. Two-thirds indicated that there were particular types of music they liked to hear in-store (though the stated preferences were very diverse) with one-third indicating no particular preference. Respondents were asked to suggest reasons for their stated in-store musical preferences, and the reasons given were in order of frequency: "Relaxing", "Soothing", "Enjoyable", "Pleasant", "Recognise", "Nice to listen to" and "Uplifting". The responses tend towards the soporific, easy-listening style rather than toward music with a strong intrusive identity. Not surprisingly, consumers identified the music they do not like to hear while shopping as being of the heavy metal, rave, loud pop or rap varieties, stating that they found them to be "Loud/Intrusive", "Disturbs concentration", "Annoying", "Confusing", "Irritating" and "Boring". Of particular interest was a question that asked if respondents could remember any of the promotions/jingles that had been played since they entered the store. A surprising 82.5 per cent of respondents were unable to recall any such advertisement being played, though slightly more than half of those who could recall an advertisement "indicated that they would be influenced to buy the item which had been promoted" (O'Shea and O'Shea, 1993: 44). The very poor levels of recall would seem to suggest that in-store music induces torpor rather than arousal or alertness. Pejorative comment would suggest that such music is "mindless", or at least bland to the point where it is lacking in any real identity. Original artists are almost never featured, though this may be for commercial reasons, and the output sometimes approaches the condition of "muzak" — the anonymous white noise that pervades lifts and hotel lobbies.

Herrington and Capella (1994) point out that a consumer's personal preference for a given musical selection or style may ultimately contribute more to behavioural response than other associated factors, a finding supported by O'Shea and O'Shea (1993). Retailers must recognise that preference appears to vary strongly by age, education, gender, ethnic background, and even marital status, if they are to utilise music in-store effectively.

Colour

Colour in itself constitutes "a complicated visual language" (Holtzschue, 1994: 104), with a range of every day applications. As Holtzschue (1994) points out, colour serves to identify by providing a way of discriminating between objects of identical form and size; colour is impressional; colour is symbolic and related to cultural experience; colour affects all of our senses in complex ways (a blue room may seem cool at 65 degrees Fahrenheit, but a pink room will feel warm at that temperature); colour is stimulating, calming, expressive, disturbing and associative.

> It pervades every aspect of our visual lives.... It embellishes the ordinary and gives beauty and drama to everyday objects. If black and white images bring us the news of the day, colour writes the poetry (Holtzschue, 1994: 104).

There is a considerable body of both psychological and physiological research into the human response to colour. However, the vast bulk of the studies conducted in relation to retailing have focused on the efficacy of colour in packaging or in food presentation. Such studies have achieved a wide currency, and many readers will be familiar in outline with studies that show a relationship between pack colour and perceived strength of coffee, and pack colour and perceived size. It is worth noting that, originally, generic products on the Irish market (Yellow Pack and Thrift) adopted the light colours which suggest a larger than actual size.

However, there is an absence of significant work into the use of colour in the creation of store environments. Notable exceptions in the research literature include Bellizzi, Crowley and Hasty (1983), who, in a controlled laboratory experiment, established that subjects reacted emotionally to warm and cool wall colours, and that colour can physically attract shoppers to a retail display. Almost all modern retail and service outlets and chains adopt a distinctive livery (e.g. The Body Shop, Spar, Centra, Woodies, Virgin Megastore, Abrakebabra), and may be heavily dependent on a colour scheme for the creation of atmosphere within the store, making the absence of research studies all the more surprising.

It is generally accepted that colours affect people emotionally, and can thus be used both to express emotion and to evoke emotion. Zelanski and Fisher (1989) point out that "bright reds, oranges, and yellows tend to stimulate us, while blues and greens often make us feel more peaceful" (28), a proposition with which anybody who has experienced the relentlessly cheerful primary colours of a fast-food environment such as a McDonald's restaurant will probably agree. Reds, yellows and oranges are the colours of fire, and are associated with warmth. There is almost certainly a physiological basis to this "... that under red lighting our bodies secrete more adrenaline, increasing our blood pressure and our rate of breathing and actually rising our temperature slightly" (Zelanski and Fisher, 1989: 28). Conversely, brown and blue will create a more calming environment, as was demonstrated in a study by Wohlfarth and Sam (1982) who found that creating a "quieter colour environment" (30) considerably changed the behaviour of severely handicapped and behaviourally disordered children, in that "the children's aggressive behaviour diminished and their blood pressure dropped" (30).

In a retail environment, the informational, expressive and symbolic aspects of colour can constitute a code that is potent and sophisticated, but nevertheless easily read and understood. As a recent trade commentator pointed out "Almost all departments are colour coded" in the modern supermarket. "Fresh fruit and veg. are usually green, suggesting fields and open space. Blue is used at fish counters, signifying the sea and freshness. Red is aggressive and gets noticed, which is why it is used to draw attention to sales and special offers" (*Shelf*life, 1995: 9). The application of the use of colour in the Irish stores of one major chain is described below.

> Colour is another vital dynamic in SPAR's philosophy. The deep red logo of a SPAR store has been successfully implanted in the consumer's mind, linking to the reputation for friendliness and service. "This isn't just an Irish but an international corporate identity for SPAR...", "SPAR consumers in Ireland can discover the familiar red logo while walking the streets of Amsterdam, Berlin or Johannesburg and feel just as easy entering the store as they can back home."
>
> The logo, therefore, has remained largely untouched down the years but other colour principals have undergone significant change. "In the past shelf colouring has been strong: that we now feel is dated. Strong colouring tended to conflict or even clash with product packaging. With brand manufacturers going for stronger, brighter, more attractive packaging we felt we should let their wares do the talking and not the store's colours."
>
> The result is that colours are now less encroaching, more subtle. SPAR's in-store palette shows a tendency for pastel shades (*Retail News*, 1995).

However, shaping consumer response through the application of colour in an environment may be less straightforward than might at first appear to be the case. There are discernible differences in the response of individuals to colour. Extroverts prefer warm colours, while introverts tend to like cool hues. Colour preference alters with age and temperament. Thus, outgoing adolescents prefer red while their more reserved peers prefer blue. The elderly have a significant preference for light colours, but yellow is the least liked colour of the spectrum. A further complication may arise from the fact that people can be attracted towards colours representing qualities which they may personally be regarded as lacking:

> Red, for instance, is usually the preference of vibrant, outgoing, impulsive people, but timid people may also be drawn to it. Those who are feeling frustrated or angry may be repelled by red (Wohlfarth and Sam, 1982: 33).

Kotler has further pointed out that there are wide and varied cultural differences in terms of colour use. For example, black is the funereal colour in the west, while white is the symbolic funereal colour in the east. Brides wear white in Western Europe, but red in India. In Imperial China, only the Emperor was permitted to wear yellow. While global communication has blurred some of these cultural differences, retailers will need to take cognisance of national differences in a multicultural society.

Towards a Gestalt

While useful work has been done, and will continue to be done, in elucidating the role of individual elements such as music and colour, it must be recognised that consumers apprehend an environment in a holistic way. Single dimensional analysis is wholly inadequate to explore the complex apprehension of experience. All of the senses combine to produce for the consumer an overall gestalt, and it is the genesis or origins of the overall store gestalt which might usefully be made the primary focus of future research.

The problem is increasingly recognised by commentators. Hackett, Foxall and Van Raaij (1993) have noted that most of the research to date has tended to be rather fragmentary in nature, and totally lacking in a common theoretical orientation. They point out that "... the complexity of the subject matter arises from the two subject areas of the 'consumer' and the 'environment' both of which are by no means simple entities", and they argue that multidimensional phenomena exist in this area of study, requiring that research studies be conducted from a multidisciplinary perspective, even though this could lead to a problem of integration. This whole area of study, especially if all aspects are to be examined in detail, involves an astonishing number of disciplines, ranging from behavioural psychology, through environmental psychology to marketing, to architecture, to geography, to sociology and also to social anthropology.

Consumer Profiles and Consumer Values

As far back as 1954, G.P. Stone had suggested a typology of shoppers involving four different types: the economic shopper, the personalising shopper, the ethical shopper and the apathetic shopper (Bellenger and Koraonkar, 1980). In a 1977 study, Bellenger, Robertson and Greenberg examined the motives of shopping-centre patrons, and proposed a category of "recreational shopper" — individuals who haunt the shopping malls of the US because they actively enjoy shopping as a leisure-time activity (Bellenger and Koraonkar, 1980).

Drawing on these insights, Solomon (1992) suggests that consumers are of five basic types, all of whom desire different kinds and standards of retail environments and atmospheres, thus making it very difficult for retailers to reach the so-called global market. These five types are as follows:

1) Economic shoppers who are very money-conscious and who will shop only in terms of getting VFM (value for money)

2) Personalised shoppers who like the idea that when they enter a retail outlet they are recognised by the sales staff

3) Ethical shoppers who like the notion of helping the smaller independent retailers and who do not support the larger chains of retailers, on principle

4) Apathetic shoppers for whom the chore of shopping is nothing more than a necessary evil

5) Recreational shoppers who simply shop because they enjoy the activity. Shoppers in this final type are in the "born to shop" category, and they are the principal protagonists of the "shopping as a leisure activity" viewpoint.

It is clear, even from the above, perhaps too narrowly-focused typology, that each type of shopper is going to have different expectations of the retail institutions that they patronise. It must also be borne in mind that the behaviour of some individual shoppers may shift across categories at different times when they are engaged in different shopping missions. Some are going to be happy with basic, utilitarian, warehouse-style interiors, while others are going to expect Place de Vendôme, Philippe Starck-like sophistication. As Bellenger and Korgaonkar (1980: 92) point out:

> The economic shopper can be attracted by a convenient location, but the recreational shopper wants more. To attract the latter

group the retailer must offer attractive décor and an exciting shopping experience. What Kotler has called "atmospherics" becomes a key to attracting recreational shoppers. The retailer should attempt to make creative use of this tool in attracting patronage.

They argue that, through using atmospherics, regional shopping malls "have built a major flow of retail traffic and a resulting high level of sales" (92). Traffic creates potential for impulse purchases. Bellenger, Robertson and Hirschman (1978), in a study of 14 merchandise lines in a large department store, had established that impulse purchases ranged from 27 per cent to 62 per cent of total sales for individual product lines, suggesting that an increase in traffic volume will always inevitably lead to increased sales volume.

The strategic issue for retailers is to determine to *whom* they are attempting to appeal and *how* store atmospherics can communicate with such target groups in order to bring them to the store and to promote particular behaviours in-store.

Somewhat more ambitious approaches to creating a typology of consumer need fulfilment have been emerging in recent years. Langrehr (1991) provocatively argues that "people buy so they can shop, NOT shop so they can buy" (428), claiming that the actual purchase of goods may be incidental to the experience of shopping. Holbrook and Hirschman (1982) view consumers as shopping for experiential and emotional reasons, and other writers have linked shopping malls with semiotic messages, consumer emotions, fantasy and dramatic performance (Langrehr, 1991). Thus, the shopping space may be seen as a theatre where consumers can fantasise playing their own roles in a drama in which the retailer's role is partly that of set designer and stage manager.

More fancifully, perhaps, the shopping space, particularly the mall, has been conceptualised as creating "sacred" space, with highly structured atmospherics based on layout, lighting etc. which sequester it from the "profane" space of everyday life. Belk, Wallendorf and Sherry (1989) point out that "the sacralization of the secular" (1) is a key process at work in contemporary society, and "for many, consumption has become a vehicle for experiencing the sacred" (1). Sacred space provides an arena for the enactment of ritual, and while it is debatable as to whether shopping behaviours have the symbolic density of meaning normally associated with ritual, certain aspects do suggest ritualistic activity. In this context, atmospheric elements (music, colour, light) take on some of the functions which they perform in other human rituals, and they may have particular importance in the patterning and sequencing of consumers' movements and actions within the store.

DEVELOPMENT OF THE CONCEPT

While the work of Kotler is of primary importance in the study of atmospherics, in helping to frame the discussion and set a research agenda, the overall progress since his 1973 paper has been disappointing. Donovan and Rossiter (1982) pointed to limitations in Kotler's approach. Chief among these was the fact that atmosphere tended to be included as a component of store image, alongside other in-store variables such as brightness, crowding and aisle width "when clearly these physical variables are antecedents of store atmosphere rather than alternatives to it" (35). Furthermore, they argue that the store atmosphere has been conceptualised as a single attribute, when in truth it is likely to be multidimensional, and no detailed investigation had been conducted into how atmosphere affects shopping behaviour within the store. An alternative framework for the discussion of the key issues, which provides the potential for a more comprehensive and integrated investigation, is that based on the work of Mehrabian and Russell (1974).

Mehrabian and Russell (1974) developed a theoretical model for studying the effects of store atmosphere on shopping behaviour. Their model, shown in Figure 28.2, is a Stimulus-Organism-Response model, and thus involves a classification of stimuli, a set of intervening or mediating variables and a classification of responses.

FIGURE 28.2: MEHRABIAN-RUSSELL MODEL

ENVIRONMENTAL STIMULI	EMOTIONAL STATES Pleasure Arousal Dominance	APPROACH or AVOIDANCE RESPONSES

Source: Donovan and Rossiter (1982): *Journal of Retailing*, 58(1): 42.

Donovan and Rossiter (1982) observe that the model is strong in the intervening variable and response areas but "leaves the problem of an appropriate stimulus taxonomy largely untouched" (36), though they maintain that, by and large, this can be rectified by subsequent researchers, and it does not invalidate the model. Hackett et al. (1993) suggest that one way forward is to develop a stimulus taxonomy for retail environments. This, in essence, means that it is necessary to develop a detailed, foolproof taxonomy which applies to all the manipulative in-store factors.

Mehrabian and Russell (1974) suggest that three basic emotional states mediate approach/avoidance behaviours in environmental situations. These emotional responses are:

- Pleasure — Displeasure
- Arousal — Non-arousal
- Dominance — Submissiveness.

Pleasure–Displeasure refers to the extent to which a person feels good or happy in a situation; Arousal–Non-arousal refers to the extent to which a person feels stimulated, alert, active or excited; Dominance–Submissiveness refers to the extent to which an individual feels in control of, or able to act in, a given situation. Subsequent researchers have tended to modify the model by deleting the Dominance–Submissiveness dimension, on the basis of insufficient evidence to support its inclusion.

Mehrabian and Russell (1974) postulate that all responses to an environment can be considered as approach or avoidance behaviours concerned with physically staying in, or getting out of, an environment, exploring the environment or communicating with others in the environment.

In summary, Mehrabian and Russell (1974) posited that an individual's perception of, and behaviour within, a specific environment are the result of emotional states created by that environment. Environmental stimuli (that is, physical features such as colour, store layout, lighting etc.) are believed to affect emotional states (pleasure, arousal and dominance), which in turn affect approach or avoidance behaviours (for example, a willingness to move towards and explore the environment, thus demonstrating a heightened propensity to buy).

Donovan and Rossiter (1982) found support for the Mehrabian-Russell model in a retailing context by investigating the relationship between emotional states induced by 11 different store environments and statements of behavioural intention in those environments. They found that store-induced pleasure was positively associated with willingness to buy. Store-induced arousal influenced the time spent in the store and willingness to interact with sales personnel. However, a crowded service environment reduced consumers' pleasure.

> The results suggest that store atmosphere engendered by the usual myriad of in-store variables, is represented psychologically by consumers in terms of two major emotional states — pleasure and arousal — and that these two emotional states are significant mediators of intended shopping behaviours within the store. The practical value of this approach is that retailers may be better able to exploit and predict the effects of in-store changes on shopping behaviour (34).

Hackett et al. (1993) suggest that the Mehrabian-Russell model needs to be tested with actual purchasing behaviour, as opposed to intended purchasing behaviour, in order for the results to have any real value. Researchers also need to bear in mind the fact that emotional reactions or emotional responses influence:

- Enjoyment of shopping in the store
- Time spent browsing and exploring the store's retail offering
- Willingness to talk to sales personnel
- Tendency to spend more money than originally planned
- Likelihood of returning to the store again, i.e. store patronage.

Nevertheless, the value of the Mehrabian-Russell behaviour model is demonstrated by its continuing application as a framework for research, as, for instance in the study by O'Shaughnessy, Heilbrunn and McLoughlin (1995), which indicated that some aspects of store atmospherics have an impact on various components of a brand's franchise.

CONCLUDING REMARKS

Atmospherics remains an under-researched area of marketing communications. While retailers are sophisticated in their approach to atmosphere creation, researchers have, by and large, ignored many of the key issues. Kotler (1973) did much to highlight the importance of atmospherics within an overall communication strategy, identifying the major elements of atmospheres and suggesting an agenda for further research. Subsequent work has been fragmented in overall approach, though the Mehrabian-Russell model (1974), as adapted and endorsed by Donovan and Rossiter (1982), does offer an integrated framework for future studies. As has been noted in this paper, sensory apprehension of atmosphere produces for the consumer an overall gestalt, and this may provide a fruitful line of inquiry, though it will demand a multidisciplinary approach on the part of investigators. There are rich insights to be garnered from the work of social psychologists, anthropologists, ethnographers, architects and marketers, and the emerging literature on hedonistic consumption can suggest both a methodology and an orientation. The uses of shopping, and the role of the retail space in the life of the post-modern consumer, have been too narrowly conceptualised to date. A more ambitious approach to the problems, involving perhaps a consideration of the sacralisation of secular experience and a fuller consideration of the affinities of much shopping behaviour to ritual, may open up new and exciting avenues of exploration.

REFERENCES

Baker, J., Grewal, D. and Levy, M. (1992): "An Experimental Approach to Making Retail Store Environmental Decisions", *Journal of Retailing*, 68(4): 445–60.

Belk, R.W. (1975): "Situation Variables and Consumer Behaviour", *Journal of Consumer Research*, 2, December: 157–64.

Belk, R.W., Wallendor, F. and Sherry, J.R. (1989): "The Sacred and the Profane in Consumer Behaviour: Theodicy on the Odessy", *Journal of Consumer Research*, 16, June: 1–38.

Bellenger, D.N. and Korgaonkar, P.K. (1980): "Profiling the Recreational Shopper", *Journal of Retailing*, 56(3): 77–92.

Bellenger, D.N., Robertson, D.H. and Hirschman, E.C. (1978): "Impulse Buying Varies by Product", *Journal of Advertising Research*, 18, December: 15–18.

Bellizzi, J.A., Crowley, A.E. and Hasty, R.W. (1983): "The Effects of Colour in Store Design", *Journal of Retailing*, 59, Spring: 21–45.

Bruner, G.C. (1990): "Music, Mood, and Marketing", *Journal of Marketing*, October: 94–104.

Donovan, R.J. and Rossiter, J.R. (1982): "Store Atmosphere: An Environmental Psychology Approach", *Journal of Retailing*, 58(1): 34–57.

Foxall, G.R. (1990): *Consumer Psychology in Behavioral Perspective*, London: Routledge.

Gardner, M.P. (1985): "Mood States and Consumer Behaviour: A Critical Review", *Journal of Consumer Research*, 12, December: 28–97.

Hackett, P.W.M., Foxall, G.R., and Van Raaij, W.F. (1993): "Consumers in Retail Environments", in Garling, T. and Golledge, R. (eds.), *Behaviour and Environments: Psychological and Geographical Approaches*, Holland: Elsevier: 1–27.

Herrington, J.D. and Capella, L.M. (1994): "Practical Applications of Music in Service Settings", *Journal of Services Marketing*, 8(3): 50–65.

Holbrook, M.B. and Hirschman, E.C. (1982) "The Experiential Aspects of Consumption: Consumer Fantasies, Feelings and Fun", *Journal of Consumer Research*, 9, September: 132–240.

Holtzschue L. (1994): *Understanding Colour. Introduction for Designers*, New York: Van Nostram Reinhold.

Keenan, J.J. and Boisi, J.C. (1989): "A Study of the Effects of Muzak Programming on Drug-store Customers", *Muzak*: RS–5.

Kotler, P. (1973): "Atmospherics as a Marketing Tool", *Journal of Retailing*, 49(4): 48–64.

Langrehr, F.W. (1991): "Retail Shopping Mall Semiotics and Hedonic Consumption", *Advances in Consumer Research*, 18: 428–33.

Mehrabian, A., and Russell, J.A. (1974): *An Approach to Environmental Psychology*, Cambridge, MA: MIT Press.

Milliman, R.E. (1982): "Using Background Music to Affect the Behavior of Supermarket Shoppers", *Journal of Marketing*, 46, Summer: 86–91.

Milliman, R.E. (1986): "The Influence of Background Music on Behavior of Restaurant Patrons", *Journal of Consumer Research*, 13, September: 286–9.

O'Dowd, K. (1995): *Shelflife*, June.

O'Dowd, K. (1995): "The Colours We Eat", *Shelflife*, March: 9.

O'Shaughnessy, S.F., Heilbrunn, B.O. and McLoughlin, D.P.J. (1995): "An Exploratory Investigation of the Impact of Store Atmospherics on Brand Franchise", paper delivered at 24th EMAC Conference on Marketing Today and for the 21st Century, France, 16–19 May, France: ESSSEC.

O'Shea, J. and O'Shea K. (1993): "The Sound of Music — A Study Conducted For Heatley Tector Ltd.", *Checkout*, May: 44.

Packard, V. (1957): *The Hidden Persuaders*, London: Longmans.

Parker, A.J. (1990/91): "Retail Environments: Into the 1990s", *Irish Marketing Review*, 5(2): 61–72.

Retails News (1995): "Giving Your Store a Facelift", An Interview with Declan Ralph, Spar Retail Manager, July/August: 28–9.

Shrimp, T.A. and Rose, R.L. (1993): "The Role of Background Music: A Re-examination and Extension", in McAlister, L. and Rothschild, M. (eds.), *Advances in Consumer Research*, 20: 558.

Smith, P.C. and Curnow, R. (1966): "Arousal Hypothesis and the Effects of Music on Purchasing Behavior", *Journal of Applied Psychology*, 50 (3): 255–6.

Solomon, M.R. (1992): *Consumer Behavior*, New York: Allyn and Bacon.

Walters, D. and White, D. (1989): *Retail Marketing Management*, London: Macmillan.

Wohlfarth, H. and Sam, C. (1982): "The Effects of Colour Psychodynamic Environment Modification upon Psycho Physiological and Behavioural Reactions of Severely Handicapped Children", *International Journal of Biosocial Research*, 3(1): 31.

Yalch, R., and Spangenberg, E. (1990): "Effects of Store Music on Shopping Behavior", *Journal of Consumer Marketing*, 7(2): 55–63.

Zelanski, P. and Fisher, M.P. (1989): *Colour for Designers and Artists*, London: Herbert Press.

Part 5

Advertising —
Effects and Outcomes

29
Advertising Effectiveness — The Holy Grail?

Peter Nash

The trade of advertising is so near to perfection that it is not easy to propose any improvement (Samuel Johnson, 1759).

Half of my advertising is wasted, but I don't know which half (Lord Leverhume, 1930).

You could say that 96% of all advertising is wasted but nobody knows which 96% (Winston Fletcher, 1992).

INTRODUCTION

In light of the fact that advertising absorbs such a large part of the communications and promotions budget, it is not surprising that a vast literature has emerged in the area of understanding advertising effectiveness. From the perspective of the client company investing in advertising, a better understanding of how advertising works will provide reassurance that its money has been spent efficiently. In addition, amongst advertising agency and marketing-research practitioners, a better appreciation of the nature of advertising effectiveness should lead to the creation of more effective advertising campaigns, thereby securing their business.

Given the number of stakeholders in the communications process with an interest in understanding how advertising works, the relatively slow progress in our understanding of the topic is surprising. As Franzen (1994) points out, the absence of a consensus view on how advertising works is not the result of any lack of scientific interest or rigour, and owes more to a lack of realism amongst many of those researching the effectiveness of advertising. In particular, there is a tension between the experience-based, pragmatic assumptions about the nature of advertising amongst practitioners, and the more abstract, laboratory-based models of communications which underlie the more academic theories of advertising effectiveness. Most recently, the focus of investigation on how advertising works has centred on the analysis of single-source data — that is, data derived from real-world tests where the consumption of advertising by individuals is measured at the same time as their purchasing patterns for selected products. The new technologies of audience measurement through peoplemeters, scanning checkouts and swipecards have made this type of real-world examination of the relationship between advertising and consumer behaviour possible. However, looking for the "holy grail" of effective advertising in the area of single-source data smacks of the logic of the well-known Sufi tale quoted by Meenaghan (1983). A mullah is found on his knees beside a lamp-post evidently searching for something. Asked what he is doing, he replies that he is looking for his key. When asked where he lost it, he replies "at home". When his somewhat puzzled inquisitor asks why he is searching under the lamp-post, he replies that there is more light there. In an analogous way, the focus of measurement of advertising effects has centred on where there is light — that is, where lines of attribution between advertising inputs and related effects can be more clearly observed.

The purpose of this paper is to review the current knowledge of how advertising works, and to describe the conditions that lead to the creation of effective advertising. The paper describes the historical evolution of models of advertising and reviews the ways in which advertising effectiveness has been measured. Central to this discussion is an appreciation of what advertising can realistically be expected to achieve, and how objectives might be set. A simple model of advertising effectiveness is presented, along with empirical findings from recent Irish advertising.

HOW ADVERTISING WORKS

Traditionally, there have been two broad schools of thought on how advertising works. The linear-sequential school sees advertising working through a somewhat mechanical series of hurdles to be overcome by consumers. By contrast, the human-needs model of advertising acknowledges that consumers buy brands for both functional and emotional benefits.

Linear-Sequential Models

The traditional view of how advertising works has been codified in a set of models collectively labelled linear sequential. The common underlying assumption of these models is that, for advertising to be effective, the consumer must go through a series of stages which are rational, logical and sequential and ultimately lead to a purchase. The three best known and influential linear sequential models are Starch, AIDA and DAGMAR (Wicks, 1989). Although these classical models of advertising are most often seen in textbooks rather than cited by advertising practitioners nowadays, the thinking behind these models (a flow process from awareness of the advertising through to some form of action on foot of awareness and exposure) still enjoys wide currency.

- Starch   Seen, Read, Believed, Remembered, Acted Upon

- AIDA   Awareness, Interest, Desire, Action

- DAGMAR   Awareness, Comprehension, Conviction, Action (Designing Advertising Goals for Measured Advertising Results).

These models suffer from a certain determinism, insofar as they view the consumer as a passive receiver of communications stimuli. In reality, consumers do not behave in the way predicted by classical learning theory, and instead of simply absorbing stimuli as transmitted, most consumers typically select and distort messages based on their experience and perceptions (Lannon and Cooper, 1983). In addition, these models imply a rationality in consumer behaviour, which leaves little room for emotion and intuition in the way in which consumers react to advertising. The simple stimulus-response mechanism implied by these models also presupposes that consumers buy brands for primarily functional reasons.

Human-Needs Models of Advertising

The humanistic model of how advertising works arises from the premise that consumers endow the brands and products that they buy and use with meanings over and above the purely functional benefits embodied in the goods (Lannon and Cooper, 1983). Certainly, rational, practical and functional factors do influence decision-making, but consumers come to advertising with an existing set of beliefs already in place. In this view of the world, brands fulfil powerful expressive and symbolic functions, such that the interaction between the consumer and the advertising is much more complicated and subtle than the process implied by the linear-sequential model.

Firms advertise brands not products, and people choose between brands on the basis of subjective, intuitive factors, rather than purely on the basis of functional differences. The humanistic model of how advertising works sees consumers as active participants in the communications process, doing things with the advertising rather than simply passively receiving the message. The implication of this model is that understanding how advertising works involves an understanding of where consumers are relative to the brand, prior to the communication. In addition, it accepts that an identical communication can be very differently decoded and processed by different consumers. Furthermore, this model acknowledges that the message that consumers get out of a communication is quite often very different from what went into it (Prue, 1991).

Clearly, both the linear model and the humanistic model provide insights into how advertising works. The learning from these very different approaches is that advertising works both at a practical (rational/overt) and a symbolic (emotional/covert) level. The formation of attitudes to the brand and consumer choice between products are influenced by rational and symbolic cues, as shown in Figure 29.1, as quoted by Lannon and Cooper (1983).

FIGURE 29.1: PRACTICAL AND SYMBOLIC ROUTES TO PERSUASION

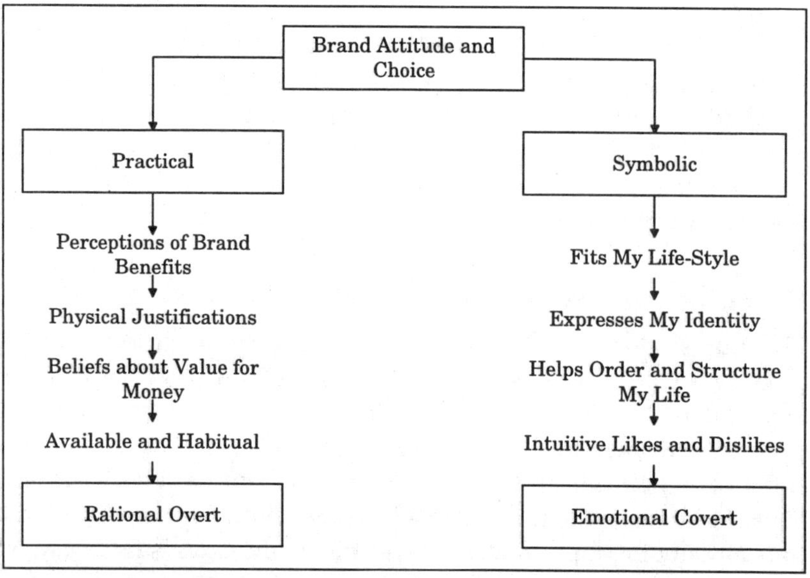

```
                    Brand Attitude and
                          Choice
                    ↓              ↓
                Practical        Symbolic
                    ↓                ↓
         Perceptions of Brand    Fits My Life-Style
             Benefits                ↓
                ↓               Expresses My Identity
       Physical Justifications       ↓
                ↓              Helps Order and Structure
      Beliefs about Value for          My Life
              Money                    ↓
                ↓              Intuitive Likes and Dislikes
      Available and Habitual           ↓
                ↓
          Rational Overt          Emotional Covert
```

MEASURING ADVERTISING EFFECTIVENESS
The Advertising-Development Process

There is a circular process associated with the development of effective advertising, beginning with advertising-strategy development, and ending in a review of possible learnings for the future (see Figure 29.2). The process leads from an exploration of the macro-marketing issues surrounding the particular product-market engagement in which the brand operates through an elaboration of the strategic issues confronting the brand. This leads to the development of an advertising brief, and the agreeing of a creative brief with the advertising agency. In turn, the creative ideas put forward by the advertising agency are pre-tested amongst consumers. Having exposed the creative execution to an audience, the material is typically assessed amongst consumers to determine the impact of the execution and the degree of wear-out over time. Arising from this, there will often be generalised learning which can be fed back into the process of developing subsequent marketing and advertising strategies. Issues

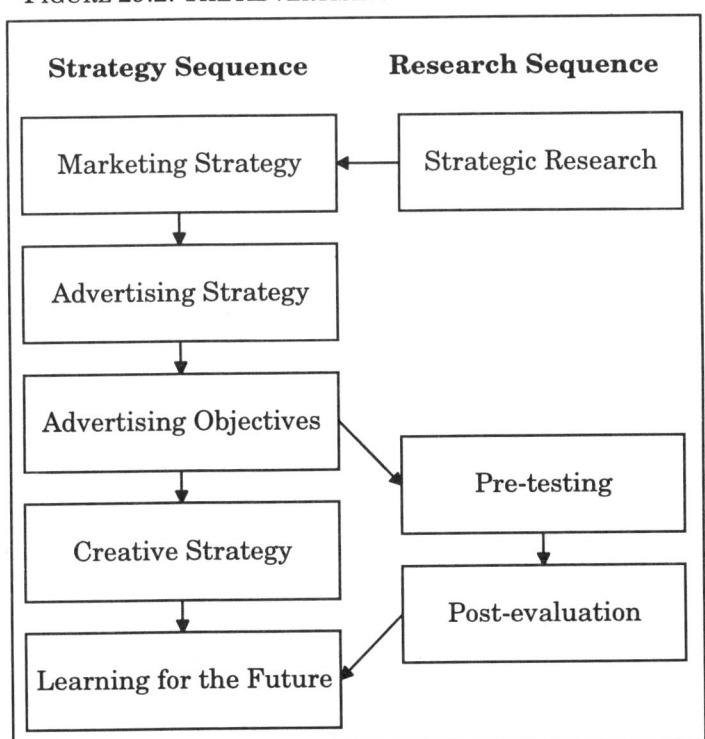

FIGURE 29.2: THE ADVERTISING DEVELOPMENT PROCESS

Strategy Sequence	Research Sequence
Marketing Strategy	← Strategic Research
↓	
Advertising Strategy	
↓	
Advertising Objectives	
↓	→ Pre-testing
Creative Strategy	↓
↓	Post-evaluation
Learning for the Future	←

shaping advertising strategy and strategy development are covered elsewhere in this volume.

Advertising Objectives

Armed with a model of how advertising works, it is only possible to measure the effectiveness of a particular campaign if the objectives of the campaign have been articulated. The traditional paradigm saw the objectives for any advertising campaign as being related to sales response, and this was the raison d'être for resourcing advertising. The linear-sequential model of advertising described above is very consistent with this view of the world. However, all available research suggests that the ability of advertising in general to call forth a sufficiently strong, measurable, sales response is quite limited (Jones, 1990). Jones has shown that advertising elasticity is typically much lower than price elasticity, 0.2 versus 1.8 respectively.

More recently, the focus of objective-setting in advertising evaluation has been linked to shifting the imagery of the brand, with any observed sales response seen as a secondary reaction. The view of advertising operating at the level of causing a re-evaluation of the brand, rather than calling forth a sales response, recognises that the processes involved at a consumer information-processing level may be more complex and less linear. In terms of imagery shifts, the process initially was seen in a stimulus-response framework. Advertising created or shifted brand imagery, which caused consumers to purchase the brand more frequently, as it was now more in line with their desired brand image.

In recent times, the paradigm of advertising causing a shift in attitudes to the brand, ultimately resulting in a purchase decision, has been somewhat discredited. In other words, it was proving difficult to show a clear relationship between advertising investments and changed brand imagery. Increasingly, advertising is seen to work through prompting *trial* of the product, with a shift in the perception of the brand occurring after trial, rather than the image shift *prompting* trial (Millward Brown, 1991). In other words, there has been a sea-change in the understanding of how advertising is believed to affect sales. It is no longer expected to cause a sales response, nor is it expected to cause a shift in the imagery of the brand, with a subsequent sales response. Rather, it is now seen to work by simply prompting trial, which confirms the image values communicated by the advertising, thus shifting attitudes, leading to the inclusion of the brand in the consumer's repertoire. In looking at advertising effectiveness, a key consideration is the sheer range of external factors which can influence both product sales and brand imagery. Figure 29.3 displays some of the influences on sales which may be at least as important as advertising.

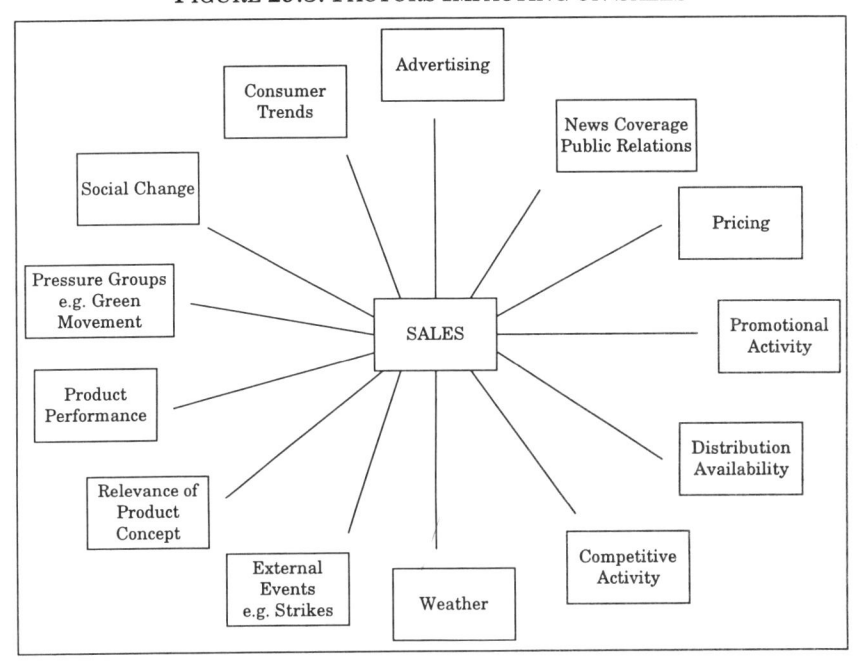

FIGURE 29.3: FACTORS IMPACTING ON SALES

(Diagram: SALES at centre, connected to: Advertising, Consumer Trends, News Coverage/Public Relations, Social Change, Pricing, Pressure Groups e.g. Green Movement, Promotional Activity, Product Performance, Distribution Availability, Relevance of Product Concept, External Events e.g. Strikes, Weather, Competitive Activity)

A NEW MODEL OF EFFECTIVE ADVERTISING
Effective Advertising is as Easy as ABC

Creating effective advertising involves teamwork between the various stakeholders in the communications process: the advertising agencies' creative team needs to be fully aligned with the client's vision of what the advertising is trying to achieve. The agency media planner needs to have sufficient resources and an understanding of the overall thrust of the proposed campaign. The client's marketing manager needs to be able to create space for the agency team to work effectively and supportively. Against this background, the process of putting in place the ABC (awareness, branding, communication) of effective advertising can proceed. Importantly, the key to effective advertising lies in the achievement of all three elements. For example, well-branded, on-target communication will be set to nought in terms of influencing consumers unless the scene has been set through the achievement of a certain threshold level of advertising awareness. Figure 29.4 shows how the three elements — A. Awareness, B. Branding, and C. on-target Communications — interact to create powerful advertising. The following section elaborates on the ABC of effective advertising.

FIGURE 29.4: THE ABC OF EFFECTIVE ADVERTISING

VISIBILITY = Awareness x *Branding*	X	COMMUNICATION
Media Spend		Communication Strategy (What to say to whom)
Media-Buying Efficiency		
Efficiency of the Ad Itself		Message
Advertising History		Empathy

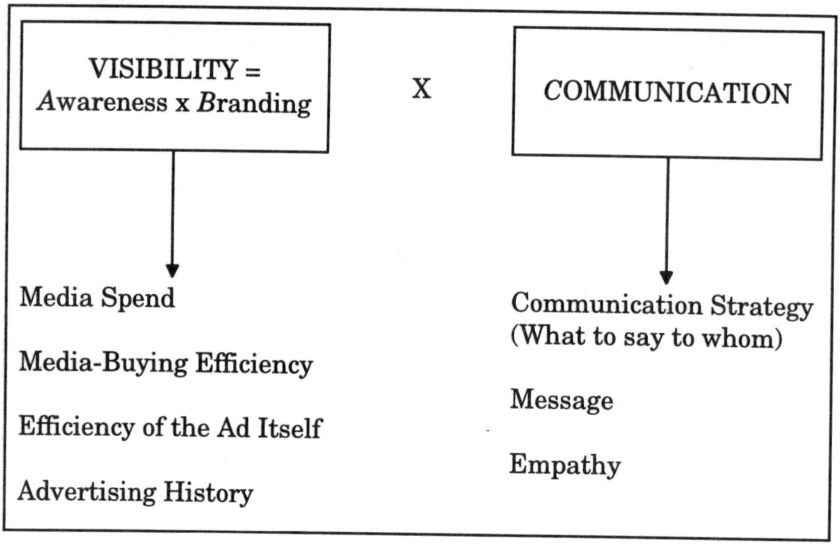

A. Creating Awareness

Creating awareness amongst consumers of a brand through advertising can be easily achieved if there is no financial constraint: irrespective of the potential of the creative material to cut through the clutter which characterises modern media, a sufficiently large spend will ensure that awareness is achieved. The characteristic of effective advertising is that it creates awareness in a cost-effective way, taking into account spending levels and patterns in the product category or relative to averages for the specific media. For example, two brands of coffee may enjoy similar levels of awareness through advertising, but one may have achieved this awareness by heavily outspending the other. In order to understand which brand is enjoying more effective advertising, we need to allow for residual memories of historical advertising (the adstock effect) and also to allow for the differing spend levels in the current campaigns. In other words, the intention is to exclude the impact of media and advertising history on the evaluation of the current campaign.

Millward Brown International has developed an advanced tracking programme which uses two inputs to provide diagnostic information regarding effectiveness in terms of creating awareness. *Media spend data* and *consumer awareness* data are brought together to model the impact of the advertising spend. The outputs from this exercise include a quantification of the adstock, the part of the awareness that the brand has been advertising, which is in fact derived from previous advertising by the brand. It also includes a measure of the relative effectiveness of individual campaigns known as the awareness index (that part of the total awareness that the brand has been advertising which is fuelled by the efficiency of the current campaign). Put simply, the awareness index is a measure of the extra awareness generated for every extra standardised media input. In the Irish advertising market, amongst those categories researched by Millward Brown, the awareness index can vary from 1 to 10, suggesting that within a category such as beer or banking there can be simultaneous campaigns which are 10 times more efficient in creating awareness than competing campaigns. The tactical significance of this is that a brand with efficient advertising can achieve the same level of awareness for a smaller spend, which is clearly highly desirable. Figure 29.5 shows the level of awareness achieved by a major beer brand as being a current television advertiser. The overall level of awareness achieved — almost 90 per cent for the brand in November/December 1994 — coincides with heavy advertising expenditure for the brand around that period as indicated by the black peaks at the foot of the diagram. This awareness is created through a combination of the historical advertising effect (the adstock level shown as the base level of 40 per cent) and the contribution of the current highly impactful creative material (the remaining proportion of the overall awareness level achieved). Quite evident from Figure 29.5 is the impact of the highly visible, creative material, which gives a huge return on each additional media pound spent.

A brand which enjoys highly-efficient advertising clearly can redeploy some advertising monies to other parts of marketing spend in a process which can lead to strong brands getting stronger, and the weak getting weaker. The key to creating awareness effectively, therefore, need not necessarily lie in the size of the media budget. However, creating awareness is a *necessary* but not a *sufficient* condition for effective advertising: effective advertising also needs strong branding and must communicate appropriate brand signals.

FIGURE 29.5: THE COMPONENTS OF ADVERTISING AWARENESS

Sampled on R.O.I.

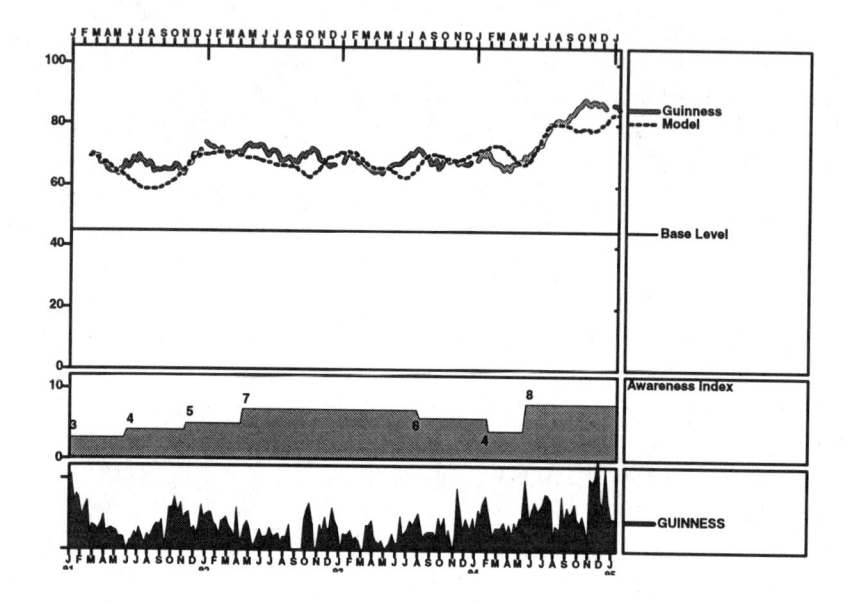

Rolling 8 weekly data

B. Branding Advertising Effectively

On the assumption that the campaign under consideration has overcome the hurdle posed by the need to generate awareness, the key to effectively creating awareness lies in having advertising creativity which cuts through the clutter in a *brand-linked* way. The lager market, for example, tends to be characterised by impactful, high-production-value advertising. Yet many lager brands fail to achieve the desired level of branded advertising awareness, not because the creative material lacks impact, but because the material fails to integrate the necessary brand references into the advertising. Classically, this leads to increased awareness that the category is being advertised but little *branded* advertising recall.

Any given commercial will contain scenes which are engaging and some footage which is perceived to be quite boring or irrelevant. It is important that the brand be associated with the more engaging sequences in the commercial, and that the engaging sequences be linked with the message in a believable and stimulating way. Recent television advertising for Harp Lager shows the effect of this so-called creative magnifier: not all sequences within the commercial are equally likely to be remembered, and it is vital that the brand be associated with the more engaging sequences within the advertisement. In Figure 29.6 it can be seen that the camel sequence (5 per cent of the length of the advertisement) actually accounts for 40 per cent of what people remember about the ad, in this instance the impact is evident, as 5 per cent of the transmission accounts for 40 per cent of what consumers remember about the ad. The learning from researching advertising and from the literature (Millward Brown, 1991) is that neither the brute-force nor the seductive approach achieves the required level of branding within commercials (see Figure 29.7). Sheer repetition of the brand name throughout the commercial will not create any association between the brand and the creative idea if there is no alignment between the two to begin with. Similarly, simply hooking a brand mention onto the end of a visually stunning and creative commercial will not create a link between the two unless the brand has some relevance to the visually stunning material. Put simply, neither *spend* nor *shout* is a substitute for the integration of the brand into the commercial.

FIGURE 29.6: THE CREATIVE MAGNIFIER

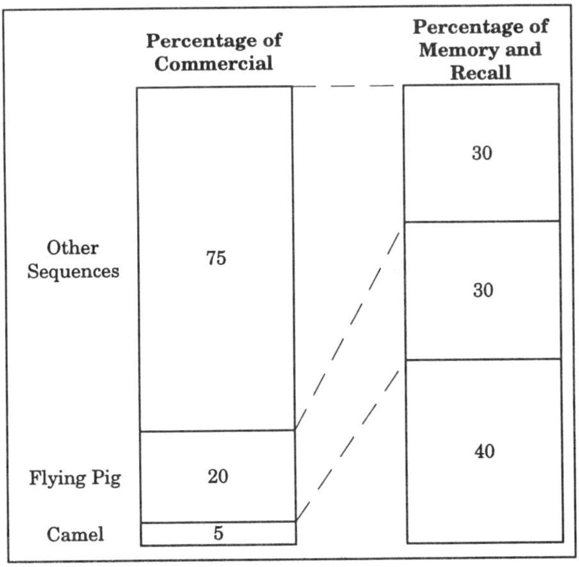

	Percentage of Commercial	Percentage of Memory and Recall
Other Sequences	75	30
		30
Flying Pig	20	40
Camel	5	

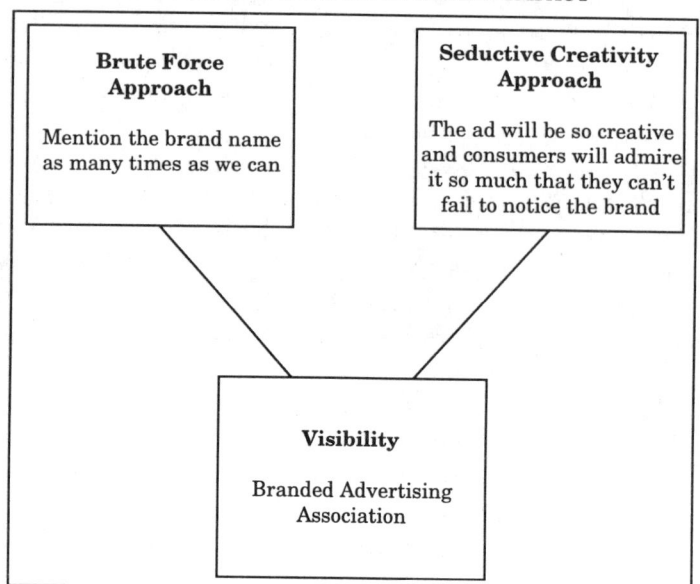

FIGURE 29.7: ROUTES TO BRAND IMPACT

```
┌─────────────────────┐      ┌─────────────────────┐
│   Brute Force       │      │  Seductive Creativity│
│   Approach          │      │   Approach          │
│                     │      │                     │
│ Mention the brand   │      │ The ad will be so   │
│ name as many times  │      │ creative and        │
│ as we can           │      │ consumers will      │
│                     │      │ admire it so much   │
│                     │      │ that they can't     │
│                     │      │ fail to notice the  │
│                     │      │ brand               │
└─────────────────────┘      └─────────────────────┘
            \                      /
             \                    /
              ┌─────────────────────┐
              │     Visibility      │
              │                     │
              │ Branded Advertising │
              │    Association      │
              └─────────────────────┘
```

C. Achieving On-Strategy Communication

In terms of a sequential communications process, the process described thus far (A and B) has generated brand-linked, impactful creative material which has gained "share of mind" amongst consumers. Creating awareness through brand-linked creativity sets up the consumer for the reception of a powerful message. The message must be delivered clearly, in an empathetic and enjoyable fashion, where any humour is presented as laughing *with* the brand rather than *at* the brand. Perhaps the most difficult stage in the pursuit of effective advertising lies in the final stage of implanting the advertising message in the mind of the consumer. All too often, highly impactful, brand-linked creative material acts as a communication vehicle for brand messages which are incorrectly processed by consumers, leading to irrelevant or even misleading take-out.

MARKETING RESEARCH CAN HELP CREATE EFFECTIVE ADVERTISING

Research is Integral to the Creative Process

The process of creating powerful advertising is intimately linked with the evaluation of advertising, a linkage which generally does not find favour with the creative chiefs of advertising agencies. Predictably, their view is that the creative process is so cerebral as to defy research, and that an injection of research into the creative process is a hindrance rather than a help. However, it is clear that marketing research has a key role to play in this area. Each of the three stages of creating powerful advertising is associated with a particular marketing-research approach. Given the modest advertising budgets of many Irish firms, and the relatively high production to air-time costs, the amount of resource available for researching advertising is quite limited. Consequently, the number of firms that systematically research this area, and the number that track advertising performance over time, is quite small.

Qualitative Research

Typically, a firm embarking on the development of a new advertising campaign will undertake some qualitative research, either before briefing the advertising agency or at some point during the development of the new creative material. The difficulty here is that qualitative research cannot shed any light on the likely impact and cut-through of the material because of the slightly hot-house nature of group discussions: group discussions do not replicate real-world advertising exposure as participants are being exposed to a variety of stimuli in a controlled environment. Once one participant cracks the advertising code or recognises the brand it is instantly communicated to all the other people in the focus group. As against this, qualitative research is an extremely powerful way of informing the development of effective branding within an advertising execution. In addition, qualitative research is unsurpassed as a way of understanding the take-out by consumers from advertising, and using group discussions at the development stage can help to turn good advertising into great advertising. In light of this, it is disappointing that Irish firms undertake so little qualitative research in the development stage of advertising. Sadly, even significant FMCG firms may only complete one modest-sized qualitative project per year.

Quantitative Research

In terms of quantitative research and its role in the development of powerful advertising, the situation is even bleaker: a mere handful of Irish firms (typically local associates or affiliates of global companies) undertake quantitative pre-testing of advertising. There are now several proprietary advertising pre-testing systems available from British research firms, but the ability of Irish firms to capitalise on these research products is again constrained by the shortage of resources needed to fine tune the advertising and promotion budget. The small scale of the local market has precluded Irish marketing-research companies from developing similar research products. Interestingly, this contrasts sharply with the international market for qualitative research, where there is a healthy demand for the leading Irish qualitative practitioners.

Advertising Tracking

Having created effective advertising — that is to say, advertising that is impactful, brand-linked and communicates the desired message — it is not enough to gain reassurance before it goes on air. It is important that the performance be monitored when aired, so as to understand how well the new material is wearing in, and to determine when the campaign is no longer working sufficiently hard for the brand. Evaluating advertising can be done formally or informally. Informal, casual, but positive, feedback from colleagues in the marketing, media and advertising milieu will be seized upon as robust evidence of effectiveness in advertising! Press mentions of a new advertising campaign, or the adoption of an advertising symbol or end-line in everyday language is often viewed as proof positive that the campaign is working well. However, this most casual method of appraising the effectiveness of advertising is really simply a measure of the success of the campaign as a media (as opposed to a brand-communication) event. At a less casual level, the Adwatch column in the *Irish Marketing Journal* (IMJ, 1995) is relied upon for feedback on effectiveness. This listing, based on unprompted consumer awareness of current advertising, is collected in a research omnibus survey and published monthly (see Figure 29.8). However, the real test of advertising effectiveness is a comparison of the objectives with the achievements at a brand level, in terms of improved brand awareness, imagery shifts and possible sales response. This requires a commitment to some form of tracking study based on an existing omnibus service or a bespoke research vehicle. At its simplest, this will require probing of brand awareness, advertising awareness, take-out from the advertising recalled and an exploration of imagery shifts which have occurred. Clearly, it makes little sense to conduct this type of investigation independently of the consumers' usage of the brand and product category in question. Most leading FMCG firms in Ireland, as well as the key financial-services players, will be routinely undertaking this type of research. A smaller number of firms will undertake dedicated advertising-tracking studies, with an emphasis on modelling advertising performance and diagnosing deficiencies in the current mix of advertising executions. Ideally, any such tracking or monitoring exercise should be continuous, as this will help to pick up any short-term effects and will help to monitor competitor activity.

FIGURE 29.8: THE ADWATCH TOP 10 ADVERTISED BRANDS

ADWATCH

	JUNE 1995	
1	(=)	GUINNESS
2	(=)	COKE
3	(=)	DAZ
4	(5)	SURF
5	(7)	BUDWEISER
6	(9)	ARIEL
7	(6)	PERSIL
8	(10)	PAMPERS
9	(-)	KELLOGGS CORNFLAKES
10	(4)	KIT KAT

Source: Adwatch (1995): *Irish Marketing Journal*, July/August: 6.

ADVERTISING EFFECTIVENESS — A LOCAL EXAMPLE

During 1994, Guinness Ireland aired a new commercial for draught Guinness, entitled *Anticipation*. Based on many years of collaboration, the genesis of this new commercial was a good example of effective teamwork involving advertising agency, client company marketing management and marketing research. The resultant execution is a good example of effective advertising at every level. The *Anticipation* execution generated a step change in the awareness that Guinness was advertising, a strong performance given the historically high awareness of Guinness as an advertised brand. Following the initial airing of the campaign, more than nine in ten beer drinkers could recall the execution. In addition, it was impossible to recall the specifics of the execution without alluding to the brand being advertised, Guinness. This is the ultimate test of the successful integration of the brand into the creative heart of the campaign. Importantly, for a big brand like Guinness, it is essential that the advertising should cause some positive reappraisal of the brand. The take-out from the *Anticipation* execution was that there were some new things to be said about Guinness, the drink, while reinforcing the existing imagery of Guinness as the pre-eminent beer brand with further endorsement as a high-quality beer, which is now becoming more popular and sociable. Despite the undoubted popularity of the actor who appeared in the execution, the hero was, and is, Guinness the brand. In terms of the rather trite assertion that effective advertising is as easy as ABC, the example of *Anticipation* shows how creating high awareness through effective creative material produced the current consumer take-out from the advertising.

FIGURE 29.9: STILL FROM ANTICIPATION

CONCLUSIONS

The single-minded pursuit of effective advertising is a legitimate objective for marketers today. The essential inputs to this process include an understanding of how advertising works, and alignment on what the advertising can be expected to achieve. However, the over-riding input must be an understanding of the market in which we operate and the nature of the players in that market.

This paper has taken market knowledge and wisdom as a given, and concentrated on reviewing salient aspects of the literature on how advertising works and what constitutes a reasonable set of objectives for advertising. The role of research in helping to create powerful advertising has been elaborated. Finally, in quoting an Irish example of effective advertising for the Guinness brand, we have shown that effective advertising hinges also on an understanding of the need for three preconditions — high levels of awareness, clear and close integration of the brand into the creative part of the advertising, and finally, on-target, unambiguous communication.

However, in a broader context, advertising is but one part of a complex armoury of communication tools deployed by modern marketing companies. The impact of all advertising — powerful and ineffectual alike — is mediated through external events, including conditions of supply and demand, as well as situational factors such as the weather and the retailing environment. In conclusion, advertising should be judged both against what it can legitimately be expected to do, and only then in the context of the wider framework of the market.

REFERENCES

Franzen, G (1994): *Advertising Effectiveness, Findings from Empirical Research*, Henley-on-Thames: NTC Publications.

IMJ (1995): "Adwatch", *Irish Marketing Journal*, July/August: 6

Jones, J.P. (1990): "Advertising: Strong or Weak Force? Two Views an Ocean Apart", *International Journal of Advertising*, 9: 233–46.

Lannon J. and Cooper P. (1983): "Humanistic Advertising, A Holistic Cultural Perspective", *International Journal of Advertising*, 2: 195–213.

Meenaghan J.A. (1983): "Commercial Sponsorship", *European Journal of Marketing*, 17(7): 5–73.

Millward Brown International (1991): *How Advertising Affects the Sales of Packaged Goods*, Warwick: Millward Brown International.

Prue T. (1991), "Recall or Response? Ad Effectiveness Monitoring: The Real Issues", *Admap*: 26(6): 38–40.

Wicks, A. (1989): "Advertising Research — An Eclectic View from the UK", *Journal of the Market Research Society*, 31: 527–35.

30
Playtime TV:
Advertising-Literate Audiences and the Commercial Game[*]

Stephanie O'Donohoe

> We never cease to be amazed at the subtleties and the understanding of the punters, the consumers in the marketplace. They've a much more finely-honed critical faculty about advertising than we often give them credit for.
>
> (Advertising Agency)

INTRODUCTION

The term "literacy" is used frequently and loosely these days, often describing people's facility with computers, film, television, or advertising. Language and literacy studies, however, suggest that it is inappropriate to study the skills of literacy in isolation: we must also ask how and why they are practised. This paper looks at the theoretical background and recent research concerning the skills and implications of advertising literacy. It argues that consumers not only understand the rules of the advertising game, but also use their understanding to play with ads in ways that practitioners may not intend and academics are only beginning to appreciate.

THE CONCEPT OF ADVERTISING LITERACY

Commenting on their increasing understanding of the vocabulary, elements and styles of advertising, Meadows (1983) described

---

[*] The young-adult research was funded by The Nuffield Foundation, with a pilot study supported by the Faculty of Social Sciences at The University of Edinburgh. Thanks are also due to Caroline Tynan and Bob Grafton Small for helpful comments.

consumers as "advertising literate". Lannon (1985) suggests that exposure to high-quality television programming may have taught people to decode complex visual imagery and make inferences from minimal cues in advertising.

The use of "advertising literacy" as a label for consumer sophistication resonated with many in the industry, inspiring articles by Drake (1984), Iddiols (1989) and others. Goodyear (1991) refers to five levels of advertising literacy, but expresses these in terms of typical advertising styles, rather than degrees of audience sophistication. She also discusses factors influencing the development of a country's advertising literacy. While such generalisations about whole countries are questionable, the suggested sources of literacy are intuitively appealing. Exposure to television, film, and advertising itself allows consumers to learn the conventions used in advertising. The level of industrialisation and consumerisation indicates the importance of added value through brand imagery: the more important this is, the greater the potential for advertising sophistication. Finally, national cultural factors favouring advertising literacy include an emphasis on trading consumer goods.

Given the lack of theorising about the nature of advertising literacy, it seems useful to turn to the discipline from which the term "literacy" has been appropriated (O'Donohoe, 1994a; Ritson and Elliott, 1995). Strictly speaking, "literacy" refers to the ability to read rather than write, and to understand rather than to produce (Graddol 1993). Indeed, Graff (1982) argues that "literacy" should be restricted to written or printed materials, as it is learned in different ways from oral and non-verbal modes of communication.

Many definitions of literacy are broader, encompassing speech, writing, viewing, and reading activities (Schieffelin and Gilmore, 1986; Buckingham, 1993). In this context, Graddol (1993: 50) defines literacy as "the ability to produce, understand and use texts in culturally appropriate ways". Advertising texts lack the formal grammar associated with verbal language, and their conventions vary to some extent across media. Nonetheless, they form a rich and complex signifying system, indicating that the concept of literacy may usefully be applied to advertising. In order to appreciate what it might mean, however, it is helpful to consider the skills that it involves.

Advertising-Literacy Skills: Previous Research

Little empirical evidence is currently available on this topic. While advertising practitioners have taken the lead in discussing it, their comments are often based on overviews of proprietary research, most of which are confidential. Details of some studies in this area are available, however, and they begin to paint a picture of advertising literacy skills across a range of ages.

In Britain, for example, Aitken et al. (1988) have demonstrated 12-year-olds' facility with complex advertising imagery, while most of Young's (1990) child respondents over the age of eight understood advertising's commercial purpose. Young addresses the issue of advertising literacy explicitly, relating it to children's acquisition of meta-linguistic competencies. More recently, a study of "television literacy" among 7–12-year-olds (Buckingham, 1993) found that even the youngest children were aware of advertising's persuasive intent. The children generally displayed technical knowledge and an understanding of narrative conventions, talking for example about hand-held camera shots or "cliff-hanger" ads. They could discuss why advertisers might have taken certain approaches, what reactions might be expected from the audience, and to whom particular ads may appeal. They made many ironic, sceptical and cynical comments about ads, sometimes drawing on negative experiences of toys or "free gifts" that they had seen advertised. They were often critical of ad characters or technical details such as the quality of acting, dubbing, and editing.

Nava and Nava's (1990) research, also discussed by Willis (1990), addressed the advertising sophistication of young working class adults. These young adults were astute at decoding complex messages, cross-references and visual jokes, as this comment reported by Willis (1990: 50) illustrates:

> You just listen carefully to the song so you can understand what the advert is trying to tell you. And when you see the pictures, you um try and work out what the song's got to do with that.

Gordon (1982) reports on a qualitative study of 18–55-year-old women. Her respondents — particularly those under the age of 24 — were aware of a range of advertising styles, mentioning categories such as "nostalgia", "comparisons", "follow-up", and "symbols linking to the brand". They had a well-developed, if somewhat cynical, set of ground rules to use in making sense of ads. For example, in the case of endorsements, "members of the public" were assumed to have been paid, and if their comments came from a genuine interview, it was assumed that the interview was edited. Turning to sex-role portrayals, respondents expected men's roles to be more varied than those for women, and men to be shown in positions of authority or superiority. Indeed, when traditional gender roles were reversed, ads were considered a "send-up", and not to be taken seriously.

More recently, Gordon's company worked with the Leo Burnett agency to examine British "mass-market" families' understanding of advertising (Rawsthorn, 1990). During a three-week period, families and marketing professionals kept a diary of their responses to television ads which made an impression on them, focusing on particular features of the ads, the extent to which they were liked, and the advertisers' likely intentions. Alan Setford, Leo Burnett's planning director, admitted to being surprised by consumers' "real depth of knowledge". They readily described advertising objectives, even using the same sort of language as the marketers: it was a consumer, for example, who referred to "a send-up of nostalgia commercials". Consumers also showed an appreciation of technical aspects of advertising, commenting on how "well-edited" ads were, or how they used "a variety of camera angles".

Advertising-Literacy Skills: Practitioners' Impressions

This section reports on exploratory research conducted in 1989 with ten Scottish-based advertising research practitioners, who worked in ad agencies and marketing research companies (O'Donohoe, 1994a). They regularly commissioned, conducted and read research on consumers' response to advertising. While such studies are not available to the public, it was thought that the practitioners involved could act as "key informants". Although their views would reflect their own professional concerns, it was thought that practitioners could offer a useful overview and insights concerning consumers' advertising literacy, and that these might suggest avenues for subsequent research among consumers themselves.

While there was some disagreement about the extent of people's understanding, the practitioners generally felt that consumers had gradually become more sophisticated and "advertising aware". This was thought to be particularly true of children and young adults, but everyone seemed to have views on advertising, and confidence in expressing them. As one agency planner put it, "They're all experts, everyone thinks they're an expert!"

The dimensions of consumer expertise which emerged in these interviews were consistent with the skills discussed above. Consumers were thought to be aware of a "spectrum of different kinds of ads". For example, they could distinguish between various "lifestyle" approaches, and between "state-of-the-art", "run-of-the-mill", and "old-fashioned" ads. They pilloried "naff" advertising, and responded to it in much the same way as "an English professor being handed a Mills and Boon novel". "Brand X" styles received particular scorn, as did "put-on" or affected approaches, which were seen as "out of touch" with real people. The practitioners also noticed how people increasingly talked about ads in a sophisticated way, "coming out with the jargon" to describe their reactions:

> They say something like "I didn't like the voice-over on that", whereas five years ago they might have said "I didn't like the man's voice" (research company).

Indeed, the use of such specialist terms in group discussions had led some researchers to worry about their recruitment procedures, in case these respondents worked in advertising. However, practitioners now accepted that "the punters" were gradually absorbing marketing and advertising terminology. Thus, ads were "targeted" at particular "segments" of the market, and "portrayed" the "lifestyle" of the "target audience" in mind.

Consumers were also considered "very sensitive to production values", and to the "look" of ads. They noticed how products were presented and how ads were shot. While they did not always know the technical terms (although their knowledge was sometimes surprising), consumers could describe a range of techniques. They might not appreciate the scale of production or media costs, but they could easily distinguish between cheap and expensive ads. "Crass" video techniques featuring products flying through the air were firmly associated with cheapness, while ads with a number of people, different sets, and good props were considered expensive. "Well-produced" ads were generally considered "classy" or "professional", and respected for that. This was generally gratifying for those in the industry. However, as Scottish agencies often dealt with lower budgets than those "down south", some practitioners lamented consumers' unwillingness to "take budgets into account" when criticising ads.

Wright (1986) coined the term "schemer schema" to describe consumers' intuitive theories about the ways in which marketers seek to influence them. The practitioners certainly believed that consumers could "have a flavour for what the advertising is trying to do", and to whom. They could distinguish between ads aimed at them and at others, and had moved beyond simplistic ideas about ads "just trying to sell something": they recognised that ads served a range of purposes, from gaining awareness to enhancing brand image. This understanding was not just an abstract one:

> ... by and large, they have no difficulty detecting what the underlying strategy of an advertising campaign usually is (research company).

In this context, a practitioner remembered a group discussion concerning an ad intended to reinforce a particular health-related behaviour. Respondents not only discussed the merits of that approach, but debated the feasibility of targeting those whose behaviour had lapsed instead. In addition to understanding various objectives, consumers tended to distinguish between "effective" and "ineffective" ads. Thus, while they often denied advertising's influence on them personally,

> ... they'll throw this back at you, the extent to which it features the brand name or the product name, whether it's selling you anything, if it doesn't tell you enough to make you go out and buy (research company).

Despite the view that consumers "can have a flavour" for advertisers' intentions, consumers were still considered to be too ready with criticism when they did not like an ad, regardless of what it was trying to do or whether they were in the target market. However, the practitioners themselves admitted to sometimes deriding ads which may well have been appropriate for their brief and target audience. Turning to advertising conventions, consumers were thought to have a good grasp of the "ground rules" of advertising. They knew that it was intended to "get a message over", and were

> ... slightly disturbed [when] an ad doesn't achieve that. It diminishes the value of the whole effort of communication if they realise it's not working (research company).

People were generally thought to accept that ads did not represent reality, although they were often willing to enter into the fantasies provided. For example, when some tourism ads were being researched, consumers objected to some showing threatening skies. It was not that they expected the weather to be constantly idyllic in the area, but they did expect some "advertising licence". Indeed, it was suggested that consumers

> ... build into their response an allowance for what the advertiser is doing, and they expect an overclaim. And if you undercut, you're discounted anyway (research company).

A related set of understood "rules" concerned the use of stereotypes. Consumers expected ads to feature "slightly idealised good-looking characters", and when ordinary people were used, they were seen to "stand out as being slightly abnormal". Groups of housewives often objected to stereotyped portrayals, and called for ads which showed men shopping or cooking. However, ads which did this were often criticised as "contrived", and role reversal "somehow often backfires". Similarly, certain product categories were criticised for "clichéd" advertising approaches, yet deviations often suffered poor recall or were considered "not quite right". This seems very surprising in view of the apparent distaste for "naff" and "run-of-the-mill" advertising. It may be that ads flouting the conventions challenged consumers' view of ads as easily pigeon-holed and dismissed, and therefore unlikely to influence them.

Turning to the sources of advertising literacy, the practitioners tended to focus on factors specific to the advertising industry. Indeed, there was a reluctance to admit that consumers had much to do with the development of their sophistication. Instead, it was argued — particularly by the advertising agencies! — that as consumers were exposed to so much good advertising, they had little option but to develop a "wide breadth of knowledge and experience" of ads:

> The British advertising industry is pretty sophisticated, and almost by definition, almost as a by-product, the British consumer is pretty sophisticated as well (advertising agency).

While the practitioners did not emphasise the way in which the mass media provided opportunities to learn advertising codes and conventions, they did observe that consumers came across a great deal of general media comment on marketing and advertising issues. Increasingly, practitioners saw particular ads, agencies and campaigns being analysed on television and radio programmes, or in articles in the press. "Young, hip and aware" consumers were thought to be particularly likely to see programmes about advertising. For example, a practitioner referred to a "youth" programme's feature on jeans advertising, which had explained how models were chosen, and previewed a forthcoming ad. Such programmes and features were thought to have given consumers a new vocabulary, a greater understanding of advertising, and perhaps a greater interest in its workings to boot. This certainly does appear to be the case, and is discussed in detail elsewhere (O'Donohoe, 1994b).

Overall, then, the skills of advertising literacy appear to revolve around the use of various cues to make inferences from ads, an understanding of specialist terminology and production techniques, and the ability to describe and evaluate a range of ads. While these emerge fairly consistently from various studies, we should also recognise that different literacy skills are likely to be acquired, valued and used in different ways by different social groups in different cultures (Gilmore, 1986; Street, 1993; Ritson and Elliott, 1995). Indeed, as we will see, considering literacy skills in isolation from the context in which they are practised would draw on a very partial and impoverished theory of literacy.

THE IMPLICATIONS OF CONSUMERS' ADVERTISING LITERACY

Commenting on the findings of the diary study conducted for Leo Burnett, Alan Setford (Rawsthorn, 1990) notes that advertisers can assume and demand a great deal of consumers. This points to the importance of creating challenging, intriguing and surprising ads, without sacrificing credibility or brand relevance. Lannon's (1992) continuum of advertising styles offers some suggestions of what this

TABLE 30.1. LANNON'S ADVERTISING-STYLE CONTINUUM

1. The Manufacturer Speaks	Similar to having a "salesman in the living room". Assumes the receiver believes that the manufacturer knows best and tells the truth.
2. The Target Group Consumes with Pleasure	Assumes viewers will identify literally or aspirationally with the people in an ad, which adds value to the product.
3. Hyperbole and Exaggeration	Flatters viewers by assuming that they understand hyperbole as an advertising convention: thus they can enjoy the fantasy and appreciate their own intelligence in recognising it as fantasy.
4. Brand Adapts Symbols and Metaphors to Express its Character	Commercials for established brands with an evolved and complex language code, flattering viewers by recognising their complicity
5. Brand Invents its Own Language	Most extreme form of flattery and assumed knowledge, as the advertiser essentially says "you now know me well so I do not have to explain myself. I can concentrate on stretching and engaging your imagination". The complicity and involvement are total.

Source: Adapted from Lannon, J. (1992): "Asking the Right Questions — What Do People Do with Advertising?", *Admap*, 27(6): 15–16.

might mean in practice. Her continuum represents the evolution of advertising as consumers have become more visually literate and adept at decoding, and as the complicity required of the viewer has increased.

According to the Scottish practitioners, one clear consequence of consumers' increased sophistication was higher expectation of a good advertising "product". Indeed, if consumers considered an ad to be entertaining or expensive, it was suggested that they might have more respect for the brand, because it was an indicator of the advertiser's confidence in it. There was also the suggestion — or hope — that sophisticated consumers of advertising might not reject campaigns which they disliked, if they appreciated that the intention was to gain awareness through irritation for example. While this would be very comforting to the practitioners, they also appreciated that ads failing to "get it right stylistically" for the target audience could lead to the brand not being taken seriously. Increasingly, advertisers were able to "get away with very little" in terms of weak propositions and poor material:

> People's experience of advertising is broader and greater, and so they are building finer filters against the bullshit part of advertising (research company).

In a sense, the advent of advertising-literate consumers made the task of advertising research easier, as consumers were more willing to take advertising seriously, get involved and discuss what particular ads were trying to do. Again, practitioners found this professionally gratifying. So far, then, it seems that the industry had little to fear from advertising-literate consumers, as long as it did its job properly. Some practitioners expressed concern, however, that consumers could use their knowledge and "professional" vocabulary to distance themselves from ads:

> ... they put up their shields and talk to you about "it's designed to do this thing and that". "And you say "does it work?" and they say "of course not, we know what it's trying to do" (research company).

In general, the practitioners agreed that consumer responses had become more self-conscious and deliberate: understanding that ads were "pitched" at them, consumers could choose to respond positively or negatively, and with cynicism or resentment at attempts to "manipulate" them. While the idea of advertising literacy facilitating greater distance or negative responses on the part of consumers worried the practitioners, it touches on a vital aspect of literacy theory which advertisers need to consider. As Maybin (1993) observes, there has been a shift away from viewing literacy in terms of skills and competencies, and towards investigating its role in social practice. Indeed, Rockhill (1987: 240) calls for research to address "how literacy is actually lived in concrete practices and daily interactions". Applying this perspective here, it seems that while we have begun to address what advertising literacy might *be*, we have hardly considered what it might *be for*: how do consumers practise the skills of advertising literacy in everyday life, and what purpose do they serve? Ritson and Elliott (1995) argue that answering this question requires an understanding of advertising-literacy practices and events. Literacy practices concern the tangible skills and purposes surrounding the "reading" of ads, while literacy events refer to the social interactions made possible by such readings.

Such a view is consistent with media uses and gratifications theory, which reverses the traditional question of what the media do to people, and asks instead what people do with the media (Katz, 1959). It sees the mass media as a resource which audiences use to satisfy various needs, and these needs or uses have been classified in a variety of ways. For example, McQuail et al. (1972) suggest that the media are used for purposes of surveillance and diversion, and to satisfy needs relating to personal identity and relationships. More recently, Lull (1990) suggested that the use of the mass media could be environmental (providing background noise, companionship, or entertainment), regulative (structuring time, activity or talk), or relational (facilitating communication, interpersonal affiliation or avoidance, social learning, and the demonstration of competence or dominance).

As O'Guinn and Faber (1991) observe, a uses and gratifications perspective on advertising is attractive, as it recognises that consumers have many different agenda, and may choose to use ads for purposes other than those intended by advertisers. Indeed, Lannon (1992: 16) has long posed "the question of what do people do with advertising: how do they use it? And what do they use it for?"

Turning to what those purposes might be, Alwitt and Prabhaker (1992) suggest that advertising serves hedonistic, knowledge, social-learning/contact, and value-affirmation functions. Others have suggested a range of purposes which advertising might serve. Thus, Crosier (1983) refers to product information, entertainment, implied warranty, value addition, post-purchase reassurance, vicarious experience, and "involvement" — the intellectual pleasure of working out puzzles or jokes. Moving away from product-related issues, Lannon (1985) discusses the aesthetic, emotional or intellectual rewards which consumers expect of advertising, while Cook (1992) argues that ads can fulfil a need for language play. In the emergent tradition of meaning-based models of advertising experience, McCracken (1987), Buttle (1991) Mick and Buhl (1992) and Elliott and Ritson (1995) have discussed how ads provide consumers with some symbolic resources for making sense of personal identities and life projects, and for facilitating social interactions and relationships.

Thus, a range of advertising uses and gratifications is possible, some of these relating loosely if at all to the business of brand choice. This chapter now considers one of the few empirical consumer studies on this topic. The issue of uses and gratifications was addressed in a broader qualitative exploration of advertising experiences, conducted among 18–24-year-old Scots between 1990 and 1991. The research involved 18 small group discussions and 16 individual interviews. Rather than imposing a set of ads on the participants, the study built on descriptions and interpretations of ads which they remembered themselves; as most of these came from television, the discussion below focuses on advertising in that medium. Further methodological details and findings are provided elsewhere (O'Donohoe, 1994a–c).

Advertising Uses and Gratifications among Young Adults

According to the criteria discussed earlier in this chapter, this study's participants were certainly advertising literate. This was demonstrated by their well-informed comments on advertising strategies, styles, conventions and imagery, and by their use of specialist terminology. In the course of the discussions, a wide range of advertising uses and gratifications also emerged. Some of these were clearly marketing-related: for example, advertising was used as a source of information, and to facilitate choice, competition and convenience. Many of the uses discussed, however, had very little to do with traditional marketing transactions. For example, commercial breaks during television programmes were sometimes seen as an opportunity to leave the room, put the kettle on, or make short telephone calls. Consistent with views of mass media serving a "surveillance" function, advertising appeared to be used as a means of scanning the environment, as well as part of that environment:

> It's almost as if advertising's become a thing like sport, and it's something you can watch, see the latest ... What's new in the cinema? What's advertising doing these days? (Male graduate worker 21–24).

Advertising was also used as a social resource, providing common ground for interaction with others. For example, the young adults often mentioned asking friends if they had "seen the latest" ad in a campaign. As one participant put it, this was a bit like talking about the weather, "only a bit more cheerful"! At another level, however, the ability to talk about and make sense of advertising was seen as a distinct if not particularly demanding social skill. Thus, someone described worrying about a Benson and Hedges ad which he could not work out, in case it cropped up in conversation and he would feel silly. This suggests that advertising-literacy skills may be related to a sense of self-esteem and social standing. There were other indications that ads were used in constructing or maintaining a sense of self: for example, by providing role models or reinforcing particular attitudes and values. In this context, an ad for Tennent's lager showed a Scot abandoning his London career in order to return home. This ad resonated strongly with the young adults' sense of national identity, as well as their personal experience of friends moving "down south" for work. The Irish version of this ad — with the main character returning to Ireland — may well resonate with its audience in similar ways, as the young exile is also a potent figure in this culture.

One final grouping of advertising uses and gratifications, which links some of the themes discussed above, is that of enjoyment. Advertising "broke up the text" in magazines, it made life richer and more colourful, and was something to look at when travelling on a bus or walking down the road. Many ads were "like wee programmes", while others were considered "more interesting" than television programmes, worth watching for "the enjoyment", "escapism", "wee stories", and "a good laugh". Certainly, advertisers are well aware of the need to entertain consumers in these ways, in order to attract attention or goodwill towards the brand. The enjoyment that the young adults derived from ads often ran much deeper than that, however. Grafton-Small and Linstead (1989) talk about "creative consumers" of advertising, while Willis (1990: 1) discusses how the "vibrant symbolic life and symbolic creativity" of young people's everyday activities helps "to establish their presence, identity and meaning" in the world. This idea of creative consumers has been taken quite literally by several spirits brands: Power's whiskey invited consumers to write in with their own offerings for the short-story campaign in the late 1980s, while Glenfiddich has recently requested semiotic analyses of the imagery in one of its ads!

High levels of creativity in the young adults' dealings with ads were certainly evident in this study, although not always in ways that advertisers would encourage. The young adults played with ads even in the research setting, often acting out scenes from them, trying on, discarding and making fun of various roles, characters, lines, and accents. Many characters were given walk-on parts, including Macbeth's witches, manipulative advertising executives, unloved traffic wardens, celebrity endorsers, and injured footballers. Phrases from ads were used as jokes among the participants in this study, and they described various instances of these being incorporated into their everyday activities:

> One of my friends uses the catch line all the time, the catch phrase and it makes me laugh (female student, 18–20).
>
> I remember when I was young we used to play this game, to see who could name the ad before it actually mentioned the product [laughter] (unemployed male, 18–20).
>
> One of my pals used to speak all the words before they'd speak them, speaking as they would speak them. Quite funny (male worker, 21–24).

The young adults also described how they sang along with their favourite (or most hated) jingles, and in several cases they performed them for the group. For example, there were many fond memories of the "Smiths Crisps" ad from many years back, and on several occasions the young adults performed the song and dance of the potatoes informing the world that "we wanna be Smi-iths Crisps"! They also remembered engaging in similar audience participation with other family members when the ad came on. If all this advertising-related play seems a little extreme, we need only think of the many (and well-rehearsed) versions of "the Guinness dance" performed on Irish floors following the Guinness's "anticipation" ad, or the way in which the reference in a Harp ad to "Sally O'Brien and the way she might look at you" invaded the Irish vernacular some years back.

In this study, various creative uses were reported for press ads, with many references to putting them into clip-frames or sticking them onto walls. One participant commented that Guinness ads generally made good posters, and someone else (a trainee accountant) regretted that he had never managed to get hold of a copy of the ad proclaiming "I used to be an accountant until I discovered Smirnoff". A female student described how, when she was younger, she had taken images from ads as the starting point for her own paintings, or used them to make collages. Some participants had literally transformed ads into pictures, by cutting out any references to the featured brand!

In general, these activities, jokes and games suggest that advertising may allow consumers to pretend, to play, to make their own fun from the raw material which it provides. The young adults in this study were also very keen to make fun of ads: indeed, it was suggested that without advertising, "there'd be less things to take the mickey out of". This was particularly evident in the case of ads which were generally accepted as "bad", "awful", "horrendous" or "tacky". Cinema advertising, particularly by local advertisers, was thought to be "so corny it's great", and "very amusing because most of them are so silly". Some extremely low-budget, "awful" television ads were also discussed with great pleasure:

— I really love, it's so cheap, the Balmore Double Glazing. It's so bad...

— I like the one for Martin's Plant Hire

— Not, oh please no, oh no!

— Oh it's awful!

— It's quite a good advert. It's just so horrible, that's why I like it (female students, 18–20).

Balmore Double Glazing ... they sing this ridiculous song and it was so terrible. The actors they got ... you could believe they were employees cos they were just so ridiculous.... Yeah, they have a sort of cult following among myself and my friends (female student, 21–24).

Clearly such ads were recognised as "bad", but for these advertising-literate consumers, this was a source of positive, almost perverse pleasure. The young adults relished the way these "awful" ads dramatically broke the conventions of "good" advertising. This in turn allowed them to congratulate themselves for their discernment (they recognised good and bad ads) and their independent spirit (they could choose to celebrate rather than denigrate bad ads, thereby subverting "the system" of advertising). This playfulness, subversiveness and self-conscious knowingness suggests that the young adults were confident players with what Davidson (1992) calls "advertising in post-modern times". It also resonates with Lull's (1990) suggestion that the mass media may be used to demonstrate competence, and indeed with Gilmore's (1986) concept of "sub-rosa literacy skills", or those owned and practised in peer settings. Observing the linguistic complexity of the games played outside an American school by students officially considered deficient in language skills, Gilmore (1986: 155) argues that such forms of play and social interaction

> ... often provide an unusually rich mode of expression for displays of language and literacy competence as well as for displays of culture and social relationships.

This perspective may help us to understand the young adults' pleasure in "horrendous" ads. Their enthusiasm in giving these cult status seems similar to the way in which some film buffs celebrate dreadful B-movies. Perhaps truly "naff" ads are the advertising industry's equivalent of *Godzilla* or Ed Wood's lifework, and are celebrated by consumer connoisseurs in that spirit. Sharing the celebration of B-movie ads with others allowed the young adults to project and collectively to reinforce an intelligent, ironic and independent self-image.

CONCLUSIONS

This chapter supports a view of advertising audiences as active, selective and sophisticated in their consumption of advertising. Examining the concept of advertising literacy, it presents evidence to suggest that its skills involve an awareness of different advertising objectives, techniques, styles and conventions, an ability to make brand inferences from a range of cues, and the acquisition of some specialist vocabulary. The practitioners taking part in the study reported here were agreed that consumers generally knew the rules of the advertising game, and had become increasingly discerning and demanding with respect to advertising. While this was not considered particularly threatening by those in the industry, there was some concern that advertising literacy might enable consumers to distance themselves from advertising's influence and disengage from its mystique. Indeed, the research on young adults' advertising uses and gratifications suggests that literacy skills may enable consumers to play games with advertising, rather than playing according to the industry's rules. Clearly, it is unwise to make sweeping generalisations about the nature and implications of advertising literacy, based on the research discussed in this paper. Nonetheless, it does seem clear that we should not only consider what advertising literacy skills might be, but also what they might be for, from the consumer's point of view. Otherwise, we will hardly begin to appreciate their implications for advertising practice.

What, then, might be the implications of active, playful, and advertising-literate audiences? Firstly, there are increasing indications that advertising theories — and methods of evaluation — need to be based on more complex and less mechanistic models of advertising response. Indeed, the term "advertising response" may be a dangerous one, as it obscures the possibility of active consumers taking the initiative and relating to ads according to their own personal agenda. Turning to the advertising planning process, researchers would do well to recognise and respect consumers' understanding of the advertising game, and to use research techniques and stimulus material to reflect that. Ads themselves can afford to be more demanding of their audience, and those producing them need to find ways of providing ostensibly non-marketing gratifications for consumers without losing sight of advertising objectives or brand strategy. While some advertisers might be tempted to produce a "Legendary Crap Ad" (Rowland, 1994a) to be consumed ironically by the target audience in ways which enhance the brand's prospects, this is quite a high-risk strategy; in any case, consumers are likely to consider such efforts far too contrived. Irony and playfulness are all very well, but these cannot simply be hijacked by advertisers without leaving creative consumers room for manoeuvre in what Ritson and Elliott (1995) remind us is "the co-creation of advertising meaning". Indeed, as Rowland (1994b: 24) observes,

> Irony is about consumers avoiding advertising's slings and arrows of intentional meaning — and finding another place from which to watch ... and laugh.

REFERENCES

Aitken, P., Leathar, D. and Scott, A. (1988): "Ten- to Sixteen-Year-Olds' Perceptions of Advertisements For Alcoholic Drinks", *Alcohol and Alcoholism*, 23(6): 491–500.

Alwitt, L. and Prabhaker, P.R. (1992): "Functional and Belief Dimensions of Attitudes to Television Advertising: Implications for Copytesting", *Journal of Advertising Research*, September/October 1992: 30–42.

Buckingham, D. (1993): *Children Talking Television: The Making of Television Literacy*, London: The Falmer Press.

Buttle, F. (1991): "What Do People Do With Advertising?" *International Journal of Advertising*, 10: 95–110.

Cook, G. (1992): *The Discourse of Advertising*, London: Routledge.

Crosier, K. (1983): "Towards a Praxiology of Advertising" *International Journal of Advertising*, 2: 215–32.

Davidson, M. (1992): *The Consumerist Manifesto: Advertising in Postmodern Times*, London: Routledge.

Drake, M. (1984): "The Basics of Creative Development Research", *International Journal of Advertising*, 3: 43–9.

Elliott, R. and Ritson, M. (1995): "Practising Existential Consumption: The Lived Meaning of Sexuality in Advertising", in Kardes, F. and Sujan, M. (eds.), *Advances in Consumer Research*, 22, Provo, UT: Association for Consumer Research.

Gilmore, P. (1986): "Sub-rosa Literacy: Peers, Play and Ownership in Literacy Acquisition", in Schieffelin, B.B. and Gilmore, P. (eds.), *The Acquisition of Literacy: Ethnographic Perspectives*, NJ: Ablex Publishing Corporation: 155–70.

Goodyear, M. (1991): "The Five Stages of Advertising Literacy", *Admap*, 26(3): 19–21.

Gordon, W. (1982): "Consumer Trends in Advertising", unpublished paper, London: The Research Business.

Graddol, D. (1993): "What is a Text?", in Graddol, D. and Boyd-Barratt, O. (eds.), *Media Texts: Authors and Readers*, Clevedon: Multi-lingual Matters.

Graff, H. [1982] (1993): "The Legacies of Literacy", in Maybin, J. (ed.) *Language and Literacy in Social Practice*, Clevedon: Multilingual Matters: 151–67.

Grafton-Small, R. and Linstead, S. (1989): "Advertisements as Artefacts: Everyday Advertising and the Creative Consumer", *International Journal of Advertising*, 8(3): 205–18.

Iddiols, D. (1989): "Unmasking the 'Advertising-Friendly' Consumer", Proceedings of the Annual Conference of the Market Research Society, Brighton: 251–61.

Katz, E. (1959): "Mass Communication Research and the Study of Popular Culture: an Editorial Note on a Possible Future of this Journal", *Studies in Public Communication*, 2: 1–6.

Lannon, J. (1985): "Advertising Research: New Ways of Seeing", *Admap*, 20(10): 520–24.

Lannon, J. (1992): "Asking the Right Questions — What Do People Do With Advertising?" *Admap*, 27(6): 17–22.

Lull, J. (1990): *Inside Family Viewing: Ethnographic Research on Television's Audiences*, London: Routledge.

Maybin, J. (1993): "Introduction", in Maybin, J. (ed.), *Language and Literacy in Social Practice*, Clevedon: Multilingual Matters: ix–xv.

Meadows, R. (1983): "They Consume Advertising Too", *Admap*, 18(7): 408–13.

McCracken, G. (1987): "Advertising: Meaning or Information?", in Wallendorf, M. and Anderson, P. (eds.), *Advances in Consumer Research*, 14, Provo, UT: Association for Consumer Research.

McQuail, D., Blumler, J.G. and Brown, J.R. (1972): "The Television Audience: A Revised Perspective", in McQuail, D. (ed.), *Sociology of Mass Communications*, Harmondsworth: Penguin.

Mick, D.G. and Buhl, C. (1992): "A Meaning-Based Model of Advertising Experiences", *Journal of Consumer Research*, 19, December: 317–38.

Nava, M. and Nava, O. (1990): "Discriminating or Duped? Young People as Consumers of Advertising/Art", *Magazine of Cultural Studies*, 1, March, 15–21.

O'Donohoe, S. (1994a): "Postmodern Poachers: Young Adult Experiences of Advertising", unpublished PhD thesis, University of Edinburgh.

O'Donohoe S. (1994b): "Leaky Boundaries: Intertextuality and Young Adult Experiences of Advertising", *Changes in Advertising and Consumption Since the 1950s*, Centre for Consumer and Advertising Studies, University of East London, September.

O'Donohoe S. (1994c): "Advertising Uses and Gratifications", *European Journal of Marketing*, 28 (8/9): 52–75.

O'Guinn, T.C. and Faber, R.J. (1991): "Mass Communication and Consumer Behavior", in Robertson, T.S. and Kassarjian, H.H. (eds.) *Handbook of Consumer Behavior*, Englewood Cliffs, NJ: Prentice Hall: 349–400.

Rawsthorn, A. (1990): "A British Perception of Commercials", *Financial Times*, 10 May: 16.

Rowland, G. (1994a): "The Cultural Significance of Legendary Bad Advertising", *Campaign*, 15 April: 31.

Rowland, G. (1994b): "It All Boils Down to Misinterpretation", letter to *Campaign*, 6 May: 24.

Ritson, M. and Elliott, R. (1995): "A Model of Advertising Literacy: The Praxiology and Co-creation of Advertising Meaning", in Bergadaa, M. (ed.), *Proceedings, 24th Conference of the European Marketing Academy*, Paris: ESSEC: 1035–54.

Rockhill, K. [1987] (1993): "Gender, Language and the Politics of Literacy", in Maybin, J. (ed.), *Language and Literacy in Social Practice*, Clevedon: Multilingual Matter: 233–51.

Schieffelin, B.B. and Gilmore, P. (1986): *The Acquisition of Literacy: Ethnographic Perspectives*, NJ: Ablex Publishing Corporation.

Street, B. (1993) "Cross-cultural Perspectives on Literacy", in Maybin, J. (ed.), *Language and Literacy in Social Practice*, Clevedon: Multilingual Matters: 139–50.

Willis, P. (1990): *Common Culture*, Milton Keynes: Open University Press.

Wright, P. (1986): "Schemer Schema: Consumers' Intuitive Theories about Marketers' Influence Tactics", in Lutz, R.J. (ed.), *Advances in Consumer Research*, 13, Provo, UT: Association for Consumer Research: 1–3.

Young B. (1990): *Television Advertising and Children*, Oxford: Clarendon Press.

31

The Social and Economic Effects of Advertising in Ireland

Caolan Mannion
Damien McLoughlin

> I think that I shall never see,
> A billboard lovely as a tree.
> Indeed, unless the billboards fall,
> I'll never see a tree at all.
> (Ogden Nash)

Advertising does not operate in a vacuum. While the intended result of the exercise might be to increase sales, brand awareness, or achieve some other marketing objective, it also has residual effects on society. Such deposits may be valuable, such as increased employment or effective dispersal of information, or detrimental, such as a weakening of the values of society, or the disruptive effects on our entertainment and leisure time. The objectives of this paper are:

- To review the main debates on the social and economic consequences of advertising and to examine them in an Irish context

- To comment on the validity of some of the claims and counter-claims

- To investigate the effect of society, through technology, on advertising.

When examining the debates relating to the effects of advertising, a contradiction arises. For convenience, many commentators have divided these effects into economic and social. In general, the economic benefits of advertising are balanced against the social consequences. Although this is an accepted dichotomy, it is not without problems. Most economic effects (such as high unemployment) have social consequences (increased poverty and associated ramifications, for example). Likewise, many social issues (such as an effort to preserve Irish culture or sense of identity) will have an effect on the economic policy being pursued by the government. While accepting these problems, we adopt this framework as the one with which academics and practitioners are most familiar and which most readily provides a framework to examine the key issues.

Advertising has been described variously as the "truth well told", or as "salesmanship in print" (Bovee and Arens, 1990: 4). A more generic definition (of which there are probably many in this collection) would describe advertising as:

> The nonpersonal communication of information, usually paid for and usually persuasive in nature, about products, services, or ideas by identified sponsors through various media (Bovee and Arens, 1989: 5).

Why does advertising exist? The question is primarily the focus of this paper. Advertising exists, say economists and business people, to sell goods, or to provide brands with identity. But it also manages to entertain, amuse, irritate, and permeate society (even if it does not intend to).

Society, for our purpose, is a group of people bounded by a common interest, be that interest geographically/psychographically (Irish society), temporally (twentieth-century society), or otherwise bound.

THE ECONOMIC EFFECTS OF ADVERTISING IN IRELAND

Advertising and the National Economy

Two issues in particular arise when one considers the impact of advertising on the national economy. The first is the role that advertising might play in stimulating economic growth, and the other is the position of the advertising industry as an employer in its own right.

When considering the relationship between advertising and economic activity, Callahan (1986: 215) identifies the argument quite clearly:

> Does advertising play a role in economic development? Does advertising cause consumption which leads to the employment of labour and capital, leading to growth in income? Or does the presence of consumption cause producers of consumer goods to compete for a share of the market, using advertising as a vital tool in this competition?

The need to understand this relationship has led to a multitude of studies. For example, for the US economy, several studies have found a procyclical relationship between advertising expenditure and the stages of the business cycle (Borden, 1944; Dean, 1950; Yang, 1964; Verdon et al., 1968). A similar effect was also observed for the West German economy for a number of different business cycles in the 1960s and 1970s (Bobel, 1982).

However, Chowdhury (1994) has suggested that the relationship observed is "fundamentally ambiguous and requires investigation". This deeper exploration is provided by Chowdhury in the form of an econometric model which examines the relationship between advertising expenditure and national income, disposable income and personal consumption expenditures. The results indicate that there are no definitive relationships between these variables and advertising expenditure.

While a large-scale examination of the Irish situation is beyond the scope of this paper, we can plot aggregate advertising expenditure figures against national income for the years 1989–93 (Table 31.1). The figures suggest some relationship between personal expenditure and the level of advertising, but really give no hint of the direction of the relationship.

TABLE 31.1: GROWTH IN TOTAL ADVERTISING EXPENDITURE BY MEDIA V. GROWTH IN PERSONAL EXPENDITURE ON CONSUMER GOODS AND SERVICES, 1989–93

	1989	1990	1991	1992	1993
Personal Expenditure*	11.3	2.7	5.1	5.8	2.8
% Change in Advertising Expenditure	14.0	6.5	6.1	9.7	8.0
Television	33.0	31.0	32.0	35.0	35.0
Newspaper	40.0	42.0	41.0	41.0	39.5
Radio	12.0	12.0	14.0	13.0	12.5
Other	15.0	15.0	13.0	11.0	13.0

* Percentage growth at current market prices.
Source: Meenaghan and Mannion, 1994 and National Income and Expenditure, Annual Reports, CSO.

The Marketing and Advertising industry is also a significant employer (see Table 31.2). In advertising, this employment is spread across advertising agencies, associated advertising specialists (media shops, consultancies and the like), production houses, and departments of larger companies (media departments in newspapers, broadcasting companies and so on). Of course, advertising also produces the fodder that keeps many marketing academics useful!

TABLE 31.2: EMPLOYMENT IN ADVERTISING IN IRELAND

	1989	1990	1991	1992
No. of Agencies*	40	38	45	41
Advertising	905	890	883	883

* Refers to the number of agencies responding to the CSO survey. This figure is likely to include all but the very smallest agencies.
Source: IAPI & CSO (1994).

It is difficult to quantify just how much employment is provided by advertising. The categories of employment in Table 31.2 deal directly with advertising, but there are also people not associated directly with the process who are kept working because of it. For instance, without advertising entire newspapers would fail. Also, a great deal of market-research activity is driven by advertising's need for market input. A further point worth noting is the changing structure of the advertising agency. While an agency in the 1960s or 1970s might have been fully integrated, an agency today is much more likely to contract out photography, typesetting and design. This reduces the headline figure of employment in the sector but emphasises the central role of advertising as a support of economic activity and employment.

The Role of Advertising in Market Entry and NPD

Although it is usually seen as a barrier to new entrants, advertising may also act as an enticement to new entrants. This dual role has been considered by Cubbin (1982).

The circumstance under which advertising may lead to new market entry relates to market positioning. When positioning a brand, a careful balancing act is undertaken to allow the new brand to position itself as closely as possible to consumer preferences, while at the same time distancing it from competition. The greater the degree of product differentiation (communicated through advertising), the greater the opportunity for unique and successful entry.

This effect can be observed in the fast-food market, for so long dominated nationally by the McDonalds and Burger King chains. These outlets expressed international and American values and boasted that the same meal could be had at any of their outlets around the world. In recent years, in Dublin and Galway in particular, the Supermacs chain has been able to position itself as the Irish fast-food chain. It advertises its Irish origins heavily, as well as the fact that much of its raw materials are purchased in Ireland — thus taking advantage of a gap in the market that was significant both from the competitive and consumer perspectives.

Advertising may also act as a barrier to trade under a number of circumstances. The first occasion is when a substantial expenditure on advertising has been made. This advertising is assumed to be sales diverting and the potential entrant expects the level of advertising to continue after entry. Such advertising creates a minimum marketing investment, which the new entrant must make in order to begin to compete on equivalent terms. An example might be the confectionery industry. When Cadbury was considering the launch of TimeOut, they had to consider the advertising levels of its two main competitors, Kit-Kat and Twix. As a result of the historical advertising spend of these two brands, Cadbury was required to spend IR£300,000 for promotion in the initial launch period of the new brand.

A second circumstance in which advertising deters entry is when consumers display more favourable demand for the incumbent's products and services. This advantage can arise for a number of reasons: the established firm's product may be superior or the market may simply believe it to be technically superior. Intel, for example, has managed to exclude competition for many years in this situation. A high-risk purchase may also lead to levels of incumbent loyalty. An example of this would be Procter and Gamble's Pampers nappy range which has been consistently in the top-ten ranking of Irish grocery brands, with sales in the region of IR£17 million, because of the high perceived risk of Irish parents. Finally, while consumers recognise that, physically, brands are similar, an existing brand may have certain positive associations which have a greater sales impact than technical evaluation. For example, the SEAT range of cars, while engineered and manufactured by Volkswagen, sells at a considerably lower price than the Volkswagen range. A new SEAT Ibiza retails at IR£10,000, while a Volkswagen Golf of similar specification will sell for IR£12,700.

Advertising and the Irish Media

By contributing revenue to broadcasting associations, newspapers, cinema, magazines, and much of the other media we interact with, advertising supports media diversity and promotes competition. This has a number of effects. More sources of information ought to be a sign of a healthy press and a healthy democracy, although it can very often mean greater conformity. However, a greater proliferation of media vehicles not only allows marketers to engage in segmentation (and thus keep their costs down), but also gives those media vehicles an opportunity to enter in the market, communicate their editorial content, and win customer loyalty (apart from the fact that some publications, such as *Buy and Sell*, are purchased simply for their advertising content — O'Donohoe, 1994).

TABLE 31.3: THE ROLE OF ADVERTISING AS A MEDIA SUBSIDY

	RTE	National Newspapers	Local Radio
Total Advertising Revenue (IR£ m)	71.44	88.0	18.1*
Total Revenue (IR£ m)	139.96	220	N/A
% of Revenue secured through Advertising	51	40	N/A

* 1993 figure.
Source: Green Paper on Broadcasting, 1995; IRTC; National Newspapers of Ireland.

RTE has gradually increased its reliance on advertising, with 51 per cent of its revenue coming from this source in 1994 (see Table 31.3), up from 44 per cent in 1986. The national newspapers have a similar level of dependence on advertising, with roughly 40 per cent of their revenue derived from advertising. The independent radio sector has also become a major force in the advertising arena. With advertising revenue of IR£18.1 million in 1993, a jump of 17 per cent from the previous year, this sector looks to be making a strong impact on the level of local advertising. What these figures clearly demonstrate is that advertising revenue plays a central role in supporting the main media in Ireland.

Table 31.4 presents an example of the Dublin market where advertising has encouraged a healthy circulation of local newspapers, with targeted journals aimed at south and north city and county. These media both allow local issues to be raised and provide advertisers with access to local audiences, facilitating more precise targeting. What the table does not show though is local papers such as *The Dublin Tribune*, *The Fitzwilliam Post* and the *Dublin Mail*, which have failed as a result of an inability to capture sufficient advertising revenue.

TABLE 31.4: DUBLIN FREE DISTRIBUTION NEWSPAPERS

	First Printed	Circulation	Publishing Frequency	Distribution
LifeTimes	1987	81,000	F/nightly	South City & County
Northside People	1987	50,250	F/nightly	North
South News	1979	51,000	F/nightly	South-East

Source: McConnell's Media Facts (1994) and Individual Newspapers.

The Advertising–Sales Controversy

A significant point of agreement between both champions and opponents of advertising is that advertising does make people buy things. For example, according to Vance Packard (1957: 11):

> Many of us are being influenced and manipulated, far more than we realise, in the patterns of our daily lives (by advertising).

Marketing professionals, in broad agreement, suggest that:

> In the long run, and often in the short run, advertising is justified on the basis of the revenues it produces (Peter and Donnelly, 1995: 133).

Unfortunately, both groups are probably wrong. In fact, researchers have been accused of running away from the problem of measuring the effect of advertising on sales (Murray, 1986: 18). Two approaches to the problem have been made. The first involves the inclusion of intermediate responses, such as advertising recall and intention to buy. This approach seemed much more actionable than attempting to make the simple sales/advertising link. Such connections tend to be more problematic. However, Murray (1986) would claim that it has been empirically established that brand awareness, attitudes towards brands and intention to buy are all related to usage.

Many of these approaches to measuring the effect of advertising on sales involve mathematical modelling. Murray (1986: 23–4) also comments on this approach:

> It has become fashionable to develop models of how advertising phenomena might operate and interact: the models either using highly restrictive constraints, which limit their practical application, or being based on intuitively "rational" assumptions to make up for the lack of empirical evidence. The word "reasonable" tends to be used when no reasons are detailed, the word "rational" tending to be used when no factual rationale is given for the assumptions used.

Although the link between advertising and sales is an opaque one, marketing effort is often equated with marketing success. While this is obviously a very over-generalised statement, it is worth noting that, in Ireland, companies with historically high levels of advertising are also market leaders. For example, the Guinness group has been consistently at or near the top in expenditure on television advertising. Its products accordingly dominate sales in the alcoholic beverage market. Coca-Cola has also been a long-term heavy advertiser on television and has a stranglehold on the cola market in Ireland (although this is under serious attack from own-labels and new brands at present. In the UK market, the Coca-Cola brand has fought back strongly with new advertising). Quinnsworth has been historically a heavy television advertiser, and has managed to continue to increase its already substantial share of the grocery market at the same time. However, it is not difficult to suggest other reasons why these brands and companies have been successful. This merely illustrates the argument of the sales/ advertising debate.

Advertising and the Consumer's Decision Process

Advertising is also a more efficient method for the dispersal of information. Companies need to communicate. In consumer markets advertising is mostly how they do it, while in business marketing, advertising also plays an important role in the communications mix. If advertising were removed from their spectrum of choices, that would not remove the need to communicate, but would simply make the process more expensive. In this situation, companies would have to resort to personal selling. Such an approach would ensure that the correct communication was made between the brand and the consumer and would also allow any queries regarding the brand to be immediately resolved. Unfortunately with the annual cost of a salesperson in 1993 running at over IR£43,000 per annum (de Búrca and Lambkin, 1993), such an approach is not feasible.

Advertising can also lead to cost-efficiencies for consumers. By informing consumers of what is available and the key differentiators of particular brands, advertising messages (though biased) often shorten (or eliminate) the search and decision processes. Fewer demands are then made on the consumer's time when it comes to making purchases. Arguably the consumer is also more informed and better able to counter the arguments of others.

The "full price" which consumers pay for a product is the actual purchase price plus the opportunity cost of search. The objective of advertising from this informational perspective is to reduce the total cost of the product. The seminal work in the area is that of Stigler (1961). According to Stigler, advertising is the modern method for identifying buyers and sellers. This identification of buyers and sellers drastically reduces the cost of search. In every consumer market there will be a stream of new buyers requiring knowledge of sellers; in addition, it will be necessary to refresh the knowledge of infrequent buyers. When price differences are large relative to the cost of search, it will pay consumers to search at a large number of establishments. If advertising lowers the cost of search, then consumers can take advantage of a given price dispersion by increasing search. Whatever the precise distribution of prices, it is certain that the increase in search will yield diminishing returns as measured by the expected reduction in the "full price" (Mixon, 1994).

Ehrlich and Fisher (1982) developed a model of the demand for advertising, which highlights the role of both buyers and sellers in influencing market demand. They argue that advertising affects the demand for goods because it lowers the gap between the market price received by the seller and the full price borne by the buyer. This gap exists because of the buyer's costs of obtaining information about the characteristics of varieties of products. This generates a derived demand for advertising by the seller as advertising reduces the time cost of consumption. What is required on the consumer side then is investment in knowledge. This investment minimises the time cost of the product. Under this scheme, profits are maximised. (Ehrlich and Fisher, 1982; Mixon, 1994).

Other variables may also affect the advertising–information flow relationship — for example, the number of brands in a given product class affects the amount of information search. As information must be gathered on additional brands, the marginal benefits of search decline as the number of brands increases (Meisel, 1979). Meisel further established, in the magazine and journal market, both that additional brands meant additional advertising (for every additional 12.5 brands introduced, the average sales to advertising ratio increased by 1 per cent) but also that consumers felt that they in fact had less information, and so began to rely on other sources of information.

In light of this trend, the need for more aggressive and attention-grabbing information may have led to a reduction in the actual information content in advertising. Beales et al. (1981) believe that legislative activity has ameliorated this advertising activity to ensure that consumers are to an acceptable degree provided with true and accurate information about products.

Advertising and Higher Prices

The relationship between advertising and price has always been a topic of contention and debate. While some would argue that with the elimination of advertising budgets the price of products could be reduced accordingly, others would say that, by stimulating competition, advertising in fact leads to lower prices.

The price of a product is affected by a number of variables: the overall level of demand for a product, the degree of consumer awareness of the price of a given product, the efficiency of the distribution method and the level of competition in the market. Based on the work of Reekie (1982), each of these variables will be examined and their effect on the price of goods highlighted.

Reekie's first contention is that advertising increases demand elasticity. Reekie rejects the first law of demand (that price varies inversely with quantity) on the basis of Demsetz's (1964, 1968) argument that this assumption ignores the way in which variations in demand increasing costs may affect the price that consumers are willing to pay for given amounts of output. In fact, consumers may be willing to pay a higher price for additional amounts of a commodity, as advertising expands. However, this price is still lower than the price under conditions of no advertising, when demand is lower and average costs much higher. This contention is supported by the work of Benham (1972) on spectacle prices in the US. In those states where advertising was banned, glasses prices tended to be from 25 to 100 per cent higher than in those states where advertising was permitted.

The second law of demand (consumers do not react to a price change immediately, so price sensitivity in the long run is greater than that in the short run) is also rejected by Reekie (1982). In fact, advertising can broadcast information about a price reduction and inform the market on the significance of a price change. Thus, demand is less elastic and average price is then higher in the absence of advertising.

The third issue addressed by Reekie is the effect of advertising on the efficiency of distribution. From any evening's viewing of television, it is obvious that most advertising is for FMCG products. Typically these are products that require little attention from retailers in the form of product information and service. Rather, these products are pulled through the channel by advertising. In order to facilitate this, prices must not complicate the pull equation. That is, retailers cannot charge prices radically different from other retailers, as consumers are typically informed via advertising. Instead, distributor profit is achieved via rapid turnover. The expectation then is that the lowest retail margins would be secured for the best-selling and most heavily advertised products. This proposal is supported by Reekie (1981) in a summary of data from the largest US food chains and 1,000 products. Table 31.5 summarises the results.

TABLE 31.5: PACKAGED GROCERY SALES, RETAIL MARGINS AND ADVERTISING BY MANUFACTURERS IN NATIONAL MEDIA

Leading Product Groups	Percentage of Retailers' Total Food Sales	Average Retailer's Margin	Advertising per Product Group (£ m)
Best Sellers	19.0	6.0	10
Moderate Sellers	19.0	11.0	3.5
Poor Sellers	23.5	12.5	0.5

Source: Reekie (1981).

The data presented in this table clearly supports the contention that those products which receive the highest advertising are also the ones which are subject to the lower retailer margins. In the words of Reekie (1982: 133):

> ... the burden of proof for the case that advertising and high prices are associated lies squarely on the shoulders of those who make the charge.

THE SOCIAL EFFECTS OF ADVERTISING IN IRELAND
Public-Service Advertising

A government can also benefit from advertising, as advertising can be used to promote a point of view. Sometimes this point of view is well accepted and not controversial — promoting voter registration, for example, or encouraging people not to drink and drive. In other instances the purpose to which governments put advertising has been open to greater question. For example, in Ireland government advertising expenditure to support the recent abortion information referendum was particularly criticised. Likewise the proposed expenditure on the forthcoming divorce referendum has created quite a deal of controversy. One may argue that these are our elected leaders, they are in office to provide direction and are not impelled to provide two sides to every story. Nor is Ireland, because of its wide and diverse sources of information, likely to become beholden to a consistent and ongoing "propaganda" campaign designed to harm democracy. (Propaganda is a loaded word because of the implication that the information communicated is tainted). In sum, government benefits, not everyone is pleased about it, but clearly it is something that the government is entitled to do and it is not morally deficient in seeking to do so.

Public-service advertising is becoming an increasingly widely used tool in government efforts to improve the lifestyle of its citizens. For Ireland it is difficult to establish a total figure for advertising expenditure across government departments. What can be done is to choose the two main spenders, the Department of Health and the Department of the Environment, and to assess their advertising spend over the past five years. Table 31.6 below shows the expenditure of both departments on advertising over the past five years.

What these figures clearly indicate is increasing interest in the use of public-service advertising as a tool of government policy. This public-service advertising can be seen to operate in two ways, firstly as a preventative promotion. In this instance, fear appeals are widely used. For example, by highlighting the "AIDS can affect anyone" theme, people can be encouraged to use condoms when having sex. A second form of public-service advertising is also often used. This is based on moral appeals. An example of this might be advertising by charitable bodies or the confidential telephone advertising which has been employed by the Northern Ireland Office.

TABLE 31.6: EXPENDITURE ON PUBLIC-SERVICE ADVERTISING, DEPARTMENTS OF HEALTH AND ENVIRONMENT IN IRELAND, 1990–94

	1990	1991	1992	1993	1994
Dept. of Health (IR£000)	751	900	1080	1080	1599
% Increase	—	20	20	—	48
Dept. of Environment (IR£000)	—	147	136	244	271
% Increase	—	—	-7.5	79.5	11

Source: Estimates for Public Services 1990–94 and the Department of the Environment.

Sports, Education and the Arts

During the summer of 1995 more than IR£10 million will be spent sponsoring major Irish sporting fixtures (Malone, 1995). The biggest sponsor of sport in Ireland is Guinness which spends in the region of IR£5–6 million per annum. This spend is spread across a number of its major brands. The core Guinness brand is backing the All-Ireland hurling championships with a three-year deal valued at up to IR£2 million (Malone, 1995). The Smithwicks ale brand is closely associated with domestic rugby and Harp has been the sponsor of the FAI cup for the past number of years. While it has been seen as difficult to evaluate the effectiveness of such campaigns from the corporate viewpoint, there are two very real opportunities for the recipients. Firstly, it allows events to be run with maximum benefit to participants. For example, the prize fund for participation in the FAI Cup could not possibly be as great without the support of Harp. Secondly, in many instances the support of a professional marketing organisation raises awareness of the event. For example, the GAA hurling championships in 1995 are supported with an excellent Guinness campaign based on the slogan "nobody said it would be easy".

The arts have also benefited from the support and sponsorship of business. For example, the attraction of international talent to an Irish piano competition would have been more difficult without the financial support of the GPA group. The additional benefit of this support is that it raises the whole profile of the event in the media and encourages ticket sales.

Many other events — rock concerts, the IRMA awards, the Chris Eubank *v.* Steve Collins fight in Millstreet — would not have been possible, or as commercially successful, without the support of business sponsors.

Subverting Society's Agenda

Just as governments and public bodies have the opportunity to advertise to demarket products or activities that they consider harmful to society, private interests have the right to respond to these attempts with advertising campaigns of their own. This response is relatively unusual, as governments will typically only use advertising to change action on something that society in general agrees is negative. One industry which is taking such action, however, is the tobacco industry and the Philip Morris brand in particular.

Over the past 25 years, smoking has become increasingly reviled and rejected as a social activity, and consequently legislated against. Irish legislators have banned smoking in sections of all restaurants, cinemas and public transport. In the US the régime is even tighter, with "smoking forbidden on eight out of ten American trains and in one in three shopping malls. In at least a dozen instances, parents who smoke have been denied custody of children in divorce cases" (Macintyre, 1995). Macintyre proceeds to speculate that "smoking may soon become, like sex, an activity that can be conducted only in private between consenting adults".

Philip Morris is directly attacking the waves of anti-smoking legislation, and through this the overall attitude to smoking amongst national and international opinion leaders. The campaign is run with full-page advertisements in international journals such as *The Economist* and *Time*. An example of the copy strategy adopted is an advertisement that lists the number of words in well-known "laws" such as the Ten Commandments (179 words), the Declaration of Independence (300 words) and Archimedes Principle (67 words), and then reports that "recent European legislation dealing with when and where you can smoke ..." amounts to 24,942 words (this advertisement can be seen in *The Economist* newspaper, 13 May 1995: 59).
While it would be overly suspicious to suggest that Philip Morris was in some way trying to subvert the course of public health policy, it is very clearly attempting to influence the passage of ongoing legislation affecting smokers. Some might applaud this as protecting freedom of speech. Others would suggest that it is an example of financial might dictating the public health agenda.

A more substantial accusation which can be levied at advertisers is the notion that they can influence editorial content of the media in which they are placed. For instance, in the United States, network television, which is entirely dependent on advertisers for revenue, can justifiably be accused of being rarely controversial and oftentimes bland, in order to attract the maximum number of viewers and build ratings for advertisers. Indeed, frequent commercial breaks have become more interesting than the programmes they support, and content which would be regarded as controversial or possibly inflammatory has been cut back or discarded entirely. Publishers have proven harder to influence: no one, for instance, would credibly claim that the editorial content of *The Irish Times*, or the *Wall Street Journal* can be affected by advertisers. Similarly, magazines which carry stinging reviews of an advertiser's product can, in the same edition, carry advertising for that product.

Advertising and Social Values

There is a vast, and not wholly conclusive, literature on the relationships of media and society and the nature of effects of media on specific groups and human values. It is within this context that the role and effects of advertising must be considered. Both the proponents and the critics of advertising agree that the practice is not value neutral. Advertising does promote values that hinge on the ability of material goods and possessions to satisfy needs and attain the "higher order" (or terminal) values mentioned by Rokeach (1974). There is a difference of opinion, however, as to what effects these value-laden messages have on their recipients. Critics of advertising argue that a continual stream of advertising and promotion has contributed to a materialist-oriented society which views the answer to all problems and needs in the continual acquisition of goods and services. Such messages have had a detrimental effect on society which has turned away from other means, such as generosity, sharing, and self-fulfilment as ways to satisfy terminal values such as "happiness" (Pollay, 1986).

Not so, say supporters of advertising. Firstly, if society truly does place a higher priority on possessions and material goods, advertising has not made the world that way. Long before advertising became commonplace, goods had a central place in many people's lives, and we hear tales of royalty or powerful people whose power derived not only from their position in life, but also from the things that they owned (McCracken, 1990). Secondly, advertising is just one source of societal communication, and cannot be said to communicate all of a society's values to its constituents. Other media and other vehicles also communicate values: these include parents, school, plays, poems, books, and a vast array of other means. Moschis and Churchill (1978) examine the socialisation process and the influence of events other than television on the value-formation process. The values promoted by other media are also accused of subverting "normal" values. Thus, books have been censored and movies and music have been criticised. Finally, it is not even clear that the values promoted by advertising are not wholly materialistic. While they do promote goods (for that is their purpose), they do so by way of reference to positive values such as generosity (the famous Cadbury's Roses ads), interaction between people ("reach out and touch someone with Telecom"), happiness ("a cigar called Hamlet"), and caring ("keep it with Kodak"). Advertising is not value neutral, but in so far as it features value-defined situations, they tend to be positive rather than negative. However, it might be argued that it trivialises selective values and reinforces conformity.

The subject of advertising to children is also contentious. Certainly children may be valid target consumers in that they purchase goods, and, more importantly, influence the purchase of many other goods, from toys to foodstuffs. This does not, however, mark them as suitable candidates for many advertising messages, some of which are restricted to certain broadcast slots in order to minimise the exposure of children (for example, in Ireland, alcohol advertising on television is shown only after nine in the evening, and cigarette advertising is banned, and so on). There is also a view prevailing that advertising in general is bad for children, for the following reasons:

- Showing advertisements repeatedly to children will instil materialist values into these "blank slates".

- Children will covet items (toys) that their parents cannot afford.

- Advertising runs contrary to many of the lessons that parents are trying to teach children (such as how confectionery destroys teeth).

- Advertising can be used to make children feel inferior or "not part of the gang", if they are missing some necessary accoutrement, such as a ninja turtle, from their assembly of toys.

Nevertheless, the Advertising Standards Association of Ireland has laid down comprehensive guidelines on how children's advertisements should be handled. They say that "direct appeals or exhortations to buy should not be made to children unless the product advertised is one likely to be of interest to them which they could reasonably expected to afford for themselves" (Advertising Standards Authority for Ireland, 1988). Further, an advertisement should not encourage children to believe that they will be inferior to other children or unpopular if they do not buy a particular product, or have it bought for them. How initiatives like these can be or actually are policed would be open to interpretation, as the messages that an adult receives from an advertisement might be different from the messages that a child receives from the same piece of communication. For example, the adult and child/youth interpretations of *The Simpsons* might be very different.

A further charge levelled against advertising is that it debases language, both by introducing new and meaningless words in the form of brand names (Lotto, FedEx, Xerox, Hoover), and, more seriously, by reducing the meaning of, and trivialising the meaning in, everyday language. For instance, to hear a new washing powder or automobile described as "the best ever", has been invoked so often and by so many as to consign the phrase and the words to an intellectual dump. Do consumers believe what they hear? Do they even hear it? A campaign is currently under way in the United States to restrict this "puffery" to entirely provable claims (Warner, 1995). Some companies, such as BMW ("The Ultimate Driving Machine") object to this movement, arguing that consumers are intelligent people and can discern fact from hyperbole. Levitt (1993) makes a similar point, saying that "consumers don't have to be especially smart not to be dumb". The issue of whether advertisers have a right even to engage in hyperbole is not addressed. The motivation for the revisions to existing laws, according to Warner (1995), is that regulators believe that decisions to purchase goods today are made far more as a result of advertising than was the case in the past. In the meantime, advertisers are clutching for ever more superlatives to heap upon their products and services. In the US, automobile dealers frequently fill the airwaves with news about their "monster extravaganza" or "never to be repeated offer", in a manner which can be frightening to the consumer, and can make consumers feel somehow derelict in their duty if they fail to check out this or that promotion. Meanwhile in Ireland, some large electrical retailers are equally profligate, claiming "till nine tonight" offers even though there are only limited numbers of stock items.

Does advertising promote "harmful" products, such as cigarettes and alcohol? Certainly it does, but such products are not illegal, nor or they illegally advertised — even when illegal and without advertising, demand has thrived (for example, during American Prohibition). Further, advertisers are restricted in the formats and times in which they can advertise these products. This is not such a clear-cut subject however. Do advertisers, for instance, encourage increased usage to current consumers, or play a role in recruiting new users, such as children? The cigarette and alcohol companies say no, that there are other factors (which there are, such as peer pressure), and that the purpose of their advertising campaigns is to redistribute the existing pie among competitors, rather than to increase the size of the pie in total.

Whether such protests of innocence are entirely believable, however, is dubious. For instance, Camel, a cigarette manufacturer, has come under strong criticism for using a child-like cartoon character as its mascot. Although Camel has denied that the mascot is a piece of "kid-bait", it has quietly withdrawn the character from circulation (Hwang, 1995).

Can Advertising Manipulate Consumer Purchase?

It is one of the great myths in marketing that by flashing the message "Coke" and "Popcorn" on a cinema screen during a movie in 1958, a significant increase in sales of these products was achieved. It is equally widely accepted that this experiment was conducted in an uncontrolled environment, and any number of external factors may have accounted for the increase in sales. Indeed, many academic researchers, having investigated this topic, have found that there is no possibility of predicting an effect in an advertising setting (e.g. Voor, 1956; Dixon, 1971, 1981; Severence and Dyer, 1973; Weintraub and McNulty, 1973; Moore, 1982; Gable, Wilkins, Harris and Feinberg, 1987; Saegert, 1987; Beatty and Hawkins, 1989).

Despite this overwhelming evidence, some authors (e.g. Key, 1972, 1976, 1980 and 1989) continue to insist that hidden or embedded messages are widespread and effective (Rogers and Smith, 1993: 10). What is perhaps even more surprising is the high and consistent proportion of the US population which believes that subliminal advertising is both engaged in and successful in marketing practice. Comparing their own study with that of authors from different populations and time periods, Rogers and Smith (1993) have found that more than half of adult Americans believe that subliminal advertising is used on a regular basis.

A more obvious problem is one of misinformation. Some European research on the general topic of misinformation is reported by Barnes (1982). On the topic of misinformation and unnecessary purchase,

Barnes reports a distinct "other people ... but not me effect". To identify this, he compares a study conducted by the then EEC and a follow-up study conducted by the Advertising Association (AA) of Great Britain. As Tables 31.7 and 31.8 below illustrate, the EEC study managed to suggest both that "advertising often misleads consumers" and that "advertising often makes consumers buy goods which they do not really need". The AA study asked individuals whether they personally were often misled, and the results were significantly different, showing advertising in a more positive, less manipulative light.

TABLE 31.7: COMPARISON OF DIFFERENT QUESTIONS ABOUT ADVERTISING AS MISLEADING (UK RESULTS ONLY)

	EEC Survey "Advertising often misleads consumers"	AA Survey "The ads you see are often misleading"	AA survey "I am frequently misled by the ads I see"
Agree Entirely	33%	29%	12%
Agree on the whole	45%	38%	16%
Disagree on the whole	13%	20%	30%
Disagree entirely	3%	8%	38%
Don't know/no reply	6%	5%	5%

Source: Barnes (1982).

TABLE 31.8: COMPARISON OF DIFFERENT QUESTIONS ABOUT UNNECESSARY PURCHASES (RESULTS FOR THE UK ONLY)

	EEC Survey "Advertising often makes consumers buy goods which they do not really need"	AA Survey "Advertising makes people buy things they do not want"	AA survey "Advertising makes me buy things I do not want"
Agree Entirely	33%	27%	4%
Agree on the whole	45%	32%	11%
Disagree on the whole	14%	16%	19%
Disagree entirely	5%	22%	65%
Don't know/no reply	3%	3%	1%

Source: Barnes (1982).

When the questions are turned into individual ones, the negativity towards advertising reduces across the board. However, the most striking result is for those who entirely disagree either that they are "frequently misled" or "[made] buy things [they] do not want".

ADVERTISING AND ANOTHER SOCIETY

While the previous analysis has focused on the effects of broadcast, mass-market media, there is currently a move toward a more narrow media format. The effects of this on marketing will be more specific targeting of marketing effort. We should thus expect different consequences of advertising to be observed.

Previously, society was defined as a group of people with something in common. Often in this debate about advertising there is an assumption that society is bounded by geographical or physical frontiers. This is not always the case and here on might give pause for thought to another society, some 20 years in existence, but which is only now gaining the attention of advertisers as it begins to become more accessible and grow at an exponential rate. The society in question is, of course, the Internet.

The Internet, described by *The Economist* (1995) as "a microcosm of society", is currently drawing the attention of a great number of companies which can advertise their wares and demonstrate their products in a forum that, thus far, has not been subject to any type of special government or social regulation, beyond those which exist for all organisations. Most industries are now represented in some fashion on the Internet, and John Patrick, Vice President of Internet Applications at IBM has said that, soon, to have an Internet presence will be as indispensable for a company as having a fax machine (Patrick, 1995). The most visible and potentially controversial part of the Internet is the World Wide Web, where graphical images and capabilities have drawn much fire from sections of society (the media, government, and various consumer groups). This, in turn, has drawn the wrath of promoters of the Internet:

> In the wake of Oklahoma City, anti-/violence/pornography/bomb downloading rhetoric is becoming the stock-in-trade of pandering politicians who wouldn't know a modem if it hit them on the head. (Rizetnikof, 1995: 33).

Despite the fact that most industries are represented on "the Web", there is also much that is of debatable value being advertised there, including gambling, pornography (*Penthouse* is the most visited site on the Web according to *The Economist* (1995)) and other examples of sedition and extremism. As of yet, none of this is subject to special regulation. Bills are now being proposed in some legislatures (the US, Singapore, New Zealand) which would restrict the information available on the Internet, though such legislation is likely to encounter at least two types of problem.

Firstly, very few people know what the Internet is. Certainly it includes the World Wide Web, but that is only its most recent incarnation. The Internet also includes E-mail communication, and subscription to newsgroup services, both of which would prove difficult to police (though perusal of E-mail messages once they have been sent is possible and has been the subject of a number of high-profile cases). In a typical month, one corporation, Hewlett Packard, sends and receives over 28 million E-mail messages. There are some 14,000 newsgroups offering discussion ranging from the latest happenings on *Melrose Place*, to how to fix your car or build a birdhouse. There are also many newsgroups of an unsavoury nature, though these are not the places where advertisers are either. Most advertisers, when considering displaying their wares on-line, turn to the World Wide Web.

The World Wide Web, the multimedia portion of the Internet, is within the control of the home-page sponsor, but that sponsor can be anyone from a respectable newspaper (*The Irish Times*), to a non mainstream political party (Sinn Féin) or a lurid publication that is in general not open to wide distribution (*Penthouse*). However, whatever is on the Internet is accessible to all

The second problem with legislating for this new medium is of a jurisdictional nature. The Internet is a global communications system. The user can travel from Ireland to the US, Russia, or Australia, with the click of a mouse, and what may be illegal or frowned upon here may never be banned in other countries to which users have access.

Although these are problems that are encountered in trying to regulate the Internet, there are reasons to believe that society need not do much more than it is already doing to keep this new medium in check. First of all, existing laws that apply to other media also apply to the Internet. Just as an obscene phone call is illegal, so too is an obscene E-mail. Just as sending a threatening letter is outlawed, so too is a threatening E-mail. Just as libel is legislated for in newspapers, such laws also apply to the Internet. The Internet is not the wild west.

Secondly, the Internet does a good job at regulating itself. E-mails, though not censored, are capable of being monitored by many of the institutions which provide them for their users. If you attempt to put forward a message on a newsgroup, which slights another member of that newsgroup, or anything that they represent, you are likely to get "flamed" (that is, inundated with dozens of messages from other citizens commenting on how bad your "netiquette" is). Further, most newsgroups have sets of rules which regulate what can be said, advertised, sold, or otherwise discussed, on a newsgroup.

The World Wide Web is currently not subject to any special regulatory measures beyond those which exist in law for all media. Yet here also, self-censorship is taking hold, though it has some way to go. Some web pages have warnings, highlighting that material ahead is of a sensitive nature, or not suitable for all viewers. On-Line services, such as America On-Line (and the imminent Europe On-Line), Compuserve, and Prodigy, are exploring, or already practise, various forms of self-regulation to keep young children from places they should not be. While not foolproof, measures enacted by these organisations should make it at least as difficult to experience undesirable parts of the Internet as it would be for them to obtain a copy of *Penthouse* or a similar magazine. Another idea would be a form of economic censorship, by charging visitors to access various web sites. If a child had to pay to access some of the more lurid parts of the World Wide Web, parents might discover sooner what is happening, and be able to put a stop to it.

The New Challenges to Public Policy

Public Policy, of course, is more interested in regulating the "conventional" world than in regulating the on-line one at present. Self-regulation practised by advertisers is intermingled with legislation enacted by government, and in both areas European influences are also at play. A look at Figure 31.1 below illustrates this dynamic.

Voluntary codes, which are adhered to by advertisers, are preferred by practitioners to government legislation. With voluntary codes, advertisers have a large input into their formation, and their supervision. This is not to say that voluntary associations take their duties lightly — far from it, they strictly record instances of grievances, investigate serious problems, and have the power to ban campaigns or censure advertisers.

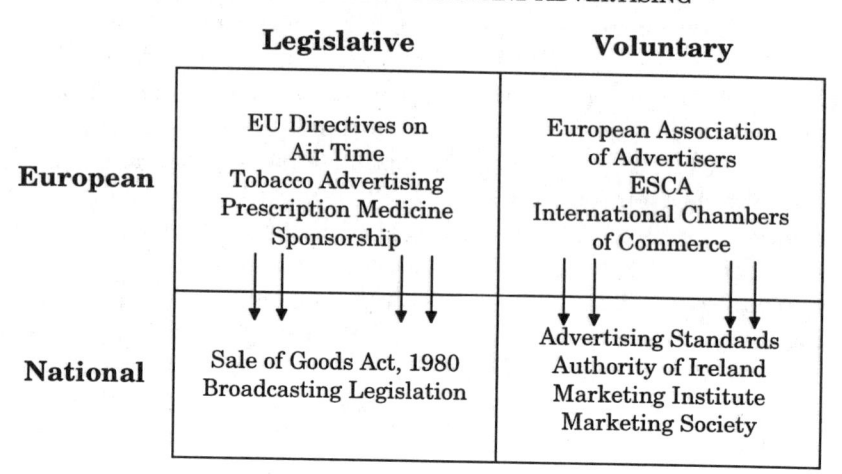

FIGURE 31.1 : PUBLIC POLICY AND ADVERTISING

	Legislative	Voluntary
European	EU Directives on Air Time Tobacco Advertising Prescription Medicine Sponsorship	European Association of Advertisers ESCA International Chambers of Commerce
National	Sale of Goods Act, 1980 Broadcasting Legislation	Advertising Standards Authority of Ireland Marketing Institute Marketing Society

CONCLUSIONS

While it is important to be aware of the costs and benefits brought by advertising, advertisers also need to know what consumers think of the exercise. Increasingly, the consumer is becoming more sceptical of the process, the claims, and the efficiency of advertising. Why is this? The volume of advertising has increased in recent years and this has been paralleled by increased "clutter". Some figures are instructive. Consider the following from Crowley (1995) with respect to the US market:

- There are seven times as many television stations today as there were ten years ago, and 43 per cent more consumer press.

- In 1990, over 1,200 more hours of television were transmitted than in 1980. In print, national newspaper advertising volumes rose by 75 per cent over the same period.

- The average adult is exposed to more than 70,000 messages per year.

Whether this clutter has been caused by advertising growth or is the result of advertising growth is unclear. The result is that consumers are forced to become more discerning in how they react to advertisements in general, and how much attention they pay to specific campaigns in particular. Advertisers have to be more creative in order to gain the attention of consumers, their advertising messages have to be transmitted more frequently in order to reach their target audience, which may be watching any of a dozen television channels, and finally, consumers are feeling more and more animosity towards advertisers, who they perceive as trying to invade every facet of their lives. Recent studies by Pollay and Mittal (1994), and Mittal (1994) give a clear impression of the frustration that consumers feel. According to these and other studies cited by the authors, consumers surveyed disliked advertising, felt that it created many undesirable effects, had some doubts about the economic benefits of the process, and were in favour of government regulation. It is up to the advertiser, or a group of advertisers, to acknowledge that a negative image exists, explore why this is so, and seek to convey a more favourable impression. By being aware of the positive and negative effects of advertising on society, advertisers should be in a better position to realise the source of consumers' fears, and how to improve the image of advertising by accentuating its positive benefits.

REFERENCES

Aaker, D., Batra, J. and Myers, J.G. (1992): *Advertising Management*, Englewood Cliffs, NJ: Prentice Hall.

Advertising Standards Authority for Ireland (1988): *Code of Advertising Standards for Ireland*, Dublin: ASAI.

Barnes, M. (1982): "Public Attitudes to Advertising", *Journal of Advertising*, 1: 119–28.

Beales, H., Craswell, R. and Salop, S. (1981): "The Efficient Regulation of Consumer Information", *Journal of Law and Economics*, 24: 491–539.

Beatty, S. and Hawkins, D.I. (1989): "Subliminal Stimulation: Some New Data and Interpretation", *Journal of Advertising*, 3: 4–8.

Benham, L. (1972): "The Effect of Advertising on the Price of Eyeglasses", *Journal of Law and Economics*, 15: 337–52.

Bobel, I. (1982): "Advertising and Economic Development", *Journal of Advertising*, 1: 237–52.

Borden, N.H. (1944): *The Economic Effects of Advertising*, Chicago: Irwin.

Bovee, C.L. and Arens, W.F. (1989): *Contemporary Advertising*, Homewood IL: Irwin.

Callahan, F.X. (1986): "Advertising and Economic Development", *International Journal of Advertising*, 5: 215–24.

Crowley, J. (1995): "A New Era of Persuasion", Chiat/Day home Page (www.chiatday.com).

Chowdhury, A.R. (1994): "Advertising Expenditures and the Macro Economy: Some New Evidence", *International Journal of Advertising*, 13: 1–14.

Cubbin, J.S. (1982): "Can Product Differentiation Deter Entry?", *Journal of Advertising*, 1: 361–73.

de Búrca, S. and Lambkin, M.V. (1993): "Sales Force Management in Ireland", *Irish Marketing Review*, 6: 53–63.

Dean, J. (1950): "Cyclical Policy on Advertising Appropriation", *Journal of Marketing*, 15: 265–73.

Demsetz, H. (1964): "The Welfare and Empirical Implications of Monopolistic Competition", *Economic Journal*, 74: 623–41.

Demsetz, H. (1968): "Do Competition and Monopolistic Competition Differ?", *Journal of Political Economy*, 76: 146–8.

Dixon, N.F. (1971): *Subliminal Advertising: The Nature of a Controversy*, London: McGraw-Hill.

Dixon, N.F. (1981): *Preconscious Processing*, London: John Wiley.

Duckworth, G. (1995): "How Advertising Works, The Universe and Everything", *Admap*, 31(1): 38–40.

Economist, The (1995): "Censorship in Cyberspace", *The Economist*, Vol. 335, No. 7909, 8 April: 82.

Ehrlich, I. and Fisher, L. (1982): "The Derived Demand for Advertising", *American Economic Review*, 72: 366–88.

Fullerton, R.A. and Nevett, T.R. (1986): "Advertising and Society — The Roots of Mistrusts in Germany and Great Britain", *International Journal of Advertising*, 5: 225–41.

Gable, M., Wilkins H.T., Harris, L. and Feinberg, R. (1987): "An Evaluation of Subliminally Embedded Sexual Stimuli in Graphics", *Journal of Advertising*, 16(1): 26–31.

Hwang, S.L. (1995): "Joe Camel is Missing...", *Wall Street Journal*, 14 July: A.1.

Kaynak, E. (1985): "Information Source Usage by Buyers of Single Detached Homes in Atlantic Canada", *International Journal of Advertising*, 4: 143–56.

Key, W.B. (1972): *Subliminal Seduction: Ad Media's Manipulation of a Not-So-Innocent America*, New York: Signet.

Key, W.B. (1976): *Media Sexploitation*, New York: Signet.

Key, W.B. (1980): *The Clam-Plate Orgy and Other Techniques for Manipulating Your Behaviour*, New York: Signet.

Key, W.B. (1989): *The Age of Manipulation: The Con in Confidence, The Sin in Sincere*, New York: Holt.

Kitchen, P.J. (1994): "The Marketing Communications Revolution — A Leviathan Unveiled?", *Marketing Intelligence and Planning*, 12(2): 19–25.

Levitt, T. (1993): "Advertising: The Poetry of Becoming", *Harvard Business Review*, March/April: 134–7.

McCracken, G. (1988): *Culture and Consumption*, Bloomington: Indiana University Press.

Macintyre, B. (1995): "The Dying of the Light", *The Independent on Sunday — Review*, 25 June.

Malone, E. (1995): "Perfect Pitch for Business", *The Irish Times — Business Supplement*, 12 May: 3.

Marsland, D. (1988): "Against Advertising — Inadequacies in the Treatment of Advertising by Sociology", *International Journal of Advertising*, 7: 223–6.

Meisel, J.B. (1979): "Demand and Supply Determinants of Advertising Intensity among Convenience Goods", *Southern Economic Journal*, 46: 233–43.

Mittal, B. (1994): "Public Assessment of TV Advertising: Faint Praise and Harsh Criticism", *Journal of Advertising Research*, 34(1): 35–53.

Mixon, F.G. (1994): "The Role of Advertising in the Marketing Process: A Survey", *International Journal of Advertising*, 13: 15–23.

Moore, T.E. (1982): "Subliminal Advertising: What You See is What You Get", *Journal of Marketing*, 46(2): 38–47.

Moschis, G.P. and Churchill, G.A. (1978): "Consumer Socialization: A Theoretical and Empirical Analysis", *Journal of Marketing Research*, 15, November: 599–609.

Murray, H. (1986): "Advertising's Effect on Sales — Proven or Just Assumed", *International Journal of Advertising*, 5: 15–36.

Nelson, P. (1970): "Information and Consumer Behaviour", *Journal of Political Economy*, 78: 311–29.

O'Donohoe, S. (1994): "Advertising Uses and Gratifications", *European Journal of Marketing*, 28: 52–75.

Packard, V. (1957): *The Hidden Persuaders*, London: Pelican Books.

Patrick, J. (1995): "IBM Internet Service Offerings", Telephone Conference, June.

Peter, J.P. and Donnelly, J.H. (1995): *Marketing Management — Knowledge and Skills*, Homewood, IL: Irwin.

Pollay, R.W. and Mittal, B. (1993): "Here's the Beef: Factors, Determinants and Segments in Consumer Criticism of Advertising", *Journal of Marketing*, 57(3): 99–114.

Reekie, W.D. (1981): *The Economics of Advertising*, London: Macmillan.

Reekie, W.D. (1982): "Advertising and Price", *Journal of Advertising*, 1: 131–41.

Rizetnikopf, L. (1995): "New Scapegoat: The Internet", *Wired*, 3(7): 33.

Rokeach, M. (1973): *The Nature of Human Values*, New York: The Free Press.

Saegert, J. (1979): "Another Look at Subliminal Perception", *Journal of Advertising Research*, 19(1): 55–7.

Severance, L.J. and Dyer, F.M. (1973): "Failure of Subliminal Word Presentations to Generate Interference to Colour Naming", *Journal of Experimental Psychology*, 101(1): 186–9.

Stigler, G.J. (1961): "The Economics of Information", *Journal of Political Economy*, 69: 213–25.

Synodinos, N.E. (1988): "Subliminal Stimulation: What Does the Public Think About It ?", in J.H. Leigh and C.R. Martin Jr. (eds.), *Current Issues and Research in Advertising*, 11(1) and (2): 157–87.

Trachtenberg, J.A. (1995): "Ads Denounce Time Warner for Rap Music", *Wall Street Journal*, 17 May: B1.

Verdon, W.A., McConnell, C.R. and Roesler, T.W. (1968): "Advertising Expenditures as an Economic Stabilizer: 1945–64", *Quarterly Review of Economics and Business*, 8: 7–18.

Voor, J.H. (1956): "Subliminal Perception and Subception", *Journal of Psychology*, 41(2): 437–58.

Warner, F.W. (1995): " Puffing Marketers Would Bear Burden of Proof if Code is Revised", *Wall Street Journal*, 17 May: B3.

Weintraub, D.J. and McNulty, J.A. (1973): "Clarity Versus Identifiability of Repeatedly Flashed Patterns", *Journal of Experimental Psychology*, 99(3): 293–305.

Yang, C.Y. (1964): Variations in the Cyclical Behaviour of Advertising, *Journal of Marketing*, 28: 25–30.

Zanot, E.J. and Pincus, J.D. (1983): "Public Perceptions of Subliminal Advertising", *Journal of Advertising*, 12(1): 39–45.